INTERNATIONA
COMPARATIVE COMPETI͠ιͺ.

This thorough appraisal of competition law and policy from an international and comparative perspective covers the role of different international organisations active in the area, the significance of multinational enterprises and, in particular, the differences between US and EU systems. Taking examples from regions such as Africa, the Middle East and Asia, Maher M. Dabbah looks at the law and policy in developing countries and at a regional level, the internationalisation of competition law and the doctrines of extraterritoriality, bilateral cooperation and multilateral cooperation as well as the relationship between competition and trade policy. The book should prove useful to anyone who is interested in gaining an insight into the international dimension of competition law and policy. It is written in language and style which make such a complex topic both possible to understand and enjoyable.

MAHER M. DABBAH is the Founder and Director of the Interdisciplinary Centre for Competition Law and Policy (ICC), Queen Mary, University of London. He also acts as a consultant to different organisations in the field and as special counsel to large businesses.

THE CAMBRIDGE ANTITRUST AND COMPETITION LAW SERIES

Series Editors

Maher M. Dabbah,
Reader in Competition Law and Director of the Inter-disciplinary Centre for
Competition Law and Policy (ICC), Queen Mary, University of London

Barry Hawk,
Professor of Law and Director of the Fordham Competition Law Institute,
Fordham University School of Law; Partner, Skadden, Arps, Slate, Meagher &
Flom LLP

Board members

Dr Werner Berg,
Partner, Crowell & Moring LLP

Professor Pierre Brooks,
University of South Africa

Professor Claus-Dieter Ehlermann,
WilmerHale

Professor Alan Fels,
The Australia and New Zealand School of Government

Professor Eleanor Fox,
New York University, New York

Professor Frederic Jenny,
Cour de Cassation, Paris

Mr Paul Lasok QC,
Monckton Chambers, London

Professor Mitsuo Mitsushita,
Nagashima, Ohno & Tsunematsu, Tokyo, Japan; Professor Emeritus,
University of Tokyo

Dr David E. Tadmor,
Partner, Tadmor & Co. Law Offices, Tel Aviv, Israel; former Director
General of the Israel Antirust Authority

Dr Cento Valjenovski,
Managing Partner, Case Associates, London

Publications within the Series consider various legal, economic and political developments related to competition law and policy. They also consider the application of competition law and policy in sector-specific as well as cross-sector contexts and deal with policy questions ranging from the formation and adoption of competition law and policy (whether at national, regional or international level) to those dealing with enforcement, and the connection between law and competition in the market place. The Series also accommodates different analytical and interdisciplinary viewpoints, such as law and economics; law and political science; law and economic geography-driven perspectives.

The Series includes publications designed to cater for academic demands as well as practitioner publications catering for the continuously evolving needs of regulators, policy-makers, and practitioners, in particular lawyers and economists (who increasingly provide advice on regulatory questions).

The editorial board of the Series welcome proposals by authors and editors who are interested in contributing to the Series through: academic monographs; revised PhD theses of high quality; practitioner texts and collections; and edited volumes.

List of books in the series

Anti-Cartel Enforcement Worldwide (3-Volume Set)
General editors: Maher M. Dabbah and Barry E. Hawk
9780521897211

A Principled Approach to Abuse of Dominance in European Competition Law
Liza Lovdahl Gormsen
9780521767149

International and Comparative Competition Law
Maher M. Dabbah
9780521516419

The International Dimension of EU Competition Law and Policy
Anestis S. Papadopoulos
9780521196468

INTERNATIONAL AND COMPARATIVE COMPETITION LAW

MAHER M. DABBAH

*Barrister; Director, Interdisciplinary Centre for Competition
Law and Policy (ICC) Queen Mary University of London*

CAMBRIDGE
UNIVERSITY PRESS

CAMBRIDGE UNIVERSITY PRESS
Cambridge, New York, Melbourne, Madrid, Cape Town, Singapore,
São Paulo, Delhi, Dubai, Tokyo, Mexico City

Cambridge University Press
The Edinburgh Building, Cambridge CB2 8RU, UK

Published in the United States of America by Cambridge University Press, New York

www.cambridge.org
Information on this title: www.cambridge.org/9780521736244

First published 2010

Printed in the United Kingdom at the University Press, Cambridge

A catalogue record for this publication is available from the British Library

ISBN 978-0-521-51641-9 Hardback
ISBN 978-0-521-73624-4 Paperback

To the ones who made everything possible:
my wonderful parents
and my brother Hassan

CONTENTS

PREFACE

Writing this book has been a very exciting and rewarding experience. The topic of international competition law and policy is one that I am very passionate about; my passion has grown over the years in parallel with the phenomenal increase in significance the topic has come to witness. International 'elements' are found nowadays in almost every single aspect of competition law and policy and this makes it necessary for everyone – whether competition officials, practitioners, judges, policymakers, business people, economists, students or others whose work has competition relevance – to develop an international-comparative perspective. This book therefore comes to make its own modest contribution to helping anyone interested in developing such perspective to do so in textbook style.

In setting out to complete the task at hand I have encountered many obstacles. First – and this is said with great pain – regretfully I sustained an extremely serious injury to my left (dominant) hand which left me simply unable to work on this book for some time. Although this was a major setback, my determination to complete the book received a major boost (and here I would like to thank Kim Hughes for the non-stop gentle reminders). A second obstacle was that – contrary to my prior (false!) hopes – life became phenomenally more (and not less) busy on the work front both within and outside ICC during the writing process: in particular, coordinating and teaching eight competition law courses attended by hundreds of students and serving as Director of the ICC have proved to be a full-time job indeed! Contrary to the hand injury however, this is an obstacle that added to the enjoyment of writing the book. A number of the courses which I teach at different institutions deal with international competition law and policy and it was extremely rewarding to have fascinating exchanges with my superb students attending these courses on many of the ideas contained in the book. I therefore would like to give a big vote of thanks to my students, especially those who have attended my courses on International and Comparative Competition Law *and* International Merger Control.

The book contains both international and comparative perspectives. I was hoping it would be a slightly bigger book and so more could go in to make the latter perspective bigger and more obvious, notably by including one or more jurisdictions. Word limit however meant that a bigger book was not possible and so I had to give a comprehensive account of the subject ensuring the existence of these two perspectives. I therefore opted to focus more on the international perspective (directly) and to include a viable comparative perspective *indirectly* which the reader will hopefully come to see when reading and reflecting on the different parts of the book. This is obviously a first edition of the book and I am hopeful that the limit set will be increased when it comes to the second edition.

I would like to thank my friends and colleagues around the world for their kind encouragement and support especially for the various international initiatives (in particular the Middle East initiative) which were launched when preparing the book and which contributed in a major way towards the book. In particular, special thanks are due to: Mr Nir Barnea, Dr Ido Baum, Professor Orna Ben-Naftali, Dr Werner Berg, Justice Yoram Danziger, Dr Tamar Gidron, Professor Barry Hawk, Professor Meir Heth, Adv. Moran Meiri, Justice Meriam Naor, Adv. Jad Nashef, Adv. Michael Naor, Dr Guy Rotkopf, Mr Avi Shobert, Adv. Dror Strum and Dr David Tadmor. I also would like to thank my former research assistant Sara Jameel who showed strong dedication to the project when she was involved in the earlier stages of its preparation. Special thanks are also due to Jamela for her help with the bibliography and tables. Finally, I would like to thank my mother and my father who have always been supportive and to whom I would like to dedicate this book.

LIST OF ABBREVIATIONS

ACCC	Australia Competition and Consumer Commission
ACFC	ASEAN Consultative Forum for Competition
AFC	ASEAN Economic Community
AFTA	ASEAN Free Trade Area
AMC	US Antitrust Modernisation Commission
ANATEL	National Telecommunications Agency of Brazil
APEC	Asia-Pacific Economic Cooperation
ASEAN	Association of South East Asian Nations
BRTI	Indonesian Telecommunication Regulatory Board
CADE	Administrative Council for Economic Defence in Brazil
CAFTA-DR	Central America-Dominican Republic-United States Free Trade Agreement
CAT	UK Competition Appeal Tribunal
CARICOM	Caribbean Community and Common Market
CBI	Central Bank of Iraq
CC	UK Competition Commission
CCJ	Caribbean Court of Justice
CCK	Communications Commission of Kenya
CCOPOLC	Competition and Consumer Policy and Law Committee
CEMAC	Economic and Monetary Community of Central Africa
CEPT	Common Effective Preferential Tariff
CERBP	Committee of Experts on Restrictive Business Practices
CFI	European Court of First Instance (now General Court of the EU)
CIS	Commonwealth of Independent States
CIT	Committee of Trade and Investment
CLP	Competition Law and Policy Committee of the OECD
CMB	Competition Monitoring Body in Africa
CNDC	National Commission for the Defence of Competition in Argentina
COMESA	Common Market for East and Southern Africa
COTED	Council for Trade and Economic Development in the Caribbean
CPDG	Competition Policy and Deregulation Group
CUA	Customs Union Agreement
DAP/MED	Department of Antimonopoly Policy of the Ministry of Economic Development of Azerbaijan

DG COMP	Directorate General for Competition within the European Commission
DGPT	Indonesian Directorate of Communications
EAC	East African Community
EC	European Community
ECA	European Competition Authorities
ECJ	European Court of Justice
ECMR	European Community Merger Regulation
ECR	European Court Reports
ECN	European Competition Network
EEA	European Economic Area
EEC	European Economic Community
EFTA	European Free Trade Area
ENP	European Neighbourhood Policy
EU	European Union
FBI	US Federal Bureau of Investigation
FCC	US Federal Communications Commission
FCO	German Federal Cartel Office
FDI	Foreign Direct Investment
FTAIA	US Foreign Trade Antitrust Improvements Act 1982
FTC	US Federal Trade Commission
GAFTA	Greater Arab Free Trade Area
GATS	General Agreement on Trade in Services
GATT	General Agreement on Tariffs and Trade
GCC	Cooperation Council of the Arab States of the Gulf
GCM	Gulf Common Market
GFC	Global Forum on Competition of the OECD
HHI	Herfindahl-Hirschman Index
IBRD	International Bank for Reconstruction and Development
ICAP	Interstate Council on Antimonopoly Policy.
ICJ	International Court of Justice
ICN	International Competition Network
ICPAC	US International Competition Policy Advisory Committee
IDA	International Development Association
IMF	International Monetary Fund
IP	Intellectual Property
IPR	Intellectual Property Right
ITO	International Trade Organisation
JFTC	Japan Fair Trade Commission
JGTC	Joint Group on Trade and Competition of the OECD
KPTC	Kenya Posts and Telecommunication Corporation
LACF	Latin American Competition Forum of the OECD

LAFTA	Latin American Free Trade Association
LAIA	Latin American Integration Association
LDC	Less developed country
LEDC	Less economically developed country
LGT	General Telecommunications Law of Brazil
MAI	Multilateral Agreement on Investment
MCIT	Ministry of Communications and Information Technology in Egypt
MDG	Millennium Development Goals
MERCUSOR	Southern Common Market
MFN	Most Favoured Nation principle of the WTO
MLA	Mutual Legal Assistance Treaty
MLAT	Mutual Assistance Treaty
MNC	Multinational Corporation
MNE	Multinational Enterprise
NAFTA	North American Free Trade Agreement
NCAs	National Competition Authorities of EU Member States
NCC	Nigerian Communications Commission
NSC	Northern Securities Company
NTC	National Telecommunications Commission of the Philippines
NTP	National Telecommunications Policy in Nigeria
NTRA	National Telecommunications Regulatory Authority in Egypt
OECD	Organisation For Economic Cooperation and Development
OECS	Organisation of Eastern Caribbean States
OEEC	Organisation for European Economic Cooperation
OFCOM	UK Office of Communications
OFT	UK Office of Fair Trading
OJ	Official Journal of the EU
PCA	Partnership and Cooperation Agreement
PTPA	Public Telecommunications Policy Act of the Philippines
R&D	Research and development
SAARC	South Asian Association for Regional Cooperation
SACU	Southern African Customs Union
SADC	Southern African Development Community
SAFTA	South Asia Free Trade Agreement
SCR	Supreme Court Review
SDE	Secretariat of Economic Law in Brazil
SEAE	Secretariat for Economic Monitoring in Brazil
SSNIP	Small but Significant Non-transitory Increase in Price
STB	Surface Transportation Board
STPC	Sudan Telecommunications Public Corporation
TAC	Treaty of Amity and Cooperation in South East Asia
TEU	Treaty on the European Union

TFEU	Treaty on the Functioning of the European Union
TPRM	Trade Policy Review Mechanism of the WTO
TRA	Telecommunications Regulatory Authority of Bahrain
TRA	Telecommunications Regulatory Authority of United Arab Emirates
TRC	Telecommunications Regulatory Commission of Jordan
TRIPS	Trade Related Aspects of Intellectual Property Rights
UCFS	Understanding on Commitments in Financial Services
UAE	United Arab Emirates
UEMOA	West African Economic and Monetary Union
UNCRBP	United Nations Conference on Restrictive Business Practices
UNCTAD	United Nations Conference on Trade and Development
USAID	United States Agency for International Development
USD	United States Dollar
USTR	United States Trade Representative
WAEMU	West African Economic and Monetary Union
WTO	World Trade Organisation

TABLE OF CASES

TABLE OF STATUTES

West African Economic and Monetary Union

TABLE OF REGULATIONS

Chapter 1

Introduction

1. Geographical expansion and increase in significance of competition law

Competition law has come to receive phenomenal attention in recent years. The field has become incredibly vast and it has come to experience a geographical expansion – in a relatively short period of time – not seen in the case of any other branch of law. Competition law is no longer an exclusive feature of the statute book of countries in the developed world: a large number of developing countries have come to adopt some form of competition law domestically and in an even larger number competition law currently ranks very high on the national agenda.[1] Many of these countries are at an extremely early stage of economic development; some of them have a notably limited experience with the concept or mechanism of a free market economy; and there are those in which even as recently as five years ago the adoption of a competition law was simply unthinkable, yet it has become a reality. Such developments are highly significant and have impacted – in most cases positively – on international trade, the way countries regulate their domestic markets, and on how firms behave and operate globally.

In parallel with the phenomenal increase in significance and geographic scope of competition law however, the question of *what is competition law all about* has mushroomed. The debate that began a number of decades ago on what the goals of competition law are or should be and what its exact role in an economy or society is remains very relevant; in some respects, the debate is even particularly heated especially when considering the interface between competition law and neighbouring fields, such as intellectual property rights[2] and industrial policy. It seems unlikely that this debate

---

[1] Chapter 6 below will consider the position in developing countries.

[2] The competition law/IP interface has attracted an incredibly vast amount of interest especially in recent years. How these two branches of law are 'linked' (if at all) and whether they are in conflict or operate in harmony are queries to which no definite

will see an end or that a 'cool-down' period will be reached in the near future. If anything, the debate is widely expected to grow and heat up even more so with the recent turbulence in the global economy and the doubts this has raised over the ability of the free market and its forces to function without government intervention.

Competition law expertise and the number of people specialising in the field has also increased considerably in recent years. This increase in expertise is very welcome and should be encouraged, especially since it could facilitate a 'globalised' understanding of competition law which is helpful in the academic arena, practice and in the work of competition authorities. However with the increase of expertise naturally come different perspectives and different attitudes and, in more ways than one, such an increase in expertise will do nothing but fuel the debate over the role of competition law and policy. On the whole, a lack of consensus remains on how one should answer the basic questions of: what should the goals of competition law be; what role should be accorded to it in an economy; and what are the exact benefits that should be sought when applying it? To this list one could understandably add the question of whether competition law should give way in certain cases to other policies or priorities (such as national security interests, employment considerations and international competitiveness of the local economy), even where the situation at hand raises competition problems.

It is important to realise however that it is *natural* for there to be lack of consensus in a field such as competition law. Even if this lack of consensus were to emerge in the form of sharp disagreements, this in fact is healthy and in some cases even necessary. Competition law has been around for many decades and arguably many centuries,[3] yet it continues to be surrounded with notable ambiguities and many of its 'components' and 'functions' remain largely unexplored and mis-understood. This must therefore persuade one to accept that a serious debate is needed in the field in order to better understand this highly interesting branch of law and the kind of role competition law and policy should perform; a serious debate will also help explore questions and issues in the field which until now have remained almost untouched.

---

answers have been given. The interface has been surrounded with controversy especially in the European Union (EU) and the USA.

[3] See M. Dabbah, *Competition Law and Policy in the Middle East* (Cambridge University Press, 2007), ch. 2.

2. A notable trend so far

Some form of competition law has been adopted in over 120 jurisdictions, all of which differ significantly in terms of their domestic or regional circumstances; though many of these jurisdictions share some important similarities. A notable trend that has come to develop in competition law literature, practice and understanding has been to view this type of law in different parts of the world with the same lenses. It is uncertain whether this indeed is sensible however, as the discussion in the following chapters will show, a huge gulf exists first and foremost in cultural perspectives across the globe on the concept and process of competition and, as a consequence, on the function and role of competition law itself. It is difficult to argue therefore that competition law throughout world regions such as Australasia, the Middle East and Africa, Europe and the Americas should be understood in the same way. Yet, experience shows that this is exactly what has been happening and what has become almost normal practice in the field: rules, practices and theories that are developed in certain parts of the world – mostly in the European Union (EU) and the USA – have come to be *forced down the throat* of countries in developing parts of the world, often with the aid of international organisations. In many cases, this has resulted in the latter facing serious difficulties, whether in relation to understanding the substantive competition rules, the functioning of the institutional structure and enforcement mechanism or building a suitable platform for coherent and sensible policy formulation. It is indeed remarkable that the real beneficiaries as a result of this 'knowledge transfer' exercise have not always been developing countries themselves but rather some 'specialists' and 'consultants' in the field. It seems not explained nor justified why some countries should take a model competition law regime of another country without careful 'local' assessment being conducted first simply because personal contacts between officials and specialists in the two – often facilitated by officials of some international bodies – make this convenient to do so. It remains to be explained why certain countries would be 'faxed over' (or perhaps in today's more common context 'emailed') a few provisions representing a slightly altered version of the competition rules of certain competition law regimes so they could incorporate them into a domestic competition law of their own.

In fairness, this trend of *copy* and *paste* (albeit objectionable in most cases) has in some way helped in turning competition law into an international phenomenon. And there is no particular desire here to be overly critical of this particular trend. In the case of many if not most countries which have come to adopt competition law in recent years however, this has been a dangerous trend, which has contributed[4] to the enormous difficulties preventing these countries from converting their competition rules into effective enforcement tools in practice in order to deal with anticompetitive situations in their domestic economies, let alone educate their public (including local businesses) on the benefits of competition and the role of competition law. A successful competition law regime in the USA or the EU for example does not necessarily mean there is going to be a successful competition law regime in countries adopting or following these model regimes. Consulting the experience of successful competition law regimes is helpful and in many cases is absolutely crucial and this must be recognised with no doubt; indeed the usual practice of many competition officials in these countries is to consult the experience of advanced regimes – such as the EU and US regimes – on a daily basis. There is nothing wrong with this. However, when it comes to adopting competition law domestically and designing a regime for enforcing this law, there is no substitute for a competition law growing from domestic roots. Competition law revolves around the idea of needing to protect the process of competition, consumers and other appropriate interests in *domestic* markets; sometimes, perhaps, this needs to include the idea of needing to facilitate this process in the marketplace. Given its concern with the process of competition, it is vital to appreciate that this process sits at the heart of the culture prevailing in the country or region concerned.[5] Determining what form and scope the local competition law should have requires an understanding of the culture prevailing in the country concerned, as well as an understanding of the particular economic, social and political circumstances of that country. Without such understanding, there is bound to be a gap – if not in the actual substantive provisions of the local competition law – certainly in the enforcement of the law; this gap will only widen through a blind copying of the competition rules of certain regimes.

3.   The competition law 'chain'

The cross-border influence of competition law as described in the comments made in the previous part is not necessarily 'bilateral', i.e. one that

---

[4] It is important to note that this situation has been *one* of many factors causing difficulties. See chapter 6 below for a list and a discussion of the different factors.

[5] See pp. 62–64 below on the importance and relevance of culture in the field of competition law.

links between only two competition law regimes. In some cases one may be able to identify a cross-border influence extending beyond being merely bilateral. The competition rules of jurisdiction or country B may be modelled on those of jurisdiction or country A and the former may be the model on the basis of which the competition rules of jurisdiction or country C were enacted.[6]

4. The lack of competition law

It is true that a large number of countries around the world have come to introduce some form of competition law domestically and in some cases also regionally.[7] The fact however remains that most countries around the world have not adopted a competition law. Some of these countries have embraced the principles of a free market without opting to legislate for protecting competition specifically in the marketplace. Some countries for many years relied on the market itself – not a body of officials enforcing a set of competition rules – to provide the forces of competition, choosing thus free trade as the appropriate competition policy and the promotion of free trade as a way to bring about desired economic benefits for their firms and citizens.[8] Other countries have somehow relied on their unfair competition law to deal with all types of market problems, whether those of anticompetitive behaviour or conduct, or those within the specific scope of unfair competition law itself;[9] and there are those countries which have laws against restrictive business or trade practices which do not necessarily seek to promote the process of competition but rather to continuously 'regulate' the behaviour of powerful firms;[10] a number of these countries for many years maintained some reservations regarding capitalism,[11] though this number has come to dwindle in recent years as can be

---

[6] For example, see how major parts of the UK competition law regime (most notably the Chapter I and Chapter II prohibitions of the Competition Act 1998) are modelled on EU competition law and major parts of the Singaporean competition law regimes are modelled on UK competition law.

[7] See chapter 7 below for a discussion on regional competition law and policy; chapter 4 below also contains a discussion on the EU competition law regime.

[8] Singapore was an example here until it adopted a specific competition law in 2005.

[9] See pp. 320–323 below. [10] See p. 17 below.

[11] Arguably, the collapse of many Asian economies in 1998 seems to have increased the fear of these countries about capitalism. See W. E. Kovacic, 'Capitalism, Socialism and Competition Policy in Vietnam' (1999) *Antitrust* 57; 'Merger Enforcement in Transition: Antitrust Controls on Acquisitions in Emerging Economies' (1998) *University of Cincinnati Law Review* 1075; 'Getting Started: Creating New Competition Policy Institutions in

seen in the case of countries like China, which has now adopted a specific competition law, the Antimonopoly Law 2007.[12]

The absence of a specific competition law from most countries may be looked at in different ways. On the one hand stands the view that competition law has come to be adopted in most if not all of the world's 'important' economies and that a sufficient number of these economies have subscribed to it, to give competition law and policy a global significance and status;[13] taking into account as well the fact that the competition rules of many of these economies have a wide extraterritorial scope making them capable of catching anticompetitive situations occurring on foreign soil.[14] On the other hand, it is arguable that the fact that many countries do not have competition laws – whilst not disputing the global significance of competition law – may produce some negative effect; for example, it may affect the chances of achieving full or meaningful 'internationalisation' of competition law through, for example, the pursuit of a multilateral agreement within the framework of an international body, such as the World Trade Organisation.[15] It would be correct to say that the exclusion of such countries might in any case (and regardless of any push towards internationalising competition law or the type of internationalisation sought)[16] affect the *role* competition law can play in a globalised economy as an effective means to address anticompetitive behaviour, conduct or transactions that impede and distort the flows of trade and investment worldwide. Even these countries themselves may be at a disadvantage here, especially in combating harmful situations. This highlights the importance of competition law and more generally international cooperation in the field for such countries. Obviously such disadvantages are not solely caused by the lack of

---

Transition Economies' (1997) *Brooklyn Journal of International Law* 403; N. S. Pakaphan, 'Indonesia: Enactment of Competition Law' (1999) *International Business Lawyer* 491; S. Supanit, 'Thailand: Implementation of Competition Law' (1999) *International Business Lawyer* 491.

[12] China adopted its long-awaited Anti-Monopoly Law in August 2007. This law entered into force in August 2008.

[13] Such a view seems to receive some strength from the fact that those economies in which competition law has not been introduced tend to – usually – follow whatever global trends emerge. However this remains highly debatable and not fully supported in practice.

[14] The extraterritorial application of competition law is examined in chapter 8 below.

[15] See chapter 10 below for a discussion on multilateral cooperation in the field of competition law.

[16] For a discussion of the process and the different types of internationalisation, see the following chapter.

competition law: in cases where a competition law regime may exist, the competition authority(ies) in this regime may be constrained due to lack of resources, whether financial or human and lack of necessary expertise or independence to take action, i.e. to be able to enforce the rules effectively.[17] Nonetheless, it is sensible to suggest that most of these 'disadvantages' should disappear if these countries are encouraged, or actually seek, to adopt competition law in their national legal orders (where they do not have such law) with the necessary institutional and enforcement mechanism, and if they are encouraged to seek international cooperation with other countries in the field.

5. Is competition law really global?

Referring to competition law as 'global' or 'international' is not unheard of; this book obviously does this. Whether in the literature, competition conferences and events, the work of international organisations or statements by competition authorities, the term *global* competition law has been used quite frequently. The point was made in the previous part that competition law can be said to have global significance. The question may be asked, however, whether competition law itself is really global? This is a highly important question and it is worth giving some thought to.

Probably almost everyone in the field would agree that this question may be answered in two ways: 'yes' and 'no'. Obviously, it is possible to say that competition law is global because, as the discussion in the previous part made clear, many nations – developing and developed, American and European, Australasian and African – have adopted some form of competition law; in addition to the fact that competition law enforcement has become increasingly international through extraterritorial assertion of jurisdiction and bilateral cooperation. On the other hand, it is arguable that competition law is not global because – apart from the fact that not all countries have adopted competition law in their domestic systems – the majority of people around the world are not familiar with competition law at all. In many parts of the world competition law is simply unknown; in others it is misunderstood and confused with laws such those on unfair competition and sport (because of the use of the word 'competition'); and there are even those world communities in which competition law – due to its association with capitalism

---

[17] See World Trade Organisation (WTO), *Annual Report* (1997).

and specifically the market mechanism – is looked at with discomfort and suspicion. There is therefore a noticeable lack of sufficient public awareness of competition law in different parts of the world; though in recent years, this awareness has been gradually increasing. There are several reasons for this increase in awareness which will be explored at different stages of the discussion in later chapters. But one important reason has been the interest of the media in the field and the almost daily reporting on competition law developments in different parts of the world. Some of these developments have an enormous global impact. Perhaps the most high-profile example here is the decision of the European Commission and the judgment of the General Court of the EU in the *Microsoft* case.[18] The case has been widely reported around the world and raised considerable interest even in some of the world's smallest communities. Astonishingly, whilst some of these communities are not at all familiar with the existence of their national competition authority – which may be located some 120 miles away – they are able to discuss the specific issues of Windows and Media Player in the case, which was decided some 2,000 miles away!

6.   The desirability of competition

Posing the question of whether competition is desirable is not a mere academic exercise. Especially in a book offering an international-comparative perspective, it would be important to ask this question. Across the world, there are variable degrees in relation to the desirability of competition. In certain parts of the world, most notably in the EU and USA the desirability of competition in the marketplace is held *almost* like an item of faith by competition officials, judges and politicians in particular. In other parts of the world however, this attitude to competition does not appear to be shared, not to mention the almost absent (free market) competition culture in some countries. In some parts of the world the idea of having competition is taken to mean a reduction in the power and influence of those few individuals or families controlling specific sectors of the local economy; it is therefore a highly undesirable and disliked idea.

---

[18] Case T-201/04, *Microsoft* v. *Commission* [2007] ECR II-3601. A more recent example of a decision that has come to attract global attention is that of the European Commission in COMP/C-3/37.990 *Intel* (2009) *Official Journal* C-227/13. The firm was fined by the Commission in May 2009 an extremely high fine totalling almost €1.06 billion.

But even if one were to eliminate the geographical reference or comparison, the question over the desirability of competition can be said to be a difficult one to answer and it is a highly debatable one. For example, looking at the almost universally acknowledged economic goals of competition law, economic efficiency and maximisation of consumer welfare,[19] it seems not everyone would agree that these goals are *impossible* to achieve without a process of competition in the marketplace. The consumer benefits of lower prices, better quality and more choice may still be realised with the existence of a single firm in the market, provided that this firm would have an interest in innovating and achieving efficiency and translating this into direct consumer benefits.[20] Certain views and theories which came to develop during the twentieth century were highly sceptical about the desirability of competition. These argued that competition considerations are not the only coordinating force within free and liberal markets, and that their dominance of the intellectual discourse of competition law *is over developed*. They also contended that coordination of private economic behaviour is also possible via other terminals such as social collusion, the creation of collectivist norms, decisions and hierarchy and the virtues of social responsibility. Furthermore, the collective intellectual influence of approaches such as those advocated by the theory of 'contestable markets'[21] and the Chicago School[22] of thought has, to a certain extent, undermined the conventional view on the desirability of competition.

Admittedly however, the chances for key consumer benefits emerging when only one firm operates in the market appear slimmer than in the

---

[19] See pp. 36–44 below for a discussion of the goals of competition law.

[20] It is worth noting the concepts of 'productive' and 'allocative' efficiency here. Productive efficiency is achieved where products are produced at the lowest cost possible. On the other hand, allocative efficiency is realised where a product is sold at the lowest price possible; the price consumers are willing to pay. See further pp. 23–25 below.

[21] The theory of contestable markets is one which has been advocated by some economists in recent years. What this theory says is that an optimal allocation of resources will be ensured provided that the market in question is contestable. Contestable in this sense means that a firm will be able to enter the market without incurring sunk costs (which the firm will not be able to recover at a future date when it exits from the market). In other words, for a market to be contestable there must be a realistic likelihood that potential competitors can easily enter the market and begin to compete when market conditions, including imperfections (caused mainly by the behaviour of firms in the market or changes in the patterns of consumer demand), provide the opportunity to do so. See W. Baumol, J. Panzar and R. Willig, *Contestable Markets and the Theory of Industry Structure* (Harcourt Brace Jovanovich, 1988); E. E. Bailey, 'Contestability and the Design of Regulatory and Antitrust Policy' (1981) *American Economic Review* 178.

[22] See further pp. 61–62 below.

situation where more than one firm exists and with some form of competition between these firms. This particular philosophy seems to have been one of the driving forces behind the dramatic change in the attitude of many countries towards the market mechanism in the last quarter of the twentieth century as can be seen from the noticeable shift on the part of those countries from monopolisation to de-monopolisation and from state control and planning to liberalisation and privatisation. This contrasts with the prevailing tendency for most of that century in many parts of the world to favour a tradition of exerting strict control over the planning and management of domestic economies. One of the major consequences resulting from this change – other than the apparent, though in light of the recent global economic crisis 'controversial', victory of capitalism over communism – has been the enhancing of the desirability of competition. This has meant that a belief came to grow that, on the whole, competition can be regarded as an effective tool for achieving important benefits for countries and their citizens, among which encouraging innovation, furthering growth and safeguarding the welfare and social development of countries came to rank high. This significant development – which has unfolded in parallel with a relentless process of globalisation and a sharp increase in the removal of hindrances to the flows of trade and investment worldwide[23] – has demonstrated a strong belief in and reliance, particularly in the developed world, on the market mechanism.[24]

7.   The 'need' for competition law

The enhancement of the desirability of competition, among other things, meant that a framework was required to afford it adequate protection. This obviously pushed competition law to the fore and contributed to the impressive increase in significance and geographical scope of the competition law as described above.[25]

Although the question over the desirability of competition can be considered to remain in contention, the question of whether competition law is needed has *very interestingly* developed into a subject of little debate and *on the*

[23] See A. Fiebig, 'A Role for the WTO in International Merger Control' (2000) *Northwestern Journal of International Law and Business* 233. See also pp. 92–97 below for a discussion on globalisation and its implications for competition law and policy.

[24] See further below at pp. 26–27 on the belief in and reliance on the market to achieve economic progress.

[25] See M. R. A. Palim, 'The World Wide Growth of Competition Law: an Empirical Analysis' (1998) *Antitrust Bulletin* 105.

whole is almost consistently answered in the positive. Perhaps the notable exceptions in this regard have been the developing of a 'public choice approach' and the question of whether the protection of competition could be achieved using other laws or policies. The public choice approach – developed in the USA in recent years in the form of 'radical' theorising – seems to have embraced a view on the need to question whether competition law has any legitimate place in a market economy. Essentially, what this approach has advocated is the need to build a strategic path hoping to return the attention of the competition law community to the first and basic principles of competition law in order to consider seriously the role of competition law.

The question of whether competition could be protected using laws or policies other than competition law and policy has been raised on a number of occasions. Some commentators have argued that enacting competition law does not guarantee competition will ensue and that competition can exist without having competition law. This argument is supported with reference to the high degree of competitiveness enjoyed by certain countries, which for many years lacked specific competition rules. In this respect, it is interesting to note how things have developed in relation to the question over the need of competition law: from the position that used to exist some years ago, namely asking whether competition law *was needed* in a given country, we have moved to a new position, namely asking why competition law is *not needed*. A presumption therefore has been created in favour of enacting competition law. Regardless of the rights and wrongs of this particular development, it is a presumption that has taken a particularly strong foothold in the field internationally.

Nonetheless, what remains in contention is the need for competition law in terms of intervention in the marketplace *in certain situations*. It would be important to be clear about one underlying function of competition law: the use of competition law must be limited to cases of market failure,[26] namely circumstances in which private forces in the market fail to sustain 'desirable activities' (in the form of competitive markets leading to greater benefits to consumers and society) or to prevent 'undesirable activities' (in the form of anticompetitive situations leading to consumer harm and an adverse effect on innovation and economic progress). A regular or heavy intervention into the marketplace using competition law can be highly damaging.[27] One

---

[26] See F. Bator, 'The Autonomy of Market Failure' (1958) *Quarterly Journal of Economics* 351.

[27] It is important to limit this view to the field of competition law. Outside the field of competition law, some form of 'regulation' may actually be highly desirable if not crucial in order to avoid highly damaging outcomes or to facilitate competitive markets. An

notable example of this is where an intervention by a competition authority in relation to the use by a firm of its intellectual property or other exclusive rights may discourage innovation by firms in the first place. The question of intervention – in terms of the depth and scope of intervention by competition authorities – is among the toughest questions facing the competition law community globally. And whilst it may not *remove* the need for having a competition law in the statute book, it raises the question over the *need* or *legitimacy* for the use of competition law in certain situations. This question is likely to continue to be raised for many years to come; and perhaps more frequently so as the field of competition law develops and its interface with other fields and policy widens and deepens.[28]

Putting these general comments on the need for competition law to one side, in practice there is a host of reasons why countries adopt competition law. These reasons include but are not limited to: the need to ensure that following a process of privatisation in domestic economies former state monopolies would not simply be replaced by private ones;[29] market globalisation and the challenges this presents in terms of the importance of protecting local consumers and firms from possible anticompetitive behaviour, conduct or transactions of multinational firms; the need to facilitate the creation of a free market economy; compliance with international obligations; and encouraging foreign investment. The existence of these different reasons means that countries have had varying experiences when introducing competition law; differences in experience also exist with regard to applying competition law in individual cases, among others.

8.   Competition law *and* competition policy

There are many situations – both in academic writing and practice – in which the terms 'competition law' and 'competition policy' are used interchangeably. It is important, however, to be aware that the two are not identical. In particular, the concept of competition policy is considerably wider than that of competition law.[30] Competition law is a body of legal rules and standards which aim at protecting the process of competition: dealing with market imperfections and restoring desirable

---

example here could be sectors such as telecommunications, water, railways, energy, transport and financial services.

[28] One such interface is the competition/IP interface which was mentioned at p. 1 above.

[29] See generally C. D. Ehlermann and L. L. Laudati (eds.), *European Competition Law Annual 1997: Objectives of Competition Policy* (Hart Publishing, 1998), pp. 150–1.

[30] See pp. 60–62 below.

competitive conditions in the market. Competition policy is concerned with the formulation of a competition law in the first place and later on its enforcement; the concept also extends to all aspects dealing with the application of competition law and covers, in addition, competition advocacy.[31] In relation to the process of application, it is worth noting how an overlap may exist between competition law and competition policy: for example, in this process a court or competition authority will set out the policy in relation to the matter at hand but at the same time it will be – in some cases – creating a competition rule or standard.

9. Similarities between competition law regimes around the world

Notwithstanding the varying experiences of countries adopting competition law, most of the world's competition law regimes share many common characteristics and features; these characteristics and features will be explored in their proper context in the following chapters, though some are worth mentioning at this stage. These include – most prominently – the prohibitions on certain types of behaviour, conduct and transactions. It is important for a competition law to include a prohibition on collusion between firms, particularly cartels aiming at market-sharing, price-fixing, limiting production and collusive tendering; in many competition law regimes, the prohibition on collusion extends to vertical restraints, namely restraints included in agreements between firms operating at different levels of the market.[32] Another important prohibition is that directed at the unilateral conduct of firms and which aims to control abuses of dominance or monopolisation. Furthermore, in most competition law regimes around the world, there is a mechanism for merger regulation aiming at controlling problematic merger operations, which may give rise to competition problems. In some regimes, the competition law chapter includes additional provisions dealing with privileges and aid given to firms by the state.[33]

All of the above-mentioned similarities concern the substance and scope of competition rules. However, similarities between competition

---

[31] See pp. 65–70 below for a discussion on competition advocacy.

[32] An example of a vertical restraint is one which seeks to fix prices or divide markets at the level of distributor(s) and/or possibly that of the supplier.

[33] See pp. 161–162 below for an example of these provisions under EU competition law regime.

law regimes around the world also exist in relation to approaches of enforcement,[34] procedural aspects and general policy views followed when applying the rules. Most competition law regimes around the world have come to develop common approaches in their analysis of different competition issues. This can be seen in light of how the economics of competition law have to some extent become 'globalised' in the treatment of horizontal mergers in the area of merger control[35] as well as with regard to the use and exercise of market definition in competition cases.[36] Obviously, such development is significant and has been particularly helpful to those – whether firms or their advisors – who often find themselves having to deal with several (sometimes many) competition authorities in different parts of the world in one and the same case. Achieving these similarities deserves particular emphasis because it has to a large extent been facilitated by bilateral cooperation[37] between different competition authorities and the useful role played by some international organisations in the field.[38]

In an era of relentless globalisation and with so many competition law regimes worldwide, similarities between these regimes are particularly welcome and can be enormously useful. They should – where relevant and possible – be fostered in order to, among other things, avoid sometimes unnecessary situations or outcomes, most notably conflicting decisions between different competition authorities in cases of concurrent jurisdiction in which the competition rules of more than one regime apply.

10.   Differences between competition law regimes around the world

The important similarities 'uniting' different competition law regimes must be looked at alongside the many differences, which continue to

---

[34] This primarily concerns judicial and administrative enforcement.

[35] Looking around the world, one is able to see a great deal of convergence in the treatment of horizontal mergers, most notably as evident from the use of the theories of 'non-coordinated effects' and 'coordinated effects'. For a discussion of these theories, see the *European Commission Guidelines on the Assessment of Horizontal Mergers* (2004) *Official Journal* C-31/5; also the guidance published by competition authorities in the UK, USA, Australia and Canada, among many others.

[36] See pp. 70–77 below for a discussion on market definition.

[37] Bilateral cooperation is discussed in chapter 9.

[38] See chapter 3 for an account of the different international organisations and their role.

form a gulf separating these regimes. These differences will be high-lighted throughout the discussion in later chapters, but it would be helpful at this stage to offer a taste of some of them. These differences are particularly worth noting because realising their existence and under-standing them is extremely vital to assessing two important things. At one end of the spectrum, this would facilitate a proper evaluation of individual competition law regimes in order to identify possible gaps in those regimes as well as key strengths, which could possibly be consulted when seeking to build or strengthen other regimes.[39] At the other end of the spectrum, identifying these differences helps identify, among other things, the challenges facing any attempt to arrive at common grounds in the field (through a process of internationalisation of competition law), whether in terms of substantive rules or procedures followed in the relevant regimes.

The existence of differences between competition law regimes in practice gives rise to two 'competing' views over how these differences should be regarded. On the one hand, it could be argued that the existence of differences must be accepted as a fact, which is inevitable in a complex field like competition law, where law, economics and politics are often mixed in the same pot. Indeed the merit of this view is highlighted by the importance of being realistic about the fact that some of the differences between competition law regimes around the world are deeply rooted in the particular legal system and the wider sociopolitical and socio-economic circumstances as well as general cul-tural patterns prevailing in the relevant country and, in some cases, differences of ideology. Moreover it is important not to exaggerate at least some of the differences between competition law regimes around the world: sometimes differences can be useful for the purposes of having a debate in the field. On the other hand, it is arguable that one must acknowledge that some of the differences can cause problems[40] in prac-tice and therefore it would important to seek ways to address these differences. As will be seen in the following chapter, one way in which an attempt has been made to do this has been to suggest internationa-lising competition law and policy.

The following four differences are in particular worth discussing here.

---

[39] Such exercise is carried out by some international organisations, most notably the Organisation for Economic Cooperation and Development (OECD); see pp. 130–141 below.
[40] See pp. 80–82 below.

(A) 'Viewing' competition and 'understanding' competition law

Perhaps the first difference that should be mentioned is the lack of consensus with respect to the meaning that should be given to the most important term in the field of competition law, namely that of 'competition'. The discussion below will consider this concept at some length and it will show how it is not clear whether there is an agreement on how the concept should be defined and understood. The lack of consensus also extends to what is considered to be 'anticompetitive' behaviour, conduct or transaction. It is not clear that the scope of this particular concept is identical in different competition law regimes and whether the treatment of different types of anticompetitive situations in these regimes is on an equal footing.[41] However, even if such consensus could be said to exist, a particular difference remains which directly affects the scope of the concept of 'anticompetitive', namely the difference over the goals of competition law and what these should be.[42] This particular difference is especially important given the 'difference' between the competition law understanding prevailing in different regimes. In some regimes, a mature understanding of competition law exists among the different communities – of enforcing authorities, practitioners and academics (and to a large extent the business community) – and the experience within these regimes with competition and competition law is very impressive. In such regimes competition policy in particular is in a constant state of change and evolution. This contrasts with the situation in (many) other regimes where there is simply a 'young' experience in the field and limited, albeit slowly developing, understanding of competition law.[43]

---

[41] See, for example, in relation to the regulation of vertical restraints and the issue of resale price maintenance. In some regimes resale price maintenance included in vertical agreements in the form of 'fixed' pricing (meaning the situation where the supplier and the distributor agree to fix the price at which the latter will resell the product) are viewed as hardcore restrictions and thus considered to have an object of restricting competition. In other regimes, this form of resale price maintenance is not seen as a hardcore restriction as such because it is considered to lack such object; though it may at the end – following the necessary economic evaluation – be considered to have an anticompetitive 'effect'.

[42] See pp. 36–44 below.

[43] See W. M. Hannay, 'Transnational Competition Law Aspects of Mergers and Acquisitions' (2000) 20 *Northwestern Journal of International Law and Business* 287.

(B)   What is the title of the law?

A second notable difference concerns how competition laws are referred to in different parts of the world. Obviously in many competition law regimes, the laws are referred to as just that: competition law.[44] In some competition law regimes, however, the laws are referred to as laws against restrictive business or trade practices, which normally are more concerned with regulating how large firms use their market muscle than with removing hindrances to free market competition.[45] In other regimes the laws are called the laws against unfair competition; and there is a third, but not final, category of countries where the law is called the competition and fair trading law or competition and trade regulation.

One may interestingly wonder whether in light of differences in names or titles of laws these laws actually mean and aim to address the same thing. This issue will be discussed in one particular context further below (in chapter 6), namely that of the competition law and policy of developing countries. For present purposes, however, it is worth observing that the laws in different competition law regimes do not necessarily have to be consistently called 'competition law' for these laws to be capable of addressing the same problematic situations *or* functioning as proper competition laws. Moreover, in some cases the difference in reference to the relevant law(s) may be merely cosmetic more than anything else without any material implication or consequence. An example here is found in the case of those jurisdictions where the law is referred to as 'competition law' and those in which the law is referred to as the law on the 'protection of competition and the prohibition of monopolistic practices'.

(C)   Enforcement

A third and in practice highly crucial difference concerns the competition law tradition and the degree of seriousness with which competition law is enforced in different regimes. In certain regimes, a weak

---

[44] Obviously in the USA the law is referred to as 'antitrust law'; see chapter 5 below which deals with the US regime

[45] Report of the American Bar Association Sections of Antitrust Law and International Law and Practice on *The Internationalization of Competition Law Rules: Coordination and Convergence* (1999).

competition law tradition exists and enforcement is either non-existent or limited whereas in other regimes building a strong competition and competition law culture and having effective enforcement are extremely important goals, which are taken very seriously, as can be seen from the actions of competition authorities and judicial enforcement in those regimes. The issues of 'tradition' and/or 'enforcement' assume huge importance in practice in light of the adverse consequences a lack of competition law tradition and effective enforcement could trigger,[46] but also because these issues have a direct link to the issue of 'independence' of competition authorities and the separation of competition enforcement and decision-making from politics. The competition authorities in certain regimes do not enjoy sufficient independence and in practice their decision-making powers and enforcement actions are subject to the approval or actions of the government or a minister. The lack of sufficient independence can enhance the political influence in a given competition law regime and possibly the 'politicisation' of enforcement and actions taken within the regime as a whole.

(D)   Institutional approaches

Finally, it would be important to highlight a fundamental difference between competition law regimes around the world relating to the issue of enforcement itself, namely that concerning the 'right' institutional approach that should be adopted. Simply put, significant divergences exist between different regimes in terms of how the competition rules should be applied and who should enforce them and as a result there is a clear lack of consensus regarding the right institutional approach to do this. In some regimes, competition enforcement is handled administratively meaning that an administrative body has full competence in conducting investigations and reaching binding (final) decisions; with of course the possibility being included to seek judicial review or appeal against these decisions.[47] In other regimes, a judicial approach is followed which means that the power to reach final decisions in relation to competition investigations is in the hands of judges who

---

[46] These consequences include uncertainty and the creation of incentives for firms to treat these countries as 'competition law havens', a situation that is likely to lead to distortions of competition in the countries concerned and may even extend beyond domestic boundaries. See D. Gerber, 'Afterword: Antitrust and American Business Abroad Revisited' (2000) *Northwestern Journal of International Law and Business* 307.

[47] The most important example is the EU competition law regime.

hear actions brought by the competition authority or the government or private parties against a firm or group of firms alleged to have committed a competition breach;[48] these actions may include seeking orders or injunctions to put an end to or prevent a particular situation and punish the offending firms or, in the case of private actions, seeking damages. Finally, there are regimes which include a specialist tribunal enjoying the power to conduct review of or hear appeal actions from decisions adopted by the competition authority(ies) and other public bodies armed with the power to enforce competition law (such as sector regulators who can take enforcement actions in their sectors).[49]

(E) Comment on the differences

It is fairly obvious why differences in institutional approaches and the title of the law exist: it is both natural and inevitable that these differences exist when countries differ in many fundamental respects, including legal culture and political system. One may wonder, however, about the other differences in *enforcement* and *how competition and competition law are viewed*. It is perfectly legitimate to ask whether such differences actually exist because of political influence or because non-competition-based considerations are taken into account when deciding actual cases. There is an argument that if different competition rules were to be enforced according to strict competition grounds the same conclusion should be reached by different competition authorities in one and the same situation. At a wider policy level, this could have a positive impact on the internationalisation of competition law: on the one hand it is highly arguable that in this case reaching consensus on internationalisation in a multilateral form would be considerably easier than would be the case otherwise, whilst on the other one could say that probably this would in fact eliminate the need for at least some internationalisation efforts, notably those seeking to build a multilateral agreement or framework since differences would not exist between different regimes.

---

[48] This is the situation prevailing in the USA. See J. P. Griffin, 'What Business People Want From a World Antitrust Code' (1999) *New England Law Review* 39; C. Bellamy, 'Some Reflections on Competition Law in the Global Market' (1999) *New England Law Review* 15.

[49] See the UK competition law regime: the Competition Appeal Tribunal (CAT) can hear such actions concerning decisions of the Office of Fair Trading (OFT), the Competition Commission (CC) and relevant sector regulators (such as the Office of Communications (OFCOM)).

11.   The concept, idea and function of competition

It would be helpful to offer an examination of the concept of competition, its underlying idea and its function in a market economy particularly since the present book deals with the 'international' and 'comparative' aspect of competition law and policy and the perspectives of different countries and competition authorities around the world when applying the law and formulating their policy.

(A)   Meaning of competition

A quick glance at any English language dictionary for the meaning of competition would show that it is defined as a process of rivalry between two or more persons. In a market context, this rivalry is directed towards the custom of people. The basic aim of every firm and businessperson in the real world is to sell their produce to as many customers as possible and to make a profit, or obtain or increase their share of the market. The dictionary meaning of competition has come to form the basis of the various definitions offered by different specialists in the field of competition law; it has also informed the understanding of the concept by competition authorities,[50] courts and specialists. However, these various definitions of the concept have somewhat diverged, especially in relation to whether the emphasis – when defining competition – should be put on it being a 'process' or a 'relationship' between market operators.[51]

At the heart of the concept of competition stands the *freedom to compete*. This means that market operators must have the freedom to compete for a process of competition to exist. In practical terms, this means that a free-market economy must exist:[52] competition is the

---

[50] See, for example, the definition given by the European Commission to the concept of competition in its *Glossary of Terms used in EU Competition Policy* (which incidentally is aimed at non-lawyers). According to the definition competition is a 'situation in a market in which sellers of a product or service independently strive for the patronage of buyers in order to achieve a particular business objective, for example, profits, sales and/or market share. Competitive rivalry between firms may take place in terms of price, quality, service or combinations of these and other factors which customers may value.'

[51] For an account of the 'different meanings' of competition, see R. H. Bork, *The Antitrust Paradox: a Policy at War with Itself* (Basic Books, 1978), pp. 58–61; see also the US case of *White Motor Co.* v. *US*, 372 US 253 (1963).

[52] See R. S. Khemani, 'Competition Policy: an Engine for Growth' (1997) *Global Competition Review* 20.

flywheel of a free economy. The spirit of a free-market economy receives its expression in many cases in the process of competition itself and normally its successful operation is measured in terms of whether a process of competition is the actual or likely result in a given situation within the sphere of economic operations. The freedom to compete means that market operators may not be forced to compete, though steps may be taken in order to promote or facilitate this. However, the freedom in this case does not extend as wide as becoming at liberty to cause harm to the process of competition or to damage its fabrics and the operation of the market as a whole.[53] Where this happens, the outcome is bound to be '*anti*' as opposed to '*pro-*' competitive.

The association of competition in the commercial world with the marketplace makes it particularly evolutionary in substance and dynamic in form.[54] This means that competition continuously evolves and is a highly dynamic process, which is conditioned by wider developments and circumstances both within and outside the marketplace. One of the most remarkable ways in which competition has evolved over the years has been in its becoming a 'global' concept. This has been facilitated by the 'adoption' of the concept by important international organisations, including the Organisation for Economic Cooperation and Development (OECD), the United Nations Conference on Trade and Development (UNCTAD), the World Bank, the International Monetary Fund (IMF) and to a large extent the World Trade Organisation (WTO), as well as by the process of market globalisation and the process of trade liberalisation, which has been sweeping through different countries around the world.

(B) Function of competition

When considering the concept of competition within the field of competition law, the main focus must be on the function of competition. It is this

---

[53] Harm in this case may be caused for example through the exploitation of consumers or customers or the exclusion of competitors through acts of collusion or monopolistic (dominance abusive) conduct as well as through harmful mergers leading to 'concentration' or damage to the competitive structure in the market.

[54] See J. M. Clark, *Competition as a Dynamic Process* (Brookings Institution, 1961), pp. 14–15; E. Mason, 'Monopoly in Law and Economics' (1937) *Yale Law Journal* 34; E. Fox, 'Competition Law and the Agenda for the WTO: Forging the Links of Competition and Trade' (1995) *Pacific-Rimely Law and Policy Journal* 1; Fox, 'Toward World Antitrust and Market Access' (1997) *American Journal of International Law* 1.

particular 'aspect' of competition that has the greatest significance in the field and that has given rise to controversy and triggered serious ideological, philosophical and scientific disagreements. The exact function that competition is meant to perform has been the subject of heated debates and disagreements especially among economists who have argued that it is not possible for the function of competition to be viewed under a single unifying concept; rather it would be important to distinguish between different notions of competition. This shows that the understanding of competition actually differs according to one's economic perception and the 'theory' or 'model' followed. Little wonder therefore that a number of notions of competition have come to be offered in order to explain its function in the marketplace. These notions range from static and customary competition to dynamic competition. Whether developing a number of notions has been a helpful contribution to understanding the concept of competition or competition law itself is a highly debatable matter.

I.   Static or customary competition

Static or customary competition can be considered as the basic form of competition. The primary concern of this notion is that in a market economy it is important to ensure the existence of optimal allocation of resources in order to meet the demand side in the market whilst incurring the lowest possible cost at any given point in time. Customary competition therefore places the interest of consumers at the heart of the market system. Adam Smith was among notable economists who spoke of the 'invisible hand' of the market mechanism to coordinate behaviour and transactions in the marketplace.[55]

II.   Dynamic competition

Dynamic competition on the other hand is a more advanced and sophisticated notion of competition than the static/customary model which involves the idea of achieving an optimal degree of innovation and *overall* economic efficiency. This in effect is what has come to be known as the 'total welfare approach', which means that the focus when considering the benefits of competition must be on the overall benefit to the market and society and not on the sole benefits to consumers.[56]

---

[55] See A. Smith, *The Theory of Moral Sentiments* (A. Millar, 1759).

[56] See P. Crampton, 'Alternative Approaches to Competition Law: Consumer's Surplus, Total Welfare and Non-Efficiency Goals' (1994) *World Competition* 55. WTO, *Annual Report* (WTO, 1997), pp. 39–40.

According to dynamic competition, competition is a continuing process, based on market innovation. This means that competitive advantages enjoyed, for example, from current market oligopolies[57] or positions of market dominance are considered as the outcome of past efficiencies and the firm(s) concerned should be entitled to make use of these efficiencies.[58] In this sense, theorists of dynamic competition – unlike those of customary competition – are not particularly concerned about the existence of economic power and an unbalanced market structure. For them, the significance must be attached to the dynamic nature of competition.

III.   Perfect competition

Perfect competition can be said to present a 'traditional' approach to the market mechanism. The idea behind this traditional approach is intended to provide a simple test, which would be easily understood by non-economists.[59] In particular, the rules of perfect competition are intended to be quite simple to apply and to facilitate the formulation of legal rules without difficulty whilst seeking to apply a common objective. This approach is built on an economic theory which pre-supposes that goods and services will be produced in the most efficient manner under circumstances of perfect competition.[60] What this essentially means is that under such circumstances a maximisation of consumer welfare will occur.[61] It is important in this context to be clear about the meaning of the concept 'consumer welfare'. When consumer welfare is maximised this means that economic efficiency – both

---

[57] An oligopoly situation is taken to exist in markets where – among other indicators or 'ingredients' – there are a few players. See G. J. Stigler, 'A Theory of Oligopoly' (1964) *Journal of Political Economy* 44; A. Ulph, 'Recent Advances in Oligopoly Theory From a Game Theory Perspective' (1987) *Journal of Economic Surveys* 149; R. C. Dolan, 'Price Behavior in Tight Oligopoly' (1984) *Review of Industrial Organization* 160.

[58] See P. Auerbach, *Competition: the Economics of Industrial Change* (Blackwell, 1988). See, however, the views of Schumpeter who emphasised the so-called creative gale of destruction, which shows that competition is not a given virtue as such: J. Schumpeter, *Capitalism, Socialism and Democracy* (Allen and Unwin, 1976).

[59] See F. M. Scherer and D. Ross, *Industrial Market Structure and Economic Performance* (Houghton Mifflin, 1990), chs. 1 and 2; D. Swann, *Competition and Consumer Protection* (Penguin, Harmondsworth, 1979), ch. 3; O. E. Williamson, *Antitrust Economics* (Blackwell, 1987).

[60] See R. Lipsey and A. Chrystal, *An Introduction to Positive Economics* (Oxford University Press, 1995); Williamson, note 59 above.

[61] See R. Lipsey and A. Chrystal, *Principles of Economic Law* (Oxford University Press, 1999).

allocative and productive (and where appropriate dynamic efficiency) – will be achieved, with the result that the wealth of society overall will be *allocated* in the most efficient way. To understand this idea it is important to discuss these three forms of efficiency.

(a) **Productive efficiency**   This form of efficiency is thought to occur in a situation where a producer is able to produce goods and services at the lowest cost possible. In this situation, the wealth of society will be expended at the lowest possible level. The producer will not be inclined to raise its prices (at least not excessively) above cost. The reason is that if it does it is very likely that customers will look for somewhere cheaper to obtain their requirements. In such a case the producer might also attract other competitors into its market. Nor will such a producer reduce its prices below cost because this means that it would be incurring a loss. The almost inevitable and, according to economists, desirable result in this situation is that the cost of producing a unit of output and the price of that unit will coincide.

(b) **Allocative efficiency**   Allocative efficiency (also known as Pareto efficiency) occurs in a situation where the marginal cost (the cost of producing an additional unit of output) and the marginal revenue (the price that the producer would obtain for a unit of production) coincide. Where this occurs, it is supposed that allocative efficiency will be achieved since consumers are able to obtain the product or service they desire at the price they are willing to pay, which in simple terms translates into being the lowest possible price; at the same time the producer is able to continue its production without incurring a loss (in a productive efficiency sense).

(c) **Dynamic efficiency**   Dynamic efficiency is thought to exist in those economies in which an appropriate balance is achieved between short- and long-term concerns and interests of the economy in question. Specifically, the focus under this type of efficiency is given to long-term concerns and interests because these relate to important components of economic developments such as investment, research and development and more generally innovation. Dynamic efficiency has been considered to be extremely important (though interestingly at the same time not necessarily possible to achieve!) because it enables an economy to respond effectively to changes in the wider economic environment and this would enable producers in particular to meet these changes whilst continuously improving economic efficiency.

IV. Workable competition

The reality of the marketplace is considerably different and oftentimes more complex than what a given economic theory advocates. This basic yet crucial fact has been recognised by many scholars who found that in practice this subjects the discipline of economics to a pragmatic pressure to attack the most serious market failures and to construct a framework within which reasonable principles will be established and reasonable behaviour on the part of both regulatory bodies and business firms will occur. As a result, the ultimate goal that must be pursued is to ensure that competition in the marketplace is working. This particular reasoning gave rise to the birth of the notion of 'workable competition'.[62]

The concept of 'workable competition' encompasses an idea that is admittedly different from a (particular) theory (of competition economics) in the sense that it is generally wider. It operates like a norm that changes according to variation in economic theorem and the conditions and structure of the market, such as shifts in the behaviour of firms, the attitude of public institutions, causes and effects of market globalisation and evolution in technological advances. Workable competition therefore presents a realistic approach to the concept of competition and *accepts* that wider circumstances – especially developments in the marketplace – condition this notion and process of competition. Proponents of the model of workable competition believe that as long as competition is workable this will be sufficient. Workable competition therefore falls short of perfect competition in that it is accepted that allocative and productive efficiency under that theory may not be possible to achieve and should not be pursued (in the fullest sense of the word).

The concept of workable competition is not frequently used in practice: usually, reference is made to 'effective' competition, which has not been defined clearly though from the use of the concept it seems fairly clear that this form of competition will be said to exist where competition produces the desired results: whether exerting effective pressure on those

---

[62] See J. M. Clark, 'Towards a Concept of Workable Competition' (1940) *American Economic Review* 241; S. H. Sosnick 'A Critique of Concepts of Workable Competition' (1958) 72 *Quarterly Journal of Economics* 380.

firms with market power or yielding consumer benefits. In light of this, one may form the impression that effective competition is another synonym of workable competition.

(C)   Comments

The entire subject of competition law has developed as such that no study of the subject which lacks an understanding of what competition actually means and what function it performs in a market economy can be justifiable, indeed possible. This means that before one could consider competition law itself – in particular what its aims should be and what role it has in the entire system of economic regulation – it is vital to understand competition as a concept, theory and process.[63] This in practice means there is a need to have an appreciation of economic concepts and principles and the importance of economic analysis: competition is entrenched in economics and economic analysis has become a key feature in the understanding of the concept and the application of competition law.

As we saw in the discussion above it is generally thought that competition is desirable. That discussion explained how the ideological debate between capitalism and communism has settled in favour of relying on markets to deliver better outcomes than state control, planning and monopolisation. This growing recognition of the reliability of markets – at the heart of which lies the process of competition – has been popular in particular among economists, who have consistently argued in favour of the desirability of competition.[64] Some economists have advocated that a successful market economy depends on the existence of competition in the market and an effective competition law and policy; a view shared by the vast majority of competition lawyers around the world. It seems that this increase in popularity has been triggered by the fact that generally monopoly does seem to lead to poor quality, restriction in output and harm to consumers. Moreover, since competition offers the consumer a greater degree of protection and choice, and since *no* suggestion that innovation is only possible in the case of monopoly (because of the existence of resources in the

---

[63] See D. Dewey, 'The Economic Theory of Antitrust: Science or Religion?' (1964) 50 *Virginia Law Review* 413.

[64] See F. S. McChesney, 'In Search of the Public Interest Model of Antitrust' in F. S. McChesney and W. F. Shughart (eds.), *The Causes and Consequences of Antitrust: the Public Choice Perspective* (Chicago University Press, 1995), pp. 25–32.

hands of the monopolist and the absence of distractions in the form of pressures from other market forces) can be sustained, it is very understandable why competition has been popular among economists.[65]

Nevertheless, it is extremely important to realise that this positive attitude to competition and the market system is not universal,[66] nor immune from serious doubts. Throughout the twentieth century – the most remarkable chapter of economic history during which the belief in the market mechanism flourished – and until the present day, the reliability of the market mechanism to deliver has been questioned repeatedly. Those who attempted to point towards the 'deficiencies' of the economic and political model of the *laissez faire* approach have not always been looked at favourably and their advocacy in favour of state intervention and increased regulation have consistently been looked at with suspicion and sometimes labelled as hidden attempts to advocate and promote 'communist' and 'socialist' ideology. The economic turbulence which came to shake some of the world's biggest financial centres in 2008 and 2009 prompting some governments – notably those of the USA and the UK[67] – to take radical measures to intervene in the marketplace simply shows that the debate over the reliability of the market system has been anything but decisively settled. Nonetheless, it is highly arguable that these serious doubts should not extend to competition and the law seeking to protect it. Indeed experience shows that competition has positive outcomes and competition law has an important role to play in developed as well as developing countries, both in creating and promoting a competitive environment and in building and ensuring public support for a general pro-competitive policy stance by different countries.

The different notions of competition which came to be developed over the years share one important 'feature', whilst of course differing in some fundamental ways. This feature concerns the ambiguity of definition and narrowness of viewpoint from which the different notions can be said to suffer. This can be seen especially in the case of the notion of perfect competition. For example, prominent scholars in the USA – most notably Robert Bork – have strongly argued that the *dominant* goal

---

[65] See D. Hay, 'The Assessment: Competition Policy' (1993) *Oxford Review of Economic Policy* 1; G. M. Hodgson, *Economics and Institutions* (Cambridge University Press, 1988).

[66] See pp. 8–9 above.

[67] Among the radical measures here are the nationalisation of two UK banks (Northern Rock and B&B) and the US government's bailout of 'Wall Street' (over $700 billion) and its intervention in the case of Freddie Mac and Fannie Mae among others.

of competition law must be the maximisation of consumer welfare. At the same time however, they appeared to have recognised that US Congress intended to implement a broader spectrum of values than the neoclassical concept of consumer welfare in the enforcement of US competition law.[68] This shows a clear 'failure' in economic theorising to appreciate that the goals advocated – most notably economic efficiency and maximisation of consumer welfare – are far from being the only, or even dominant, goals of competition law.[69] In fairness, economists have made an important contribution to the understanding and application of competition law. However they have proved to be simply unable to develop viable rules and theories suitable for the economic reality of markets and taking into account the implications of variability of business strategies and commercial planning as well as different market behaviours and structures. This inability has been heightened by the fact that economists have not been the most consensus-building community in the world of competition law. Even in relation to the most basic aspects of competition, different economic approaches speak of identical issues differently.[70] Economists have also ventured into a somewhat imaginary world when developing their notions of competition and economic theories which are intended to be used when applying competition law and have – mostly in relation to the notion of perfect competition – quite overlooked the fact that this model of competition does not seem to be possible to realise because markets are disorganised

---

[68] See R. H. Bork, 'The Role of the Courts in Applying Economics' (1985) *Antitrust Law Journal* 2.

[69] The academic criticism of this goal is extensive. See P. C. Carstensen, 'Antitrust Law and the Paradigm of Industrial Organization' (1983) *University of California, Davis Law Review* 487; E. Fox, 'The Modernization of Antitrust: a New Equilibrium' (1981) *Cornell Law Review* 1140; E. Fox, 'The Politics of Law and Economics in Judicial Decision Making: Antitrust as a Window' (1986) *New York University Law Review* 554; R. H. Lande, 'Wealth Transfers as the Original and Primary Concern of Antitrust: the Efficiency Interpretations Challenged' (1982) *Hastings Law Journal* 65; J. May, 'Antitrust Practices in the Formative Era: The Constitutional and Conceptual Reach of State Antitrust Laws, 1880–1918' (1987) *University of Pennsylvania Law Review* 495; L. Orland, 'The Paradox in Bork's Antitrust Paradox' (1987) *Cardozo Law Review* 115; R. Pitofsky, 'The Political Content of Antitrust' (1979) *University of Pennsylvania Law Review* 1051; F. M. Rowe, 'The Decline of Antitrust and the Delusions of Models: the Faustian Pact of Law and Economics' (1984) 72 *Georgetown Law Journal* 1511; L. B. Schwartz, '"Justice" and Other Non-Economic Goals of Antitrust' (1979) *University of Pennsylvania Law Review* 1076; J. J. Flynn, 'Antitrust Jurisprudence: a Symposium on the Economic, Political and Social Goals of Antitrust Policy' (1977) 125 *University of Pennsylvania Law Review* 1182.

[70] See D. Hay 'Competition Policy' (1986) *Oxford Review of Economic Policy* 1.

in substance, complex in structure, and are far from being capable of generating any strains of perfect competition. In this context, it is essential that the discipline of economics becomes more receptive to the importance of other disciplines in the field. The picture that has come to develop regarding the relationship between different disciplines in the field shows the disciplines of law and political science taking full account of the importance of economics and the various economic interpretations but reveals little evidence of the reverse. Economists should be encouraged to remain aware of the fundamental policy questions continuously facing lawyers and the policy designs offered by political scientists. It has become an established fact that the appropriate design of policy is crucial to the successful operation of competition law and policy.[71] Given the important role economics plays in the field of competition law, being aware of policy questions and designs would help economists not only identify *the* inevitable tensions with the disciplines of law and politics but also understand the continuing interactions between economics and politics in particular.

A final point that should be considered in relation to the function of competition is to the evergreen debate about whether competition is an end in itself or a means for attaining some other objective. The answer to this question does not seem to be particularly easy. Nor has the debate been definitely settled in favour of a particular view. One view – which seems to be the more acceptable one – is that competition is a means to achieve economic prosperity and ensure economic fairness in the marketplace.[72] Competition, therefore, is not an ultimate goal in itself, but rather an instrument to enhance the welfare of people and ensure a proper functioning of markets. Protecting competition through law and policy would make little sense if it were not believed that competition would help to achieve such goals. The other less acceptable view seems to be that competition is an end in itself.[73] This view might be

---

[71] See R. Gilpin, *Political Economy of International Relations* (Princeton University Press, 1987); M. E. Porter, *The Competitive Advantage of Nations* (Macmillan, 1989); K. Ohmae, *The Borderless World: Power and Strategy in the Interlinked Economy* (Harper-Collins, 1994).

[72] This seems to be the prevailing view, according to many scholars. See Bellamy, p. 16, note 48 above; Ehlermann and Laudati, pp. 123–4, note 29 above.

[73] It is interesting to note the judgment of the European Court of Justice delivered on October 2009 in Case C-501/06, *GlaxoSmithKline Services* v. *Commission* [2009] ECR 0000 in which the Court ruled that the purpose of EU competition rules is to protect 'not only the interests of competitors or of consumers, but also the structure of the market and, in so doing, competition as such'.

justified with reference to the US competition law regime, for example, in the case where Jeffersonian or atomistic competition is simply pursued to the end of having many small, independent businesses. Indeed, this was a motivation behind the Celler-Kaufer Act 1950 when US Congress amended the merger provisions of the Clayton Act 1914.[74] It could be argued, however, that this can be reduced to an argument that competition is a means to achieve some other purpose, since in this case it is striving for perfect competition and thus maximising consumer welfare. Equally though this idea of having a thriving small business culture seems to be an end in itself.

12. Competition law: concept, framework, goals, characteristics and nature

Many aspects of competition law have given rise to serious disagreements among those who deal with competition law in one way or another. More likely than not, any debate on competition law is liable to end in a disagreement or at least lack of full consensus; such is the 'unique' nature of competition law which simply always invites debate. The inevitable competition law debates and probable disagreements extend to the concept of competition law, the framework within which it should operate, the goals that should be sought when applying the law and whether there is a political perspective to competition law. In relation to the actual application of competition law, the debate and lack of consensus have extended to a variety of important issues, such as those dealing with economic analysis.

(A)   The 'concept' of competition law

There are a number of observations that could be made about the 'concept' of competition law on which almost everyone would agree. The first – and most basic – of these observations relates to the wording of competition law: competition law is generally negative and prohibitory in wording.[75] This is obvious since competition law does not *directly* encourage competition or force firms to compete, but rather seeks – through the employment of specific rules – to prevent or

---

[74] See pp. 244–245 below.
[75] See H. First, 'Antitrust Law' in A. B. Morrison (ed.), *Fundamentals of American Law* (Oxford University Press, 1996); Bork, p. 70, note 51 above.

eliminate any situation deemed harmful to competition and in this way protect competition; this covers a variety of situations stretching from those of anticompetitive behaviour and abusive conduct to problematic merger operations.[76] In the EU, for example, Article 101(1) of the Treaty on the Functioning of the European Union (TFEU) (ex Article 81(1) EC) provides that collusion between firms is *prohibited* and Article 102 TFEU (ex Article 82 EC) states that abuse of dominance is also *prohibited*.[77] In a similar manner, section 1 of the Sherman Act 1890 in the USA declares that entering into practices in restraint of trade or commerce is *prohibited* and section 2 of the Act makes it clear that monopolisation or attempts to monopolise are also *prohibited*.[78] In none of these provisions is there any mention of 'encouraging competition' or of 'compelling' firms to compete. Nevertheless, arguably the use of competition law to protect competition has been widened, at least on some occasions, to encompass the idea of *ensuring* that firms compete.

Another 'consensus-oriented' point that could be made about the concept of competition law is that competition needs law as a form of expression. Over the years, an overall view has emerged to this effect: protecting competition by law is considered to be important in order to guarantee the benefits of the market mechanism. This can be seen especially in light of how the enforcement of competition law has over the years helped eradicate harmful situations, principally hardcore cartels and serious abuses of dominance.

The fact that law is used to protect competition has raised a number of questions, some of which are highly interesting whilst others have been remarkably difficult. It is widely accepted that over the years the idea of competition has adapted to, among other things, evolving intellectual influences within the discipline of economics as well as legal and political changes; and to a certain extent to cultural and social changes, some of which shaped the idea of competition from the outset. As a result, it has become endlessly debatable as to what form a law aimed at protecting competition should take and what its scope should be. Among the recurring questions concerning the scope of competition law the following have always ranked high: whether

---

[76] This definition corresponds to other definitions employed by different writers. See D. P. Fidler, 'Competition Law and International Relations' (1992) *International and Comparative Law Quarterly* 563.
[77] See p. 161 below   [78] See pp. 238–243 below.

competition law should be concerned with regulating uses of power by large firms *or* with the removal of hindrances to free competition; whether it should (and in practice it is actually used to) protect competitors *and/or* the process of competition;[79] and whether it is or should be more concerned with the interests of consumers *than* the interests of producers. The fundamental differences between competition law regimes around the world as described above – such as those concerning the type of procedures and mechanisms that should be relied on to enforce competition law – have rendered such questions more interesting but they have also made them more difficult.

Quite frequently reference will be made in the present book to a 'competition law regime'. It is useful to note that the concept of regime in this context includes all of the following three different components: a process of competition; competition law; and competition policy.

(B)   Framework of competition law: common or typical provisions

Across the world, the competition rules of different regimes feature a number of common or typical provisions, which in practice serve as the 'avenues' through which competition law protects competition and which centre around addressing key concerns.

I.   Prohibition on 'collusion' in horizontal and vertical situations

The most important of these provisions is the one which seeks to ensure that firms do not harm, prevent or distort competition through collusion with their actual or potential competitors. In broad terms, such provision prohibits horizontal agreements, practices or conspiracies between independent firms, such as those aiming at price-fixing, market-sharing, output limitation, bid-rigging or other important aspects of the firms' competitive interaction. These situations are commonly referred to as 'cartels' and considered to be among the most serious breaches of competition law. However, it is important to note that the simple fact that a horizontal agreement is entered into is not necessarily objectionable nor should such an agreement be treated with suspicion simply because it is an agreement between competitors: some horizontal agreements are particularly beneficial to competition and consumers and

---

[79] See pp. 59–60 below.

mostly they lead to pro-competitive outcomes. The most obvious examples of these agreements are those concerning research and development (R&D), specialisation and standard-setting.[80] These agreements are generally not prohibited but they may be subject to specific regulation.[81] The prohibition on collusion normally extends to non-horizontal or vertical agreements, namely those agreements entered into between firms operating at different levels in the economy or market. The most common type of these agreements is a distribution agreement entered into between a supplier and a distributor. Vertical agreements are very common in practice and they are less likely to harm competition than horizontal agreements principally because of the absence of a relationship of actual competitors between the parties. Nonetheless, they may feature certain anticompetitive restraints and in practice could lead to harmful outcomes, particularly in economies in transition or developing ones. For example, a vertical agreement may contain a resale-price maintenance clause, an export ban or restrictions on sale to certain customers or other distributors. As a result, the agreement may lead to a reduction of inter-brand and/or intra-brand competition.[82] Hence, vertical agreements may also be addressed under competition law. This may take the form of an instrument seeking to regulate these agreements by outlining those restraints which would be exempted and those which would not and setting out a particular threshold – taking the form of the market share held by the supplier and/or the distributor – which determines the scope of the exemption under the relevant instrument.[83]

---

[80] For a good discussion of these types of agreements, see the *European Commission's Guidelines for the Assessment of Horizontal Cooperation Agreements* (2000) *Official Journal* C-3/2. Note however the problem which may arise in situations of standard setting in the context of access by firms to foreign markets which is discussed at p. 587 below.

[81] In several jurisdictions, a block exemption approach is adopted to these types of horizontal agreements. See, for example, EU Block Exemption Regulations: Regulation 2658/2000 on the application of Article 81(3) of the Treaty to categories of specialisation agreements (2000) OJ L 304/3 and Regulation 2659/2000 on the application of Article 81(3) of the Treaty to categories of research and development agreements (2000) OJ L-304/7.

[82] Inter-brand competition concerns competition between different products whereas intra-brand competition concerns competition in relation to one product. In the case of the latter, this will be competition between different distributors handling the same product.

[83] See, for example, the EU block exemption regime for vertical agreements; see further chapter 4.

II.   Prohibition on abuse of dominance
or monopolisation

A second common provision found in competition laws around the world is that dealing with the business phenomenon of abuse of dominance or monopolisation. There are many situations in which a firm or firms that enjoy a position of economic power or strength may be able to harm competition individually or collectively through acting unilaterally. The prohibition on abuse of dominance assumes enormous significance in practice and is considered to be complementary to the prohibition on collusion. However, it is a provision that has given rise to serious difficulties and has provoked controversies. On the one hand, determining whether the prohibition should bite in a particular case requires establishing first and foremost the existence of a dominant position or economic strength. In most, if not almost all, cases this is never an easy task especially since it requires defining the relevant market.[84] On the other hand, there is a difficulty in establishing a coherent policy[85] on how interventionist a competition authority should be in relation to the way in which firms choose to build a position of market power or make use of this power. Achieving economic strength is usually extremely challenging and requires considerable investment and phenomenally hard work by the firm(s) concerned. It should be (and in practice it is generally) accepted that when a firm achieves such a position by winning the competitive struggle lawfully it should not be punished for its superior performance. However, there is no reason to believe that this means that economic strength may be employed by the dominant firm or firms for example to prevent or restrict competition from existing or to prevent or restrict potential competitors from entering the market. In practice, the 'use' of dominance or economic power is subject to carefully crafted provisions in competition law which are employed to strike a balance between legitimate behaviour (which often is referred to as attempts to 'meet' competition) and illegal behaviour (which is abusive and aims to 'defeat' competition) on the part of a dominant firm.

---

[84] See pp. 70–77 below concerning the exercise of market definition.
[85] See the *European Commission's Guidance on Enforcement Priorities in Applying Article 82 of the Treaty to Abusive Exclusionary Conduct by Dominant Undertakings* (2008); the Canadian Competition Bureau, *Information Bulletin on the Abuse of Dominance Provisions as Applied to the Telecommunications Industry* (2008); T. Hoppner, *Abuse of Market Dominance: The Refusal to Supply Competitors under Article 82 EC* (VDM Verlag Dr. Muller Aktiengesellschaft & Co. KG, 2009).

III.   Regulating mergers

In most but not all competition law regimes around the world there is an instrument seeking to control merger operations or situations. A merger (also referred to sometimes as 'concentration' or 'combination') may occur in a variety of ways, through: amalgamation (the pure merger situation) where two or more firms merge to become a single entity; acquisition of control, whether sole or joint control of a firm; and the creation of a full-function joint venture, an autonomous, independent entity by two or more firms which is intended to operate on a lasting basis. Firms might elect to merge in order to become more efficient, something that will improve market conditions and structures, thus generating greater benefit to consumers. But some mergers may have anticompetitive effects: they may intend to reduce or lessen competition in the market and to artificially create or strengthen a dominant position which is not based on superior economic performance achieved through lawful means.[86] The creation of a merger may lead to a decrease in the number of competitors in the market, thus enabling the merged entity to – unilaterally or through coordinated strategy with remaining firms on the market – cause adverse effects on the market. Merger regulation is therefore an important instrument for the purposes of maintaining a particular market structure, which would facilitate effective competition.

There are several types of merger operations which may fall within the scope of competition law. These include horizontal mergers, vertical mergers and conglomerate mergers;[87] in addition to the full-function joint venture situation.

IV.   Other provisions

In some competition law regimes, the rules contain provisions dealing with business phenomena or situations other than those mentioned

---

[86] For an analysis of this concept of economic performance see M. Dabbah, 'Conduct, Dominance and Abuse in "Market Relationships": Analysis of Some Conceptual Issues Under Article 82 EC' (2000) *European Competition Law Review* 45.

[87] It is important to note that the same merger operation may have 'horizontal', 'vertical' and 'conglomerate' elements. The classification of these elements depends on the relationship between the merging firms: whether they are competitors (horizontal merger or element); whether they are firms operating at different levels of the market (vertical merger or element); or whether there is neither a horizontal nor vertical relationship (conglomerate merger). Moreover, conglomerate mergers can be of: market extension type (the merging firms make the same product in different geographic areas, with no overlap between these); production or product line extension type (where the merging firms make complementary products); or pure conglomerate (no relationship or link between the products of the merging firms).

above. For example, there may be a provision dealing with state aid: situations in which a government grants 'aid' – such as privileges or benefits – to national firms which puts them at a competitive disadvantage vis-à-vis foreign firms. This has particular significance in 'regional' settings where different countries may have committed themselves to a principle of non-discrimination and have accepted the effectiveness and applicability of the relevant regional competition rules in their own legal systems.[88] Moreover, the relevant competition law may contain a prohibition on collusion or abuse of dominance by public firms or in relation to those sectors of the economy which have general interest;[89] though in other regimes the competition law may simply remove such firms or sectors from the scope of it altogether.[90] Finally, in some competition law regimes the scope of the rules may extend to situations which many do not regard as 'competition' issues but which in many cases arguably do have competition relevance; for example, the rules may cover situations of price regulation or trade regulation.[91]

(C) The goals of competition law

Perhaps no aspect of the field of competition law has given rise to a more heated debate than the issue of the goals of competition law. The question of what the goals of competition law should be is simply one of the oldest and most important questions in the field which has branched out beyond the national level towards the regional and international levels.[92] This question – notwithstanding the phenomenal literature dealing with it and the attention given to it by competition authorities and courts, not to mention the views on how it should be answered – has remained to the present day simply unanswered. In fairness, this should not be highly surprising given the remarkable changing nature and state of competition and its continuing evolution which have contributed to the particularly fluid nature of competition law. There is a difficulty in unveiling the 'identity' of competition law and determining what its goals should be in a single competition law

---

[88] The most notable example here is the EU; see Art. 107 TFEU (ex Art. 87 EC).

[89] See Art. 106 TFEU (ex Art. 86 EC).

[90] See, for example, Art. 19 of the Law on Competition and Monopolistic Practices 2005 of Egypt.

[91] See pp. 321–323 below for a discussion of the situation in which competition rules may be mixed with these elements in the same law.

[92] See Ehlermann and Laudati, p. 3, note 29 above.

regime, let alone attempting to do this across a global spectrum by considering all competition laws around the world.[93] One may wonder whether this difficulty is possible to overcome, if this is at all a desirable thing to do. Nevertheless, it should be acknowledged that determining what the goals of competition law are is a precondition to a number of important things: rationalising competition policy;[94] building a body of coherent rules; and ultimately guaranteeing a proper functioning of a competition law regime.[95]

I. What is required?

A search for the goals of competition law requires, among other things, an awareness of why the relevant competition law regime was established, what legislative intent stood behind the enactment of the rules in the regime and how the regime has developed. A word of caution however is necessary in relation to the issue of legislative intent. The search for the goals of competition law is not confined strictly to the search of legislative intent behind the formulation of the law. One ought to realise too that other factors have, or are capable of having, a direct impact on how the search for goals should be conducted and what its results are likely to be. For this reason, a heavy emphasis amongst lawyers on legislative intent could lead to a great narrowness of viewpoint.[96] The issue of legislative intent is pertinent for discovering the motivation behind the enactment of a particular competition law by a group of legislators at a particular time. This point deserves specific emphasis because competition law does not stand in isolation but rather stands within a wider framework, which includes not only all components of the relevant competition law regime but also social, economic, cultural and political elements prevailing in the country concerned. This means that competition law belongs to an order, where different disciplines, factors and interests are interwoven and which all evolve constantly, and all according to changes related to the relevant time

---

[93] See R. H. Bork, *The Tempting of America* (Sinclair-Stevenson, 1990), pp. 331–3.

[94] See Bork, p. 50, note 51 above.

[95] A proper functioning of a competition law regime includes the need to have legal certainty for the 'subjects' of competition law, most notably business firms so they could plan their behaviour, conduct or operations with more confidence and consider all the implications from those.

[96] See J. J. Flynn, 'The Reagan Administration's Antitrust Policy, "Original Intent" and the Legislative History of the Sherman Act' (1988) 83 *Antitrust Bulletin* 259.

period.[97] Even within the same jurisdiction, changes may occur over time. These include changes in the mix of goals of competition law, the extent to which public intervention is acceptable and those related to acceptable assumptions about the marketplace. One must not lose sight of the fact that market conditions are not static, rather they may be influenced by various currents and so the understanding of competition law changes accordingly. Thus, placing a particular emphasis on legislative intent would lead to overlooking the importance of other issues, which are crucial in determining the goals of competition law.

There is limited evidence that establishing awareness of the reasons for enacting a competition law and building a competition law regime and the way in which this regime has developed has been attempted in all parts of the world. In the USA this has been done and this perhaps explains the superiority of American scholarship in the field of competition law. In the EU – the USA's rival for world dominance in the field of competition law – this has not been done to the same extent.[98] In other parts of the world, such efforts have been far less noticeable and in the case of many regimes they have been simply non-existent. However, even if one is to ignore the lack of awareness in this respect, there is no consensus on the issue of goals and what these should be. Several goals have been claimed in the name of competition law and the 'possibilities' here range from economic to social to even wider (political) goals. Some of these goals have been recognised throughout all competition law regimes around the world; most obviously the goal of enhancing economic efficiency and maximising consumer welfare. Other goals have consistently been the subject of uncertainty; most remarkable are the goals of protecting competitors, in particular small and medium firms,[99] the goal of promoting consumer welfare in a non-technical sense and the goal of safeguarding democratic values and principles in the marketplace. Finally, there are those goals that have been unique to particular parts of the world or special sectors of the economy, for example: the use of competition law as a means of facilitating the move from monopolisation to de-monopolisation and from state control and planning to liberalisation and privatisation as has been the case with several countries in Africa, the Middle East and

---

[97] See Report of the American Bar Association, note 45 above.
[98] See D. Gerber, *Law and Competition in Twentieth Century Europe* (Oxford University Press, 1998).
[99] See Bellamy, note 48 above.

Latin America;[100] the goal of furthering market integration among regional communities as has happened in the EU; and the goal of safeguarding the public interest, such as ensuring the plurality of the media, protecting employment or furthering regional development within countries through creating jobs and investment opportunities.

The lack of clear consensus on goals may be considered to not generally matter very much to the extent that it is thought that on the one hand competition is 'good' (and on that basis it should be encouraged) and on the other all anticompetitive restraints are 'bad' (and on that basis they ought to be condemned and eradicated).[101] However, not all countries believe that competition is good and in some of those countries, even where a competition law regime has been built, competition and competition law and policy do not seem to be taken seriously. This state of affairs adds to the importance of the debate on what the goals of competition law should be and makes it particularly necessary to consider the issue of goals.

II. Identifying the different goals

When considering the goals of competition law it is vital to adopt an 'open-mind' approach. In addition to having an appreciation of the fact that different competition laws around the world do have different goals, it needs to be acknowledged that under a particular competition law regime, different provisions may aim to achieve different goals which may in turn all fall along a spectrum of different policies.[102] This means that when identifying the goals of competition law, one must consider the various provisions of the relevant competition law and analyse them in terms of the policies underlying them.

Over the years, many goals have been advocated under competition law. The 'list' of goals that has emerged is not exhaustive however, nor does the fact that a particular goal appears on the list indicate that such a goal is definitely conclusive. Broadly speaking, the different goals – as referred to in statements of political institutions, decisions and statements of competition authorities, judgment of courts and the work of academics and practitioners – may be divided along the lines of three categories: economic, social and political.

---

[100] See further chapter 6 below.
[101] B. Doern and S. Wilks, *Comparative Competition Policy* (Oxford University Press, 1996).
[102] See WTO *Annual Report* (1997), p. 39. Also, see Bellamy, note 48 above, where the author talks about competition law being placed in 'a broader social compact'.

(a) **Economic goals**   The first category includes goals that concern primarily issues of economic efficiency and maximisation of consumer welfare. Achieving economic efficiency and maximising consumer welfare are today considered the main goals of competition law. As we saw above, economic efficiency is measured in terms of productive, allocative and in some cases dynamic efficiency. There is little consensus on which of these types should be emphasised in the actual application of competition law. Conversely, there is no total consensus that the best way to measure welfare in the field of competition law should be in terms of consumer benefits: it has been argued that the more appropriate welfare standard to be used in the field of competition law should be that of total welfare, namely as long as welfare is maximised in a total sense, and not necessarily in a consumer-specific context, this should be sufficient. The *consumer welfare versus total welfare* approach remains a highly contested matter in the field of competition law. In most competition law regimes, the declared approach is that of consumer welfare and in some regimes a heavy emphasis has come to be placed on consumer interests in the enforcement of competition law which can be seen in light of how certain competition authorities are either *mandated* with consumer protection or make specific efforts to *advocate* that they are both a 'competition' and 'consumer' body.[103] However, what is interesting to ask is whether the authorities in those regimes embracing a consumer welfare standard consistently follow such a standard in their actual practice. It seems to be that this has not always been the case and this has been partly caused by the lack of sufficient consensual decisiveness on the part of economists on the issue of goals.

For the discipline of economics, economic efficiency and the max-imisation of consumer welfare are the underlying aims of competition law. The general assumption among economists is that enhancing economic efficiency – in order to achieve lower prices, increase choice, and improve product quality for the benefit of the consumer – is the primary purpose of competition law. Leading US economists, such as Bork, for example, have argued that in the USA the only legitimate goal of competition law is the maximisation of consumer welfare and there-fore competition, for the purposes of competition law analysis, must be understood as a term of art signifying any state of affairs in which

---

[103] Notable examples include the US Federal Trade Commission, the Australian Competition and Consumer Commission, the UK Office of Fair Trading and the European Commission.

consumer welfare cannot be increased by judicial decision-making.[104] Bork has also argued that when it enacted the Sherman Act 1890,[105] US Congress intended the courts to take into account when deciding competition cases only that value which has come to be known today as consumer welfare. To put this point another way, according to Bork, the policy the courts were intended to apply was the maximisation of wealth or consumer want satisfaction. This, in Bork's opinion, requires courts to distinguish between agreements or activities that increase wealth through efficiency and those that decrease it through harmful practices or situations.[106]

Beyond the specific goals of economic efficiency and maximisation of welfare, the category of economic goals includes those of the promotion of trade, facilitating economic liberalisation (including privatisation) and enhancing the development of a market economy.[107] These goals are particularly relevant in relation to those countries with economies in transition. These countries often include competition law in the relevant legislative package of 'economic modernisation' measures,[108] which are specifically adopted to facilitate a process of liberalisation in different sectors of the economy and ensure that harmful anticompetitive outcomes would not arise from this process.

(b) Social goals   The second category of social goals covers a variety of situations, including the idea of consumer protection other than in the above-mentioned technical sense of economic efficiency and maximisation of consumer welfare. The possible social goals or values which may be sought in the application of competition law include: safeguarding the consumer from undue exercise of market power; the dispersion of

---

[104] See Bork, p. 51, note 51 above.   [105] See below for an account of the Act.

[106] See R. H. Bork, 'Legislative Intent and the Policy of the Sherman Act' (1966) *Journal of Law and Economics* 7.

[107] See E. Fox and L. A. Sullivan, 'Antitrust – Retrospective and Prospective: Where are We Coming From? Where are We Going?' (1987) *New York University Law Review* 936; K. G. Elzinga, 'The Goals of Antitrust: Other Than Competition and Efficiency, What Else Counts?' (1977) 125 *University of Pennsylvania Law Review* 1191; L. A. Sullivan, 'Economics and More Humanistic Disciplines: What are the Sources of Wisdom for Antitrust?' (1977) 125 *University of Pennsylvania Law Review* 1214; J. F. Brodley, 'The Economic Goals of Antitrust: Efficiency, Consumer Welfare, and Technological Progress' (1987) *New York University Law Review* 1020.

[108] These measures include laws and regulations, such as privatisation law, intellectual property law, corporate governance regulations and commercial agency laws and sectoral rules (especially in the fields of telecommunications, gas and electricity).

socio-economic power of large firms; safeguarding the opportunities and interests of small and medium-size firms; the protection of democratic values and principles; the protection of 'public interest' and important non-economic values; and ensuring market fairness and equity mainly though wealth distribution in society.[109] An approach to competition law which embraces a social goal or objective *rests* on an antipathy towards the risks of private power and receives legitimacy from the principles of justice and economic equity in a market democracy. Former US President Franklin Roosevelt once warned that the liberty of democracy can be threatened if the people tolerate the growth of private power to a point where it becomes stronger than their democratic state itself.[110] In this context, competition law in the USA has been seen by many as an instrument to ensure that such a situation would not arise.[111] For this reason, the primary concern of competition law should not be to achieve economic goals but rather safeguard important social and economic values which are seen as underlying the legislative history of the first competition instrument in the USA, namely the Sherman Act 1890.[112]

(c) **Broader (political) goals**   Advocating or even discussing the existence of a third category of wider political goals may at first glance appear to be questionable. At a basic level, this category may be considered to overlap with the category of social goals and at least some of the goals within the category may be considered to be of social and not political 'orientation'. Furthermore, both lawyers and economists are always keen to 'remove' competition law from any political context: lawyers are usually concerned over a political connotation to competition law which is often seen as a perfect recipe for uncertainty and controversy whereas economists always vehemently argue against developing any political dimension to competition law because this is seen amongst other things as a threat to the prominence economists enjoy in the

---

[109] G. Amato, *Antitrust and the Bounds of Power* (Hart Publishing, 1997), pp. 2–3.

[110] Franklin D. Roosevelt Library, New York, File 277.
   It has been argued, however, that principles of fairness and equity normally advantage inefficient firms and disadvantage the most efficient ones. See F. H. Easterbrook, 'The Limits of Antitrust' (1984) 63 *Texas Law Review* 1; Briggs, Pogue, Recheteller and Whiting, 'Interview with James Miller chairman of FTC'. Furthermore, there seems to be some indication that these principles have ceased to be taken into account under US competition law; see *NYNEX Corp.* v. *Discon, Inc.* 119 S. Ct. 493 (1998).

[111] See further the discussion in chapter 5.   [112] See Lande, note 69 above.

field. Nevertheless, it cannot be denied that there is a political dimension to competition law and competition enforcement in particular: many competition authorities may find themselves influenced in their decisions by political considerations; several situations may arise in practice in which decisions by politicians prevail over decisions of the competition authority;[113] some political decisions simply mean that competition law will be pushed to one side; and in some competition law regimes the primary actor is a politician who simply plays a leading role in determining the enforcement agenda and actions in individual cases.[114] The political dimension also extends to the recognised goals of competition law in certain parts of the world. These goals relate to wider *overriding* political aims, such as those relating to the process of integration in communities based on economic unions and free trade areas, the promotion of national interests globally and enhancing the international competitiveness of domestic firms and industries as well as dealing with particular national issues such as economic developments, financial stability and soundness, unemployment and safeguarding important interests, such as those of plurality of the media and social security.

The justification for recognising a third category of goals for competition law along such wider political lines is grounded – other than on the recognition of these goals in some jurisdictions[115] – by the fact that competition law is related to experience.[116] As will become apparent in light of the discussion in chapter 4, the situation in the EU furnishes an illustrative example in this regard. In the case of the EU, competition law is recognised as an important tool in achieving the goal of market integration and there are many cases in practice in which what led to a finding of anticompetitive situation was not the actual or likely decrease in economic efficiency or minimisation of consumer welfare but rather the view that the situation hindered the single market objective and amounted to an actual or potential affront to this goal.[117] Therefore,

---

[113] See, for example, the mechanism of ministerial authorisation in the German competition law regime under which where the German Federal Cartel Office (FCO) blocks a merger the merging parties may seek 'authorisation' from the relevant minister which if granted would result in the decision of the FCO being reversed and the merger cleared.

[114] See the discussion in chapter 6 in relation to developing countries.

[115] See M. Dabbah, 'The Internationalisation of EC Competition Policy' in I. Akopova, B. Bothe, M. Dabbah, L. Entin and S. Vodolgin (eds.), *The Russian Federation and European Law* (Hopma, 2001).

[116] See M. Lerner (ed.), *The Mind and Faith of Justice Holmes: His Speeches, Essays, Letters, and Judicial Opinion* (Random House, 1943), pp. 51–4.

[117] See pp. 164–165 below.

when examining competition law, one ought not to generalise about the classification of goals: the manner in which competition law is interpreted and applied in different jurisdictions demonstrates that there are many situations in which it can be used, other than the above-mentioned categories of economic and social goals.[118] These situations as we noted can relate to specific sectors in the national economy, or even interstate sectors within a regional setting.[119]

III.   A brief comment on the classification of goals

The three broad categories of goals identified above are somewhat *in competition* with each other;[120] the categories are therefore not fully compatible and they cover diverse interests. This has a number of consequences in practice, the most notable of these is the difficulty in making such diverse interests consistent or converge with one another. For this reason, forging common grounds and fostering international standards in the field become harder to achieve and this has implications specifically for the internationalisation of competition law[121] and within it the process of convergence and harmonisation between different competition law regimes more particularly.[122]

(D)   Characteristics of competition law

A discussion on the goals of competition law should be complemented with one on 'characteristics'. A number of characteristics of competition law are important to outline, namely: prohibition; regulation; exemption and exclusion; and penalties.

I.   Prohibition

The first characteristic of competition law that should be mentioned is that of prohibition. The discussion above showed how competition law is prohibitory in nature and negative in its wording. A legal provision containing prohibition is interpreted liberally and applied extremely widely in practice in the field of competition law. On occasion this

---

[118] For a comparative study see *Competition Policy in the OECD Countries* (OECD, 1986).

[119] See C. D. Ehlermann, 'The Contribution of the EC Competition Policy to the Single Market' (1992) 29 *Common Market Law Review* 257.

[120] See E. U. Petersmann, 'Legal, Economic and Political Objectives of National and International Competition Policies: Constitutional Functions of WTO "Linking Principles for Trade and Competition"' (1999) 34 *New England Law Review* 145, 155.

[121] See chapter 2.   [122] See the discussion in chapter 10 on this process.

means that the relevant competition authority or court applies the prohibition despite the fact that literally the provision does not cover the relevant situation by relying on the 'spirit' of the prohibition to condemn the behaviour, conduct or operation at hand. An example of this is where the prohibition – on the basis of its wording – extends only to 'agreements' or 'contracts' whereas in the relevant situation the competition authority or court is unable to point towards the existence of any form or an agreement but may believe that a form of coordination of competitive behaviour between independent firms exists.[123] Another example is found in those cases where a prohibition on abusive conduct may be used to control merger operations, taking the view in this case that the contemplated merger may lead to substantial lessening of competition or strengthening of market power, and this in itself may be considered to be an abuse of market power.[124]

II.   Regulation

Competition law contains an element of regulation. A regulatory approach is adopted in relation to business phenomena where it would

[123] A recent case in point is the *Cement Cartel* investigated by Egyptian Competition Authority (ECA) and ruled on by the Egyptian Criminal Court in August 2008. Among other things, the case shows that the ECA is willing to infer from that circumstances than an 'agreement' exists. In this case the ECA conducted a comprehensive study on the Egyptian cement market following a request received by the Minister of Trade and Industry so as to find out whether unjustified increases in price were the result of anticompetitive conduct. After collecting a wealth of information on the output and production capabilities of cement companies and data from governmental and non-governmental bodies the evidence was examined and analysed in both legal and economic terms. The ECA finally concluded that there was a cartel in the cement market involving agreements between cement producers on prices and to restrict the marketing of products. The ECA in the case went beyond finding positive evidence of an agreement to looking at the economic reality of the situation and on that basis it concluded that the situation in question amounted to an infringement of the prohibition on collusion. See M. Dabbah, jurisdictional chapter on 'Egypt' in M. Dabbah and B. Hawk, *Anti-cartel Enforcement Worldwide* (Cambridge University Press, 2009).

[124] Perhaps the most high-profile case in which this has occurred is Case C-6/72, *Continental Can* v. *Commission* (1973) ECR 215, judgment of the European Court of Justice. The European Commission had ruled that the proposed acquisition by a subsidiary of the Continental Can group fell within the scope of Art. 102 TFEU (ex Art. 82 EC) which prohibits an abuse of a dominant position; the case arose at a time when the EU competition law regime lacked a specific merger control instrument, which ultimately came to be adopted in 1989 (Regulation 4064/89). In its judgment, the ECJ – although disagreeing with the conclusions of the Commission in the case – upheld that Art. 102 TFEU could be used to control merger operations notwithstanding the absence of any reference to such operations in the wording of the Article.

be necessary to conduct an analysis in order to determine the anti-
(harmful) and pro- (beneficial) competitive effects. This is normally
used in the areas of merger control and vertical agreements. The use of
regulation is in such areas a more sound alternative to an approach
embedded in outright prohibition, what is usually termed a *per se*
approach. It enables a competition authority or court to take into
account the beneficial aspects or effects in the relevant situation and
this can be decisive in reaching a decision of compatibility with the
relevant provision(s) of the law; in this case the competition authority
follows what is referred to in some jurisdictions as *a rule of reason*
approach.[125]

III.   Exemption and exclusion

The availability of an exempting provision in a competition law is vital
for certain situations – notwithstanding their anticompetitive effect – to
be declared ultimately not to be within the scope of the prohibition
because of crucial benefits outweighing such effect. The issue of exemption overlaps with that of 'regulation' and in some competition
law regimes the exemption is operated within the framework of a
'Regulation'.[126] In practice, granting or obtaining an exemption depends
on the types of pro-competitive aspects present in the relevant situation
and whether these satisfy the exemption criteria set out in the relevant
provision. Normally, these criteria are worded in vague language and in
some cases they allow for non-competition considerations to be taken
into account. A notable example of such vague wording includes references to: consumers obtaining a 'fair share' in the relevant beneficial
situation whereas a notable example of a criterion arguably allowing
non-competition considerations to be taken into account includes references to 'technical and economic progress' and 'international competitiveness'. Obviously, vagueness in terminology can be said to invite legal
uncertainty though in fairness it should be noted that the exempting
provisions are normally interpreted and applied *restrictively*; this is
unlike the approach followed with regard to prohibition itself as noted
above.

---

[125] The US competition law regime furnishes a good example of a regime which employs a
rule of reason approach and a *per se* approach. See pp. 240–242 below.

[126] See, for example, the EU competition law regime which has a number of 'block
exemption Regulations'. The word 'Regulation' in this context however refers to the
name of the instrument; see p. 162 below.

A highly practical and pragmatic approach that some competition authorities follow in practice in relation to exemptions is that of the adoption and use of block exemptions. A block exemption represents a collective approach to a type or types of situation and takes the form of a 'Regulation' or 'Communiqué', among other forms of legislative instruments. Essentially the approach followed in these instruments is one that seeks to set out restrictions which are never tolerated and are therefore 'black-listed' because they are perceived to be anticompetitive (hardcore restrictions). This includes restrictions aiming at harmful practices such as those of price-fixing and market and customer allocation. The relevant instrument may also contain a list of provisions which must be present in a given situation in order to benefit from block exemption. This is normally referred to as a 'white-list'. In recent years, the approach incorporated into block exemption instruments has become more economic-based and usually focuses on the 'effects' of the situation (and thus does not require the existence of white-list clauses). This economic (and pragmatic) approach can be seen especially in light of the use of market share thresholds in determining the applicability of the relevant block exemption instrument.[127]

In addition to exemptions, it is possible for a competition law to contain a number of exclusions, which may concern a variety of sectors of the economy, different types of firms or different kinds of business phenomena. For example, it is possible that the prohibition on collusion may not apply to vertical agreements because a legislative decision was made to exclude these from the scope of the prohibition; or to exclude certain merger operations from the same prohibition; or to exclude certain regulated industries from the scope of the competition rules altogether. Finally, as we noted above certain types of firms may be excluded from the scope of the competition law.[128]

IV. Penalties

The availability of penalties in a competition law regime and the ability of a public body – whether a court or a competition authority – to impose penalties in actual cases is extremely crucial in order to, among

---

[127] See, for example, EU Regulation — on vertical agreements which contains a market share threshold of 30%, namely the supplier and the buyer must have a market share of less than 30% in order to benefit from block exemption; this is in addition to other important conditions, such as that the agreement is a vertical agreement within the meaning of the Regulation and that it contains no hardcore restrictions.

[128] See note 90 above in relation to Art. 19 of the Egyptian competition law.

other things, guarantee the effectiveness of the relevant regime and establish its credibility. Penalties in the field of competition law come to perform a double or even treble function. On the one hand, penalties are important to impose in cases where a competition breach occurs in order to punish those harming competition and consumers; related to this idea is that of 'compensating' those injured as a result of the breach. Secondly, penalties have an important deterrent effect in order to ensure that those (including the punished firms or individuals in question) who might entertain the idea of committing an infringement of the competition rules would think again.

Depending on the competition law regime in question, a number of penalties may be at the disposal of the competition authority or court. The main penalty relied on by competition authorities or courts, is that of a fine, which may be imposed on firms and individuals depending on the regime in question. Fines may be criminal or civil and this too depends on the approach to competition law breaches followed in the relevant regime. In any case however, fines imposed in competition cases can be extremely high. High-profile cases of enormous amounts of fines imposed on firms include the fines imposed by the European Commission on the US firms, Microsoft and Intel for committing an abuse of their dominant position as well as those fines imposed by the Commission in many cartel cases.[129]

In addition to fines, the rules in the relevant competition law regime may provide for imprisonment of individuals who participate in serious competition breaches, such as where these individuals commit a cartel offence, by acting dishonestly and participate in the creation or implementation of a cartel.[130] The availability of imprisonment as a penalty can have a serious impact on the decision of an individual to participate in the cartel: the thought of spending a number of years in prison can focus the mind much more than the thought of facing a fine, especially when this is imposed on the firm; moreover it has serious personal and family consequences and is in many cases a perfect recipe to ruin a high-flying career as a business person.

Other penalties may include divestiture taking the form of a break-up[131] of the relevant firm or even suspending the business activities of

---

[129] See the European Commission's website for details about fines imposed in cartel cases: http://ec.europa.eu/competition/cartels/overview/index_en.html.

[130] See as an example the UK competition law regime, specifically s. 188 of the Enterprise Act 2002.

[131] Especially in the USA, one is able to find evidence of orders made for breaking up firms. One of the most notable earlier examples is the order made in 1904 by the Supreme Court against Northern Securities Company (NSC).

the offending firm.[132] Needless to say that these are draconian penalties and in practice – although they may be ordered – it is likely that ultimately political opposition may prevail in this case or the decision ordering the penalties may be reversed on appeal by (higher) courts. Finally the possibility may be provided for disqualification of corporate directors found to have participated in or to have been responsible for a competition infringement.[133] A disqualification order in this case would prevent the relevant person from filling the position of a director in any firm in the relevant regime for a certain period of time. Like imprisonment – though arguably it is not as serious as that at personal or family level – the possibility of being disqualified in this manner can have an effective deterrent effect.

(E) The interdisciplinary nature of competition law

A final issue to be considered in this part concerns the nature of competition law. Competition law is interdisciplinary in nature and this basic yet crucial point concerning both the concept and function of competition law is one that has lacked sufficient recognition in the literature. No study of competition law would be meaningful and no understanding of the subject could be complete without realising this unique nature of competition law. The fathers of the concept of competition law in most parts of the world have been politicians, not commercial lawyers or even economists.[134] Politicians coined and championed the 'idea' underpinning the concept of competition law: the idea of using law to protect competition and act against harmful business behaviour, conduct or operations. This is of course very interesting given the prominent role that lawyers and economists have come to play in formulating and applying competition law, not to mention the role played by political scientists in designing the institutional structure within different competition law regimes.

The involvement of the politician, the lawyer, the economist (and the political scientist) makes competition law a special type of law with true multi- or interdisciplinary characteristics. However, the interdisciplinary nature of competition law extends beyond this and 'connects' with the branch of business management and administration. It was noted

---

[132] See Dabbah, note 3 above, for a discussion of relevant regimes in the Middle East which contain such provision.

[133] See the UK regime as an example which contains such disqualification instrument; see in particular s. 204 of the Enterprise Act 2002.

[134] See Amato, p. 2, note 109 above.

throughout the discussion on the concept of competition above how the idea of competition itself and its protection is special in nature. This 'idea' is found in the overlap between these different disciplines.

The involvement of various disciplines in the field of competition law makes the subject very complex. Nonetheless, such involvement is particularly necessary for an effective operation of a competition law regime. The practice in different competition law regimes with regard to the application of competition law and the formulation of competition policy has relied primarily on the skills of lawyers and economists. The skills of lawyers and economists are vital for an effective and successful enforcement of competition law. However, one ought to remember that the administration of competition law and policy also involves the exercise of bureaucratic politics and also requires business acumen. There is ample evidence indicating that the priorities and importance attached to the enforcement of competition law and the design of competition policy in many countries is dependent on political choices made by ministers and government officials acting in a variety of capacities. An adequate understanding of competition law and policy therefore requires insights from political science and public administration to complement the legal and the economic perspectives. It is regrettable that this third intellectual strand within the field has received little systematic analysis.[135] Furthermore, it is vital for lawyers and economists in particular to have solid business acumen when handling competition issues, whether in policy formulation or enforcement situations or when delivering advice to firms in individual cases.

The interdisciplinary nature of competition law has a revolving movement. At each spin, a new discipline enters and this means that each discipline needs to be sensitive to the importance of the discipline(s) in front. Put in a concrete manner, this means that an intriguing interrelation exists between the different disciplines and each may be considered to come both before and after other disciplines. Lawyers need to be aware of fundamental economic theories, the business reality of the market, the political reality surrounding a competition law regime and institutional designs when attempting to understand competition law, applying its provisions in real cases and engaging in and evaluating various competition policy debates. It is obvious that embracing competition and relying on the market mechanism (with or without a mechanism of regulation) is a political decision; the operation of the market is the result of business

---

[135] See Doern and Wilks, pp. 3–4, note 101 above.

decisions and strategies and this requires an appreciation of how business people tend to think and operate; competition is concerned with the marketplace and for this reason economic analysis is vital when measuring market power and determining the effect on competition resulting from business behaviour, conduct or operations; and the particular institutional architecture established within a competition law regime can have a decisive impact on how competition law is enforced and this heightens the importance of political science in the formulation of policy decisions which are reasonable and which would help in applying the law in a sensible way.

13.   Enforcement: actors, considerations, policy approaches and culture

Ultimately, what matters in the field of competition law is not the exact wording of the law, the comprehensiveness of its provisions and how *beautifully* it is drafted. In fact in cases where the constitution or basic law or the different economic laws in the relevant jurisdiction bring within their scope situations of collusion or abusive conduct it may not matter very much whether a specific competition law exists in the relevant regime. The crucial element of a competition law regime is enforcement. What matters is whether there is actual enforcement and whether efforts are made to, among other things, fight and eradicate harmful situations and regulate others, where it would be necessary to do so. Enforcement presents the real test in determining the effectiveness of a given competition law regime. Without enforcement, the competition rules would be reduced to being what they are in fact: ink on paper.

Establishing an effective enforcement mechanism is a top priority for many competition authorities. In some cases, this can be a personal ambition of those heading the relevant competition authority as well as their staff of officials. This is perhaps the most challenging task those working within competition authorities face in their public career. Establishing this mechanism is not automatic even with the availability of financial resources and competition expertise: the highest hurdle that must be cleared is that of 'getting it right'. Experience in the field shows how even some of the world's most mature competition authorities are likely to stumble and as a result 'get it wrong'. Remarkable examples here include serious defeats suffered by the European Commission before the EU Courts on a number of occasions;[136] the UK Office of Fair Trading's public apology to the supermarket chain Morrisons and the payment of £100,000 in addition to costs to Morrisons in order to settle the defamation action launched by Morrisons;[137] and the failed judicial actions by US competition authorities on a number of occasions.[138] Of course all of these examples can be 'explained' on the ground that they have been extremely rare (and indeed they are) and on the ground that inadequate reasoning or economic analysis was adopted by the relevant competition authority or inappropriate supervision of the officials within the relevant authority[139] or that the matter or finding was simply rushed through without carrying out a proper vetting of the finding in the case. Nevertheless, these examples show the difficulty in ensuring that competition authorities 'get it right'.

A number of issues have direct bearing on the issue of enforcement and these need to be considered not only in the context of the present discussion on enforcement but equally importantly in practice when seeking to establish an enforcement mechanism in the relevant regime.

(A) Is policy design and formulation relevant?

Competition law is one of those fields in which policy is more important than the exact wording of the law. In simple terms, the true emphasis must be on policy formulation and design because when one gets the policy 'right', the law will almost naturally slot into place. Insufficient focus on policy formulation and design, on the other hand, can simply mean that the law will end up being all over the place. Such is the unique nature of competition law itself. However the question that must be asked is what is meant by policy design or formulation and how is this achieved in practice.

When designing policy approaches the main focus must be put on the question of what is the main goal(s) sought in the name of competition

[136] See as an example the judgments delivered in merger cases by the European Court of First Instance (now General Court of the EU) in 2002 and 2003: Case T-342/99, *Airtours* v. *Commission* [2002] ECR II-2585; Case T-310/01, *Schneider Electric* v. *Commission* [2002] ECR II-4071 and Case T-80/02, *Tetra Laval* v. *Commission* [2002] ECR 4519.

[137] The OFT apology was issued on 23 April 2008. See Press Release 54/08, available at www.oft.gov.uk/news/press/2008/54–08.

[138] See chapter 5.

[139] In the Morrisons situation, the problem reportedly arose from the conduct of a non-competition official even who wanted to add their own 'stamp' to the case!

law in the relevant regime. A policy approach advocating continuous intervention in the marketplace may be suitable to a regime that aims at continuous regulation of the use of market power by large firms but would not be suitable in the case of a regime which favours overwhelming reliance on the market mechanism with minimal intervention. Perhaps the most important aspect of policy design and formulation is that of intervention: in what circumstances should intervention occur. The question of intervention is important not only for the purposes of ensuring legal certainty and predictability in the relevant regime but also in light of limited resources enjoyed by competition authorities. It is a widely accepted proposition that a competition authority cannot investigate anything and everything and in practice many competition authorities enjoy *discretion* over the decision whether to launch an investigation in a given situation or not.[140] This discretion is important to have in order to enable a competition authority to prioritise in handling its work. Nevertheless, in relation to those areas in which competition authorities typically intervene, it is vital to set out the policy on intervention in clear terms. One such area is that of regulation of conglomerate mergers: a competition authority will need to determine, using a well-defined and consistent policy approach, whether these mergers will be regulated or whether they are simply operations deemed not to give rise to serious competition problems and as a result they should fall outside the scope of the relevant merger rules; another arguably more important area meriting such clarity of terms regarding intervention is the area of abuse of dominance or monopolisation which has come to receive particular attention by key competition authorities in recent years.[141]

Admittedly, the question of intervention can be said to be difficult to determine in the abstract and arguably this is something that requires reliance on experience from practice. In the real world, an abundance of knowledge is available in the form of academic literature, decisional practice of competition authorities and jurisprudence of courts. For many competition authorities all of these sources of information are without a doubt an important substitute for actual experience, which requires a long time to build. As such, they present such competition authorities with a second best world and have enormous credibility in practice as a reliable approach towards designing a clearly formulated policy on intervention.

---

[140] This discretion was acknowledged and upheld by many courts in different competition law regimes, most notably the EU competition law regime; see chapter 4 below.

[141] See the European Commission's *Guidance paper*, note 85 above.

(B)   Political perspective

A fundamentally important point is that it is difficult to separate competition law from a political perception at any one time. The 'politics' of
competition law receives expression in a variety of ways. A common
factor to these ways is the manner in which public institutions give legal
expression to the goals of competition law, whether in the actual wording
of the law but more importantly in the way they interpret, apply and
enforce these instruments.

The roots of the political perception of competition law grew originally from how competition law was seen as a response to an important
problem of democracy.[142] Some commentators have sought to explain
that this point concerns how private power may be employed to
infringe not only the freedom of other individuals, but also the balance
of public decisions which may become vulnerable in the face of such
power.[143] Competition law therefore is seen as a tool to safeguard
against such use of power in order to ensure that principles of liberal
democracy are safeguarded.[144] Nonetheless, in doing so it seems that an
apparent inconsistency may be triggered between two perspectives on
the role of competition and competition law. The idea of competition is
rooted in the freedom of firms to carry out their business in a manner and
ways they consider best suited to further their personal interest.
However, competition law can limit this freedom. At first sight, this
limitation seems to be inconsistent with the idea of competition and its
dynamic and democratic values. This apparent inconsistency results
in a balance being struck between two sets of considerations and the
interests associated with them. One is concerned with the interests of
those whose freedom is limited by the law, which is a short-term consideration. This consideration is normally prevalent in jurisdictions
where public authorities are hostile to dominant firms and assume that
such firms have, and will use, economic dominance to harm small competitors or consumers. The other relates to the interests of those whose freedom is, or may be, limited by the actions of others, in the case of
anticompetitive practices of firms. This is a long-term consideration because

[142] See generally E. K. Kintner, *An Antitrust Primer* (Macmillan, 1973).
[143] Amato, p. 2, note 109 above.
[144] Amato, p. 3, note 109 above. Reference is made to the principles of liberal democracy
because this dilemma really has its roots entrenched there. See J. Locke, *Two Treatises of
Government* (Cambridge University Press, 1988), p. 118.

it takes into account the consequences for those whose freedom would be limited over time, should the law fail to address the limitation on their freedom or the source of harm to their interests. To put this point another way, the balance is essentially between the bounds of public power and private power and the relationship between these two forces. As we noted above, as a corollary of this the question arises whether the market can be relied on to address competition concerns and to provide the important benefits sought in the name of competition law in the long term, or whether there is a need for public intervention to address such concerns in the short term. This question reveals an interesting aspect of competition law: the law is about who should hold power over making various types of decisions that affect the market and its functioning. Two independent views can be put forward in this context. One view might be that each firm should have the right to decide and formulate its own policy in the hope that self-interest and the public interest will somehow coincide. On the other hand it might be thought that public authorities should take a more active and interventionist approach into the marketplace. An example of the latter approach is furnished by the way in which many competition authorities opt for a wide view of situations falling within the different competition law prohibitions and then exempt certain situations.[145]

The issue of decision-making – or more commonly, the making of important commercial decisions – is central to any debate in the field of competition law: from the stage when enacting competition legislation is contemplated to the stage at which a competition law regime is established, which includes enforcement efforts, and ultimately to the stage at which international cooperation in the field may be pursued.[146] The relevance of the issue resides in the query of whether governments and competition authorities or business firms should be the key players at these various stages.

(C)   Beneficial v. harmful intervention

In regulating the conditions of competition in the market, the 'invisible hand' of competition may, at times, be replaced with the more visible hand of public institutions.[147] Whilst it is understandable that this is

---

[145] See pp. 44–47 above for a discussion on the issues of prohibition and exemption.
[146] See chapters 9 and 10 which deal with bilateral and multilateral cooperation respectively.
[147] See note 55 above and accompanying text for a reference to this concept as coined by Adam Smith.

inevitable in some cases,[148] especially to address anticompetitive situations in the market, it seems that public intervention can generate some uncertain implications. These uncertain implications are a source of difficulty. First, the opposing perspectives of competition law described in the previous section can exist in two different jurisdictions. For example, as the discussion in chapters 4 and chapters 5 shows this seems to be the case with the EU and the USA. Secondly, the perspective within one jurisdiction may change over time.[149] In the USA, for example, it would appear that a change in administration in Washington can have an impact with regard to the application and enforcement of US competition law.[150] If one traces these uncertain implications to their origin, it becomes apparent that the reason different perspectives on competition law and policy exist arises from the way competition law is applied by public institutions. Leading officials in former US administrations expressed some very strong views over the functioning of US competition authorities, such as the Federal Trade Commission (one of the authorities responsible for competition law enforcement in the USA), describing the officials in those authorities as individuals who are hostile to the business system, to free trade, and who sit down and *invent* theories that justify more meddling and interference in the economy and the marketplace.[151] Therefore, there is an important issue in the relationship between the law, as it appears in statute, and the way it is applied by institutions in practice. This relationship has been examined by a few scholars, who have explained that in this relationship competition law, as it appears in the statute, defines and configures power relationships, and, in turn, public institutions manipulate the statute and its interpretation in order to achieve institutional, other political and even personal goals.[152]

Competition law is subject to political influence. The politics of a competition law regime is apparent from the manner in which competition authorities apply their domestic competition law, whether in the way the goals of competition law receive legal expressions in the statutes

---

[148] See Fox, note 69 above.   [149] See also Kintner, pp. 228–32, note 142 above.

[150] See p. 256 below.

[151] See remarks of David Stockman, former Director of Office Management and Budget and a leading official in the Reagan Administration in *Chicago Tribune*, at A-1, cols. 2–3, 23 February 1981.

[152] See D. Gerber, 'The Transformation of European Community Competition Law' (1994) *Harvard International Law Journal* 97; D. K. Tarullo, 'Norms and Institutions in Global Competition Policy' (2000) *American Journal of International Law* 478.

or in their guidelines and policy statements based on these statutes. Some commentators have observed that three modes of such political expression exist: the core of competition policy and its objectives; the extent and nature of non-competition policy goals that are allowed by statute to be considered in decision-making; and exemption provisions.[153] These expressions of course are not set in stone and may vary from one jurisdiction to the next. A prominent way in which politics and its influence are apparent in the field of competition law concerns the manner in which the application of competition law is handled and the way competition cases are decided. It seems that potentially there is a very long distance between competition law and its outcomes. A competition case may begin with a complaint to a competition authority which may be followed with an investigation by the latter. The investigation may then lead the competition authority to warn the defendant firm(s) and in some cases perhaps this will trigger an enforcement action, which in turn may bring the case before the court or specialist tribunal for a ruling.[154]

The question of intervention by competition authorities is one that inevitably will continue to be raised and debated. The question assumes high importance especially in relation to those industries which tend to be inherently in continuous changing mode. These include the high-technology sector. Indeed it is legitimate to ask whether it is sensible for competition authorities to revert to aggressive enforcement in such sectors given that such actions themselves could lead to distortions in the market. There is serious disagreement over the optimal industry structure in relation to these sectors and this often is a major trigger of disagreements over competition enforcement as can be seen from disagreements between the USA and the EU over cases involving competition enforcement against firms such as Microsoft, Intel, Boeing and McDonnell Douglas and General Electric and Honeywell International. Indeed, a serious disagreement also exists with regard to what competition authorities actually seek to achieve when intervening in these cases: do they seek to maintain optimal industry structures or traditional attitudes against foreign producers? History in particular shows that there is a belief that limiting competition – and perhaps going beyond this to encourage collaboration between firms – can actually help with expansion of industries and facilitating technical and economic

---

[153] See Doern and Wilks, p. 15, note 101 above.
[154] See Doern and Wilks, p. 14, note 101 above.

developments.[155] In other words, there is lack of consensus on what competition authorities actually object to when intervening in competition cases arising in certain sectors of the economy and what it is they seek to achieve.

A final point worth making concerning the question of intervention is that in some cases one forms the impression that competition authorities are too anxious to impress and to show others how good they are. To this end, these authorities either set themselves a target of an over-ambitious number of investigations which they do everything possible to meet and many times they fail to do so,[156] or rush into actions, which are not well-founded and which on occasions could lead to an 'apology'.[157]

(D)   The involvement of different actors

In competition law enforcement a number of actors may be involved. These include: (first of all) competition authorities themselves; law courts or specialist tribunals; sector regulators; governments (or individual ministers); public prosecutors; and consumer or professional associations; of course to this list business firms should be added.[158] As different players and interests are involved in the field of competition law, there is a possibility that competition authorities become subject to political pressures; and their decisions may be overturned or at least shaped up by politicians.[159] Voices in some quarters have argued that distancing competition authorities from these pressures is favourable from a legal standpoint.[160] It can be said that it is important to ensure that decisions regarding the investigation and prosecution of particular cases would be consistent with consideration of 'natural justice' or

---

[155] See as an example of encouraging such collaboration the Japanese experience; also the Austrian experience which is discussed at pp. 63–64 below.

[156] This can be seen in the case of the widely alleged UK Office of Fair Trading's 'promise' to handle 50 cases in the first year following the introduction of the Competition Act 1998 which the UK Competition Appeal Tribunal was led to believe would result in considerable work for the latter though at the end this was not the case.

[157] See note 137 above and accompanying text.

[158] One may also add to the list bodies active in lobbying and promoting special interests and where relevant also international organisations.

[159] See p. 43 above.

[160] See A. O. Krueger, 'The Political Economy of Rent-Seeking Society' (1974) *American Economic Review* 291; J. M. Buchanan, 'Rent Seeking and Profit Seeking' in J. M Buchanan, R. D. Tollison and G. Tullock (eds.), *Toward a Theory of the Rent Seeking Society* (Texas A and M University, 1980).

procedural fairness. There is no doubt that injecting more considerations of fairness and justice will reduce the influence of politics. This can have a positive impact on the issue of making important commercial decisions in the market. Ensuring an adequate degree of independence can also help to ensure the administration of competition law and policy leads to a sensible body of case law and rules emerging over the long term. Distancing competition law enforcement from political pressures also seems to be desirable from the point of view of institutional structure. The idea here is to foster the independence of competition authorities, establish the standing of foreign firms in domestic competition law regimes and introduce non-discrimination principles.[161]

(E)   Protecting competitors

The question of whether competition law aims to protect competition or competitors has been posed on numerous occasions. The question directly arises from the issue of the purpose and goals of competition law. Some commentators have argued that this question may lead the competition law community down dangerous paths[162] – as has happened in a number of jurisdictions – with the emergence of two different groups: one that believes the purpose of competition law, in particular the prohibitions on collusion between firms and abusive conduct, is to protect the freedom of (non-colluding or small) firms, and another that believes that the aim of the law is to protect the process of competition.

Competition authorities on the whole consistently maintain that in their enforcement efforts their primary concern is with protecting competition as a process and consumers and they do not seek to protect competitors. Some competition authorities often make this point in order either to answer or to thwart criticism that in their enforcement actions they clearly give weight to protecting local competitors at the expense of foreign ones. This has been the case as far the European Commission is concerned: the Commission has been accused on a

---

[161] See R. A. Posner, 'The Federal Trade Commission' (1969) *Chicago-Kent Law Review* 48. Posner noted that the politicisation of competition law at the US Federal Trade Commission was due to its dependence on Congress. Note also the old proposal in the EU to establish an independent non-political competition authority in order to separate political regulatory powers from decisional ones; see C. D. Ehlermann, 'Reflections on a European Cartel Office' (1995) *Common Market Law Review* 471; A. Pera and M. Todino, 'Enforcement of EC Competition Rules: a Need for Reform?' (1996) *Fordham Corporate Law Institute* 125.

[162] See Ehlermann and Laudati, p. 12, note 29 above.

number of occasions by US politicians in particular to be driven by an interest to protect EU-based firms in the face of competition from US firms;[163] claims which the Commission has forcefully denied.

The question has been raised as to whether it makes sense to draw a distinction between protecting competition and protecting competitors. Some views have been put forward that one ought to be less concerned about this distinction because protecting competition should include within its ambit protecting competitors (who provide competition), and vice versa: an effort to protect competitors includes protecting competition. This means that the distinction is not one of idea but rather of terminology and literal expression. It has been argued that the direct objective of competition law is to address competition impediments and that the economic conditions differ from one country to the next in exactly the same way the measures to cure those impediments themselves differ.[164]

(F)   What is competition policy?

It was said above that competition law and competition policy are not the same. In practice there is a 'journey' that needs to be made from competition law until competition policy is reached.

Competition policy covers the issue of enforcement, understood in broad terms to include actual enforcement in individual cases as well as formulating an approach on the issue of intervention to groups of certain situations or one that is design to determine the scope of the rules;[165] it should also be taken to extend to the actual steps taken to adopt competition law as well as competition advocacy efforts.[166] It is therefore possible that competition policy could exist without competition law. Ultimately what must be important is competition policy in terms of determining the crucial functions and issues covered under the concept; nevertheless, the existence of competition law can have a direct impact on this. At the heart of the concept of competition policy therefore sits the issue of intervention by public authorities in various situations, such as those of market imperfections and market failures.[167] Inevitably therefore, the concept is seen as anchored

---

[163] See, for example, claims made in the wake of decisions adopted by the European Commission in *GE/Honeywell International* (prohibiting the merger between these two firms) and *Microsoft* (finding an abuse of dominance on the part of the firm).

[164] See Ehlermann and Laudati, p. 21, note 29 above.

[165] An obvious example on determining the scope of the rules would be the issue of exclusions and exemptions; see pp. 46–47 above.

[166] See pp. 65–70 below for a discussion on competition advocacy.   [167] See p. 11 above.

in politics and includes within its ambit the exercise of discretion by competition authorities and in some cases governments in the enforcement of competition law.

The fact that competition policy can exist without competition law presents a particular difficulty in determining what type of public policy amounts to competition policy. Normally, when public policy considerations are injected in the marketplace, analytical dilemmas appear.[168] It is difficult to decipher which of the public policies should be called competition policy when the majority of such policies are actually or symbolically capable of affecting the process of competition in the market. There is a query as to whether it should be industrial policy, trade policy, consumer protection policy, other types of social policy or only public policy, that should expressly be named competition policy. A simple survey of the situation in various countries by a competition law enthusiast would reveal that in some countries the policy is called competition policy, but in others it is part of the industrial, trade or even the consumer protection policy of the country concerned. As a result of globalisation, the distinction between these policies has become a fine one. Perhaps the way to reconcile such differences in position is to accept that competition policy potentially has a very wide scope, encompassing all policies that affect the conditions of competition.[169] Accepting or rejecting such a suggestion for reconciliation is a central point to any examination of competition law, especially in an international context when dealing with the interface between competition policy and other policies.[170]

Leaving the dilemma of searching for the appropriate form of public policy to one side, the issue of public intervention in order to regulate economic behaviour is itself, prima facie, a source of difficulty. This is an issue that was discussed above. In the present context, however, it is interesting to observe in this regard the paradox of mainstream economic theorists where, on the one hand, they discourage public regulation of industrial policy but, on the other hand, they are less sceptical as far as public regulation of competition policy is concerned. As early as the 1930s, during the time of economic depression in the USA, some of the first Chicago school scholars called for an outright dismantling of 'gigantic' firms and persistent prosecution of firms

---

[168] See Amato, p. 2, note 109 above.   [169] See Fidler, note 76 above.

[170] See, for example, chapter 11 which includes an account of the relationship between competition and trade policies.

which conspired or colluded to fix prices, share markets and limit output. Those scholars argued that competition law must prohibit and the government must effectively prevent firms or groups of firms from acquiring substantial market power, regardless of how that power may appear to be exercised. The scholars argued that the US Federal Trade Commission must become the most powerful of all government bodies. In the view of some people however this call is quite interesting, and ironic, since it is open for argument that the economic depression during that period may actually have been caused by competition law enforcement.[171] The Chicago school of thought has been particularly prominent in supplying a great deal of the existing US competition law ideology.[172] The school's 'successful' life span covers the last three decades.[173] During these recent times however, unlike neoclassicism theory, the school has become a 'symbol' for advocating a more relaxed approach to competition law. From a critical stance, therefore, it seems that there is lack of consensus and inconsistency amongst economists on how competition policy should be viewed, and whether it can be seen to offer a reliable explanation of the behaviour of firms in the market. Economists for example disagree over the nature and extent of competition that should be encouraged through intervention by competition authorities in the marketplace. But despite this lack of consensus there seems to be recognition among economists that competition is needed to deliver the benefits available from the market and that it is desirable to encourage competition and adopt law(s) to protect it.[174]

(G)   The importance of culture

Culture – understood in a wide sense – plays an important role in the enactment of competition law and more importantly in the shaping of its enforcement. There is an undeniably cultural dimension to the field of competition law which seems to have grown from the cultural perspective of competition. This cultural dimension is often identified

---

[171] See H. C. Simons, *A Positive Program for Laissez Faire: Some Proposals for a Liberal Economic Policy* (Chicago University Press, 1934), p. 43.

[172] See pp. 253–255 below.

[173] See the review of the School's theoretical influence in W. F. Shughart, 'Be True to Your School: Chicago's Contradictory Views of Antitrust and Regulation' in F. S. McChesney and W. F. Shughart (eds.), *The Causes and Consequences of Antitrust: the Public Choice Perspective* (Chicago University Press, 1995), pp. 323–40.

[174] See Doern and Wilks, p. 1, note 101 above.

in terms of the historical perspective of competition law which is considered to shed light on how competition law has developed and informs us of how it will continue to evolve. This dimension shows how competition law has its own political idea and philosophy and how competition law enforcement depends on the prevailing culture within the relevant regime. This issue will be explored in later chapters dealing with the EU and US competition law regimes and the topic of competition law and policy in developing countries. Competition law in almost all existing regimes around the world originated from a particular political idea or a political philosophy[175] which indicates a fundamental point about competition law: that it is extremely difficult to separate competition law from the political, historical and cultural framework in which it is set up.

The general opposition towards monopoly and restrictive practices engaged in by firms is a very old one.[176] Efforts in both the Eastern and Western worlds were made several centuries ago to fight anticompetitive situations. This has included clear judicial statements condemning such situations.[177] However what history shows is that the perception of competition law and competition has shifted over the years and in some cases this shift was between two extreme ends of the spectrum: from one at which competition was considered to be an 'evil' force to the other at which competition is seen as a 'virtue'. This can be explained with reference to one of the most crucial historical experiences in the field of competition law, namely the Austrian experience which during the nineteenth century in particular played a crucial role in supporting the creation of competition law culture in Europe as a whole. Austria had already identified competition concerns and attempted to address them even before the debates which led to the adoption of the first competition legislation in Europe and in other parts of the world took place. The increase in the popularity of competition in Austrian society became obvious in the middle of the nineteenth century. During that time, the liberals in Austria acquired political power following years of

---

[175] See p. 54 above. [176] See Dabbah, chapter 2, note 3 above.
[177] See the early UK case of *Dyer's* (1414) YB 11 Hen 5 of 5, 26.20 CONG. REC. 1167 (1889). In the latter case of *Darcy* which was decided in 1602 the common law of England consolidated its stance towards monopoly. In that case, the King's Bench Division held that monopoly leads to poor quality, harms consumers and restricts competition. In the centuries that followed, this common law view had a far-reaching effect both within the UK and abroad. For example, the view was mentioned in the debates leading to the enactment of the Sherman Act 1890 in the USA; see pp. 238–243 below for an account on the Act.

aristocratic leadership. This increase in popularity was paralleled by events which led to the creation of the first parliamentary democracy in Austria. However, soon this popularity was challenged and eventually vanished with the economic depression which hit Austria in 1873 and which lasted for several years. This sharp turn of events *discredited* the idea of competition and turned it into an *evil force* in the eyes of many. The support for unhindered and free competition was converted into suspicion of its forces and ultimately resulted in support for monopolisation and state intervention, control and planning in the marketplace. In the last quarter of the nineteenth century, the scene began to witness the creation of cartels, which escalated in both number and power at the time. The first industries to witness cartelisation were the main ones, such as coal and steel. But this activity soon spread to other areas in the final years of that century. During that period, cartels were viewed as a natural and inevitable stage in the development of capitalism rather than a problem that needed to be combated. As the twentieth century approached, there was a change of attitude towards viewing cartels. This was promoted in part by the changing values and change in the political climate. Cartels came to be seen as a means by which big businesses were able to exploit and hurt the public at large. With this new awareness coming to light, political and intellectual movements developed which began to call for dealing with cartels by enacting an appropriate and effective legislation for fighting such harmful practices;[178] although the question of how and whether this was at all possible was largely unanswered. The effect of cartels was very uncomfortable and many of the elections at town/city, regional and national levels in Austria at that time were fought on the issue of cartels. Some commentators have argued that the new attitude towards cartels provided the seeds for the development of competition law in Austria and for a competition law tradition in Europe.[179] These developments contributed a great deal towards bringing about the remarkable shift in perception: competition was no longer seen as an evil force.

14.   The boundaries of competition law

The boundaries of competition law remain simply unclear in many respects. This includes important aspects such as the extraterritorial

---

[178] At that time there was already legislation dealing with cartels in Austria but that legislation was not effective.

[179] See Gerber, p. 43, note 98 above.

assertion of jurisdiction and the relationship between competition law and intellectual property rights and between competition policy and other public policies, most notably industrial policy. One way in which the lack of clarity could be reduced or eliminated is through competition authorities and courts setting out in clear terms the policy approach to be adopted on these issues in their decisional practice, case law or administrative guidance. Especially in the area of extra-territorial assertion of jurisdiction, it is often impossible to know where the boundaries of local competition rules lie when applying these rules in cross-border cases, such as those of international cartels and trans-national mergers. In the absence of clarification of the policy approach adopted by competition authorities and courts, the boundaries of competition law will remain the subject of debate and argument.

15. Competition advocacy

The view, as stated above, that competition law is directed towards dealing with anticompetitive situations that are designed to reduce consumer welfare and which result in inefficient use of resources would bring one close to assuming that such practices constitute the only source of harm to competition. However, under no circumstances should this be seen as a valid assumption: harm to competition can also result from the way in which various public policies are formulated and implemented and institutional arrangements are designed;[180] in addition to the likelihood of harm resulting from intervention by public bodies in the market as highlighted above. Anticompetitive situations may easily be facilitated by various government interventions and non-intervention in the marketplace. One country, for example, may grant legal monopoly to its firms; it may limit in other ways the number of competitors in the market; it may introduce unduly restrictive rules and regulations; or it may decide not to deal with anticompetitive situations or give wide exemptions or exclusions to these. For this reason, the question arises whether the mandate of a competition authority should extend beyond mere enforcement of competition law towards competition advocacy.

---

[180] To support the above discussion on the desirability of the involvement of various disciplines in competition law and policy, this is one instance in which the expertise of political scientists would be needed.

(A)   Using competition advocacy

There is a great deal of merit in the view that competition authorities must take part in the formulation of economic policies of countries, especially those which may adversely affect competitive market structures, business conduct and transactions, and economic performance. To this end, a competition authority must act like a competition advocate, a role through which it can particularly encourage government policies that would reduce barriers to entry, facilitate deregulation, promote trade liberalisation and enhance competition or at least ensure that competition will not be harmed by the government action. As a corollary, a competition authority will be able to minimise unnecessary government intervention in the marketplace, something which is regarded as a highly desirable ability for a competition authority.

(B)   Is competition advocacy necessary?

Competition advocacy should enable a competition authority to have a greater say on how various public policies should be shaped, as well as affording it the opportunity in some cases to propose different alternatives or modified version of existing government or legislative proposals that would be less detrimental to competition, specifically to economic efficiency and consumer welfare. In this regard, competition advocacy can become a safety valve in a competition law regime that would ensure against not only anticompetitive practices, but also lobbying and economic rent-seeking behaviour by various interest groups, which seem to be common in the field of competition law. Of course, the desirability of these ends cannot be denied since they are bound to help achieve greater accountability and transparency in economic decision-making mechanisms and promote sound economic management and business principles in both public and private spheres.[181]

(C)   Competition advocacy and enforcement

Certain links seem to exist between competition advocacy and the enforcement of competition law. Enforcement is widely seen as an effective tool for fostering competition, breaking down barriers to

---

[181] See Doern and Wilks, pp. 334–7, note 101 above.

entry, increasing economic efficiency and protecting consumer welfare. It is important to note however that the importance attached to enforcement should not necessarily mean that competition advocacy should be relegated to a marginal role. In all events, competition advocacy can enlarge the benefits that may accrue from competition law enforcement. Hence, competition advocacy can be seen to be complementary to competition law enforcement. This is particularly so in developing economies or those in transition. Such economies normally feature markets which, in their early stages of development, tend to be concentrated and sometimes dominated by one or a few large firms that may engage in anticompetitive behaviour or extensive lobbying practices. The aim of competition advocacy in this instance is to promote conditions that will translate into more competition in the market without a direct intervention on the part of a competition authority or the government generally. The role of a competition authority as a competition advocate in these situations can be contrasted with that of a competition authority operating in a regime that subjects firms in the market to close and continuous supervision. It is simply argued that the latter approach is not (at least not always) entirely satisfactory since it is more resource-intensive, and the justification for it is hardly compelling because it means that the competition authority in this case would be reverting to continuous and in many situations unnecessary intervention in the marketplace.

Competition advocacy exists in several jurisdictions throughout the world. Looking at the examples furnished by those jurisdictions it would be possible to conclude that competition advocacy can be based on both explicit (statutory) and implied (informal) grounds. In some jurisdictions competition authorities enjoy a certain mandate to submit their views on specific matters to the relevant ministry or regulatory agency or other public bodies.[182] In other jurisdictions, legislation may be silent on the role of the competition authority under such circumstances. In such a case, and provided that a competition authority is not prohibited under legislation from participating, a competition authority should – through its law enforcement role – actively seek opportunities to make the case for competition in the public forum; competition law regimes in France, Germany, the EU and the USA furnish a good example of

---

[182] These countries include Canada, Italy, the Republic of Korea, Russia and South Africa. See B. Doern, 'Canadian Competition Policy Institutions and Decision Processes' (1996) in Doern and Wilks, pp. 71–7, note 101 above.

this being done by competition authorities.[183] Undoubtedly, the benefits which active competition advocacy generates to the economy and to consumers can be guaranteed to be significant, or at least as substantial as those accruing from more traditional competition enforcement.

(D)   Establishing public awareness

A wider role for competition advocacy can be found in the public sphere. The successful establishment of a market economy requires the fostering of a competition culture. Both consumers and the business community need to be educated on the values of competition and competition law and on how these will benefit them. A competition authority has an important role to fulfil in this educational process. In several jurisdictions the public does not have sufficient experience with competition law and policy or an appreciation of the desirability and benefits which enhanced competition could bring them.[184] To an extent, however, this may be understandable, since the first experience the public may have with free markets is likely to be negative, not positive. In planned economies or those in transition the liberalisation of markets often is accompanied by disruption, misallocation and inefficient use of resources, unemployment and a high increase in prices of goods, especially in those economies which were formerly controlled economies. Under these circumstances, competition advocacy can be particularly helpful, but the task of a competition authority in building public support for competition law and policy is especially challenging. Much here can depend on the conditions of competition in the market and the role of a competition authority in the formulation of wider economic policies of the country since the economic environment in which firms operate is conditioned by many economic policies and the degree of competition in an economy can be strengthened or weakened according to the way in which these policies are developed and applied.

---

[183]   See R. Sturm, 'The German Cartel Office in Hostile Environment' and G. Peters, 'United States Policy Institutions: Structural Constraints and Opportunities' in Doern and Wilks, pp. 187–96 and 42–9 respectively, note 101 above. In the USA, a competition advocacy programme was adopted by the Federal Trade Commission in the 1980s; see A. C. Celnicker, 'The Federal Trade Commission's Competition and Consumer Advocacy Programme' (1988–9) *Saint Louis University Law Journal* 379.

[184]   Many Middle Eastern and African countries can be mentioned as an example here: looking at these regions, it is easy to observe the obvious lack of information amongst citizens and businesses in different countries on the desirability and benefits of competition.

Engaging in competition advocacy seeking to enhance public awareness is especially important in developing economies. The comments made here can be seen as more relevant to such economies and to young competition law regimes than ones which are mature and well developed.

To ensure a greater degree of transparency and accountability, and to embark on a true educative process, a competition authority should, where possible, bridge any (possible) existing gap between the work it conducts and the public. To this end, it is recommended that a competition authority seeks to conduct its work openly in public. The author admits of course that this proposition is subject to significant limitations, since in the investigation of most competition law cases a competition authority is subject to a strict requirement of confidentiality relating to the handling of information obtained during the course of investigation. To the extent possible, however, a competition authority should attempt to make information about its work publicly available. This can be done by ensuring that enforcement decisions are regularly published in bulletins, newsletters and crucially nowadays on the Internet (primarily the website of the relevant authority), so that interested parties (such as practitioners, other public bodies, regional authorities, business associations and the firms concerned and the academic community) who are affected by competition enforcement can be made aware of the policy approach adopted by the authority and key developments. Additional effective educational tools for making the public more aware of competition and competition policy can include publicising summaries of decisions in competition cases in the media, press conferences and press releases. Another more technically difficult tool is the formulation of guidelines on specific areas of competition law and policy. These tools have been employed by competition authorities in several jurisdictions,[185] especially in key areas such as merger control. The value of these guidelines, especially for firms who wish to observe the law, can be appreciated in the light of the fact that the language of competition law in most jurisdictions is sparse and general and the provisions of the law are usually not sufficiently detailed to offer appropriate guidance.

Another way in which a competition authority can bring its work closer to the public is through organising competition law workshops,

---

[185] See, for example, the extensive guidance published by the European Commission, the UK Office of Fair Trading and the US Antitrust Division and Federal Trade Commission.

conferences and seminars to promote an understanding of the role of competition and to show how its enforcement activities further such goals.[186] Through such fora, a competition authority will be able to demonstrate how competition benefits competitors, customers and consumers; how producers in competitive markets are forced to respond to demands of their consumers; and how competition results in the most efficient allocation of market resources. Competition law enforcement will thus be enhanced when a competition authority is successful in making the members of its community understand and support the concepts of competition, competition law and competition policy. Such members are not confined to the business community and consumers. They may well include competition lawyers, academics with expertise in business and economics, bodies and associations acting for consumers and other interest groups, policymakers and politicians.

16. Market definition and economic analysis

The first part of this chapter demonstrated quite vividly the increased economic approach to competition policy over the years, especially during the last quarter of the twentieth century. This increase has had many important consequences. One of these consequences has been placing the important issue of market definition at the centre of the process of applying the competition laws of many jurisdictions. The aim of this part is to demonstrate the relevance of the issue of market definition. The discussion of this issue will be in fairly brief terms and simply comes to ensure that this chapter would be complete through offering the reader – especially the student of the subject – an account of some of basics about market definition.

(A) The purpose of market definition

Competition law is concerned with *problems* which may result from a firm or firms possessing or exercising market power. Market power does not exist in a vacuum but in relation to a market, and as will be

---

[186] Several domestic competition authorities and other organisations dealing with competition law and policy have over the years engaged in such programmes. Several competition authorities host meetings attended by officials of competition authorities from around the world, competition law days and public hearings to which they invite members of the public, firms, practitioners, consumer organisations and academics.

seen below, the relevant market. This is an idea which may not be very difficult to understand in theory. In practice, however, the task of market definition – meaning the means by which the relevant market is identified or defined – can be very complicated and daunting.

Given the importance of the use of market definition in measuring economic strength, it is hardly surprising that market definition has come to occupy central stage in competition law analysis. Defining the relevant market enables the identification of situations giving rise to competition concerns and the measuring of a firm's or firms' market power; it also makes it possible to identify and learn about the actual competitors and the market shares of such firm(s). It is the case that in most competition law regimes the rules cannot be infringed unless firms have some degree of market power. Therefore, the application of the rules also requires a proper definition of the relevant market.

(B) The increasing significance of market definition

It should not be difficult to conclude from the above that market definition is not an end in itself but rather a *means* to an end; nevertheless it is worth emphasising this. The need to define the relevant market, and the method and approach for doing so, have been parts of the competition law and policy of some jurisdictions from their inception. In the EU, for example, defining the relevant market has always been a necessary step in the application of central provisions in the EU competition law chapter, in particular Articles 101 and 102 TFEU (ex Articles 81 and 82 EC) but perhaps more crucially the EU Merger Regulation, Regulation 139/2004.[187]

Over the years, there has been a progressive adoption of a more sophisticated economic approach in the application of competition law by many competition authorities around the world. As a result of this important development, the significance of market definition has increased at a phenomenal rate. To take the example of the EU, prior to 1989 the European Commission was called upon to define the relevant market in 20 or 30 cases per year, since that year the Commission has had to define the relevant market in hundreds of cases per year; the significance of the year 1989 is that it was the year in which Regulation 4064/89, the original (now old) Merger Regulation, was adopted.[188]

---

[187] See pp. 161–162 below.
[188] This Regulation was replaced by the current Regulation, 139/2004 on 1 May 2004. See further chapter 4.

Following the adoption of a specific mechanism for merger control, the Commission was forced to develop a more methodical approach to market definition. Indeed, it would be very fair to say that most of the expertise of the Commission in market definition over the last 20 years has been derived in the area of merger control. In light of the radical and significant changes in the EU competition law regime which have occurred in the last ten years, the significance of market definition has increased dramatically and is likely to continue to do so in the future.[189]

The increased relevance of the notion of market power and, therefore, the use of market definition as a tool to identify it, have meant that all those whom competition law affects or who have to deal with competition law have to familiarise themselves with the exercise. This includes firms, their advisors and competition authorities. But competition authorities have come to carry an additional responsibility, namely to provide a clarification of their policy and approach to market definition. This, in a way, is part of the competition advocacy task of competition authorities which was considered above. The US competition authorities and the European Commission have been among the first to accept and bear this additional responsibility, publishing administrative guidance on market definition in the 1990s.[190] Administrative guidance on market definition, despite lacking the binding force of the law, is of considerable importance, in that it has rendered public the procedures that competition authorities follow and the criteria and evidence on which they rely when approaching the issue of market definition. Such guidance also increased the transparency of the practice and policy of these competition authorities and reduced compliance costs for firms. The provision of clear guidance is particularly relevant in light of the fact that in many competition law regimes, firms are self-reliant and must self-assess their compliance with the competition rules.[191]

---

[189] See, for example, the increased economic approach adopted by the European Commission in many Regulations, notably Regulation 330/2010 on vertical restraints. This approach is bound to increase in scope and importance as can be seen from areas of EU competition law, such those of IP licensing.

[190] See chapters 4 and 5 for such guidance, especially the *European Commission's Notice on Market Definition* (1997) *Official Journal* C-372/5 and the US *Horizontal Merger Guidelines*.

[191] A notable example here is found in the case of the US and EU competition law regimes; see chapters 5 and 4 respectively.

(C) Basic principles of market definition

Among the dimensions of market definition are: the relevant product market dimension and the relevant geographic market dimension.[192] These are the most important dimensions and it is to these dimensions that the discussion now turns.

I. Relevant product market definition

Generally, the definition of the relevant product market is carried out using a classical 'constraints' approach. In essence this approach rests on the notion that there are three main sources of competitive constraint upon the exercise of market power by firms: demand substitutability, supply substitutability and potential competition. These concepts will be explained in the discussion that follows.

(a) **Demand substitutability** Demand substitutability concerns a determination of the range of products (B, C and D) readily available to which consumers or users of product A can actually switch because of substitutability between these products.

In order to measure demand substitution, a number of factors may be relied on. The aim in taking these factors into account is to consider what similarities, if any, may exist between a particular product and its 'actual' or 'potential' substitutes. The principal factors which have been used for this purpose are: physical characteristics, intended use and price.[193] Of these factors, many competition authorities put particular emphasis on the third, though courts in some and the same jurisdiction have shown a preference towards looking at all the three factors and not just price.[194] When looking at price, many competition authorities use a hypothetical quantitative test, known as SSNIP (Small but

---

[192] Other dimensions also exist. For example, the temporal market, which shows that in some cases it is important to take into account a particular time or season of the year when deciding whether products can serve as substitute for one another.

[193] It is important to note that the list of facts is not necessarily exhaustive. For example, one may identify factors such as customer habits and preferences which may be relevant in determining substitution between products.

[194] See, for example, how in the context of EU competition law, while the European Commission emphasised price when defining the relevant market, the European Court of Justice has focused also on the physical characteristics of the products and intended use. See, for example, the case of Case 27/76, *United Brands* v. *Commission* [1978] ECR 207.

Significant Non-Transitory Increase in Price) test. This test derives its origins from the US competition law regime. The question that this test poses is whether the customers would switch to readily available substitutes in response to a hypothetical, small (usually in the range of 5 per cent or 5 to 10 per cent), permanent and relative increase in the price of the product(s) under consideration. If customers would so switch, these available substitutes are included in the relevant product market. The SSNIP test helps to identify a set of products small enough to allow permanent increase in relative price that would be profitable (i.e. the increase would not trigger a switch on the part of customers to other products). This set of products is what is commonly referred to as a relevant product market for the purposes of competition law.[195]

(b) **Supply substitutability**   Supply substitutability entails identifying firms who are able to switch production to the relevant product as a response to a price increase of this product. If it is considered,[196] this always happens after considering demand substitutability. Supply substitutability should only be taken into account when the switch in production will occur within a period that does not imply a significant adjustment of existing assets of the (switching) firm. In practice, this means within a short period of time.

(c) **Potential competition**   The third element, potential competition, is not taken into account at the market definition stage. Instead, competitive constraints coming from potential competition will be assessed at a later stage of the process: the stage of measuring market power of a particular firm.

---

[195] The SSNIP test is not free from limitations. One such limitation is the 'cellophane fallacy'-type of situation, where the price is at such a level that any further increase would trigger a switch. The application of the SSNIP test in such a case would look as if the theoretical price increase was not profitable and, hence, would lead to overly wide relevant market being defined. This is a limitation which at least some competition authorities take into account when defining the relevant market in a competition case. See, for example, the approach followed by the European Commission as can be seen from its *Notice on Market Definition* (1997).

The cellophane fallacy doctrine was identified in a US case dealing with the product: *United States* v. *E. I. du Pont de Nemours & Co.*, 351 US 377 (1956).

[196] There are many situations in practice in which supply substitutability is not considered. The leading candidate case where it is actually considered is where demand substitutability does not yield reliable results on substitutability.

II. Relevant geographic market definition

The relevant geographic market comprises the area in which the firms concerned are involved in the supply and demand of the relevant products, in which the conditions of competition are sufficiently homogeneous, and which can be distinguished from neighbouring geographic areas because, in particular, conditions of competition are appreciably different in those areas. In identifying this area, the SSNIP test may be used. Essentially, what the test seeks to answer in this context is whether the customers of a particular firm would switch to readily available substitutes or firms located elsewhere in response to a hypothetical, small (in the range of 5 per cent or 5–10 per cent), permanent and relative increase in the price of the product(s) under consideration. If the answer to the question is in the positive, these areas will be included in the relevant geographic market.

The SSNIP test, however, may not be fully decisive in this context and for this reason looking at additional elements may be helpful and relevant in identifying an area where conditions of competition are sufficiently homogeneous. Factors like past evidence of diversion of orders to other areas, the examination of the customers' current geographic pattern of purchases and trade flows are, of course, very relevant. In addition, the nature of demand for the relevant product may in itself determine the scope of the geographical market. Factors such as national preferences or preferences for national brands, language, culture and lifestyle, and the need for a local presence are all important in defining the appropriate relevant geographic market. Furthermore, barriers and switching costs for firms located in other areas may also be taken into account. Perhaps the clearest obstacle for a customer to divert its orders to other areas is the impact of transport costs and transport restrictions arising from provisions of national legislation. The size and nature and value of the relevant product(s) and the physical geographic characteristics of some countries or regions can have a serious impact on transport costs and hence on the scope of the geographic market. Moreover, the existence or absence of regulatory barriers (e.g. those arising from public procurement, price regulations, quotas and tariffs limiting trade or production, technical standards, legal monopolies, requirements for administrative authorisations, or other regulations) is very important for geographic market definition.[197]

---

[197] See, for instance, the two decisions adopted in 2001 against Deutsche Post by the European Commission where the scope of the markets was defined as national because

Geographic market definition would vary according to the relevant geographical location. For example, one can imagine that in the EU, which is a union of independent countries, the exercise would be far more complex than, for instance, in a single country, where issues such as market integration, cultural/linguistic differences, regulatory barriers or national preferences are not relevant as in the case of the EU. Unlike the case with the EU, these differences do not prevent the competition authority, and where relevant the courts, of a single country from reaching the conclusion that the relevant geographic market is local. On the contrary, there are many examples of cases where very narrow geographic markets were defined. In the USA, for example, in some cases the relevant geographic market was defined as the metropolitan areas of one or two states.[198]

(D)   Market definition in practice

In practice, the starting hypothesis for a competition authority's analysis in a particular case – particularly in merger cases – is the market definition provided by the parties to the case. For example, in the case of the EU, a substantial part of a document called Form CO (the notification form for mergers) is devoted to market definition issues. The European Commission asks and expects the firms concerned to define the relevant product and geographic markets and to provide very detailed additional information to allow it to examine the definition given by the parties.

In addition to the information provided by the parties, a competition authority may seek to rely on market studies carried out by independent bodies, such as consumer associations and consultant firms, as well as seek the views of customers and competitors of the parties: this includes asking them in appropriate cases to answer the SSNIP test. Both

---

entry was impossible in view of the existence of exclusive rights or fiscal monopolies. See Cases COMP/36.915 and COMP/35.141 (2001) *Official Journal* L-125/27.

[198] See, for example, the case of *Dairy Farmers of America – Sodiaal* (2001) 1 Trade Cases 73, 136; the market was defined as the sales of branded stick and branded whipped butter in the Philadelphia and New York metropolitan areas.

At the same time, however, there are examples which may be found where the relevant geographic market has been defined as the whole country, two or more countries, almost all of the world and the whole world (i.e. a global market – see, for example, the 2007 decision of the Japan Fair Trade Commission's decision in the *TDK Corporation/Alps Electric Co. Ltd* merger finding that the relevant geographic market for magnetic heads was global).

customers and competitors receive from a competition authority requests for information, sometimes very detailed, so as to assist the competition authority in defining both product and geographic markets. Of course, competitors in particular might sometimes be tempted to influence the competition authority in one or another direction and normally, but not necessarily always, competition authorities are aware of that. Some competition authorities, such as the European Commission, the US Antitrust Division, the Federal Trade Commission, the UK Office of Fair Trading, the German Cartel Office, the Canadian Competition Bureau and the Australian Competition and Consumer Commission, among many others have enough experience to be able to distinguish between objective facts and subjective opinions and are therefore not unduly influenced in their assessments. Competition authorities in other jurisdictions, especially in developing countries or those operating in young competition law regimes, on the other hand, do not necessarily enjoy the same, or similar, experience; in addition such authorities are generally constrained by many factors such as lack of resources and expertise. As a result, their ability to distinguish between objective facts and subjective opinions is limited if not rendered virtually non-existent.

In some cases the parties, as well as competitors or customers, support their views with econometric analyses that try to show whether correlation exists between the prices of different products or that try to estimate cross-elasticity between different products. If data is abundant and reliable (which is normally the case for mass consumer goods) these studies can contribute positively to a competition authority's own analysis. They do not necessarily substitute, however, other more traditional aspects of the analysis.

On the basis of all this information, a competition authority should usually be in a position to delineate the relevant markets or, at least, the few alternative possible relevant markets. In fact, in view of the limited resources of most if not all competition authorities in the world, competition authorities define markets (in exact terms) only when strictly necessary. In EU merger control, for instance, if none of the conceivable alternative market definitions for the operation in question give rise to competition concerns, the European Commission normally leaves the question of market definition open.[199]

---

[199] See, for example, *Schibsted Multimedia AS/Telenor Nextel AS/Telia AB* [1999] 4 CMLR 216. The Commission has left the definition of the relevant market open in a large number of merger cases.

Chapter 2

The internationalisation of competition law: concepts, ideas, options and players

1. Attention given to the process

The internationalisation of competition law is a topic that has received considerable attention particularly in recent years.[1] Most of this attention has emerged within the academic arena; though one must not overlook the important work of certain international organisations and competition authorities which have contributed significantly towards enhancing this attention. The origins of the 'idea' of internationalisation date back to the 1940s and 1950s when concentrated efforts were made at that time to create an International Trade Organisation (ITO) and later build a competition agenda within the United Nations.[2] This no doubt makes the topic an old one. Over the intervening half a century or so however it has constantly remained a feature of current debate in the field and new ideas and proposals have continuously emerged seeking to identify what the 'next' step(s) should be in the field for the purposes of internationalising competition law. These ideas and proposals have not been confined to a particular area of competition law and policy nor indeed to a particular body, country or forum: initiatives seeking to internationalise competition law have covered different aspects of the field and have been either launched or supported by international organisations, scholars and key competition authorities as well as by many countries around the world. The majority of these initiatives have proposed furthering the internationalisation of competition law through existing international organisations such as the World Trade

---

[1] This includes an abundance of literature which has dealt with this topic. See M. Dabbah, *The Internationalisation of Antitrust Policy* (Cambridge University Press, 2003) for a detailed bibliography of sources on the topic. The specific wording of 'internationalisation of competition law' should be understood widely in this book to include also the term 'internationalisation of competition policy'.

[2] See pp. 542–544 below.

Organisation (WTO), the Organisation for Economic Cooperation and Development (OECD), the United Nations Conference on Trade and Development (UNCTAD) and the International Competition Network (ICN) which have already developed some agenda or programmes dealing with competition law and policy. The idea of utilising existing international organisations clearly carries considerable merit and is worth looking at in detail. The following chapter will therefore examine the involvement of international bodies and their contribution to the internationalisation debate. For present purposes, it would be sufficient to acknowledge that in many respects the work of these bodies has been extremely detailed and has gone beyond a general examination of the topic of internationalisation towards making specific recommendations and building specific programmes for achieving meaningful internationalisation. Many of these recommendations and programmes have made an impressive contribution towards: understanding the prospects of building cooperation among countries and between them and existing international organisations; offering suitable fora for competition officials from different countries to meet and discuss issues of common interest; and overall facilitating convergence between different competition law regimes. The achievements of the ICN, the OECD and UNCTAD in particular have been notable in this regard.

2.   The what, why and how of internationalisation

(A)   Meaning of internationalisation

The exact meaning of the concept of internationalisation in the field of competition law depends on the context in which it is used and the intended use of the concept. Most instances in which the concept has been employed show a narrow interpretation of the concept as a vehicle to achieve a specific set of highly ambitious ideas, such as the idea to conclude a binding multilateral agreement in the field or create a world competition authority. A narrow interpretation of the concept has not been particularly helpful and to an extent it has contributed towards some alienation and resistance to a push towards internationalisation: the impression created as a result of advocating such specific ideas that the process would entail loss of sovereignty and limitation of competence on the part of countries and their authorities in the field has itself resulted in the creation of anti-internationalisation camps. Moreover, at a conceptual level a narrow understanding of the concept does not match the nature of the concept itself. Internationalisation is a wide concept and it should be used and understood in a wide sense. In the context of the present book it is taken to refer to *all* options through which competition law or its enforcement come to have an international dimension. To identify the meaning of the concept therefore it would be important to consider all of these options; something that is done in section C below.

(B) Why internationalise?

One of the main points made in the previous chapter concerned the various differences between competition law regimes around the world.[3] As we remarked, some of these differences are extremely serious. Accepting the existence of *all* these differences as a fact – which neither should nor can be challenged – is in itself neither an attractive nor valid proposition. Among other things, some of these differences – if not addressed – can give rise to serious problems; and to a large extent these problems already exist. These problems are of different types and nature. Some of the problems concern the actual characteristic of competition law as a *national* (or where relevant, regional) regulatory mechanism. As such, competition law is subject to limitations, affecting its capability to address all anticompetitive situations which have transnational dimension. The relentless process of globalisation has turned many markets – and as a result the behaviour, conduct and transactions of firms active in such markets which are likely to give rise to such situations – global or at least widely transnational. The process of globalisation has increased the number of cross-border business transactions among firms and countries and has enabled the former to establish a presence in different countries with the consequence that their behaviour and conduct (in addition to transactions) even when occurring in one location can vibrate across the world. Such an important development has meant that competition authorities may not necessarily be suitably equipped – whether with the appropriate vision or resources – to deal with situations transcending their domestic boundaries. In the case of some competition authorities however, the possibility may be open to revert to either of two options to deal with the situation: assert jurisdiction over the situation *extraterritorially* or rely on an existing mechanism for bilateral cooperation. Neither of these options may

---

[3] See pp. 14–19 above.

be ideal or indeed sufficiently effective. In the case of the former,[4] an extraterritorial assertion of jurisdiction by the competition authority or court concerned would give its competition law or enforcement actions a wide reach and this means that this law may end up being used to regulate individuals, firms and transactions in other countries. There is solid evidence to support the view that competition law enforcement by a score of domestic competition authorities in the world has become increasingly extraterritorial over the years. Although there is merit in the claim that anticompetitive situations with cross-border elements should not go unregulated or unpunished, it is doubtful that this development should be regarded as acceptable when such enforcement would interfere with the prerogatives and orders of other countries. Furthermore, there has been a remarkable spread of competition law around the world: the previous chapter noted that over 120 jurisdictions have adopted some form of competition law. The possibility is very much alive for a given situation to fall within the scope of a number (if not many) of these competition laws. The application of the competition laws of different countries in the same situation can trigger conflicts between those countries. Apart from the damage that may be caused to the relationship between the countries themselves (and more seriously their competition authorities), conflicting results and the situation of overlap of jurisdiction more generally are damaging to firms, who are normally anxious about the application of more than one domestic competition law to their situations.[5] In relation to the second option of bilateral cooperation on the other hand, this option itself – notwithstanding its important benefits – suffers from shortcomings, which may render the efforts of a competition authority to have a cross-border anticompetitive situation addressed not particularly effective.[6] It should be clear therefore that the existing differences between countries in the field of competition law and specifically those concerning current competition law enforcement give rise to a variety of problems of legal, regulatory, business and diplomatic types. In response to this situation, the internationalisation of competition law has been proposed in order to seek, among other things, effective ways to deal with these problems. In this regard, it may be interesting to observe how the field of competition law and policy has come to be

---

[4] See chapter 8 for an examination of the doctrine of extraterritoriality. See also E. Fox, 'Global Problems in a World of National Law' (1999) *New England Law Review* 11.

[5] See pp. 106–110 below for the different concerns of firms.

[6] See chapter 9 which deals with bilateral cooperation.

regarded as an *exception* by many who have reservations about the value or point in seeking cooperation between countries in the arena of international economic regulation.[7] It seems that the core principles of competition law and policy are considered to support the fundamental goal behind creating a globalised economy, namely ensuring open and free markets by removing restrictions which could impede access by foreign firms to local markets. For this reason, seeking international cooperation and coordination has come to be viewed as not only necessary for the purposes of avoiding or solving the kind of problems mentioned above but also for the purposes of promoting this fundamental goal of global economic integration.

(C)   How to internationalise?

I.   The complexity of the concept

At the core of the concept of internationalisation lie a number of ideas. Many of these ideas are very similar in terms of what they aim to achieve. In relation to some ideas however, these differ fundamentally and in essence represent different 'visions' of how *competition law enforcement* in particular should be handled in a globalised economy. It is understandable that differences here should exist when these visions are promoted by different entities and groups. To be fair this also reflects the nature of internationalisation, which is a very complex concept and process encompassing competing national interests and divergent 'world views' of different countries on even the most basic issues in the field of competition law,[8] such as how competition should be viewed and what should be the goals of competition law; let alone the highly *delicate* issues of what role international institutions should have in the process, how this role could be politically justified and to what extent the involvement of international bodies will lead to international pressures onto the concrete functioning of domestic institutions (mainly competition authorities and courts) or possibly limitation of national sovereignty. These delicate issues in particular tend to 'condition' the meaning of the concept of internationalisation and in practice they prescribe the options to pursue it. Equally important however – and what the comments made here on the complexity

---

[7] See F. S. McChesney, 'Talking 'bout My Antitrust Generation: Competition for and in the Field of Competition Law' (2003) *Emory Law Journal* 1401.

[8] See pp. 14–19 above for an account on the differences between countries.

of the concept show – is that there are legal as well as political implications for the internationalisation of competition law. Indeed choosing a particular option of internationalisation depends on how much countries would be willing to achieve a political agreement under which they would forgo national interests in favour of pursuing global welfare and common rules and shared objectives.[9] Determining this requires a highly complex analysis of how much each country believes it would benefit and lose in this case. This however can be extremely difficult to quantify. Good illustrations here can be found in the case of export cartels, which have almost universally benefited from unconditional support by their home countries and are usually exempted from the prohibition on collusion between firms in domestic competition laws.[10] Export cartels are considered to be good (or at least not problematic) from a national perspective given their use as a means of penetrating foreign markets and facilitating a transfer of wealth from foreign consumers to national producers.

Understanding the concept and process of internationalisation boils down to one's particular viewpoint of what internationalisation entails, why it is needed and how it could be achieved. This would explain why there is more than one view in relation to the what, why and how to internationalise. It is important to recognise the existence of different views which, among other things, shows that it is possible to pursue and achieve internationalisation in a variety of ways or options. None of these options are perfect and therefore choosing or advocating a particular option depends on identifying the disadvantages or limitations from which each of the options suffers and weighing these in a sensible and pragmatic manner. Needless to say in this respect the existence of differences in how the internationalisation of competition law is viewed has the *potential* to invite resentment towards the concept itself and in practice can derail efforts seeking to achieve internationalisation; not to mention the potential for sharp disagreements between the world's advance competition law regimes or an attempt by some of them to employ the process of internationalisation as a way to impose their standards on less-developed competition law regimes or countries which lack competition law. All of these likely possibilities show that

---

[9] See A. Guzman, 'The Case for International Antitrust' (2004) *Berkley Journal of International Law* 355.

[10] See J. A. Rahl, 'An International Antitrust Challenge' (1989) *North Western Journal of International Law and Business* 98.

there may be serious challenges facing an attempt to reach common ground in relation to internationalising competition law.

II.   The examples in brief

The point was made in this and the previous chapter that the idea to internationalise competition law has been motivated by differences existing between countries in the field of competition law and the need to address these differences. However, in advocating internationalisation, differences have come to surface with regard to the way 'internationalisation' should be viewed and the best option(s) to pursue it. This has resulted in a number of 'examples' of internationalisation which may conveniently be split into three *non-rigid* categories: unilateralism, bilateralism and multilateralism. These three examples represent different strategies in the field. On the whole, they seek to achieve different objectives and are intended to operate in different ways, but one should realise that they may also overlap in terms of their 'end result', namely creating an international dimension to competition law and policy.

The discussion here will offer only an outline of the unilateral, bilateral and multilateral options; they will be discussed comprehensively in chapters 8, 9 and 10.

(a) **Unilateralism**   The idea of unilateralism embodies the use of domestic competition laws to deal with situations involving foreign elements through assertion of jurisdiction *extraterritorially*. The doctrine of extraterritoriality has provoked deep controversies in the field of competition law due to its perceived 'intrusive' nature into the affairs of other countries. Nonetheless, extraterritorial assertion of jurisdiction has become standard practice in the field and to a large extent the doctrine can be said to be inherent in the competition rules of different regimes.[11]

It may appear a little bit surprising to classify the doctrine of extraterritoriality as one option of internationalisation given its potential to cause problems when the process of internationalisation is understood by most people as a process that comes to solve problems. This is understandable. However, this is where the open-mindedness deemed to be necessary when looking at the concept of internationalisation itself is most useful: internationalisation should be understood as a

---

[11] See in particular pp. 456–461 below which contains a discussion of the situation under EU merger control.

process through which competition law and enforcement assume an international dimension. There is no doubt that the doctrine of extra-territoriality fits this description. At the same time, it should be recognised that extraterritoriality makes it possible in many cases to address anticompetitive situations, which otherwise would escape being caught. In this sense, the doctrine offers a tool to deal with competition problems of a cross-border nature.

In most typical situations, extraterritorial assertion of jurisdiction by competition authorities and courts has occurred in order to deal with adverse effects on competition in local markets, or to open up foreign markets and deal with possible anticompetitive practices, which may be considered to be hindering the access of local firms to those markets. This has given extraterritoriality its characteristic as an enforcement tool. Understanding unilateralism along these lines of extraterritoriality has been the common approach to this option. However, a unilateral approach – with or without the use of extraterritoriality – can also involve an attempt to promote local competition rules and standards and spread their influence beyond national boundaries as well as an effort by certain competition authorities to engage in giving advice to different countries on introducing competition law or the provision of assistance or training to the competition authorities of these countries. This means that there may be an 'advocacy' function to a unilateral strategy in the field of competition law.

(b) Bilateralism   The bilateralism option primarily revolves around erecting a mechanism for *bilateral* cooperation between two competition authorities or jurisdictions around the world. Generally this cooperation takes the form of a formal bilateral agreement, which addresses a host of issues concerning the enforcement of the competition rules of the parties. It is common for such agreements to contain provisions on comity,[12] information-sharing and coordination of enforcement efforts. Since the 1990s, these agreements have come to incorporate a principle of positive comity,[13] which may also be used informally in practice in the absence of a formal agreement – what is commonly referred to as *de facto* positive comity cooperation.

---

[12] See pp. 496–500 below for a discussion of the concept of comity.
[13] See, for example, the EU–US agreements discussed at pp. 501–505 below. Other bilateral agreements also have been entered into by different countries; see chapter 9 for an account on these agreements.

It is possible that bilateral cooperation may be achieved without a formal *competition-specific* agreement being in place but instead with a general economic cooperation agreement, a free trade agreement or an association agreement. Bilateral cooperation therefore should be understood as all means through which the competition authorities of two jurisdictions engage in some form of cooperation in actual competition cases including coordination of enforcement efforts; in some cases, bilateral cooperation may exist on the basis of a dialogue[14] or a memorandum of understanding[15] between two jurisdictions or their competition authorities specifically.

(c) **Multilateralism**   The third option of multilateralism is the most complex of the three options. It contains a number of ideas and over the years several variants of the option have emerged. These variants however do not necessarily offer rigid alternatives: in many cases they actually overlap. In broad terms, it is possible to divide the multilateral option into two forms: multilateralism achievable through *binding* obligations and multilateralism achievable through *non-binding* obligations. The obligations in this case should be understood to apply to countries. The difference between these forms is enormous because among other things the former is considered to pose greater 'threats' to national sovereignty than the latter, which relies on the use of instruments of *soft law*, i.e. instruments in the form of guidelines, recommendations or best practices and principles which lack binding force. Both of these forms of multilateralism will be discussed below.[16] However, it would be helpful to highlight the several variants of multilateralism some of which actually have linking points to the two forms mentioned here.

First, there is the idea of convergence and harmonisation among the domestic competition laws of different regimes so that common rules and standards could emerge from this process.[17] Convergence and harmonisation are usually two terms that 'go together' in the field of competition law and in many cases they are used interchangeably. A difference however exists between them. Harmonisation denotes the process through which different competition law regimes end up adopting the same rules or

---

[14] See, for example, the Declaration on the Start of a Dialogue on Competition by the EU and China Terms of Reference of the EU-China Competition Policy Dialogue (2003), available at http://ec.europa.eu/competition/international/legislation/china.pdf.

[15] See the memorandum of understanding concluded in 2009 between the EU and Brazil, available at http://ec.europa.eu/competition/international/bilateral/brazil_mou_en.pdf.

[16] See chapter 10.   [17] See pp. 562–567 below.

standards. This could happen in two ways: the first is when a centre of gravity is created at a higher level – whether regional or international in the form of a treaty or agreement – the operation of which leads to the parties harmonising their domestic rules with this treaty or agreement; the second way in which harmonisation could be achieved is where the centre of gravity in this case will be the rules of a (strong) competition law regime and these rules will be transplanted into another (weaker) competition law regime. The reference is made to 'strong' and 'weaker' competition law regimes because normally this is required for such a transplant to occur; equivalent (more acceptable) terms could be 'developed' and 'developing' or 'mature' and 'young' competition law regimes. Convergence on the other hand refers to the situation in which different regimes move towards each other through a change in their respective position or their domestic rules. The variant of convergence and harmonisation may be pursued and achieved through binding and non-binding obligations, though in recent years the popular model which has come to flourish is the 'soft convergence', i.e. the ICN model of achieving convergence through non-binding commitments.[18]

The second variant of multilateralism involves creating a detailed international competition law code to be adopted by countries. This code was proposed in 1993 when a group of scholars – known as the Munich group – produced such an instrument.[19] A multilateral code may be based on a binding agreement or obligations or it may be voluntary in nature and lack such binding basis.

Finally, there is the extremely ambitious variant of establishing an international competition law regime with a framework of autonomous international institutions, some form of a world competition authority.[20]

This list of variants is not exhaustive; it is very possible that more can be imagined or will come to light in the future. However, these are the main, principal and important ones which have emerged over the years; of course one could also argue that regional cooperation or even sub-regional cooperation should come within the scope of the multilateralism option.[21]

3.   The hurdles facing internationalisation

The whole idea of internationalisation and all efforts seeking to further it face enormous challenges in both theory and practice, notwithstanding

[18] See the account on the ICN's soft convergence at pp. 573–578 below.
[19] See pp. 545–547 below.   [20] See the discussion at pp. 120–130 below in relation to the WTO.
[21] See chapter 7 which deals with regional cooperation in the field of competition law.

the expansion of the pro-internationalisation camp over the years, especially in light of the legal, business and political problems triggered by competition law enforcement in its present form. At a basic level, it is important to be aware of the reservations expressed by the anti-internationalisation camps, which remain a strong force raising a number of fundamental questions and concerns, including: the claim that there is lack of sufficient clarity with regard to the best option to pursue internationalisation; the question of whether it is really possible or realistic to achieve some of the options, especially those seeking to make available multilateral solutions on a binding basis; and even the question of whether it is really necessary to internationalise competition law through a multilateral option given that it may be argued that the competition law community has on the whole coped fairly well in addressing all challenges triggered by international competition issues.

However, even if one were to consider the above reservations as merely 'psychological' or 'theoretical' and thus possible to overcome, in practice the barriers facing internationalisation efforts are enormous. *First*, there are political barriers. Any internationalisation move requires the consent of countries which can never be guaranteed for a number of reasons: other than the concerns over sovereignty, many countries consider there is a high cost or even a risk inherent in internationalisation, and many are not convinced about the real benefits they would enjoy through opting for 'global welfare'; nor do they believe that these benefits compensate for the cost or risk involved. *Secondly*, there are technical barriers in the form of lack of expertise and capacity on the part of the vast majority of competition authorities and countries more generally. Regardless of the particular form of internationalisation to be pursued, it seems to be necessary that competition law will need to be adopted by all countries and competition authorities around the world will need to develop their expertise and build their capacity as a first step before the internationalisation options taking multilateral or even bilateral forms can be pursued in a meaningful way. *Thirdly*, there are other types of barriers caused by lack of consensus on whether within an international setting the focus should be exclusively on consumers without considering the position of producers. Such lack of consensus is all the more serious because universally there is not total agreement on the most suitable welfare standard to be used in the field of competition law, namely whether it should be consumer welfare standard or one that is based on total welfare.[22] *Moreover* there is the difficult question of how can distortions of competition and discouragement of innovation be avoided when seeking internationalisation or international cooperation in the field, especially since countries do not share common interests and whatever bargaining process will take place may lead to some interests being favoured over others with the ultimate result being that such serious outcomes may arise. *Fourthly*, there are hurdles caused by the fact that the reality is extremely complex because of the involvement of important non-state actors, principally multinational firms and special interest groups. In the case of some countries they are in a weak position when compared to multinational enterprises that, other than their significant lobbying power,[23] enjoy enormous bargaining power vis-à-vis those countries. This power can in some cases receive expression in the form of threats by those multinational firms to desert these countries which in some cases the countries concerned have no choice but to submit to. *Finally*, one ought to mention the hurdles caused by how the international enforcement actions of different competition authorities are viewed: when home and foreign competition authorities take action in cross-border competition cases – as the European Commission has done in high-profile cases such as *Microsoft*, *GE/ Honeywell* and *Boeing/McDonnellDouglas* – questions arise whether this is about punishing foreign firms, favouring local competitors and supporting and promoting national champions.[24]

4.   Sovereignty and the internationalisation of competition law

The concept of sovereignty can be seen as sitting at the centre of the enactment, application or enforcement of competition law. The idea of protecting competition – the core of competition law – is, in many ways, closely linked to national interests and a variety of economic, political and social considerations featuring high on the agenda of countries. In practical terms, protecting competition requires competence to act and to intervene in the marketplace. This competence is part of the general

---

[22] These standards were discussed in the previous chapter.

[23] See p. 114 and p. 117 below.

[24] In almost all of these cases the European Commission, because of its strict enforcement actions, has been attacked on the ground of 'disguised protectionism' and protecting EU-based competitors and furthering the single market objective rather than seeking to uphold competition in strict terms.

prerogatives and powers enjoyed by countries by virtue of the fact that they are sovereign. It should not be at all difficult to imagine therefore that the concept may have considerable implications for the process of internationalisation of competition law, especially when pursued through binding commitments. This is particularly so given that from a national perspective the view held by certain countries has been that a form of internationalisation of competition law – with binding commitments – amounts to a direct limitation of their national sovereignty. One does not need to go further than the position of a country such as the USA to be able to see that such perspective has always been alive.[25]

It would not be unreasonable to suggest that internationalising competition law through several of the options identified in the previous part presupposes some kind of limitation on the sovereignty of individual countries. For example, using binding obligations to pursue internationalisation in a multilateral fashion would certainly require such a limitation; this can be seen most remarkably in light of how the creation of EU competition law regime – as part of a 'new legal order of international law' – involved limitations on the sovereignty of individual member states. At the other end of the internationalisation spectrum, a unilateral approach – through reliance on an extraterritorial assertion of jurisdiction by a country in the field of competition law – may be deemed to encroach upon the national sovereignty of other countries. As the discussion in chapter 8 will demonstrate, the most frequent argument in the diplomatic protests lodged against reliance by countries – especially by the USA – on the doctrine of extraterritoriality in the field has been that the extension of jurisdiction by those countries over foreign firms in competition cases transcending national boundaries infringes the sovereignty of other countries. The reverse side of the same coin shows however that *arguably* reliance on the doctrine of extraterritoriality in the field of competition law seems to be triggered by sovereignty concerns. It would not require a great deal of imagination to think of a situation in which the sole justification for the extraterritorially enforcement of competition laws is the need to protect competition and consumers in local markets and safeguard wider national interests. Not infrequently such interests have been identified as a defence of national sovereignty. Curtailing reliance by individual countries on the doctrine of extraterritoriality can be regarded – albeit indirectly – as a kind of

---

[25] See J. P Griffin, 'What Business People Want from a World Antitrust Code' (1999) *New England Law Review* 39.

limitation on the sovereignty of the countries concerned to address what they perceive as harmful situations.

These different 'perspectives' – some of which are conflicting – make the issue of sovereignty a particularly complex one in the field of competition law; especially so in the process of internationalisation of competition law. On the one hand, the process may be perceived by certain countries as *sovereignty-limiting* whilst on the other hand, due to the *sovereignty-infringing* probability in extraterritorial enforcement, the process may be seen as offering an option under which this could be avoided. These conflicting views need to be balanced carefully; an exercise which is difficult and in itself complex to undertake. Achieving this balance depends primarily on the extent to which sovereignty will *actually* be limited in the process. One thing appears to be clear: the process is unlikely to involve the relinquishment of sovereignty *in absolute terms*. In other words, it would not be possible to argue in a sensible way that the process implies countries would absolutely lose their sovereignty, a point that has ample support from the case of the different treaties establishing originally the European Community, and later the EU. Under none of these treaties have the member states of the EU lost their sovereignty totally: as was acknowledged by the EU's highest judicial authority – the European Court of Justice – in its early jurisprudence, the limitation of sovereignty of member states occurred in *limited* fields. None of the options for the internationalisation of competition law – including the multilateral one through binding commitments – involves a far-reaching commitment as the creation of the EC or the EU. The process of internationalisation of competition law therefore may not be seen as being wholly incompatible with the concept of sovereignty. It would not be correct to assert that the process necessarily causes countries to no longer be considered sovereign or for them to be deprived of the power legally to act independently in the field.

Perhaps what is required is an appreciation that the concept of sovereignty has evolved at a conceptual level as far as its use in contemporary political practice is concerned. The evolution of sovereignty in this case may be possible to observe in light of the process of relentless globalisation, which has placed countries – economically at least – on a path towards progressive integration or *centralisation* in many fields whilst at the same time witnessing a process of progressive *decentralisation* of power and authority. As a result of this development, some fundamental pillars supporting the concept of sovereignty may seem to be in need of adjustment given that one may query whether countries are actually *fully sovereign* in relation to markets in modern times anyhow, without going through a process of internationalisation of competition law. Many markets have become truly global and extremely wider than individual countries or regions. Even in the case of some 'local' markets, these feature technological development, which in part is drawn from the home country and in (perhaps a larger) part required from outside. When one considers these phenomenal market developments – as part of the wider process of globalisation and specifically the high level of interdependence between countries this has come to facilitate – the question of whether countries remain fully sovereign in economic areas probably is not possible to answer with an absolute 'yes' and at any rate calls for serious debate.

5.   Globalisation and its relevance

(A)   *The meaning of globalisation*

Globalisation is one of the most frequently used concepts in all areas of economic regulation and trade policy. Since the 1990s, it has become an extremely popular slogan used in many cases without actually reflecting on what it means or what its connotations are. It is unclear when exactly the concept was coined. One thing that is certain is that the concept is not the product of the trade liberalisation the world has come to witness following the creation of the WTO in 1995; there is evidence that the concept is older than this: some people regard it as a 1980s concept, others see it as a 1960s concept and there are those who argue that the 'roots' of globalisation extend to the nineteenth century and even the sixteenth century.[26] What almost everyone agrees on is that there is a history of globalisation in the world but the dominant use of the concept since the 1990s has been pretty much modern with a strong economic flavour.

It is extremely challenging to capture globalisation in a single, unified definition and in fairness it is probably true that the concept is not susceptible to such a definition. Globalisation is a multi-tiered, multi-dimensional and multi-faceted concept that embodies an extremely long process of human evolution. Instead of searching for a definition of globalisation one should concentrate on attempting to understand the

---

[26] See D. O. Flynn and A. Giraldez, 'Born Again: Globalization's Sixteenth Century Origins (Asian/Global Versus European Dynamics)' (2008) *Pacific Economic Review* 359.

concept in the particular context it is used. As globalisation has come to unfold over the years a number of contexts have come to develop in which globalisation operates. These contexts include cultural, political, social, technological, and of course a wider economic context, with which most people have come to associate globalisation. In its economic context, globalisation is considered to provide a 'fusion' of national economies converting them into a global one. Despite the differences between these contexts of globalisation, they share a common ground, namely the fact that they concern a 'transformation' of *national* (or where relevant *regional*) phenomena into *global* phenomenon through a process of integration.

(B)   Is globalisation a natural process?

It is critical to an understanding of globalisation to appreciate that it is not a *natural* phenomenon or process; in this regard globalisation is similar to free trade and competition, both of which are not natural phenomena. Globalisation is a process that follows from political choices and decisions adopted by governments and relevant supranational authorities; sometimes this process could include influence by international bodies and organisations, some of which are the product of the concept of globalisation and were created specifically to support the process, most notably the WTO, UNCTAD, the World Bank and the International Monetary Fund (IMF). Political decisions – as well as those processes through which government policies are formulated – have facilitated the creation and actual existence of globalisation. These decisions and processes also determine the extent and level of globalisation. In this respect, it is important to note that globalisation – especially when viewed as an erosion of national identity – could be considered to be *politically* not acceptable.

In its economic and market context, the political decisions and processes facilitating globalisation described above are widely considered to reflect a newer, late 1990s, approach to markets and state regulation. This approach stands in complete contrast to the approach largely witnessed in the years preceding the last two decades or so of the twentieth century. The discussion in the previous chapter demonstrated quite succinctly how the global economy witnessed dramatic changes in a remarkably short period of time, including the reduction and elimination of state control and monopolisation; favouring the market mechanism; and opening domestic markets to foreign trade and investment. Many people identify the process of globalisation with these important developments and vice versa.

(C)   The pros and cons of globalisation

There is no shortage of pro- and anti-globalisation movements and trends around.[27] Arguments in favour of globalisation have always existed and many interest groups and countries regard globalisation as one of the best products in history to advance the common good in the world and to create interconnection between different peoples in order to distribute benefits, which would not be possible to deliver throughout the world otherwise. In this respect, globalisation has been viewed as critical to economic development and progress and advancing important causes in other arenas. At the same time, many anti-globalisation movements have expressed extremely strong views against what they see as a perfect recipe for unfair concentration as opposed to equitable distribution of wealth around the world and manipulation of the 'weak' at the hands of the 'strong'. It is beyond the scope of our discussion to engage in a detailed examination of these arguments and of the *virtues* and *vices* of globalisation. Whether globalisation is a good or bad process has always been a highly debatable issue; it is unlikely this will be settled at any point in the future. There is certainly an argument that globalisation would be considered a good thing in so far as it leads to improvement in economic conditions and standards (including standards of living) within different countries, especially developing ones. There would be little sense in attacking or opposing globalisation (not least for the sake of it) if consumers worldwide (in both developed and developing countries) were able to enjoy better quality of products and services, more choice and lower prices. In this way, globalisation can have positive effects, which must be welcomed, encouraged and supported. From a competition law perspective, globalisation can actually help achieve many of the goals

---

[27] It may be worth noting that pro- and anti-globalisation movements may actually be formed depending on geographical location. For example, in one and the same country – such as the USA – pro-globalisation voices may be heard loud and clear in one part of the country in which politicians and businesses attach huge importance to the export of products as the main engine for economic growth and achieving political influence internationally; the picture in another part of the country may be radically different and anti-globalisation voices may be dominant because globalisation could facilitate the closure of factories in the relevant part and the loss of employment for many following a decision by the relevant businesses to move to 'nearby' foreign locations in order to make use of, among other things, cheaper labour and favourable tax regimes, etc.

strived at in the enforcement of the law and it is not outrageous to suggest that globalisation can deliver these benefits even in the absence of competition law or competition enforcement: in such situations, provided markets are open, the existence of globalisation could facilitate effective competitive constraints by foreign firms on possible anticompetitive conduct and the behaviour of local firms in these markets and promote competition to the benefit of local consumers. At the same time, globalisation has facilitated the emergence of 'global competition', a process through which – with the technological advances and positive learning processes many firms have come to enjoy – competition in many global markets has been enhanced and promoted quite significantly.

Having said that, there is also a counter argument that globalisation is not a virtue. As we noted above, there is a certain degree of discomfort and scepticism over globalisation in many quarters. Different groups, including some consumer groups, anti-capitalist groups and some developing countries have come to regard globalisation as a process used by developed countries and their (powerful) firms to impose their standards on these groups and to suppress and constrain their freedom. Many anti-globalisation movements – such as those opposed to corporate globalisation and those who seek to establish global justice in the world – see globalisation as a means towards exploitation of consumers (especially those of disadvantaged countries), a cause of loss of employment and a strategy aimed at weakening the position of important groups within countries, such as those of workers' unions and alliances. In this case, and if indeed there is truth behind this, it would be difficult to advocate or defend globalisation.

(D) The effects of globalisation on the field of competition law

The most relevant context of globalisation to the field of competition law is that of market globalisation, which has been particularly fostered by advances in technology and the elimination of barriers hindering the flows of trade and investment worldwide.[28] The globalisation of different national and regional markets raises a number of challenges in the field of competition law. A specific challenge that is worth mentioning is the one faced by competition authorities which could be presented in the

---

[28] See generally M. Walters, *Globalization* (Routledge, 1995); J. H. Dunning, *The Globalization of Business: the Challenges of the 1990s* (Routledge, 1993).

form of a question: how can competition authorities ensure that the global integration of markets leads to and maintains competitive outcomes, thus making globalisation both economically more efficient and socially more acceptable? There is no easy or simple answer to this question but it is believed that the way in which competition authorities choose to enforce competition law – and specifically their efforts to build international cooperation in the field – has an important role to play in ensuring the 'efficiency' and 'acceptability' of globalisation and especially in avoiding resentment to globalisation and a favouritism towards protectionism, whether as a general stance by countries or as a backlash to globalisation.

Globalisation has led to an increase in the number of competition law issues that transcend national boundaries. The sequence in this regard is an easy one to follow. As markets and competition become increasingly international, so do anticompetitive situations. These situations may occur in different fields, including air or sea transport, software products, pharmaceuticals, fuel, steel, glass, aluminium and telecommunications, among others; and they may be in a variety of forms such as export cartels, international cartels and conspiracies, vertical restraints, abuse of market dominance and harmful mergers. The economic effects of these practices can easily pierce national boundaries and are not constrained by the existence of *invisible* territorial hindrances. For example, a number of firms may collude on a product market that extends beyond national boundaries. The collusive behaviour in this case will have an effect throughout *that* market. Similarly, a single firm enjoying dominance in the manufacture and distribution of its products throughout the world may be able to achieve the same result unilaterally, namely through abusing its dominant position and affecting competition in the relevant market. The same is also true with regard to international mergers which, when implemented, produce effects in more than one country and which normally require the approval of several competition authorities before they can be implemented. Competition law practice and literature are full of examples covering such, or similar, scenarios. In all of these scenarios, the anticompetitive situation affects the interests of consumers on the *relevant* market[29] and, as a consequence, the country and communities of which they are part. It should therefore be clear why domestic competition authorities would want to regulate such situations;

---

[29] See pp. 70–77 above for discussion on the relevant market and how this is defined in the field of competition law.

though it is clear that legal and political hurdles affecting their endeavour may arise along the way.

The situations identified above in their nature lead to the transfer of wealth from consumers to producers; and in an international context the transfer of wealth will be from consumers in one country to producers in another. Regardless of whether one or more domestic competition authorities are able to intervene in these situations, whether they will intervene and how they will do that, it is beyond doubt that such situations give rise to fundamental legal, economic and political problems with which the internationalisation of competition law is concerned. It can be seen therefore that globalisation has very significant implications for competition law in the global economy. Globalisation has made it almost inevitable to change competition law and policy. In this regard, the internationalisation of competition law can be seen as a response to market globalisation; a direct relationship thus exists between the two. Indeed, globalisation has had a direct impact in the field of competition and has made it necessary to 'change' how competition law and policy are understood and how they are enforced. Arguably, a globalised economy should be seen in parallel to globalised competition law solutions, which is what the process of internationalisation is all about.

6.   The interaction between different disciplines

The nature of the topic of internationalisation of competition law – conditioned primarily by the special nature of competition law itself[30] – makes it necessary to gain insights from various disciplines when debating the topic or attempting to analyse the process of internationalisation. The topic – like the field of competition law more generally – has been dominated by lawyers and economists.[31] Obviously, there are important legal and economic dimensions to the internationalisation of competition law and these have justified the heavy involvement on the part of lawyers and economists in the debate. Almost all thoughts formulated and ideas put forward on how competition law and policy could be advanced at the international level have been the product of work undertaken by lawyers and economists; lawyers in particular – whether operating within domestic, regional or international organisations or the

---

[30] See pp. 49–51 above.   [31] See p. 50 above.

medium of academic debate and writing – have been influential in the shaping of the debate.

Nonetheless, the legal and economic dimensions – whilst of major significance – are not the only dimensions that one must be aware of in the process of internationalisation: additionally, one must realise the importance of politics (and specifically political science), business management and administration and arguably even economic geography. The discussion above highlighted the strong political dimension to the process. By involving the specific discipline of political science one will be better able to understand a key component of internationalisation which is at the centre of thinking of political scientists: how decision-making power is allocated and transferred between different levels, principally the national and supranational level and what role(s) the governments of countries and international organisations play in formulating public policies. Economic geography is important to consider because it gives perspective on how the issue of location, distribution and spatial organisation of economic activities throughout the world influences attempts to build global standards in areas of economic regulation; which is of direct relevance to the process of internationalisation of competition law. These different disciplines – in addition to law and economics – offer valuable insights to understanding the internationalisation of competition law and which enable one to analyse the topic in its proper context. There is mutual interest between the members of these disciplines in this process – and arguably an overlap between some of the disciplines[32] – which could be highlighted by constructing adequate dialogues between these disciplines.[33] For this reason, adopting an interdisciplinary approach to a study on the internationalisation of competition law is highly desirable and worth encouraging. What one must remain aware of is the involvement of different actors in the process which gives rise to a number of issues, such as: the design of *international institutions and organisations* and their functioning in the field of competition law; the regulation of the behaviour, conduct or transactions of *multinational enterprises*; the influence by and on national sovereignty of

---

[32] For example, it can be said that the work of economists has expanded over the years to include elements traditionally considered to be within the scope of study of economic geography (i.e. the work of geographers).

[33] On constructing dialogues between different disciplines, see generally J. Weiler, 'Community, Member States and European Integration: is the Law Relevant?' (1982) *Journal of Common Market Studies* 39; R. Pryce, *The Politics of the European Community* (Butterworths, 1973).

countries; the advocacy of consumer rights and interests by *consumer organisations*; the involvement of *regional blocks* and *their supranational bodies*; and the role played by the special *public bodies* of countries such as *competition authorities* and *courts*. The role of these different actors will be discussed in the following part. What is important to note in the present context however is that *institutions* – national, regional and international – require specific attention when examining the internationalisation of competition law because of the important contribution they actually and potentially can make both to advancing and hindering the process. This is not just a matter of conducting a legal analysis but also involves studying policy processes, which are at the heart of the topic of internationalisation of competition law.[34]

Other than the enthusiasm of lawyers and economists for internationalising competition law and their contribution in this regard, the topic has not received sufficient attention from the members of other disciplines, such as political science or economic geography. It seems that economic geographers have not identified competition law as a specific field to be considered in the international context. Political scientists on the other hand whilst giving some attention to the field, have not pushed their work to the stage of materialising into systematic work. They have therefore left the field (and the topic of internationalisation) to lawyers and economists.[35] It is not fully clear why this has happened: whether the domination of the field by lawyers and economists has discouraged or perhaps rendered it virtually impossible for the members of other disciplines from entering the 'debate' and undertake work in the field; whether the latter simply have had little interest in doing so; or whether economists and lawyers have gradually enlarged their specialisation and expertise and in doing so ventured into areas traditionally studied by members of the other disciplines. Whilst there may be some evidence that lawyers have engaged in institutional design and policy formulation in the field of competition law and economists have expanded the scope of their work to consider issues of spatial organisation of economic activities, it seems quite inevitable that they will stall when faced with complex questions of institutional design in an international setting

---

[34] See M. Staniland, *What Is Political Economy?: a Study of Social Theory and Underdevelopment* (Yale University Press, 1985); D.C. North, *Institutions, Institutional Change and Economic Performance* (Cambridge University Press, 1990); M. Granovetter, 'Economic Action and Social Structure: the Problem of Embeddedness' in M. Granovetter and R. Swedberg (eds.), *The Sociology of Economic Life* (Westview Press, 1992).

[35] B. Doern and S. Wilks, *Comparative Competition Policy* (Oxford University Press, 1996), p. 4.

dealing with international politics, especially when it comes to determining what is politically acceptable in the process of internationalisation and how political bargaining between the different players and interest groups need to be handled;[36] questions which are as distant from traditional legal and economic analysis and theories as one can be. The process of internationalisation cannot therefore be looked at as a mere legal debate; nor can the process be completed with ideas put forward by lawyers or even economists: there is a need to involve other disciplines and specifically to have concrete and empirical studies conducted to examine institutional issues and the political reality in the internationalisation landscape.

A simple example that would illustrate the scope for input and contribution by political scientists in particular can be found in relation to the issue of cooperation. A central question concerning cooperation in the field of competition law – whether in bilateral or multilateral form – is whether cooperation can help strengthen the position of competition authorities who might feel weak vis-à-vis strong multinational firms who would not comply with the orders or actions of these authorities. Political scientists have an important role to play here in order to test the validity of theories and views formulated by lawyers and inform any study on internationalisation about the real benefits of cooperation and the likelihood of their occurrence in practice. One such view is that cooperation would actually strengthen competition authorities (including those of developing countries) in terms of capacity building and building their expertise.[37]

7. The different players: their role, contribution and perspectives

The world has come to change dramatically over the past 20 years in particular. Many of the changes that began in the 1990s have not reached

---

[36] Doern and Wilks, pp. 4–5, ibid. The authors argue that their assertion is not intended to be dismissive of law and economics disciplines, or to imply that academic lawyers or economists invariably overlook political factors. They merely (and it seems rightly) emphasise 'a systematic bias and an understandable, if regrettable, narrowness of viewpoint' on the part of either discipline.

[37] Arguably small competition authorities and developing countries have benefited from the work of international bodies such as UNCTAD, the ICN and to a certain extent the OECD. Also bilateral cooperation has been beneficial to the parties concerned enabling them to improve their practices and make their enforcement more efficient as can be seen from key examples such as the US–EU cooperation and the Australia–New Zealand cooperation. See pp. 501–506 below.

full maternity and remain highly dynamic and continue to accelerate at a phenomenal rate. Today's world is one of continuous and fast transition, especially in the economic arena. This has major implications for governments, business firms, wider communities, international bodies and various special interest groups. In addition to the many opportunities this gives rise to, it also poses formidable challenges. The process of internationalisation of competition law can be said to be caught in the middle of these changes and this gives rise to a number of questions. These questions concern: identifying *who are the major players* in this process and *how the relationship between them should be understood*; determining *who among these players should lead and ultimately decide on the type and extent of internationalisation to be pursued*; and figuring *whether entrusting the decision-making role to one player or particular group of players as opposed to another player or group would affect the process.*

(A) The players

The different players who have been involved or likely to have a role in debates on the internationalisation of competition law and efforts to further the process include: countries; multinational firms; special interest groups; international organisations; and regional organisations and bodies. In this section, the role of the first three players will be discussed; the role played by the latter two – namely international and regional actors – will be discussed in later chapters.[38]

I. Countries

The use of the concept of countries when dealing with the internationalisation of competition law needs to be handled with particular care because several entities within countries have some form of involvement in the process. Countries are made of an executive (which may or may not include the relevant competition authority(ies)), judicial and legislative branch. Putting competition authorities to one side, these three branches may not always share the same view in a field like competition law, let alone when it comes to considering the internationalisation of

---

[38] Chapter 3 will consider the role of international organisations and chapter 7 will consider the role of regional organisations. It is also worth noting that chapter 4 will consider the EU competition law regime, which obviously is the world's only effective and fully operational regional competition law regime.

competition law; the situation is not any different – in terms of unity of views – when competition authorities are taken into account. In the case of some countries, a regional organisation of which they are part may exist within which a supranational authority may be given competence to act in the field of competition law – something that will only make things more complex and harder when it comes to considering the perspectives of countries in the process.

(a) **Governments** Governments play an important role in the internationalisation of competition law. Especially in relation to bilateral and multilateral options, government approval and consent is vital before the country concerned (or its competition authority(ies)) is able to participate in such initiatives. This requires the making of political decision(s) or the initiation and completion of policy processes. Even in relation to the unilateral option, whether in assessing extraterritoriality or advocating local competition standards or actively engaging in the provision of technical assistance at an international level, governments have decisive control. Other than the involvement of governments in the legislative process and the adoption of laws, government control the budget and determine what resources would be devoted to competition law activities. For example, when it comes to technical assistance competition authorities usually do not have the resources (unless specifically made available by governments) to engage in such activities. In practice, therefore many competition authorities simply 'respond' to technical assistance requests by other competition authorities but the necessary funding will usually be provided by the latter or more likely by an international body; a few competition authorities providers of technical assistance offer funding.

The role government plays in the field of competition law and the area of economic regulation more generally is highly interesting. When governments conduct international negotiations in these fields they seek to protect national interests. Nonetheless the concept of national interests is quite vague and can be problematic, especially in the context of internationalisation of competition law because the 'different' interests covered under the concept may not coexist in full harmony and it can easily happen that a particular interest or one set of interests would dominate.

(b) **The legislative branch** The legislative branch in different countries assumes specific responsibilities in the process of internationalisation of competition law, primarily relating to legislating and the approval of actions taken or proposed by the executive branch. In some regimes, the international functions of the competition authority are subject to close vetting and approval by parliament. In certain countries – notably the USA – the legislative branch includes a special parliamentary committee devoted to competition law and policy.[39] In these countries, parliamentary sessions can sometimes witness extremely heated and well-argued exchanges on competition law, especially when a new competition law (or laws seeking to resist the influence of foreign competition laws in the country)[40] is being proposed or an amendment to the existing competition rules is tabled before parliament. In most parliaments around the world however, little attention is given to competition law and policy and exclusive competence is enjoyed by the government in the field.

(c) The judiciary   In many competition law regimes, courts can exert strong influence on the policy direction of the country concerned in relation to the process of internationalisation of competition law. Particularly when it comes to assertions of extraterritoriality some courts have defined the scope of jurisdiction within which these assertions may be made (and as a result have widened the geographic reach of local competition rules) or at the other extreme *block* such assertions by foreign countries.[41] Courts therefore can be said to play an important role in the internationalisation of competition law. Indeed it is possible to find concrete examples of how courts can help or even take the lead to establish supranational competition law regimes; notably the role played by the European Court of Justice in establishing EU competition law regime.[42]

(d) Competition authorities   Competition authorities – whether actual or potential – can be key actors in mustering support for internationalising competition law. Competition authorities are well placed to realise problems calling for internationalisation and for suggesting and advocating ways in which these problems may be overcome.[43]

---

[39] See the US Senate Subcommittee on Antitrust, Competition Policy and Consumer Rights.

[40] See pp. 472–475 below in relation to blocking laws.

[41] See the discussion in chapter 8 below in the context of the doctrine of extraterritoriality.

[42] See in particular pp. 172–174 below.

[43] One of the important factors in ensuring the impressive success of the ICN is the fact that its membership is made of competition authorities.

II. Multinational enterprises

(a) **The term**   The term 'multinational' firm, enterprise, company or corporation is not one that came to be coined only recently; notwithstanding the fact that the *environment* within which such entities operate – i.e. a globalised economy – largely is a twentieth-century product. There is ample evidence pointing to the existence of such entities as early as 1602.[44] It is less certain however how the concept should be understood and when an entity would truly be a multinational enterprise (MNE) or multinational company or corporation (MNC): whether this will be so when an entity conducts its economic activity or has a corporate structure in more than *one* country or in a *few or more* countries; whether the existence of production facilities in *foreign* countries without a corporate structure or engaging in the supply or sale of products in those countries would suffice; whether the business and legal form of the entity is relevant; and whether the term covers both private and state-owned enterprises. In other words, although the understanding is that a cross-border element must exist in the structure or economic activities of a multinational enterprise, there is uncertainty as to whether the existence of this element is sufficient in itself to make such entity a multinational enterprise *and* how many countries are needed to amount to 'multi' in this case. There is therefore a problem of definition[45] and over the years 'competing' views on how the term should be defined have emerged in the work of scholars[46] and international organisations.[47] In the present context, a wide and loose definition will be adopted in line with the prevailing understanding of the term 'multinational enterprise': an entity active in production or distribution in two countries, regardless of the way it is structured[48] and financed. The emphasis is put here on *behavioural* more than *structural* elements because this would 'fit' within the context of the discussion on internationalisation of competition law.

---

[44] Scholars often mention the Dutch East India Company as an example of the world's first multinational enterprise. This company was set up at the beginning of the seventeenth century and armed by the Parliament of the Netherlands with a 'monopoly' to engage in activities in colonialised Asia.

[45] See P. T. Muchlinski, *Multinational Enterprises and the Law* (Oxford University Press, 2007).

[46] See N. Hood and S. Young, *The Economics of the Multinational Enterprise* (Longman, 1979).

[47] See the definition put forward by the OECD in its *Guidelines for Multinational Enterprises* (OECD, 1976); and see UNCTAD *Report of Eminent Persons* (UNCTAD, 1974).

[48] See Muchlinski, note 45 above, for an account on different structures.

This is not to say however that structural elements may not be relevant as far as a competition law analysis of situations stretching beyond national boundaries is concerned. Indeed there are many situations in which structural elements could pave the way for internationalisation, the most obvious of which is found in the 'single economic group' doctrine, namely where a competition authority will be able to impute liability to a parent firm located in a foreign jurisdiction where a subsidiary under the control of such parent which operates in local markets engages in anticompetitive behaviour, such as participating in a cartel situation. As the discussion in chapter 8 below will show, this doctrine has served as a basis for extraterritorial assertion of jurisdiction by competition authorities.[49]

Traditionally, the understanding developed that for an entity to 'leap' towards and acquire a multinational status it would need to go through a long process of gradual expansion which starts first with consolidating the entity's position in its home market; sometimes this could be through the conferring of a monopoly status on such an entity by the state, which would also support the entity in its penetration or capturing of foreign markets. The Internet revolution however seems to have somewhat altered this understanding. The creation of the Internet has meant that the global reach of certain entities – notably those in the high-technology or general services sector – may be achieved in a short period of time (sometime almost instantly as soon as operations are started) and regardless of the size of the entity. Such entities are sometimes referred to as 'micro multinationals', i.e. small entities which through the use of the Internet can begin their business operations in different countries around the world as opposed to in a single (home) country.

(b) Competition issues caused by MNEs   When discussing MNEs and their role in the field of competition law, an association is usually made between MNEs and anticompetitive situations. It should not be thought however that the behaviour, conduct or transactions of MNEs naturally or inevitably give rise to competition problems. In fact there are many situations in which MNEs may operate in a pro-competitive manner: the behaviour, conduct or operations of MNEs may invite, facilitate and enhance both price and non-price competition in global and local markets alike.

---

[49] See, for example, how the European Commission asserted such jurisdiction in the *Wood pulp* case, discussed at pp. 453–454 below.

Nonetheless, MNEs may cause competition problems at two different levels. First, they may cause problems at the level of behaviour and conduct often taking the form of: cartelisation; harmful partial-function joint ventures;[50] vertical restraints; and abuse of dominance. Secondly, competition problems may arise at a structural level through MNEs opting to structure themselves through merger operations so as to acquire (or strengthen their) dominance, lessen competition, cause foreclosure[51] in the relevant market and create barriers to entry and as a result be in a 'better' position to harm competition.

The recognition that competition problems may arise as a result of conduct or behaviour by MNEs emerged in the first half of the twentieth century. Even at that time, concentrated efforts came to be made at the international plane to address such problems and to seek to regulate the behaviour of MNEs, most notably the draft Havana Charter which aimed at establishing an International Trade Organisation and later on the adoption of the *Set of Principles and Rules for the Control of Restrictive Business Practices* within UNCTAD. The *Set* includes a specific call for MNEs to refrain from engaging in harmful anticompetitive conduct or behaviour as can be seen in section D(3) and (4) of the *Set*.[52]

(c) **The concerns of MNEs**   The reverse side of the coin however shows that MNEs have several concerns over the way in which competition law is enforced at present, which the process of internationalisation may be seen as capable of addressing. Among these concerns the following are worth noting.

First, there is the concern over lack of uniformity between different competition law regimes which is seen as a characteristic of current competition law understanding and enforcement around the world. Lack of uniformity has been considered to be problematic with business behaviour, conduct and operations increasingly transcending national boundaries. The proliferation of competition law around the world has

---

[50] The distinction here is made specifically between partial function and full function joint ventures, which amount to merger situations in the field of competition law. The former are taken to stand on the basis of 'cooperation' agreements between firms; see above.

[51] Foreclosure may be in the form of excluding competitors, whether actual or potential ones.

[52] Section D(3) deals with anticompetitive agreements and section D(4) deals with abuse of dominance. UNCTAD and the *Set* are discussed in further details in the following chapter.

meant that in parallel such situations increasingly become subject to the jurisdiction of more than one domestic competition authority.[53] Many of these authorities differ fundamentally even on some of the basic issues which means that lack of uniformity in approach is quite inevitable. This is something firms seriously dislike in practice because they prefer uniformity in the way in which their competition cases are handled and decided by different competition authorities. Firms are aware that such lack of uniformity could lead to material differences in outcome of investigations. In some cases they even *fear* the lack of uniformity because of the real possibility that the authorities may reach strikingly conflicting decisions over the legality of the same practice.[54] This is the gravest concern firms have in practice, especially in merger cases. It may be worth noting here that the issue of assertion of jurisdiction by competition authorities in these cases is directly linked to the possibility of conflicting decisions: where a merger case, for instance, could potentially fall within the jurisdiction of two or more competition authorities, a lack of exercise of jurisdiction by one competition authority reduces the possibility of conflicting decisions. This means that firms can be concerned about multi-jurisdictional merger review though many firms simply accept this as a fact and would be content with this state of affairs as long this does not translate into conflicting decisions at the end. Thus firms are not so much concerned about the mere possibility of more than one competition authority asserting jurisdiction over a particular operation as much as they are concerned about the possibility that between these authorities a lack of uniformity may exist leading to inconsistent outcomes.

Nevertheless, one needs to bear in mind that reaching conflicting decisions in certain cases may be inevitable, mainly due to differences in the legal standards employed by different competition authorities, which can give rise to inconsistencies,[55] and those concerning the structure of the relevant market and the levels of its concentration. For

---

[53] A particularly high-profile example of a record number of jurisdictions in which a merger had to be notified is the *Exxon/Mobile* merger which occurred in 1999. Another operation, the *MCI/WorldCom* transaction in 1997, was reviewed by more than 30 competition authorities in the world; see A. Frederickson, 'A Strategic Approach to Multi-Jurisdictional Filings' (1999) *European Counsel* 23.

[54] See the mergers cases of *Shell/Montedison* (1994) *Official Journal* L-332/48 and *Boeing/McDonnell Douglas* (1997) *Official Journal* L-336/16.

[55] See D. Wood and R. Whish, *Merger Cases in the Real World: a Study of Merger Control Procedures* (OECD, 1994).

example, the market in country A may be an oligopolistic and highly concentrated market unlike in country B. When it comes to regulate a merger operation under the competition rules of both countries one should expect that the competition authorities concerned are very likely to form different views over the same operation. Additionally, conflicting decisions may be triggered due to the fact that non-competition considerations may be taken into account whether by only one or all of the competition authorities concerned. These considerations may relate to industrial policy or could be based on political calculations and interests.

Secondly, there is the concern over diplomatic conflicts between countries. Obviously, the assertion of jurisdiction by more than one competition authority and the reaching of inconsistent results by those authorities in a particular case affect the firms concerned in a direct way. For instance this could mean that the firms will not be able to implement their merger operation. Beyond this however inconsistent outcomes may lead to international conflicts between the countries concerned which will go beyond the field of competition law and extend to industrial policy. Firms are generally concerned about the prospect of being caught in such conflicts, where it is normal for industrial policy considerations and other considerations to override competition policy considerations. Moreover, they are concerned about situations in which their business operations beyond national boundaries may be adversely affected. In other words, firms may encounter difficulties in the future where the governments concerned may decide to engage in 'retaliatory' policies or adopt a protectionist stance as a result of which these firms might suffer.

Thirdly, there is the concern over differences in procedure. Competition law regimes around the world differ in terms of the procedures used in applying and enforcing the rules within the regime. These differences relate to a number of aspects of competition law and policy, ranging from how firms could or must notify their operations, conduct or behaviour to the relevant competition authorities, to how these authorities go about conducting their investigations and to how enforcement will be carried out where this becomes necessary. Some of these differences are very fundamental. Differences are especially worth highlighting in the field of merger control. Merging firms can be anxious about the length of time required for different competition authorities to reach a decision on a particular operation because delays in decision-making may be harmful to their interests. These firms usually would favour speedy decisions in merger cases which are taken within similar timeframes. The literature and practice in the area of merger control are full of examples supporting this.[56] Nonetheless, it should be noted that under certain circumstances such firms may request or agree to a delay in the procedure before the competition authority in order to serve their interests.[57]

Fourthly, there is the concerned over increase in costs. Multi-assertion of jurisdiction by different competition authorities increases the burden and expense imposed on MNEs of having to comply with the laws of different jurisdictions.[58] In some cases firms may incur an unnecessary expense notifying their merger operations in several jurisdictions without their operations actually producing an impact on competition in those jurisdictions or simply because they want to be on the safe side. Some of these firms never hear from the competition authorities concerned; a fact that is used to show the wasteful nature of regulation in these cases.

Finally, firms are generally concerned about situations in which one competition authority may hand over confidential information about those firms to another authority within the framework of bilateral cooperation, which may exist between them. The fear is that the latter may use or cause this information to be used for economic espionage. Also, there is an anxiety when information is handed over to a jurisdiction which allows private actions.[59] These actions are considered to be a 'rogue elephant' because private plaintiffs in these actions are not under the same constraints as competition authorities, for example, regarding breach of confidence. So, there may be a risk of confidential information being disclosed to other firms and individuals. Having said that, it is important to note that in the case of competition authorities brought together by bilateral cooperation agreements, such agreements as a rule prevent the disclosure of confidential information without the consent of the proprietor of the information (i.e. the disclosing firm) or

---

[56] See Griffin, note 25 above.

[57] This is, for example, the case where the firms would want to secure a positive outcome from the competition authority by proposed commitments or remedies to address possible anticompetitive concerns identified by the authority or where the delay would enable the firms to sort internal matters without ultimately jeopardising or completely derailing the flow of procedure. See, for example, Regulation 139/2004 in the field of EU merger control which provides for 'stop-the-clock' option in some cases; see p. 162 below.

[58] See remarks by Philip Condit, CEO of Boeing Corporation, about the conflicting results reached by the EU and the USA in the *Boeing/McDonnell Douglas* merger, Press Release 'Boeing Responds to European Commission Recommendation' (July 1997).

[59] Private actions are allowed under the US competition law regime; examined in chapter 5 below.

clear authorisation under an international treaty.[60] Notwithstanding these safeguards, firms and their legal advisors sometimes sense that an exchange of confidential information between two competition authorities must have occurred discreetly!

III.   Special interest groups

The term 'special interest groups' may be understood liberally to refer to a number of forces, extending from lobbyists with specific agenda, to producers, importers and finally to consumer groups. In this section, the focus will be given to the latter.

Offering an account on the role and perspective of consumer groups in relation to the process of internationalisation is not an easy task mainly because the views within these groups easily diverge, especially on issues such as that of internationalisation. Additionally, it can be said that insufficient attention has been given to this issue specifically to be able to offer a unified or 'global' perspective of consumers which can stand the test of critical assessment and evaluation.

Perhaps the widely assumed view has been that the interests of consumers in a global economy would be maximised if competition rules as wide as markets were introduced, i.e. if a process of meaningful internationalisation of competition law would be opted for. This view seems to be based on the understanding that building a global 'vision' in the field of competition law would better facilitate the appraisal of positive as well as negative impacts of international operations of firms on the interest of consumers in different countries. Important international organisations such as the OECD, World Bank, the WTO and Consumers International[61] have in recent years devoted attention – in varying degrees – to consumer interests in global markets, as well as advocating ways to protect those interests. A clear consensus has been emerging, especially at the WTO and the OECD, that introducing international competition rules and standards would enhance the welfare and interests of consumers in global markets. Both the OECD and WTO have called on countries to make competition and trade policy more responsive to the interests of consumers and to take those interests into account especially when consumers are located beyond national boundaries.[62]

---

[60] See chapter 9 below for a more detailed discussion.
[61] See www.consumersinternational.org.
[62] See *New Dimensions of Market Access in Globalizing World Economy* (OECD, 1995), p. 254; WTO *Annual Report* (WTO, 1997), p. 75.

The argument in favour of internationalisation of competition law (leading to international competition rules) aside, it would be actually correct to say that in the first place attention ought to be given to the process of globalisation itself and determining what views consumer groups hold in relation to the process. As noted above, globalisation occupies an important place in the whole process of internationalisation. There has been a heated debate on whether globalisation itself in general would benefit consumers.[63] It may be of interest to note the position of pro- and anti-globalisers. The former tend to assume markets are competitive, including markets in developing countries and those in transition. According to pro-globalisers, liberalisation of trade and furthering globalisation will benefit consumers. Anti-globalisers, on the other hand, have adopted a different stance, arguing that liberalisation would have the opposite effect, namely leading to damaging monopolies in different markets and this can only herald bad news for consumers, especially those located in markets in which little choice is available in the form of products made by local rivals.

(B)   Countries v. markets and countries v. multinational enterprises

It may be worth making a few comments on the highly interesting relationship between two major actors discussed above and to attempt to trace the origins from which this relationship has actually evolved.

It is probably clear to everyone that the topic of MNEs has witnessed a remarkably interesting transition over the years. This transition has spanned different areas: from those dealing with corporate and tax law to economic regulation. As a result, many important and challenging questions have arisen concerning MNEs which are undoubtedly crucial to examine, as can be seen from leading works on the topic.[64] In the present context however, our focus is on the field of economic regulation, in which the transition has occurred in large part due to the wide recognition that emerged in the last quarter of the twentieth century that MNEs – not markets – are the appropriate 'counterparts' of countries in a globalised economy.

Traditionally, the field of economic regulation was analysed on the basis that two 'actors' existed: the state and the market or countries and

---

[63] See pp. 92–97 above for a discussion on the concept and process of globalisation.
[64] See Muchlinski, note 45 above.

markets. The reason why such thinking prevailed for a long time is fairly easy to explain. Until at least the last quarter of the twentieth century, the state dominated the field of economic regulation and appeared as the sole actor. For many years – notwithstanding MNEs existed in some form or another – it was felt that countries did not have to be quite concerned with MNEs since the 'regulation' was understood in its *market context*. This position however came to change dramatically especially in the last quarter of that century with many countries embracing the market mechanism. One of the direct outcomes of this shift on the part of countries was the emergence of private actors; many of which became MNEs with the process of globalisation accelerating at phenomenal speed. With the emergence of MNEs, the traditional approach of viewing economic regulation as a relationship of *countries v. markets* began to appear quite inaccurate and in need of more than just a cosmetic adjustment. It became obvious that 'markets' were not actors but structures and they had to be substituted by MNEs. As a result, the field of economic regulation has come to be analysed along the lines of *countries v. MNEs*, as we noted above the two most important actors in the field. This has been a dramatic change with double impact: *first* it has signalled the emergence of business firms as important 'non-state'/'non-country' actors[65] serving as a driving force towards achieving technical and economic progress and furthering the process of globalisation; and *secondly* it has meant that MNEs would become a primary 'target' of economic regulation in order to deal with problems caused by their behaviour or conduct.

The contrast between countries and MNEs could not be stronger. The former are expected to protect, in addition to their territories and security, the public interest. The latter on the other hand exist to promote their self-interests. In an economic regulation setting this could lead to a clash between these two forces: in seeking to protect the public interest (and specifically competition and consumers in their markets), the regulation by countries of the conduct, behaviour or transactions of MNEs could mean that such self-interests must be constrained. At the same time however these two forces may operate in a complementary manner and the regulation by countries (or lack of it) could promote these self interests. To put the point in another way, the relationship that exists between countries and MNEs in the field of economic regulation in

---

[65] See M. Dabbah, 'The Internationalisation of Competition Law and MNEs as Non-State Actors in the Process' (2003) *Non-State Actors and International Law* 1.

general and that of competition law in particular is extremely complex and is far from being possible to analyse along simplistic lines. It seems that five strands in particular need to be analysed when considering this relationship.

I.   Growth of MNEs and regulation of their activities

First, one needs to appreciate that the growth of MNEs has, over the past two decades or so, been matched by phenomenal growth in government regulation of economic activities of MNEs. This has included the regulation of such activities outside national boundaries.[66] The theory and practice of different disciplines, including political economy, have felt comfortable with this development and in many cases have even supported it. Especially in situations where the activities of MNEs were deemed to be restrictive – for example by reverting to practices which would exploit consumers or limit the economic freedom of market operators – it was accepted that countries could and should intervene to prevent this. In other words, as economic activities in the marketplace developed and expanded, the sovereign powers of countries developed and expanded in parallel in order to regulate these activities. It seems that this particular 'ideology' was developed out of what many scholars professed was the existence of a contrast between the country and the market as opposed to states and MNEs. Scholars of political economy in particular have argued that underlying the country are the concepts of territory, loyalty, exclusivity and the monopoly of the legitimate use of power and that this should be contrasted with markets, which are associated with the concepts of functional integration, conceptual relationships and expanding interdependence with consumers.[67] This contrast appears to have captured the thinking and imagination of these scholars and has led them to conclude that countries and markets have fundamentally different ways of arranging and directing human relations. The perceived tension between them therefore was seen as having a

---

[66] Some scholars have argued that the fact that the activities of MNEs can be regulated and the fact that this may place them in a weak position, promotes rather than excludes adopting a cooperative approach when examining the relationship between countries and MNEs. See J. M. Stopford and S. Strange, *Rival States, Rival Firms* (Cambridge University Press, 1991).

[67] See the interesting views of Jackson about markets and their relationship with countries, noting in particular that 'markets can be very beneficial, and, even when not beneficial, market forces demand respect and can cause great difficulties when not respected'. See J. H. Jackson, *The Jurisprudence of GATT and the WTO* (Cambridge University Press, 2000), p. 6.

profound impact on the course of modern history and as such it has become a crucial problem in the study of political economy.[68] In this way, the idea of regulating the economic activities of MNEs seems to have originated from the formerly existing contrast between countries and markets which included the idea of 'market' regulation.

II. The transfer of sovereignty

Secondly, it seems that with the economic activities of firms increasingly becoming more global, the relationship between countries and MNEs is subject to continuous change and evolution. It has been argued that for the last three decades there has been an unprecedented transfer of *sovereignty* from countries to MNEs with the consequence that the concept of sovereignty can be said to be 'losing' its political (international or supranational) attribute and seeping away downwards into the invisible order of business power.[69] Such a conclusion seems to have been drawn from the fact that MNEs are able to evade or circumvent the laws of countries, and therefore economic regulation in certain jurisdictions. With an increased process of globalisation, MNEs can employ their personnel and corporate structure to drain know-how away from one country to another in less time than it takes to tell a tale. As some commentators have convincingly argued, it is total futility to talk about a 'US firm' or a 'German firm' when the factories of the firm are located in Malaysia, its IT programmes in India and its executives are recruited worldwide.[70] The effect of this situation can mean a number of things. On the one hand it can mean that firms may choose to operate in jurisdictions with lax competition law enforcement and avoid those jurisdictions in which competition law is enforced seriously. On the other hand, it can mean that MNEs may exert decisive control over how the competition rules are enforced in certain jurisdictions. As we will see in chapter 6 below, MNEs may – through threats, intimidation to exit from the jurisdiction or lobbying to exert political influence on governments, individual politicians or competition officials – force a

---

[68] See R. Gilpin, *The Political Economy of International Relations* (Princeton University Press, 1987), pp. 10–11.

[69] See L. Eden, 'Bringing the Firm Back in: Multinationals in International Political Economy' in L. Eden and E, Potter (eds.), *Multinationals in Global Political Economy* (Macmillan, 1993).

[70] See R. J. Weintraub, 'Globalization Effect on Antitrust Law' (1999) *New England Law Review* 27.

government or the competition authority into a position of having to opt for lax enforcement or to engage in no enforcement at all.

III.   Penetrating foreign markets

Thirdly, it is important to appreciate the *interlocking* which could happen between countries and 'their' MNEs in the context of opening and penetrating foreign markets[71] and enhancing the international competitiveness of the local economy. The political ideology of many politicians and governments as a whole is that a global economy makes it important for all forces of society to unite and support one another. This ideology has been particularly apparent in relation to the business phenomenon of mergers and the reliance on various tools such as direct 'government intervention', 'economic patriotism' and 'national champions'.

IV.   MNEs as part of the problem and solution

Fourthly, as noted above in the context of the present chapter it is all the more crucial to be aware that MNEs can be considered to be both part of the problem and solution when considering the question of internationalisation of competition law. In a large part, internationalising competition law has arisen in order to deal with the cross-border anticompetitive behaviour, conduct and transactions of MNEs. The other face to the internationalisation coin however shows that MNEs have an important role to play in this process, which would address a number of concerns they have over the way competition law is currently enforced around the world. These concerns were considered above.[72]

The existence of these two faces to the internationalisation coin raises the question of whether MNEs are really in favour of internationalising competition law. This question cannot be answered with a simple 'yes' or 'no'. The answer really is: it depends on the type of internationalisation one has in mind. Internationalisation can be seen as offering an answer to the different concerns MNEs have, as identified above, and in this way the process is looked at very favourably and considered to be necessary by many MNEs. On the other hand, some types of internationalisation may not be considered to be helpful from the perspective of many MNEs

---

[71] See R. Vernon, *Sovereignty at Bay: the Multinational Spread of US Enterprises* (Longman, 1971), pp. 231–47; R. Vernon, 'Sovereignty at Bay: Ten Years After' (1981) *International Organisation* 517. See further the discussion in chapter 8 below which deals with how the jurisdictional reach of domestic competition laws has been extended beyond territorial limits.

[72] See pp. 106–110.

especially those types of internationalisation which would not really serve the interests of MNEs.

In simple terms, one cannot say with certainty whether MNEs or which particular industrial sectors will support or resist the move towards greater internationalisation of competition law. Different MNEs appear to have different views. There is a need therefore to know more about the views and needs of MNEs in light of any efforts seeking to further the process of internationalisation. All that exists at the moment is a presumption that certain sectors of the economy – especially those that are conditioned by global developments such as the electronic commerce sector – would favour pursuing the internationalisation of competition law in order to develop common rules and standards and therefore reduce the uncertainty, expense and general concerns MNEs operating in these sectors are subject to under the current climate of multi-assertion of jurisdiction.

V. Single or shared perspective of internationalisation?

Finally, any debate on the internationalisation of competition law can never be complete without adequately identifying the (country and non-country) actors in this process and a proper consideration of their role. This point must be made abundantly clear. The process of internationalisation opens a number of questions in this respect. One question that has central importance is whether countries should be considered the principal actors in this process. In other words, whether the process should be considered from a *single* (countries) or *shared* (countries and possibly MNEs) perspective.

The way in which the debate on the internationalisation of competition law has developed shows that it has had an almost one-sided perspective, namely that of countries. Countries are viewed as the major (sometimes even the sole) players in the process. The reason why such a view has come to be formed is fairly simple to explain: countries are considered to have the final say on whether to support the process of internationalisation and whether it can actually be furthered at all, let alone deciding what the exact type of internationalisation or its extent should be. The basis on which this power stands is the concept of sovereignty, which arms countries with the supreme power to exert control within their territorial boundaries. Key developments – principally the emergence of MNEs as crucial players and central elements in the study of international political economy and domestic policy formulation – have mandated however that the internationalisation of competition law needs to be considered at least from a shared perspective.[73] A shared perspective here refers to on the one hand the perspective of countries and on the other that of – primarily – the business community; but also international organisations and possibly where appropriate also the views of other interest groups such as consumer bodies. As we noted above, sovereign countries are not the only actors in the process and there are other forces from above and below. MNEs are the most influential of these forces especially since their growth has made the concept of sovereignty questionable: the question of who or what exerts supreme power within a particular territory which for many years was answered automatically as 'countries' may not be that straightforward in relation to some areas – such as economic regulation – in today's world; as we argued above, obviously the ability of MNEs to engage in threats to exit or withdraw from certain countries or to engage in lobbying in order to politically influence how the competition rules of these countries would be enforced offers a good example in this respect.[74] The lobbying ability of multinational firms or firms more generally can be a major problem. In some cases firms simply need not collude or abuse their power individually when they are able to achieve the same result by pressing governments.[75] Beyond this of course MNEs exercise power in a profound functional sense simply and directly because they play a role in enhancing the economic prosperity of countries.

The recognition that the process of internationalisation needs to be considered from a shared as opposed to single a perspective is very sensible and should not be viewed as being a challenge which comes to undermine the position of countries as decision-makers. The fact is that the internationalisation of competition law is in part a response to the globalisation of markets which in turn is a direct result of the operation of firms in markets beyond national boundaries. It is therefore a natural thing that one needs to take into account the role of firms within the

---

[73] See Fox, note 4 above; Griffin, note 25 above.

[74] See M. Olson, *The Logic of Collective Action* (Harvard University Press, 1965); D. C. Mueller, *Public Choice* (Cambridge University Press, 1979).

[75] A good example of how this could be the case can be seen in light of what happened in the sugar industry in Nepal. In 1998 Nepal sugar producers approached the government and persuaded it to impose import tariffs on Brazilian sugar because they were able to supply local markets themselves. The government responded in the positive and as a result of the imposed tariffs no more Brazilian sugar was entering Nepal. The domestic sugar producers then approached the government again and lobbied for an increase in the price of sugar. Astonishingly the government complied and as a result consumers in Nepal came to pay higher prices.

process[76] as well as that of other actors. The following chapter will explain the role of international organisations and will demonstrate among other things that, considering their role, views and actual and potential contribution, international organisations are crucial for the purposes of understanding and fully analysing the process of internationalisation. Some international organisations have played an increasingly vigorous role in cultivating and shaping competition law and policy as well as other related or neighbouring laws and policies.

(C) The need for comprehensive debate

There is one final comment which is important to make concerning the involvement of the different players in the internationalisation process. In the short to medium term, it must be realised that the topic of internationalisation of competition law would benefit from a comprehensive debate. The debate should focus on but more crucially be directed towards the recognition of the necessary involvement of different actors in the process and giving due weight to their interests, concerns and views in general. The debate must involve government officials from different countries, firms, non-governmental organisations (including specifically consumer groups), competition authorities, international bodies and other interested parties who should come together to discuss the role of competition law and policy in a global economy. This debate should take place within different fora: at an international level as part of the proceedings of international organisations, such as the OECD, UNCTAD and the ICN (within which admittedly some useful debates have taken place); at a regional level; and at a national level, whether within government advisory groups or academic institutions serving as a platform for public discussions of competition law and policy.

[76] See Weintraub, note 70 above.

Chapter 3

The involvement of international bodies and organisations in the field of competition law and policy

As we saw in chapter 1, the end of the twentieth century witnessed a remarkable proliferation of competition law regimes around the world. As we noted, many of these regimes share important similarities, though fundamental differences do exist between them not least in terms of their experience with the concept of competition and with competition law and policy; equally, differences amongst the different jurisdictions exist in relation to how the process of internationalisation of competition law should be conceived.[1] As was noted in the previous chapter, while the 'international competition policy scene' has not witnessed the conclusion of binding commitments on the part of countries,[2] various mechanisms and proceedings within different international fora have been instituted through which consultations, debate and sharing of information and experience between competition authorities in particular have been occurring.[3] It is through these mechanisms and proceedings that the internationalisation of competition law has mostly continued to gain renewed impetus. They have especially provided support to those in favour of internationalisation to push the whole idea forward; despite the emergence of serious setbacks over the years which derailed various internationalisation efforts on more than one occasion.[4] The different

---

[1] See p. 82 above.

[2] See A. Fiebig, 'A Role for the WTO in International Merger Control' (2000) *Northwestern Journal of International Law and Business* 233.

[3] See generally S. W. Waller, 'The Internationalization of Antitrust Enforcement' (1997) *Boston University Law Review* 343.

[4] See E. Fox, 'International Antitrust: Cosmopolitan Principles for an Open World' (1998) *Fordham Corporate Law Institute* 271; J. Halverson, 'Harmonization and Coordination of International Merger Procedures' (1991) *Antitrust Law Journal* 531; E. U. Petersmann, 'International Competition Rules for the GATT-MTO World Trade and Legal System' (1993) 7 *Journal of World Trade Law* 35; Fiebig, note 2 above.

mechanisms and proceedings referred to here are particularly note-worthy because most of them have emerged within the framework of international organisations, which have played a major role in keeping the internationalisation debate alive and in furthering the understanding of competition law globally, as well as in spreading competition law itself around the world and helping many countries build much-needed capabilities to enforce it. In this respect, international organisations have an important *role* in consolidating the global understanding of competition law and policy and furthering the international agenda in the field, especially through initiating new or expanded international efforts, which are structured in a flexible and sensible manner in order to recognise and address 'remaining' differences between countries. In this regard, it would be important to realise that countries lack the ability to deal with the major issues here themselves.

In this chapter the different international organisations active in the field of competition law and policy will be identified and discussed in outline. The discussion in the chapter will focus on what contribution these bodies have come to make to understanding competition law and furthering it at the international level by offering an account of their work and agendas. The chapter will consider the institutional capabilities of these international organisations and reflect, where relevant, on what their future directions in the field should be; where relevant, the chapter will assess the existence of unused potential of international organisations and how such potential can be turned into actual capabilities to push the global competition law agenda forward.

1.   The World Trade Organisation (WTO)

(A)   General

In this section, the WTO will be introduced in broad terms. The reader's attention is drawn to chapter 11 which examines the different WTO agreements, which can be said to have competition relevance.

The WTO is a unique international organisation and rule-making body with a mechanism for dispute resolution. The WTO deals with trade between its member countries and it has rules and principles in place for this purpose. With the Marrakesh Agreement, in January 1995 the WTO came to succeed the General Agreement on Tariffs and Trade (GATT), which was concluded in October 1947 by 23 countries. Today the WTO has a very wide membership base including 153 developing and developed countries; currently some 30 countries hold 'observer' status within the WTO.[5] At present, the body of trade agreements comprising the WTO consist of 18 multilateral agreements: in relation to 16 of these agreements all WTO members are parties whilst to the other two agreements only *some* WTO members are parties.[6]

(B) Functions

As its main goal, the WTO seeks to facilitate the smooth, free, fair and predictable movement of international trade and to establish parity amongst countries by, among other things: acting as a forum for conducting trade negotiations; concluding and administering trade agreements; settling trade disputes between WTO members; and reviewing the national trade policies of different countries. Like the GATT, the WTO deals principally with trade-distorting acts of governments providing an extremely broad framework of rules dealing with trade between its members. Thus, the WTO rules, except those on anti-dumping, have not been focused on the behaviour of private firms. Instead, the WTO has adopted a comprehensive set of rules obliging member governments to observe common non-discrimination principles and market-opening commitments which are included in different schedules.

Since its creation through the Marrakesh Agreement, a *revolution* – which one may conveniently term as the WTO revolution – has come to unfold both within the WTO and within the environment in which it operates: on the one hand, considerable expertise has come to be acquired by its professional staff and it has come to enjoy centrality as a forum for negotiating binding rules governing the economic conduct of countries; on the other hand, the forces of free trade (with a few exceptions) have come to bulldoze through borders and barriers bringing them down and enabling many countries to reap crucial economic benefits as a result. Almost everyone agrees on this. However, hardly any agreement has materialised in relation to the exact relevance competition law has within the WTO, the role that the WTO can play in the field and the chances for a *concrete* WTO competition law agenda to emerge whether in the near or distant future.

---

[5] A list of all these countries can be found on the WTO's website, www.wto.org.
[6] Namely, these are: the *Agreement on Trade in Civil Aircraft* 1980 and the *Agreement on Government Procurement* 1981.

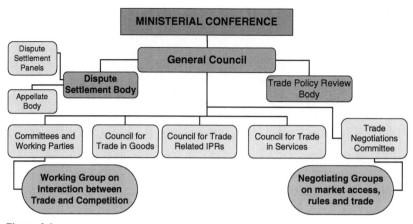

Figure 3.1

(C)   Structure and committees

Figure 3.1 is produced for the benefit of the reader. This section will not provide an account of all the bodies and divisions featuring in the diagram. Three bodies however are worth describing here: the Ministerial Conference; the General Council; and the Dispute Settlement Body. For our purposes, specifically the *Working Group on Interaction between Trade and Competition Policy* is of particular relevance and importance. It will be discussed further below when addressing the competition law 'context' of the WTO.

I.   Ministerial Conference and General Council

The WTO Ministerial Conference, the organisation's highest institutional body, meets approximately every two years and in the meantime the General Council conducts the WTO's business. Both bodies are made up of representatives from every member of the Organisation and decisions are usually made with the consent of the entire membership before being ratified by the members' parliaments domestically. WTO activities are also supported by a Secretariat which is led by the WTO Director-General.

II.   Dispute Settlement Body

As noted above, the WTO has a mechanism for dispute resolution attached to the General Council. Within this mechanism a WTO member may launch an action against another WTO member for breach of a WTO rule or perhaps more accurately the 'non-implementation' of a WTO commitment by the latter; such action in practice takes the form of a complaint to the WTO Dispute Settlement Body and this may lead to a ruling delivered by a WTO Panel or the WTO Appellate Body. If this ruling is in favour of the complaining member, such member may be effectively authorised to 'retaliate' against the other member. Over the years, the WTO dispute resolution mechanism was used to deal with situations which had interesting competition law questions, most notably the *Kodak/Fuji* case concerning the dispute between the USA and Japan which will be dealt with below.[7]

(D)   Involvement in the field of competition law

I.   Origins and roots

The WTO's explicit engagement in the field of competition law began in 1996, one year following its creation when the *Working Group on the Interaction between Trade and Competition* – what is widely known as the *Singapore Group* – was set up to explore the relationship between competition policy and trade policy and explore the possibilities for introducing some form of competition law framework or agenda within the WTO.[8] In its work initially the Group focused on what was deemed to be the core principles of interface between these two important policies:[9] transparency; non-discrimination; procedural fairness; voluntary cooperation; capacity building; and limitations on hardcore cartels. The roots of this WTO engagement however can be said to extend to one decade before the Singapore Group was set up: to the Uruguay Round negotiations, which took place between 1986 and 1994, and which led to the Marrakesh Agreement establishing the WTO.

II.   The Singapore Group's work

The Singapore Group has made a major contribution to the initiation of a debate on a WTO competition law agenda which can be seen in light of numerous studies conducted and reports published on the matter.[10] The

---

[7] See pp. 609–614 below.
[8] The EU has also been a driving force behind the idea of building an international framework for international competition rules within the WTO. Particularly important to note here are the efforts of the European Commission and former (late) Commissioner for Competition, Karel Van Miert in establishing the *Singapore Group*; see p. 123 below.
[9] Chapter 11 focuses on the interface between competition and trade policy and discusses it in detail.
[10] Most of these studies and reports can be found online, such as on the WTO's own web page which is a good source of information.

contribution of the Group however must be looked at in light of the actually modest mandate it would have: in setting up a specific group for evaluating how trade policy interacted with competition policy, the intention was to provide a forum for *discussion* without any signal that formal negotiations between WTO members on a competition agreement would definitely ensue. Nonetheless, the Group's input has been important in facilitating the participation of several WTO members in this debate and many of them have made helpful submissions to the WTO on the issue. The WTO itself has had an output in the form of accounts on competition law produced as part of its Annual Reports; not to mention the abundance of academic and non-academic literature, which came to be poured in through journals, books and reports of different types.[11] In practice however this debate has remained what it actually is – a debate – and insufficient progress has come to be made in practice in the form of taking concrete steps towards building such an agenda. Perhaps the only occasion on which the WTO community came fairly close to taking a concrete step was at the 4th Ministerial Meeting – the Doha round – in 2001 when it was agreed to *include* competition policy in the Ministerial Declaration and to start formal negotiations on competition policy within the WTO framework following the 5th Ministerial Meeting, namely the Cancun round which would occur in 2003. This particular Declaration established a 'vision' of a bright future for a WTO competition law agenda especially in light of how specific it was in terms of setting out the topics on which negotiations would take place, including, among other things: hardcore cartels; offering support to competition authorities of the developing world through capacity building; and cooperation between countries and specifically between their competition authorities in the field. The remarkable failure of the Cancun round in 2003 however delivered a fatal blow to the Doha round efforts and achievements with the decision taken to *exclude* competition policy from future trade negotiations at the WTO.

III.   Competition relevance of WTO rules, principles and decisional practice

The exclusion of competition policy from trade negotiations does not mean however that the WTO rules themselves lack any competition

---

[11] See P. Marsden, *A Competition Policy for the WTO* (Cameron May, 2003); and M. D. Taylor, *International Competition Law – A New Dimension for the WTO?* (Cambridge University Press, 2006).

relevance; and some of the cases handled by the WTO arguably had a strong competition dimension.[12] Many of the WTO's key provisions feature a competition law 'component', as will be seen from the discussion in chapter 11 below. In this respect therefore the WTO cannot be considered to be a body that is wholly alien to the field of competition law. It is true that the WTO is a trade body, but competition law is not totally absent from the ambit of its rules or the scope of its work. One might conveniently mention here the work of the GATT, which existed prior to the creation of the WTO. Under the GATT several cases had arisen where countries claimed that other countries supported or fostered anticompetitive behaviour and conduct by firms that foreclosed access to the local markets of the latter. This happened despite the fact that the GATT (as with the WTO) was not designated as an intended forum for handling such claims; not to mention of course the fact that international trade rules within the GATT did not hold different GATT members' governments accountable for the actions of private firms. In this way, the GATT did not contain a multilateral set of rules that make governments responsible for market access-restraining practices of firms; i.e. those cases in which hindrances to the access to local markets by foreign firms take the form of anticompetitive behaviour (such as cartels or vertical restraints), conduct (such as abuse of dominance or monopolisation) or transactions (such as harmful mergers). Nevertheless, neither the GATT nor the WTO should be seen as lacking the features necessary to achieve competition law objectives.[13] Indeed, the basic non-discrimination principles of national treatment, Most-Favoured-Nation (MFN) and transparency that underpin the WTO support the operation of impartial competition law regimes at national level within WTO members. Furthermore, a domestic policy framework that ensures that private firms do not, through private arrangements, restrict the flow of trade and investment that countries worked hard towards achieving is equally important to support the international

---

[12] As noted above, the *Kodak/Fuji* dispute is a perfect example. See pp. 609–614 below for a detailed discussion of the case.

[13] See P. Nicoliades, 'For a World Competition Authority' (1996) *Journal of World Trade Law* 131; M. Matsushita, 'Reflections on Competition Policy/Law in the Framework of the WTO' (1997) *Fordham Corporate Law Institute* 31; F. Weiss, 'From World Trade Law to World Competition Law' (2000) *Fordham International Law Journal* 250; E. U. Petersmann, 'Proposals for Negotiating International Competition Rules in the GATT–WTO World Trade and Legal System' (1994) *Aussenwirtschaft* 231; P. Marsden, '"Antitrust" at the WTO' (1998) *Antitrust* 28.

trading system, on which the whole WTO idea obviously rests. In these ways, the two policy frameworks – namely trade policy and competition policy – are complementary.[14] As will be seen, this conclusion will be made very clear in the discussion in later chapters of the book.[15]

As noted above, competition law concepts appear in several WTO agreements. These include:[16] the *Basic Telecommunications Agreement* and specifically the *Telecommunications Reference Paper on Regulatory Principles of the Negotiating Group on Basic Telecommunications*;[17] the *General Agreement on Trade in Services*;[18] the *General Agreement on Tariffs and Trade*; the *Agreement on Trade-Related Investment Measures*;[19] the *Trade-Related Aspects of Intellectual Property Rights*;[20] the *Agreement on Government Procurement*; the *Agreement on Technical Barriers to Trade*; and the *Accounting Disciplines Agreements*. The actual competition-relevance of all of these agreements however is not something on which everyone absolutely agrees. The matter therefore is highly debatable and depends on how expansive or narrow one's interpretation of the rules contained in these agreements is.[21]

IV.   The view of firms on the activities of the WTO

As noted in the previous chapter, firms (and particularly multinational enterprises) are important players in all competition law regimes and the process of internationalisation of competition law and policy more generally; and in respect of the WTO it is interesting to note here how they view the role of the organisation. Within different fora around the world, many in the business community have repeatedly voiced their scepticism about the necessity and productivity of competition policy negotiations at the WTO;[22] although it should be also noted that there have been those

---

[14] See H. M. Applebaum, 'The Coexistence of Antitrust Law and Trade Law with Antitrust Policy' (1988) *Cardozo Law Review* 1169.

[15] See in particular chapter 11 which addresses the complementarities between the two policies.

[16] These agreements are discussed below at pp. 599–607.

[17] See Section 1.1 of the *Fourth Protocol to the General Agreement on Trade in Services* (GATS).

[18] See Arts VIII, IX and IX:2.   [19] See Art. 9.

[20] See, for example, Art 41 of the Trade Related Aspects of Intellectual Property Rights (TRIPS).

[21] See pp. 606–607 below.

[22] See, for example, some of the views emerging from within *Business Roundtable* in the USA. Business Roundtable is an association comprising of the chief executive officers of some of the United States' leading companies. See www.businessroundtable.org/about.

in favour of such development. A particular reason for scepticism in this context has been the perceived difficulty in building international consensus in the field of competition law which is considered to be a major precondition to establishing any form of international competition law framework, especially within the WTO. Even if such consensus were to be considered to be achievable, it has been thought that any resulting WTO agreement in the field of competition law is bound to be imbalanced because WTO members are not at the same or similar levels of development: the fact that the WTO brings within its membership many developing countries has been considered to be a primary potential hurdle in the face of achieving the required balance in such future agreement. This is an interesting perspective because the fact that the WTO's membership contains developing countries is widely regarded as a distinctive advantage for the organisation when considering the potential it has to reach a multilateral agreement in the field of competition law.

It seems that different business associations and bodies[23] consider that instead of pushing for a multilateral WTO competition agreement, a more appropriate role for the WTO would be to engage in educational work by establishing a new work programme to assist countries in developing their competition law and policy domestically, to act as an 'information bank' and to provide technical assistance to different competition authorities on enforcement and related matters.[24] Thus, although there is not a *full* rejection across the business community globally of the idea of introducing binding WTO obligations in the field of competition law, the widespread belief is that a basis for building an international competition law agenda within the WTO has yet to be established and that it would be premature to consider adopting new international competition rules within the WTO and bring those within the scope of different WTO tools, most notably its dispute settlement mechanism.[25]

---

[23] See, for example, the views of the International Chamber of Commerce and the US Council for International Business among others.

[24] It is interesting to observe here that such views on educational role coincide with those put forward by some WTO members over the years; see pp. 558–560 below.

[25] It is important however to note the fact that firms sometimes may prefer using the WTO dispute resolution mechanism in competition disputes (even in the absence of WTO competition rules) because they may form the view that – in their own specific situation – they may be able to turn their competition 'complaint' into a trade issue through lobbying their own government and thus enhance their chances of securing a successful result. See pp. 609–614 below for a discussion of this is the kind of attempt made by Kodak in its efforts to push for action to be taken against Fuji.

V.   Reasons for lack of serious WTO impact

Notwithstanding the competition law relevance of WTO rules and principles and its decisional practice as well as the clear determination to build a competition law agenda within the WTO – as evident from the creation and work of the Singapore Group – extremely limited impact has been made in practice. Indeed the entire WTO competition law future has been thrown into doubt and the Singapore Group has become inactive.[26]

A number of reasons can be identified as to why the WTO is considered to have failed. One major reason that must be mentioned here concerns the perceived *unsuitability* of the WTO in both its *nature* and *adjudicatory mechanism*. These two aspects will be discussed in turn.

(a) **The binding nature of the WTO 'mechanism'**   The WTO embodies an approach based on hard law,[27] namely one that has as its foundations binding rules and commitments imposed on different WTO members. Such a hard law nature presents a major obstacle for WTO members to commit themselves to an agreement in the field of competition law because of what many of them perceive as a serious risk to be bound by a suboptimal set of rules and standards; especially because of the lack of sufficient legal basis within the WTO framework for competition concepts to flourish.[28] Given the nature of the WTO rule-making mechanism and general operation, many WTO members are reluctant to surrender to the consequences of such a mechanism and general operation, which can easily lead to WTO rules and standards in the field being imposed on them; not to mention the inevitability – as many countries see it – of final WTO rules being drafted at the lowest common denominator because of the major differences between countries in the field of competition law and outside of it. For these members the WTO rule-making mechanism and general operation make them lose the feeling of comfort and control (and the discretion!) they currently enjoy in the field of competition law, namely the ability to legislate or amend existing legislation whenever they see fit and as frequently as

---

[26] See p. 597 below.

[27] The discussion in chapter 10 below will consider hard law instruments and how they differ from soft law instruments.

[28] See R. Howse and K. Nicolaidis, 'Legitimacy and Global Governance: Why Constitutionalizing the WTO is a Step Too Far?' in T. Cottier and P. C. Mavroidis (eds,) *The Role of the Judge in International Trade Regulation: Experience and Lessons for the WTO* (University of Michigan Press, 2003).

they wish in order to meet national demands and interests. Such freedom is absent within the WTO framework, which is characterised by striking rigidity and in practice can resemble a nightmare because of the well-known difficulties in conducting trade negotiations within the WTO and agreeing rules and standards. The operation of the WTO mechanism in the field of competition law can be more impossible than difficult and serious doubt is felt by many WTO members as to whether any progress can be made if at all. Within a global setting in particular the need for a change of approach or policy in the field of competition law will be all the greater. Given that the field of competition law is usually considered to be a short- to medium-term concern with regard to the requirement for change[29] – unlike the area of trade policy which can be considered to be a long-term one in this regard – the WTO's vast membership and hard law approach present a major problem.

The serious concerns of WTO members as described above usually mushroom when the inevitable limitations of sovereignty[30] as a result of introducing competition law within the WTO mechanism are taken into account. The limitation of sovereignty is itself a major concern even for those WTO members who enjoy strong standing in the field of competition law, notably the USA. US views over the years have consistently shown a resistance to such a limitation because of concerns over loss of discretion, which is seen as vital for the purposes of a proper functioning of a competition law regime. The concern over limitation of sovereignty is, in the case of some WTO members with little or no experience in the field of competition law, even graver because of their fear that the hard law nature of the WTO mechanism will enable WTO members with strong competition law regimes simply to impose their desired rules on the former.

(b) The WTO's dispute resolution mechanism   The WTO system includes a vital and unique element: its dispute resolution mechanism. This mechanism however is built and intended to deal with disputes between WTO members. Private parties are unable to launch actions under the mechanism and their only hope to bring an issue before a WTO panel at present is through lobbying and persuading their national governments to do so on their behalf. The success in this case however

---

[29] As noted in chapter 1, the field of competition law must respond to changes and evolution in the marketplace which are – simply put – continuous and never-ending.

[30] See pp. 89–92 above for a discussion on the issue of sovereignty.

cannot at all be guaranteed especially given: the difficulty encountered sometimes in appointing a dispute resolution panel;[31] the extremely high cost involved in starting a WTO dispute resolution action; the risk of friction in relations between the members concerned which is likely to be caused as a result; and above all the fact that WTO members can only complain if there is a breach of WTO rules and competition issues do not fit this description.[32] Introducing a competition law dimension to the WTO is bound to be problematic as far as the WTO dispute resolution mechanism is concerned. It is difficult to imagine a situation in which private parties will enjoy standing in this case, whilst at the same time it is difficult to imagine a situation in which it would be suitable to exclude private parties from having recourse to this mechanism.

2. The Organisation for Economic Cooperation and Development (OECD)

The OECD – which was set up in 1961 – brings together 34 countries who are among the world's most developed nations. The origins of the OECD can be traced to the Organisation for European Economic Cooperation (OEEC), which was formed in 1947 to administer American and Canadian aid following the Second World War. The OECD provides a forum for its members' governments where they can meet for discussions and consultations in order to compare policy experiences and perspectives, seek answers to common problems, identify good practices in different economic fields and coordinate domestic and international policies. The OECD also plays an important leadership role in proposing solutions and global response when challenges arise in the global economy, such as the recent global economic crisis.

The composition of the OECD, in that its main membership is composed of developed nations, has attracted particular criticism of the organisation and its actual ability to play a meaningful role in advancing competition law at the international plane. In particular the argument here has centred around the fact that developing countries are effectively excluded from what the latter themselves have come to view as an organisation of wealthier nations. Such argument has particular merit especially when considering that the most pressing issue in internationalising competition law and policy may be considered to be the need to introduce and strengthen competition

---

[31] See, for example, what happened in the *Kodak/Fuji* dispute, pp. 609–614 below.

[32] See G. C. Shaffer, *Defending Interests Public-Private Partnerships in WTO Litigation* (Brookings Institute, 2003)

law and policy in different countries, the vast majority of which are developing countries. To be fair, however, it is very arguable that it is this particular composition of the OECD which has in fact enabled the OECD to build its considerable wealth of expertise in the field of competition and eventually to offer the benefits of this expertise to many competition authorities in the developing world: more than 70 developing and emerging market economies have come to benefit from this wealth of expertise in one way or another. Indeed one might wonder how the OECD's agenda (in terms of its focus and direction) and actual output would have turned out to be if it did not enjoy this particular composition.

(A) Scope of work

The OECD is not a competition body, but rather an international organisation involved in 'economic cooperation and development' with a strong competition law branch. The majority of the OECD's activities lie in fields outside of competition law: its overall mission is to help the world economy develop by sustaining economic growth and employment and raising the standard of living while maintaining financial stability. Indeed, a coherent competition law agenda came to be developed within the OECD some two decades ago following its inauguration in 1961.

Over the years the OECD has played a leading role in the field of competition law, in particular through encouraging and assisting countries and their competition authorities to seek and achieve effective and efficient enforcement of their domestic competition rules; it has also played an important role in enriching the debate on internationalisation of competition law and suggesting ways in which this process could be promoted in a meaningful and practical way.[33] Through its key role in the field, the OECD has become far more than an important forum within which certain countries engage in a process of consultation on the operation of their domestic competition law regimes: it has also served as a rich source of technical assistance and an invaluable bank of information to many countries with young competition law regimes, as well as those in the process of introducing or planning to introduce competition law and policy into their domestic legal systems.[34] In particular, the OECD has been helpful to

---

[33] In 1976, the *Guidelines for Multinational Enterprises* as revised were adopted which deal with a variety of competition law and policy issues. See also OECD *Declaration on International Investment and Multinational Enterprises* (1976).

[34] See Lloyd and Vautier, *Promoting Competition in Global Markets: a Multi-National Approach* (Edward Elgar, 1999).

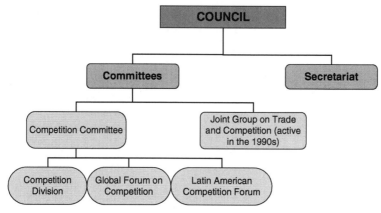

Figure 3.2

national judges and officials in competition authorities in such countries who are keen on developing their understanding and decisional mechanisms and practices when handling competition cases. In more ways than one, the OECD has made a tremendous contribution towards spreading competition law around the world. It has shown important leadership, displayed open-mindedness and shown remarkable willingness to 'join forces' in undertaking a variety of competition law projects with other international bodies, including those with relatively modest competition law agenda. For example, it has been active in designing collective competition projects with the World Bank.[35]

(B) Structure and committees

Figure 3.2 gives an overview of the OECD institutional structure as far as its involvement in the field of competition law is concerned.

I. The Council

The OECD's decision-making powers are concentrated in the Council, the supreme body armed with responsibility for overseeing the OECD's work and for determining its strategic direction and agenda. The Council is composed of one representative from each of the OECD members and a representative from the European Commission.

---

[35] More up-to-date information is available at www.oecd.org and www.worldbank.org.

Permanent representatives to the OECD meet regularly and take decisions by consensus but ministerial level meetings occur only once a year; it is at these ministerial meetings that key issues are discussed and the OECD's priorities are set. The work mandated by the Council is executed by the OECD Secretariat, a strong body with some 2,500 staff, which include economists, lawyers, scientists and other professionals with appropriate qualifications. The Secretariat also supports the activities of the OECD committees and it carries out its work according to the directions received from the Council.

II.   Committees

The OECD Committees are formed in respect of specific policy areas including science, financial markets and education, as well as competition; there are some 200 Committees at present within the OECD which are composed of representatives from the OECD countries. Each year senior officials from member countries' national governments or administrations attend committee meetings to request, review and contribute to the work undertaken. In the field of competition law, the OECD conducts its work through an important committee: the Competition Committee; another committee that should be mentioned is the Joint Group on Trade and Competition (JGTC) which was particularly active in the 1990s. The Competition Committee is supported by the Competition Division.

(a) **The Competition Committee**   The Competition Committee has its roots in the Competition Law and Policy Committee (CLP) and many times it is referred to with this long title. The CLP was set up in 1987, though it was not a wholly new committee: prior to 1987 the CLP effectively existed and was known as the Committee of Experts on Restrictive Business Practices (CERBP), which was established by the OECD's predecessor, the OEEC in 1953. The Competition Committee is made up of representatives of domestic competition or enforcement authorities of OECD members and it is the main committee with competition law involvement.

The aim of the Competition Committee is primarily to promote common understanding and cooperation among competition authorities within the OECD family and even beyond.[36] This is carried out through meetings of officials of competition authorities from OECD countries and in some cases those of non-OECD members. These meetings have played a

---

[36] See www.oecd.org/about/0,3347,en_2649_37463_1_1_1_1_37463,00.html.

key role on many important fronts; perhaps the most notable of these is the convergence these meetings have facilitated between the competition laws of the relevant regimes, as well as convergence between some of these regimes and those in existence in non-OECD member countries. The Competition Committee has made extremely important contributions over the years. Its work has included four branches focusing on: competition analysis and enforcement; capacity building; economic issues; and sectoral regulation. The *first* of these involves conducting discussions on current issues before participating competition authorities, helping those authorities improve their enforcement functions, increasing international cooperation between them and supporting them in enhancing their analytical strengths. This work has been conducted mainly through publishing regular reports (most notably the famous and extremely helpful Country Reviews) and holding discussion groups. Among other things, this work has enabled the Competition Committee to offer the OECD family a common platform on which they will be able to bring their understanding of competition law and policy closer together. The *second* capacity building branch has grown out of a programme started in 1990 and which has carried into effect the creation of a number of regional OECD centres.[37] The *third* branch of economic issues arguably has a wider scope than competition law and focuses on issues of economic growth and efficiency, as well as seeking to improve market performance. *Finally*, the sectoral regulation branch deals with: ways in which different countries handle the regulation of special sectors;[38] how the competitive structure of the sectors can be improved; how they can be made more productive; and how they can facilitate greater maximisation of consumer welfare. The OECD has conducted some interesting work on this front, especially in the 1990s[39] which, among other things, offered a helpful guide to developments in different countries and how the latter determined the parameters of the relationship between competition authorities and sectoral regulators in relation to the sectors.

(b) The JGTC The JGTC is a younger and less known committee than the Competition Committee: it was only established in 1996, thus

---

[37] The OECD has regional centres in Hungary (a joint venture with the Hungarian Competition Authority) and Korea (a joint venture with the Korean Government).

[38] These sectors include telecommunications; gas and electricity; water; railways; aviation; postal services, and banks, among others.

[39] See the comprehensive OECD study on the *Relationship between Regulators and Competition Authorities* (OECD, 1999).

coinciding with the creation of the WTO Singapore Group.[40] The JGTC was particularly active in the last four years of the 1990s and during this time it pursued a different strategy from that undertaken by the Competition Committee as explained above. In particular, it focused on fostering the understanding of member countries on issues relevant to the interface between competition and trade policy.[41] To this end, it conducted numerous important studies and published several reports focusing on understanding the relationship between these two policies and their tools. The JGTC has facilitated meetings between officials of competition enforcement authorities and trade policymakers to develop a common understanding regarding the framework for addressing matters of interest to both competition and trade policy communities. This served as an important forum in the 1990s in studying possible future directions in which competition law could be internationalised.

(C)   Notable work in the field of competition law

The OECD's role and the types of activities that it undertakes have changed over time. For example, traditionally, Competition Committee meetings have been an opportunity for senior competition officials from OECD members to meet and discuss issues of substantive law and areas of potential cooperation. However, now the focus is more on cooperation between competition authorities of OECD members and a number of OECD measures have been adopted to address this issue and to bring it to the forefront of Competition Committee's business.

Among the OECD's notable work in the field of competition law, the following are worth highlighting.[42]

I.   Peer review

One key function of the Competition Committee has been to provide peer reviews of member countries' competition law regimes through which the OECD seeks to evaluate competition law regimes around

---

[40] See p. 123 above. It is the case however the JGTC has been much more active than the WTO Singapore Group and has made a greater contribution to clarifying the interface between competition policy and trade policy, a topic which represents the main point of focus for both bodies.

[41] The important relationship between competition and trade policy will be examined in chapter 11 below.

[42] In addition to the different strands of the OECD work discussed here, one should also note its work on the competition/trade policy interface. This latter strand however will be discussed at pp. 590–592 below.

the world and recommend ways in which their effectiveness may be improved further. Peer reviews serve as outside diagnostics of the strengths and weaknesses of such regimes by describing the country's current system and analysing how well it works in practice and also importantly making general and specific suggestions for improvement in the legislation and institutional structure within the relevant regime and enforcement efforts by the relevant authority(ies).

The peer review process serves to better assess the current situation and future direction of a country's competition law regime. The process begins with an OECD staff member, or a consultant, preparing the review; any given review will focus on the cases that have arisen in that country and institutional issues within the domestic legal and political systems. Once the review is finalised, the results of the review will be delivered by way of presentation. During this presentation competition authorities from different countries will have the opportunity to raise questions with the country under review and that country is given an opportunity to respond. The way in which peer reviews are structured is a deliberate attempt to foster development: a number of the comments and issues highlighted in the any given review is likely to be applicable to other countries confronting similar issues and the discussions that take place during the presentation can provide hints as to methods to structure enforcement priorities or particular approaches that can be adopted.

It should be noted that peer review is a non-binding exercise which means that the country under review is not obliged to follow or incorporate any of the conclusions or recommendations made. However, the reviews have the potential to facilitate change in the relevant regime by advocating the idea that change is necessary, for example by stressing that the creation of more severe penalties is an effective deterrent against potential infringements of competition law. Reference to a negative review conducted by the OECD can serve as a powerful tool in providing an impetus for legitimate domestic change. Furthermore, the desire to comply with the recommendations arising out of the reviews is fortified by the potential 'shaming' a member may feel subject to; the Competition Committee is not unique among OECD agencies in conducting reviews and there is no doubt that a member would feel embarrassed if it is given a poor review across several sectors.

II.   Technical assistance and advocacy

Since the early 1990s, the OECD has been undertaking its own technical assistance programmes. These are important efforts which have resulted in benefits to many competition authorities around the world. The OECD technical assistance initiatives have increased significantly in recent years and now – via its competition centres in Asia (Korea) and Central Europe (Hungary) – the OECD provides training and conferences for competition officials in those regions.

The OECD has also been heavily involved in the area of competition advocacy.[43] Increasingly, its efforts are particularly effective, especially through *indirectly* attacking anticompetitive government practices.

III.   OECD competition fora

In more recent years, the OECD created important competition fora within the Competition Committee, notably the *Global Forum on Competition* (GFC) and *Latin American Competition Forum* (LACF). These two important initiatives have enabled the OECD to expand its peer reviews to include a number of non-member and non-observer OECD countries. Both the GFC and the LACF are noteworthy for how the OECD has expanded its 'reach' to include competition authorities from around the world at different levels of development. This has increased the number and spectrum of voices at the OECD.

The GFC is mandated to contribute to the global development of competition law in various ways. It is intended to be a forum in which: OECD's members' experiences and best practices can be effectively disseminated; non-members' conditions, views and experiences can be divulged; the different approaches between developed and less-developed competition law regimes can be addressed; larger networks of government officials with similar understanding can be developed; and policy dialogue can be entered into with contributions from the private sector.

The LACF, as the name suggests, focuses solely on Latin America. At each annual forum senior officials from countries in the region along with international experts discuss issues of competition policy that are of interest to them. Although none of the countries which participate in this forum are members of the OECD, each forum features a peer review of one of the countries in the region.

IV.   Recommendations, best practices and studies

The OECD has produced many important studies and produced a number of Guidelines, Best Practices, Guiding Principles and Recommendations

---

[43] See above for a discussion of competition advocacy.

over the years and these have had a direct positive impact in the field of competition law globally. Among these, the following are important to note:[44]

- *Guidelines for fighting bid rigging in public procurement* (2009);
- *Recommendation on competition assessment* (2009);
- *Recommendation of the Council concerning merger review* (2005);
- *Best Practices for the formal exchange of information between competition authorities in hardcore cartel investigations* (2005);
- *Guiding principles for regulatory quality and performance* (2005);
- *Recommendation of the Council concerning structural separation in regulated industries* (2001);
- *Recommendation of the Council concerning effective action against hardcore cartels* (1998);
- *Recommendation of the Council concerning cooperation between member countries on anticompetitive practices affecting international trade* (1995);
- *Recommendation of the Council for Cooperation between Member Countries in Areas of Potential Conflict between Competition and Trade Policies* (1986).

Competition authorities around the world – regardless of whether they have ever participated in OECD proceedings or not – pay special attention to various OECD output and many of them use this output as a highly authoritative source in the field; competition law experts, whether academics or practitioners also view OECD output with the same regard.

Among the different OECD products mentioned above, it is worth noting the *Best Practices for formal exchange of information between competition authorities in hardcore cartel investigations* which were adopted in November 2005 and which have received particular attention in the competition law community. The *Best Practices* recognise the importance the OECD places on the need to fight hardcore cartels and build an effective anti-cartel enforcement through what may be considered to be a 'network' between different competition authorities within which exchange of information may occur. They encourage the exchange of information and the simplification of the process to the greatest extent possible in order to avoid any unnecessary burden being caused for competition authorities themselves and to facilitate the effective and

---

[44] The OECD website contains a full list of all the recommendations, guidance and best practices produced over the years.

timely exchange of information. Obviously, in practice such a mechanism may be subject to serious limitations, most notably: the likely reluctance on the part of a country or a competition authority to exchange information with another; the fact that there will be a need for the recipient authority to give safeguards as to how it will go about making use of the information received; and the need to ensure that no negative consequences will follow for firms or individuals concerned, in particular those who submit information to the 'transmitting' competition authority voluntarily. All of these limitations appear to be recognised in the *Best Practices*, which show that they will only apply, i.e. information will be exchanged, where: the information being exchanged comes from private sources; the would-be transmitting competition authority is prohibited from disclosing the information in question; or the disclosure of the information can only occur if authorised in certain circumstances under an international agreement or treaty or the domestic law of the country concerned. The *Best Practices* deal with safeguards for the formal exchange of information including highlighting what should be done for this purpose. They also discuss and cover the issue of legal professional privilege,[45] which can be extremely important when conducting investigations in cartel cases, in addition to paving the way towards ensuring transparency in the process of exchange of information. The *Best Practices* in many ways build on previous OECD recommendations in the field, including the *1998 Recommendations* on fighting hardcore cartels.

Beyond the field of anti-cartel enforcement, the OECD has produced other recommendations dealing with a variety of important topics in the field of competition law including: multinational enterprises;[46] bilateral cooperation between competition authorities;[47] and cooperation between countries in relation to the interface between competition and trade policies. A notable publication in relation to the latter is the *Recommendations for cooperation between member countries in areas of potential conflict between competition and trade policies* (1986). These *Recommendations* encouraged participating countries not to distort competition through abusing unfair trade laws, to take into account the effect of export/import restrictions on competition and trading partners when considering the approval of such restrictions, to ensure that their

---

[45] This concerns communications between a firm and its lawyer(s) and other types of information considered privileged.
[46] See chapter 2, note 47.   [47] See pp. 509–510 below.

procedures are transparent and to notify other countries of the antic-ompetitive behaviour of their domestic firms.

V. Roundtable discussions

OECD staff prepare discussion documents to facilitate roundtable discussions between senior representatives – often the heads – of the different competition authorities. In these discussions, competition authorities' representatives are given the opportunity to present their views on a large number of issues; recent discussion topics have included the important topic of efficiencies in merger analysis; how competition authorities can more effectively guide the private sector in respect of monopolisation issues; and plea bargaining settlements of cartel cases. The OECD's role in these discussions is as facilitator; it invites outside presenters to explore the issues at hand.

Roundtable discussions are of particular use in helping participants to assess their existing understanding and approach to a given issue or topic in light of high-quality contributions made by some of the world's leading competition authorities. The consensus between the participants should not be understated nor seen as a mere agreement without any material consequences: in fact the results obtained from roundtable discussions carry considerable value and as far as the OECD is concerned they have formed a basis for the development of different Recommendations, as mentioned in the previous section.

VI. Contribution to convergence

A major contribution made by the OECD has resulted through its active role in encouraging *soft convergence*[48] amongst the competition law regimes of its member countries. Arguably this convergence has been facilitated by the unique membership of the OECD: as mentioned above it consists of most, if not all, of the world's developed countries – almost all of which have strong competition authorities and rich expertise in the field of competition law more generally. As such, and as one can expect, greater convergence in procedural and substantive law between the regimes concerned has been unfolding; in itself, this is an outcome that could contribute towards the internationalisation of competition law perhaps more notably through convergence and harmonisation at an international – not

---

[48] See further below at pp. 569–578 for a discussion of soft law instruments (non-binding commitments) and their contribution to convergence; for an explanation of the concept of convergence (and harmonisation), see p. 86 above.

only OECD – level. This contribution by the OECD is all the more important given the various limitations – institutional or otherwise – from which the organisation actually suffers and which constrain its ability to play a more expansive role in developing an international approach to competition law policy; not least the fact that it has such a limited and unique membership. Indeed, the failure of the negotiations on a Multilateral Agreement on Investment (MAI) at the OECD has cast some doubt over the OECD's ability to serve as a forum for the pursuit of a form of internationalisation of competition law that could lead to negotiating and concluding any possible international agreement in the field. Notwithstanding these limitations, the OECD deserves to be looked at in a positive light and one should recognise the strong experience it enjoys in a wide range of competition and trade policy issues, let alone general economic and consumer matters which are highly relevant not only in the actual design of competition law and policy but also when it comes to applying and enforcing the competition rules within different regimes. Its contributions should be regarded as extremely valuable, especially in light of its efforts on the convergence front.

3.   United Nations Conference on Trade and Development (UNCTAD)

UNCTAD was formed in 1964 and today has 173 member countries. At its heart, UNCTAD seeks to promote the integration of developing countries into the world economy whilst maintaining development efforts; it carries under its wings a closely guarded commitment to promote the interests of developing countries for their own sake. The work undertaken by UNCTAD aims to foster development by shaping current policy debates and thinking on development with the overarching desire to ensure that domestic policies and international action are mutually supportive in crafting sustainable development.

(A)   Functions

UNCTAD has three main functions: it acts as a forum for intergovernmental deliberations aimed at consensus-building among its member countries; it undertakes research, policy analysis and data collection for the purpose of debates; and it provides tailored technical assistance to developing countries. Given that the nature of its work involves close analyses of trade policies, UNCTAD's venturing into the field of competition law was nothing but a natural and short walk, which was orchestrated by its developing country members. The Conference first entered the field in 1973 when it began its negotiations on how best to control restrictive business practices. It seems that at the outset of the negotiations three important goals guided UNCTAD's work in the field of competition law: a desire to facilitate a more efficient and more equitable globalised economy using globalisation-sensitive competition rules; an interest in enhancing competitiveness and energising the economic growth of developing countries by spreading a competition-based culture; and championing consumer interests through an effective application of competition law leading to better quality products, more choice in the marketplace and lower prices.

(B) Structure

Figure 3.3 gives a general overview of the structure of UNCTAD. Among the different UNCTAD 'arms', it is important to note the *Intergovernmental group of experts on competition law and policy.*

I. The Quadrennial Conference

The Conference is the highest decision-making body of UNCTAD and it meets once every five years. At the Conference, member states make assessments of current trade and development issues, discuss policy options and formulate global policy responses. The Conference also determines UNCTAD's priorities and mandate. The Conference essentially serves a political function in that it allows intergovernmental consensus to be built

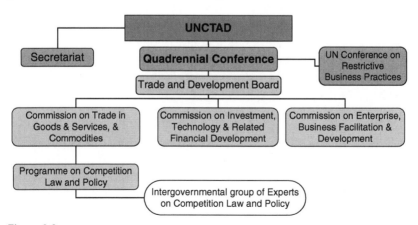

Figure 3.3

as to the issues at hand. Competition law and policy discussions are a feature of the work conducted at each Conference.

II. The Trade and Development Board

The Trade and Development Board guides UNCTAD's work. The Board meets at least once a year. All member states of UNCTAD are able to 'sit' on the Board and accredited intergovernmental and non-governmental organisations enjoy observer status.

The yearly meetings of the Board are held as 'regular' sessions but ad hoc policy and institutional matters can be dealt with up to three times a year in 'executive' sessions.

III. The Commission on Trade in Goods and Services and Commodities

UNCTAD's *Commission on Trade in Goods and Services and Commodities* deals with a host of trade issues, but the ambit of its work extends to competition law and policy. The Commission meets once a year to address these issues. The decisions taken by the Commission are considered to reflect the collective political will of UNCTAD's membership because they are made by consensus.

IV. The Intergovernmental Group of Experts on Competition Law and Policy (The Intergovernmental Group)

The Intergovernmental Group plays an important role within setting the agenda of UNCTAD in the field of competition law and policy. The Intergovernmental Group meets to discuss ways of improving worldwide cooperation on competition policy 'implementation' and enhancing convergence through dialogue based on the UN *Set of Principles and Rules for the Control of Restrictive Business Practices.*[49] Specifically, through its 'Expert' meetings, the Group facilitates the input of academics, practitioners and the private sector. This input is especially important to support the work of the Commission on Trade in Goods and Services and Commodities by allowing government representatives participating in Commission proceedings to take advantage of and benefit from this input.

V. The Secretariat

The UNCTAD Secretariat consists of 400 staff members divided into five divisions; four divisions provide technical assistance to UN organisations

---

[49] See www.unctad.org/en/docs/tdrbpconf10r2.en.pdf. The *Set* is discussed below.

and the remaining division interacts with organisations of the UN system, non-governmental organisations, the private sector and universities.

(C)   Notable UNCTAD achievements

I.   The UN Set

(a) **Origin and provisions**   The UN *Set of Multilaterally Agreed Equitable Principles and Rules for the Control of Restrictive Business Practices* is in essence a multilateral agreement or perhaps more specifically a multilateral code of conduct on competition policy that: provides a set of *equitable rules* for the control of anticompetitive practices; recognises the *development* dimension of competition law and policy; and provides a framework for *international operation* and *exchange* of best practices.

The work to adopt the Set was initiated by the United Nations Conference on Restrictive Business Practices (UNCRBP), which was convened under the auspices of UNCTAD following the adoption of Resolution 33/153 of 20 December 1978 by the UN General Assembly. UNCRBP met in Geneva the following year pursuant to an UNCTAD Resolution though it was not able to complete its work during that meeting. A resumed session was requested and granted and UNCRBP met again about four months later where it adopted a resolution approving the Set and submitted it for adoption by the General Assembly. The General Assembly adopted the Set at its 35th session in December 1980.

The negotiations concerning the Set were conducted for eight years before the UN General Assembly came to adopt it. These negotiations were instrumental in developing the aims of the Set as can be seen from the way in which the negotiations were structured, which was within three different groups: *Group B*, made up of industrialised countries; *Group D*, comprising principally socialist countries; and *Group 77*, containing developing/less-developed countries. It should be highlighted that Group 77 played a prominent role in the drafting of the Set even though it featured relatively 'weaker' economic UNCTAD member states. The Set aims to ensure favourable treatment of developing countries by offering them a shield against the harmful restrictive business practices of multinational firms. It provides that countries should improve and enforce their laws on restrictive business practices, and that they should consult and cooperate with the competent authorities of countries adversely affected by restrictive business practices. In effect the protection for developing countries as envisaged by the Set takes a declaratory form, requiring multinational firms to respect the domestic laws on restrictive business practices of the countries in which they operate. Looked at in light of its substance and the time at which it was introduced, the Set represents a remarkable effort towards adopting a comprehensive multilateral agreement in the field of competition law. Perhaps this reveals the Set's key strength. However, this strength is said to have been overshadowed by, among others, four obvious facts: that the Set is voluntary; that it is not binding; that it has not been recognised as a source of public international law; and that since 1981 it has not evolved into a dynamic body for the treatment of competition law issues with an international dimension.

The Set was not intended to be mere ink on paper, nor was it designed to operate in the abstract. It was in fact hoped to have a brush with the process of implementation within the domestic competition law regimes of member countries. For this purpose, the Intergovernmental Group was assigned the task of monitoring the Set's implementation. Through the functioning of the Group an annual forum came to take place within which multilateral discussions are conducted, and consultations occur and views are exchanged on a variety of matters related to the Set.

(b) Review of the Set at United Nations Conferences   The Intergovernmental Group's meetings are not the only forum of regular occurrence that deals with competition matters; every five years since the adoption of the Set, a Review Conference is held at which the heads of competition authorities and senior officials from developed and developing countries meet. Review Conferences have been held in 1985, 1990, 1995, 2000 and more recently in 2005. These Review Conferences offer, among other things, an important opportunity for competition authorities from around the world to foster bilateral and regional cooperation between them, share experience (particularly in relation to best practices), discuss capacity building and technical assistance programmes under the auspices of UNCTAD and to examine ways in which these authorities can strengthen their enforcement mechanisms and efforts. In particular it is worth mentioning the 4th Review Conference 2000, at which a Resolution was adopted in the field of competition law following a review process of the Set. The Resolution reaffirmed the validity of the Set, recommended that the UN General Assembly 'subtitle' the Set for reference purposes as the 'UN Set of Principles and Rules on Competition' and issued a new call for member countries to *implement* the Set. The Resolution also deals specifically with the issue of cooperation between competition authorities. It recognises the importance of bilateral cooperation agreements in this regard, though arguably it somehow played down the importance of and need to enhance regional as well as global competition initiatives, especially as far as small and developing countries are concerned. Nonetheless, the Resolution requested that the UNCTAD Secretariat examine the possibility of formulating a model cooperation agreement on competition law and policy as based on the Set. This important achievement was supplemented at the Review Conference in 2005 which expanded UNCTAD's role as a suitable international forum within which consultations and efforts seeking cooperation can take place. The Conference also underscored UNCTAD's commitment to providing technical assistance to developing countries with interest in the field of competition law. Other achievements within the Conference worth noting include revision to the UNCTAD *Model Law on Competition* and arranging ad hoc peer review exercises.

The adoption of the Resolution demonstrated a strong belief in the need to design future strategies to internationalise competition law. Indeed this came at a time when the whole idea of internationalisation and the movement towards it was benefiting from a strong momentum.[50] And this seems to have encouraged and facilitated important UNCTAD efforts, including a study dealing with the extent to which developing countries suffer from anticompetitive practices, which hinder their opportunities to develop and become competitive. This study, which was completed in 2008, attracted the interest of several important competition authorities, including the European Commission. Among the issues the study aimed to address are those concerning lack of consumer awareness about unfair and anticompetitive practices. The study strives to explore the various ways in which competition law and policy can help address some of the problems of developing countries and make such countries less vulnerable to anticompetitive practices. The study argues that practices of this nature increase the costs for the economies of those countries, increase their inefficiencies and dent their chances of enhancing their international competitiveness.[51]

(c) **Model Law on Competition** The Model Law on Competition was adopted in order to provide countries with a source of reference when drafting or amending domestic competition laws. It is related to the Set

---

[50] At that time, among other things, there were fresh hopes for serious and promising progress to finally introduce a concrete competition law agenda within the WTO.

[51] The full findings of the study can be found at www.unctad.org/en/docs/ditcclp20082_en.pdf.

and can be said to be based on different elements within the Set. The Model Law has been amended and updated since its adoption, most notably at the 4th Review Conference 2005 as noted above when the Model Law was expanded to include the area of merger control.

II. Voluntary peer review

Like the OECD's Competition Law and Policy Committee, UNCTAD has come to attach particular importance to peer review exercises in recent years. As noted above, these exercises are voluntary and are conducted by different competition law experts with the aim of providing an objective assessment of a given competition law regime for the purpose of identifying shortcomings and offering suggestions and technical assistance to deal with these. UNCTAD however can be said to be well placed to conduct 'unique' peer review exercises: because of its 'development' perspective and rich experience in working with developing countries, it is able to focus in its peer review process on the development dimension of competition law and policy. Countries which have been the subject of voluntary peer review in recent years include Benin, Jamaica, Kenya, Senegal and Tunisia.

III. Technical cooperation and capacity building

UNCTAD runs a programme seeking to offer developing countries and those economies in transition valuable assistance in terms of capacity building and technical cooperation. The programme has five different strands, including the peer review process which was discussed in the previous section: the legislation strand through which UNCTAD assists developing countries in adopting or amending their domestic competition laws in a manner that would be best suited to their own circumstances and needs; the institutional strand which focuses on creating new domestic institutions or improving the institutional structure of existing ones; the capacity-building strand which seeks to ensure effective enforcement within the relevant regime; and the advocacy strand the aim of which is to promote competition cultures in developing countries.

IV. Training activities

UNCTAD's training activities seek to educate and provide a variety of audiences in the developing world – specifically judges, policymakers, competition and consumer officials and the private sector – with competition law expertise. These activities are usually carried out at UNCTAD's offices in Geneva or on the ground, in the relevant country.

Many of the activities have an element of university style 'teaching' and 'tutoring'.[52] A large number of them also focus on the basics of competition law and policy because of the lack of any form of knowledge or understanding in the field of competition law on the part of the participants.[53] Others however are more 'advance' and tend to be concerned with arming participants with the skills necessary for the implementation of a competition law or the carrying out of legislative reform activities;[54] some programmes involve having specialists in the field meet with judges in various developing countries and discuss competition cases, which are pending in the relevant regime.

It is also worth mentioning UNCTAD's training activities in the context of the of the *Contribution of Competition Policies to the achievement of the Millennium Development Goals (MDGs)*, which are an integral part of UNCTAD's involvement in the field of competition law and which come to highlight the emphasis UNCTAD places on the need to formulate and enforce competition and consumer protection laws in a 'pro-poor' manner, that is through ensuring an efficient allocation of resources that would lead to poverty reduction in developing countries. In recent years, UNCTAD has organised several training programme conferences in collaboration with local competition authorities and other institutions of the relevant countries.[55]

V.   Regional cooperation

Chapter 7 below deals with regional cooperation, a part of the field of competition law which has been receiving increased attention around the world, partly because of the contribution made by international organisations and certain competition authorities, such as the European Commission. UNCTAD has been one of the key international organisations with particular interest in this topic. For example, in recent years it has carried out quite extensive research and studies on the topic and has also been conducting a number of capacity-building activities in a

---

[52] See, for example, the distance learning course on competition law for practitioners.

[53] See, for example, the course on the *formulation of a competition law and policy* which is usually attended by politicians (ministers and members of parliaments), judges and heads of universities or academic faculties.

[54] See, for example, the programme on the *implementation of a competition law and policy*.

[55] See, for example, the programmes offered jointly with: the Romanian Competition Council and Romanian Chamber of Commerce and Industry in Romania (March 2005); the Department on Antimonopoly Policy of the Ministry of Economic Development (DAP/MED) of the Republic of Azerbaijan in Azerbaijan (September 2005); and the Czech competition authorities in the Czech Republic (November 2006).

'regional' context which seek to help different developing countries in their efforts to build a network for regional cooperation in the field of competition law; a specific focus has been given to the African continent.

VI.   Other contributions to competition law

Other UNCTAD key works and efforts have focused on specific topics of interface between competition law and policy and other related areas, such as intellectual property rights.

4.   The International Competition Network (ICN)

(A)   General

The International Competition Network (ICN) was launched in 2001 as a multilateral initiative seeking to offer an imaginative response by competition authorities worldwide to the challenges presented to competition law enforcement in a globalised economy resulting from the phenomenon of market globalisation and the proliferation of competition law regimes worldwide.[56] The ICN initiative was founded by several competition authorities, but the key ones that played a prominent role in this regard were the US Department of Justice, the US Federal Trade Commission and the European Commission. In one way, it would be accurate to say that the initiation of the ICN was facilitated through the close and positive cooperation that has come to be established between the USA and the EU in the area of competition law, particularly since around the mid-1990s.[57] Nonetheless, the ICN was from the very beginning and has grown to be much more than being about three competition authorities: currently the ICN's membership includes 112 competition authorities; a membership base that is bound to widen in the years to come with new competition law regimes becoming established and new competition authorities inaugurated and admitted to the Network.

It is open to debate however whether the ICN can be considered to be the product of the year 2001. Many argue that the actual origins of the ICN are found in 1993 in the Munich Group of scholars who attempted at that time to draft a multilateral code on competition law.[58] Regardless of the year in which the ICN roots took hold, creating the ICN was an extremely novel and remarkable development. For the first time

---

[56] See www.internationalcompetitionnetwork.org.
[57] See below at pp. 501–505 in relation to bilateral cooperation between the two regimes.
[58] See p. 542 below and pp. 545–548 below.

competition authorities from around the world came together to discuss and share ideas in a meaningful way on their difficulties and problems in addressing international competition issues and to seek ways in which they may improve their domestic regimes and achieve convergence between their procedural and substantive rules. Nowadays the ICN is widely considered as the best medium within which competition authorities from different economies and world regions can interact in a meaningful and fruitful way. A large number of these authorities view the ICN as the most significant aspect of their international cooperation; as we shall see one direct implication of this has been that the argument in favour of pursuing internationalisation 'options' based on binding multilateral commitments – most remarkably within the WTO framework – have been weakened considerably.

(B) Functions

The ICN is very much *after* achieving convergence and development of domestic competition law regimes around the world. For this purpose, it holds annual conferences; establishes working groups; makes a vast array of documents available on its website for no charge (including guidelines and best practices); and conducts workshops for its members. As can be seen from Figure 3.4, the ICN's structure directly reflects these functions and ensures that there are no superfluous bodies creating bureaucracy and hindering its ability to reach members and offer assistance.

(C) Structure

I. Overview

The whole composition and structure of the ICN are highly interesting. First, the ICN members are exclusively competition authorities – from both the developed and developing world – something that has

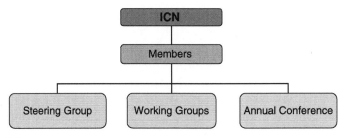

Figure 3.4

contributed enormously towards it accumulating considerable wealth and expertise and achieving some outstanding results in a relatively short period of time. Among other things, a unique membership such as this has enabled the ICN to focus exclusively on competition law, thus eliminating the possibility of distraction or having progress on competition issues being linked to progress being made in other fields. Secondly, in part this success has also been facilitated by the way in which the ICN has been operating: in a project-oriented manner and through steering and working groups. Thirdly, the ICN in essence is a virtual network[59] of competition authorities (and specialists who occasionally participate in its proceedings and work) which does not have a permanent secretariat, such as the case with other international organisations. It is an independent body however with no structural links to any already existing international organisations, regardless of whether or not these are dealing with competition policy.

II.   Steering Group

The ICN Steering Group consists of 15 elected members divided as follows: three *ex officio* annual conference host members serve for three years (the year before they host, the year of the conference and the year following the conference) and the remaining 12 members, who serve for two years, are recommended by the outgoing Steering Group subject to member consensus. When recommending future members, the key consideration governing the outgoing Steering Group's choice is that the Steering Group should reflect the geographic diversity of the ICN's membership. The Steering Group meets in person after each annual conference and then as frequently as considered necessary to perform its functions. Not all 15 members need be present at the meetings, as the quorum is set at eight.

The Steering Group implements some decisions of the ICN annual conference and has a quasi-supervisory role over the ICN's Working Groups by establishing the membership of Working Groups and reviewing and initially approving the projects and work plans the Working Groups devise. It also devises 'best practices' which can either be used in practice by competition authorities or as a tool to support change in domestic competition law regimes.

III.   Working Groups

The membership of the ICN Working Groups comprises representatives of ICN members and other participants a particular Working

---

[59] A great deal of ICN work is done via email communications and telephone conferences.

Group Chair may appoint, thus including industry experts and academics. Each Working Group enjoys a degree of autonomy in that they can determine the nature and ambit of their responsibilities within the parameters set by the Steering Group.

IV. Annual conference

There is no definite composition of each ICN annual conference; each year it can vary in terms of the developing country members who are in attendance, invitees from international organisations and competition law experts. A speculative list of participants is penned by the *Annual Conference Planning Committee* to be put to the Steering Group for approval. This Committee also comes together to create a draft agenda for that year's conference. The agenda generally focuses on reports from and progress within Working Groups and the future work programme of the ICN.

(D) Success and notable projects

The phenomenal success of the ICN can be in part explained with reference to the sensible and pragmatic approach it has come to develop as part of its 'project-oriented' way of doing business. Over the past nine years of its existence the ICN has not sought a wholesale or top-down approach to achieving harmonisation. Especially in the field of merger control, it has adopted a gradual approach towards drafting 'best practices' in the design and operation of merger control regimes worldwide. The best practices have taken the form of recommendations and they have addressed a host of merger control issues: from merger notification to principles of transparency and procedural fairness.[60]

Initially, the focus of the ICN work was placed on specific topics in the field, namely multi-jurisdictional merger control and competition advocacy;[61] to the almost total exclusion of anti-cartel enforcement and abuse of dominance. The latter areas however came to be added to the ICN's

---

[60] See pp. 573–577 below for a discussion of different ICN recommendations.

[61] Competition advocacy was discussed in some detail at pp. 65–70 above. Hence, the concept should hardly require any further explanation at this point. Competition advocacy is dealt with by a separate working group within the ICN. The group's main work has revolved around examining ways in which distortions to competition caused by public intervention in the marketplace can be addressed. The scope of the work of the group is expected to expand with time to cover other important areas. Other topics that have been discussed include capacity building, consumer outreach and the competition law enforcement in regulated sectors.

agenda. In particular, in relation to cartels the ICN has been looking at the conduct and value of investigations by competition authorities into uncovering and punishing cartels. Among its main priorities here, the ICN has been keen to assist competition authorities in improving their operational and practical skills for the purposes of constructing effective anti-cartel enforcement regimes. A number of ICN 'workshops' have been held during which the topic of fighting cartels was discussed and a manual on anti-cartel enforcement techniques has been produced; in addition to a 'template' on anti-cartel enforcement. More recently, attention has also shifted to the topic of abuse of dominance and monopolisation.

5.   The World Bank

The World Bank is not a bank in the common sense of the word; it is akin to a cooperative, in that its 185 member countries are shareholders (and therefore its owners). These shareholders are represented through the Board of Governors, which is the ultimate policymaker at the World Bank (see Figure 3.5). Two different institutions make up the organisation: the International Bank for Reconstruction and Development (IBRD) and the International Development Association (IDA). Working in tandem, IBRD and IDA provide financial assistance to developing countries for a variety of purposes.

(A)   Functions

The functions of the World Bank have changed considerably in the years since its inception in 1944: its mission once related solely to post-Second World War reconstruction and development but this has now evolved to focus on the alleviation of global poverty whilst retaining an interest in other areas that form part of the global challenges faced by the world.

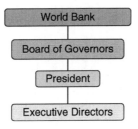

Figure 3.5

In relation to competition law and policy, the World Bank's contribution is by way of research and the publication of Working Papers aimed at facilitating public discussion and also working with the governments of developing countries on specific competition law projects, such as those aimed at conducting a review of the relevant competition law regime and offering training and teaching programmes on competition law.

(B)   Structure

As noted above, the Board of Governors of the World Bank is the highest body within the Bank with responsibility for among other things policy formulating. The Board is composed, generally, of the ministers of finance or development from the World Bank's member countries. As the Board meets only once a year at the Annual Meeting of the World Bank, specific duties are delegated to 24 Executive Directors who work on-site at the Bank. These Executive Directors are selected in different ways: each one of the five largest shareholders[62] appoints an Executive Director to promote their interests and the remaining 19 represent the interests of the other member countries. Meetings of the Board are chaired by the President of the World Bank, who is by tradition a US national. The President also oversees the day-to-day running of the World Bank, working alongside vice presidents who are in charge of regions, sectors, networks and functions.

(C)   Notable projects

In light of the Bank's broad field of interest, which prioritises many issues above competition law and policy, it is not surprising that there are no notable projects to highlight. As noted above, however, the World Bank has a clear ethos of supporting competition law regimes of developing countries. Nonetheless, it appears that the Bank has conceded the position of 'global authority' on competition law and policy to other international bodies such as the OECD, UNCTAD and the WTO.

6.   Comments

The field of competition law and policy has benefited enormously from the involvement of the five international organisations discussed in this

---

[62] These are France, Germany, Japan, the UK and the USA.

chapter. Their contribution therefore must be recognised and they should be given credit for taking on some challenging tasks and building ambitious agendas. In particular the work of these organisations should be recognised as far as developing countries are concerned: these countries have benefited greatly from the financial and logistical support, training, capacity building and technical assistance received from or via these organisations. This work has also been beneficial at a wider level: the organisations have served as important fora for dealing with international competition law and policy issues. In this respect, as noted in the previous chapter, the ICN, OECD, UNCTAD, WTO (and to lesser extent the World Bank and the IMF) are all important actors in the process of internationalisation of competition law and the global competition law landscape. Specifically, the work of the OECD, UNCTAD and the ICN should be noted here because of the success they have achieved in bringing about a degree of (soft-law) convergence in the field globally.[63]

Among all benefits and contributions brought about by the involvement of international organisations however, perhaps the one that is most important of all has been the creation of a 'network' within which different competition authorities – both bilaterally and multilaterally – have come to talk to one another, consult on policy and enforcement issues and learn from best practices in the field. This has facilitated the building of trust and confidence between different competition authorities which are extremely useful to have in practice, especially where enforcement actions are being considered or undertaken by two or more authorities in one and the same situation. When *competition authority A* has confidence in *competition authority B* and the regime within which the latter operates this is bound to affect its decision to rely on the latter to take action in a given situation, share information with the latter or otherwise support the latter in its investigation of a situation. In other words, the existence of confidence can help turn a mechanism of bilateral cooperation[64] – especially when based on positive or negative comity – into a viable and effective tool in practice which can lead to efficient use of enforcement efforts by the authorities concerned and also benefits to the firms under investigation.[65]

A serious question worth asking is what the future directions for the involvement of the ICN, OECD, UNCTAD and the WTO in particular

[63] See chapter 10 for a discussion on soft law convergence.
[64] See chapter 9 for a discussion on the mechanism of bilateral cooperation.
[65] See pp. 509–512 above.

should be in the field of competition law. Answering this question requires, first, an appreciation of the limitations from which all of these bodies suffer. As noted in various places in the discussion above all of these organisations suffer from serious (and different) limitations. For example, the OECD's involvement in the field – through the work conducted within the Competition Committee – has been particularly helpful in forging links between the competition law regimes of the OECD's member countries, between competition and trade authorities and, to an extent, between the competition authorities of member countries and non-member countries. However, given the OECD's membership, a 'negative' perception of the Organisation has developed and it is seen as club for the world's advanced nations. Furthermore, notwithstanding the important analytical work the OECD has been conducting in the field, its output is not seen by many countries as receptive to the particular needs of non-member countries, especially those with new competition law regimes. Due to such limitations and others, the OECD is considered to fall well short of providing a proper forum for building a global competition agenda. Interestingly, the WTO – by way of comparison – does not suffer from such limitations and additionally enjoys a dispute resolution mechanism, which the OECD obviously lacks. But the WTO of course suffers from other serious limitations, most notably the fact that it is a WTO body without a recognised or formal competition agenda.

As a result of the limitations associated with the different organisations, it is understandable why it has been argued that a fresh consideration of competition law and its place in the global economy appears to be necessary.[66] Specifically, what appears to have been lacking are recognised norms in different areas within the field of competition law as well as norms concerning the interface between competition law and other areas, especially that of trade policy. Undoubtedly, the work of these organisations has been extremely valuable – and continues to be so – in furthering the scope and idea of the internationalisation of competition law.[67] Nevertheless, it is obvious that it is necessary at present to expand on the agenda, institutional capabilities and mechanisms of these organisations, if the process of internationalisation is to receive the adequate

---

[66] See generally M. Dabbah, *The Internationalisation of Antitrust Policy* (Cambridge University Press, 2003).

[67] See J. Shelton, 'Competition policy: What Chance For International Rules', speech delivered at the Wilton Park Conference (24 November 1998).

treatment and proper consideration it deserves. One crucial way in which this can happen is through greater collaboration between the different organisations and support given by one institution to another. Collaboration in this case would be particularly important for the purposes of enhancing efficiency in the way in which these organisations conduct their work in the field. It can be achieved through proper consultations which could lead to division of responsibilities and assigning to each organisation the task(s) best suited to its expertise, composition, resources and outlook. This collaboration and division of responsibility has been lacking so far. It is true that some of these organisations have been offering support to other organisations. For example, UNCTAD has been working closely with the OECD and the ICN and, to a lesser extent, the WTO following the Doha round in 2001 and the promising prospects it created for a greater WTO involvement in the field of competition law. Similarly the ICN has embraced a philosophy of cooperating with the WTO, the OECD and UNCTAD. However, one wonders whether the efforts of all of these organisations have been properly *orchestrated* and whether there has been too much overlap in the activities they have been carrying out, notably those of capacity building, technical assistance and competition advocacy. Institutional rivalry might have been a factor here and it is understandable that each of these organisations has an interest in expanding its involvement and ensuring its print in the field. In seeking such recognition, however, these organisations risk failure to achieve the best outcome in the most efficient way for each of these activities. The organisations are not in a position to build the global agenda in the field of competition law individually. And they actually place themselves in a position that is far from the goal when too much overlap in their activities and tasks is created; not to mention the non-efficient use of scarce resources that is likely to arise. Coordination between the different organisations and a division of responsibility are vital in enhancing the prospects for success. Each of the organisations enjoys strengths and quality which are unique to it and which are not shared by the other organisations. These strengths will guarantee the relevant organisation greater impact in the field of competition law when coordination of involvement is opted for. The other face of the same coin shows that this organisation will, through opting for coordination, avoid the risk of being pushed to a secondary role and position as a result of a more successful effort by another organisation. For example, notwithstanding UNCTAD's extremely strong links with very young competition authorities in the developing world, many competition authorities in the developing world feel more interested in establishing links with the ICN and the OECD because of the greater wealth of expertise available within these two authorities and because they are seen as 'norm-building' bodies. This point must not be seen as a criticism of UNCTAD or a failure to recognise its important work however; nor should the point be understood that these competition authorities are necessarily totally right in their view; UNCTAD's efforts must be recognised and applauded. Ultimately however, competition authorities make their own individual choices and preferences and this is one factor that simply cannot be ignored when comparing between the 'appeal' different international organisations have in the field of competition law.

Chapter 4

EU competition law regime

This chapter will consider the competition law regime of the European Union (EU), a regime that has come to acquire huge significance and dominance within both Europe and globally; in spite of the state of stagnation and the divisive conflicts which the regime witnessed at certain stages of the early existence of the European Community.[1] This significance of the regime can be seen in light of, among other things, how a large number of countries around the world have adopted local competition rules based on the key provisions of EU competition law, notably Articles 101 and 102 of the Treaty on the Functioning of the European Union (TFEU);[2] these countries include both developed and developing ones. Beyond serving as a global 'model', the EU competition law regime has served as a valuable source, which many competition authorities frequently use for insights into how competition issues are analysed and to learn about recent trends and developments in the field.[3]

---

[1] Obviously a distinction is made here between the EC and EU; the latter was created in 1992. See generally P. P. Craig and G. De Burca, *EU Law* (Oxford University Press, 2009). It is important to note however that this chapter – like the present book more generally – refers mostly to 'EU' and not 'EC' and does so also in a retrospective sense (unless the context otherwise demands specific reference to EC).

[2] Formerly, Arts 81 and 82 EC. These articles have been renumbered following the coming into force of the Lisbon Treaty on 1 December 2009. Tables of equivalence of the new numbering of the provisions on competition and the texts of the Treaty on the Functioning of the European Union, the Treaty on the European Union and Lisbon Treaty can be found at the following link: http://europa.eu/lisbon_treaty/full_text/index_en.htm.

[3] One should in this respect mention the enormous amount of literature which has been published on EU competition law and policy in books and articles. Notable standard books (in addition to the literature mentioned throughout the chapter) include (non-exhaustively): P. M. Roth and V. Rose (eds.) *Bellamy & Child: European Community Law of Competition* (6th edn., Oxford University press, 2008); J. Faull and A. Nikpay, *The EC Law of Competition* (Oxford University Press, 2007); A. Jones and B. Sufrin, *EC Competition Law: Text, Cases and Materials* (Oxford University Press, 2007); R. Whish, *Competition Law* (Oxford University Press, 2008); M. Furse, *Competition Law of the EC and UK* (Oxford University Press, 2008); B. J. Rodger and A. MacCulloch, *Competition Law and Policy in the EC and UK* (Routledge-Cavendish, 2009); M. Dabbah *EC and UK*

EU competition law is highly fascinating and its enforcement mechanism – especially with the radical reform introduced in 2004[4] – provides a model of a highly successful regional competition law regime, especially when one considers the close relationship between the European Commission – the main EU body in charge of competition enforcement – and national courts and national competition authorities of the member states. The regime stands on deeply strong 'intrinsic' and 'extrinsic' elements that make it worth considering as a model to be used in any context in which some form of supranational regime – whether regional or international – is considered.[5] The regime also contains a unique experience supported by a rich background, especially on the relationship between law and politics. Indeed the political significance and influence of the regime has been as extensive as its economic and legal impact.

1. Building the EU competition law regime as a 'European' idea

Europe – whether in terms of the inception of the original European Economic Community (EEC) or the coining of the concept of the European Union (EU) in the early 1990s – has been about 'ideas'. Ideas are important in the European context, because the EU only develops, and progress in any field within it is only made, when ideas themselves are developed and advanced.

There has been no other field in which European ideas have been more important and influential – whether within the EU or internationally – than the field of competition law and policy. Within the EU itself, competition law plays a hugely important role in bringing about key benefits to European citizens, whether in terms of lower prices, better quality of products or more choice. It is widely recognised that competition law in Europe arose as a result of political and economic necessity unique to the Continent.[6] The purpose behind introducing competition

---

Competition Law: Commentary, Cases and Materials (Cambridge University Press, 2004); V. Korah, *An Introductory Guide to EC Competition Law and Practice* (Hart Publishing, 2007); A. Albors-Llorens and J. Goyder, *Goyder's EC Competition Law* (Oxford University Press, 2009).

[4] See pp. 192–197 below.

[5] See generally Gerber, *Law and Competition in Twentieth Century Europe* (Oxford University Press, 1998).

[6] See A. D. Neale and D. G. Goyder, *The Antitrust Laws of the United States of America: a Study of Competition Enforced by Law* (Cambridge University Press, 1980), p. 439; G. Amato, *Antitrust and the Bounds of Power* (Hart Publishing, 1997), p. 2.

law within the framework of the Treaty of Rome 1957 was to support the political idea behind the Treaty, namely to establish not only a single market within which goods, services and persons will be able to move freely but also ultimately to create an ever closer union among the peoples of Europe.

Internationally, EU competition law has come to play an equally important role and an impressive international dimension has been developed to the whole interpretation, application and enforcement of the EU rules on competition. Building an international dimension to EU competition law has been the result of a very specific European idea: promoting the single market and strengthening the EU, turning the EU competition law regime into a dominant regime on the world stage which different nations can consult for lessons, and helping internationalise competition law as a whole.

2. The EU chapter on competition and relevant legislative framework

(A)   Articles 101–109 TFEU

The competition rules of the EU pursue 'multi-purpose' objectives and in practice perform a number of functions. The rules are contained in Chapter 1 of Title VII of TFEU. The chapter in turn contains nine Articles, Articles 101–109 TFEU. The first of these provisions – Articles 101[7] and 102[8] TFEU – respectively deal with the business phenomenon of collusion between firms and abuse of dominance. Article 106 TFEU deals with public firms or those to which special or exclusive rights are granted by member states and those 'entrusted with the operation of services of general economic interest or having the character of a revenue-producing monopoly' and provides that these will be subject to the rules contained in the Treaty, in particular those featuring in the chapter on competition. Articles 107–109 TFEU deal with state aid, aid

---

[7] Article 101 TFEU in para. 1 prohibits agreements, decisions by associations of undertakings and concerted practices which restrict competition and which affect trade between Member States. By virtue of Art. 101(2) TFEU, any agreement, decision or concerted practice which is caught by para. 1 of the Article is declared void; however, the prohibition may be declared inapplicable in the case of agreements or practices which satisfy the requirements of the third paragraph of the Article.

[8] Article 102 TFEU is directed towards any abuse by one or more undertakings of a dominant position in the Common Market or a substantial part of it which may affect trade between Member States.

granted by member states which harms or poses a threat to competition by 'favouring' certain firms or the manufacture of goods.

(B)   Regulations

Other relevant legislative instruments in the field of competition law include many Regulations, which form a body of secondary legislation.[9] These include Regulation 139/2004,[10] the Merger Regulation, which deals with mergers or as referred to in the Regulation itself 'concentrations with Community dimension' and Regulation 1/2003,[11] the Modernisation Regulation, which plays a key role in the implementation and enforcement of Articles 101 and 102 TFEU. There are also a number of Regulations which function as block exemption instruments and which deal with particular category or categories of situations, such as Regulation 330/2010 (vertical restraints),[12] Regulation xxx/2010 (specialisation),[13] Regulation xxx/2010 (Research and Development),[14] Regulation 772/2004 (intellectual property licensing)[15] and Regulation 800/2008 (state aid).[16]

(C)   General Treaties Articles

In addition to these key competition instruments there are important additional general provisions, which are of supreme importance in EU competition law regimes. These include Articles 3,[17] 4,[18] and 5 of the Treaty on European Union (TEU) and Article 18 TFEU. Article 3 TEU contains the objectives of the Union. The Article provides that the 'Union shall establish an internal market. It shall work for the sustainable development of the EU based on balanced economic growth and price stability, a highly competitive social market economy ...' Article 4(3) TEU sets out the duty on member states to ensure the fulfilment

---

[9] Secondary legislation with competition relevance also exists in the form of Directives. See, for example, the Trade Mark Directive 89/104 (1989) *Official Journal* L-40/1.

[10] (2004) *Official Journal* L-133/31.   [11] (2003) *Official Journal* L-1/1.

[12] (2010) *Official Journal* L-102/1.   [13] (2010) *Official Journal* L-xxx (number tbc).

[14] (2010) *Official Journal* L-xxx (number tbc).   [15] (2004) *Official Journal* L-123/11.

[16] (2008) Official Journal L-214/3.

[17] This Article has replaced in substance former Art. 2 EC (which has been repealed following the entering into force of the Lisbon Treaty).

[18] See in particular para. 3 of the Article which has replaced in substance Art. 10 EC (which has been repealed following the entering into force of the Lisbon Treaty).

of all their obligations under the Treaties or arising from actions taken by EU institutions. Article 5 TEU – the subsidiarity principle – deals with the division of competence between the two important levels within the EU: the higher Union level and lower national level. The Article provides when action in a particular situation would be better attained at the Union as opposed to national level.[19] Article 119 TFEU provides that the activities of the Union and of member states shall be conducted in accordance with the principle of an open market economy with free competition. Article 18 TFEU contains the 'anti-discrimination' principle, which has particular importance in the field of competition law especially to ensure that there will be no discrimination on the part of member states on the ground of nationality. Finally, it is important to note the *Protocol on the Internal Market and Competition* which refers to the idea of 'a system ensuring that competition is not distorted'.[20]

(D)   Administrative guidance

It may be worth noting here the existence of an extensive body of guidance issued by the European Commission over the years. Although the different guidelines and notices do not form part of the competition chapter itself and the legislative framework for the protection of competition more generally *nor* do they have the binding force of the law, they do play a hugely important role in practice in explaining the scope and application of the different Articles and Regulations and how they operate in practice. Among the most notable guidelines and notices are: the *Notice on market definition* (1997);[21] the *Notice on agreements of minor importance (de minimis)* (2001);[22] the *Guidelines on transfer of technology* (2004);[23] the *Modernisation*

---

[19] Paragraph 3 of the Article provides as follows: 'Under the principle of subsidiarity, in areas which do not fall within its exclusive competence, the Union shall act only if and in so far as the objectives of the proposed action cannot be sufficiently achieved by the Member States, either at central level or at regional and local level, but can rather, by reason of the scale or effects of the proposed action, be better achieved at Union level.'

[20] Under the old Art. 3(g) EC this was one of the activities of the Community. In the process of Lisbon Treaty negotiations this idea was subject to some heated debate, in particular there was an attempt to signal that by shifting the idea from a Treaty Article to a protocol, somehow the competence of EU institutions in the field of competition would be reduced and this would give Member States a greater say in regulating competition matters (at national level).

[21] (1997) *Official Journal* C-372/5.   [22] (2001) *Official Journal* C-368/13.

[23] (2004) *Official Journal* C-101/2.

Package (2004);[24] the *Guidelines on horizontal mergers* (2004);[25] the *Notice on cartel leniency* (2006);[26] the *Guidelines on non-horizontal mergers* (2007);[27] the *Guidelines on vertical restraints* (2010);[28] and the *Guidelines on horizontal agreements* (2010).[29]

3. The special characteristics of EU competition law

There are many characteristics to EU competition law which make it a unique type of law especially when compared to the competition laws of other regimes. EU competition law is enforced in a special context, namely the goal of market integration and therefore it has a market-integrating aspect. In this context, the law belongs to a wider 'system', designed to eliminate barriers between EU member states and enhance the creation of a single (internal) market.[30] Since the inception of the original EC Treaty and specifically the coming into force of the competition provisions in 1962, the law has come to be widely recognised as fundamental to furthering this single market goal,[31] initially in the form of the Common Market and later to establish the Internal Market.[32] Attaining this goal required not only eliminating restrictions imposed by member states, but also ensuring that those restrictions would not be 'replaced' by private restraints resulting from the behaviour or conduct of private firms, because both were considered capable of harming this goal. For this reason, and others, competition law was

---

[24] The Modernisation Package was published alongside Regulation 1/2003. It contains a number of notices and guidelines, including: *Notice on cooperation within the Network of Competition Authorities* (2004) *Official Journal* C-101/43; *Notice on cooperation between the Commission and national courts* (2004) *Official Journal* C-101/54; *Guidelines on effect on trade between Member States* (2004) *Official Journal* C-1010/81; *Notice on handling of complaints by the Commission* (2004) *Official Journal* C-101/65; *Guidelines on the application of Article 101(3) TFEU (ex Article 81(3))* (2004) *Official Journal* C-101/97; *Notice on informal guidance relating to novel questions (guidance letters)* (2004) *Official Journal* C-101/78.

[25] (2004) *Official Journal* C-31/5. [26] (2006) *Official Journal* C-298/17.

[27] (2007) *Official Journal* C-265/7. [28] (2010) *Official Journal* C-130/1.

[29] (2010) *Official Journal* L-xxx (number tbc).

[30] See Report of American Bar Association on *Private Anticompetitive Practices as Market Access Barriers* (2000).

[31] Many commentators share the view that competition policy is regarded as the most fundamental and successful of EU policies. See L. McGowan and S. Wilks, 'The First Supranational Policy in the European Union: Competition Policy' (1995) *European Journal of Political Research* 141.

[32] See B. E. Hawk, 'Antitrust in the EEC – the First Decade' (1972) *Fordham Law Review* 229; U. W. Kitzinger, *The Politics and Economics of European Integration: Britain, Europe, and the United States* (Basic Books, 1963), pp. 22–58; the European Commission 23rd Report on Competition Policy (1993), p. 88.

introduced within the EU framework to address such concerns and this has contributed towards competition law becoming of central importance in the EU.[33] Over the years, numerous occasions arose on which practices were declared as having an anticompetitive 'object' because they were considered to be an affront to the single market objective.[34] Associating competition law with the single-market integration goal has meant that the law has developed in many ways that depart from the 'traditional' approach, which can be observed in different competition law regimes around the world. This has meant that EU competition law contains not only the economic goals of enhancing efficiency and maximising consumer welfare, but also a wider (political) goal.[35] EU competition law therefore has a variety of goals and this reflects a 'European' regulatory approach to competition which has well-founded supranational attributes. These attributes were confirmed in a groundbreaking judgment of the European Court of Justice (ECJ) in *Van Gend en Loos* which was a non-competition case. In this early decision, the Court spoke clearly about a 'new legal order of international law', which included both EU member states and their nationals and which meant that the member states have limited their sovereign rights, albeit within limited fields.[36] Adopting and using competition law in this legal order offers an example of internationalisation of competition law and policy.

---

[33] See P. Massey, 'Reform of EC Competition Law: Substance, Procedure and Institutions' (1996) *Fordham Corporate Law Institute* 91.

[34] See the landmark judgment of the ECJ in Case 58/64, *Consten and Grundig* v. *Commission* [1966] ECR 299: confirming a decision of the European Commission that an exclusive distribution agreement between Grundig (supplier) and Consten (distributor) imposing an export ban on the latter had an anticompetitive object under Art. 101 (1) TFEU (ex Art. 81(1) EC).

[35] See the discussion above in relation to goals. See Mendes, *Antitrust in a World of Interrelated Economies: the Interplay between Antitrust and Trade Policies in the US and the EEC* (Editions de l'Université de Bruxelles, 1991).

[36] Case 26/62, *NV Algemene Transporten Expeditie Onderneming van Gend en Loos* v. *Nederlandse Administratie der Belastingen* [1963] ECR 1.

The question of legal personality and nature of the EU (the EC at the relevant time) has also been considered on other occasions by the ECJ. The following characteristics of the legal order established by the EU have been emphasised by the ECJ. By contrast with ordinary international treaties, the EU created its own legal system which became an integral part of the legal systems of the Member States. By creating a Union of unlimited duration, having its own institutions, its own legal capacity and capacity of representation on the international plane and real powers stemming from a limitation of sovereignty or a transfer of powers, the Member States have limited their sovereign rights. This limitation of Member States sovereignty is permanent. Case 6/64, *Costa* v. *ENEL* [1964] ECR 585, at 593. See how this view of the ECJ corresponds to EU legislation. Article 356 TFEU states that the Treaty is concluded for unlimited duration.

4. The nature of EU competition law

Notwithstanding the unique characteristics of EU competition law regime which as we saw in the previous part sets it apart from other competition law regimes around the world, EU competition law shares at least one common thread relating to its nature with the competition rules of many countries, namely the fact that it was *desired* neither by lawyers nor by economists, but by politicians and by 'scholars' who saw vital importance in safeguarding the pillars on which democratic regimes stood; for these scholars competition law in Europe was seen as the appropriate response to 'a crucial problem of democracy'.[37] The existence of such an underlying political perspective to EU competition law means that it is difficult to detach the law from a particular political idea at a particular point in time.[38] The creation and, arguably, the way in which EU competition law has come to develop show that it is as much about politics as law and economics. For this reason, EU competition law furnishes a good example of how competition law is *interdisciplinary* in nature and supports the view that a study on competition law and policy ought to be approached in an interdisciplinary manner.[39]

The existence of a political perspective to EU competition law can be also seen from the way in which the policies underlying the different provisions of the Treaty on the Functioning of the European Union (in particular Articles 101 and 102 TFEU) have changed according to changes in time and political thinking, despite the fact that the wording of these provisions has remained the same since their adoption in 1957. These changes reflect the existence of a political component in the nature of EU competition policy, especially at the level of EU bureaucratic politics and decision-making in competition cases, where compromises may be reached between competition policy and other types of policies, such as industrial policy.[40] It is perhaps not surprising that these changes have come to occur in a regime

---

[37] See Amato, p. 2, note 6 above.   [38] See pp. 62–64 above.

[39] See pp. 49–51 above for a discussion of the interdisciplinary nature of competition law. Also, see M. Dabbah, 'Measuring the Success of a System of Competition Law: a Preliminary View' (2000) *European Competition Law Review* 369.

[40] See I. Maher, 'Alignment of Competition Laws in the European community' (1996) *Yearbook of European Law* 223.

Former (late) Commissioner Karel Van Miert once said, competition policy 'is politics'; quoted in B. Doern and S. Wilks, *Comparative Competition Policy* (Oxford University Press, 1996), p. 254. For an illustration of the kind of compromises in question in the Commission decisional practice, see *Aérospatiale/Alenia/De Havilland* (Case IV/M.053) [1991] *Official Journal* L-334/42; [1992] 4 CMLR M2; *Ford/VW* [1993] *Official Journal* L-20/14; [1993] 5 CMLR 617.

that has supranational characteristics and which originally was subjected to influence of fundamentally different 'perceptions' of competition law by member states. Whilst some of the founding member states considered EU competition law to be 'juridical' on the basis that it formed a body of legal rules, other member states considered the main EU competition rules as policy statements, which had the function of the European Commission in its enforcement and decision-making tasks in the field of competition law.[41] The existence of these different perceptions and the fact that they were advocated by key member states resulted in two competing and conflicting views of competition law and competition: the former which emphasised the 'juridical' perception saw competition law and the competition as an end whereas the latter perception of policy statements and guidance considered them to be a means to further a variety of policies. In practice EU competition law and policy had to develop on the basis of striking a balance between these perceptions. This was not always an easy task and nor does it appear that the right balance was struck over the years. These perceptions remain alive and continue to be promoted to the present day as can be seen from the heated debate within the framework of the Lisbon Treaty negotiations over the idea of a 'system of undistorted competition' and whether it should continue to be contained in a Treaty Article or relegated to a protocol.[42]

5. The institutional structure within EU competition law regime

Establishing a 'new legal order of international law' within the framework of the EU required the creation of new autonomous institutions, which would be armed with the necessary mandate to interpret, apply and enforce EU law. To this end, a number of EU institutions were established. Originally, two of these institutions, namely the European Court of Justice and the European Commission, came to play a central role in interpreting and enforcing EU competition law and in formulating competition policy in the EC. In 1989 a third EU institution was created, namely the European Court of First Instance which has been playing an important role in offering the necessary judicial review of

[41] See Gerber, p. 346, note 5 above (footnotes omitted).

This, in turn, raises the issue of the seriousness of competition law beyond national boundaries. Initially, some Member States believed that EU law, in general, and EU competition law, in particular, could be enforced seriously under such circumstances, whilst others held a completely opposite view.

[42] See note 20 above.

Commission decisions. Almost all the meaning of EU competition rules has been supplied by these important institutions; consequently, they also provoked the most controversy surrounding the application of rules.[43]

(A)   The European Commission

Using law to protect competition in the EU meant there had to be clear 'severance' of the law from all domestic links and influences. This was seen as important in ensuring that the law would fulfil its primary function, namely to address harmful situations extending beyond national boundaries of individual member states. This effectively necessitated a marginalisation of member states and their institutions in order to enhance the chances for the flowering of a 'culture of competition' in the EU.[44] At the same time, it made it absolutely vital to have an enforcing Union institution at the heart of the new supranational regime, which – to put things in historical perspective – was extremely novel and highly revolutionary. The basic case was therefore made for 'centralising' EU competition law regime through concentrating the necessary powers of enforcement in the hands of the institution, which was supposed to act on behalf of the Union itself, the European Commission; this case however came to be well made in practice through important judgments adopted by the ECJ in its early case law. Arguably, this was a policy choice echoing the lack of trust on the part of the Commission in the ability or willingness of the different actors in member states – whether judges, administrative bodies, lawyers or the business community – to apply EU competition law whether correctly or in good faith.[45]

---

[43] For example, the employment of Art. 102 TFEU (Art. 82 EC) by the Commission and the ECJ has made it difficult to decipher the aims of the provision. See M. Dabbah, 'Conduct, Dominance and Abuse in "Market Relationship": Analysis of Some Conceptual Issues Under Article 82 EC' (2000) *European Competition Law Review* 45; V. Korah, 'Tetra Pak II – Lack of Reasoning in Court's Judgment' (1997) *European Competition Law Review* 98. More recently, clarification has been purportedly supplied especially through guidance issued by the Commission: see the *Guidance Paper on Article 82 EC* (December 2008).

[44] L. S. Forrester and C. Norall, 'The Laicization of Community Law: Self-Help and the Rule of Reason: How Competition Law is and Could be Applied' (1984) *Common Market Law Review* 11.

[45] See M. Hutchings and M. Levitt, 'Concurrent Jurisdiction' (1994) *European Competition Law Review* 123; M. Reynolds and P. Mansfield, 'Complaining to the Commission' (1997) *European Counsel* 34.

In terms of being a logical choice however, it made complete sense to put the Commission at the heart of the regime. It was clear from the beginning that applying EU competition law required fundamental changes not only in terms of how business behaviour and conduct were viewed but also significant alterations in the way such behaviour and conduct were carried out. In particular it was necessary to broaden the enforcement viewpoint in order to capture all the implications and consequences for business behaviour and conduct, even where the situation in question appeared to have pure national attributes. For example, where an agreement is entered into between a producer and a distributor, both of whom are incorporated and based in a single member state which contains an export ban preventing the distributor from selling to firms in other member states, competition in the single market can be harmed even if competition in that member state would not be affected at all.[46] It would have been virtually unrealistic to expect that member states would have developed such a wider viewpoint, whether because they are unable or unwilling to do so. The European Commission, on the other hand, naturally enjoyed such viewpoint and the fact it had experienced legal and economic experts in competition law at its disposal – unlike the majority of founding member states – made it a more suitable institution and more qualified to decide cases with legal, economic and political significance to the Union as a whole. More crucially, because competition law was not known as a field and because it was important to 'respond' to the economic growth the EC witnessed in the first 15 years of its existence (which corresponded to the exact aim of the Treaty of Rome as expressed in the old Article 2 EC), centralised enforcement of EU competition law was the only sensible option to guarantee consistency in the application of the law. This was enormously vital in the context of provisions such as Article 101(3) TFEU (ex Article 81(3)), which afforded business firms an opportunity to benefit from an exemption from the prohibition contained in Article 101(1) TFEU (ex Article 81(1) EC). The exact role and function of Article 101(3) TFEU were remarkably uncertain in the early years following 1962 when Articles 101 and 102 TFEU were implemented especially given that the main aim of the EU (or the EC at that time) was clearly to further the goal of market integration. As a centralised institution, the Commission was in the best position to establish uniform application of EU competition rules throughout the member states, promote market integration by preventing the erection of private barriers and

---

[46] See note 33 above.

create a body of rules acceptable to all member states and the industry as fundamental to the proper functioning of the single market.[47]

The process of institutional centralisation was initiated by the old Regulation 17/62, a measure that proved to be very difficult to draft because of the differences in position which existed between the founding member states at that time.[48] The Regulation came to establish the powers of the Commission in enforcing Articles 101 and 102 TFEU and specifically defined the role of the Commission in EU competition law regime.[49] As explained below, the Regulation however has been replaced by a new Regulation, Regulation 1/2003 which has introduced radical reform to the enforcement mechanism within the regime.[50]

(B)   The General Court of the EU

The creation of the General Court of the EU (GCEU) in 1989 was done because having a specialist court was seen as important in order to ease the workload the ECJ was under and introduce a judicial review mechanism of first instance to vet decisions adopted by the Commission.

The GCEU has grown to become a major actor in EU competition law regime over the years. It is difficult however to judge whether the existence of the GCEU has been positive in terms of reducing the workload of the ECJ and consolidating EU competition law as a whole. On the one hand, it is highly arguable that the GCEU's contribution has indeed been significant in ensuring that the decisional practice of the Commission is subjected to effective scrutiny and its existence has reduced the burden on the ECJ given the number of cases in which the judgment of the GCEU was the final say on the relevant matter without any involvement of the ECJ. The GCEU has during its two decades of jurisprudence produced several commendable judgments which show the importance of the Commission's discretion in the field of competition law but which more crucially confirm that the use

---

[47] See the Commission White Paper on *The Modernisation of the Rules Implementing Articles 85 [now Article 101 TFEU] and 86 [now Article 102 TFEU] of the EC Treaty* (1999) *Official Journal* C-132/1, para. 4.

[48] (1962) *Official Journal* L-13/204. See V. Korah, *An Introductory Guide to EC Competition Law and Practice* (Sweet & Maxwell, 1994); Deringer, 'The Distribution of Powers in the Enforcement of the Rules of Competition and the Rome Treaty' (1963) *Common Market Law Review* 30.

[49] Note, however, that with the adoption of a specific Regulation (originally Regulation 4064/89 and now Regulation 139/2004) for merger control Regulation 17/62 was rendered inapplicable to mergers. See pp. 177–192 below.

[50] See pp. 192–197 below.

of discretion by the Commission is being subjected to close scrutiny. In *Italian Flat Glass* v. *Commission*, for example, the GCEU held that the Commission should bear the burden of proof in competition cases and that this required standard is not satisfied by the Commission merely 'recycling' the facts of the case.[51] A similar attitude by the GCEU can be seen from its decision in *PVC*, where the GCEU lamented the sloppy decision-making process of the Commission.[52] In an important case, *European Night Services* v. *Commission*,[53] the GCEU annulled the Commission decision, emphasising the obligation on the Commission to set out the facts in individual cases and considerations having decisive importance in the context of its decisions. The GCEU stated that while the Commission was not required to discuss the issues of law and facts and the considerations which led it to adopt its decision, it is required under the Treaty to make clear to the GCEU and the firms concerned the circumstances under which it has applied EU competition rules. Thus, when a Commission decision applying EU competition law lacks important analytical data – which is vital in competition cases and to enable the GCEU to establish whether an appreciable effect on competition exists – such as reference to market shares of the firms concerned, the Commission is not entitled to remedy such defect by adducing for the first time before the GCEU such data.[54]

On the other hand, the fact is and remains that judgments of the GCEU are subject to appeal to the ECJ and there have been many cases in which an appeal action has occurred or was at least attempted and on certain occasions the judgment of the GCEU was set aside, whether partially or in its entirety. Moreover, there appears to be some kind of uncertainty concerning how 'certain' interpretations offered by the GCEU are in the absence of a decision by the ECJ itself[55] and what is the exact 'direction'

---

[51] Joined Cases T-68, 77 and 78/89, *Società Italiana Vetro* v. *Commission* [1992] ECR II-1403; [1992] 5 CMLR 302.

[52] Joined Cases T-79/89, T-84–86/89, T-91–92/89, T-94/89, T-96/89, T-98/89, T-102/89 and T-104/89, *BASF AG* v. *Commission* [1992] ECR II-315; [1992] 4 CMLR 357.

[53] Cases T-374–5 and 388/94 [1998] ECR II-3141; [1998] CMLR 718.

[54] For example, the GCEU annulled the Commission decision in the case of *Airtours* because the GCEU believed that the Commission did not supply sufficient evidence in support of its decision. See Case T-342/99, *Airtours plc* v. *Commission* [2002] ECR II-2585.

[55] A notable example here can be found in the Case T-201/04, *Microsoft* v. *Commission* [2004] ECR II-4463. The GCEU in the case introduced significant modifications to the application of Art. 102 TFEU in refusal to supply situations. It has been felt however that these modifications would need to be confirmed by the ECJ. See Vesterdorf, 'Article 82 EC: Where Do We Stand After the Microsoft Judgment?' (2008) *ICC Global Antitrust Review* 1, available at: www.icc.qmul.ac.uk/GAR/GAR2008/index.htm.

of different GCEU cases. In its case law over the past two decades, the GCEU has produced several judgments, which make it difficult to discern the direction in which its jurisprudence has been moving. For example, against the good judgments referred to above which show the GCEU's interest in vetting the Commission's use of discretion stands a line of cases in which the GCEU has not been inclined to interfere with the use of wide discretion by the Commission, especially with regard to the imposition of fines and mitigating circumstances.[56] This attitude by the GCEU may seem quite surprising in the light of the purpose for which the GCEU was established. Some commentators have argued that the very creation of the GCEU as a court of both first and last instance for the examination of facts in cases brought before it is an invitation to undertake an intensive review in order to ascertain whether the evidence on which the Commission relies in adopting a contested decision is sound. Despite this view, however, there is no reason to believe that the EU competition law regime suffers from lack of effective judicial control at least at the level of the GCEU. Looking at the area of merger control, for example, since the introduction of specific merger control tools in 1989, only an extremely small number of mergers – which represent less than one per cent of all notified cases to the Commission to date – were prohibited by the European Commission. Of these few decisions by the Commission, about half came before either the GCEU or the ECJ. In some of those cases, the GCEU annulled the decision of the Commission and the latter's decisional practice was subjected to strong scrutiny and criticism.[57] Thus it seems that there is sufficient evidence to support the view that, on balance and bearing in mind that exceptions can be found, there seems to be effective judicial control in the EU competition law regime; the existence of the GCEU has clearly contributed towards that.

(C) The European Court of Justice

The European Court of Justice (ECJ) sits at the top of the judicial pyramid within the EU competition law regime and the EU more generally. The

---

[56] See Case T-7/89, *S. A. Hercules Chemicals NV* v. *Commission* [1991] ECR II-1711; [1992] CMLR 84; Case T-69/89, *Radio Telefis Eireann* v. *Commission* [1991] ECR II-485; [1991] 4 CMLR 586.

[57] See the CFI judgments in Case T-342/99, *Airtours plc* v. *Commission* [2002] ECR II-2585, Case T-77/02, *Schneider Electric* v. *Commission* (22 October 2002) and Case T-5/02, *Tetra Laval BV* v. *Commission* (25 October 2002).

ECJ enjoys a unique role in the regime which rests in part on the tasks that were originally allocated to it and more remarkably in part on the 'self-made' role the ECJ has given itself as an intellectual leader. This leadership was facilitated partly due to the state of political sclerosis from which the EC suffered from the late-1960s to the early-1980s when the EC was considered to lack any sense of direction and effective leadership to set the agenda for the future and partly due to the teleological vision which the ECJ relied on in its jurisprudence.[58] Following a teleological reasoning in the interpretation of EU law meant that the ECJ was able to look beyond the wording and literal interpretation of the different provisions in the law towards considering the policies or objectives underlying these provisions; in the field of EU competition law this has meant giving expression to market integration as a key goal in the application of the competition rules.

In addition to its key contribution to the understanding of EU competition law within its particular context, the ECJ drew in the early case law a jurisprudential line, which showed how it viewed the availability of a centralised institution – the Commission – to achieve this goal as necessary. The ECJ interpreted EU competition law in a specific way in order to enhance the powers of the Commission and place it at the centre vis-à-vis member states and their domestic competition authorities and courts. In this way the ECJ provided the Commission with 'windows of opportunity' where the ECJ would look beyond the facts of a particular case, confirming its willingness to support particular policy developments or approach by the Commission.[59] In giving the Commission an opportunity to strengthen its grip on competition enforcement in the EU, the ECJ contributed towards strengthening EU competition law. This has been a highly fascinating jurisprudential line because it makes it arguable that the ECJ has moved well beyond a juridical function and performed a political role: first through pushing extremely hard towards the wider

---

[58] See D. Gerber, 'The Transformation of European Community Competition Law' (1994) *Harvard International Law Journal* 97, 127–30. See also generally J. Bengoetxea, *The Legal Reasoning of the European Court of Justice* (Oxford University Press, 1993); B. Van der Esch, 'The Principles of Interpretation Applied by the Court of Justice of the European Communities and their Relevance for the Scope of the EEC Competition Rules' (1991) *Fordham Corporate Law Institute* 223, 225–34; M. Dabbah, 'The Dilemma of Keck – the Nature of the Ruling and the Ramifications of the Judgment' (1999) *Irish Journal of European Law* 84.

[59] See J. Goyder, *EC Competition Law* (Oxford University Press, 2002), pp. 578–82.

political goal of market integration;[60] and secondly in assuming a substantial policy-making role in establishing a competition law regime beyond national boundaries.

(D) Domestic courts

EU competition rules are directly applicable which means they become part of the legal system of the member states without this being conditional upon any action taken by the member states. The rules are also directly effective, meaning that they may be invoked by individuals, whether as claimant or defendant, in the domestic courts of the member states.[61] In this way, domestic courts have a very important role to play in applying EU competition law regime. In the early years of the existence of the regime however there was little evidence of this role. At that time domestic competition law regimes functioned almost exclusively on the basis of enforcement by administrative institutions.[62] For this reason, those firms or individuals who were concerned about anticompetitive situations had little motive and indeed saw little benefit in launching judicial actions to seek a remedy for harm caused to them as a result of such situations. For such potential claimants, it made more sense to complain to national competition authorities or the Commission: complaining was easier, less expensive and less uncertain than litigation in courts and the Commission in particular had established a policy of 'attracting' potential complainants.[63] Furthermore, an inclination to opt for a complaint as opposed to judicial action was enhanced by the obvious lack of clarity of the way in which EU competition law was supposed to be applied in domestic courts.[64] In later years however the role of national courts began to increase

[60] See Craig and De Burca, note 1 above; A. W. Green, *Political Integration by Jurisprudence: the Work of the Court of Justice of the European Communities in European Political Integration* (Sijthoff, 1969).

The flip-side of this argument is that a political topic has been 'judicialised'. This would, of course, raise the question as to whether this is desirable or inevitable.

[61] See the case of *van Gend en Loos*, note 36 above.

[62] Also, it was obvious that anticompetitive activities of firms could affect markets in more than one Member State. Hence, it was not possible for domestic courts to regulate such activities when they affected markets beyond national boundaries.

[63] See R. Whish, 'Enforcement of EC Competition Law in the Domestic Courts of Member States' (1994) *European Competition Law Review* 60; L. Hiljemark, 'Enforcement of EC Competition Law in National Courts – the Perspective of Judicial Protection' (1997) *Yearbook of European Law* 83.

[64] See D. F. Hall, 'Enforcement of EC Competition Law by National Courts' in P. J. Slot and A. McDonnell (eds.), *Procedure and Enforcement in EC and US Competition Law* (Sweet & Maxwell, 1993), p. 42; R. Rittler, D. Braun and F. Rawlinson, *EEC Competition Law – a*

and recently it has been particularly enhanced since the introduction of the Commission's modernisation programme in 2004:[65] unlike under the old enforcement regime, national courts now additionally have the power to apply Article 101(3) TFEU.

Because the EU framework provided for an involvement by national courts in the enforcement of EU law, it was necessary to establish a channel through which national courts could 'communicate' with the ECJ in order to help them handle the application of the law through receiving vital guidance on how different provisions of EU law should be interpreted. To this end, the Treaty itself provided for a preliminary ruling procedure under Article 267 TFEU (ex Article 234 EC), which gives the domestic *courts* and *tribunals* of member states the chance to enter into a dialogue with the ECJ, subject to limitations expressed in the Article, on all aspects of EU law. This provision has been very useful in the context of EU competition law not only in starting and developing this dialogue but also in getting domestic courts to become more engaged in the application of the competition rules of the EU. Under the provision, a domestic court can ask the ECJ to give an interpretative ruling in relation to a matter of EU competition law that has arisen in the course of proceedings before the domestic court. Whenever this request is made, the ECJ aims to avoid ruling on questions of fact, which fall within the jurisdiction of the domestic court. The function of the ECJ is rather to lay down, in the abstract, the principles of EU competition law to be applied to the case in question.

(E) National competition authorities

In the early years of the development of EU competition law regime, national competition authorities (NCAs) of member states had no 'presence' in the regime. Apart from the centralised role of the Commission, which arguably left little scope for involvement on the part of NCAs, some member states lacked competition rules[66] and as a result there was no national competition authority or authorities to speak of in those

---

Practitioner's Guide (Kluwer, 1991), p. 718; G. Cumming, 'Assessors, judicial notice and domestic enforcement of Articles 85 and 86' (1997) *European Competition Law Review* 370; C. Kerse, *EC Antitrust Procedure* (Sweet & Maxwell, 1994), pp. 81–2; Kerse, 'The Complainant in Competition Cases: a Progress Report' (1997) *Common Market Law Review* 230; I. Van Bael, 'The Role of National Courts' (1994) *European Competition Law Review* 6.

[65] See below.

[66] One such Member State is Italy. See M. Siragusa and G. Scassellati-Sforztine, 'Italian and EC Competition Law: a New Relationship – Reciprocal Exclusivity and Common

member states. This situation has come to change dramatically over the years with all member states giving serious attention to competition law and with the Commission's modernised enforcement of Articles 101 and 102 TFEU. The outcome of these developments has been that NCAs have come to be recognised as important actors in the enforcement of EU competition law. The most notable recognition here has been on the part of the Commission itself as can been seen in particular in light of its efforts to create the European Competition Network (ECN).[67]

6. The relationship between EU and domestic competition laws

(A) The influence of EU competition law within the Union

The relationship between EU and domestic competition laws is worth looking at from a number of perspectives. Apart from the legal and economic perspectives,[68] there is a political perspective to this highly interesting relationship which exists because the relationship concerns political factors as much as legal and economic ones. This perspective is interesting to consider in light of the influence EU competition law had on the domestic competition laws of member states. For example, it is worth noting how a number of member states have in recent years 'modelled' their relevant domestic competition rules on Article 101 and 102 TFEU[69] and have amended their regimes in order to bring them closer to Regulation 139/2004;[70] in the case of some member states, EU competition law has had profound influence on the decision of these member states to adopt domestic competition laws. Equally important, it is worth noting the fact that as part of their accession to the EU, those member states which joined in 2004 and 2007 adopted domestic competition rules based on EU competition law; for almost all of these countries competition law came to be taken seriously as a result of the influence of EU competition law and

---

Principles' (1993) *Common Market Law Review* 93; F. Romani, 'The New Italian Antitrust Law' (1991) *Fordham Corporate Law Institute* 479; B. Cova and F. Fine, 'The New Italian Antitrust Act *vis-à-vis* EC Competition Law' (1991) *European Competition Law Review* 20.

[67] See pp. 194–197 below for a discussion of the ECN.

[68] See Massey, pp. 117–21 note 33 above; J. Temple Lang, 'European Community Constitutional Law and the Enforcement of Community Antitrust Law' (1993) *Fordham Corporate Law Institute* 525.

[69] See, for example, how the UK modelled the Chapter I and Chapter II prohibitions contained in the Competition Act 1998 on these Articles.

[70] A good example here is Germany.

the concentrated efforts of the European Commission in this respect. EU competition law has been highly influential as a 'model' on which the competition rules of many member states have come to be based. Nevertheless, the issue of influence goes much deeper than a simple and general statement that there has been such influence. The issue requires careful assessment of the complex relationship between the EU competition law regime and domestic competition law regimes of member states, in particular a look at how this relationship began in the early years of the existence of the EC and how it has developed since those early years.

(B) The years prior to modernisation: 1957–2004

I. The jurisdictional competence criterion

During the early years of the existence of EU competition law regime, the relationship between EU competition law and domestic competition laws of member states was a particularly vague one. This could have hardly been surprising given the lack of clarity on the scope of 'obligations' member states had within the framework of the EU (particularly originally in creating the E(E)C) and whether this meant that there was a surrender of national sovereignty. It was therefore important that the necessary clarification be offered and this finally emerged in the case law of the ECJ. Essentially, the position the ECJ saw fit to adopt was to rule that the relationship between EU and domestic competition laws stood exclusively on a jurisdictional competence criterion,[71] a 'two-barrier theory'.[72] This theory, which defined the respective areas – EU and domestic – of competence, 'conditioned' the basic components of the relationship between both sets of laws. It provided that EU competition law was applicable wherever there was an effect on trade between member states.[73] This therefore left it open to member states to apply their domestic competition laws (or general relevant laws) as they saw fit in situations extending to their domestic territories or markets, provided that such action did not conflict with EU competition law; in case of conflict, EU competition law would – according to the ECJ's own doctrine of supremacy – prevail over conflicting national rules.

---

[71] See Kirchner, 'Competence Catalogues and the Principle of Subsidiarity in a European Constitution' (1997) Constitutional Political Economy 71.

[72] Case C-148/68, Walt Wilhelm v. Bundeskartellamt [1969] ECR 1.

[73] See J. Faull, 'Effect on Trade Between Member States and Community: Member States Jurisdiction' (1989) Fordham Corporate Law Institute 485.

A characterisation of this relationship along the lines of existence or lack of effect on trade between member states would in the circumstances have been expected to ensure a smooth relationship and eliminate the possibility of any form of coordination between the two spheres. The situation in practice however did not reflect such expectation. On the one hand, 'grey' situations came to arise over the years in which an 'overlap' of jurisdiction was found to exist, namely situations in which both EU competition law and domestic competition laws could be said to be applicable and this raised the serious question of what level action is better taken at. On the other hand, the possibility of coordination between the two spheres was not totally excluded; for example in the early-1970s in particular, it was clear that domestic courts could apply most provisions of the EU competition law.[74] Admittedly, however, it seems there was no particularly strong appetite for such coordination and on the whole actors within both EU and domestic competition law regimes were not quite motivated to consider coordination. This lack of motive can be attributed to several factors, the most important of which was the existence then of certain limitations on the competence of domestic courts and national competition authorities to enforce competition law generally;[75] as well as their lack of power to apply Article 101 (3) TFEU since Regulation 17/62 reserved this power for the Commission's exercise only.[76] This limitation on the ability of domestic courts and domestic competition authorities to apply EU competition law in its entirety pushed them to the sidelines as opposed to pulling them towards the centre of the regime. As was noted above, in the early years firms and individuals aggrieved by anticompetitive situations felt discouraged from seeking to enforce EU competition law, in particular Article 101 TFEU, in domestic courts. The 'must take into account' scenario for such potential claimants was this: supposing a domestic court would find the Article 101(1) TFEU prohibition applicable in the relevant situation, the possibility was open to the defendant firm(s) to apply to the Commission for an exemption under Article 101(3) TFEU and in fact *convince* the Commission to issue such exemption which would effectively render the legal action meaningless and simply a waste

---

[74] See Case 127/73, *Belgische Radio en Televisie et al.* v. *SV SABAM and NV Fonier* [1974] ECR 51, paras 16 and 17; [1974] 2 CMLR 238.

[75] See J. Bourgeois, 'EC Competition Law and Member States Courts' (1993) *Fordham International Law Journal* 331.

[76] See Art. 9 of the Regulation.

of time and money. The situation was the same in relation to coordination between EU and domestic spheres of competence through the channel of enforcement by national competition authorities of EU competition law.[77] However, whilst this channel was indeed open, the fact that national competition authorities also lacked competence to grant exemptions under Article 101(3) TFEU,[78] combined with some of them even lacking authority under their domestic laws to apply EU competition law in the first place, meant that this option was even less popular than the courts' option.

II. The centralisation and decentralisation debate

The relationship between EU and domestic competition laws, including the division between their respective spheres of competence, was not the focus of any proper debate in the period between 1957 and the early-1980s, whether at academic or policy-making levels. The relevant legal literature during that period offered insufficient attention to this relationship and there was hardly any exposition of the issues at its heart, or a concerted effort to discuss the 'way forward'. The situation was no different with regard to the agenda of the European Commission and Commission officials somehow did not consider the matter to be a priority.[79] As a result, the general impression formed was that there was clear satisfaction with the status quo and this translated into hardly any consideration in practice of whether a change in the formal relationship between EU and domestic competition laws was necessary in terms of expanding the coordination between their spheres of competence.

That position came to change noticeably from the mid-1980s however with a change of thought regarding this relationship beginning to appear on the horizon.[80] A number of factors mobilised this change

---

[77] Notice on Cooperation between the Commission and National Competition Authorities in Handling Cases Falling within the Scope of Article 85 and 86 EC (1996) Official Journal C-262/5. This Notice is no longer valid as it has been replaced under the Modernisation Package – see note 24 above for the current Notice.

[78] It was obvious that a national competition authority might have expended its resources to bring an action under Art. 101(1) TFEU over which it did not have ultimate control. See M. A. Fernandez Ordonez, 'Enforcement by National Authority of EC and Member States' Antitrust Law' (1993) Fordham Corporate Law Institute 629.

[79] It seems that the reason for this relates to the economic difficulties during that period, with the Oil Shock, as well as political sclerosis at international level generally.

[80] During this period, there was a change of economic conditions and political consensus within the EU was growing.

and made it possible. The different economic difficulties, such as those of the oil shock, were easing and the period of stagnation from which the Union suffered until that time was clearly coming to an end as can be seen in light of the revival of the process of market integration marked by the introduction of the Single European Act 1986. Effectively, all this gave the clearest of indications that it was no longer possible to maintain a formal division of competence along the lines of the jurisdictional competence criterion and that it was necessary to 'revisit' this criterion and its suitability to a reinvigorated Community, which was now heading towards a higher degree of integration. It was therefore only legitimate and necessary to ask whether there was a need for a fundamentally more cooperative and integrated framework for EU law in general, and for the EU competition law regime in particular. This spawned the existence of what has materialised as a central debate in EU competition law and policy, namely the *centralisation/ decentralisation* debate. The former was seen as a *centripetal* process which, as noted above, led to concentrating enforcement powers in the field of competition law at the Union level, i.e. in the hands of the Commission. Different factors led to this perspective. One motivation was the concern on the part of officials of the Commission. Decentralisation on the other hand represented a completely different perspective which relied on a *centrifugal* process that advocated the delegation of authority to the national level. The decentralisation process entered the EU competition policy scene around the mid-1980s,[81] when the Commission began properly to consider the need to involve national courts and national competition authorities in applying EU competition law.[82] Several factors contributed to this trend. Most significantly it was apparent that the Commission was unable to meet its responsibilities under the regime because: first, there was a lack of resources, mainly caused by financial and political factors; secondly, there was a possibility (one may say it was a fact)

---

[81] Prior to this, the Commission was hesitant about decentralisation, because it was thought: *first*, it would reduce the capacity of EU institutions to influence the development of EU competition law regime; *secondly*, it would afford Member States the opportunity to use it to further their own objectives and individual interests; and *thirdly*, it would increase the risk of inconsistencies within the system. See J. Meade, 'Decentralisation in the Implementation of EEC Competition Law – a Challenge for the Lawyers' (1986) *Northern Ireland Law Quarterly* 101.

[82] See Commission 13th and 15th Reports on Competition Policy (1983) and (1985), paras 217 and 38 respectively.

that the EU in the mid-1980s was going to expand geographically;[83] and thirdly, one cannot overlook the fact that the Commission saw involving national courts and national competition authorities as an important way to strengthen the link between EU competition law regime and its constituents. The case for decentralisation became even more pressing with major events that took place in the late-1980s and early-1990s. These events included the collapse of the Soviet Union in 1989,[84] the signing of the Treaty on European Union in 1992[85] and the impending accession of more countries during that period.[86] All of these developments within and outside the field of competition law pushed decentralisation to prominence within the Commission. Broadly speaking, three options readily presented themselves of how decentralisation could be achieved. These included: an enhanced role for national courts to apply EU competition law; a deeper involvement by national competition authorities to enforce EU competition law; and encouraging greater reliance by national courts and national competition authorities on domestic competition laws.

(a) The application of EU competition law by domestic courts Pursuing decentralisation through the national courts of

---

[83] In 1986 Spain and Portugal acceded, and the accession of more countries such as Sweden, Finland and Austria was appearing on the horizon. Also, the accession programme included countries which upon acceding had either no competition law or had competition law regimes at a very early stage of development. This meant that firms and future officials in those countries had to be informed about competition law concepts, and this was thought likely to cause an increase in both the financial and educational burdens of the Commission.

[84] The changing situation in Central and Eastern Europe meant that the Commission had to at least consider the possibility of expanding its membership to include certain Central and Eastern European countries where the concepts of competition and competition law were unfamiliar. See pp. 208–214 below.

[85] The TEU introduced the principle of subsidiarity, which was mentioned earlier – see note 19 above and accompanying text. It is important to note that the principle of subsidiarity did not require changes in the EU competition law regime. However, it has played a central role in the relationship between EU and domestic competition laws, and in this form it entered the centralisation/decentralisation debate. See B. P. B. Francis, 'Subsidiarity and Antitrust: the Enforcement of European Competition Law in the National Courts of Member States' (1995) *Law and Policy in International Business* 247; R. Alford, 'Subsidiarity and Competition: Decentralized Enforcement of EU Competition Laws' (1994) *Cornell International Law Journal* 275; R. Wesseling, 'Subsidiarity in Community Law: Setting the Right Agenda' (1997) *European Law Review* 35.

[86] See note 83 above.

member states was almost a 'natural' course of action for the Commission. This option proved to be highly attractive to the Commission in order to 'relieve' the burden that had come to be imposed on it by its heavy workload and foster meaningful compliance with EU competition law at the national level. Obviously the Treaty of Rome 1957 itself had already catered for a 'dialogue' to occur between national courts and the ECJ – through the preliminary ruling procedure in the former Article 234 EC (now Article 267 TFEU) – and this offered a safety valve in maintaining consistency in how EU competition law would be interpreted. Among other things, deepening the involvement of national courts was seen as something that would not require a change to the 'two-barrier theory'; the Commission also felt this would not require any loosening in its control over the enforcement of EU competition law. It was not at all surprising therefore that the Commission would favour this option as can be seen from its efforts in the late 1980s and early 1990s to encourage legal actions in national courts.[87] The response to the Commission's efforts was not quite as encouraging however.[88] The Commission contemplated a number of ways in which it could show its seriousness and determination to pursue this option. It found that clear guidance should be provided on its 'approach' to this form of decentralisation and for this reason it adopted its *Notice concerning Cooperation between the Commission and Courts of the Member States with Regards to the Application of Articles 85 (now Article 101 TFEU) and 86 (now Article 102 TFEU)*, which was issued in 1993.[89]

Nevertheless, even with the adoption of the Notice the views remained mixed on the Commission's efforts with the latest effort being viewed in some quarters as radical.[90] The Notice was fairly clear with regard to the Commission's efforts to encourage private actions and the importance the Commission attaches to the issue of compliance.[91] It strongly heralded the principle that cases with no particular political, economic or legal significance for the EU should, as a general rule, be handled by national

---

[87] See C. D. Ehlermann, 'The European Community, its Law and Lawyers' (1992) *Common Market Law Review* 213.

[88] See R. Wesseling, 'The Commission Notices on Decentralisation of EC Antitrust Law: in for a Penny, Not for a Pound' (1997) *European Competition Law Review* 94.

[89] (1993) *Official Journal* C-39/6. This Notice is no longer valid. For the current Notice which deals with the relationship, see note 24 above.

[90] See A. J. Riley, 'More Radicalism, Please: the Notice on Cooperation Between National Courts and the Commission in Applying Articles 85 and 86 of the EEC Treaty' (1993) *European Competition Law Review* 93.

[91] See paras 15 and 16 of the *Notice*.

courts or national competition authorities.[92] In order to clarify the role of national courts, the Notice offered procedural guidelines for national courts to follow in handling the application of EU competition law. It specified the factors that national courts should consider when deciding cases and the steps they should take.[93] Essentially, national courts were directed under the Notice to base their decisions on EU competition law to the extent it is possible for them to predict how the Commission, and possibly the European Courts, would decide relevant cases. The Notice recommended that domestic courts take into account, in addition to the judgments of the European courts, the decisional practice of the Commission under the block exemption Regulations. However, there was a great deal of scepticism over the Notice, especially during the first year of its existence. Primarily, considerable doubts existed with regard to whether the Notice would lead to a significant increase in the utilisation of national courts as a proper forum to enforce EU competition law. There was little belief that the Notice could fundamentally alter the situation on the ground: it was clear that the general attitude of firms with regard to the risks and uncertainties attached to legal actions brought before domestic courts.[94] As a matter of fact, this scepticism continued throughout the Notice's existence. There is no doubt that some hurdles remained in the face of this type of decentralisation, such as those relating to domestic courts' lack of competence to issue individual exemptions.[95] Despite this scepticism, it can be said that, on the whole, the Notice was a positive step forward in coordinating the relationship between the Commission and domestic courts.

(b) Application of EU competition law by national competition authorities   The second variant of decentralisation relates to national competition authorities directly enforcing EU competition law. For many years, there was relatively little incentive on the part of the Commission to advance this variant. Several reasons may be suggested for this lack of

---

[92] Note that the *Notice* was issued at virtually the same time as the subsidiarity principle was introduced, and this seemed to suggest – as remarked in note 85 above – that the Commission was here applying the principle within EU competition law regime. See para. 14 of the *Notice*.

[93] See paras 17–32 of the *Notice*.

[94] See C. D. Ehlermann, 'Implementation of EC Competition Law by National Antitrust Authorities' (1996) 17 *European Competition Law Review* 88.

[95] See G. Marenco, 'The Uneasy Enforcement of Article 85 EEC as Between Community and National Levels' (1993) *Fordham Corporate Law Institute* 605.

enthusiasm. For a number of years the Commission viewed this variant of decentralisation as being more complex and more uncertain than decentralisation via national courts. The Commission thought this option would have rendered inevitable the orchestration of the relationship between national competition authorities and itself through coordination in the decision-making between officials of those authorities and its own officials. This was seen as risky because each set of officials enjoys a degree of discretion and each is receptive to policy considerations and responds to pressures of the competition law regime within which it operates.[96] Another reason for this lack of enthusiasm is that national authorities showed little interest in enforcing EU competition law rather than their own national competition laws.[97] Furthermore, the fact that most national competition authorities had limited resources and experience, coupled with the fact that some member states, notably Italy, did not even have competition law regimes,[98] let alone the fact that major differences existed between national competition laws and EU competition law, contributed to a large extent to this lack of enthusiasm.

Despite this obvious reluctance by the Commission to pursue this variant of decentralisation, and the equally evident lack of incentive on the part of national competition authorities to apply EU competition law, the Commission issued a *Notice on Cooperation between the Commission and National Competition Authorities in Handling Cases Falling within the Scope of Article 85 (now Article 101 TFEU) and 86 (now Article 102 TFEU) EC* in 1996 ('the 1996 Notice').[99] The 1996 Notice, which indicated the willingness of the Commission to consider seriously this type of decentralisation, specifically referred to the principle of subsidiarity – which allocates the competence between Union and national levels – as a justification for increased transfer of competence, albeit in a limited manner, to national competition authorities.[100] The 1996 Notice explained that if, by

---

[96] The Commission also thought that this could impose significant additional costs on the Commission as well as interfere with its capacity to control efforts to protect competition in the EU.

[97] To a certain extent, this is understandable because they lack competence to issue individual exemptions under Art. 101(3) TFEU. They are primarily responsible for the development and enforcement of their own domestic competition laws, and their competent performance is likely to be judged in light of the fulfilment of this task.

[98] See note 66 above and accompanying text.

[99] (1996) *Official Journal* C-262/5. This Notice is no longer valid. For the current Notice (the European Competition Network notice), see note 24 above.

[100] In the light of this allocation principle, the competence of the Commission or the relevant national competition authority to act was determined by the size and effect of

reason of its scale or effects, the proposed action can best be taken at the higher level, it is for the Commission to act. If, on the other hand, the action can be taken satisfactorily at national level, the competition authority of the member state concerned is better placed to act. Whilst clearly of value, this allocation of competence principle – as introduced in the 1996 Notice – was limited in terms of its sphere of operation and application, mainly due to the lack of competence of national competition authorities to grant exemptions under Article 101(3) TFEU.

The 1996 Notice showed that the Commission had at that time come to recognise the importance of cooperation with national competition authorities. It showed the benefit of such cooperation, especially to avoid duplication of competition enforcement.[101] The 1996 Notice did not, however, fundamentally change the attitude of domestic policymakers to think more positively with regard to the process of decentralisation. It is clear, in light of the 1966 Notice, that making this type of decentralisation more viable required further significant steps on the part of the Commission towards consolidating its efforts in this direction; the Commission eventually took these steps when it adopted Regulation 1/2003 and established the European Competition Network.[102]

(c) National competition authorities applying their own competition laws   A third variant of decentralisation is for national competition authorities to continue to apply their own national competition laws, but to do so more frequently.[103] Naturally, this variant of decentralisation was little discussed, mainly because the Commission in particular and the competition community in Europe more generally always used

---

the agreement, practice or conduct in question. The Commission took the position that where the main effects of situation are within one Member State, the domestic competition authority of that Member State may handle the case. Nevertheless the Commission reserved to itself the right to take a case where it considered that it had important political, economic or legal significance – for example, if it raised new points of law or if it involves conduct or behaviour in which another Member State had a particular interest. This position has to a large extent survived into the Commission's Modernisation programme; see pp. 192–197 below.

[101] The Notice aimed to avoid the possibility that domestic competition authorities would have expended effort and resources in cases which the Commission would ultimately take out of their area of competence.

[102] See pp. 194–197 below.

[103] See P.-V. Bos, 'Towards a Clear Distribution of Competence Between EC and National Competition Authorities' (1995) *European Competition Law Review* 410.

the term 'decentralisation' to mean only the decentralised application of EU competition law. Nevertheless, two reasons have often been used to explain why this variant should also be considered. First, an increase in the application of national competition laws by competition authorities of member states responds to the values and concerns attached to the principle of subsidiarity. These values and concerns reduce the centralisation of power at EU level and increase the authority of member states to protect competition, where they can do so, at least as effectively as the Commission. Secondly, to the extent that national competition authorities satisfactorily protect competition by relying on domestic competition laws, the Commission would accomplish its objectives without drying up its resources any further. Increased reliance on domestic competition laws in such cases may also avoid many of the difficulties that might arise when the Commission and one or more domestic competition authorities apply EU competition law.

In spite of the above factors, it can be argued that an increased reliance by national authorities on their domestic competition laws is controversial. For over 42 years (1962–2004: the relevant years) the Commission sought to establish EU competition law as the basis of market integration. An increased reliance on domestic competition laws was seen as a step in the opposite direction which was liable to reverse this process, with the potential to reduce the superiority and authority of the Commission. Affording domestic competition authorities the opportunity to advise the business community, make important commercial decisions and decide on the norms to be followed by firms was considered to be a challenge to the superiority of the Commission. In addition, there appear to have been doubts within the Commission about the extent to which domestic competition laws may be relied on to protect competition at least as satisfactorily as when EU competition law is applied (by the Commission). Such doubts may be considered to be justified given that during early times in particular restrictions on competition were often considered to have cross-border effect. These restrictions were considered to be a possible infringement of the laws of more than one member state and therefore might create conflicts among member states as well as create costs in both time and resources for both national competition authorities and the firms involved. A member state was not regarded as necessarily able effectively to address restrictions which had effects in more than one member state, because it was not guaranteed that it would have unlimited, or even in some cases sufficient, access to information and evidence in other member states to be able successfully to prosecute anticompetitive situations under domestic competition rules.[104]

It was thought, however, that the concern triggered by these factors could be eliminated to the extent that domestic competition authorities would enforce similar substantive competition rules in similar ways. There is no doubt that the closer national competition law regimes are, the easier it should be to develop means of distributing authority between the EU level and the national level, especially in difficult cases and those involving regulating evidentiary matters. Furthermore, the more similar these regimes are, the more meaningless the distinction between EU and domestic competition laws becomes. The net result is that applying domestic competition law through national competition authorities will be less objectionable.

(C)   The harmonisation with EU competition law

I.   The shift towards harmonisation

A final 'phase' characterising the pre-modernisation years 1962–2004 which is worth noting concerns the closer relationship which began to emerge at some point as a result of the *harmonisation* of the competition laws of member states with EU competition law. The renewed confidence between the mid-1980s and the early-1990s in achieving the goal of single market integration – as evidenced through the introduction of the Single European Act and the Treaty on European Union in 1986 and 1992 respectively – opened a new chapter in the EU competition policy scene: since that time, several member states have either introduced new competition rules similar to the EU rules or altered their existing laws so as to bring them more into line with those rules.[105] Interestingly, this shift towards greater

---

[104] There was also the argument that increased reliance by national competition authorities on their domestic laws would have undermined the supremacy of EU competition law and the values of the one-stop-shop principle which has been prominent in EU merger control – see Art. 1 of the current (Regulation 139/2004) and former (Regulation 4064/89) Merger Regulation.

[105] As stated in note 69 above, one such Member State is the UK.

The discussion below will not deal with the situation in individual Member States. For that, see the following literature: P. Wessman, 'Competition Sharpens in Sweden' (1993) *World Competition* 113; J. Ratliff and E. Wright, 'Belgian Competition Law: the Advent of Free Market Principles' (1992) *World Competition* 33; S. M. Martinzez Lage, 'Significant Developments in Spanish Antitrust Law' (1996) *European Competition Law Review* 194; T. Liakopoulos, 'New Rules on Competition Law in Greece' (1992) *World Competition* 17; K. Stockmann, 'Trends and Developments in European Antitrust Laws' (1991) *Fordham Corporate Law Institute* 441.

harmonisation was more the result of initiatives on the part of certain member states than the result of the decentralisation efforts on the part of the Commission. Accommodating competition rules of a similar type to EU competition law enabled a member state to demonstrate its support to some of the founding fathers of the EU, such as France and Germany, who were pursuing further integration. Such a member state could expect that such support would be appreciated by other supporters of these initiatives. Countries seeking future accession to the EU in the 1990s, expressed an interest in 'harmonising' their laws with EU competition rules. Member states such as Sweden, Austria and Finland were in various stages of accession at the relevant time, and by enacting competition laws similar to EU competition law they could demonstrate their support for the integration efforts of existing member states and of EU institutions. The relevant period also witnessed an intensifying battle for foreign investment among member states. This development encouraged businesses to follow a domestic legal environment that was not significantly different and was not more stringent than that of the EU. The 'definite' possibility in the early-1990s that certain countries were likely to accede to the EU added more vigour to the views of the business community: business firms in different member states emphasised that they and interstate commerce would benefit from operating within a legal environment characterised by uniformity in competition rules in different member states. Such arguments were strengthened when it became clear at the relevant time that in the near future the EU was set to expand phenomenally to include 25 and possibly 27 member states; this finally happened in 2004 and 2007 respectively. Other factors that seem to have contributed towards the harmonisation of domestic competition laws of member states with EU competition law include the increased willingness on the part of national competition authorities of different member states to learn from each other *and* a growing recognition throughout Europe of the value of competition. The latter development can be seen from the way in which the market mechanism has become more dominant in the EU which made it necessary to adopt national measures to protect its dynamics and ensure its proper functioning. To some extent, this provided an ideological shift: it reflected a growing awareness of the need for economic reinvigoration throughout Europe and that increased competition was the most likely means of fostering strong and healthy economic environments. In many ways, EU competition law regime was seen as the perfect model to follow and this enhanced the drive towards harmonisation.

II.   Types of harmonisation

Harmonisation within the EU competition law regime has occurred in two different contexts. The first is substantive law or textual harmonisation,[106] under which there has been an increase in following the wording and framework of Articles 101 and 102 TFEU. In some cases, some domestic laws, such as the French law,[107] merely followed the basic framework of these provisions, whilst others, such as the Swedish laws, adopted their terminology.[108] The second is institutional and procedural harmonisation. In this sense, viewing the EU competition law regime as a model is more ambitious than its textual counterpart: procedurally, significant differences remain between EU competition law regimes and the competition law regimes of many member states. Nevertheless, general patterns of change at the institutional level in domestic competition law regimes have been to move towards more judicial characteristics and institutions that are inclined towards more judicial roles. An increasing number of national competition authorities have adopted roles that involve interpretation, application and enforcement of domestic competition rules, unlike the position under the administrative control regimes, which previously existed in the relevant member states. To this end, national competition authorities have increasingly, for example, been given greater independence from political influence.

III.   Stages of harmonisation

Harmonisation in the EU context has mainly involved two stages. The first is the adoption at the national level of similar patterns of harmonisation towards EU competition law. The second stage concerns efforts to coordinate between EU and national competition law regimes. The interaction between these stages was expected to play a central role in shaping the future relationship between EU and domestic competition laws especially since further integration within the EU called for increasingly integrated competition law regimes. The interaction of the stages of harmonisation was expected to help clarify the future dynamics of such integration, in particular whether the EU and member states would move beyond the mere formal jurisdictional criteria established in the early years.[109]

---

[106] See H. Ullrich, 'Harmonisation Within the European Union' (1996) *European Competition Law Review* 178.

[107] See generally F. Jenny, 'French Competition Law Update: 1987–1994' (1995) *Fordham Corporate Law Institute* 203.

[108] See M. Widegren, 'Competition Law in Sweden – a Brief Introduction to the New Legislation' (1995) *Fordham Corporate Law Institute* 241.

[109] See p. 177 above.

The picture which was expected to emerge from the further integration of different competition law regimes placed the EU competition law regime at the heart of the development of competition law in Europe generally and held the regime as a centre of gravity to which national competition law regimes are primarily connected. This was not expected however to push the 'two-barrier theory' to the sidelines: it was expected that this theory would continue to constitute a key element, as the question of competence to investigate and decide in a particular competition case – the Commission or the relevant national competition authority – was expected would continue to be a central issue. What later developments revealed however is that this is a difficult (and largely political) issue because there was a fear that the Commission's power and authority may be threatened with the greater involvement of national competition authorities. Political conflicts were expected therefore to remain alongside the boundaries of the decisional practice in the field: the fact that decision-makers in the Commission and in member states were thought to be generally committed to different and sometimes inconsistent policy and personal objectives was expected to enhance the likelihood of such conflicts.

IV. The horizontal and vertical elements

The process of harmonisation and its consequences revealed the existence of two dimensions in the relationship between EU and national competition law regimes. The first is a vertical dimension which concerns cooperation between the EU and national levels. This dimension includes factors such as the extent to which Commission officials and those in national competition authorities share common interests and forge institutional means to pursue and protect such interests. Whilst policy-makers at either level share the common goal of protecting the process of competition, they often diverge with regards to the best means of achieving this goal. Also, it is not clear whether their interests coalesce with regard to other goals and values. No doubt establishing a common intellectual and communicative base for pursuing common interests between the EU and national competition law regimes was never going to be an easy project to undertake. The second dimension may be termed 'horizontal' and concerns cooperation at the national level. This dimension connotes the prospects of national competition authorities creating close links between themselves. This however was expected to depend on the extent to which these authorities perceive common interests. Also, the extent to which they are willing and able to create means to pursue such interests – independently of the 'vertical dimension' – was expected to be another important factor in this regard.

For many years, there was little awareness of the importance of these dimensions or even their existence. This appears to have been mainly caused by the fact that over those years competition law was examined exclusively from the perspectives of individual – EU or national – competition law regimes; it was in fact more the EU perspective than the national one. Very few, including lawyers, economists and policymakers, had good knowledge of similar experiences and common and shared problems and solutions between the different regimes.[110] The situation however began to change in the early 1990s and towards the end of that decade the change accelerated with the Commission's – at that time – proposed Modernisation programme, which was finally put into effect on 1 May 2004. The change in this case attracted particular attention to the importance of these dimensions. The Modernisation programme and in particular the creation of the European Competition Network (ECN)[111] increased the importance of these dimensions and their 'integration' with each other.

V.   Comment

The harmonisation of national competition laws with EU competition law seems to carry various implications for the separation between EU and national levels. In marking a new departure for the traditional EU/member state relationship, this harmonisation has furnished an important example of how EU membership and this 'new legal order of international law' affected the national legal order. This impact can be seen in light of the fact that harmonisation has even been considered by member states, which, on more than one occasion, seemed unwilling to shift from their well-established competition law regimes to the EU model.[112]

Obviously harmonisation is not necessarily free from difficulties. Even with the existence of a comprehensive textual and procedural harmonisation, there can still be scope for divergence between the EU and national competition law regimes on the one hand and among the latter themselves on the other, in so far as policies underlying EU and national

---

[110] Gerber, p. 3, note 5 above.   [111] See pp. 194–197 below.

[112] See S. Held, 'German Antitrust Law and Policy' (1992) *Fordham Corporate Law Institute* 311; R. Bechtold, 'Antitrust Law in the European Community and Germany – an Uncoordinated Co-existence?' (1992) *Fordham Corporate Law Institute* 343.

competition laws may differ.[113] It is true that such disparity may not present a difficulty if there is sufficient flexibility at the national level to accommodate the grounding of EU competition law within domestic legal orders and if the competition laws – EU and domestic – reflect general underlying principles. Still, divergence may prove problematic where the direct consequence of harmonisation leads to obfuscation in the relationship between EU and national competition laws, with the more subtle differences between the two not being considered.

Harmonisation may increase interest at the domestic level in developments at EU level (and this has indeed happened in recent years), which may promote more two-way traffic between them. Moreover, it can be seen as a vote of confidence in the EU competition law regime. At the same time, responsiveness to the domestic legal culture in different member states has inevitably led to nationally specific competition laws, albeit ones with a common genesis (as a result of harmonisation).[114] Furthermore, harmonisation may eventually allow for a better division of competence between EU and national spheres, but it is not completely clear that it can eliminate all problems associated with overlapping jurisdiction and legal uncertainties. This last point is particularly worth considering within the new structure created under the Commission's Modernisation programme, to which the discussion in the following section is devoted.

(D)   The modernisation era

I.   The White Paper on Modernisation

On 28 April 1999, the Commission introduced its *White Paper on the Modernisation of the Rules Implementing Articles 85 (now Article 101 TFEU) and 86 (now Article 102 TFEU) EC.*[115] The White Paper presented a fundamental rethink by the Commission on the EU competition law regime which according to the Commission had 'worked so well' but which was 'no longer appropriate for the Community of today with 15

---

[113] See B. Bishop and S. Bishop, 'Reforming Competition Policy: Bundeskartellamt – Model or Muddle' (1996) *European Competition Law Review* 207.

    Given that EU competition law is shaped by policies underlying it, harmonisation of domestic competition laws within EU competition rules depends not only on formal adoption of text and procedure of EU competition law regime at domestic level, but ultimately on the convergence of those policies.

[114] See A. Jacquemin, 'The International Dimension of European Competition Policy' (1993) *Journal of Common Market Studies* 91.

[115] (1999) *Official Journal* C-132/1; [1999] 5 CMLR 208.

member states, 11 languages and over 350 million inhabitants'.[116] The Commission offered in the White Paper some reasons for the proposed revision – albeit in incomplete terms. At paragraph 5 of the *White Paper*, the Commission provides that the reasons for this rethink reside in Regulation 17/62 'and in the external factors to the development of the Community'. Furthermore, at paragraph 10 of the White Paper, the Commission explained that the regime existing under that Regulation was no longer adequate to meet the challenges facing the EU. The Commission believed that it was essential to adapt the regime as it existed at that time in order to remedy the problem of resources, to relieve businesses from unnecessary costs and bureaucracy, to enable the Commission to pursue more serious competition law infringements and to stimulate a simpler and more efficient system of control.

According to the Commission, the time became ripe in the late-1990s for introducing shared responsibility with national courts and national competition authorities in the enforcement of EU competition law, including the determination of whether the criteria of Article 101(3) TFEU are satisfied. This meant that national courts and national competition authorities would be able to apply Article 101 TFEU in its entirety, rather than just Article 101(1) TFEU and the provisions of the block exemptions. It therefore proposed that the notification and exemption system in Regulation 17/62 should be abolished and replaced by a Council Regulation, which would render the criteria in Article 101(3) TFEU directly applicable without a prior decision of the Commission. This proposal was intended to leave the Commission in a position to concentrate its priorities, such as combating international cartels and serious abuses of dominance. This did not, of course, mean that the Commission would relinquish being the guardian of EU competition rules. On the contrary, the Commission made it clear in the White Paper that it will continue to observe how these rules are applied by national courts and national competition authorities. This was expected to involve asserting jurisdiction in particular cases, namely those with legal, economic and political significance for the EU.

The proposals of the Commission as set out in the White Paper were radical, especially the Commission's proposal to abandon its monopoly to grant Article 101(3) TFEU exemptions. However, for firms and those advising them ending the notification and authorisation system provided a relief. One of the problems with that (old) system was that, for the

---

[116] See para. 5 of the Paper.

majority of agreements, obtaining an individual exemption from the Commission required a notification to it. The Commission had suffered for many years from a lack of resources and a shortage of staff to keep up with the increasing number of notifications and for this reason the system was flawed. The proposals in the Paper had the effect of abandoning the notification procedure completely. Notification would not be possible under the new 'modernised' regime, which the White Paper clearly aimed to create. Under the new regime firms were supposed to be responsible for making their own assessment of the compatibility of anticompetitive situations with EU competition law in the light of the relevant legislation and case law within the EU competition law regime.[117]

Abandoning notification was expected to be an issue of particular challenge to firms and their legal advisors. Nonetheless its consequence was thought to help harmonise the position of the EU on competition law exemptions with that in the USA, where firms have to be more self-reliant[118] – an aspect which incidentally was expected to have a direct positive effect on the internationalisation of competition law.

II.   Regulation 1/2003

The Commission's reform efforts finally culminated in the adoption of its Modernisation Regulation, Regulation 1/2003 and the accompanying Modernisation Package.[119] The Regulation replaced Regulation 17/62 and, among the fundamental changes it has made to the enforcement of Articles 101 and 102 TFEU, opened a new chapter in the relationship between EU and national competition law regimes. The Regulation incorporates the changes the White Paper proposed. Many of these changes are worth highlighting.

(a) **The European Competition Network**   The Regulation established the European Competition Network which Recital 15 of the Regulation describes as 'a network of public authorities applying the [EU] competition rules in close cooperation'. As part of the Modernisation Package the Commission published a *Notice on Cooperation within the Network of Competition Authorities.*[120] Like other Notices and guidelines published by the Commission, the Notice lacks the binding force of the law and so it

---

[117] See para. 77 of the Paper.
[118] The following chapter deals with the US competition law regime.
[119] See note 24 above.   [120] See note 23 above.

is not binding on national competition authorities; nonetheless, the national competition authorities of all of the EU member states have committed themselves to abiding by the principles of the Notice.

A number of the principles covered under the Notice are important to note. The Notice shows that the ECN is intended to serve as forum within which the Commission and national competition authorities have the opportunity to address issues of common interest, coordinate their enforcement efforts and ensure an efficient allocation of resources. To realise a proper functioning of the forum and achieve these objectives, the Notice provides for mechanisms for *case allocation* and *information sharing* between the members of the ECN.

In relation to case allocation, the Notice makes clear that case allocation comes to ensure an efficient allocation of tasks between the Commission and national competition authorities and between national competition authorities themselves.[121] Case allocation also comes to achieve effective and consistent application of EU competition law. The Notice coins a key principle vital for case allocation namely that of 'well-placed authority'. The Notice shows that a well-placed authority is the authority – whether the Commission or a national competition authority – that is most appropriate to investigate the case at hand.[122] In determining this, the Notice provides that three cumulative conditions must be considered and satisfied: (a) the agreement or practice has substantial direct actual or foreseeable effects on competition within the territory of the relevant authority and is implemented within or originates from its territory; (b) the authority is effectively able to bring to an end the entire infringement; and (c) it can gather, possibly with the assistance of other authorities within the ECN, the evidence required to prove the infringement.[123] Obviously, among other things, the idea here is to have – as a preferred option – a single authority dealing with a given case.[124] Nonetheless, it is recognised that in some cases more than one authority may be become involved which means that parallel actions of enforcement would be inevitable. This is particularly so where the situation in question produces substantial effects in the territory of more than one authority and where action by a single authority would fall short of addressing the situation. In such cases of parallel action the relevant

---

[121] See pp. 189–192 above in relation to the discussion on vertical and horizontal harmonisation.
[122] See para. 6 of the Notice.   [123] See para. 8 of the Notice.
[124] See recital 18 of Regulation 1/2003.

authorities are required to coordinate their enforcement actions and are advised to designate one of them as 'lead authority'.[125]

There are cases in which the European Commission itself would be considered to be the well-placed authority. This is, for example, where the situation in question produces effects on competition in more than three member states;[126] it is therefore envisaged that cases would be transferred to the Commission from the national level if it appears to the relevant national competition authority(ies) that action in the case is better taken by the Commission. Other circumstances making the Commission well placed to handle a case include those: where other provisions of the EU law are closely 'linked' to the case; where national competition authorities are unable to agree on which authority among them is better placed to handle the case; and where these provisions may be exclusively or more effectively applied by the Commission; as well as those circumstances in which the interest of the EU requires the adoption of a Commission decision to develop competition policy in the EU;[127] the latter situation is particularly relevant when a new competition issue arises or when it is vital to ensure effective enforcement.[128]

With regard to information sharing within the ECN, Regulation 1/2003 and the Notice provide that information sharing is essentially for ensuring a proper functioning of the ECN and its forum of competition authorities, in particular to facilitate cooperation and smooth allocation and re-allocation of cases. Under Article 12 of the Regulation, the Commission and the national competition authorities are able to share information, including confidential information *for the purposes of applying* Articles 101 and 102 TFEU.[129] Clearly Article 12 is of extreme importance especially in the context of Article 22 of the Regulation. Under the latter provision the Commission or a national competition authority may request another national competition authority to carry out inspection

---

[125] See para. 13 of the Notice.   [126] See para. 14 of the Notice.

[127] It is important to note that transferring a case to the Commission does not mean that there may not be interaction with national competition authorities: Art. 11(5) of the Regulation shows that consultations between the Commission and national competition authorities may take place.

[128] See para. 15 of the Notice.

[129] Under Art. 28(2) of the Regulation, information acquired or exchanged by the Commission and national competition authorities which is subject to the obligation of professional secrecy cannot not be disclosed. Article 28(2) implements the provisions of Art. 339 TFEU which forbids the disclosure of 'information of the kind covered by the obligation of professional secrecy, in particular information about undertakings, their business relations or their cost components'.

or other fact-finding measure on its behalf. It is also possible for simultaneous inspections to be carried out in different member states following which the information gathered by one authority can be shared with another authority. This coordination between authorities is especially important when carrying out simultaneous 'dawn-raids' in cartel cases as can be seen from the recent flat glass cartel case.[130]

The Notice also contains additional points which have particular relevance to key provisions of the Regulation, such as Article 11 of the Regulation. Among these points is the obligation imposed on members of the ECN to inform one another of investigations and pending investigations under the Article.

(b) Article 11 and the mechanism of cooperation   Article 11 of the Regulation deserves mention since it complements many of the powers and provisions described in the previous section and deals with cooperation between the Commission and national competition authorities and courts. The Article can be said to be inspired by Article 4(3) TEU.[131] According to this Article, the application of EU competition rules will be on the basis of close cooperation between the two sides. The provision also states that national competition authorities and courts are required to inform the Commission at the outset of any proceedings involving the application of Articles 101 and 102 TFEU opened by them. Furthermore, national competition authorities and courts are expected to consult the Commission prior to adopting a decision under these provisions requiring an infringement to be terminated, accepting commitments by firms or withdrawing the benefit of one of the block exemptions. This obligation includes submitting to the Commission, no later than one month before a decision is adopted, a summary of the case and any related important documents. The Commission also reserves the right to request any other relevant documents. Finally, the provision states that where the Commission has decided to initiate proceedings, national competition authorities will be relieved of their competence to apply Article 101 and 102 TFEU. The Article clearly shows therefore that the Commission sits at the top of the pyramid of enforcement of these two Articles.

---

[130] See Commission Press Release IP/07/178, 'Commission fines flat glass producers €486.9 million for price fixing cartel' (28 November 2007).
[131] See pp. 162–163 above for a brief explanation of Art. 4(3).

III. Private enforcement

A private enforcement mechanism does not exist under EU competition law regime. The only possibility that is open for potential claimants who are interested in seeking damages against firms in breach of Articles 101 and 102 TFEU is to launch their actions under national laws of EU member states. However, on 3 April 2008, the European Commission published its long-awaited *White Paper on damages actions*.[132] The White Paper sets outs a broad range of measures aimed at ensuring that all victims of anticompetitive behaviour are able to obtain full compensation for harm suffered by them. The 'policy' on private enforcement under EU competition rules however will take some time to become coherent and this is something that will be watched with considerable interest not only within the EU, but also around the world.

7. The significance and influence of the EU competition law regime beyond the single market

It was noted above that the European Commission is the world's only effective supranational competition authority. This position has meant that the Commission was in a good position to develop several years ago a constructive international outlook and vision. This – along with the fact that the EU competition law regime itself is a supranational regime – has enabled the building of a very impressive 'international' dimension, which is considered to be among the success stories of the EU in the field of competition law. Indeed this international dimension can be said to be inherent in the actual characteristics of the regime as a whole and the Commission as an EU institution. Nevertheless, one must not overlook an important development, which can be said to have underpinned this success story, namely the impressive 'intrinsic' dimension, which was discussed above. There is no doubt that the outcome of the Commission's efforts towards decentralisation – as they eventually emerged in the form of its Modernisation programme – carries enormous importance as a development enabling the Commission to focus on

---

[132] *White Paper on Damages Actions for Breach of the EC Antitrust Rules*, COM(2008) 165 (2 April 2008). Prior to the publication of the White Paper, the Commission had published its *Green Paper on Damages Actions for Breach of the EC Antitrust Rules*, COM(2005) 672 (19 December 2005). The latter Paper opened a full process of consultation on the views of the Commission.

dealing with extremely harmful practices – such as hardcore cartels and serious abuses of dominance – which often have a cross-border element. As a result this development has come to support the international dimension of EU competition law even further. So the success the Commission achieved 'at home' in ensuring an effective and well-coordinated enforcement of EU competition rules has been important in advancing the role of the regime on the world stage. In particular this success has been a factor influencing the decision of policymakers in third countries to use the EU competition law regime for insights and guidance when they consider adopting competition laws or changing their existing ones; or even when competition officials around the world seek guidance on how to approach a particular issue in a given competition case or learn what topics are 'hot' and 'current' in the field of competition law. The number of non-member states that have adopted competitions laws on the basis of EU competition law has increased phenomenally over the years. Some of these countries have in recent years acceded to the EU and others are edging slowly towards future accession, but there are other ones which bear no relation to the EU, whether in geographical or other terms.[133] Such a development highlights an important role for EU competition law, and its growing success and influence present an opportunity that the Commission has been keen to exploit in several ways.

These important points notwithstanding, it is vital to appreciate the challenge for the Commission especially in relation to advocating the EU competition law regime internationally and pushing ahead with its vision for internationalising competition law in the form of a binding multilateral agreement using the regime as a 'model' – something the Commission has been highly passionate about. Certain countries simply have not been willing to subscribe to the Commission's vision of internationalisation. The USA, for example, has been a forerunner in this respect because the common sentiment held by successive competition law 'administrations' on the other side of the Atlantic was that such vision has little to offer from the perspective of a competition law regime which celebrated its centenary two decades ago.[134] To a certain extent,

---

[133] See the Commission 28th Report on Competition Policy (1998), pp. 116–18.

[134] It is worth noting however that US competition authorities have on occasions adopted 'aspects' within the EU competition law regime and incorporated elements from this regime into their decisional practice; see p. 516 below for an example. Moreover, many competition officials and lawyers in the USA hold the EU competition law regime and the European Commission in high regard and attach enormous weight to its actions and decisions.

this reaction is understandable because the USA has an extremely well-established tradition of competition law and policy. However, this reaction has some serious implications for the internationalisation of competition policy. The fact that the US competition law regime is strong, and that US policymakers have been mostly unwilling to consider the EU position as the best way in which competition law may be internationalised means that the Commission will find it hard to advocate internationalisation on the basis of the principles and ideas developed in the EU competition law over the years. The USA does not regard the EU competition law regime – which provides a model of internationalisation of competition law – as a useful example of how to develop a global framework in the field of competition law. This can be seen from the number of occasions over the years on which the USA has rejected proposals put forward by the EU.[135] This situation has led to a conflict of views between the USA and the EU which seems to constitute a hurdle in the face of internationalisation of competition law.

In building the international dimension of the regime, the European Commission has relied on three important strategies: a unilateral strategy (relying on extraterritorial assertion of jurisdiction); a bilateral strategy (revolving around bilateral cooperation with individual countries and blocks of countries); and a multilateral strategy (seeking to promote multilateral solutions and initiatives at world level).

(A)   The doctrine of extraterritoriality

As we noted above, competition law in the EU has primarily been about protecting competition and consumers and furthering market integration. In seeking to achieve these goals, the European Commission has sought to punish all types of anticompetitive situations, regardless of the nationality or place of incorporation of the firm(s) concerned. In the same way the Commission applied EU competition law to address the behaviour, conduct and transactions of EU-based firms, it has also relied on extraterritorial application of the competition rules to ensure that anticompetitive conduct, behaviour and transactions of non-EU firms will be controlled and regulated where competition and trade in the EU are likely to be adversely affected; hence the ability of

---

[135] See D. Gerber, 'The US–European Conflict Over the Globalisation of Antitrust Law' (1999) *New England Law Review* 123.

the Commission to investigate and punish the abusive conduct[136] and eradicate cartel activities[137] involving non-EU firms and regulate mergers between non-EU firms (including blocking such mergers, as happened in the merger between US firms General Electric and Honeywell international in 2001). Chapter 8 will discuss the doctrine of extraterritoriality at length and consider the EU perspective on extraterritoriality.

(B)   The bilateral strategy

A second way in which the international dimension of the EU regime has been built has been through a mechanism of bilateralism. The Commission has developed two strands within its mechanism of bilateralism: *first*, specific, competition-focused bilateral cooperation agreements involving the European Commission and other competition authorities around the world (such as the 1991 and 1998 EC–US Agreements);[138] and *secondly*, general bilateral relations established between the Commission and third countries or blocks of countries which contain a competition component. This strand includes things like: Free Trade Agreements; Association Agreements (such as those entered into with Candidate countries before they join the EU);[139] Partnership and Cooperation Agreements (such as that with the Russian Federation); Euro-Med and Neighbourhood agreements with Mediterranean countries; and the European Economic Agreement (EEA) which brings together the EU and the European Free Trade Area (EFTA) under a single umbrella.[140]

The European Commission has always placed particular emphasis on bilateralism. Through bilateralism, the Commission has been able to foster meaningful cooperative relationships with key competition authorities, most importantly US competition authorities. This has been vital because the EU and US competition law regimes are the world's most important regimes and because many cases in practice fall within the

---

[136] See the investigations conducted and action take by the Commission against firms such as Microsoft and Intel in recent years.

[137] The Commission's anti-cartel enforcement practice is full of examples, see http://ec.europa.eu/competition/cartels/what_is_new/news.html.

[138] The agreements are considered at pp. 501–505 below.

[139] See the Commission 25th Report on Competition Policy (1995), para. 221; D. Kennedy and D. E. Webb, 'The Limits of Integration: Eastern Europe and the European Communities' (1993) *Common Market Law Review* 1095.

[140] See J. Stragier, 'The Competition Rules of the EEA Agreement and their Implementation' (1993) *European Competition Law Review* 30.

concurrent jurisdiction of the Commission and US competition authorities. So building meaningful cooperation is very important in practice in order to, among other things, reduce the risk of conflicts and engage in a constructive dialogue on specific issues in competition cases. As the discussion in chapter 9 will show, these are benefits not only for the Commission and US competition authorities, but also for businesses themselves. Firms are always anxious when their operations or behaviour are subjected to review by more than one competition authority. This involves higher cost for them (in terms of time and resources) and the possibility of inconsistent outcomes does affect them in a material way.[141] At the same time, bilateralism has enabled the Commission to advocate and spread EU competition rules and standards globally. As we noted before, looking around the world one could see remarkable evidence of this: many regimes have simply adopted competition rules which are closely based on EU competition law.

I.   Competition-specific bilateral cooperation

Bilateral cooperation will be discussed extensively in chapter 9 below; this will include a consideration of examples of competition-specific bilateral cooperation. The most prominent of these examples is the US–EC cooperation agreements of 1991 and 1998 which will be discussed extensively; other examples include the EU–Canada[142] and the EU–Japan[143] cooperation agreements, and the EU–China dialogue.[144]

II.   General bilateral relations

The Commission has given particular attention to its bilateral links with: candidate countries (through Association Agreements), the Russian Federation (through the Partnership and Cooperation Agreement), Middle Eastern countries (through the Euro-Med and Neighbourhood Agreements) and third countries around the world in Asia and Africa

---

[141] See pp. 106–110 for a fuller account on the concerns of business firms.

[142] Council and Commission Decision of 29 April 1999 concerning the conclusion of the Agreement between the European Communities and the Government of Canada regarding the application of their competition laws (1999) *Official Journal* L-175/49.

[143] Council Decision of 16 June 2003 concluding the Agreement between the European Community and the Government of Japan concerning co-operation on anticompetitive practices (2003) *Official Journal* L-183/12.

[144] See the *Terms of reference of the EU–China competition policy dialogue* (2004) available at: http://ec.europa.eu/comm/competition/international/bilateral/cn2b_en. pdf. Negotiations for a comprehensive EU–China Partnership and Cooperation Agreement began in January 2007.

(through Free Trade Agreements). In all of these relations, competition law features very prominently and the different agreements contain rules and standards which are modelled on the basis of EU competition law, notably Articles 101 and 102 TFEU; in some cases the 'modelling' extends to the Merger Regulation, Regulation 139/2004.

The way in which competition law elements have flourished within the framework of these agreements is highly fascinating. First, when the agreement in question is concluded it will have competition provisions which are almost identical to those of the EU. Secondly, when the agreement becomes *implemented* the other party ends up introducing or changing its competition rules so they become compatible with the competition provisions of the agreement. As a result, in most cases the competition rules of the other party will indirectly be modelled on EU competition law. This is hugely important, not least psychologically. During times when there is healthy rivalry between the EU and the USA in particular, having so many countries with competition rules based on those of the EU is an important victory for the EU and European Commission in particular. This point can be illustrated with reference to the developments leading to the accession by Central and Eastern European nations to the EU in recent years. Throughout the 1990s – following the collapse of the Soviet Union – there was a race between the EU and the USA to the doorstep of many of these countries. Competition law was at the very forefront of this race. Psychologically, politically and strategically, it was important for the Commission to emerge victorious here and at the end it did: all of these countries ended up adopting competition laws based on the EU model. Now, 'legally' it was not crucial for these countries to follow the EU model in order to have successful competition law regimes. But this was a condition set for accession; i.e. without having a competition law in place (and one that is based on EU competition law) these countries would not have fulfilled the criteria for accession.

Such strategy of bilateral cooperation has been an effective means for the international influence of EU competition law to grow. It is worth noting here that such influence can be seen even in the case of the USA (with US competition authorities on occasions using EU competition law-based concepts)[145] and the EEA (with EU competition law sitting at the centre of the operation of the EEA and the application of the rules, and influencing the competition law regimes within EFTA: whether the

---

[145] See note 134 above and p. 516 below.

EFTA regime itself or those of its member states, such as Norway, Iceland and even Switzerland, which is not part of the EEA).

(a) **The EEA Agreement**   The Agreement on the European Economic Area (the EEA Agreement) came into force on 1 January 1994. The original contracting parties to the Agreement were the E(E)C, the European Coal and Steel Community and the then 12 EU member states, on the one hand, and five European Free Trade Association (EFTA) countries, Austria, Finland, Iceland, Norway and Sweden, on the other. Upon the accession of Austria, Finland and Sweden to the EU in 1995, Iceland and Norway were left as the only EFTA countries. The number of EFTA countries was subsequently increased to three in May 1995 when Liechtenstein became a party to the Agreement. Nowadays the EEA brings together the 27 EU member states and these three EFTA member states.

The broad objective of the EEA Agreement is to establish a dynamic and homogeneous EEA, based on common rules and equal conditions of competition. To this end, the cornerstone policies and principles of the EC, as well as a wide range of accompanying EU rules and policies, were incorporated into the Agreement. Among the most important of the policies and principles which have been incorporated are those in the areas of free movement of goods, persons, services and capital, competition, public procurement, social policy, consumer protection and the environment. Secondary EU legislation in areas covered by the Agreement has also been incorporated into the Agreement by means of direct references in the Agreement to such legislation.

Three independent legal systems have in effect been established following the signing of the EEA Agreement. First, there is EU law which applies to the relations between member states within the EU. Secondly, there is the EFTA system which applies to the four EFTA member states (including Switzerland). Thirdly, there is the EEA Agreement which applies to relations between the EU and EFTA sides as well as between the EFTA member states themselves (excluding Switzerland). This state of affairs has meant that for the EEA to be viable the EEA regime and the EU regime in particular need to develop in parallel and be applied and enforced uniformly. To this end, the Agreement provides for decision-making procedures for the integration into the EEA of new secondary EU legislation and for a surveillance mechanism to ensure the fulfilment of obligations under the Agreement and a uniform interpretation and application of its provisions. Under the

Agreement a Joint Committee – which is made up of representatives of the contracting parties – was established. This Committee is responsible for the introduction of new rules within the EEA. The surveillance mechanism, however, is arranged in the form of a two-pillar structure of independent bodies of the two sides. The implementation and application of the Agreement within the EU is monitored by the European Commission, whereas the Surveillance Authority is responsible for carrying out the same task within the EFTA pillar. In order to ensure a uniform surveillance throughout the EEA, the two bodies are expected to cooperate, exchange information and consult each other on surveillance policy issues and individual cases.

The two-pillar structure also applies to the judicial control mechanism, with the EFTA Court exercising competences similar to those of the ECJ and the GCEU with regard to, among other things, the surveillance procedure regarding the EFTA countries and appeals concerning decisions taken by the EFTA Surveillance Authority.

(i) The EFTA Surveillance Authority   The EFTA Surveillance Authority (the 'Authority') was established under the *Agreement between the EFTA Countries on the Establishment of a Surveillance Authority and a Court of Justice* (widely referred to as the 'Surveillance and Court Agreement'). This agreement, among other things, contains basic provisions on the Authority's structure and lays down its tasks and competences. The Authority is managed by a college of three members, all of whom are appointed by common accord of the governments of the EFTA countries for a period of four years which is renewable. At the head of the Authority stands a president, who is appointed in the same manner, for a period of two years. The members are completely independent in carrying out their duties. They are supposed not to seek or take instructions from any government or other body and they are expected to refrain from any action incompatible with their duties. In this sense, the members are supposed to be individuals whose independence is beyond doubt and who are not vulnerable to any sort of compromise.

The main task of the Authority is to ensure that the three EFTA member states fulfil their obligations under the EEA Agreement. In general terms, this means that the Authority is under a general surveillance obligation, namely to ensure that the provisions of the Agreement, including the protocols and the acts referred to in the Annexes, are properly implemented in the domestic legal orders of the EFTA member states and that they are correctly applied by their authorities.

In the field of competition law, the Authority has extended competence, including a range of tasks of an administrative character which
supplements those vested in the Authority with regard to general
surveillance and which fully reflects the extended competences of the
European Commission in these fields. These tasks mainly relate to
the practices and behaviour of firms in the marketplace. Thus, the
Authority is expected to ensure that the competition rules of the
Agreement are complied with, notably the prohibitions on anticompetitive behaviour and on the abuse of market dominance by firms. To
ensure that the Authority is able to carry out such tasks, it possesses
similar powers to those enjoyed by the European Commission, namely
the power to, among other things, make on-the-spot inspections,
impose fines and periodic penalties and, in the case of an infringement,
make a decision compelling the firms concerned to bring the infringement to an end.[146]

(ii) The EFTA Court   The EFTA Court has jurisdiction with regard to
EFTA member states, which are parties to the EEA Agreement. The
Court is mainly competent to deal with infringement actions brought
by the EFTA Surveillance Authority against an EFTA member state with
regard to the implementation, application or interpretation of an EEA
rule. The settlement of disputes between two or more EFTA member
states, hearing appeals concerning decisions taken by the EFTA
Surveillance Authority and the giving of advisory opinions to domestic
courts in EFTA member states on the interpretation of EEA rules are also
within the general competence of the Court. Thus, the jurisdiction of the
Court mainly corresponds to the jurisdiction of the ECJ – as described in
the previous part of the present chapter.

The EFTA Court consists of three judges, one nominated by each of
the three EFTA member states. The judges' appointment is by common
accord of the governments of those countries for a period of six years.
The judges elect their president for a term of three years. In addition to
the regular judges, there is also a system of ad hoc judges, the purpose of
which is to cater for situations where a regular judge cannot sit in a
particular case. The judgments of the Court – unlike in the case of the
ECJ – are delivered on a majority basis. The procedure followed by the

---

[146] See Regulation 1/2003 for details of the powers enjoyed by the Commission in relation
to the enforcement of Arts 101 and 102 TFEU.

Court is laid down in the Statute of the EFTA Court and in its Rules of Procedure.

(iii) The competition chapter of the EEA Agreement The EEA Agreement contains several important provisions dealing with competition matters which are worth mentioning. Articles 53, 54 and 59 of the EEA Agreement mirror Articles 101, 102 and 106 TFEU. The control of concentrations, which is modelled on the basis of Regulation 139/2004, is incorporated in Article 57 of the Agreement. By virtue of Article 60 and Annex XIV of the Agreement most of the EU Regulations concerning competition law have been incorporated, subject to certain modifications, in the EEA system. Article 61 of the Agreement contains a mirror provision of that found in Article 107 TFEU. It is also important to note the relevance of the Surveillance and Court Agreement and the different Protocols and Annexes of the EEA Agreement.[147]

It would appear in light of the above that the body of EU law (*acquis communautaire*) was adopted in the EEA Agreement. It seems that this was a response instigated by the Commission to the globalisation of international trade,[148] and the pressure the latter created for increased coordination in competition policy between different competition authorities.[149] In light of this, the competition rules contained in the Agreement apply where there is an effect on trade between an EFTA member state and the EC. The Agreement however does not require signatories to adopt EU competition rules into the domestic legal order.

The EEA Agreement provides for consultation procedures between the parties on the competition rules therein. These rules, according to the ECJ in its judgment in *Wood Pulp*, could in no way preclude the integral application of EU competition law.[150] Indeed by looking at the EEA Agreement and its particulars of Protocols and Annexes, it is clear there is a supremacy enjoyed by the EU competition law regime and the

---

[147] See, for example, Protocols 21 and 24 and Annex XIV which deal with the topic of merger control.

[148] See generally T. Jakob, 'EEA and Eastern Europe Agreements with the European Community' (1992) *Fordham Corporate Law Institute* 403; S. Norberg, 'The EEA Agreement: Institutional Solutions for a Dynamic and Homogeneous EEA in the Area of Competition' (1992) *Fordham Corporate Law Institute* 437.

[149] Commission 25th Report on Competition Policy (1995), section V.

[150] Case 89/85 etc., *A. Ahlström Osakeyhtio and Others* v. *Commission* [1988] ECR 5193; [1988] 4 CMLR 474.

Commission in competition cases. This can be seen from the area of merger control where if a concentration (merger operation) has an EU (Community) dimension and EFTA dimension, the operation will fall within the competence of the European Commission. The ECJ's view on the non-precluded integral application of EU competition law is also the view held by the Commission. This view is reinforced by the extraterritoriality doctrine which was upheld by the ECJ in the same judgment, and which gives the Commission jurisdiction to act under EU competition rules whenever an anticompetitive agreement or conduct, despite originating from outside the EU, is implemented within the EU.[151]

(b) Association agreements[152]   *(i) General overview*   The EU has entered into a number of association agreements, within and outside Europe. The three tables below list a number of these agreements with: candidate countries; Western Balkan countries; and Mediterranean countries. Obviously these agreements differ in terms of their exact objectives and the function they are expected to perform. For example, association agreements with candidate countries are intended to have a bigger role to play than those concluded with other countries given their status as 'pre-accession' agreements. In particular, a shift towards these agreements was an expression of the serious transition experienced by the countries concerned in both political and economic terms. The willingness of these countries to become associated with the EU showed a strong desire on their part to establish closer links with the EU: many of these countries came to attach huge significance to these links as an opportunity to help them reap the benefits of European integration. This also made sense because of the geographic proximity between these countries and the EU and the existence of many shared values and increasing interdependence between them.[153] On its part, the EU welcomed such a development, which the European Commission in

---

[151] See pp. 453–455 below.

[152] The discussion here will also deal with what are called 'Stabilisation and Association' agreements.

[153] All these Association Agreements have been conceived with a view to substantially contributing to enabling the countries to strengthen their links with the EU, both in economic and political terms. The question whether this must necessarily lead to future accession to the EU however cannot be considered to be definitely answerable in the positive; nonetheless, such a step was always aspired to by all associated countries who became EU Member States in 2004 and 2007 and it seems to be aspired to by existing candidate countries. For a general discussion, see Jakob, pp. 429–34, note 148 above;

particular had worked hard to achieve. This was considered to be an extension to some of the important goals the EU sought to promote, namely promoting democratic values, a market-oriented economy, the rule of law and respect for human rights.[154] Through concluding association agreements with these countries the EU was able to support the political and economic changes in these countries.

(ii) Content of the agreements   Association agreements are generally very comprehensive in their coverage of different fields. They provide for almost all aspects of economic activity, political dialogue and cultural cooperation in addition to trade, commercial and economic cooperation. The main areas covered by the agreements include political dialogue at the highest level possible, free movement of goods, workers, establishment, services, payments, capital, competition law and other economic provisions, approximation of laws, economic, cultural and financial cooperation and institutions. Competition law usually occupies an important position in these agreements. The primary objective behind the competition provisions of the agreements is to prevent distortions of competition within the framework of the agreements. On this basis, the provisions can be expected to help the relevant countries establish or strengthen local competition law regimes and thus forge closer relations with the EU; in the case of candidate countries the closer relations were/ are intended eventually to achieve integration into the EU. In this way, competition law is given an important *supporting* role: to support efforts towards cooperation or integration. It is perhaps not unusual for competition law to play a supporting role in the context of such agreements. After all, the EU experience itself furnishes an example of how competition law can be employed to support market integration and complement provisions prohibiting restrictions on free movement of goods, services and persons, among others.[155] Thus, on the basis of the EU experience itself it was considered to be very logical for the free trade provisions contained in association agreements to be supplemented by competition

---

G. Marceau, 'The Full Potential of the Europe Agreements: Trade and Competition Issues: the Case of Poland' (1995) *World Competition* 44.

[154] See T. Frazer, 'Competition Policy after 1992: the Next Step' (1990) *Modern Law Review* 609.

[155] See in particular the complementarities between a provision like Art. 101 TFEU and Art. 34 TFEU (which deals with free movement of goods). The complementarities in this case exist not only in relation to the functions these two Articles perform in practice but also in the jurisprudence of the ECJ under both Articles which shows significant 'cross-borrowing' of concepts coined under both Articles (especially in relation to the doctrine of exhaustion of intellectual property rights); see Dabbah, ch. 6, note 3 above.

provisions, in order to prevent private trade barriers from distorting harmonious economic relations between the parties.

(iii) The status of EU competition rules in the framework of the agreements As noted above, generally the competition provisions of the agreements are worded very closely on the basis of EU competition rules, primarily Articles 101 and 102 TFEU.[156] The agreements usually provide for implementation of these provisions in order to ensure successful operation of the agreements and effective cooperation between the parties.[157] An assessment of these provisions in individual cases is intended to be carried out following the assessment established in the EU competition law regime. This further highlights the 'primacy' of EU competition rules within the framework of the agreements. Nonetheless, the agreements do not provide for comprehensive guidance on who should enjoy competence in handling different cases, the European Commission or the relevant authority of the other party to the agreement; this issue of determining competence to act can give rise to various complex issues, which have been discussed elsewhere.[158]

(iv) The annual conference with candidate countries An annual conference is held between the Commission and candidate countries which aims at an assessment of the areas covered under the association agreements. Competition law often occupies centre stage at this important event; in particular issues of how to ensure effective enforcement by the countries concerned. The annual conference has come to be regarded as an event of extreme importance in the competition law diaries of the

---

[156] For a translation of the statutes and a detailed analysis of the implementation of these provisions see J. Fingleton, E. Fox, D. Neven and P. Seabright, *Competition Policy and the Transformation of Central Europe* (CEPR, 1995), ch. 4 and Appendix 2.

[157] In the case of Association Agreements, the rules necessary to implement the competition provisions were agreed to be established by the Association Councils within a period of three years. See, for example, the implementing rules for the application of the competition provisions applicable to firms provided for in Art. 33(1)(i) and (ii) and 33 (2) of the EU–Poland Interim Agreement (1996) *Official Journal* L-208/24. See M. Blässar and J. Stragier, 'Enlargement' (1999) *European Community Competition Policy NewsLetter* 58; T. Vardady, 'The Emergence of Competition Law in (Former) Socialist Countries' (1999) *American Journal of Comparative Law* 229; K. Van Miert, 'Competition Policy in Relation to the Central and Eastern European Countries – Achievements and Challenges' (1998) *European Community Competition Policy NewsLetter* 1.

[158] See M. Dabbah, *The Internationalisation of Antitrust Policy* (Cambridge University Press, 2003), pp. 121–30.

Commission and candidate countries. In general, it is a policy-oriented event, focused in particular on the development of EU competition law and on how to ensure the full and proper enforcement of its rules in candidate countries. It has served to demonstrate the necessity of a timely application of EU competition law for a successful accession, and has reconfirmed the commitment of the Commission and candidate countries to enhancing cooperation in the field of competition law. The Conference has also helped the Commission in evaluating the situation in all candidate countries, especially those that have been having difficulties in completing their negotiations on the competition law chapter with the Commission. The Conference has also served as an appropriate medium for the Commission to convey the message to candidate countries that a candidate country can be ready for EU membership only if its public authorities and firms have become accustomed to a competition discipline such as that of the EU well before accession. As far as the Commission is concerned, each candidate country is required to demonstrate that it has the necessary legislative framework in place; it has established the necessary administrative capacity; and it has established a credible enforcement record.

(v) Tables of agreements
Agreements with Candidate countries

Agreement with	Type and date of the agreement	Comment
Croatia	Stabilisation and Association 2004	The Agreement provides among other things in Title VI, for: approximation of Croatia's existing laws to EU law, including gradual approximation to the Union *acquis communautaire* (Article 69); and incompatibility of business phenomena of collusion, abuse of dominance and competition distorting state aid with the operation of the agreement where they affect trade between the EU and Croatia (Article 70).

		Article 70 also shows the importance attached to effective competition law enforcement by Croatia and provides for the creation of an operationally independent body armed with the necessary power to deal with and regulate state aid. The Croatian Competition Act 2003 and associated secondary legislation have gone a long way in aligning Croatian competition laws with those of the EU.
Macedonia	Stabilisation and Association 2004	The Agreement contains similar provisions to that found in the Agreement with Croatia, e.g. the approximation of laws (Article 68) and incompatibility of anticompetitive behaviour (Article 69). The provisions of the Agreement have been implemented by the Law on Protection of Competition 2005 and the Law on State Aid 2003 of Macedonia.
Turkey	Association Agreement 1963	The Agreement, along with the protocol added in 1970, provides for strengthening of trade between the EU and Turkey and for a three-stage process to establish a Customs Union; Decision 1/95 of the EU Association Council (the Decision) addressed competition as part of the final stage. Chapter IV, Section II of the Decision states that

anticompetitive agreements/ collusion (Article 32), abuse of dominance (Article 33) and competition-distorting state aid (Article 34) are incompatible with the Customs Union. Any practices which fall within the prohibitions are to be determined in accordance with the criteria the EU applies in deciding cases under Articles 101, 102 and 107 TFEU (Article 35). The approximation of laws is provided for in Article 39 and cooperation between Turkey and the European Commission in the form of exchanging information is provided for in Article 36.

If the EU, or Turkey, consider that the rules to be implemented in furtherance of the Agreement are unable to deal with an incompatible practice, or in the absence of such rules, either party may take unilateral measures to remedy the situation following consultation with the Joint Customs Union Committee (Article 38).

Turkey has, on the whole, yet to fulfil its obligations under the Decision but its national competition laws have been aligned with those of the EU.[159]

---

[159] See M. Dabbah, *Competition Law and Policy in the Middle East* (Cambridge University Press, 2007), ch. 4.

Agreements with Western Balkan countries

Agreement with	Type and date of the agreement	Comment
Albania	Stabilisation and Association 2006	Title VI of the Agreement prohibits anticompetitive agreements/ collusion, abuse of dominance and state aid which may have an effect on trade between Albania and the EU (Article 71(1)). The criteria established by the EC in applying Articles 101, 102, 106 and 107 TFEU are applicable when determining whether a practice is incompatible with the Agreement (Article 71(2)). Albania is also obliged to establish an 'operationally independent public body' to oversee the implementation and enforcement of the provisions of the Agreement within four years under Article 71(3) and (4). Albania's Law for the Protection of Competition 2003 implemented the Agreement.
Montenegro	Stabilisation and Association 2007	The competition provisions contained in Title VI, Article 73, are, if not largely similar, almost identical to those in the Stabilisation and Association Agreement with Albania. However, in respect of state aid, Article 73(7)(a) provides that all state aid granted by Montenegro within five years following the adoption of the Agreement is deemed to fall within the justifying circumstances referred to in Article 107(3) TFEU.

Other bilateral links

Agreement with	Type and date of the agreement	Comment
Algeria	Euro-Mediterranean Association Agreement 2005	Article 41 of the Agreement prohibits anticompetitive agreements/collusion, abuse of dominance and state aid which may have an effect on trade between Algeria and the EU and Annex 5 to the Agreement includes provisions relating to cooperation between the competition authorities in the EU and Algeria
Brazil	Framework Agreement for Cooperation 1995	The Agreement provides for the strengthening of cooperation and consultation between Brazil and the European Commission in respect of international issues of mutual interest, such as trade, finance, investment and technology (Article 2). Though there are no specific competition provisions, the parties agreed to facilitate trade transactions as far as possible and to endeavour to reduce and eliminate obstacles to trade in Article 5(1)–(2). Cooperation in respect of investigations into dumping and subsidisation activities is required by Article 5(5), with the investigating authority being obliged to meet requests for information that will be used to determine its decision before such a decision made.

		The European Commission concluded in October 2009 with a Memorandum of Understanding with Brazil which seeks to promote closer cooperation in the field of competition between the Commission and Brazilian competition authorities.
Chile	Association Agreement 2002	Title VII of the Agreement establishes the way in which the EU and Chile will cooperate and coordinate the activities of their respective competition authorities; coordination of activities is specifically stated not to impinge on decision-making autonomy (Article 175). Cooperation extends to the notification of actions (Article 174), consultation (Article 176), the exchange of non-confidential information (Article 177) and technical assistance (Article 178).
China	Declaration on the Start of Dialogue on 2003	The Dialogue acts as a permanent mechanism for consultations and transparency between China and the EU in respect of competition matters.
Egypt	Euro-Mediterranean Association Agreement 2004	Article 35(1) of the Agreement deals with competition policy and prohibits anticompetitive agreements/collusion between undertakings, abuses of a dominant position and state aid where such practices affect trade between the EU and Egypt.

		Egypt implemented the Agreement with its Law on Protection of Competition and Prohibition of Monopolistic Practices 2005.
Faroe Islands	Agreement between the EU, the Danish Government and the Faroe Islands 1996	One of the aims of the Agreement is to 'provide fair conditions of competition for trade' between the parties (Article 1) and this has been provided for by prohibiting anticompetitive agreements/ collusion, abuse of a dominant position and state aid where such practices affect trade between the EU and the Faroes (Article 25 (1)).
		If a practice is found to be incompatible with the Agreement, the party concerned must inform a Joint Committee of all relevant information and provide assistance so as to allow the Committee to examine the case and eliminate the practice (Article 29).
Israel	Euro-Mediterranean Association Agreement 2000	Article 36 of the Agreement prohibits anticompetitive agreements/collusion, abuses of a dominant position and state aid where these may affect trade between the EU and Israel. Article 37 provides that by the end of the fifth year following the adoption of the Agreement, all state monopolies of a commercial character will cease to be discriminatory in respect of the procurement and marketing of goods.

		No implementing rules are in force; a competition law regime exists in Israel.
Jordan	Euro-Mediterranean Association Agreement 2002	Article 53 contains provisions similar to those found in Article 36 of the Agreement between the European Commission and Israel, except that (like Montenegro) all state aid granted by Jordan within five years following the adopting of the Agreement is deemed to fall within the justifying circumstances referred to in Article 107(3) TFEU (Article 53(4)(a)) and the gradual liberalisation of public procurement is expressed as a key objective (Article 58).
Korea	Cooperation Agreement 2009	The Agreement regulates cooperation between the European Commission and the Korean Fair Trade Commission by providing for: the reciprocal notification of cases where they may affect the important interests of the other party (Article 2); the possibility of coordinating enforcement activities and the rendering of assistance in enforcement activities (Article 3); the possibility of allocating enforcement actions (Article 4); the exchange of non-confidential information (Article 7); and regulating bilateral meetings (Article 8).

Lebanon	Euro-Mediterranean Association Agreement 2006	Article 35 of the Agreement prohibits anticompetitive agreements/collusion, abuses of a dominant position and state aid where these may affect trade between the EU and Lebanon. There is currently no specific competition law in Lebanon, but a draft competition law has been prepared and awaits being enacted.
Mexico	Economic Partnership, Political Coordination and Cooperation Agreement 2000 (also known as the 'Global Agreement')	The Agreement provides for the notification of enforcement activities, the exchange of information, conflict avoidance and the coordination of enforcement activities.
Moldova	Partnership and Cooperation Agreement 1998	Under Article 48 of the Agreement, the parties agree to address or remove restrictions on competition caused by private firms or state intervention in so far as they may affect trade between the EU and Moldova (Article 48(1)). A Trade and Industry Sub-Committee was established to oversee the implementation of the competition provisions of the Agreement; the Sub-Committee acts as an official forum for consultation and cooperation between the EU and Moldova.

Morocco	Euro-Mediterranean Association Agreement 2000	Article 36 of the Agreement prohibits anticompetitive agreements/collusion, abuses of a dominant position and state aid where these may affect trade between the EU and Morocco. However, like Montenegro and Jordan, special provisions apply in respect of state aid, particularly in respect of the reorganisation of steel products (Article 36(4)).
Palestine	Euro-Mediterranean Interim Association Agreement on Trade and Cooperation 1997	Article 31 of the Interim Agreement prohibits anticompetitive agreements/ collusion, abuses of a dominant position and state aid where these may affect trade between the EU and Palestine.
Russian Federation	Partnership and Cooperation Agreement 1997	Under Article 53 of the Agreement, the parties agree to address or remove restrictions on competition caused by private firms or state intervention in so far as they may affect trade between the EU and Russia. This objective is to be attained by ensuring the existence and enforcement of laws addressing competition restrictions (Article 53(2)). Article 55 also provides for the approximation of laws, including competition legislation.
South Africa	Agreement on Trade Development and Cooperation 1999	The Agreement provides that appropriate measures can be taken by either side, after

		consultation with the Cooperation Council, if it is considered that a certain practice has not been adequately dealt with and is harmful to its interests.
Switzerland	Agreement on Air Transport 1999	In the field of air transport, the European Commission is directly competent to initiate an investigation and order investigative measures, such as dawn raids, in Switzerland against Swiss enterprises suspected to have entered into an unlawful anticompetitive agreement.
Tunisia	Euro-Mediterranean Association Agreement 1995	Article 36 of the Agreement prohibits anticompetitive agreements/collusion, abuses of a dominant position and state aid where these may affect trade between the EU and Tunisia. However, like Montenegro, Jordan and Morocco special provisions apply in respect of state aid, particularly in respect of the reorganisation of steel products (Article 36(4)). No implementing rules are in force.
Ukraine	Partnership and Cooperation Agreement 1997	Under Article 49 of the Agreement, the parties agree to address or remove restrictions on competition caused by private firms or state intervention in so far as they may affect trade between the EU and Ukraine. This objective is to be attained by ensuring the

existence and enforcement of
laws addressing competition
restrictions (Article 49(2)).
Article 51 also provides for the
approximation of laws,
including competition
legislation and the provision of
technical assistance to the
Ukraine.

(c) **Partnership and Cooperation Agreements** Partnership and
Cooperation Agreements (PCAs) exhibit some similarities with
Association Agreements, though they also differ in several ways; one of
these ways should be obvious from the title of these agreements: a PCA
shows that this is more an agreement between 'partners' and not an
agreement between the EU and a country 'associated' to it. The EU has
entered into three such agreements with the Russian Federation (1994),
Ukraine and Moldova. Among these agreements, the PCA with the
Russian Federation is considered the most significant. This Agreement
follows from an earlier Trade and Cooperation Agreement between the
EU and the former USSR which was concluded in 1989. The latter
agreement was, within less than two years, however regarded as unsuitable for developing the relations between the parties. In entering into the
PCA, the EU opted for a much looser framework in political, legal and
economic terms than those contained in Association Agreements
because it was concerned about the uncertainties in the transformation
process in Russia and due to geopolitical considerations. Nevertheless,
from the perspective of the parties, the Agreement indicated that Russia
was no longer a 'state-trading' country but one with an economy in
transition.[160] The Preamble to the PCA also referred to a 'political
conditionality' clause, declaring that the parties are convinced of the
paramount importance that must be accorded to the rule of law and
respect for human rights.

---

[160] See generally M. Maresceau and E. Montaguti, 'The Relations Between the European
Union and Central and Eastern Europe: a Legal Appraisal' (1995) *Common Market Law
Review* 1327.

III.   Comment

The Commission's initiatives on a wider level in Europe have led to the conclusion of different types of agreements between the Commission and many neighbouring countries. These initiatives have enhanced the importance of the EU competition law regime. As the Commission has linked some of these agreements – i.e. Association Agreements concluded with candidate countries – to the objective of future accession to the EU,[161] it has placed itself, and the EU, in a superior bargaining position. Including an approximation of law requirement in those agreements has meant that EU competition law has become remarkably transposed into different legal systems and traditions. Arguably, this should be seen as one of the main successes of the EU competition law experience. Accommodating EU-like competition law in Central and Eastern European countries seems to indicate that EU competition law continues to be of importance in achieving further integration. Thus, the EU has expanded in geographic terms, whilst at the same time it has maintained the rules and principles on which it was originally based and which have contributed to its development since its creation. This seems to have equipped the Commission with the confidence and experience to advocate EU competition law thinking beyond all EU and European boundaries.

(C)   Multilateral efforts

The final strand in the international dimension of the EU competition law regime is the Commission's strong support for multilateralism in the field. The Commission's efforts towards creating a wider, multilateral framework of competition policy beyond the EU and Europe have been quite substantial.[162] It is most remarkable that the Commission – despite being the only effective supranational competition authority in the world – has consistently pushed for multilateral solutions to international competition problems.

I.   Involvement with the work of international bodies

The Commission's multilateral efforts date back to the early 1990s. In 1994, the *Wise Men Group*, a group of experts, commissioned by the late Karel

---

[161] See the Commission's document on 'The Enlargement Negotiations after Helsinki' MEMO/00/6 (February 2000).

[162] See Commission 25th Report on Competition Policy (1995), section V; Commission 28th Report on Competition Policy (1998), pp. 118–20.

Van Miert (then Commissioner for competition within the Commission), made some interesting proposals in order to strengthen the multilateral framework of competition rules and to promote international cooperation in the field. The Group recommended building multilateral cooperation in response to changes in the global economic environment and the challenges posed by these on the competition law front.[163] It recommended creating a fully fledged international instrument, including an adequate enforcement structure, a core of common principles and a positive comity provision.[164] The Group also put forward a proposal for a dispute settlement mechanism that could be used to settle disputes between member countries regarding their compliance with rules and principles of the instrument.[165] As early as 1996 – almost immediately following the creation of the World Trade Organisation (WTO) – the Commission pushed very hard for developing a competition mandate within the WTO, as can be seen in light of the setting up of the Singapore Group in 1996 to study the relationship between competition and trade policy. As we noted above, little progress however has come to be made in developing a competition agenda within the WTO framework and, as things stand, the whole idea is on indefinite hold.[166]

The little progress made within the WTO framework however has not stopped the Commission from believing that multilateralism is the best way forward and from exploring other options outside the WTO. The Commission has been particularly active within international organisations, especially the Organisation for Economic Cooperation and Development (OECD), the United Nations Conference on Trade and Development (UNCTAD) and the International Competition Network (ICN). Within the former, the Commission has provided important expertise to help support the work of the OECD in the field. It has championed the good cause of offering technical assistance to many young competition authorities around the world in order to enable them to enhance their enforcement mechanisms and advance their expertise in the field. The Commission has also supported the work of UNCTAD and has endorsed its Set and its approach.[167] An interesting feature of the Set relates to its terminology, which seems to be closely related to that of EU competition law, such as the concepts of

---

[163] See pp. 80–82 above for the challenges and problems calling for internationalisation of competition law.
[164] See pp. 496–500 below for a discussion on the concept and principle of positive comity.
[165] See 'Competition policy in the new trade order: strengthening international cooperation and rules' COM(95) 359, available at: http://europa.eu/index_en.htm.
[166] See p. 597 above.   [167] See pp. 144–146 above for a discussion on the Set.

'dominance' and 'abuse'. This, along with the fact that the Set emphasises the importance of institutional dimensions, and the interaction between these and substantive provisions, as is the case with the EU competition law regime, makes it clear that EU competition law has played a central role in the development of this Set. Finally, the ICN provides a notable example of multilateralism on the part of the European Commission, which was instrumental (as a founding member) in creating the Network in 2001. As we saw,[168] the ICN is a virtual network of competition authorities with emphasis on soft-law convergence; in other words, seeking to arrive at common standards to be used in different regimes through means that lack binding force and by different competition authorities voluntarily adopting those standards within their domestic regimes.[169] The ICN has been a phenomenal success and the Commission can take particular pride in its achievement here.

II. Other examples of concrete efforts by the Commission at world stage

The Commission's multilateral efforts towards the internationalisation of competition law have been the result of several factors, including those relating to increased globalisation, the emergence of the EU as a world player and phenomenal geographical expansion (through the accession of different countries) in recent years, as well as the need – as identified by the Commission – to build a global order within the field of competition law. These efforts of the Commission have not been confined to advocating the idea of multilateralism and building necessary frameworks for pursuing the idea (as we saw in the previous section), but have extended to making concrete contributions in terms of offering technical assistance to countries willing to introduce competition laws and policies within their domestic economies. It should not require a great deal of convincing for one to accept that building a competition law regime, with effective competition law and policy and credible and transparent enforcement bodies, is a formidable task. Constructing such a regime is integrally linked to broader private sector development strategies. When developing countries and those in transition consider adopting competition laws within their domestic legal systems, one of their main concerns normally revolves around the lack of sufficient resources and the necessary expertise.[170] The European Commission has over the years

---

[168] See p. 151 above.   [169] Chapter 10, pp. 569–578 below deals with soft law convergence.
[170] See pp. 317–319 below.

made it clear that it understands this concern and therefore has expressed a willingness and shown readiness to offer assistance and support in terms of organising and financing important projects in countries and regions interested in adopting competition law and policy; indeed, this initiative by the Commission should be seen in parallel to similar initiatives by other important competition authorities, such as those in the USA and Japan and important international organisations, such as UNCTAD. During the last decade or so, the Commission has organised training sessions for competition officials from candidate countries for EU accession, Latin and Central America, Africa and the Middle East. Of these projects, it is worth mentioning the cooperation project between the Commission and the Common Market for East and Southern Africa (COMESA).[171] The aim of this project is to develop a regional competition policy in Africa and to focus on capacity-building in the enforcement of competition law by competition authorities within COMESA. The project has come to assume great significance. The project is based on the recognition that competition policy is one of the trade-related areas of cooperation between the EU and COMESA and a crucial part of the overall integration of COMESA and its welfare-enhancing objective. As a result of the project, member countries of COMESA have been able to enjoy a greater capacity in formulating and enforcing local competition laws. This includes developing clear and transparent competition rules, credible institutions with recognisable competition law expertise and effective enforcement.

III. Association of European Competition Authorities

The Commission and the national competition authorities of EU member states participate in the Association of European Competition Authorities (ECA). Other members of the ECA include the competition authorities of Norway, Iceland, Liechtenstein and the EFTA Surveillance Authority. One of the major functions of the ECA is to offer a platform for the member competition authorities to discuss a variety of issues dealing with the application and enforcement of competition law; the discussions also extend to cooperation between competition authorities especially in the field of merger control.

---

[171] For an account on COMESA see pp. 382–385 below.

Chapter 5

US competition law regime

1. Introduction

The US competition law regime is one of the oldest and most influential regimes in the world. Many people consider that the first legislation in the field of competition law enacted in 'modern times' was the US Sherman Act, the first federal competition law adopted in 1890.[1] Naturally, therefore, the US competition law regime has a rich history and actors within the regime – whether US competition authorities, the judiciary, academics and practitioners – have phenomenal experience in the field of competition law. The contribution made by all of these actors over the past 100 or so years has been hugely important in advancing competition law to its current position of global significance. The admirably vast output by American scholars in particular must be acknowledged.[2] Many global developments in the field have US

---

[1] It is important to note however that competition law roots can be traced in Canada to the *Act for the Prevention and Suppression of Combinations in Restraint of Trade* which was adopted in1889; the substantive provisions of this Act were later incorporated into the first *Criminal Code of Canada* in 1892.

[2] An enormous amount of competition law literature exists in the USA, mostly in the form of scholarly articles. Many books (of which a considerable number are 'casebooks' – typical of US academia and practice) also exist. Notable works (non-exhaustively) include: P. Areeda, L. Kaplow and A. S. Edlin, *Antitrust Analysis: Problems, Text, Cases* (Aspen Publishers, 2004); E. Fox, L. A. Sullivan and R. J. Peritz, *Cases and Materials on United States Antitrust in Global Context* (Thomson West, 2009); A. I. Gavil, W. E. Kovacic and J. B. Baker, *Antitrust Law in Perspective: Cases, Concepts and Problems in Competition Policy* (Thomson West, 2008); E. Gelhorn and W. E. Kovacic, *Antitrust Law and Economics in a Nutshell* (Thomson West, 2004); D. J. Gifford and L. J. Raskind, *Federal Antitrust Law: Cases and Materials* (Anderson Publishing Co., 2002); J. E. Kwoka and L. J. White, *The Antitrust Revolution: Economics, Competition, and Policy* (Oxford University Press, 2003); H. Hovenkamp, *Federal Antitrust Policy: the Law of Competition and its Practice* (Thomson West, 2005); E. T. Sullivan and J. L. Harrison, *Understanding Antitrust and its Economic Implications* (LexisNexis, 2003); R. J. R. Peritz, *Competition Policy in America, 1888–1992: History, Rhetoric, Law* (Oxford University Press, 1996).

roots: whether in relation to economic analysis[3] and the use of economics in the field more generally or the design and use of important tools, such as the leniency programme in the area of anti-cartel regulation to mention but a few. Little wonder however that the American approach and thinking in the field of competition law and policy has been and continues to be extremely influential.

2.   A brief historical perspective

In order to be able to understand the US competition law regime, in particular how it has developed over the years and what function it performs in the present time, it is crucial to become familiar with its roots, which as noted above extend to the nineteenth century. That century witnessed a wide spread of anticompetitive practices in many US industries. Notable in this regard is the situation in the transportation of goods sector, which was dominated by railroad companies, which used to charge excessive and disproportionate prices. These prices were excessive because they exceeded what the customers of those companies could charge for their produce, and disproportionate because the prices did not correspond to the value of the service the companies rendered. These anticompetitive practices maximised the personal profit of their creators while being detrimental to the public interest. The trend during the nineteenth century was to form trusts, which were orchestrated by influential figures such as John Rockefeller. Trusts were operated by a body of trustees, who had legal control over them and who held stocks in competing firms and who as a result were able to manage the affairs of the industry concerned. Being in such a powerful position, the trustees were able to eliminate competition between the firms they were running. It was against such injurious and uncomfortable practices that the term 'antitrust' was created and the main legislation on the subject matter, the Sherman Act 1890, was passed.[4] Under this 'new' piece of legislation it was rendered illegal to enter into contracts in restraint of trade or to monopolise, or attempt to monopolise, a market.[5]

---

[3] See in particular pp. 73–74 above for a discussion on the use of the SSNIP test when defining the relevant market in competition cases.

[4] For a good account of the political perspective of the Sherman Act and other US antitrust laws see generally E. K. Kintner, *An Antitrust Primer* (Macmillan, 1973); also the literature mentioned in chapter 1, note 69.

[5] See pp. 238–248 below for a discussion of the two main pillars of the Sherman Act 1890: s 1 and s 2.

There has been a huge debate for many decades now over what actually inspired the enactment of the Sherman Act. Some people have argued in favour of the view that the Act had been inspired on economic efficiency grounds: obviously the interest here being to give the Act the strong economic context the US competition law regime has come to be associated with.[6] Whether this is true or not is something that is very much open to speculation. However, such view is not as strong as that advocating that the Act was actually inspired by Jefferson's democratic ideal of a society of equal and independent citizens, subject only to democratically legitimate power and thus the desire to stand up to and fight and defeat wrongful acts and situations, namely the trusts!

The Sherman Act 1890 was an improvement on the common law position existing prior to its enactment because it enabled a public authority to take action against firms engaged in anticompetitive activities whilst also enabling anyone injured by those activities to bring an action against such firms.[7] The Act was expected to be very effective in fighting anticompetitive practices. In reality, however, the Act did not live up to such expectation. The years following the enactment of the Act witnessed distinguished prominence of competition law: such prominence was seen in presidential campaigns for 1912; the presidential election of that year – won eventually by Woodrow Wilson – was fought mainly on the competition law front. Two years later, the post-Sherman Act long legislative activity began with the adoption of two significant pieces of legislation: the Clayton Act 1914 and the Federal Trade Commission Act 1914.[8]

3. A regime of 'contexts'

The brief historical overview given in the previous part serves to show the existence of more than one context for the US competition law regime, most notably a social but also a political context.[9] To these one must add the economic context (see part 7 below) because of the way in which US competition law and policy have developed and the use of economic analysis in applying different competition rules under the regime. In this respect, the US experience in the field of competition law has been quite unique. More importantly, however, the existence of

---

[6] See pp. 250–256 below on the economic context and foundations of the regime.
[7] See pp. 256–264 below for the private enforcement branch of the US competition law regime.
[8] The two Acts are discussed at pp. 244–245 below.   [9] See part 8 below.

these different contexts has fuelled the impressive debate the US competition law regime has witnessed – whether in enforcement, judicial or academic circles – in relation to its different aspects, including even some of the basic questions such as: what goals should be sought under US competition law? This debate – whilst admittedly causing many frictions and divisions of opinion among the US competition law community – has certainly helped advance the regime and enabled the US competition law experience to develop into one of the most mature experiences in the world. For this reason, acquiring some awareness of this experience would be invaluable especially in the context of a debate on the internationalisation of competition law. Most commercial phenomena that cause competition problems have, at some stage, been considered by US courts and competition authorities. Such phenomena have also been the subject of extensive comments by US scholars and academics. The end result has been an abundance of case law and literature, which have been extremely valuable in understanding and furthering the understanding of so many people in the field of competition law. Furthermore, one can never overstate how economic analysis has also become influential in US competition law. Chapter 1 of the book demonstrated how an appreciation and understanding of economic doctrines and theories is an extremely essential component for competition lawyers to understand. The US competition law experience has been invaluable in demonstrating that competition law does not exist in a vacuum. The experience shows that competition law is an aspect of the social and economic policy of the system to which it belongs, and as such it reflects the tensions and the preoccupations of that system at any time.

4. The US federal legal system in brief

To many non-US observers, the US legal system is extremely complex and simply too difficult to understand. A similar feeling is shared by many observers who attempt to study the US competition law regime. Obviously, the perceived difficulty is triggered in part by the fact that the system is made up of federal and local (state) components. This chapter will focus on the former components of US competition law regime and as a result it will not consider the local, state laws in the field of competition law. In this part of the chapter a brief overview is offered of the US federal legal system for the benefit of readers who may not be familiar with the topic.

The roots of the US legal system date back to the US Constitution, which was ratified in 1788. Among other things, the Constitution established a federal system of government within which power was distributed between a national government (the 'federal' government) and the individual state governments. The remit of the federal government is confined to issues of national concern, including the regulation of commerce between states and with other nations whereas individual state governments deal with matters of local concern. The federal government has three branches – the legislative, executive and judicial – which operate on the basis of two fundamental principles, among many others: the principle of separation of powers and the principle of checks and balances with each branch having authority to act on its own, to regulate the other two branches and be regulated by the other branches. All of these branches have performed crucial roles in the development of the federal legal system generally and the US competition law regime particularly.

(A)   The legislative branch

The bicameral US Congress is the legislative branch of the federal government comprised of the lower House of Representatives and the higher Senate, both being required to approve a bill before it becomes law. The House of Representatives is made up of representatives from each state in proportion to that state's population whereas in the Senate each state has two representatives regardless of a state's population. The US Congress has always played a key role in the competition law scene in the USA through: legislating important laws on which the US competition law regime has come to be established and advanced; contributing to the debate in the field of competition law through its hearings; and monitoring the activities of US competition authorities, in particular the US Federal Trade Commission.[10]

(B)   The executive branch

The power of the executive branch is vested in the President of the United States of America, though in practice it is delegated to the Cabinet and other officials, depending on the field within which the relevant power(s) fall. The members of the Cabinet are responsible

---

[10] See pp. 236–237 below for an account on the Federal Trade Commission.

for the administration of different government departments, including the Department of Justice of which a special division deals with the field of competition law, namely the Antitrust Division.[11] Each department of state has considerable regulatory and political power, being solely responsible for executing federal laws and regulations.

(C) The judicial branch

The highest court in the federal court system is the US Supreme Court, which is made up of nine justices. The Supreme Court deals with matters relating the federal government, disputes between states and questions of interpretation of the US Constitution. The Supreme Court has been quite active in the field of competition law and has delivered a number of important judgments. It has on occasion shown a noticeable degree of judicial activism, through which the Court has helped clarify many aspects of US competition law.[12]

Beneath the Supreme Court are the courts of appeals, with 11 numbered 'circuit' courts operating on a geographical jurisdictional basis. The district courts are below the courts of appeals and are the general trial courts for federal law, be it civil or criminal. Both appeals and district courts have played an important role in marking the outer-boundaries of US competition rules, especially with regard to the doctrine of extraterritoriality.[13] A separate court system exists for each individual state, but these deal solely with state laws and they have their own rules and procedures.

It is understandable why US courts have played such an important role in US competition law regime. First, the regime is judicially enforced and so the courts are given the power to decide cases and rule on the applicability of competition rules in different situation. Secondly, a quick glance at the language of US competition laws would show that it is generally drafted in broad terms with a distinct 'common law-like' nature, which means that – beyond it being necessary for judicial clarification to be given to legislative provisions – courts are naturally afforded a wide discretion in their application of the statute. The exercise

---

[11] See below for a discussion on the Antitrust Division (widely referred to in the US especially among practitioners as 'Justice').

[12] See, for example, the clarification offered by the Court in relation to exact scope of s 1 of the Sherman Act 1890 which prohibits anticompetitive behaviour; see further below.

[13] See chapter 8 for a discussion on judgments delivered by these courts in key cases dealing with this doctrine.

of this discretion has over the years been directly influenced by the many debates witnessed on the US competition law scene on the aims and scope of competition law and policy in the US and current economic assumptions in an attempt to align the law with the perceived goals of competition law.[14]

5.   US competition authorities

The US competition law regime is unique in that there is dual enforcement at the federal level with the involvement of two different authorities: the Antitrust Division of the Department of Justice (Antitrust Division) and the Federal Trade Commission (FTC).[15] The roles and duties of these two authorities overlap to some extent and, naturally, this unique structure has resulted in complexities and criticisms arising over the years. It is worth mentioning here the review of the institutional structure of the US competition law regime which was launched in 2004 by the especially formed Antitrust Modernisation Commission (AMC) as part of a process that sought to identify whether, in light of various developments the US competition law regime has come to witness, US competition laws needed modernising. The AMC and its final report will be discussed further below.[16]

(A)   The Antitrust Division[17]

The Antitrust Division is part of the Department of Justice and is thus part of the executive branch of the federal government. The Division is headed by the Assistant Attorney General for Antitrust and its sphere

---

[14] See the work of major scholars such as Bork and others, cited in chapter 1 above, at notes 68 and 69. For a discussion on the issue of goals of competition law, see pp. 36–44 above.

[15] The Antitrust Division and the FTC however are not the only actors within the US competition law regime. Obviously, as noted before the regime is judicially enforced and this means that courts have an important role to play. Also, as will be seen below the regime allows for private enforcement and this means that private litigants are also important actors. Beyond this, it is important to note the role played by individual state attorneys who only bring actions under state laws (which generally parallel the federal laws) for conduct occurring wholly within their own state. Finally, one should be aware of the role played by sectoral regulators, especially in the field of merger control (such as the Federal Communications Commission (FCC) and the Surface Transportation Board (STB)).

[16] See pp. 268–274 below.

[17] An organisational chart of the Division is available at: www.justice.gov/atr/org.htm.

of activity relates to criminal and civil enforcement under two key pieces of legislation, namely the Sherman Act 1890 and the Clayton Act 1914 through litigation.[18] With regard to the former branch of enforcement, the Division enjoys exclusive competence under the Sherman Act. Criminal enforcement ranks high on the Division's agenda as can be seen from its fight against cartels: the Division attaches enormous significance (and resources) to its efforts to unearth and prosecute as many cartels as possible.[19] The task of criminal enforcement within the Division is assigned to the Criminal Enforcement Group, which is led by a Deputy Assistant Attorney General who reports to the Assistant Attorney General (the person who heads the Division). The Group is also responsible for determining the Division's policy on criminal enforcement. The Deputy Assistant Attorney General and the Division's Director of Criminal Enforcement supervise investigations and litigation conducted by attorneys and support staff located in the Division's National Criminal Enforcement section in Washington DC and in seven 'field' offices found in the following US cities: Atlanta; Chicago; Cleveland; Dallas; New York; Philadelphia; and San Francisco.

It is important to note that the scope and the legal foundation of the Division's work extend beyond the traditional boundaries of the field of competition law. Especially in the area of anti-cartel enforcement, the Division utilises instruments other than US competition rules such as those laws prohibiting the submission of false statements to federal authorities, perjury, and conspiracies to defraud the USA. In recent years, the Division has stepped up its enforcement of the laws on obstruction of justice and perjury; this can be seen from a simple comparison in enforcement efforts between the 1990s and years after 2000: during the former, the Division prosecuted two corporations and seven individuals for obstruction offences whereas since 2000, the Division has prosecuted no fewer than 11 corporations and 23 individuals for obstruction offences.[20] It would be correct however to describe this kind of enforcement work as either independent of or supplementary to competition law enforcement and not a substitute for the latter.

---

[18] These two Acts are discussed at pp. 238–245 below.

[19] See speech delivered by Scott Hammond, Deputy Assistant Attorney General for Antitrust: 'Recent Developments, Trends, and Milestones in the Antitrust Division's Criminal Enforcement Program', as part of the 56th Annual Spring Meting of the American Bar Association Section of Antitrust Law (Washington, October 2008), available at: www.usdoj.gov/atr/public/speeches/232716.htm.

[20] See ibid.

The Division works in collaboration with a variety of investigative authorities and public bodies and interacts with others. First, there is close collaboration with the FTC as can very notably be seen from the field of merger control. Secondly, Division attorneys work with the Federal Bureau of Investigation (FBI) agents to investigate criminal matters: the latter may conduct a variety of operations, which support the Division's work, for example in relation to gathering incriminating evidence in cartel investigations using its tools of undercover operations. Thirdly, the Division's Office of International Affairs works with the Department of Justice's Foreign Commerce Section to coordinate discovery and investigations of international cartels with foreign authorities. Fourthly, while Division attorneys conduct the majority of criminal competition law proceedings, the Division may refer investigations and litigation to individual US Attorneys,[21] especially those matters that are of a local character that involve situations of price-fixing, bid-rigging or similar forms of collusion. Finally, given that US federal courts hear and decide competition cases brought by the Division, the Division must carry out its role as prosecutor which involves establishing in court the facts and the breach of the competition rules law as well as demonstrating that there is justification for seeking the relief in the relevant enforcement action.

The competence with which the Division pursues civil and criminal actions means that it may choose to pursue the former instead of the latter even in those situations which are considered to fall within the scope of the latter. Specifically, the Division may do so in cases where: the relevant law is surrounded with confusion; the issues of law or fact in the case are truly novel; it is established by way of clear evidence that the persons under investigation were not aware of, or did not appreciate, the consequences of their actions.[22] When determining its course of action in these cases, the Division will pay close attention to the anticompetitive impact of the situation: where it is not significant, civil as opposed to criminal action will usually be preferred. In proceeding on grounds of civil enforcement, the Division in these cases will seek a court order prohibiting future infringements by the persons concerned and requiring them – normally the firm(s) in question – to undertake

---

[21] US Attorneys are located in each federal district of the United States and are responsible for prosecuting criminal cases brought by the federal government.
[22] See D. I. Baker, 'To Indict or Not to Indict: Prosecutorial Discretion in Sherman Act Enforcement' (1977–8) *Cornell Law Review* 405.

steps to remedy a situation in order to put an effective end to the anticompetitive situation.

The Division enjoys broad powers when carrying out its functions in the field of competition law. This includes the power to seek and gather information and carry out investigations; as noted above, the Division may seek the assistance of other authorities in its pursuit of prosecuting criminal competition law violations. The Division may seek and obtain search warrants,[23] conduct covert taping and electronic surveillance of suspected cartel participants with the assistance of federal law enforcement authorities including the FBI[24] and seek the issuance of a grand jury subpoena.

(B)   The Federal Trade Commission[25]

The FTC is an independent body established in 1914 under the Federal Trade Commission Act. The FTC reports directly to the US Congress. It is headed by five commissioners, one of whom is appointed as Chairman, who are nominated by the President of the USA and confirmed by the Senate. Each commissioner serves a seven-year term and, so as to maintain political impartiality, no more than three commissioners may be of the same political party. The President may remove a Commissioner only for 'inefficiency, neglect of duty, or malfeasance' (which has never occurred).

The FTC's work in the field of competition law is conducted within its Bureau of Competition. The FTC has both prosecutorial and adjudicative roles: like the Antitrust Division, the FTC investigates and

---

[23] The Division may apply for search warrants when there is probable cause to believe: (i) a crime has been committed; (ii) documents or other evidence of the crime exist; and (iii) such evidence is at a particular location. The application for a search warrant is made to a magistrate in the judicial district where the 'property' is located and is often obtained with the assistance of the FBI.

[24] See speech delivered by Scott Hammond, Deputy Assistant Attorney General for Antitrust at the OECD: 'Caught in the Act: Inside an International Cartel' (October, 2005).

The Antitrust Division's ability to eavesdrop on conversations of suspected cartel participants was strengthened in 2006 when the US Congress added criminal violations of the Sherman Act to the list of crimes that can be investigated with the use of court-ordered wiretaps. Court authorisation for such wiretaps is required when no party to the discussion provides prior consent to the recording. The Division may wiretap discussions without court authorisation, however, if it obtains the consent of one of the participants.

[25] An organisational chart of the FTC is available at www.ftc.gov/ftc/ftc-org-chart.pdf.

brings enforcement actions for infringement of competition law[26] through civil litigation in federal courts. The FTC may bring administrative proceedings (also known as 'Part III Proceedings') in its adjudicative role. Like the Division, the FTC enjoys discretion in its work. For example, it does not necessarily have to launch civil litigation in all cases brought to its attention: if the FTC is convinced that there has been an infringement of the law, it may seek voluntary compliance by entering into a consent order with the infringer.[27]

In practice, the work of the FTC is not confined to the field of competition; the FTC also has a Bureau of Consumer Protection in addition to the Bureau of Economics, which provides support to the Bureau of Competition. The Bureau of Competition's main work arises out of the review of notified mergers under the Clayton Act 1914 though it does look at other business phenomena for possible anticompetitive effects. The Bureau's position on 'what to investigate' is founded on the view that the FTC takes formal enforcement action under the law when this is considered to be necessary so as to protect consumers. Beyond its enforcement work, the Bureau also has an important research role in making reports and legislative recommendations to Congress and acting as a resource on competition topics, for example, by publishing guidance to businesses in cooperation with the Antitrust Division.[28]

6. US competition laws

US competition rules belong to a wide web of laws; in addition there is a considerable body of administrative guidance[29] that has been published by US competition authorities over the years as well as a body of

---

[26] See s. 5 of the Federal Trade Commission Act 1914. This includes infringement of ss. 1 and 2 of the Sherman Act 1890 and ss. 3, 7, 7A and 8 of the Clayton Act 1914. See further below for a discussion of these two Acts and these particular sections.

[27] In signing the consent order, the infringer does not need to admit that it had infringed the law; as the case may be, it merely undertakes to stop the disputed practice as outlined in an accompanying complaint or it undertakes to resolve anticompetitive aspects of a proposed merger.

[28] See below.

[29] Publishing guidance comes to serve a number of important purposes, including enhancing transparency in the work of the authorities and reducing the compliance costs on the part of businesses with the competition rules. Over the years, the authorities published guidance covering different areas, ranging from licensing of intellectual property right to the application of the competition rules in an international context (what is called international operations) to the healthcare industry; guidance has also been published in the field of merger control, notably the *Horizontal Merger Guidelines*

studies and reports either produced or commissioned by the authorities.[30] There are 18 laws which have competition relevance, though of varying degrees of importance.[31] Out of these laws, three particular *chief* federal competition laws are particularly worth noting, namely: the Sherman Act 1890, the Clayton Act 1914 and the Federal Trade Commission Act 1914. These three pieces of legislation will be discussed below; in addition to others. Three other important Acts however, namely the Foreign Trade Antitrust Improvements Act (FTAIA) 1982,[32] the International Enforcement Assistance Act 1994[33] and the Trade Act 1974[34] will be discussed in later chapters.

(A)   The Sherman Act

As noted above, the Sherman Act 1890 was the first federal piece of legislation adopted in the USA in the field of competition law. The Act contains two important pillars, on the basis of which US competition law enforcement was first initiated and has developed over the years, namely section 1 and section 2. These two provisions are discussed further below. The Sherman Act criminalises the infringement of its provisions by making such acts felonies. As felonies, the penalties attached to violations of the Act are severe and vary according to when the offence in question was committed because of the changes brought in by the Antitrust Criminal Penalty Enhancement and Reform Act of 2004. For infringements occurring before 22 June 2004, individuals can be fined up to US$350,000 and/or be imprisoned for up to three years in a federal prison for each offence; for legal bodies the fine may be up

---

(1992) and *Non-horizontal Merger Guidelines* (1984). A debate and 'revision' project was launched by the Antitrust Division and FTC in the field of merger control in 2009 seeking to revise and update the Horizontal Merger Guidelines – see www.ftc.gov/opa/2009/09/mgr.shtm; see p. xxx below.

[30] See, for example, the Report of *the International Competition Policy Advisory Committee* (ICPAC) produced in 2000, discussed at pp. 266–267 below.

[31] These are: the Sherman Act 1890; Wilson Tariff Act 1894; Clayton Act 1914; Federal Trade Commission Act 1914; Anti-dumping Act 1916; Webb-Pomerene Act 1918; Tariff Act 1930; Robinson-Patman Act 1936; Trade Act 1974; Antitrust Procedures and Penalties Act 1974; Hart-Scott-Rodino Antitrust Improvements Act 1976; Export Trading Company Act 1982; Foreign Trade Antitrust Improvements Act (FTAIA) 1982; Local Government Antitrust Act 1984; National Cooperative Research Act 1984; National Cooperative Research and Production Act 1993; International Enforcement Assistance Act 1994; and Antitrust Criminal Penalty Enhancement and Reform Act 2004.

[32] See pp. 447–449 below.   [33] See pp. 517–519 below.   [34] See pp. 616–620 below.

to US$10 million. Individuals committing an offence on or after 22 June 2004 can be fined up to US$1 million and be sentenced for up to ten years in prison for each offence and legal bodies can be fined up to US$100 million. Some offences carry an even higher threshold for fines by amounting to twice the gain or loss involved in the particular case. These fines may be increased: courts are allowed to impose a fine that is equal to twice the defendant's gain or the victim's loss resulting from the offence.[35] The penalties for violating the Sherman Act are not confined to fines and imprisonment: other penalties include debarment[36] and corporate probation.[37]

I. Section 1: anticompetitive behaviour

Section 1 of the Sherman Act states '(e)very contract, combination in the form of trust or otherwise, or conspiracy, in restraint of trade or commerce among the several States, or with foreign nations, is declared to be illegal'.[38] Even in the early years when the application of section 1 arose, US courts considered that given the absolute nature of the prohibition contained in the section, it was crucial that the scope of the

---

[35] See *United States Code*, 18 USC § 3571(d).

[36] This applies to contractors and prevents the debarred contractor from receiving contracts from the federal government. See *Federal Acquisition Regulation* (2008).

[37] The *Sentencing Guidelines Manual* recommends that corporate probation be imposed on organisations under several circumstances, including: (1) if it is necessary to secure payment of restitution, enforce a remedial order, or ensure completion of community service; (2) the fine is not paid in full at the time of sentencing and restrictions are necessary to safeguard the organisation's ability to make payments; (3) the organisation has at least 50 employees or was required by law to have an effective compliance and ethics programme but does not have such a programme; (4) the organisation engaged in similar misconduct within the previous five years, as determined by a prior judicial adjudication; (5) high-level personnel participated in the current offence and in similar misconduct within the previous five years; or (6) if it is necessary to ensure that changes are made within the organisation to reduce the likelihood of future criminal conduct. The period of probation must be between one and five years. Probation must include the condition that the organisation not commit another federal, state, or local crime during the term of probation, and must require either restitution or notice to the victims of the offence. Probation violations may result in an extension of probation, the imposition of more restrictive conditions, or revocation of probation and a resentencing of the corporation; see note 272 of the *Guidelines*.

[38] Section 3 of the Sherman Act 1890 prohibits the same behaviour as does s. 1, but it applies to restraints of 'trade or commerce in any Territory of the United States or of the District of Columbia, or in restraint of trade or commerce between any such Territory and another, or between any such Territory or Territories and any State or States or the District of Columbia, or with foreign nations, or between the District of Columbia and any State or States or foreign nations'.

prohibition be confined to certain and not all situations of restraints of trade, namely *unreasonable restraints* of trade.[39] A line of judicial pronouncement during those years clearly showed that the 'true test of legality (being) whether the restraint imposed is such as merely regulates and perhaps promotes competition or whether it is such as may suppress or even destroy competition'.[40] On the basis of this test and judicial reasoning, two different approaches came to develop with regard to the application of section 1 in practice: one requiring the application of a *rule of reason* before determining whether a given situation was unlawful and another relying on *per se* prohibition under which a situation will be deemed to be illegal without any assessment of the situation being undertaken. It is important to bear in mind however that these two approaches are not confined to the application of section 1 of the Sherman Act, but are used in applying other aspects of US competition law as well.

(a) **The *rule of reason*** Under the *rule of reason* approach, a court is required to weigh 'all the circumstances of a case in deciding whether a restrictive practice should be prohibited as imposing an unreasonable restraint on competition'.[41] Therefore, a court must examine all conceivable circumstances before determining the legality of a particular restraint where conduct does not consist of a *per se* offence.[42]

The rule of reason approach is more suitable for practices that fall within a 'grey' area, i.e. those which do not clearly harm competition by their object or even effect. Courts applying the rule of reason will: (a) examine whether the restraint has substantial anticompetitive effects, including whether the restraint at issue has market impact, in that it raises prices, reduces output, limits choice, or diminishes quality; (b) examine any evidence of pro-competitive aspects of the restraint;

---

[39] In *Standard Oil Co. of New Jersey* v. *United States*, 221 US 1, 60 (1911) it was stated that: 'since the enumeration addressed itself simply to classes of acts, those classes being broad enough to embrace every conceivable contract or combination which would be made concerning trade or commerce or the subjects of such commerce, and thus caused any act done by any of the enumerated methods anywhere in the whole field of human activity to be illegal if in restraint of trade, it inevitably follows that the provision necessarily called for the exercise of judgment which required that some standard should be resorted to for the purpose of determining whether the prohibitions contained in the statute had or had not in any given case been violated.'

[40] See *Board of Trade of the City of Chicago* v. *United States*, 246 US 231, 238 (1918).

[41] See *Continental T.V., Inc.* v. *GTE Sylvania, Inc*, 433 US 36, 49 (1977).

[42] See below for a list of *per se* offences.

and (c) weigh the anticompetitive effects against the pro-competitive effects of the alleged restraint.[43] The rule of reason approach fits well with a number of the typical characteristics of competition law given that it rests on the 'idea' that only those situations which are harmful and detrimental to competition should be prohibited and in most cases this is decided by looking at the actual effects produced in the relevant situation.

(b) The *per se* approach   In some situations, the use of the *rule of reason* approach would not be appropriate because the behaviour in question is manifestly anticompetitive and so should be deemed to be illegal *per se*. This means that there is no need for a court to examine whether the behaviour in question unreasonably restrains trade or harms competition and consumers: the mere existence of the behaviour will be enough to fall within the section 1 prohibition. A number of situations in practice would fit this description; perhaps the most obvious ones are those involving price-fixing,[44] market-sharing,[45] restriction of output,[46] bid-rigging,[47] or concerted refusal to supply[48] among competitors. Although following a *per se* approach does not require a detailed assessment of the situation (as is the case with the rule of reason approach), in practice an application of the approach is not a straightforward matter. In particular, it is important to note that the manner in which the approach operates is overly formalistic and quite rigid and this involves a risk of mechanical operation in certain

---

[43] See *Leegin Creative Leather Products, Inc.* v. *PSKS, Inc.*, 127 S. Ct. 2705, 2712–13 (2007); *Ind. Fed'n. of Dentists*, 476 US 459 (1986); *Bd. of Trade*, 246 US 238.

[44] See *United States* v. *Trenton Potteries Co.*, 273 US 392 (1927). In *Leegin Creative Leather Products, Inc.*, the US Supreme Court overruled the previous (decades long) categorisation of vertical price restraints as *per se* illegal; vertical price restraints must now be evaluated under the *rule of reason*.

[45] See *Palmer* v. *BRG of Ga., Inc.*, 498 US 46, 49–50 (1990) (agreements between competitors to not compete in other's territories are *per se* illegal); *United States* v. *Sealy, Inc.*, 388 US 350, 357–58 (1967) (horizontal agreements to allocate territories are unlawful and it is unnecessary to examine the restraints' justification or reasonableness).

[46] See *Broad Music, Inc.* v. *CBS*, 441 US 1, 19–20 (1979); *United States* v. *Topco Assocs., Inc.*, 405 US 596, 607–08 (1972).

[47] See *United States* v. *Wf Brinkley & Son Construction Company Inc.*, F783 F.2d 1157 54 USLW 2508, 1986–1 Trade Cases 66,963 (1986).

[48] See cases such as *FTC* v. *Ind. Fed'n. of Dentists*, 476 US 447, 458; *United States* v. *Gen. Motors Corp.*, 384 US 127, 145–46 (1966); and *Klor's, Inc.* v. *Broadway-Hale Stores, Inc.*, 359 US 207, 212 (1959) all of which demonstrate that a boycott or concerted refusal to deal by competitors are *per se* illegal.

cases with the result that the beneficial or pro-competitive effects of the situation may be overlooked and beneficial and pernicious behaviour on the part of competitors may be deterred. It is understandable therefore that US courts have emphasised the need to exercise caution before coming to the conclusion that a given situation should be labelled *per se* illegal. In *Sylvania*, for example, it was stated that 'departure from the rule-of-reason standard must be based upon demonstrable economic effect rather than ... upon formalistic line drawing'.[49] US courts also repeatedly held that following the *per se* approach is suitable where the situation 'facially appears to be one that would always or almost always tend to restrict competition and decrease output'.[50]

(c) A 'mental' element   Looking at section 1, it is clear that there is no reference to intention or the state of mind of persons whose behaviour falls within its scope. This can be considered to be a shortcoming of the provision given that it provides for criminalisation.[51] For this reason, in its pronouncements on section 1, the US Supreme Court took particular care to ensure that section 1 would not be out of line with one of the important general requirement underpinning US criminal law, namely the *mens rea* element. The Court did this by introducing a requirement of criminal intent for criminal prosecution under section 1. Such intent is determined by establishing – in the Court's words – that the 'defendant's conduct was undertaken *with knowledge* of its probable consequences'.[52] Lower courts applying section 1 have interpreted this statement by the Supreme Court to mean that, in criminal cases involving *per se* violations of the section, all that must be shown is that the defendant knowingly entered into a conspiracy to commit the offence; it is therefore not necessary to show that the defendant *intended* the actual anticompetitive effects or to unreasonably restrain trade.[53] As the Second Circuit Court of Appeals explained, in *per se* section 1

---

[49] See *Continental T.V., Inc.* v. *GTE Sylvania Inc.*, note 41 above.

[50] See *Broad. Music, Inc.* v. *CBS*, 441 US 1, 19–20 (1979); *United States* v. *Topco Assocs., Inc.*, 405 US 596, 607–8 (1972).

[51] See by comparison s. 188 of the UK Enterprise Act 2002 (providing for a criminal offence in the UK competition law regime) which refers to dishonesty.

[52] See *United States* v. *U.S. Gypsum Co.*, 438 US 422, 438–44 (1978) (emphasis added).

[53] See *United States* v. *Giordano*, 261 F.3d 1134, 1142–44 (2001); *United States* v. *Brown*, 936 F.2d 1042, 1046 (1991); and *United States* v. *Cooperative Theatres of Ohio, Inc.*, 845 F.2d 1367, 1373 (1988).

criminal cases, 'a requirement that intent go further and envision actual anticompetitive results would reopen the very questions of reasonableness which the *per se* rule is designed to avoid'.[54]

II.   Section 2: unilateral conduct and monopolisation[55]

Section 2 of the Sherman Act is an important companion to section 1 because it can catch situations which may not necessarily be possible to bring within the scope of the prohibition in the latter. Section 2 makes it unlawful for any person to 'monopolize, or attempt to monopolize, or combine or conspire with any other person or persons, to monopolize any part of the trade or commerce among the several States, or with foreign nations'. Section 2, in effect, deals with unilateral conduct amounting to an abuse of a dominant position.[56]

Traditionally, the approach followed when applying section 2 was established on the premise that once the possession of market power in a particular market was established any conduct having the purpose or effect of protecting or increasing that power was prohibited *per se*, regardless of whether the conduct was a natural consequence of the power.[57] However, the more modern approach which slowly came to emerge later was that the emphasis must be placed on the *anticompetitive effect* of the conduct and not on the mere existence of market power.[58] This means that for a position of 'monopoly' to be deemed illegal under the section, the firm concerned must have acquired or maintained this position through anticompetitive means, such as through the suppression of competition in the relevant market. Thus, situations in which the monopoly position is acquired or maintained through 'growth or development as a consequence of a superior product, business acumen, or historical accident'[59] cannot be considered to fall within the scope of the prohibition in section 2.

---

[54] *United States* v. *Koppers Co.*, 652 F.2d 290, 2 n.6 (1981).

[55] See also the discussion at pp. 268–274 below in relation to recent developments and the 'section 2 Report'.

[56] See Art. 102 of the Treaty on the Functioning of the European Union which talks about abuse of a dominant position; see p. 161 above.

[57] See *United States* v. *Aluminum Co. of America*, 148 F.2d 416, 431 (1945); the case is considered below in the context of the doctrine of extraterritoriality. See pp. 433–434 below.

[58] In this respect the position under s. 2 has been harmonised with that under equivalent provisions under competition law regimes around the world, most notably EU competition law regime.

[59] See *United States* v. *Grinnell Corp.* 384 US 563 (1966) obiter at 570–71.

(B)   The Clayton Act 1914

The Clayton Act 1914, as amended, is a civil statute and therefore provides only civil recourse for violations of its provisions. The procedure for actions initiated under the Clayton Act differs depending on which of the two enforcement authorities – the Antitrust Division or the FTC – is pursing an action within the Act's framework; this issue will be looked at in further detail below as will the provisions relating to private enforcement actions.

I.   Sections 7 and 7A: merger control[60]

Sections 7 and 7A of the Act are extremely important provisions in that they provide the tool for controlling mergers in the US competition law regime. Section 7 prohibits mergers or acquisitions that 'substantially lessen competition or tend to create a monopoly'. Before the mid-1970s, a market share based presumption of illegality was blindly employed by US competition authorities and courts in the application of section 7 but now other factors are taken into account, including efficiency enhancing consequences, with 'evidence of market concentration simply (providing) a convenient starting point for a broader inquiry into future competitiveness'.[61]

Section 7A was inserted following the reform of the Clayton Act in 1976.[62] The section introduced a requirement of mandatory pre-merger notification in the case of those merger operations meeting the thresholds stipulated in the section.[63]

II.   Section 2: discrimination

In 1936 section 2 of the Clayton Act was amended by the Robinson-Patman Act with the effect of prohibiting price discrimination that would lessen competition. Indeed the section is fairly widely referred to as the 'Robinson-Patman Act section'. The latter act is discussed below. It is worth noting here section 2(a) which prevents sellers from discriminating in price between buyers of similar 'commodities of like

---

[60] For a comprehensive examination of these sections and the US merger control regime see M. Dabbah and P. Lasok, *Merger Control Worldwide* (Cambridge University Press, 2005); also the US chapter in the second (cumulative) supplement of this work (2007).

[61] See *United States* v. *Baker Hughes, Inc* 908 F.2d 981, 984 (1990).

[62] See the Hart-Scott-Rodino Antitrust Improvements Act 1976.

[63] A recent review of the section was undertaken by the Antitrust Modernisation Commission. See further below at pp. 268–272.

grade and quality'. The prohibition therefore does not extend to services. Moreover, US courts have interpreted the provision so that it applies only to *interstate* commerce.[64] Section 2(c) extends to non-price discrimination by prohibiting the grant or receipt of gratuitous commissions and brokerage fees. Infringement of section 2 is not only the concern of sellers because section 2(f) prohibits a buyer from knowingly inducing or receiving a discriminatory price as prohibited by the section.

(C)   The Federal Trade Commission Act 1914

As noted above, the Federal Trade Commission Act created the FTC. Aside from this, however, the Act introduced an operative provision within US competition law regime – contained in section 5 of the Act – to prohibit unfair methods of competition and unfair or deceptive acts or practices in or affecting trade. Though section 5 generally covers conduct prohibited by the Sherman Act and Clayton Act, 'unfair' has in this context been defined widely by the courts to include conduct which runs counter to established public policy and may cover conduct which is not necessarily an infringement of the Sherman Act or the Clayton Act.[65] Like the Clayton Act, an infringement of section 5 does not carry any criminal penalties.

(D)   Robinson-Patman Act 1936

The legislative history of the Robinson-Patman Act had a particular flavour from the retail grocery market in the USA. The Act came to address a problem in this sector arising out of the significant market power certain large (chain) retailers enjoyed vis-à-vis the suppliers in the market which led to small retailers being placed at a competitive disadvantage compared to those large retailers. It was considered imperative therefore to compel suppliers to treat all retailers equally in order to prevent anticompetitive harm to small market operators. This became one of the main goals behind the Act. At the same time, the Act was also adopted in order to deal with a 'reverse' situation: whereby suppliers are able to *price discriminate*[66] between their buyers in a way that causes

---

[64] See *Gulf Oil Corp.* v. *Copp Paving Co., Inc.*, 419 US 186 (1974).

[65] See *Federal Trade Commission* v. *Sperry & Hutchinson Co.*, 405 US 233, 244 (1972).

[66] The prohibition on price discrimination is contained in s. 2(a) of the Act. This however does allow for justification of a 'discrimination' practice (see in addition also s. 2(b) of

competitive harm to specific rivals of the suppliers. In modern competition law context, this has become known as a foreclosure situation.[67]

The adoption of the Act has been one of the triggers in the US competition law regime of the debate on whether competition law comes to protect competition or competitors.[68] Obviously, the 'context' within which the legislative history of the Act came to flourish has been influential in forming the view that the Act has a strong social connotation and seeks to protect competitors. Such aim has been seen by many in the USA as objectionable, not only because of such social connotation but also because of the risk the Act allegedly created for protecting inefficient competitors.

The Act has not generated extensive case law in relation to the issue of price discrimination. Nonetheless, looking at the available case law one is able to see the difficulty encountered in establishing an infringement of the Act. A notable recent example is found in the case of *Volvo Trucks North America Inc.* v. *Reeder Simco GMC Inc.*[69] This was a case that arose out of a private action[70] by Reeder, a dealer of Volvo trucks in the USA against Volvo alleging discrimination by the latter: according to Reeder, Volvo offered other dealers more favourable terms and in this way it was placed at a competitive disadvantage in relation to the acceptance of bids submitted to retailers: the latter adopted the practice of soliciting bids from different dealers and they made a decision on which bid to accept following receipt of all bids (what is referred to in practice as 'competitive bidding'). In its judgment, the US Supreme Court decided that Reeder's action should fail because according to the Court under the Act it was a requirement to show that the defendant (in this case Volvo) engaged in discriminatory practices between dealers competing to resell its product to the *same retail customers*. In the Court's opinion, Reeder's claim was not founded on competition between Volvo dealers for the same retail customers and as such it was not valid under the Act.

---

the Act): on the basis that the supplier by dealing with a buyer who is offered the lower price (the favoured buyer) was able to reduce its cost.

[67] See, for example, the *Guidance paper* published by the European Commission in relation to the enforcement of Article 102 of the Treaty on the Functioning of the European Union (ex Article 82 EC), mentioned in chapter 4, at note 43.

[68] See above for a discussion of this debate.

[69] (04–905) 546 US 164 (2006) 374 F.3d 701.

[70] The Act is enforceable primarily by the FTC but private actions have also emerged over the years and have made an important contribution to building the jurisprudence on discrimination under the Act.

(E) The National Cooperative Research Act of 1984

During the mid-1980s it was felt that joint research and development projects needed to be promoted and encouraged to so as to enhance the international competitiveness of the USA, the main reason behind the shortfall of such projects considered as being the fear of prosecution should the joint venture be judged anticompetitive and the potential for private treble-damages actions. The National Cooperative Research Act, as amended, deals with these concerns by stating that all research and development joint ventures (including production joint ventures) were to be examined individually and analysed on a 'reasonableness' basis and that the amount of damages recoverable from private actions in respect of joint ventures notified to the competition law agencies would be limited to actual damages.

(F) The Export Trading Company Act 1982

Under this Act, the Secretary of Commerce, with the agreement of the Attorney General, may issue an export certificate to an association of persons who wish collectively to export goods or services from the USA provided that their actions will not likely result in a 'substantial lessening of competition or restraint of trade within the United States nor a substantial restraint of the export trade of any competitor of the applicant'. These certificates cover specific conduct and grant the recipients immunity in respect of any civil, criminal or competition law actions arising out of the specified conduct.

(G) The Local Government Antitrust Act 1984

This Act limits the remedies available to those challenging the legality of local government conduct in light of competition laws by prohibiting the recovery of monetary damages; injunctive relief is still available. It applies to the acts of 'any local government, official or employee thereof acting in an official capacity'.

(H) Hart-Scott-Rodino Antitrust Improvements Act 1976

The Act was mentioned above in the context of the discussion on the Clayton Act 1914 and the specific amendment it has made to the latter.[71]

---

[71] See p. 244 above.

(I) Antitrust Criminal Penalty Enhancement and Reform Act 2004

The Act introduced changes (upwards) to the penalties which may be imposed in the case of violations of the Sherman Act 1890. These changes were discussed in relation to the Sherman Act.[72]

(J) Antitrust Procedures and Penalties Act 1974

This Act, among other things, established avenues giving US courts a greater involvement in the conclusion of consent decrees or orders reached between US competition authorities and firms involved in situations falling within the scope of US competition rules; it also provides for increased fines in cases of infringements of the Sherman Act 1890.

(K) Webb-Pomerene Act 1918

The Act provides that associations engaged in export trade as well as agreements entered into by such associations do not come within the scope of the prohibition in the Sherman Act 1890 in so far as the situation does not produce anticompetitive effects in the USA and does not restrain the export trade of a domestic competitor of the association in question.[73] The Act operates by way of an application made by the association to the FTC for exemption.

(L) National Cooperative Research and Production Act 1993

This Act provides for the use of a *rule of reason* approach as opposed to a *per se* approach in evaluating horizontal cooperation agreements, in the form of research and development and cooperative joint ventures. Such agreements may be notified to the Department of Justice and the FTC; where this has been done the Act eliminates the possibility of treble-damages remedy[74] against the parties to the agreement in question. This means that any possible private action for recovery will be limited in terms of what may be recovered to actual damages.

---

[72] See pp. 238–239 above.   [73] Only goods, merchandise and wares are covered by the Act.
[74] See pp. 256–264 below for a discussion of the remedy and private enforcement in US competition law regime more generally.

(M) Anti-dumping Act 1916

This Act is vaguely worded. It aims to prohibit anti-dumping practices. It renders unlawful situations where a person imports or assists in importing any items into the USA and causes these to be imported or sold within the USA at a 'price substantially less than the actual market value or wholesale price of such articles, at the time of exportation to the United States, in the principal markets of the country of their production, or of other foreign countries to which they are commonly exported after adding to such market value or wholesale price, freight, duty, and other charges and expenses necessarily incident to the importation and sale thereof in the United States'. For the prohibition to apply in a given case however, one must show that the act in question was done with the intent to: destroy or injure an industry in the USA; prevent the establishment of an industry in the USA; or restrain or monopolise any part of trade and commerce in such items in the USA. An infringement of the Act is punishable by a fine and/or imprisonment.

(N) Wilson Tariff Act 1894

Section 8 of the Act prohibits situations of collusion[75] between two or more persons or corporations either of whom is engaged in 'importing any article from any foreign country into the United States' where such collusion is intended to operate in 'restraint of lawful trade or free competition in lawful trade or commerce, or to increase the market price in any part of the United States'. According to the section, such situations are declared to be contrary to public policy, illegal, and void.

(O) Tariff Act 1930

This is an 'unfair competition' Act. It includes a prohibition on 'unfair methods of competition and unfair acts' in imports into the USA. The prohibition also applies to the sale of these articles following importation, where in the situation there is a threat or effect to: 'destroy' or cause substantial injury to a local industry; prevent the establishment of such an industry; or lead to monopolisation of trade or commerce

---

[75] The section refers to 'combination, conspiracy, trust, agreement, or contract'.

in the USA.[76] The Act also contains prohibition on situations where the import involves an infringement of intellectual property rights.

Because of its declared prohibitions the Act has been considered to be controversial and it has been argued that it amounts to an infringement of WTO rules.

7. Economic 'context' and foundation in US competition law regime

As we saw in the previous chapter, in the EU competition law and policy have played a vital role in promoting the integration of the common market and the national economies of EU member states. Among other things, the use of competition law in this context has given rise to extremely heated debate on the European (and even the US) side of the Atlantic. By comparison, no such role has been played by competition law in the USA: the US economy has been fully integrated since 1789 and this renders a role of competition law for this purpose simply irrelevant. Nonetheless, the purpose and goals of competition law and policy in the USA have been debated for a long time; looking ahead, this debate is unlikely ever to see an end. On the contrary, judged on the basis of recent and current developments as well as likely future directions in relation to competition law enforcement, the debate is set to be fuelled, especially with the general economic climate in the USA, and is globally continuing to change.

The debate mentioned in the previous paragraph has been largely economics-based. Over the years, many theories have come to be developed advocating the use of a particular type of economic approach and thinking in the field of competition law; some of these theories even extended to fundamental questions concerning intervention in the marketplace and the goals of competition law. Two main schools of thought however have dominated the debate, namely the Chicago school and the Harvard school. Although based on 'theories', the influence of these two schools of thought, especially the former has been anything but theoretical: in applying US competition law, US courts have over the years delivered judgments interpreting the competition rules in a manner and tone that have revealed the influence of 'current' economic thinking during the relevant time in these judgments. This

---

[76] See s. 337 of the Act.

observation is also very possible to make in relation to the practice of US competition authorities. Interestingly, it can be said that the majority, if not all, of US judges, competition officials and even practitioners and academics are mentally oriented in a way that shows them extremely committed to identifying everything they do or say in their line of work with a particular school of thought with a particular desire to show consistency in following such school of thought under all circumstances: arguably this reveals a notable degree of conservatism and not quite a liberal approach because they are not particularly open to suggestions that situations may arise which may disturb the pattern supplied by and followed under a particular school of law because in the circumstances of these situations the foundations of another school of thought would be more appropriate to follow.[77] Beyond US boundaries, one can also see the influence of the Chicago school of thought in competition law regimes around the world: the interpretation given to competition rules and the approach followed when enforcing these rules in many regimes clearly shows that the relevant competition authorities and courts follow this school of thought and its teachings. Indeed, the Chicago school of thought has been a great American product used almost globally.

In the discussion below, we will consider the Harvard and Chicago schools of thought.

(A) The Harvard school

The Harvard school of thought is based on a 'structuralist' approach[78] to competition law and its enforcement. The influence of this school of thought was particularly prominent in the application of US competition laws from approximately around the mid-twentieth century and it lasted until the 1970s. This can be seen from the interventionist attitude on the part of US competition authorities during that time and the heavy use of the *per se* approach to the application of the competition

---

[77] A good example that could be used to illustrate this is the debate over whether competition is a means or an end and the 'supremacy' of consumer welfare as a standard; see above. Arguably, one of the things that the recent global economic crisis showed was how a 'traditional' approach pushing for consumer welfare and emphasising competition is not probably always sound to adopt and that goals such as research and development should be equally sought in appropriate cases.

[78] Under this approach, the focus is on the structure of the market and industry. See in this regard the reference by the European Court of Justice in its recent landmark judgment in Case C-501/06, *GlaxoSmithKline Services* v. *Commission* to the structure of the market and the need to protect it; see chapter 1 above, at note 73.

rules with little regard to consumer welfare. In following a structuralist approach, the emphasis was put on the structure of the relevant market or industry as the main criterion in determining how likely anticompetitive behaviour is in the relevant market. For example, it was considered that the more concentrated the market is – i.e. among other things, the fewer the number of firms operating in this market – the higher the likelihood that the firms in question will engage in anticompetitive behaviour (such as through collusion). Markets which present such structural problems therefore were considered to provide fertile grounds for firms operating in them to exercise market power in a way that would help them maximise their personal profits. Essentially therefore the model on which the school of thought was based is that you could not rely on the market itself to deliver without adequate intervention by public authorities. Thus, in the absence of proper intervention market failure was considered to be inevitable.[79]

The Harvard school of thought attached considerable importance to legislative intent behind the Sherman Act 1890 and the Clayton Act 1914. Its followers relied quite heavily on what they considered to be Congress' sole purpose behind adopting competition law in the USA: namely, the need to combat the growing economic and political power of large market players, such as the United States Steel Corporation (which controlled two-thirds of steel production in the early-twentieth century and prided itself on its size rather than its efficiency or power of innovation). Heavy intervention in the marketplace – which the school advocated – was something which Harvard scholars considered Congress *intended* in passing first the Sherman Act and later the Clayton Act. One of the slogans used by the school was that the goal of competition law was to protect competitors and not competition. It considered that this was the interpretation that should be followed in light of the broad language used in the law and the risk to small and medium-size firms raised by the existence of economic power enjoyed by their larger competitors.[80] In following this line of thinking and reasoning, it was considered to be vital to employ competition law to regulate the economic power of big firms in the market and even to restrict the growth of such firms; no attention was given to the benefit consumers may enjoy in this case.

---

[79] See pp. 11–12 above for a discussion of the concept and phenomenon of market failure.
[80] See T. Dilorenzo, 'The Origins of Antitrust: an Interest-Group Perspective' (1985) *International Review of Law and Economics* 73.

As noted above, the Harvard school of law enjoyed influence during one of the crucial times of the twentieth century and its impact on judicial approach and thinking in some of the leading cases delivered by US courts around that time was clearly evident. A notable case in this regard is *United States* v. *Aluminium Company of America* (*Alcoa*), which is considered in the context of the doctrine of extraterritoriality in chapter 8 below.[81] In the case, the court found that the firm breached section 2 of the Sherman Act 1890 because it used its market power to engage in *aggressive* competition. In the relevant market, this resulted in an increased choice of products and lowering prices for consumers! In *Brown Shoe Co.* v. *United States*[82] the Supreme Court prohibited a merger under section 7 of the Clayton Act 1914 between two shoe manufactures stating that the paramount issue in the case was to protect small businesses against potential abuses of power by larger firms, despite acknowledging that the merger would allow the firms to 'market their own brands at prices below those of competing independent retailers'. It is highly arguable that this particular statement by the Supreme Court points rather unquestionably to the influence of the Harvard school even outside the boundaries of the Sherman Act 1890: as noted, this was a merger case decided under the Clayton Act 1914.

(B) The Chicago school

The influence of the Harvard school of thought – as outlined in the previous section – began to see an end by the late 1960s. One of the major factors leading to this was the perceived disparity in the application of competition laws arising out of the Harvard school approach. In particular, it was considered to be unsatisfactory that the approach effectively meant that the conduct of a firm with lower market shares would be permissible but that same conduct if performed by a firm with more market power would not without sufficient attention being given to the conduct itself to see whether in fact it was competition enhancing. Moreover, the approach was considered to have resulted in a highly undesirable deterrent effect on firms engaging in aggressive competition. Such factors among others resulted in discontent with the Harvard model and the ground was set for the Chicago school of thought to take root.[83]

---

[81] See pp. 433–434 below.   [82] 370 US 294 (1962).
[83] Some would attribute the rise of Chicago itself to the demise of Harvard.

The Chicago school of thought developed on foundations, which could not be more different from those on which the Harvard school of thought flourished. As a result, the approach and ideology advocated by the two schools of thought 'clashed' on a number of important fronts. At a basic level, Chicago scholars contended that the main purpose behind competition law was to increase the efficiency rather than to protect individual – small and medium-size – competitors against the exercise of market power by large firms. One particularly prominent Chicago scholar was Robert Bork whose work helped expand the influence of the school both within and outside the USA.[84] Economic efficiency according to Bork and his fellow Chicago scholars should be defined in terms of wealth maximisation. Because of the emphasis being put on economic efficiency, it was considered that the attention when applying the competition rules should be given to protecting competition because it was thought that through this 'consumer welfare' was possible to achieve, namely lower prices, better quality and more choice.[85] As noted in chapter 1, Bork believed that the only legitimate goal of competition law was the maximisation of consumer welfare; no other possible goals of competition law were relevant.[86]

Another front on which the Chicago school of thought came to clash with the Harvard school of thought was the question of intervention in the marketplace. Chicago scholars saw no validity in the Harvard thinking that unless intervention by public authorities in the market occurs, market failure was bound to occur. The Chicago school contended that actually markets can be relied on to deliver important benefits to consumers and that intervention should occur only in exceptional cases, when market failure occurs.[87] In supporting their theory Chicago scholars developed (arguably highly questionable!) assumptions that consumers are able to make rational choices when choosing their own course of action with regard to what product to buy and what price to pay for it and that they enjoy sufficient information for this purpose.

---

[84] See pp. 27–28 above.

[85] As we saw in chapter 1, a consumer welfare standard is distinguished from a total welfare standard. It is worth noting however that there is not quite complete consensus that what the Chicago school of thought advocated was strictly speaking a consumer welfare standard; see E. Fox and L. A. Sullivan, 'Antitrust – Retrospective and Prospective: Where are We Coming From? Where are We Going?' (1987) 62 *New York University Law Review* 936.

[86] See chapter 1, at note 68 and accompanying text.

[87] See E. Fox, 'The Battle for the Soul of Antitrust' (1987) *California Law Review* 917.

The influence of the Chicago school of thought reached an extremely high degree of prominence in a relatively short period of time due to the prominence achieved by its scholars, most notably Bork, as can be seen from his appointment as a judge. Furthermore, one cannot ignore the global reach the school came to acquire in competition law regimes as noted above. Little wonder therefore that the Chicago school brought about a transformation of US competition law regime which is most evident in the shift in judicial attitude and the move away from the *per se* approach and presumption of illegality towards the *rule of reason* approach. This in practice meant that the focus had come to be put not on the mere existence of economic power but on the use of this power and whether the behaviour or conduct in this case is harmful or beneficial. It is crucial to bear in mind however that although the Harvard school has seen its demise with the rise of the Chicago school, this does not mean that the *per se* approach itself has no place in US competition law. There are cases in which a *per se* approach would be justified, most notably those of hardcore cartels. Furthermore, it cannot be said that a 'structuralist' approach has no role to play. The structure of the market, including the important issue of concentration, is of fundamental importance in competition law analysis as can be seen most notably in merger analysis; nonetheless this analysis does not rest on unjustified presumptions as those on which the Harvard school is based.

(C) Comment

As can be seen from the above discussion, the Harvard school of thought was considered to suffer from some serious drawbacks, which in the eyes of many people meant that the school was out of touch with reality and as such had no place in the 'modern' field of competition law. Nevertheless, the school has been considered to have made one particular notable contribution, which some people consider gives it an advantage over Chicago school of thought: the Harvard school is considered to have provided *certainty* for firms with regard to how the competition rules are likely to be applied in a given situation and the *ability* for the courts to use presumptions of illegality. The Chicago school by contrast is considered to have made the task of courts – whether the judges or juries – and the competition authorities much harder because it placed the task of deciding complex economic issues through the application of the *rule of reason* at the heart of the application of US competition law. In the eyes of some people therefore the shift from Harvard to Chicago led to a loss of certainty and this has been said to have reduced the deterrent effect of the competition rules. Obviously, all this is a matter of argument and there is no sufficient evidence that has been relied on in practice to support such points. At their best therefore such arguments show that Chicago school is not immune from criticism which is a valid proposition especially when one considers the heavy reliance on occasion by the school on too much theorising and use of assumptions.[88]

8.   The 'other' context: the role of politics

The economic context of US competition law has been extremely obvious and has become extremely dominant over the years in the discourse in the US competition law regime. Nonetheless, the regime does not exclusively have an economic context: it is important to be aware of another crucial context, namely the political context of the regime. Politics in the field of competition law in the USA does play a major role: whether in the *legislative process* or *enforcement actions* taken by US competition authorities. In relation to the *former*, one must bear in mind that it was to fight the trusts phenomenon, break up powerful firms and monopolies such as Standard Oil and US Steel monopolies that the various US competition laws were passed. In relation to the *latter*, one can usually use the type of Administration in Washington DC and political 'setting' in Congress as a highly reliable yardstick to predict how effective or relaxed enforcement is likely to be for a period of four or eight years, i.e. the *guaranteed* or *possible* length of time of an Administration.[89]

9.   Private enforcement

One of the major characteristics of US competition law regime is its reliance on private enforcement of the rules in relation to which the USA has a long history. Private actions in the field of competition law are considered to be an integral part of competition law enforcement and

---

[88] See, for example, the use of three assumptions mentioned above and the 'theorising' discussed in chapter 1.

[89] See pp. 272–273 below with regard to the withdrawal by the 'section 2 of the Sherman Act 1890 report' from the Bush administration era by the new head of the Antitrust Division under the Obama administration.

they have been consistently encouraged by US competition authorities and courts. Obviously, the fact that the regime features judicial enforcement and the fact that a litigation culture prevails in the US legal system as a whole with the relevant procedural rules (including those dealing with contingency fees and class actions)[90] have helped enormously in developing a private enforcement mechanism in the field of competition law. This point is worth emphasising because of the difficulty in establishing a viable tool of private enforcement.[91]

The reliance on private actions in the US competition law regime as both an independent strand of competition enforcement and a supplementary tool to public enforcement in the regime has on the whole been considered as a positive development carrying considerable advantages, whether in terms of relieving the burden on the Antitrust Division in particular or providing those who suffer competition harm with an avenue to seek compensation[92] or offering redress to a wrong (especially where the relevant competition authority chooses not to investigate the situation). At the same time however this reliance has raised some fundamental questions about possible negative 'side-effects', most notably the risk of seriously undermining the deterrent effect of enforcement within the regime given that guilty firms may end up settling cases with potential plaintiffs and thus avoid litigation in court and the risk of high damages, including treble-damages awards.[93] Undermining deterrence within the regime has been considered to be a serious matter because of the potential risk inherent in it of discrediting the regime. This no doubt is a serious point calling for careful assessment. To some extent the Antitrust Modernisation Commission dealt with this point in its Report. The Commission concluded that deterrent effect and ability to directly compensate victims of anticompetitive situations worked well in private enforcement though it did suggest a legislative improvement to improve the mechanism further.[94]

---

[90] See pp. 261–263 below.

[91] See, for example, the European Commission's experience in relation to this topic which was discussed at p. 198 above.

[92] Obviously public enforcement – however effective and regardless of the type of penalties it leads to, whether financial or otherwise – does not compensate those who suffer harm as a result of anticompetitive behaviour or conduct.

[93] See pp. 258–260 below.

[94] The Commission recommended in its report, among other things, the adoption of a law that would apply to all competition cases, which involve joint and several liability which would allow non-settling defendants to obtain a reduction of the plaintiffs' claims equal to the amount of the settlement or the allocated share of liability of those defendants who

Four different issues are worth discussion when dealing with private enforcement under US competition law regimes: damages claims; injunctions; class actions; and limitation periods.

(A) Damages claims

First, damages actions are possible under US competition law by virtue of section 4 of the Clayton Act 1914 which gives private parties who have suffered loss due to a competition law infringement the power to launch such actions in federal courts. This in effect is the treble-damages remedy: plaintiffs are able to bring actions against the offending firm(s) and obtain three times their actual damages; damages are automatically trebled under section 4. Claimants in damages actions may also recover their court fees.[95]

A major goal behind the section 4 enforcement mechanism was to create – what is widely referred to among US competition specialists – 'private attorneys general' in order to achieve the very purpose behind private enforcement as outlined above, namely enhancing and supplementing the whole enforcement within the US competition law regime and offer victims of competition law infringements a proper tool to seek redress. Actions under sections may be launched by 'any person', a term interpreted widely to include: firms; associations[96] existing under or authorised by US law or the laws of any US territories as well as the laws of any state or any foreign country. However, potential claimants under the section must show that they suffered actual injury in their 'business or property'. Such injury includes pecuniary losses from paying a price for goods or services that was artificially inflated by the anti-competitive behaviour or conduct.[97] It can also include injury to a non-existing business, which is at a planning stage, provided there is clear evidence of intent, capability and sufficient resources to become operational, i.e. to enter the market.[98] It is worth noting the judgment of the

---

do settle, whichever is higher. See chapter 3 of the Commission Report, *Civil and Criminal Remedies*.

[95] See pp. 490–493 below in the context of the doctrine of extraterritoriality for an account on the treble damages doctrine, especially how it is perceived around the world.

[96] See *Cates* v. *IT&T*, 756 F.2d 1161, 1173 (1985); *Coast* v. *Hunt Oil Co.*, 195 F.2d 870 (1952).

[97] See *Reiter* v. *Sonotone Corp.*, 442 US 330, 339 (1979).

[98] See *Grip-Pak, Inc.* v. *Ill. Tool Works, Inc.*, 694 F.2d 466, 475 (1982); *Martin* v. *Phillips Petroleum Co.*, 365 F.2d 629, 633 (1966); *Arista Records LLC* v. *Lime Group LLC*, 532 F. Supp. 2d 556, 568 n.13 (2007).

US Supreme Court in *Brunswick Corp*[99] which offers a definition of the term 'injury' in this context. According to the Supreme Court, the term should be understood as 'injury of the type the competition laws were intended to prevent and that flows from that which makes defendants' acts unlawful'.[100] This means in practice that injury for the purposes of section 4 must be caused by behaviour, conduct or any other situation prohibited under US competition law. This crucial requirement under the section can be seen to be made of two sub-requirements: the requirement that the claimant must show both that the competition law infringement was a material cause of the harm suffered;[101] *and* the requirement that the claimant suffered an injury in the circumstances. Essentially therefore this means that the general rule that actions may be started by 'any person' is not quite accurate because in practice not every 'person' can enjoy standing to bring and succeed in a private action for damages under the US competition law regime. Over the years, three categories of persons nonetheless have been established to have standing and they offer examples of typical situations in which section 4 actions are likely to benefit from admissibility: first, customers of firms engaging in cartel activities who are considered to be most likely persons to suffer injury from such activities as a result of, for example, increased prices;[102] secondly, competitors may be granted standing when they challenge conduct that reduced competition by excluding them from the market (situations of anticompetitive foreclosure);[103] thirdly, suppliers have been granted standing when they challenged a buying cartel's anti-competitive conduct that resulted in depressed prices for the suppliers' goods or services.[104] Beyond these recognised categories, the question of standing under section 4 is highly debatable and at best is surrounded

---

[99] See *Brunswick Corp.* v. *Pueblo Bowl-O-Mat, Inc.*, 429 US 477 (1977).

[100] Ibid. at 489.

[101] See *Zenith Radio Corp.* v. *Hazeltine Research, Inc.*, 395 US 100, 114 n.9 (1969); *Blue Tree Hotels Inv., Ltd.* v. *Starwood Hotels & Resorts Worldwide, Inc.*, 369 F.3d 212, 220 (2004); *Maddaloni Jewelers, Inc.* v. *Rolex Watch U.S.A., Inc.*, 354 F. Supp. 2d 293, 306 (2004).

[102] See *Atl. Richfield Co.* v. *USA Petroleum Co.*, 495 US 328, 334 (1990).

[103] See *Matsushita Elec. Indus. Co.* v. *Zenith Radio Corp.*, 475 US 574, 586 (1986) which concerned a predatory pricing conspiracy.

[104] *See Knevelbaard Dairies* v. *Kraft Foods, Inc.*, 232 F.3d 979 (2000); *Int'l Casings Group, Inc.* v. *Premium Standard Farms, Inc.*, NO. 04–1081-CV-W-NKL, 2005 WL 2319834, (2005). Outside this context however suppliers to market participants have trouble bringing competition law claims because their injuries are considered too secondary and indirect to amount to an 'injury' in this case; see *Serfecz* v. *Jewel Food Stores*, 67 F.3d 591, 597 (1995).

with ambiguity. A highly notable example of how this is so is furnished by 'indirect purchasers', namely those who did not purchase directly from the defendant(s). In a major ruling by the US Supreme Court in the case of *Illinois Brick Co. v. Illinois*,[105] it was held that indirect purchasers do not have standing to bring damages claims for illegal overcharges allegedly passed on to them through the distribution chain. In this case, the Court felt that to rule otherwise would invite seriously undesirable and adverse consequences. In particular the Supreme Court was concerned about: first, the risk that actions by indirect purchasers would expose defendants to multiple liability from claimants at different levels of the distribution chain; secondly, the risk that permitting recovery by indirect purchasers would 'transform treble-damages actions into massive efforts to apportion the recovery among all potential plaintiffs that could have absorbed part of the overcharge from direct purchasers to middlemen to ultimate consumers'; and thirdly, the desirability and need for enhancing effectiveness of competition law enforcement 'by concentrating the full recovery for the overcharge in the direct purchasers rather than allowing every plaintiff potentially affected by the overcharge to sue only for the amount it could show was absorbed'.[106] This ruling of the Supreme Court has not been particularly welcomed and it has triggered different responses seeking to limit its effect. Notably, lower federal courts have created exceptions[107] to the ruling enunciated and a number of states passed what are known as 'Illinois Brick-repealer statutes', which expressly grant indirect purchasers standing to bring section 4 actions. In addition, some state courts have held that the ruling in *Illinois Brick* does not apply to their states' laws. Currently, roughly half the states, including New York and California, permit indirect purchasers some cause of action for damages.[108]

(B) Injunctions

The second strand of private enforcement under US competition law regime is found in section 16 of the Clayton Act 1914 which offers an equitable remedy for relief. The section provides that '(a)ny person,

---

[105] 431 US 720 (1977).   [106] See paras. 730–741 of the judgment.

[107] Namely, the cost-plus contract, the ownership or control exception, and the co-conspirator exception. However, the Supreme Court has never approved these exceptions, and they have been applied sparingly.

[108] Interestingly, the Antitrust Modernisation Commission recommended that the ruling in *Illinois Brick* be overruled; see the Commission's report, pp. 267–70.

firm, corporation or association shall be entitled to sue for and have injunctive relief ... against threatened loss or damage by a violation of the antitrust laws ... when and under the same conditions and principles as injunctive relief against threatened conduct that will cause loss or damage is granted by courts of equity'. In order to launch an action seeking an injunction under section 16, the claimant must have standing. The issue of standing in this case has been understood on the whole along the lines of the issue of standing under section 4 of the Clayton Act 1914[109] in the context of damages actions with one significant difference however: under section 16 there is no requirement for a claimant to show that it has suffered actual injury. In line with the particular wording of the section, such claimant need only demonstrate the existence of a significant threat of injury from an impending infringement of the competition rules or from a current infringement that is likely to continue to occur.[110] Whilst this section 16 creates a broader framework within which to launch private actions, it is important to note that relief given under the section must be narrowly tailored to address the egregious conduct, and should not be so broad as to inhibit legitimate behaviour or conduct. This means that an injunction should be based on significant *causal link* between the competition law infringement and the enjoined conduct.[111] It is not enough simply to require that the defendant comply with the competition laws:[112] a proper injunction should identify specific prohibited behaviour or conduct.[113]

(C) Class actions

Class actions represent a third (significant) strand of private enforcement under US competition law regime. These actions are governed under rule 23 of the *Federal Rules of Civil Procedure* which provides for *certification* of class actions. For a class to be certified under rule 23, it must be shown that the action:

---

[109] See above.

[110] See *Zenith Radio Corp.*, 395 US at 130; *In re Warfarin Sodium Antitrust Litig.*, 214 F.3d 395, 399 (2000).

[111] See *In re Microsoft Antitrust Litig.*, 333 F.3d 517, 533 (2003); *Berkey Photo, Inc.* v. *Eastman Kodak Co.*, 603 F.2d 263, 292–93 (1979).

[112] See *Hartford-Empire Co.* v. *United States*, 323 US 386, 410 (1945).

[113] See *Pub. Interest Research Group of N.J., Inc.* v. *Powell Duffryn Terminals Inc.*, 913 F.2d 64, 82–83 (1990).

- *first*, is 'so numerous that joinder of all members is impracticable':[114] there is no specific number of class members needed to meet this requirement though proposed classes exceeding 40 members are usually sufficient;[115]
- *secondly*, involves 'questions of law or fact common to the class';[116]
- *thirdly*, the claims and defences of the class *representatives* must be typical of the claims or defences of the class:[117] a class representative's claim is generally considered typical 'when it is alleged that the same unlawful conduct was directed at or affected both the named plaintiff and the class sought to be represented';[118] and
- *fourthly*, the class representative must 'fairly and adequately protect the interests of the class'.[119] When determining the question of adequacy and fairness, considerations must be had of the qualification and experience of the attorney representing the claimant (including the ability to litigate the matter in question) *and* whether the claimant has interests antagonistic to those of the class.[120]

It is not uncommon, nor unheard of that members of a proposed class action possess competing interests with respect to the relief sought;[121] in practice this is an issue which arises quite frequently.[122] This may raise a particular issue in the face of certification of a class. It is worth noting rule 23(b) here, in particular paragraphs 2 and 3. Under the former paragraph, certification of a class is possible in the case of actions seeking injunctive relief (discussed in the previous section) where this is appropriate. A key issue in addressing the appropriateness of class certification under the paragraph is whether an injunctive class is appropriate in cases seeking primarily monetary relief. US courts however are in disagreement on this issue. Some courts have resolved the issue by certifying a class action under the paragraph with respect to the requested injunctive relief only whilst using paragraph 3 of rule

---

[114] Fed. R. Civ. p. 23(a)(1).   [115] See *Stewart* v. *Abraham*, 275 F.3d 220, 226–27 (2001).

[116] See r. 23(a)(2).   [117] See r. 23(a)(3).

[118] *In re Data Access Sys. Sec. Litig.*, 103 F.R.D. 130, 139 (1984).   [119] See r. 23(a)(4).

[120] *Jones* v. *United Gas Improvement Corp.*, 68 F.R.D. 1, 21 (1975). The evaluation of class counsel under r. 23(a) was supplemented by the addition of r. 23(g) in 2003. The latter rule is intended to guide the court in assessing proposed class counsel as part of the certification (of the class) decision.

[121] There is an abundance of examples of this situation in the case law. See *Amchem Prods., Inc.* v. *Windsor*, 521 US 591, 626–27 (1997); *Bradburn Parent/Teacher Store, Inc.* v. *3M*, No. Civ. A. 02–7676, 2004 WL 414047, at *9 (2004); *Telecomm Tech. Servs., Inc.* v. *Siemens Rolm Commc'ns, Inc.*, 172 F.R.D. 532, 544–45 (1997).

[122] *S. Snack Foods, Inc.* v. *J & J Snack Foods Corp.*, 79 F.R.D. 678, 680 (1978).

23(b) for certification of class actions for damages.[123] Paragraph 3 allows the aggregating of a large number of small damages actions that would not be economical to bring as individual actions. A class may be certified under the paragraph where the requirements mentioned above are met and in the circumstances questions of law or fact common to class members outweigh those questions affecting only individual members *and* a class action is the superior method for fairly and efficiently resolving the case at hand. This means that in these cases there is a common thread running through the entire class.

(D) Limitation period

The final strand of private enforcement of US competition law that should be discussed concerns the issue of limitation period. Section 4B of the Clayton Act 1914 establishes a four-year limitation period for private actions.[124] A limitation period typically begins to run when the claimant suffers an injury caused by a competition law infringement.[125] This should not be considered to be a rule that is set in stone however given that there are three specific situations in which the running of the limitation period can be 'tolled' for 'equitable' reasons. First, under the doctrine of fraudulent concealment, the limitation period may be tolled where the defendant wrongfully concealed the infringement in question and it would not have been possible to uncover the infringement through an exercise of reasonable diligence.[126] Secondly, the limitation period may also be tolled by launching a class action given that in such cases, there will be – in the words of the Supreme Court[127] – a suspension of 'the applicable statute of limitations as to all asserted members of the class'.[128] The rule on suspension aims at preserving the efficiency and economy of litigation created by class actions. Thirdly, the limitation period may be tolled under section 5(i) of the Clayton Act 1914 where civil and criminal actions brought by

---

[123] See *Jefferson* v. *Ingersoll Int'l, Inc.*, 195 F.3d 894, 899 (1999); *Seawell* v. *Universal Fid. Corp.*, 235 F.R.D. 64, 67 (2006).

[124] 15 USC § 15b.

[125] See *Zenith Radio Corp.* v. *Hazeltine Research, Inc.*, 401 US 321, 338 (1971); *In re Nine West Shoes Antitrust Litig.*, 80 F. Supp. 2d 181, 191 (2000).

[126] See *Kan. City* v. *Fed. Pac. Elec. Co.*, 310 F.2d 271, 277 (1962); *Nine West*, 80 F. Supp. 2d at 192.

[127] *American Pipe & Construction Co.* v. *Utah* 414 US 538 (1974).

[128] *Ibid.* at 554; *see also Arneil* v. *Ramsey*, 550 F.2d 774, 782 (1977).

the Antitrust Division or the FTC are pending. For this to occur however there must be an *actual* civil or criminal action[129] which is brought by the Antitrust Division or the FTC to prevent, restrain or punish an infringement of US competition law and the private action in the case *must be based* in whole or in part in the action brought by the authorities. When these criteria are met, the limitation period will be suspended for up to one year following the conclusion of the action by the authorities.

10.   International outlook

Like the EU competition law regime, the US competition law regime too has come to feature an international outlook, created by US competition authorities, courts, Congress and to some extent the government. Notable similarities can be identified between the two regimes, specifically the fact that both regimes have developed a strong extraterritorial dimension for assertion of jurisdictions in situations extending beyond their 'geographical' boundaries and the fact that they have converged in the importance they attach to bilateral cooperation – especially as a means of extending their influence.[130] Both of these points will be discussed below and the EU and US perspectives will be examined in detail.[131] At the same time however, major differences in outlook have come to emerge between these two regimes. The present part will consider the US perspective on a number of issues; the EU perspective was considered in the previous chapter.

(A)   Multilateralism

The USA has not shared the EU's huge enthusiasm for pursuing multilateral cooperation on the basis of binding commitments. US competition authorities in particular have on occasions shown a certain

---

[129] The term proceeding for this purpose does not cover investigations conducted by the authorities; see *SCM Corp.* v. *Xerox Corp.*, 463 F. Supp. 983, 987 n.7 (1978).

[130] See p. 293 above in relation to the EU–US rivalry; also chapter 9 below in relation to the use of bilateral cooperation for this purpose.

[131] Chapter 8 considers the doctrine of extraterritoriality and chapter 9 deals with bilateral cooperation. It is important to note however that whilst the reference here is to 'similarities', as we shall see the two regimes have differed in their 'approach' – see in particular in relation to the US 'effects' doctrine and EU 'implementation' doctrine in the context of extraterritorial assertion of jurisdictions.

degree of scepticism over the real value of even debating such an option because the fairly consistent approach which has been followed by them over the years is that the competition law community around the world has not reached the stage where one could regard such an option as really viable or necessary. As noted in other places in the book,[132] US competition authorities have objected to the EU's push towards building a competition agenda within the WTO, though some (short-lived) signals indicating a different line of thinking in the US approach appeared at around the time of the WTO Doha round in 2001.[133]

The US objections to concluding binding multilateral agreement or rules in the field of competition law have been grounded in its concerns over 'limitation' of sovereignty which is bound to result from signing up to such agreement or rules; what has on occasions even been considered to amount to a 'loss' of sovereignty.[134] On the other hand, one ought to highlight the strength of the US competition law regime and the overall success of Congress, the courts and the competition authorities in building a strong international enforcement dimension within the regime through heavy reliance on the doctrine of extraterritoriality; this particular strategy has been 'complemented' by US competition authorities developing some extensive bilateral links with major trading partners and allies. In this way, the regime has been seen as fully equipped to deal with all competition problems likely to face US consumers, producers and the economy as a whole; something that has rendered a binding multilateral option unnecessary.

US competition authorities however have not dismissed the multilateral option in its entirety. As we saw in chapter 2, they were among the founders of the International Competition Network and its multilateral approach of non-binding commitments and major sponsors of its work though they have not shown an equal enthusiasm towards UNCTAD's same approach of non-binding commitments. The USA has also been an active contributor within the OECD work and deliberations. In these two particular respects, US competition authorities can be said to have made an important contribution to the policy debate in the international competition law scene.

---

[132] See p. 129 above and pp. 556–557 below.   [133] See p. 557 above.

[134] See pp. 89–92 above for a discussion on the issue of sovereignty and the variants of 'limitation' and 'loss' of it.

(B) Free trade agreements

The USA has entered into a number of key free trade agreements, within which competition law is very prominent. This includes most notably the (trilateral) North America Free Trade Agreement (NAFTA) which is discussed in chapter 7.[135] Important bilateral free trade agreements worth mentioning include the US–Singapore agreement[136] which was extremely influential towards Singapore adopting a specific competition law domestically.

(C) An integrated competition-trade approach

Some components of the international dimension of US competition law regime show that there has been a 'link' established between competition policy and trade policy. In particular, an integrated – competition-trade – approach has arguably been opted into on occasions to deal with competition problems facing US firms in foreign markets. A high-profile case demonstrating this is the *Kodak/Fuji* dispute (which involved an action by the USA against Japan before the WTO because of alleged harm suffered by Kodak as a result of Fuji's alleged anticompetitive conduct);[137] another illustration can be found under section 301 of the Trade Act 1974.[138]

In November 1997, then US Attorney General Reno, and then Assistant Attorney General for Antitrust Klein formed a special committee of experts, the International Competition Policy Advisory Committee (ICPAC), to examine what new tools and concepts were needed to address competition policy issues that were appearing on the horizon in the global economy. An important part of ICPAC's work was devoted to the question of whether an integrated competition-trade approach is a viable option to consider for dealing with all competition problems in the global economy. In its final report (which was produced in February 2000) however, whilst ICPAC evaluated the available approaches under competition policy and trade policy to deal with such problems it concluded at the end that no particular approach is appropriate to respond to all international competition problems,

---

[135] See p. 403 below. NAFTA is not the only 'regional' agreement that can be mentioned: the USA is also party to the Asia-Pacific Economic Community (APEC); see pp. 396–397 below.

[136] The agreement was concluded on 6 May 2003; it entered into force on 1 January 2004.

[137] See pp. 609–614 below.   [138] See pp. 616–620 below.

especially those facing US firms beyond US boundaries. Specifically, ICPAC argued against applying the trade methodology when dealing with conduct, behaviour or transactions of firms beyond US borders: ICPAC stated doing so creates a risk that firms operating within the USA and others in foreign markets will be subjected to different standards with the consequence being adverse for the latter; this was seen as something liable to trigger parallel actions by other countries, something that US firms were considered to be highly likely to suffer from.

(D)   The FTC's international programme

The FTC operates a highly sophisticated international programme in the field of competition law. The programme has a number of objectives including: supporting the international enforcement efforts of the FTC; enhancing bilateral cooperation; and facilitating convergence in the field especially in policy approaches for the purposes of developing best practices. The programme has deep roots extending to 1982 when an International Antitrust Division was established within the FTC Bureau of Competition; this Division was replaced in 2007 by the Office of International Affairs.

Additionally, the FTC (and the Antitrust Division) engages in extensive technical assistance activities.[139] As noted in chapter 3 above, technical assistance and capacity-building programmes are very expensive. The FTC has for the past two years self-funded its technical assistance activities but it has also received funding from the federal government, in particular from the US Agency for International Development (USAID). FTC's provision of technical assistance is directed at competition authorities with young experience in the field of competition law. Among the countries which have benefited from FTC technical assistance activities in recent years are: China, Egypt, India, Mexico, Peru and South Africa. Within these activities, FTC officials may spend a few months in the host competition authority for the purposes of training officials at the latter[140] *and* officials of foreign competition authorities may spend time at the FTC as international fellows or international interns observing how the FTC conducts its work so they can gain a valuable insight into competition enforcement

---

[139] In its recommendations, the Antitrust Modernisation Commission showed support for technical assistance activities and recommended their continuation.

[140] This is also something which Antitrust Division officials are engaged in.

which can be extremely useful to them when they return to their home competition authorities.[141] In recent years, competition authorities from over ten countries have sent officials to the FTC and FTC officials have visited many young competition authorities; in addition to spending time at leading competition authorities (most notably the European Commission) as part of the staff exchange programme between the two.

(E)   Department of Commerce's contribution

The Department of Commerce – through its Commercial Law Development Programme[142] – has been engaged in sponsoring foreign competition officials so they can attend competition law conferences and events around the world. It has also collaborated with foreign governments for the purposes of facilitating the provision of technical assistance to competition authorities in these foreign jurisdictions and holding joint events and programmes. A notable beneficiary of these activities in recent years has been the Egyptian Competition Authority.

11.   Some recent developments

The competition law scene in the USA has witnessed some interesting developments on the policy front in recent years. Out of these, it is worth noting the work of the Antitrust Modernisation Commission, the change in Administration in Washington DC and the recent work begun on revising the *Horizontal Merger Guidelines* (1992).

(A)   The Antitrust Modernisation Commission

I.   General

The Antitrust Modernisation Commission (AMC) was formed by the US Congress in 2004 pursuant to the Antitrust Modernisation Commission Act of 2002 to examine whether US competition laws were in need of an overhaul and what changes could be made to the

---

[141] Such hosting of foreign officials has been made possible by the US SAFE WEB Act 2006.

[142] Full details about the programme and specific competition activities within it are available at: www.cldp.doc.gov.

current regime should a modernisation of the rules be needed.[143] The Commission consisted of a total of 12 members with the President, Senate and House of Representatives each appointing four. After three years of meetings and hearing views from interested parties the Commission delivered the *Antitrust Modernisation Commission Report and Recommendations* in April 2007.[144]

As noted in the Report, the impetus behind the formation of the AMC was the recognition by Congress that in the twenty-first century competition 'increasingly involves innovation, intellectual property, technological change, and global trade' and the acknowledgement that current competition laws in the USA may need to evolve alongside the evolving nature of competition to remain effective. However, as the parameters of the AMC's work extended to assessing, in general, current competition laws and policy the AMC also evaluated the effectiveness of dual federal enforcement – meaning by the Antitrust Division and the FTC – by using merger control as a good case study.

II. The problems and advantages of dual enforcement

The existence of more than one competition authority – which operate in parallel as the case in the USA as opposed to ones which carry different function and are complementary as the case in the UK[145] – in a competition law regime is often considered to offer a near perfect recipe for difficulties. Many observers of the US competition law regime have not infrequently argued that the involvement of two different authorities is a complex feature of the regime and causes a great deal of confusion and, not to mention the potential such institutional structure has to undermine the effectiveness of the regime because of the additional financial costs, time and burdens that are a natural consequence of firms having to deal with more than one authority. Some people consider the added financial costs in particular to be highly objectionable because they are likely to be passed down the chain, ultimately reaching

---

[143] Antitrust Modernisation Commission Act of 2002, Pub. L. No. 107–273, § 11051–60, 116 Stat. 1856, amended by Antitrust Modernisation Commission Extension Act of 2007, Pub. L. No. 110–6, 121 Stat. 61.

[144] Antitrust Modernisation Commission *Report and Recommendations* (2007) available at: http://govinfo.library.unt.edu/amc/report_recommendation/toc.htm.

[145] In the UK competition law regime – taking the area of merger control and market investigations as examples – the Office of Fair Trading acts as a first phase authority and refers the matter (within the framework of the rules contained in the Enterprise Act 2002) to the Competition Commission, which acts as an in-depth or second phase authority.

consumers. However, even if such a development is unlikely and firms are willing to shoulder without protest all financial costs incurred during investigations by the two US competition authorities, the fact that the latter may be involved in the same situation is considered to enhance as opposed to minimise uncertainty. Moreover, it has been considered that the involvement of more than one authority carries a serious risk of inefficiency by wasting public resources in duplicating work.

In its Report, the AMC, even in light of the above concerns and others, made no recommendations as to changing the dual federal enforcement system in place. The AMC however accepted that having a single authority would be 'superior institutional structure', but it cited lack of evidence as to the duplication of effort between the Antitrust Division and FTC, excessive costs and significant disruption to operations (should a move from two authorities to one occur) as factors weighing against a move to a single authority.[146] Instead of directing its efforts at issues surrounding the creation of a single authority, the AMC thus focused its study and recommendations on areas particularly thought to suffer from the dual enforcement structure. Obviously one of these areas relates to the field of merger control. Two aspects of US merger control can be used to illustrate: the mechanism of pre-merger notification and the different approaches followed by the Antitrust Division and FTC when seeking injunctions to block merger operations. These two issues will be considered in turn.

(a) **The requirement of prior notification**   As discussed above, the Hart-Scott-Rodino Antitrust Improvements Act 1976 inserted section 7A of the Clayton Act 1914 and established the federal pre-merger notification mechanism, under which parties involved in a merger operation must notify any merger meeting the thresholds stipulated in the section to *both* the Antitrust Division and the FTC. As both authorities have concurrent jurisdiction to review notified mergers, they decide between themselves which authority will formally investigate the relevant merger operation through a 'clearance process' whereby one authority requests leave from the other to investigate the operation and the other agency 'clears' the request. Thus, even before an investigation can begin, the parties to a merger operation – for whom time is often of the essence – must wait while the authorities go through this process of allocating jurisdiction which can take more than 30 days.

---

[146] See chapter II.A, pp. 129–30 of the Commission's report.

The AMC considered this issue carefully and the problems which this situation gives rise to in practice. It suggested that a clearance agreement be entered into between the authorities on similar lines to an abandoned memorandum of understanding which was reached between the two authorities in 2002.[147] Though this memorandum stipulated that a decision should be made within ten days, the AMC recommended that the new agreement should provide that all clearance issues are to be resolved within 'a short period of time' after the notification of the merger, using nine calendar days as an example.

(b) Injunctions While the Antitrust Division and the FTC have essentially the same powers to seek injunctions from the courts to block mergers, the legal basis on which their powers stand derive from different statutes and each authority takes a different approach when seeking blocking injunctions.[148] In practice, the Antitrust Division tends to consolidate proceedings in accordance with rule 65(a)(2) of the *Federal Rules of Civil Procedure*, which allows the hearing on an application for preliminary relief to be combined with a trial on the merits, by seeking permanent and preliminary injunctions against mergers it deems anticompetitive. Thus, when an action is initiated by the Antitrust Division it can be resolved in a single appearance before a judge and the merging parties may proceed with the deal if a permanent injunction is not granted and the Antitrust Division does not appeal. The FTC, however, cannot consolidate proceedings and it only seeks preliminary injunctions in federal district courts because, for the FTC, a preliminary injunction aims to preserve the *status quo* pending a trial before an FTC Administrative Law Judge; the opportunity to consolidate proceedings afforded by rule 65 is not available. Therefore, in the absence of a stay, if the FTC fails to obtain preliminary relief it may continue to pursue permanent relief in administrative *Part III Proceedings* leaving the merging parties in limbo for a lengthy period of time (sometimes over a year).

To deal with the issues mentioned in the previous paragraph, the AMC suggested that changes are needed so that the standards applicable

---

[147] The memorandum was abandoned after Congress voiced opposition to the allocation of mergers on the basis of sectors.
[148] The power of the Antitrust Division is found in s. 15 of the Clayton Act 1914 whereas the power of the FTC is found in s. 13(b) of the Federal Trade Commission Act 1914, along with the Administrative Procedure Act 1946 and the *FTC Rules of Practice*.

to each authority when seeking the grant of a preliminary injunction are the same and that the FTC be prohibited from pursuing administrative litigation in merger cases where the Hart-Scott-Rodino Antitrust Improvements Act 1976 applies.[149] It also recommended that the FTC adopt a policy whereby, on seeking injunctive relief, it will to seek both preliminary and permanent relief and endeavour to consolidate the proceedings provided an appropriate schedule may be drawn up with the merging parties.

(B)   The Obama Administration and the withdrawal of the 'Section 2 Report'

In January 2009, a fundamental change occurred in the political scene in Washington with the departure of the Bush (Republican) Administration after eight years in office and the swearing in of the new Obama (Democratic) Administration. This change was highly anticipated as likely to translate into a fundamental change in the US competition law regime.

As was remarked in the introductory part of this chapter, the US competition law regime is one of the world's most robustly enforced regimes in the world. Interestingly however this reputation was cast in doubt during the Bush Administration years. People have variably cited different facts and figures to support the view that a reduction in the level and extent of competition enforcement occurred between the years 2001–09. For example, it is thought that the total number of cases which was investigated by the Antitrust Division dropped quite significantly: in 1999 (the closing stages of the Clinton Administration) the Division investigated 346 cases, which was significantly higher than the 208 cases investigated by the Division in 2008 (the closing stages of the Bush Administration).[150]

Moreover, it has been pointed out that during the eight-year term of the Bush Administration the Division failed to file a single monopolisation – section 2 of the Sherman Act 1890 – case. This seemingly lax attitude has been considered by different people to be attributable to different things, including an alleged strict adherence to the Chicago

---

[149] These changes were thought to be best achieved by amending s. 13(b) of the Federal Trade Commission Act 1914.

[150] See the Ten Year Workload Statistics available at www.usdoj.gov/atr/public/workstats.pdf.

school, under which as we saw markets are considered to work better when left alone and with minimal intervention by public authorities. Putting this to one side however, what is clear is that under the Obama Administration a sharp departure appears to be highly likely from the approach and policy to competition law prevailing during the Bush Administration. One of the major indications of this 'change' – other than the President's pre-election statements on the competition issues – can be seen in the choice of the person to head the Division. Christine Varney was appointed as Assistant Attorney General for Antitrust Division and one of her early actions in her first three months in office was an important step, which gave rise to a big debate almost all over the world: on 2 May 2009 Ms Varney withdrew the 'Section 2 Report', which offered consumers, businesses, courts and practitioners a guide to the Antitrust Division's policy in respect of monopolisation cases. She stated that the Report – which had been introduced prior to her term in office – raised too many hurdles to competition law enforcement and that the withdrawal 'is a shift in philosophy and the clearest way to let everyone know that the Antitrust Division will be aggressively pursuing cases where monopolists try to use their dominance in the marketplace to stifle competition and harm consumers'.[151]

(C)   Revising the Horizontal Merger Guidelines

The *Horizontal Merger Guidelines*[152] were adopted jointly by the Antitrust Division and the FTC in 1992. They came to offer guidance on how horizontal mergers are appraised under section 7 of the Clayton Act 1914 and highlight the circumstances under which the authorities are likely to show concerns over a horizontal merger operation.

For some time however, a view has been taking foothold that it would be necessary to revise and modernise the Guidelines; indeed the Guidelines themselves make it clear that they are to be revised from time to time. Action was finally taken when new administrations became constituted within the Antitrust Division and the FTC: the authorities announced their intention to revise the Guidelines in order to ensure that they offer the business community, lawyers and the courts accurate guidance. A process of consultation was started in late

---

[151] See Department of Justice Press Release available at www.usdoj.gov/atr/public/press_releases/2009/245710.htm.
[152] The *Guidelines* are available at the Antitrust Division's homepage.

2009 and seminars were held to discuss the different aspects of the Guidelines and identify ways in which they can be improved. From the authorities' perspective, their particular interest is to consider: the use of direct evidence when evaluating horizontal merger; the use of the hypothetical monopolist test when defining the relevant market;[153] the use of market concentration standards and thresholds;[154] and the viability of introducing within the Guidelines guidance on merger remedies.

---

[153] See pp. 70–77 above.

[154] Several competition authorities consider the issue of market concentration when evaluating mergers, using a well-known test called the Herfindahl-Hirschman Index (HHI). For a discussion of what this test involved and how it is applied in practice, see the European Commission's *Horizontal Merger Guidelines*, mentioned in chapter 4, at note 25 (and accompanying text).

Chapter 6

Competition law and policy in developing countries

1. Introduction

The phenomenal geographical expansion of competition law in recent years has been most noticeable in the developing world. As we noted in the first chapter, this expansion has occurred against the backdrop of the economic transformation witnessed worldwide and which has led to an increased reliance on the market mechanism. The impact of this shift has been particularly felt in developing countries, many of which have been taking remarkable steps in replacing their centrally planned economies with ones based on free-market philosophy. Considerable work however remains to be done in many parts of the developing world in this regard in order to bring about meaningful and sustainable privatisation, which could in turn contribute to advancing economic and technical development; an equal if not greater amount of work is needed in the field of competition law.

(A)   What is meant by 'developing countries'?

The question of what is a 'developing country' and whether this is an appropriate way to describe a country that is not developed itself can be discussed in a chapter of its own if not an entire book. Some people would argue that the use of the concepts of *developed* and *developing* countries may not be the best way to categorise countries and for this reason many international institutions, governments and people have shown a preference towards the term 'less developed countries' (LDCs)[1] to describe countries which are not developed; and there are those who use the term 'newly industrialised countries' to refer to these countries. Other terms in use include economies 'in transition' or 'emerging'

---

[1] Sometimes the term less economically developed countries (LEDCs) is also used.

economies. In this chapter however the term 'developing countries' is used with full awareness of the existence of alternative terms as highlighted in this paragraph. This is simply done because the focus in the chapter is on the topic of 'competition law' in these countries and not on issues of definition.

The table below lists those countries which are widely regarded as developing countries;[2] the table also indicates the existence or absence of specific competition law in the relevant country.[3]

Name of country	Relevant competition law
Afghanistan	—
Albania	Law No. 9121 of 28 July 2003 for the Protection of Competition
Algeria	Competition Ordinance 2003
Angola	None, though draft bill introduced in 2004 is waiting to be enacted into law
Antigua and Barbuda	No specific law but provisions dealing with competition can be found in the Protection Against Unfair Competition (Intellectual Property) Act 2006 and the Telecommunications Act 2007
Argentina	Competition Defence Act 25,156 of 1999; also note the existence of: Decree 89/2001; Decree 396/2001; and Resolution of the Secretariat of Technical Coordination 100/2004
Armenia	Law on the Protection of Economic Cooperation 2000 (as amended)

[2] It is arguable that other countries which are not listed in the table are also developing countries.

[3] In some developing countries only a single piece of legislation deals with competition and is thus the main competition law in the relevant country; in others however a number of instruments exist none of which is strictly speaking a proper competition law but all of which have competition relevance whilst there are those countries in which other instruments with competition relevance exist *in addition* to the competition law. The table below lists all of these various instruments where relevant. It is also important to note that sectoral laws and regulations may exist in the relevant country which have competition relevance; most notable here is the telecommunications sector which is discussed below in part 10 of the chapter.

Azerbaijan	Law on Antimonopoly Activity No. 526 of 1993 (as amended). The following laws are also worth noting: Law on Natural Monopolies No. 590-IG of 1998; Law on Unfair Competition No. 62 of 1995; Law on Protection of Consumer Rights; Law on Advertising 1997
Bahamas	No specific laws at present though a Utilities Regulation and Competition Authority Bill has been proposed to deal with the utilities sector
Bahrain	No specific law but general provisions exist in the Constitution and the Law of Commerce
Bangladesh	Draft Competition law 2008 soon to be adopted. A Monopolies and Restrictive Trade Practices (Control and Prevention) Ordinance however has existed in the country since 1970
Barbados	Fair Competition Act 2003, CAP.326.C
Belarus	Law on the Prevention of Monopoly Activities of 1992; there is also a Law on Natural Monopolies of 2002
Belize	—
Benin	Law No. 90–005 of 1990 Setting the Conditions for the Exercise of Trade Activities in the Republic of Belin; an Ordinance is also in existence since 1967 which deals with price regulation, namely the Ordinance on the Regulation of Prices and Stocks 1967
Bhutan	None at present but a draft Consumer Protection Bill adopted in 2007 does contain some competition provisions
Bolivia	Supreme Decree No. 29519 Regulating Competition and Consumer Protection SIRESE Law 600 of 1994
Bosnia and Herzegovina	Act on Competition of Bosnia and Herzegovina, Official Gazette of BiH No. 48/05
Botswana	No specific competition law but provisions dealing with competition can be found in the Industrial Property Act and the Telecommunications Act 1996

Brazil	Brazilian Competition Act, Law 8884/94, as amended; also it is worth noting the Resolution 20 of June 9 1999; Law 8.137 of 27 December 1990; Law No. 10.446 of 8 May 2002; Law No. 75, May 20, 1993; CADE Resolution 15/98; and CADE Resolution 18/98
Brunei Darussalam	Monopolies Act, Cap. 73 1932 (dormant)
Burkina Faso	Law No. 033–2001; Law No. 15/94/ADP 1994; Regulation No. 03/2002/CM/UEMOA on dominant positions; Regulation No. 04/2002/CM/UEMOA on state aid; Directive No. 02/2002/CM/UEMOA on cooperation between members of the West African Economic and Monetary Union
Burundi	None, though a competition law is planned to be introduced in due course
Cambodia	Law Concerning Marks, Trade Names and Unfair Acts of Competition 2002
Cameroon	Competition Act 1998
Cape Verde	No specific law yet but the Preamble to Decree Law No. 2/99 sets out the principles of competition policy for the country and led to the creation of a competition authority.
Central African Republic	—
Chad	—
Chile	Competition Law Decree 211 of 1973; also note Law No. 181.20
China	Anti-monopoly Law of the People's Republic of China 2007. Note that other instruments are also in existence in China which have competition relevance.[4]
Colombia	Article 333 and 334 of the Constitution; Law 256 of 1996 on unfair competition; Law 155 of 1959 on restrictive business practices; Bill on Competition (not yet enacted)

---

[4] See the chapter on 'China' in M. Dabbah and P. Lasok, *Merger Control Worldwide* (Cambridge University Press, 2005).

Comoros	—
Congo DR	—
Costa Rica	Law on the Promotion of Competition and Consumer Protection No. 7472; Executive Regulations to the Law on the Promotion of Competition and Effective Consumer Protection and amendments No. 25234-MEIC of 1996
Côte d'Ivoire	Competition Act, Law No. 91–999 of 1991 (dormant); Law No.97–10 of 1997 (dormant)
Croatia	Law on Protection of Market Competition 2003, Official Gazette No. 122/03; Regulation on Agreements of Minor Importance, Official Gazette No. 51/2004
Democratic Republic of the Congo	—
Djibouti	No specific law at present but a Commercial Code 2009 is to be submitted to the National Assembly which may potentially contain competition law in pursuit of the International Monetary Fund recommendations
Dominica	—
Dominican Republic	Law No.42–08 on the Defence of Competition
Ecuador	Executive Order 16–14 2009 incorporating Decision 608 of the Andean Community on competition
Egypt	Law No. 3/2005 concerning the Protection of Competition and the Prohibition of Monopolistic practices; Executive Regulations for the Law concerning the Protection of Competition and Prohibition of Monopolistic Practices
El Salvador	Competition Law 2004; Executive Regulatory Provisions to the Competition Law 2004
Equatorial Guinea	—
Eritrea	—
Estonia	Competition Act (*Konkurentsiseadus*) RT I 2001, 56, 332, as amended

Ethiopia	Trade Practice Proclamation No. 329/2003
Fiji	The Commerce Act 1998; Fair Trading Decree 1992 (as amended)
Gabon	—
Gambia	Competition Act 2007
Georgia	Law on Monopoly Activity and Competition 1996, as amended
Ghana	Protection Against Unfair Competition Act No. 589/2000
Grenada	—
Guatemala	No specific competition law but Articles 119(h) and 130 of the Constitution, Articles 340 and 341 of the Criminal Code and Articles 361 and 362 of the Commercial Code contain competition provisions
Guinea	—
Guinea-Bissau	—
Guyana	Competition and Fair Trading Act 2006
Haiti	No specific law but the Act of July 1954 on intellectual property rights contains provisions on unfair competition
Honduras	Law for the Defence and Promotion of Competition No. 357–2005
Hungary	Act LVII of 1996 on the Prohibition of Unfair Market Practices and Restriction of Competition, as amended; Act IV of 1978, The Criminal Code, as amended
India	Competition Act 2002, as amended
Indonesia	Law No. 5 Concerning Prohibition of Monopolistic Practices and Unfair Business 1999 (some articles are currently under review and unenforceable)
Iran	No specific law, though various provisions which have competition relevance exist, including Articles in the Constitution
Iraq	—
Jamaica	Jamaican Fair Competition Act 1973, as amended; Consumer Protection Act 2005

Jordan	Competition Law No. 33/2004; note also the Trade Secrets and Unfair Competition Law No. 15/2000
Kazakhstan	Law on Competition and Restrictions in Monopolistic Activities 2006
Kenya	Competition Bill 2009 (not yet enacted); Trade Practices, Monopolies and Price Control Act, Cap. 504
Kiribati	—
Kuwait	A new competition law was adopted in 2007; also note Decree No. 68 of 1980 Commercial Law which contains some provisions with competition provisions
Kyrgyzstan	Law about Natural Monopolies in the Kyrgyzstan Republic; Law about the Limitation of Monopolistic Activity, Development and Protection of Competition; Rule of the National Commission on Security and Development of Competition
Lao PDR	Decree 15/PMO on Trade Competition 2004
Latvia	Competition Law 2002, as amended
Lebanon	High Commissioner's Order No. 2385 of 1924, 'Laws & Systems of the Commercial and Industrial Property in Lebanon', as amended; Law No. 31 for the year 1967 authorising the Government to enact promulgating decrees to combat high prices and monopoly; Promulgating Decree No. 32 for the year 1967 on anti-monopoly and high prices. A comprehensive competition bill has been prepared but little progress has been made over the past a few years to enact it into law
Lesotho	No specific competition law but economic entities are regulated under the provisions of the Industrial Property Order No. 5 of 1989 and a law is being formulated within WTO guidelines
Liberia	—
Libya	None yet, though a draft competition law is expected to emerge soon

Lithuania	Law on Competition of 1999, as amended; Merger control (secondary) legislation; Antitrust (secondary) legislation
Republic of Macedonia	Law No. 04/05 on Protection of Competition 2005, as amended
Madagascar	Law on Competition and the Malagasy Commission 2005 (not yet implemented by Decree)
Malawi	Competition and Fair Trading Act 1998
Malaysia	No specific competition law but many different laws can be used to regulate activities, including the Trade Descriptions Act 1972; the Companies Act 1965; and the Control of Supplies Act 1961. See also the Provisions in the Guidelines for Regulation of Acquisitions of Assets, Mergers and Takeovers and the Malaysian Code on Takeovers and Mergers 1998 which have competition relevance
Maldives	—
Mali	Ordinance No. 92/021/P-CTSP of 1992
Mauritania	No specific laws but provisions of the Commercial Code 2000 relate to pricing and competition
Mauritius	Competition Bill VI of 2003
Mexico	Federal Economic Competition Law 1993, as amended
Moldova	Law on the Protection of Competition 2000; Antimonopoly Law 1992
Mongolia	Unfair Competition Law 1993, as amended; Consumer Protection Law 1991
Montenegro	Law on Protection of Competition 2005
Morocco	Law No. 06–99 on Free Pricing and Competition
Mozambique	None yet but a draft competition law is expected to surface soon
Myanmar	No specific law but a competition authority exists – the Myanmar Commission for the Supervision of Business Competition

Namibia	Competition Act 2003
Nepal	Competition Promotion and Market Protection Act 2007
Nicaragua	Law No. 601 on the Promotion of Competition 2006
Niger	—
Nigeria	Draft Competition Bill 2002 not yet implemented
Oman	The Law of Trademarks, Trade Data Undisclosed Trade Information and Protection from Unfair Competition No. 38/2000
Pakistan	Competition Ordinance 2007; Competition Commission of Pakistan (Conduct of Business) Regulations 2007; Competition (Leniency) Regulations 2007; Competition (General Enforcement) Regulations 2007; Competition Commission (Investment and Expenditure) Regulations 2007; Competition Commission (Appeal) Rules 2007
Panama	Anticompetitive Competition Practices (Unfair Competition) Law No. 29 of 1 February 1996, as amended
Papua New Guinea	Independent Consumer and Competition Act 2002
Paraguay	A draft Law for the Defence of Competition has been in existence for a number of years. The bill submitted to Parliament was rejected in 2008 but the matter returned to the legislative table in 2009 for further discussion
Peru	Law No. 701/1991 Against Monopolistic, Controlist and Restrictive Practices, as amended (Free Competition Law); Market Access Law; Law No. 26876/1997 Antitrust and Anti-oligopoly Law for the Electricity Sector
Philippines	No specific competition law but provisions can be found in the Philippine Constitution 1997, the Price Act 1992, and the Intellectual Property Code 1997.

Poland	Act of 16 February 2007 on Competition and Consumer Protection; Act on Countering Monopolistic Practices of 1990
Qatar	Law on Protection of Competition and Prohibition of Monopolistic Practices 2006
Russia	Law No. 135/2007 on the Protection of Competition; Law No. 147 on Natural Monopolies (a new version was due in 2008); Law No. 117 on the Protection of Competition in the Financial Services Market; Law No. 148–1 on Competition and Limitation of Monopolistic Activity in the Commodities Market
Rwanda	None yet though a law is in contemplation
Saint Kitts and Nevis	—
Saint Lucia	Law for the Protection Against Unfair Competition 2001
Saint Vincent and the Grenadines	Fair Competition Act No. 24 of 2004
Samoa	No specific competition law but individual sectors are addressed using different legislative instruments some of which have competition relevance. See, for example, the Telecommunications Act 2005, Part VI
São Tomé and Príncipe	—
Saudi Arabia	Competition Act 2004
Senegal	Law on Prices, Competition and Economic Disputes No. 94–63 of 1994; Decree No. 96–343 of 1996 on Law No. 94–63
Serbia	Law on Protection of Competition 2005
Seychelles	—
Sierra Leone	—
Solomon Islands	No specific laws but sectors look to be regulated individually in the future
Somalia	—
South Africa	Competition Act No. 89 of 1998, as amended
Sri Lanka	Fair Trading Commission Act No. 1 of 1987, as amended
Sudan	—

Suriname	No specific competition laws but provisions exist in Articles 390 and 400 of the Penal Code and a law was being developed with CARICOM in 2008
Swaziland	—
Syria	Competition and Antitrust Law No. 07/2008
Tajikistan	Law on Competition and Restrictions to Monopoly Activities on Goods Markets 2000; Law on Natural Monopolies 2001
Tanzania	Fair Trade Practices Act 2003
Thailand	Trade Competition Act 1999
Timor-Leste	—
Togo	WAEMU Community competition law replaced national legislation in 2003
Tonga	Protection Against Unfair Competition Act No. 2 of 2002
Trinidad and Tobago	Fair Trading Act 2006
Tunisia	Competition and Prices Act 1991–64
Turkey	Law on the Protection of Competition No. 4054, as amended
Turkmenistan	—
Uganda	None, though a draft law was formulated in 2004
Ukraine	Law on Protection of the Economic Competition 2001, as amended; Law on the Antimonopoly Committee of Ukraine 1993
United Arab Emirates	A draft Competition Law was still being discussed in 2009 but has yet to be enacted
Uruguay	Law No. 18,159/2007 on the Promotion and Defence of Competition
Uzbekistan	Law on Competition and Restriction of Monopolistic Activity 1996; Law on Natural Monopolies 1997
Vanuatu	—
Venezuela	Law for the Promotion and Protection of Free Competition 1992; Regulation No. 1 of the Pro-competition Law 1993. A new Competition Bill was discussed in 2006
Vietnam	Competition Law 2004

Yemen	Law No. 19 of 1999 on Encouraging Competition and Prevention of Monopoly and Commercial Fraud; A draft Law on Competition Protection and Monopoly Prevention was formulated in 2006 but has not yet been adopted
Zambia	The Competition and Fair Trading Act 1994
Zimbabwe	The Competition Act 1996, as amended

(B) An overview of this chapter

The topic of competition law and competition policy and their role in developing countries has attracted considerable attention in recent years, no doubt rightly so. An abundance of literature – in the form of books, scholarly articles and reports by various bodies and organisations – has come to emerge in which the topic has been examined;[5] this has been necessary in order to promote the understanding of the topic, though it remains the case that perhaps all the themes and questions underpinning the topic remain largely unexplored and the need for a comprehensive work in the form of a book or several books would be a welcome thing indeed. Many people – whether those who specialise in the field of competition law or in other (related) fields – who have not had the chance to deal with the topic find it incredibly fascinating. However those who have had such an 'opportunity' would perhaps all agree the topic is extremely challenging because among other things it raises many questions, which specialists may not necessarily have previously encountered in their line of work, regardless of the knowledge and expertise gained from dealing with competition law and policy in the developed world. In this respect, it is important to emphasise the fact that the topic of *competition law and policy in developing countries* and that of *competition law and policy in the developed world* differs significantly. The first hurdle those who approach the former topic need

---

[5] See, for example, the following contributions: T. Stewart, J. Clarke and S. Joekes, *Competition Law in Action: Experience from Developing Countries* (International Development Research Centre, 2007); L. Cernat and P. Holmes (eds.), *Competition, Competitiveness and Development: Lessons From Developing Countries* (UNCTAD, 2004); P. Cook, R. Fabella and L. Cassey, *Competitive Advantage and Competition Policy in Developing Countries* (Edward Elgar, 2007); M. Gal, *Competition Policy in Small Market Economies* (Harvard University Press, 2003).

to 'clear' in order to ensure a proper understanding of it, is *not* to make too many assumptions based on knowledge gained from experience (however rich) with the latter topic. In practice this hurdle is not often cleared and the tendency to opt for many assumptions is rather widespread. This situation adds to the challenges surrounding the topic. In particular, a person who aims to advocate what competition law and policy in the developing world should be like or how they should be approached or handled would need, as a result, to also show why there is no room for making such assumptions and the damage doing so actually causes; admittedly, this damage can be quite substantial especially when one considers the psychological impact assumptions have on the thinking of those who specialise in competition law and policy in developing countries – in particular competition officials in these countries who can be easily influenced in their thinking and outlook. There is also the risk here that major difficulties may be caused, whether at the legislative stage itself or later on when it comes to application of the rules and enforcement by the relevant competition authority or court.

Developing countries have unique circumstances and interests and these make the competition law 'question' a particularly difficult one to deal with. This chapter will consider these circumstances and interests and offer numerous examples from practice in order to explain all of the crucial aspects of the topic. These examples will be taken from different regions around the world. The chapter will consider the topic in the *context* of the present book. It will therefore not aim to advocate what role or function competition law and policy should have in developing countries or present a 'thesis' on the topic. Rather, the aim is to highlight a number of aspects related to the topic and raise and consider several issues which are of interest to students, academics, practitioners and policymakers. The discussion offered here is not intended to be exhaustive nor is it intended as a complete critique of the topic. As noted above, a comprehensive study of the topic would be highly valuable and this chapter is not aimed at producing this study, which indeed would require an entire book!

2. The different 'aspects' of the topic

There are a number of aspects to the topic of *competition law and policy in the developing world* which may conveniently be presented in the form of the following (non-exhaustive) questions:

- How have competition law and policy come to be spread around the developing world?
- Do developing countries need competition law and policy?
- What would be the most suitable form of competition law and policy for the economies of developing countries?
- Does it make sense or is it necessary to follow 'models' from the developed world when introducing competition law in a developing country?
- What challenges do developing countries face in adopting specific competition rules?
- What benefits do competition law and policy have for developing countries and their citizens?
- Can the adoption of competition law actually be counterproductive and harm developing countries?
- What would a developing country need in order to ensure a proper functioning of its competition law regime?
- What role do, and what role should, consumers play in the competition law scene of developing countries?

Needless to say these are far from being easy-to-answer questions and it should be acknowledged that they can and do – when raised – trigger heated debate, which in relation to many of the questions has never been settled and as a result lack of consensus remains among different people, whether competition or non-competition specialists.

In the discussion below these questions will be discussed and critically assessed.

3. The spread of competition law around the developing world

As noted above, in recent years competition law has come to spread very rapidly around the developing world. Many developing countries – in which competition law was simply unthinkable only a few years ago – now have competition legislation in place;[6] some of these countries have

---

[6] See, for example, countries such as China (which introduced specific competition law in 2007) and Saudi Arabia (which adopted its competition law in 2004). Perhaps these two countries furnish remarkable examples because of: the political monopolisation which exists in the former and its solid 'communist' approach for many years to regulating the economy (see M. Williams *Competition Policy and Law in China, Hong Kong and Taiwan* (Cambridge University Press, 2004); M. Dabbah 'The Development of Sound Competition Law and Policy In China: an (Im)Possible Dream?' (2007) *World*

been making concentrated efforts towards building vigorous enforcement of their competition rules and their competition authorities in particular have been engaged in active competition advocacy to ensure that competition and competition law are taken into account within the work of the executive and legislative branches *and* to educate business firms, consumers and the public at large on how competition benefits them, why competition law is needed and what role they have as players in the local competition law regime.[7] However, others have not engaged in the development of their competition law and policy with such enthusiasm.

For the largest part of the twentieth century, most if not all developing countries gave insufficient and inadequate recognition to the concept and idea of competition and the need to protect it.[8] This 'negative' development unfolded in remarkable contrast to the way in which competition came to be viewed within the developed world:[9] at the relevant time when developing countries moved in the direction of liberalisation and privatisation, a different trend prevailed in the developing world which showed a move towards more monopolisation and state control and planning in different sectors of domestic economies. This often took place through strengthening the economic and political control of a few powerful families and individuals in key sectors of the economy. This has led to strong 'concentration of wealth' in the hands of a few and appears to have minimised the prospects for a fair and equitable distribution of wealth within society; in competition law specific terms this enhanced the chances for harming and even eliminating competition because, among other things, competition was not given proper attention or considered worthy of protection.

The insufficient and inadequate recognition given to the value of competition within different developing countries, among other things, resulted in the absence of specific competition laws and policy in these countries: adopting competition law under these circumstances was considered to run contrary to the developments leading to this state of affairs but at any rate was not considered to be necessary. The situation

---

Competition 341; M. Furse, 'Competition Law Choice in China' (2007) *World Competition* 323); *and* the family-oriented strong control and ownership of the whole economy in the latter (see M. Dabbah *Competition Law and Policy in the Middle East* (Cambridge University Press, 2007), at pp. 198–207).

[7] See above for a discussion on competition advocacy and its benefits.

[8] See Gal, note 5 above.

[9] See the discussion in chapter 1 above and chapter 4 and 5 which deal with the EU and US competition law regimes respectively.

began to change at the beginning of the 1990s[10] in particular with considerable attention being given by an increasing number of developing countries to the value of competition and the need to develop competition law and policy domestically. Despite the clear benefits arising out of this change of attitude on the part of developing countries, it should be stressed that this development may, in some cases, be nothing more than a response to international pressure, both within and outside the field of competition law, rather than a gradual internal or national awareness within those countries. It seems this has happened, mainly but not exclusively, due to: international obligations;[11] encouragement by third countries and international organisations;[12] a desire by some of those countries to join regional blocks and communities;[13] and the process of globalisation.[14] The fact that competition law and policy has not been truly 'home-grown' in some developing countries has had an impact on the substantive competition rules in such countries, most notably with regard to the substantive, legal components.

Developing countries have increasingly come to adopt competition laws with modern elements which have been borrowed in the vast majority of cases from competition law regimes in the developed world and the competition rules and standards developed by international organisations;[15] by looking at the experience of developed nations with competition law and policy many developing countries have come to associate having a competition law and policy with economic progress,

---

[10] See A. Singh and R. Dhumale, *Competition Policy, Development and Developing Countries* (South Centre Working Papers, 1999), pp. 7–9.

[11] See, for example, how Syria's accession to the WTO has been conditioned upon the country meeting several requirements. One of these requirements concerned changes to Syria's economic laws and introducing a specific competition law domestically. See also efforts by Sudan in recent years to adopt competition law as part of several economic and structural reforms seeking, among other things, to comply with the rules and standards of international bodies, especially the World Bank and the IMF.

[12] Notable in this regard are the efforts of the European Commission, the Organisation for Economic Cooperation and Development (OECD), the World Bank and the United Nationals Conference on Trade and Development (UNCTAD).

[13] This is demonstrated by efforts of various countries since the 1990s to join the EU and at more global level the World Trade Organisation (WTO); see above for a discussion of the accession of several central and eastern European countries to the EU.

[14] A good example is furnished by Egypt's enactment of its Law on the Protection of Competition and the Prevention of Monopolistic Practices 2005.

[15] This includes most notably the UNCTAD's *Set of Multilaterally Agreed Equitable Principles and Rules for the Control of Restrictive Business Practices* and *Model Law*; both available at www.unctad.org. See above for a discussion on the Set and the Model Law.

sustained growth, modernisation of domestic economies and building a market economy.[16] This 'belief' seems to be held by a number of developing countries, which are currently in the process of enacting domestic competition legislation.[17] This important development has occurred in parallel to the wave of deregulation which covered a number of key sectors throughout the developing world in recent years.[18] Although this belief has, among other things, pushed the competition law 'question' high on the agenda of national governments throughout the developing world – which is undoubtedly a feat – problems may arise where a firm conviction in this belief is the only, or main, motivation in adopting a competition law. For example, if a developing country views the introduction of competition law as a 'quick-fix' for problems related to but distinct from competition, or as a 'shortcut' to economic growth and development, there is potential for competition law and policy to be easily disregarded when they are no longer seen as conducive for the attainment of such non-competition goals. Therefore, it is vital that developing countries truly appreciate the objectives of competition law and policy.

Adopting competition law in developing countries is now considered to be crucial for the purposes of supporting these countries in developing a free market economy and for making the shift from a controlled economy towards privatisation and liberalisation. Two particular groups of actors have played an influential role in spreading such thinking and emphasising the need for effective, genuine competition law and policy. These are international organisations and some of the world's major competition authorities.

---

[16] See J.S. Hur, 'The Evolution of Competition Policy and its Impact on Economic Development in Korea' in Cernat and Holmes, note 5 above.

[17] See, for example, efforts by countries such as Lebanon, Sudan and the United Arab Emirates and others which recently came to adopt competition law, such as Kuwait and some African countries.

[18] The most notable example here has been the telecommunications sector. See, for example, the key steps taken by the following countries for the purposes of liberalising the sector and enhancing competition within its boundaries: Kenya (with the adoption of the Kenya Communications Act 1998); Nigeria (with the deregulation process started in 1992 and the creation of the Nigerian Communications Commission); Oman (with the deregulation occurring following accession to the WTO in 2000 and the adoption of the Telecommunications Regulatory Act 2002); the Philippines (with the liberalisation in the 1990s and the adoption of the Public Telecommunications Policy Act No. 7925); Brazil (with the creation of the National Telecommunications Agency, *Nacional de Telecomunicações* (ANATEL) in 1997); and Saudi Arabia (with the partial privatisation following the adoption of the Telecommunications Act 2001).

(A) The involvement of international bodies

When considering the proliferation of competition law around the developing world it would be remiss to ignore the role of different international organisations. In the case of most developing countries, competition law has not been considered *naturally* by these countries taking the initiative to introduce domestic competition rules themselves. In this regard, it was noted above that developing countries have had a different experience from that of many developed countries. Many developing countries have been 'introduced' to competition law and in some cases even forced to adopt it by international organisations.[19]

Several international bodies and organisations have played a highly influential role in the field of competition law within developing countries. Whether in the adoption of competition legislation,[20] the setting up of institutional structures to enforce the competition rules or the review of existing competition law regimes,[21] some of the world's leading international organisations have positioned themselves at the very centre. On the whole, this has been useful and the involvement of international organisations brings to developing countries a host of key benefits; not least the opportunity to 'connect' with the developed world and thus benefit from the vast experience and expertise developed countries enjoy in the field of competition law. Over the years, many developing countries have benefited from such connection in terms of receiving technical assistance, being supported in terms of capacity building within their local competition authorities and learning about best practices in the field.[22] These benefits are hugely important for such countries given their limited experience in the field of competition law and should be welcomed as a constructive role played by international organisations. Nonetheless, the involvement of international organisations has not always been constructive and can sometimes be problematic, especially from the perspective of developing countries themselves. For example, certain developing countries do on occasions feel that the relevant international organisation is

---

[19] Another notable example, in addition to the recent example mentioned in note above can be found in the case of Indonesia: the country was forced to adopt a specific competition as a condition imposed by the IMF for granting the country the financial aid it sought.

[20] See in particular the work of UNCTAD and the WTO.

[21] See the involvement of the World Bank, UNCTAD and to an extent the OECD.

[22] See below for a discussion on capacity building and technical assistance offered by UNCTAD.

imposing itself on them and forcing them to accept foreign rules and standards in the field by acting almost *unilaterally* whereas their preference would be to engage in a *dialogue* with the international organisation in order to better understand what is expected of them and to have an opportunity to make their concerns known. Many times developing countries are given no such opportunity and end up simply obeying the orders of the organisation in question given that the latter controls the funds needed to receive the technical assistance and the contacts with foreign specialists in the field.

The major players among international organisations who have been influential in this process of spreading competition law around the developing world are: UNCTAD; the IMF; the WTO; and the World Bank.[23] They enjoy unique positions, which have enabled them to – in different ways – effectively exert influence on different developing countries and encourage or force them to consider competition law. The role and different activities conducted by these organisations were explored in chapter 3 above.

(B) The involvement of major competition authorities

A number of competition authorities have played a role in the development of competition law and policy in developing countries. A notable involvement in this regard has been that of the European Commission, which – as we saw in chapter 4 – has worked hard in building an international dimension to the EU competition law regime and which has in turn enabled it to play a major role in the decision of several developing countries to adopt competition law, especially in Central and Eastern Europe, the Balkan countries, the Mediterranean Basin, Africa, but also beyond. The European Commission is also active in influencing the enforcement of competition law in many developing countries and contributes towards ensuring that such enforcement would be effective.

---

[23] It may be worth noting here the International Competition Network (ICN), which includes within its 'network' developing countries. Given the nature of the ICN's work and focus however it has not given developing countries a great deal of attention; nor have the competition authorities of these countries contributed significantly to the ICN's work. On the other hand, it is also important to note that the OECD has had involvement in the developing of competition law and policy in developing countries, though this has not been particularly extensive. The OECD has conducted some peer review work; in addition to issuing some helpful guidance and recommendations to developing countries and running some training programmes for the competition officials of several of these countries.

A similar contribution is also made by other key competition authorities, such as the US Federal Trade Commission (which we considered in chapter 5);[24] other important competition authorities involved in this work include the Japan Fair Trade Commission.[25]

The involvement of major competition authorities has led, on occasion, to a process of 'approximation of laws', namely some form of obligation or expectation at least that the developing country concerned would bring its competition laws closer to those of the relevant (advance) competition law regime.[26] This issue and process of approximation is open to debate with regard to whether it is beneficial or harmful to the interest of the developing countries concerned. Approximation may be a major precondition for the developing country to achieve closer economic links with the relevant jurisdiction. In effect this could mean an obligation on the developing country to introduce competition rules similar to those found in the relevant jurisdiction and not just an 'alignment' obligation, i.e. for the developing country to align its competition law with that of the latter. The requirement of approximation may even be given a narrow meaning by imposing a requirement on the developing country to follow not only the wording of the law but also judicial practice and relevant case law of the jurisdiction in question.

The process of approximation may take the form of quite 'aggressive' parachuting-in of competition laws from the developed world into developing countries. This indeed happens not infrequently. As we saw above,[27] such parachuting-in can be seen as part of the rivalry between major competition authorities, primarily those of the USA and the EU to expand their international influence in the field of competition law; this can sometimes be inspired by 'ideological' thinking and conviction on the part of competition officials in these authorities as well as by a desire to make it easier for their 'domestic' firms to operate in the 'targeted' countries, namely through ensuring that a similar regulatory environment to that prevailing in their home country would also exist in the latter. The parachuting-in of competition law has been very much driven by the internal agenda of the EU and the USA rather than the needs of the countries concerned, who appear to

---

[24] See pp. 267–268 above.
[25] See, for example, the international programme in operation by the JFTC.
[26] See the use of this tool in the context of EU accession by several countries; pp. 202–204 above.
[27] See p. 203 above.

be relegated to mere pawns in the play between more influential competition regimes: it happens even though EU and US competition laws themselves are not always the best models to be followed.[28]

However, the potential controversy concerning the involvement of foreign competition authorities in the development of competition law and policy in developing countries should not detract from the hugely valuable contribution these bodies make. Indeed, their involvement can bring about some very beneficial outcomes, especially at capacity building and technical assistance levels. Competition authorities within key competition law regimes – most notably the EU, US and Japanese regimes (but also other ones around the world)[29] – offer international technical assistance and capacity building programmes aimed at assisting other young(er) competition authorities, especially those of developing countries. These programmes usually take the form of secondments of officials from the former authorities to the latter and also having staff from the latter carry out visits to the former in order to experience first hand how competition cases are handled in practice.

4.   The should/should not debate

The phenomenal expansion of competition law around the developing world has received mixed reactions in different quarters. This part of the chapter will aim to highlight a number of those arguments *in favour* and *against* building competition law regimes in developing countries. Before doing so however, it would be worth highlighting the reality prevailing in most parts of the developing world, and the transition seen in different developing countries especially in recent years which has helped promote competition law and policy in these countries.

It should not be surprising at all that many parts of the developing world are regions with an abundance of economic opportunities. The potential of many developing countries to do extremely well in the economic arena – whether locally, regionally or even globally – is simply huge. In the real world this has not been quite apparent due to the fact

---

[28] Part 5 below discusses the issue of best model of competition law for developing countries.

[29] See, for example, the programmes run by the Korea Fair Trade Commission and the Turkish Competition Authority.

that developing countries face enormous challenges which are caused by major adverse phenomena such as poverty, illiteracy and conflicts (which often result in bloodshed);[30] to this non-exhaustive list of causes one may add natural disasters and sometimes harsh climate conditions. Many people would agree that the majority of causes of the challenges facing developing countries however are government- and/or man-made.[31] Nonetheless, the existence of the different challenges should make one appreciate two things: on the one hand, things like competition law and policy can quite often be easily brushed to the sidelines or pushed towards the bottom of the relevant government's list of priorities; on the other hand, the causes make it particularly important to appreciate the remarkable skills enjoyed by many citizens in the developing world to achieve economic prosperity and to seek innovative ways towards promoting enterprise and improving the productivity of their own nations and their regions as a whole.[32] Notwithstanding the adverse impressions – whether self- or non-self-inflicted – often formed regarding the developing world, many of these countries have rich traditions and their citizens enjoy a strong desire to advance knowledge and a particular interest to contribute in a meaningful way.[33]

For many years, local economies in the developing world were largely underdeveloped and suffered due to the lack of adequate infrastructure, technological developments and expertise to be able to promote meaningful economic activities; a state of affairs that remains to exist in some form or another. This situation has, however, come to change in recent years and a noticeable economic transformation has been unfolding throughout many parts of the developing world; though it should be noted that this transformation has not achieved full maturity. As noted above, many developing countries have been making serious efforts in order to facilitate privatisation within different sectors of their domestic economies;[34] trade

---

[30] See part 6 below for an account on the challenges facing developing countries.

[31] Obvious examples of causes here include corruption, misguided politics (often leading to internal divisions) and exploitation of national resources in the hands of a few individuals or families.

[32] See W. Carlin, S. Fries, M. Schaffer and P. Seabright, *Competition and Enterprise Performance in Transition Economies: Evidence from a Cross-Country Survey* (Centre for Economic Policy Research, 2001).

[33] A high-profile example here can be seen in the case of the Indian people.

[34] See furthermore part 10 below which refers to the telecommunications sector.

liberalisation;[35] foreign direct investment;[36] and establishing technologically advanced and services-based economies are some examples of such efforts. The engagement in these initiatives by different developing countries has created fresh hopes for building a generally enabling, transparent and non-discriminatory environment – resting on the idea of having a process of competition – within which domestic and foreign investment can flourish. These hopes have been strengthened with the economic and structural reform programmes set up by different developing countries (often with the help of international bodies) and the enactment of crucial laws and the formulation of key economic policies as part of these programmes.[37] Among these laws and policies, competition law and policy have received particular emphasis. This has also helped place the topic of competition law and policy high on the national (political and economic) agenda of many developing countries.

(A)   The arguments in favour

The decision of different developing countries to adopt some form of competition law has been welcomed as crucial for the purposes of helping those countries achieve a number of important benefits, including the ones discussed here below.

I.   Fighting harmful practices

Many developing countries suffer from 'effective monopolisation' of the different sectors of the domestic economies at the hands of a few firms, individuals and families; a situation that in competition law terms is considered to give rise to possible harms to competition and consumers and in *socio-economic terms* is considered to give rise to a concentration of wealth within society. The monopolisation of the local economy in this manner may occur regardless of whether a centrally

---

[35] See 'Global Trade Liberalisation and the Developing Countries' (IMF, 2001), available at www.imf.org; 'Trade Liberalisation and Economic Reform in Developing Countries' (UNCTAD, 2005), available at www.unctad.org; S. Edwards, 'Openness, Growth and Trade Liberalisation in Developing Countries' (1993) *Journal of Economic Literature* 1358; R. Dornbusch, 'The Case for Trade Liberalisation in Developing Countries' (1992) *The Journal of Economic Perspectives* 73.

[36] See De Mello, 'Foreign Direct Investment in Developing Countries and Growth: a Selective Survey' (1997) *Journal of Development Studies* 1.

[37] See pp. 333–336 below for a discussion of these programmes.

controlled or free market economy exists and it may take the form of collusion among the firms operating in the relevant market or an abuse of dominance by a single firm.[38] Obviously, this presents a serious obstacle to efforts aimed at introducing competition legislation in these countries; a similar obstacle may hamper actual efforts seeking enforcement of existing competition rules.[39]

Where such effective monopolisation is found, the fabrics of competition would be seriously damaged. Even if 'other' firms (i.e. ones who are not monopolising the market) exist they may seriously struggle to gain any foothold in the competitive process and to expand their presence; indeed not infrequently, such firms may find themselves at the mercy of the holder(s) of monopoly position or more powerful rivals – a state of affairs which in itself could lead to the extinction of competition. For example, any such firm may find that they have little choice but to engage in a cartel activity with a more powerful competitor in order to guarantee some form of survival; in the real world, threats by powerful firms against smaller competitors forcing them to behave in a certain way or even to eliminate the latter from the market are not unheard of.[40]

II. Attracting foreign direct investment

The issue of foreign direct investment (FDI) carries particular economic and political importance in developing countries.[41] In some cases, discussing or facilitating FDI is not a matter of bilateral relations between the 'invested-in' (developing) country and the 'foreign' investing country or firm(s): international organisations can play a key role in this context and so the relationship would be 'tri-' or 'multi-' lateral.

Whether FDI is uniformly welcomed by all developing countries is something that can be considered the subject of some debate.[42] What

---

[38] See the discussion in part 6, sections (H)(i), (ii) and (iii) respectively for an account on the phenomena of collusion and abuse of dominance.

[39] The relevant competition authority – if one exists – may lack either the will *or* power to enforce the rules in these cases (for example where the authority is not the decision-maker in the competition law regime and lacks independence to act). See further below for a discussion of the issue of independence.

[40] Competition law practice around the world is full of examples here. See in particular EU competition law regime, especially in the area of abuse of dominance under Art. 102 TFEU (particularly cases such as C-62/86, *Akzo* v. *Commission* [1991] ECR I-3359 and C-395 and 396/96 P, *Compagnie Maritime Transports Belge* v. *Commission* [2000] ECR I-365 which concern threats made towards competitors).

[41] See De Mello, note 36 above.

[42] See Dabbah (*Middle East*), p. 5, note 6 above.

seems to be fairly clear however is that – at any rate – FDI does not enjoy an unconditional, open-door attitude by all developing countries. In some countries FDI – although welcomed – is subjected to strict conditions laid under the law such as those requiring that it must lead to economic growth, technological development, improvement in the quality of goods or services, increase in employment opportunities, or boost in the country's entry into world markets. In some cases, the relevant law may have additional strict conditions aimed at ensuring that the firm engaged in FDI would not come to enjoy a monopolistic position in local markets. In other countries, the welcoming of FDI by the relevant developing country is not genuine but rather is superficial and comes to satisfy the relevant international organisation, where the latter is pushing the country concerned to accept foreign participation in its local markets.[43] That said, there are many developing countries in which FDI is looked at in an extremely positive way for the purposes of bringing about economic and technological developments and in order to enhance the competitiveness of the local economy. To this end, some countries have taken well-tailored measures such as creating industrial free zones, which are designated areas featuring customs and duty-free movement of goods and services.[44] A number of incentives are provided for foreign firms operating in the free zones ranging from tax and custom duties exemptions to easing restrictions on currency transfer. Some countries have gone even further and have also adopted specific investment laws and taken structural steps, such as establishing a specific ministry in order to oversee the implementation of the law and to develop and promote foreign investments, so as to enhance the incentives of foreign entities to invest in local markets.[45] This positive attitude towards FDI, however, comes in varying degrees and in some developing countries it is quite extreme and extends to giving foreign

---

[43] This welcoming could be in the form of inviting foreign firms to acquire stakes in public firms. At the same time however the relevant country would impose such extensive conditions on the potential acquirer that would simply frustrate the latter and bring it to change its 'expression of interest' to 'expression of no interest'.

[44] Industrial free zones exist in many developing countries around the world and there is consensus that their existence facilitates greater FDI in the relevant country.

[45] See, for example, the creation of the Ministry of Investment in Sudan which was set up in order to: improve the investment environment in Sudan; facilitate the investment procedures; execute strategies and policies of investment; issue licences to investment projects; provide relevant information to investors; organise workshops, forums and conferences to highlight the advantages of investing in Sudan; and develop relations with international organisations to facilitate exchange of information.

firms – often with the backing of their home governments – a free hand in the host country simply because the door is opened too widely and unconditionally. Indeed, the country concerned may even encourage such foreign participation at the expense of its own firms. Some evidence may be found that such an attitude could easily lead to manipulation of the country concerned at the hands of the foreign firm(s) and this may well discourage investment by firms from other foreign countries.[46]

The exact relationship between competition law and policy and FDI in general and in relation to developing countries in particular has attracted divergent views. At one end of the spectrum, there is the view that the existence of the former – with its aim to guarantee competitive markets – would encourage the latter. Therefore, according to this view foreign firms and investors are expected to be attracted to a competitive environment, especially one in which competition rules exist and are consistent with or similar, both in letter and application, to those prevailing in major jurisdictions, most notably the EC and the USA. At the other end of the spectrum, there is the view that foreign firms and investors might be more inclined to invest in countries where the national government maintains a 'protectionist' policy of state control and planning in relation to certain sectors of the economy with an imperfect competition environment. The belief is that these firms will be able to benefit from such a stance by national governments and be guaranteed the advantages of a quiet life, especially when they opt to choose acts of monopolisation over competition.[47]

It is important to note that these views have been suggested on the assumption that FDI is possible in the relevant jurisdiction(s): as noted above, not all developing countries have maintained a (consistent) policy (at least) of allowing foreign participation in all sectors of the

---

[46] Perhaps the most obvious example here is the involvement of many Chinese firms in the African continent. Many of these firms are fully supported by the Chinese government – whether through subsidisation or another way – and this puts them at a noticeable advantage vis-à-vis local firms; notably this enables them to out-bid the latter because they are able to meet the conditions set out in the relevant bid. In some cases these conditions are set in accordance with a political agreement between the governments concerned or as a result of political pressure from the Chinese government. There are many countries who decline to invest in African countries which have heavy involvement with Chinese firms. As a visiting foreign Minister of Trade and Industry told an African leader during their meeting: 'Mr President, thank you for the opportunity but our companies never go where Chinese companies operate.'

[47] See B. Hoekman and H. L. Kee, *Imports, Entry and Competition Law as Market Disciplines* (Centre for Economic Policy Research, 2003).

economy. Nonetheless, the prevailing position, even globally, has increasingly been in favour of allowing and encouraging such participation and this position has been adopted by a very large number of developing countries in recent years. With the heavy emphasis placed on FDI in many developing countries, there has been a growing recognition that competition law should be adopted and utilised for the purposes of encouraging FDI in the local economy of these countries.[48] In some developing countries competition law is being used as one of the main tools to attract and foster foreign participation in the local economy. It is probably true that developing countries on the whole appear to have embraced the former view (competition law will attract FDI) as opposed to the latter view (foreign firms prefer the absence of competition law) on the relationship between competition law and FDI identified above.

III. Fighting poverty

Developing countries suffer from a serious poverty problem, which in actual fact also exists, albeit to a considerably lesser extent, in the developed world. Poverty, when present, can cause many serious problems for individual citizens, society and the relevant country as a whole. One of those problems that has competition law relevance is high prices. An increase in the price of different products – whether goods or services – has a more serious impact on poor communities because the members of these communities may be forced to sacrifice important opportunities and qualities of life, such as education, in order to be able to afford these goods or services. In the alternative – equally bad – scenario, these communities may simply have to 'accept' that these goods and services are outside their reach.

In simplistic terms, reducing poverty requires that the poor be empowered, given productive employment and increased access to resources. The success of any initiatives seeking to achieve this is intrinsically linked to the way in which markets function; as the World Bank stated: 'Markets work for the poor because poor people rely on formal and informal markets to sell their labour and products, to finance investment, and to insure against risks. Well-functioning markets are important in generating growth and expanding opportunities for poor

---

[48] Notable examples here are Egypt, Jordan, Lebanon, Libya, Sudan and Syria and the United Arab Emirates. In all of these countries a strong link has been identified between competition law and FDI.

people.'[49] The term 'well-functioning markets' denotes the presence of competition and the absence of distortion of the competitive structure of markets and it is clear that unless these characteristics are addressed, poverty will – in spite of other efforts – continue to be a serious problem facing developing countries.

IV. Complementing efforts seeking to promote corporate governance

The topic of corporate governance is one that was neglected for many years in most developing countries and has only recently come to receive particular attention and focus in different parts of the developing world.[50] Many developing countries are turning their attention to this topic having realised that corporate governance is a crucial factor in attracting foreign investment and enhancing investor confidence.[51] Additionally, with the strong interest on the part of many developing countries for increased integration into the global community, closer attention has come to be given to the need to improve corporate governance domestically. In doing so, these countries are following the examples furnished by developed countries and taking note of the guidance, general principles and codes of practices which have come to be produced by key international organisations, most notably the World Bank and the IMF.

Competition can play a major role in enhancing corporate governance.[52] It would not be difficult to think of a situation in which a firm that is subject to no competitive pressure whatsoever – whether from within or from outside the market – and is the only or one of very few firms in the market could easily become inefficient and its management become lax in their approach, with no real drive for innovation or 'burning desire' for efficiency, especially in cases where such a firm is able to charge for its products whatever price it desires. In such a situation, the management of the firm would feel comfortable and safe in the knowledge that the firm is unlikely to be 'threatened' or its quiet

---

[49] World Development Report (WDR) 2000/2001: *Attacking Poverty*, available at: http://web. worldbank.org/WBSITE/EXTERNAL/TOPICS/EXTPOVERTY/0,,contentMDK:20194762~ pagePK:148956~piPK:216618~theSitePK:336992,00.html.

[50] See A. Dignam and M. Galanis, *The Globalisation of Corporate Governance* (Ashgate Publishing, 2009).

[51] Note however that in the case of some developing countries this attention has been brought about by international organisations. The World Bank has had a particular involvement in this regard.

[52] A. Dignam, 'The Role of Competition in Determining Corporate Governance Outcomes: Lessons From Australia's Corporate Governance System' (2005) *Modern Law Review* 68.

life disrupted, and one adverse consequence that may follow from this situation is a tendency towards or even an engagement in anticompetitive behaviour or abusive conduct. Furthermore, in these situations firms tend to have access to capital through local and international banks. Among other things, such access to capital enhances the economic power of these firms, arms them with a significant business advantage and may even reduce their drive for efficiency further. Hence, the widely held belief is that competition can address this undesirable situation and on the whole it can deliver key benefits in terms of enhancing economic efficiency – notably productive efficiency – in the market and lead to maximisation of consumer welfare.

The focus which has come to be given to corporate governance in different developing countries has nonetheless been narrow in its scope, being devoted almost exclusively to *intrinsic* factors of corporate governance, namely issues such as the need to protect shareholders' interest, adherence to codes of conduct by senior corporate management and general issues dealing with conflict of interest among the officers of a firm. However, it is crucial to appreciate that corporate governance is equally concerned with *extrinsic* factors, most notably the environment in which the firm conducts its business activities and the type of economy prevailing in the relevant country. For this reason, the existence of conditions conducive for competition under the umbrella of such factors can lead to good practices of corporate governance and may in some cases be rather vital to achieve this.

Corporate governance in developing countries may be improved significantly through enhancing competition in local markets. To achieve this however, those countries not only need competition legislation in place but also need the necessary mechanism for its effective enforcement. This would necessitate the existence of an independent competition authority with the necessary capabilities and powers to conduct investigations and reach binding conclusions. It would also require a system of checks and balances with an effective judicial branch and the formulation of public policies that do not hinder competition. In relation to the latter, a pro-competitive institutional structure and the function of competition advocacy can play a major role. The following section will consider the issue of pro-competitive institutional structure.

V. Pro-competitive institutional structure

Competition authorities – but also other public authorities – of developing countries have an important role to play in promoting competition and building an environment in which competition and economic growth, as opposed to anticompetitive situations, will flourish. The approach being suggested here involves creating institutional structures and designs which are pro-competitive. This approach would entail building institutions, which operate in an efficient and transparent manner, by introducing and implementing suitable, clear and user-friendly rules and guidelines which will be of huge value to business firms and their legal advisors and also to consumers. These rules and guidelines must be suitable to the specifications of the local economy and the legal system in use; they must be clear in order to support legal certainty; and they must be user-friendly in order to ensure that they offer the necessary help and comfort to firms and other parties with direct or individual concern under the relevant competition law regime. Above all, to build their pro-competitiveness these institutions will need to design and implement concrete action plans for the purposes of removing artificial barriers to entry in local markets and those facing trade and investment more generally, most notably barriers caused by government rules and regulations as well as those caused by the anticompetitive behaviour and conduct of firms operating within the relevant market(s).

(B) Arguments against

The proliferation of competition law around the developing world has been received with a certain degree of scepticism. The reservations about the value of competition law in the developing world seem to be based on the view that the chances for competition law to play a role in the absence of a free market economy are slim.[53] In many developing countries there is lack of independence on the part of local competition authorities from the executive branch of government and such authorities are subject to political influence and control; and in most if not all developing countries matters other than competition law are given higher priority. A concern that sometimes arises in practice in this regard is over whether there is any justification for devoting resources to the field of competition law. All these points have led to the scepticism mentioned here.

---

[53] See W. Carlin, J. Haskel and P. Seabright, 'Understanding the Essential Fact About Capitalism: Markets, Competition and Creative Destruction' (2001) *National Institute Economic Review* 67.

(C)   Comment

The two sets of competing views have their respective merits. In fairness however, the majority view has evolved in favour of different developing countries adopting competition legislation. Indeed, the entire 'look' at the debate over the value of competition law and policy in developing countries has witnessed a shift from what used to be the common question of *why do developing countries need competition law* to what has become the common question of *why developing countries do not need competition law*. In this way, the onus has shifted from having to demonstrate the need for competition law in a particular developing country to having to demonstrate why competition law should not be adopted in the country. As such, a 'presumption' has been created in favour of developing countries adopting some form of competition law and this has as a result made it less necessary to ask whether developing countries need competition law.

5.   What would be the most suitable law or model for developing countries?

A serious question that has always been posed but never quite answered is *what type* of competition law would be suitable for developing countries. This is perhaps one of the most difficult questions facing anyone in charge of or involved in the designing of a competition law regime in a developing country. It is hugely important to pay particular attention to this question.

It was noted above how an increasing number of developing countries came to embrace and introduce 'modern' competition laws, based in large part on the 'models' in existence in the developed world. The two models which have been most dominant here and most used are the EU and US competition law regimes.[54] There is a risk however that is attached to this development as far as developing countries are concerned, namely that modern competition laws have been introduced

---

[54] This can be seen from the wording of competition laws of developing countries and the practice adopted in enforcing these laws. Looking at some of these laws one clearly sees the 'US' and EU' elements and to some extent even the 'Canadian' element. Some of these laws are quite US-centric whilst others are quite EU-centric. In relation to some countries, the legislative developments are highly fascinating: for example, these may begin with the first 'draft' of the law being US-centric and when this draft becomes final it may end up being quite EU-centric. See the (long) legislative history of the Chinese Anti-monopoly Law 2007.

and developed in these countries without sufficient understanding on their part of what competition entails or what its role in the economy should be. Thus, the legislative developments in the field appear to out-step the maturing and developing of competition as a concept, as free-market ideology and as a culture.

The competition law 'conception' of developed countries and their advanced economies is not necessarily ideal for developing countries, which mostly are small, emerging market economies.[55] In the former economies – other than the fact that the legislative history of competition law is different from that of the latter – competition law and policy operate within a much more dynamic economic and political environment and on the whole have developed according to competition-specific considerations and patterns.[56] Developed countries have, by and large, first developed competition laws and policies and then modified these (where relevant) in the light of international agreements and developments in the global economy more generally. This has not been the experience of developing countries, many of which have adopted competition law either under or in the light of such agreements and developments.

Nonetheless, the following of models from the developed world by developing countries has been defended as a sensible step, which would – in addition to giving them the chance to forge closer economic links with the relevant developed jurisdiction – enable them to ensure and protect effective competition in local markets. The practice has also been defended as being desirable from the point of view of firms because this will relieve them of the burdens associated with having to deal with different competition laws; this has both substantive law and procedural benefits.[57] As such, the parachuting-in of competition laws from the developed world into developing countries may not necessarily be objectionable. At the same time, however, the need for adopting competition laws *within* the domestic legal order of developing countries – i.e. for the laws to develop from local roots – seems to

---

[55] See M. Gal, 'The Ecology of Antitrust Preconditions for Competition Law Enforcement in Developing Countries' in Cernat and Holmes, note 5 above.

[56] See F. Vissi, 'Challenges and Questions around Competition Policy: the Hungarian Experience' (1995) Fordham International Law Journal 1230.

[57] Among these benefits are: using similar substantive analysis to determine the applicability of the relevant laws in the relevant situation *and* enhanced certainty and reduction in cost which are likely to emerge from following similar procedures in different competition law regimes.

be important in the context of these new market economies. The adoption of rules consistent with the cultural and institutional context of the country concerned is seen as more desirable because such rules are more readily accepted by those who apply them and to whom they apply than the rules parachuted-in from the developed world. Thus, the attention should be given to effectiveness of the rules when it comes to enforcement – something that is regarded as more fundamental than a simple exercise of 'modelling'.

When considering the question of what is the best model for developing countries to follow in the field of competition law, two particular issues deserve some close attention. These two issues will be considered in turn.

(A)   Means and end debate

The enormous efforts made in recent years to examine the topic of competition law and policy in developing countries has included an attempt to analyse and understand the concept and phenomenon of competition in these countries. Nonetheless, what seems to be clear is that a crucial question remains quite untouched and as a result this has caused a degree of uncertainty to remain, namely whether competition should be considered as a means to an end or an end in itself.[58] This uncertainty can be seen in the case of many developing countries. The experience of different developing countries shows that competition has been considered as both a means to an end *and* as an end in itself. On the one hand, a declared goal within the competition law regimes of these countries is to have competition in the domestic economy and to use competition law in order to ensure this would happen. On the other hand, in practice competition has been treated as a tool to achieve a variety of objectives, ranging from economic efficiency and the maximisation of consumer welfare to ensuring economic development, sustainable growth and protecting wider social and political objectives.

(B)   Similarities in policy approach

Competition law within different developing countries has developed along different but, at the same time, similar lines. In those countries in

---

[58] See pp. 29–30 above.

which some form of competition law has been introduced, the law even bears different titles. However, differences between developing countries in the field of competition law exist not only in relation to the name and wording of the laws, but also in relation to how these laws are actually enforced. Despite these differences, most developing countries can be said to have an interesting form of law and competition policy which, when placed under a magnifying glass, appears to be a policy that includes all policies aiming to achieve trade liberalisation in a wide sense, prevent barriers to entry to the market and facilitate markets which are contestable.[59] All of these issues have come to receive expression in the formulation and implementation of competition policy in different developing countries; in fact these factors also feature among the goals expressed in the laws of some of these countries. Thus, competition policy seems to have been given a wider framework, which is additionally defined by issues of market access and removal of barriers hindering trade and investment, and even industrial policy considerations. In this way, governments in developing countries have come to use competition law for the purposes of enabling them to achieve a change of outfits: from a situation of state control and planning with the state acting as a 'controller' to the situation of a free market economy with the state acting as a 'regulator' of behaviour and practices of private firms.

Another similarity of policy approach among different developing countries revolves around a heavy degree of intervention in the marketplace and giving domestic competition rules a social 'orientation'. There appears to be a particular interest in regulating prices of certain commodities in particular[60] as well as the behaviour of powerful firms in the market. This particular regulatory approach – which differs from the *laissez-faire* approach seen in many Western countries – shows competition law as being a tool for not merely protecting competition but also helping create and promote competition within a mechanism of extra-regulatory function available to the government. The model of competition regulation that has come to be used in those countries therefore appears to be unique and interesting given that apparently an increasing number of developing countries have come to embrace the belief in the market mechanism and the desirability of competition in

---

[59] See p. 9 above for a discussion on the theory of contestable markets.
[60] See, for example, the price regulation instrument in existence in many developing countries.

the marketplace as a tool for the purposes of economic development. However these countries have been reluctant totally to relinquish their control of the market and as a result they seem interested in reaping the benefits of competition without a readiness to accept the risks that may flow from it, such as a possible increase in price to reward additional innovation and investment on the part of firms and difficulties created for inefficient firms which might struggle in a climate of heated rivalry. Indeed, this shows that competition has not been fully accepted by all developing countries, many of which have shown little interest in abandoning their heavy price-regulation mechanism.[61] One may wonder however whether this should be understandable given the lack of market stability and the questionable maturity and responsibility of private firms to seek economic efficiency and refrain from behaviour or conduct harmful to consumers, competition and the public interest at large.[62] Many would argue that it is perhaps necessary to have some price regulation in the case of certain commodities such as milk and bread especially, as was considered above, poverty is a common feature in many developing countries. In many developing countries these are considered to be hugely essential as basic products and leaving them to free market forces may lead to an *increase* as opposed to a *decrease* in prices and to *exploitation* as opposed to *welfare maximisation*, not only due to the risks of anticompetitive behaviour or abuse of dominance but also because the price of these products is susceptible to a change upwards even in the absence of harmful practices. It is thought that a change of this nature would prove extremely damaging to consumers in developing countries.[63] The possibility for intervention by the government to regulate prices *in exceptional cases* should not therefore be considered as objectionable. It is important to note the emphasis in this proposition, however: intervention should be an exception rather than the rule, and the issue of price regulation may certainly be considered as controversial and problematic in relation to other sectors or commodities.

---

[61] Some exceptions however can be found. See further at p. 361 below.

[62] See V. Chetty, *The Place of Public Interest in South Africa's Competition Legislation* (American Bar Association, Section of Antitrust Law, 2005).

[63] It is possible to see the seriousness of such an outcome in light of the changes in the market for wheat and the 'sharp' increase in the price of bread seen in Europe witnessed especially in 2006. See, for example, 'Bakers set to raise price of a loaf', *Financial Times* (15 August 2006).

6. The challenges facing developing countries

The decision and actual effort to introduce a new competition law in a developing country can be subject to serious challenges, which often prove to be daunting and highly frustrating.

(A) The involvement of the government in the local economy

In some developing countries, the government plays a major role in different sectors of the economy. From the relevant government's point of view this is crucial in order to protect the greater good of the people and to ensure that market developments adhere to the principle of social responsibility, which private forces generally have no appreciation of. The government would normally defend their decision to play a major role on the ground that the people are in favour of government control and feel greater security and protection with the government running and regulating the economic affairs of the country. However, non-governmental views in developing countries across-the-board dispute this and hold that the public in fact is not content with sustained government control over the economy; and at any rate they would contend that the public is never given an adequate opportunity to have a say in this matter.

The government's involvement in different economic sectors can present several problems; on the whole, such involvement has the potential to hinder the development of the private sector and the emergence of a process of competition in local markets. First, the manner in which certain sectors may be structured could render competition neither possible nor workable. For example, participation by private local firms in the relevant sector may to a large extent be made conditional upon securing loans from local banks. The issuance of such loans however may be surmounted with numerous difficulties, which could mean that local contractors are unable to bid for and secure large construction projects. On the other hand, as noted above, the government may favour attracting foreign participation by firms who – due to subsidies granted to them by their home country(ies) – are able to submit extremely low bids and as a result oust any possible local competition in the bidding process. The irony would not be lost that in effect this may be considered as a form of anti-dumping, which may be prohibited by the local rules of the country concerned.[64] Secondly, the government may operate a price-fixing and market/customer-sharing mechanism in relation to sectors in which some privatisation has been introduced. Notable examples here include the transportation sector,[65] which may feature in some developing countries public firms, political 'party-affiliated' firms[66] and private firms. As a result, free market competition may be absent in the relevant sector(s). These sectors may even be structured in such a way that the government is in fact in full control of the sector. Transport firms operating within the sector – whether public, party-affiliated or private – would have little choice but to abide by measures adopted by the government in the sector.[67]

(B) Political factors

Enormous political hurdles may exist in the face of efforts seeking to introduce or strengthen domestic competition rules in developing countries. Indeed these hurdles can exist regardless of the type of political regime in existence, i.e. regardless of whether in the relevant country a dictatorship or a democratic regime prevails and regardless of whether the local economy is centrally planned or not. Even if a democratic regime is in existence, the government may be in the form of a 'coalition' between many political parties who may not necessarily see eye-to-eye on a hugely important step, such as whether and how to introduce a competition law or enforce existing competition rules. The phenomenal importance of this step can be seen in light of the fact that the decision to adopt a competition law sits at the heart of *either* the move towards a market economy *or* the efforts to ensure the

---

[64] These anti-dumping provisions may be contained in a trade law, unfair competition law or even in the relevant competition law. On the latter, see the Ethiopian Competition and Trade Proclamation 2003, in particular Art. 11 thereof.

[65] See M. Dutz and A. Hayri, 'Inappropriate Regulation and Stifled Innovation in the Road Freight Industry: Lessons For Policy Reform' in G. Amato and L. L. Laudati (eds.), *The Anticompetitive Impact of Regulation* (Edward Elgar, 2001), pp. 245–61.

[66] These are generally private firms but with strong political affiliation and loyalty to the ruling party or person/family in the relevant country.

[67] One example from the real world of dictating conditions by government is where the government operates a market-sharing scheme, under which private firms may be excluded from certain routes with the bizarre excuse that they may use trucks with heavy loads on relevant roads and as a result damage the roads, i.e. the infrastructure itself.

proper functioning of an existing market economy. There is not a more intractable ideological disagreement that arises between political factions than the 'state of affairs' underpinning such a step. The effort required to achieve the political blessing of a single party or person in the case of a non-democratic regime or that of more than one political party in a democracy can be enormous and instances of failure are perhaps more common than those of success in these cases. In practice this effort needs to be particularly concentrated and guided by a careful strategy given that considerable lobbying (mostly by special interests) may be taking place behind the scene which oftentimes has serious influence on the actual decision eventually taken by politicians; this is especially so in relation to the question of how wide the scope of the new competition law should be and what situations or persons should be caught within the net of its rules. The scope of the law may be effectively controlled in a variety of ways through the particular definition given to key terms and concepts featuring in its provisions.[68] A careful strategy is also needed on the enforcement front, given that lobbying may lead to politicians choosing lax or ineffective enforcement of the competition rules in the relevant competition law regime. The lobbying will be particularly effective in those countries which are notorious for corruption; many developing countries fit this description.

When dealing with political constraints, one must consider the phenomenon of short-lived governments. In some parts of the developing world, elected or appointed governments or politicians do not survive for long and are sometimes replaced shortly after their inauguration. This presents huge difficulties for competition law development and enforcement, especially where a minister – often the minister responsible for trade, industry or the economy – sits at the heart of the relevant competition law regime. Among other things, such a short tour as a government or a minister minimises the prospects for the formulation and design of a coherent, long-term and sustainable competition policy. At another level, this means that sometimes decisions in actual cases may not be reached at all or if a particular minister comes to a particular conclusion, for example that a particular situation is anticompetitive, this may be reversed by his successor before a final decision is reached. This shows the importance of having an independent competition authority, though achieving this in practice may be a highly challenging task

---

[68] See below in relation to the discussion on the scope of competition law.

which, whilst not necessarily impossible to execute, can take a considerably long time.[69]

(C) Fixing institutional parameters

It should be noted that even if the initial hurdle of convincing politicians and receiving their blessing to adopt competition law in the country concerned is cleared, enormous and numerous hurdles are faced in determining the parameters of the institutional structure within the new competition law regime. It was noted above that introducing a competition law and designing a competition policy for developing countries are important steps, though seeking to promote competition solely through these two steps might not be sufficient: developing countries are unique countries and for this reason the approach to competition law should be suited to the size and type of their domestic economies and their particular geographic location.[70] The unique political, social and cultural circumstances of these countries make this all the more important. Developing an appropriate institutional framework must be sensitive to all these factors and circumstances.[71]

Several difficult questions often arise when considering the issue of institutional parameters in the context of introducing or enforcing competition law in developing countries. Usually these questions are dealt with in a manner that would ensure *as opposed to* avoid political influence or intervention. This particular outcome may be recognised in the relevant competition law by giving politicians a statutory basis to play a crucial role in the actual decision-making process in competition cases; alternatively, it may occur in the form of political pressure put on competition officials in their work by telling them what to investigate; how to investigate; and, quite crucially, what not to investigate.

Among the difficult questions which usually arise when determining institutional parameters are:

---

[69] See the discussion below in relation to the question of independence.

[70] See M. Gal, 'Does Size Matter: the Effects of Market Size on Optimal Competition Policy' (2001) *The University of South Carolina Law Review* 1437.

[71] See Boza, 'Tailor Made Competition Policy in a Standardised World: a Study From the Perspective of Developing Economies' in IDRC report *Tailor-Made Competition Policy in a Standardising World: The Experience of Peru* (Instituto Apoyo and Ciudadanos al Día, 2005).

- Who should have sole responsibility for enforcing the law?
- Should the person or body in question be independent or part of the executive branch? Should courts have a role to play in the enforcement of the law?
- What type of expertise is needed to apply the law and to operate the regime, and how could it be achieved?
- What resources (including human and financial resources) should be made available?
- In the case of where more than one actor is involved in the operation of the competition law regime – the competition authority, a minister, the government as a whole, the office of public prosecutor/attorney general and courts – how can one ensure that *bureaucracy* of the regime would not derail enforcement actions?

Answering these questions *correctly* can have an enormous positive effect on the type of competition law regime that would emerge in practice.[72] At any rate however, the answers given to these questions – whether right, wrong, or in between – will both directly and indirectly lead to an impact on the wider economy, society and culture in the country concerned. Conversely, the answers themselves may actually be conditioned by the patterns of the relevant economy, the existing forces of society and the prevailing culture in the country concerned.[73]

Three specific issues under the umbrella of institutional parameters deserve particular focus: the issue of structure, composition and powers of the relevant competition authorities; the issue of resources; and the issue of judicial control.

I.   Structure, composition and powers of the competition authority

Competition authorities in many developing countries are established as 'investigating' bodies but without effective powers: they have bite but no teeth. The structure and composition of these authorities often suffer from major problems. First, the competition authority may lack the independence needed to be able to conduct its work and to reach final conclusions because the law may reserve considerable powers to

---

[72] See Kovacic, 'Getting Started: Creating New Competition Policy Institutions in Transition Economies' (1997) *Brooklyn Journal of International Law* 403.

[73] As we will see in relation to the discussion at p. 320 below, culture has a particularly important role to play in the field of competition law, most notably so in the developing world; see also pp. 62–64 above.

the relevant ministry and minister who plays a key role in the regime and who enjoys executive powers over the work of the competition authority and is the decision maker in actual cases.[74] Secondly, the composition of the competition authority may be highly controversial and problematic due to the high-level ranking of those serving as members of the authority, many of whom are occupied by non-competition work and are simply unable to give competition cases and work the necessary focus and attention and as a result competition law and policy issues are likely to be sidelined and possibly even overshadowed by non-competition matters. Thirdly, the composition of the competition authority may not be adequately balanced and may not reflect the relevant sectors given the exclusion of representatives of the private sector from the board within the relevant competition authority.[75] Fourthly, the work of the competition authority may not be sufficiently constant to lead to effective enforcement of the competition rules: the meetings which the competition authority is supposed to hold may not be sufficiently frequent to enable effective competition law enforcement and robust competition policy to take foothold in the country concerned;[76] or the quorum required by law before a decision can be reached may seldom be met in practice due to the absence of members of the board.[77] Finally, in some countries, there is a practice of 'doubling' officials which means that those who handle the work of the competition authority also work in related areas within relevant government bodies, often the ministry for trade and industry. It is doubtful whether this practice enhances the chance for competition law enforcement to be promoted. On the contrary: the chances for effective enforcement in this case are slimmer because an official can be easily over-stretched and be less productive when operating on Monday and Tuesday as a competition official and Wednesday to

---

[74] Many examples may be found here. See in particular the position under the competition law regimes of: Egypt; Saudi Arabia, Jordan, Ethiopia. As we noted above, in the absence of a statutory basis for political role, political influence may be exerted in different ways on competition officials.

[75] See the discussion in part 7 below with regard to the role of consumers in developing countries.

[76] See as an example the position under the Saudi Arabian competition law regime.

[77] One particular competition law regime that has suffered from such difficulties is the Egyptian regime. There have been a number of competition cases in which the Egyptian Competition Authority was unable to reach a decision over a considerable period of time because of the insufficient number of members the Authority's board present at every board meeting.

Friday as a trade official. In other words, having a 'hybrid' role of officials as competition officials and trade officials affects the extent and quality of the work conducted. Given that the officials do not exclusively focus on competition cases they are not in a good position to prioritise between their tasks and/or to give competition cases adequate focus and attention. There is no better alternative here other than to have officials being given exclusive focus on competition law and policy.

Interestingly in many cases competition officials in developing countries are aware of most if not all of the shortcomings mentioned in the previous paragraph. Admirably they try to do as much as they can to remedy the situation but they are not always successful because of the hurdles they often face; some of these hurdles were discussed above.[78] Perhaps this is where the input of influential international organisations – most notably the World Bank – can be particularly helpful. International organisations can play a leading role in advocating the view that a competition authority should be independent from the government with a separate budget and sufficient resources and in providing the relevant country with a suitable institutional model. In this regard, there are several alternatives regarding institutional structure and composition which may be suitable for developing countries. A particularly suitable option to pursue would be to create the position of a *chairman* of the authority along with an advisory board which could be made up of representatives of both the *public* and *private* sector. The chairman would be a person who enjoys expertise in competition-related fields and would be responsible for the running of the competition authority. Another possibility would be to have a *board of directors or commissioners* in place but to assign to it the responsibility of policy formulation. A position of *director of competition* could then be created within the competition authority; this director would be a qualified person responsible for the day-to-day operations of the authority. However, one should still recommend the creation of an advisory committee made up of representatives of different sectors to advise the director. Regardless of which option is chosen, competition officials should operate within *independent* and *autonomous* units which are clearly identifiable from the relevant ministry and the government more generally. With regard to the involvement of a minister in the field of competition law, it would be sensible to recommend that

---

[78] See pp. 311–313 above in relation to political hurdles.

decisions by the competition authority should not be subject to the approval of such a minister,[79] though it may be made possible for ministerial authorisation to be sought in cases where the parties disagree with the decision of the competition authority. Such authorisation may be given on *narrow* (highly exceptional) grounds such as those of international competitiveness or economic development.[80]

II. Lack of resources

The lack of sufficient resources – whether human (including expertise) or financial – is a serious hurdle facing the enforcement efforts of many competition authorities in the developing world. In particular, local markets in developing countries often lack competition expertise and if this were to be available, it is very likely that this expertise will not be attracted to working for the 'newly created' or 'toothless' local competition authority, especially when private practice offers a better career prospect and a more handsome financial gain. Those who decide to join the authority – whether experts of competition law or not – often do not stay around for long and in some cases leave almost as soon as they join. As a result, many competition authorities in the developing world are understaffed which means that the handful of officials (which in some cases is as few as four!) in the authority are far from being capable of handling the huge task of establishing a solid basis of effective enforcement. Effective enforcement in this case would require having the necessary staff of lawyers and economists, investigators (who will be able to conduct physical investigations at the business premises of firms and conduct interviews with various parties) and case-handlers (who will be in charge of building individual cases and managing their progress from the moment an investigation is opened until the decision-making stage). Some developing countries are extremely vast in terms of both geography and the size of the population, which may be very diverse in the case of the latter. This obviously necessitates the existence of competition authorities with adequate size to be able to execute their responsibilities. Equally important, competition expertise needs to be injected within the competition authorities

---

[79] See how decisions of the National Commission for the Defence of Competition (CNDC) of Argentina are ratified by the Secretariat of Domestic Commerce within the Ministry of Economy.

[80] The mechanism of ministerial authorisation is found in the German competition law regime in the area of merger control; see chapter 1, at note 113.

of developing countries. In many cases such action is rather urgent. Expertise can be achieved in one of two ways, preferably using both simultaneously: first, through training sessions aimed at equipping the staff of these competition authorities with a good understanding of competition law and policy, including sessions dealing with competition law practice within key jurisdictions and sessions dealing with appropriate case studies on how different provisions of the law are applied which include a consideration of the analysis – in both legal and economic terms – that often needs to conducted. Secondly, the relevant competition authority should seek to establish close relations with foreign competition authorities both within and beyond the relevant region within which its home country is located. As we saw above, a number of leading competition authorities operate well-established international technical assistance and capacity-building programmes, from which competition authorities of developing countries can benefit.

When a shortage of staff and expertise is coupled with the high cost involved in pursuing cases – especially those in the form of international cartels, cross-border abuse of dominance or anticompetitive transnational mergers – the likely outcome will be that enforcement will not take place; this likelihood turns into a near certainty with the existence of limited budgets, which are 'characteristic' of competition authorities in developing countries. It is worth noting here that an investigation in one or more foreign jurisdictions and even a finding of a competition law breach does not necessarily offer such an authority a better chance in these cases because it will still have to establish both the existence of the prohibited behaviour or conduct and its adverse effects on competition and/or trade in local markets in accordance with local law. Indeed the existence of foreign investigations may have the opposite outcome for local enforcement, namely 'free-riding' or at least complete reliance on the former. It is debatable whether this is sensible. On the one hand, it may be considered sensible where the foreign investigation can put an end to the infringement and the harmful situation as a whole; this is clearly beneficial from a local perspective. Indeed the attitude of certain competition authorities and courts is that it would *not* be sensible to do otherwise.[81] From the

---

[81] See, for example, the view of the Israel Antitrust Authority in a case which was brought before the Israel Supreme Court (sitting as a High Court of Justice) Case 6623/03, *Oded Lavie* v. *Director of Antitrust Authority* (2003). According to the authority it made no

relevant competition authority's perspective, this is also probably desirable in order to avoid a situation in which it reaches a conclusion different from that of its foreign (more powerful) counterpart; in these cases the authority may prefer the role of an 'assisting' or 'supporting' authority by conducting certain investigatory tasks or handing over certain information in its possession to the foreign competition authority, provided of course that the latter is not prevented under domestic law. On the other hand, it is arguable that it is not sensible because there may be cases in which the foreign action taken may not necessarily address the local adverse effect produced as a result of the situation. In fairness, however, it is usually the case that the enforcement by foreign authority(ies) would mean that the harmful situation – notably international cartels and cross-border abuse of dominance – would be eliminated throughout the world but exceptions may nonetheless exist, for example where the cartel is structured in such a complex way to have independent elements confined to specific jurisdictions.

III. Judicial contribution and control

Providing for the possibility of appeal and/or judicial review under competition law is an important safeguard in the relevant regime. However in some cases this judicial control in the developing world is given to the highest court in the country without first going through the lower judicial tiers, i.e. lower courts or tribunals. This makes it important to ask whether such an approach to judicial control and supervision is appropriate. Arguably, judicial review should be conducted at first instance before reaching the highest court in the country. Moreover, there is the question of whether judges in developing countries enjoy the relevant expertise and ability to vet competition decisions. The answer given to this question is usually in the negative. It is often said that judges lack specialisation in general and cannot be expected to vet decisions adopted by the competition authority or the government itself for that matter. Indeed, in some developing countries the judicial branch in general terms is considered to suffer from a rather illogical situation, namely lack of experience caused by the fact that the relevant individuals join the bench when they are inexperienced and often leave for private practice when they are experienced.[82] This no doubt impacts on the quality of judicial supervision within the relevant

---

sense to bring an action against the abusive conduct of a firm when this conduct was brought to an end globally as a result of the action by a foreign competition authority.

[82] See, for example, Ethiopia.

competition law regime, which is bound to suffer from a major short-coming as a result. The situation is particularly serious in those developing countries in which judicial enforcement is the bedrock on which the competition law regime in the country stands.

(D) Lack of sufficient awareness of competition

People in developing countries lack sufficient awareness of the concept of competition in its *economic* sense. In some of these countries, the concept of competition is not particularly compatible with the prevailing culture, which – by way of contrast from the ideology of competition – may be closer to unfair competition than competition law. For example, throughout almost entire regions in the world, the prevailing culture has been to understand competition as a means to 'defeat' a competitor not on the merit through legitimate means but rather through recourse to tactics and practices of defaming and undermining the competitor. The famous example of 'a man ate his tomatoes and rumours have it this has made him impotent' is one of those that could be cited here. A practice seeking to discredit a competitor does not need to be confined to making allegations against such competitor or engaging in fraudulent behaviour and dishonest practices but could easily extend to engaging in practices such as predatory pricing and rebates.[83] The 'mentality' of defeating competitors can be seen even in those developing countries in which privatisation was introduced in parts though not all of the relevant sector(s) of the economy. In these countries the remaining public firm may seek to undermine the new private operators for a number of reasons, one of them is to 'show' the superiority of the public sector.[84] Moreover, in some countries the prevailing culture favours cooperation and collaboration on the part of market operators whether through business associations and alliances or through other means.

(E) Too much or too little competition?

Even if one were to assume that awareness of the concept of competition exists throughout the developing world, highly inconsistent views can

---

[83] For an explanation of predatory practices see chapter 11, note 13. Rebates can take different forms. One notable example is loyalty rebates: offering customers a rebate if the customer would obtain all of his requirements from the firm offering the rebate.

[84] For a particular example see Dabbah (*Middle East*), p. 278, note 6 above.

be found in developing countries with regard to how much or how little competition exists in local markets. At one end of the spectrum, some views maintain that competition is simply 'non-existent' in the relevant country due to the fact that the government exercises full control over different sectors of the economy and the fact that there is no private sector as such. At the other end of the spectrum, some views complain that there was 'too much' competition in some sectors and that this is highly damaging because it means that in the relevant sector(s) supply outstrips demand. Indeed, some of these views sometimes go further by advocating that the government should step in and address this problem by *limiting* competition.

The fact that views are as diverse as these makes it quite difficult to determine the true 'state of play' in local markets in developing countries which in practice can only be done by undertaking relevant economic analysis and review. Needless to say, however, in relation to sectors in which there is deep government intervention or a monopoly it would be difficult to talk about competition existing or playing an effective role.

(F)   The unique formula of competition and non-competition considerations

In many cases, competition authorities in developing countries are not in the position, often enjoyed by their counterparts in the developed world, of being concerned solely with competition-based considerations. Competition cases before them can easily involve non-competition considerations, such as those related to employment and general economic developments, to which the involvement of foreign firms in particular is thought to contribute. Often competition authorities in the developing world face a serious dilemma presented by the unique formula of competition and non-competition based considerations because either they feel that they should not ignore these considerations or simply they are forced not to do so because of political pressure. The field of merger control in particular offers an example of this dilemma.

The bundling of (or as a reverse action, the difficulty in severing) competition and non-competition issues gives rise to difficulties in different contexts. For example, the relevant competition law may not deal exclusively with competition law and policy: the law may contain elements extending beyond competition law towards trade policy, unfair competition, anti-dumping and price regulation. As such, the 'competition law' content can be easily 'diluted' – something that is bound to impact on the effectiveness of the competition provisions of the law and their application in practice. In particular, the mixture of competition law and non-competition law provisions is bound to cause confusion over the exact purpose and function of the law.[85] Experience in this regard shows – in a rather undisputable fashion – that in *nascent* or *developing* competition law regimes, where the competition law provisions are mixed with unfair competition provisions in particular, the latter tend almost always to obscure the significance and role of the former.[86] This has a serious repercussion in practice: as a result the competition authority in the relevant regime usually ends up handling mostly unfair competition cases as opposed to competition cases and it is hardly surprising that this happens.[87] The confusion described here has also arisen in those developing countries in which a *separate* law exists for dealing with unfair competition. A fairly widespread impression that existed for many years in many parts of the developing world is that unfair competition rules could be used as an instrument to fight *all* harmful competition practices and that by fighting such practices competition will simply exist. In this respect, it can be thought that a legal framework seeking to protect competition in these countries has fairly old foundations – extending in some cases to the early parts of the twentieth century.[88]

---

[85] One of the aspects in relation to which confusion may be caused here concerns the question of whether the relevant competition law aims at protecting competition or protecting competitors.

[86] In Tunisia for example there used to be a great deal of confusion over the role of the Competition Council with the majority of cases referred to the Council being unfair competition cases. The situation however has come to improve dramatically with the Council taking the initiative of explaining in its decisions the differences between unfair competition and competition law.

[87] See the position in relation to Ethiopia. It is understood that since the creation of the Ethiopian Competition Commission, the Commission has received a total of 45 complaints, which concern trade and unfair competition issues. Investigations have been opened into the majority of these complaints and in the case of eight complaints the Commission was able to conclude its investigation and reach a final decision; these decisions are apparently archived in the Ministry of Trade and Industry and have not been publicised. Thus, the Commission has received no competition complaints and it has not conducted a single competition investigation since its creation.

[88] Lebanon, for example, adopted rules on unfair competition in 1924. Of course one may also cite here the 'implementation' of the Paris Convention for the Protection of Industrial Property 1833 as amended by different developing countries over the years. Two particular provisions of the Convention may be worth noting which are contained in Art. 10A of the Convention. The first, Art. 10A(2), of the Convention defines unfair competition as 'any act of competition contrary to honest practices in industrial or commercial matters'. The second,

In fairness however, in recent years the confusion caused by the existence of unfair competition law or unfair competition provisions in a competition law has shrunk considerably but as seen from the discussion above it has not totally disappeared. This 'improvement' has occurred partly due to the elevation of the concept of free competition in developing countries and the increase in familiarity with competition law. Nonetheless, more work remains necessary, especially at grass-roots level, in terms of facilitating a cultural transformation in mentality and ideology among both business and ordinary people in the relevant regime. This is where competition advocacy becomes a highly crucial and desirable tool for competition authorities and for public authorities in developing countries to revert to in order to achieve a change in thinking and to build a robust competition culture.[89]

(G) Manipulation at the hands of other countries and their firms

Many developing countries are manipulated at the hands of other countries and multinational enterprises. The government of a developing country may not always be the 'commander in chief' in relation to its own affairs, especially in the political sphere but also in economic and social ones. Even if a competition law is enacted or exists in the relevant country serious dilemmas may be encountered by the government concerned over how vigorous local competition law enforcement[90] can or should be and what role it should facilitate – through a process of competition – for its local firms. Such dilemmas are often caused because of the bargaining power some multinational or at least foreign firms (with the backing of their home governments) enjoy vis-à-vis the local government of the country concerned.

The risk of manipulation is particularly high in the case of those developing countries which attach special importance to foreign direct investment and the need to attract it.[91] In such case – using the example of the construction sector – the relevant developing country may prefer

---

Art. 10A(3), establishes three categories of cases that have to be prohibited in particular, namely 'acts of such a nature as to create confusion, false allegations of such nature as to discredit a competitor and indications which are liable to mislead the public'. Neither of these provisions however is a competition law tool.

[89] See pp. 65–70 above.
[90] See below in relation to enforcement in an extraterritorial context, which is not the focus of the present section.
[91] See pp. 298–301 above for a discussion of the issue of foreign direct investment and its relationship with competition law.

foreign participation over participation by local firms and this can lead to direct harm to competition in different contexts. A simple scenario taken from the real world may be used as an illustration.[92] In one developing country the government followed a policy of attracting foreign participation and put hurdles[93] before local firms who were interested in bidding for large construction projects, which included road construction. Foreign firms were – quite naturally – able to submit extremely favourable bids due to subsidies enjoyed by their home government. They were also able to avoid the hurdles faced by local firms since these did not apply to them. However, with the lack of sufficient knowledge on the part of the foreign firm of, among other things, the geography and climate of the relevant country and due to sub-standard work conducted at low-cost the relevant project was not completed according to the right specifications. This meant that with the heavy rain the country experiences in the winter period, the road built was absolutely flooded which meant that goods could not be transported on the relevant road. Traders at the different points of destination who sold the goods in question in this case were able to raise prices because of the high demand and the limited availability of stock.

The competition law scene within developing countries appears to be highly influenced by external trade relations concluded by the domestic governments of these countries. In the case of some countries, almost exclusively, the government's desire to accommodate foreign interests appears to determine the parameters of competition and competition policy. This is a deeply troubling situation given that the domestic competition law regime would not under these circumstances be afforded the opportunity to take its natural course for development and progress, including ensuring effective and impartial enforcement within the regime. This problem remains regardless of how 'perfect' or 'watertight' the relevant competition rules of the relevant law are in terms of drafting and wording. Hence, what is required in this case is a more sensitive government approach to competition and competition policy and a recognition that an almost *unconditional* offer to foreign firms and their home governments to participate in local markets is

---

[92] This example comes from a case this author handled in practice.

[93] One of these hurdles concerns the need to have access to funds. Local construction firms almost always need to secure and obtain loans when undertaking large construction projects. However, the banks from which funds may be obtained can impose a condition demanding the existence of collaterals as security. Local firms however may not be able to provide collaterals up to the level demanded by the banks.

not necessarily in the relevant country's best interest and the interest of its consumers; nor is this unconditional offer in fact necessary in order to have participation by foreign firms in local markets: it would be reasonable to expect such participation to emerge even on a 'conditional' basis given that many of these firms need developing countries as much as (perhaps even more) than the latter need them.

(H) The wording of the law

The scope of a competition law may be effectively controlled in a variety of ways: narrowing down the meaning of the 'entities' caught under the law so for example an 'undertaking', a 'person' or 'company' (i.e. the entities whose behaviour, conduct and transactions the law seeks to address) may be defined as non-public actors, thus putting public entities outside the scope of the law, or it may be considered to exist only where the entity in question does not lack power to decide independently;[94] limiting the types of practices which may be caught under the law, for example through giving an exclusion to vertical agreements or certain types of vertical arrangements (such as outlawing market-sharing practices but allowing resale price maintenance);[95] or narrowing down the forms of 'collusion' between firms in the market. Another option in which the scope of the law may be controlled is through introducing a wide set of exemptions, such as exemptions for certain types of cartels (most notably crisis or export cartels) and/or a set of 'exclusions', which would place certain business phenomena beyond the scope of the law.

The competition laws of developing countries quite characteristically carry the features mentioned above, which in practice have resulted in limiting the scope of these laws and hindering the ability of the relevant competition authority to enforce the law effectively. A number of issues in this respect are worth highlighting.

I.   The prohibition on collusion

One may find examples throughout the developing world of the prohibition on anticompetitive behaviour omitting any reference to forms of

---

[94] See, for example, Art. 9 of the Egyptian Law on the Protection of Competition and Prevention of Monopolistic Practices 2005 which provides that the law does not apply to 'public utilities'; also Art. 3 of the Turkish Competition Law on the issue of power to decide independently.

[95] Under resale price maintenance, the supplier is able to impose a particular resale price, which the distributor will have to follow.

collusion other than 'written' or 'oral' *agreements* or *contracts*. This omission is problematic given that in practice it is bound to limit the ability of the competition authority to uncover situations of collusion. In competition law practice, a competition authority should have the ability to make use of additional concepts or tools (other than that of an agreement) to prove the existence of anticompetitive behaviour. These concepts include 'concerted practice', 'conspiracy', 'decision' by an association of firms or undertakings etc.[96] A competition law provision which makes sole reference to an 'oral' or 'written' anticompetitive *agreement* or *contract* renders it effectively impossible for the competition authority to prove the existence of collusion between firms where the authority is not able to point towards the existence of an agreement, whether oral or written. Some developing countries have remedied this situation by amending their laws following the receipt of appropriate expert advice to include a particular mention of other forms of collusion, in addition to agreements or contracts. In other countries, the competition authorities and courts may employ 'teleological' reasoning and interpret the prohibition to catch all forms of collusion. This situation can be problematic however and at any rate such interpretation may prove 'impossible' if the competition authority is unable to prove the existence of an 'agreement' up to the required standard.

II. Vertical restraints

In a large number of developing countries local markets feature many vertical restraints. Vertical restraints are those included in vertical agreements, i.e. agreements between firms operating at different levels of the market (such as those entered into between a supplier and a distributor). The provisions of the competition laws of developing countries however quite prominently lack adequate mechanisms for dealing with vertical restraints. It is true that these provisions may contain some reference to vertical restraints. But this reference usually falls short of providing sufficient clarity on the policy approach to vertical agreements and being, perhaps more crucially, a proper tool for the competition authority itself to engage in the regulation of vertical agreements. It is of little wonder therefore that the area of vertical restraints – notwithstanding its significance – has largely been given insufficient attention in the developing world.

---

[96] See, for example, Art. 101 TFEU (see p. 161 above) and section 1 of the US Sherman Act 1890 (see pp. 239–243 above) which make reference to some of these terms.

III.   Abuse of dominance and monopolisation

The prohibition on abuse of dominance is one that carries fundamental importance in the field of competition law. The competition laws of developing countries however seem to suffer from lack of sufficient clarity in this area. For example, the relevant provision of the law may provide that no person may carry on trade which gives an opportunity to control a relevant market for goods or services, or to limit access to a relevant market or otherwise unduly restrain competition, having or being likely to have adverse effects on market development.[97] This particular wording does not make it clear that there is a prohibition on the abuse of a dominant position. In fact, it is arguable that according to this wording it is possible to condemn the mere holding of a dominant position, a proposition which would be both difficult and wrong to defend.[98] Furthermore, one may find examples in the competition rules of developing countries according to which things like the unfair imposition of an excessively low selling price amounts to an abuse of a dominant position. In the field of competition law, normally lower prices in themselves would be condemned only where this amounts to predatory pricing[99] or where the lowering of the price causes discrimination or is used to bring about foreclosure, such as to exclude competitors or prevent their entry to the relevant market. It is not clear from such wording however that the situation described therein is intended to cover predatory pricing or any of these harmful situations. This is all the more so in the case of those laws which would provide in other provisions for a prohibition of predatory pricing: prohibiting a sale at a price that does not cover production cost to eliminate competition.[100]

Another difficulty found in the case of some of the competition laws of developing countries concerns the establishing of a dominant position in the first place. These laws may simply provide for an automatic finding of dominance in a case where a firm has a market share of 50 per cent in which case the firm may be even considered a 'monopoly'.

---

[97] See also the use of terms such as 'complicating' practices of competitors which feature in the Egyptian competition law regime.

[98] It is important to note that under competition law the prohibition is on the *abuse* of a dominant position. This means that it is permissible to hold a dominant position as long of course as this position was acquired or is maintained through legitimate means, such as through innovation and efficiency.

[99] See further chapter 11, note 13.

[100] See Art. 11(2)(i) of the Ethiopian Competition and Trade Proclamation 2003.

IV. Merger control

The competition rules of many developing countries do not extend in their scope to the area of merger control: indeed, a merger control mechanism has not been adopted in every jurisdiction in which a competition law regime has been introduced. Accordingly, situations where the structure of the market may be altered as a result of merger operations in a way that causes an adverse effect on competition may go unregulated or uncontrolled under the relevant law. It would be fair to add however that this is probably not a deficiency as such. Nonetheless, it is normally very difficult to establish why merger control is omitted from the competition rules of developing countries; competition officials and policymakers in these countries normally struggle to come up with a plausible explanation of why their local rules do not provide for a merger control mechanism and whether this omission should be remedied.

V. Exemptions and exclusions

Exemptions or exclusions are not unheard of in different competition law regimes around the world. The function of these provisions is to render certain prohibition provisions of the law – particularly those aimed at collusion – inapplicable in certain situations. However, the concern one normally develops when considering these provisions in the competition rules of developing countries is the vast size and wide scope of the commercial activities reserved for the government and as a result the almost certainty that the competition law prohibitions may be rendered virtually inapplicable in most if not all cases. Furthermore the exemption criteria in particular may be worded in extremely general language and an open-textured wording here may prove difficult to handle in practice and affects legal certainty. These exemption and exclusion provisions therefore are likely to hamper the utilisation of the competition law as an instrument for protecting competition, safeguarding consumer welfare and promoting economic development in the relevant country.[101]

VI. Procedural matters

The competition rules and the competition law regimes of developing countries as a whole lack a sufficiently developed mechanism of procedural rules dealing with issues such as conducting investigations,

---

[101] See D. Nkikomborirak 'Exemptions and Exceptions: Implications For Economic Performance: the Case of Thailand' in Cernat and Holmes, note 5 above.

holding oral hearings and communicating the findings of competition investigations to the relevant parties. Such a mechanism however is a vital component of a competition law regime and is of huge significance in practice to the parties subject to proceedings by the competition authority as well as to third parties with a relevant interest in those proceedings.

The reverse side of the same coin, however, may show that the relevant competition authority actually enjoys some key powers, such as the power to enter business premises or ask questions. These powers need to be exercised with greater safeguards. The competition rules of developing countries however normally lack such safeguards and, more generally, clarity over the exercise of the different powers in all situations. For example, the law may provide for entry into premises by competition officials showing their 'competition authority's ID'.[102] A more appropriate method of exercising the power however would be for those seeking entry to produce 'written authorisation' by the competition authority and where force is to be used to gain entry, this authorisation should be obtained in the form of a warrant from a judge.

(I) Enforcement-specific challenges in an extraterritorial context

As we will see in chapter 8 below, extraterritorial assertion of jurisdiction has become an established feature of the competition rules of different countries, including developing ones. The experiences of the EU and USA (the most prominent examples in relation to the use of extraterritoriality) along with those of several other countries show that their competition authorities are able to exercise jurisdiction extraterritorially and that firms subject to this assertion of jurisdiction have in different cases (save for exceptional circumstances) complied fully. This assertion of jurisdiction has also been upheld by the highest courts in the relevant jurisdictions.[103]

---

[102] See Art. 15(1)(c) of the Competition and Trade Proclamation of Ethiopia. Under Art. 17 of the Egyptian Law on Protection of Competition and Prohibition of Monopolistic Practices 2005, whosoever is authorised by decree of the Minister of Justice as a 'Law Official' automatically has the right to access books and documents in 'any governmental or non-governmental quarter' and gain whatever information (presumably) they deem necessary for the investigation of a case before the Egyptian Competition Authority.

[103] See pp. 432–446 and pp. 453–454 below regarding the position adopted by the US Supreme Court and the European Court of Justice. The pronouncements of these two important courts

Notwithstanding the existence of a credible and fully functioning competition law regime, the ability of a competition authority of a developing country to assert jurisdiction in this manner is highly questionable and is uncertain at best. This means that it is not necessarily the case that whenever a foreign situation produces effects or impacts within the domestic boundaries of such a country the relevant competition authority will be able to take action. A number of factors can be mentioned in support. The competition authority may face serious obstacles in accessing relevant information as part of its investigation. Such information may be located abroad and it can be simply impossible for such an authority to obtain this information: the firm(s) concerned may refuse to comply with the orders of the authority and refuse to hand over the relevant information. It is worth noting here that the existence of a bilateral cooperation agreement with the jurisdiction in which the information is located does not necessarily guarantee a better outcome; there can be more than one reason as to why 'cooperation' in this case may not be more than ink on paper.[104] Nonetheless, even if the competition authority is able to obtain the necessary information and reach a conclusion finding an infringement it can still face serious problems in enforcing its decision where there are no assets belonging to the firm(s) concerned in local markets. The prospects for such an authority to succeed in seeking enforcement through the courts of the foreign jurisdiction do not appear to be real because there can be a difficulty in persuading the relevant court to enforce the findings. This difficulty mushrooms where fundamental differences exist between the two jurisdictions, whether in terms of being civil and common law jurisdictions or in terms of one jurisdiction allowing for criminal penalties whereas the other allows only for civil penalties. Indeed a number of illustrations can be found from practice, most notably the decision of the UK House of Lords in *Huntington* v. *Attrill*.[105] In this case, the House of Lords emphasised that the 'rule that

---

on the topic of extraterritoriality have been crucial in the recognition enjoyed by the doctrine;

[104] Note in particular the possibility that the other authority in possession of the information or in whose jurisdiction the information is located may reach an agreement with the firm(s) concerned – through for example a consent decree – under which the firm(s) will cooperate fully with this authority and hand over all information in its/their possession in return for the authority undertaking not to share this information with foreign competition authorities. See the *Vitamins cartel* case investigated by a number of competition authorities around the world for a good illustration.

[105] [1893] AC 150 at 157.

the courts of no country execute the law of another applies not only to prosecutions and sentences for crimes and misdemeanors, but to all suits in favour of the state for the recovery of pecuniary penalties for any violation of statutes for the protection of its revenue or other municipal laws, and to all judgments for such penalties'. In a later case, *Government of India v.Taylor*,[106] it was noted that an 'explanation of the rule thus illustrated may be thought to be that enforcement of a claim for taxes is but an extension of the sovereign power which imposed the taxes, and that an assertion of sovereign authority by one state within the territory of another, as distinct from a patrimonial claim by a foreign sovereign, is (treaty or convention apart) contrary to all concepts of independent sovereignties'. These statements were followed in the UK Court of Appeal's judgment in *United States of America v. Inkley*,[107] in which the Court of Appeal held that it had no jurisdiction to enforce an action by a foreign state to enforce in the English courts the execution of its own penal laws.

Furthermore, the competition authority in question may appear to be more like a featherweight boxer standing in the face of a heavyweight one, i.e. the relevant foreign firm(s) are very likely to be multinational with significant power and influence when compared to the power and influence of the competition authority in question. This power and influence will be all the greater in cases where the situation is perceived to produce an effect only in the relevant developing country but not anywhere else, including those jurisdictions with powerful competition authorities. In this case, one of the options available to the firm(s) concerned would be simply to decide not to operate in the developing country if the local competition authority would put up stiff resistance or persist in seeking to control the situation; or the firm(s) concerned may simply threaten to exit from the local market if such resistance or persistence occurs. This is especially so in merger cases, in which the authority may decide to regulate the merger involving the multinational firm(s) through, among other things, imposing conditions;[108] as a result of this the firms concerned may feel that simply withdrawing from the market and avoiding such regulation is more beneficial to their business interests than continuing to operate in this market and face regulation. The same thing however may occur in the case of other types

---

[106] [1955] AC 491 at 511.   [107] [1989] QB 255.
[108] In merger control language this amounts to 'conditional clearance' of the merger.

of business phenomena, be they abusive conduct[109] or collusive beha-viour. In the area of abuse of dominance, an interesting situation may arise concerning the use of intellectual property rights[110] by dominant foreign firms. In situations where the relevant competition authority seeks to order the firm to license its intellectual property rights to local firms the former firm might prefer to sacrifice the local market in favour of maintaining its technological advantage. A threat by the firm to put this into practice can present the relevant competition authority with a serious situation. It is little wonder therefore that in these cases there is hardly any effort on the part of the competition authorities of developing countries seriously to consider asserting jurisdiction extraterritorially let alone attempting to prohibit a large cross-border merger operation or seek to penalise foreign behaviour or conduct, whether in the form of abuse of dominance or collusion.

(J)   Chances to enter into bilateral cooperation agreements

A likely consequence from the enforcement-specific challenges as described in the previous section is that the chances of the competition authority or authorities in question will be extremely limited for the purposes of persuading potential partners – in particular more advance competition authorities – to build bilateral links, especially in the form of bilateral agreements.[111] The existence of the challenges may encourage a perception to develop that the authority or authorities in question do not enjoy sufficient credibility in terms of competition enforcement.

(K)   Conflicts

Many parts of the developing world are regrettably serious trouble spots and suffer from extremely bitter (and deadly) conflicts, which often lead to grave consequences. In some of these parts, natural dis-asters sometimes strike with brutal force. This is a very painful reality

---

[109] A particularly high-profile example here can be found in the *Microsoft* case. Notwithstanding its efforts to reach a settlement with the European Commission, Microsoft took hardly any notice of the calls from a number of competition authorities, which sought to conclude with Microsoft settlements on exactly the same terms as those between it and the European Commission.

[110] Patent rights furnish the most obvious example here. Many multinational firms enjoy many and important patents.

[111] Bilateral cooperation is considered in detail in chapter 9.

haunting most if not all of the developing world. The existence of such circumstances means that they are – in terms of the agenda of the local government and in the eyes of the public – a number one priority. As a result, insufficient serious attention comes to be given to economic development and much less to the need and benefits of competition law. Nonetheless, attention is given in some cases because at some point it may be realised that with these conflicts continuing to boil, they become seen as part of the everyday reality and however painful this is they end up being taken for granted.

(L) Self-erected challenges

Some of the challenges that often face developing counties are self-erected: some of these countries set themselves highly ambitious targets in the economic arena which often prove unattainable. For example, some countries have what may be regarded as fairly well-established declarations concerning their desire to embrace the market mechanism and introduce liberalisation in the local economy. These declarations have extended in some cases to the introduction of developmental plans[112] and/or adoption of structural adjustment programmes[113] of the kind normally introduced with the help of the International Monetary Fund (IMF) and the World Bank. These plans and programmes – which are often set for time cycles between four to five years in duration – normally seek to set the country concerned on a course towards a more market-oriented and liberal economy through promoting privatisation, foreign investment and deregulation. Other aims underpinning these programmes may include reducing budget deficits and even deregulating controls on prices, profits which firms may make and exports. In practice, however, little success is achieved for the purposes of turning these declarations into reality or for the purposes of implementing these plans and programmes and many of these countries with such self-imposed programmes remain a long way from achieving the set goals.

---

[112] See, for example, the development plans launched by Iran in 1989 which came to 'rehabilitate' the economy; facilitate privatisation by reducing government involvement in the economy and transferring state-owned enterprises to the private sector; and liberalise trade. Some of the Development Plans have also placed special emphasis on competitiveness, boosting productivity and eliminating monopolistic behaviour and practices.

[113] A good example here can be found in the 1991 structural adjustment programme which Iran imposed on itself and Sudan's Structural Adjustment Programme.

An outcome that sometimes emerges from such an approach can be that of contradiction. Indeed, in some of these countries the constitution is supreme and plays a major role in establishing not only the culture and tradition of the country but also the economic policy to be followed. One can easily find a clear and strong tendency towards nationalisation and the exclusion of foreign participation in the local economy which blatantly contradicts the drive towards the liberalisation and privatisation sought under the self-imposed structural programmes.[114] To complicate the situation even further, constitutional provisions may – at the same time – provide for a prohibition of monopolistic practices,[115] or at least for the operation of the economy in accordance with free market principles.[116]

Putting the issue of contradiction to one side, in the absence of specific competition law, developmental plans and structural programmes – with or without the existence of laws or regulations[117] – have been relied on to lay the foundations of a competition policy in some countries.

---

[114] See, for example, Arts 44 and 81 of the Iranian Constitution. According to the former 'all large-scale and *mother* industries, foreign trade, major minerals, banking, insurance, power generation, dams and large-scale irrigation networks, radio and television, post, telegraph and telephone services, aviation, shipping, roads, railroads and the like' (emphasis added) are to be governed by the State. Article 81 forbids 'concessions to foreigners for the formation of companies or institutions dealing with commerce, industry, agriculture, services or mineral extraction' a provision which effectively prevents multinational or foreign firms from doing business in Iran. It is also worth noting Art. 153 which also forbids 'any form of agreement resulting in foreign control over the natural resources, economy, army or culture of the Country as well as other aspects of the national life'.

[115] See Art. 43 of the Iranian Constitution.

[116] See Art. 25 of the Iraqi Constitution; Art. 21 of the Basic Law of Palestine provides that the 'economic system in Palestine shall be based on the principle of free market economy'; and Art. 8 of the Constitution of Sudan 1998 provides that 'the State shall promote the development of national economy and guide it by planning on the basis of work, production and free market, in a manner fending off monopoly, usury and fraud, and strive for national self-sufficiency for the achievement of affluence and bounty and endeavour towards justice among states and regions'.

[117] The most obvious examples of these laws are those which seek to regulate mergers, especially those in sectors such as banking. The laws in question may provide for a fully fledged mechanism of control and may even employ a 'competition-based' test for determining whether or not a merger should be allowed to proceed. See Art. 23 of the Iraq Banking Law 2004 which provides that no merger, consolidation, acquisition or assumption of liability can take place without the prior approval of the Central Bank of Iraq (CBI). The CBI must be notified 90 days in advance by any bank intending to undertake the above transactions and be given such information as it requires. The CBI will not approve a request for a merger, consolidation, acquisition or assumption of liability which would 'substantially lessen competition'.

These plans and programmes normally contain rules seeking to promote competition in economic activities. They can provide for things like the 'reorganisation' of state-owned entities through divestiture, dissolving or even merging. The government will be given the power to adopt the necessary measures for this purpose. These measures however are not well suited to effect full and complete protection of free competition because no proper institutional structure, or at least a designated authority with the necessary powers, to enforce the rules effectively, is in place. This is the case despite the fact that these plans often lay down rules for the 'regulation' of monopolies and promotion of competition in economic activities, for example through: abolishing all monopolies and monopolistic practices; promoting competition in key sectors, such as post and telecommunication, transportation and insurance; and seeking to enhance the productivity and efficiency of these entities and to regulate prices in order to prevent price increases.[118]

What the above points help to establish is that there seems to be 'solid' evidence that many developing countries which lack specific competition rules attach importance to the process of privatisation for the purposes of having a successful competition policy: it is believed that an enhancement of the private sector will enable the country or countries concerned to enhance competitiveness both domestically and internationally.[119] Indeed, in the case of some countries greater efforts have been made to remove all forms of price controls and to allow prices in all sectors of the local economy to be determined by the market forces of supply and demand in order to liberalise the economy.[120] Whether this may be regarded as a *sensible* or *extreme* approach to deregulation is debatable. It would probably be more sound for deregulation to occur in steps as opposed to taking the form of a single and 'catch-all' step because there can be a risk that such a step could lead to a negative impact on the economy with a dramatic increase in the price of goods and services which can easily aggravate the living conditions of citizens; not to mention the risk of

---

[118] See L. Achy and L. Sekkat, *Competition, Efficiency and Competition Policy in Morocco* (International Development Research Centre, 2005)

[119] See Art. 116 of Chapter 14 of the Iranian Development Plan 2000–2004 which highlights the importance of strengthening the competitive potential of the country in international markets.

[120] See, for example, the three-Year Economic Salvation Programme (1990–1993) introduced by the Sudanese government in order to 'reform' the economy.

increase in unemployment.[121] In any event, experience shows that it would be difficult if not impossible to push through an agenda calling for full liberalisation and decreased government control over the economy to occur in one go. At best, one may be able to make the case for *gradual* liberalisation and to present the benefits and advantages which may follow from the government promoting competition in local markets. In this situation, the relevant competition authority (if one exists) and relevant international bodies may be appropriate vehicles to use to make the case.

7. The role of consumers

Consumers play a key role in any given competition law regime. Therefore, the creation and running of organised consumer activities – often in the form of setting-up consumer associations – is considered to be highly crucial in ensuring that the interests and concerns of consumers receive adequate expression in the policy formulation and enforcement tasks of public authorities, including competition authorities.

Throughout the developing world, consumer associations have come to be set up over the years; though these associations appear to be facing major challenges and difficulties, most notably a lack of adequate support from the government and a lack of sufficient resources to enable them to engage in meaningful work aimed at enhancing consumer awareness and 'defending' the position of consumers in the country concerned. It is blatantly clear that some of these associations do recognise the value and significance of competition law and policy and try in so far as possible to undertaking some work in the field.[122]

---

[121] See, for example, the widespread view formed about the negative effects of Sudan's Structural Adjustment Programme (SSAP) (mentioned in note 113 above) on the local economy.

[122] The most commendable example this author has seen throughout the world is the Ethiopian Consumer Association which has two highly enthusiastic managing directors and secretary who operate with extremely modest resources out of a simple shed in Addis Ababa. The contribution of the association is all the more impressive with the knowledge some of its members are able to display in the field of competition law and which has been built through self-research and self-teaching methods. Their passion for building competition law in their country and for spreading competition advocacy is overwhelming especially in light of how they are apparently harassed and 'chased out' of local markets whenever they attempt to campaign on a competition platform, but they go back the following day!

In some developing countries, the relevant competition law provides for some of the members of the competition authority to be selected from consumer associations. In some cases however there is little evidence of the government being particularly in favour of including this reference in the law and that the reference in fact is inserted following pressure from international organisations or as a result of brave efforts by individual public officials. Even where the law may mandate the appointment of consumer representatives, this appointment may not necessarily occur, at least not in a short term of five years.[123]

The lack of participation by a consumer association in the work of the relevant competition authority can be said to limit the potential of effective competition enforcement in developing countries given that such participation would be expected to lead to the competition authority being utilised to launch competition investigations and/or engage in meaningful competition advocacy tasks to educate the public on the value of competition and competition law and policy.

8. Developing countries and the process of internationalisation

We saw in chapter 3 above that developing countries were the driving force behind the adoption of the *Set on Multilaterally agreed Rules and Principles* of UNCTAD. In this way, developing countries can be said to have supported the idea of internationalisation. Whether they remain among its supporters and whether internationalisation can be said to be in the interest of developing countries is something that can be considered to be open to debate. Probably it is correct to say that internationalisation – especially in the form of bilateral but more relevantly multilateral cooperation – carries significant benefits for developing countries. The 'limitation' on the benefits of internationalisation however is that many developing countries lack either a specific competition law or where such law exists, a proper functioning competition law regime. Furthermore, it is uncertain whether a process of convergence and harmonisation[124] would benefit developing countries and their competition authorities. Convergence and harmonisation can be beneficial for businesses in terms of dealing

---

[123] The author here is relying on an example of a regime in which the government has, on purpose, consistently delayed the appointment of a consumer representative since the relevant competition law came into effect.

[124] See pp. 86–87 above and pp. 562–567 below for a discussion on convergence and harmonisation.

with the 'problems' and 'concerns' raised by concurrent jurisdiction.[125] For developing countries however a risk is attached to convergence and harmonisation because this process could easily lead to rules and standards being imposed on them. In other words, through convergence and harmonisation there can be a top-down approach as opposed to a bottom-up approach, which would allow competition law in these countries to grow from local roots. Such a generalisation in relation to convergence and harmonisation however should be qualified: as we shall see in chapter 10 the process of convergence and harmonisation when pursued through soft law instruments does not necessarily involve an 'imposition'; nonetheless, it will in the case of developing countries have an element of a top-down approach since it is quite unlikely that developing countries would make material contribution to the developing of such instruments. Within the International Competition Network framework, for example, competition authorities of developing countries have a limited scope to offer the necessary expertise to develop different sets of agreed principles and policy recommendations. The bargaining position of developing countries may not be as strong as that of developed countries when operating within multilateral fora.[126] One may cite the UNCTAD as an example of how the bargaining position of developing countries can be strong. The limited impact of UNCTAD's Set however shows that the strong bargaining position of developing countries within UNCTAD has not led to material results in their favour.

9. Sectoral regulation

It would be helpful to select a sector of the economy which has come to enjoy particular attention in the developing world and to consider how this sector has come to be regulated in different developing countries. The telecommunications sector[127] is being selected here because it

---

[125] See pp. 80–82 above.

[126] Some authors have suggested that developing countries may enjoy a stronger position through the use of 'trade-in' or 'trade-off' strategies. For example, within the ICN framework developing countries could agree in return for concessions in the field of merger control to receive concessions in other areas such as those of abuse of dominance. It is not very clear however whether this is realistic as a proposition and to what extent it can be workable in practice.

[127] The term 'telecommunications' is usually defined in a broad manner and encompasses many different forms of content including any process which enables a telecommunications

furnishes an excellent case study of a mechanism for regulating competition being in place in a regulated sector. Interestingly, as we shall see such mechanism exists in certain developing countries even though a specific competition law is absent from such countries. In some countries the mechanism in existence is extremely well developed – at least in terms of substantive rules – and represents a 'competition law', albeit one tailored for the telecommunications sector. The particular attention given to the telecommunications sector in competition law terms in developing countries should not perhaps be surprising: the attention has come to be given in light of international influence as a result of the involvement of key international organisations, most notably the WTO which has given the telecommunications sector special focus within its framework.[128]

(A) General

The telecommunications sector assumes particular importance in developing countries. The sector offers a very interesting case study on the benefits of competition and the necessity of regulation and how these two components are actually balanced in developing countries. This sector also offers a case study on the 'challenges' which many consider to be peculiar to developing countries.

The telecommunications sector generally displays a heavy degree of governmental control in developing countries. The growth and demand for telecommunications services throughout the developing world has become phenomenal. In most countries, the sector features a single firm as the sole licensed telecommunications operator. In all countries, an autonomous and independent telecommunications regulator has been set up. In form therefore the functions of regulation and operation in the sector are separated and are handled by different entities. In practice however this is not quite the case: de facto these two functions may be brought together within the auspices of the relevant ministry and decisions on these functions are reserved for the relevant minister.

In recent years, governments in developing countries have displayed attitudes, which have given rise to 'inconsistent' signals with regard to

---

entity to relay and receive voice, data, electronic messages, written or printed matter, fixed or moving pictures, words, music or visible or audible signals or any control signals of any design and for any purpose by wire, radio or other electromagnetic, spectral, optical or technological means.

[128] See pp. 605–606 below.

the issue of privatising the telecommunications sector and injecting competition within the different elements of the provision of telecommunication services in local markets. On the one hand, declarations have been made favouring privatisation in this key sector. On the other hand, steps in practice have not matched such declarations: indeed these have revealed that the relevant governments are not in favour of opening the telecommunications sector to competition and/or seriously considering privatising the telecommunications operator.[129]

The sole telecommunication operators in many developing countries are powerful entities enjoying a monopoly position in the sector; this monopoly position appears to have been afforded under the relevant laws. Sometimes the government seeks a path towards internal restructuring of the national telecommunications operator in order to 'make it efficient' and to enable it to 'capture' the market. The government's plans in this case are usually to strengthen the national operator and its grip on the market before other operators may be allowed to enter the sector. Sometimes, rather oddly, the operator itself appears to be operating within two 'self-imposed' deadlines: first to achieve efficiency and capture the market within a short time of one or two years and secondly to convert itself into the best telecommunications operator in the relevant continent over a period of five to ten years. These deadlines are usually known and even approved in advance by the relevant government.

The powerful position enjoyed by the sole telecommunications operator can easily lead to the marginalisation of the telecommunications regulator's role and its influence over the sector. Effectively, the regulator may not be able to issue licences to other parties even if it considers this to be in the best interest of consumers. This leaves the regulator simply paralysed in carrying out its functions: the regulator cannot compel the operator to act in a particular way or to even force it to submit relevant

---

[129] See, for example, developments in Ethiopia. It is understood that about seven years ago the government of Ethiopia publicised its intention to sell part of the Ethiopian Telecommunication Corporation (the main telecoms operator in the country) to private firms and that in fact a bidding process was opened through which several bids were received. It appears that this process was abandoned and in fact cancelled at the end. According to the government none of the bidding parties were able to meet the conditions set by it; it seems those conditions were particularly difficult and required the potential acquirer furnishing particularly strong capabilities of administrative, technical and financial nature with the result that no telecommunications operator in the world would have been able to meet them. In this way, the government can be said to have frustrated the bidding process even before it had actually started.

information where that is needed. Nor can the regulator revert to revoking the operator's licence given that such action, even if it were possible, would effectively bring about a total 'shut-down' in the provision of telecommunications services throughout the relevant country.

The status quo in the telecommunications sector in many developing countries is highly problematic from a competition point of view. It is clear that a sole operator is not capable of meeting the huge demand for telecommunication services in these countries, many of which are simply vast. By introducing competition not only would this demand be satisfied, in fact it would also bring about development in terms of better quality and a greater range of products and services, enhanced choice overall and lower prices. Under a climate of a single or main operator, the chances are particularly high for the operator to handle developments within the sector along the lines of *basic* concepts of supply and demand without employing sound economic analysis or innovation thinking and strategy. An example here can be found in an operator's decision to lower the price of pre-paid SIM cards for mobile phones which has happened in a number of developing countries in light of the low demand for this product. Interestingly, this reduction does not necessarily signal that the reduced price is beneficial to consumers since it may have been the case that the original price was excessively high and that the reduction in this case has simply left the price at a level that is 'high'; a determination on this matter however would only be possible once the particulars of cost are known. The problem however is that a telecommunications operator may not furnish any details on particulars of cost, not even to the telecommunications regulator in the relevant country.

The general view therefore is that opening the telecommunications sector to competition is bound to bring about key consumer benefits and also make the incumbent operator itself much more efficient.[130] Normally, allowing competition into the telecommunications sector is one of the least risky steps taken by governments from a competition point of view. This is because operators are admitted to the sector following the issuance of a licence by the regulator, who reserves the power to cancel or amend such licence in case the operator in question engages in anticompetitive behaviour or abusive conduct or in the case of a breach of other terms of the licence.

---

[130] See in this regard the discussion on the relationship between corporate governance and competition law.

(B) Some examples

It would be useful to consider a number of examples from different developing countries around the world.

I. Bahrain

The WTO, of which Bahrain has been a member since 1995, obliged Bahrain to open up its telecommunications sector and end monopolies in the sector by 2005. Accordingly, Bahrain adopted the Telecommunications Law, which entered into force in 2003.[131] The aim of this Law is to liberalise the telecommunications market and it set up the Telecommunications Regulatory Authority (TRA) to regulate this process. Among the various duties of the TRA listed in Chapter III of this Law, is the duty to 'promote effective and fair competition among new and existing licensed operators'; thus the Authority is empowered to make such regulations, orders and determinations as it considers necessary for the promotion of competition. Chapters IX and XVI of the Law are dedicated to issues relating to competition, which are considered to be rather progressive and new even to the entire Arabian Gulf region as a whole. Chapter IX provides the timetable for introducing competition in the telecommunications sector by issuing licences to other firms, thereby ending the monopoly of Batelco which had been the sole telecommunications service provider in Bahrain since 1981. Article 65 of the Law details the anticompetitive behaviour which is prohibited. Any act or omission of a licensed operator, which will have the effect of materially preventing, restricting or distorting competition in the Bahraini telecommunications sector, is prohibited. This includes any agreement, arrangement, understanding or concerted practice which prevents, restricts or distorts competition in the market, abuse of a dominant position by a licensed operator and anticompetitive changes in the structure of the market, especially anticompetitive mergers and acquisitions. For this purpose, dominant position is defined as 'the Licensee's position of economic power that enables it to prevent the existence and continuation of effective competition in the relevant market through the ability of the Licensee to act independently, to a material extent, of competitors, subscribers and users'. However, the Law exempts from the

---

[131] The Law was adopted under Legislative Decree No. 48 of 2002 and is available at the website of the Telecommunications Regulatory Authority at www.tra.org.bh.

prohibition on anticompetitive practices those agreements which promote economic or technical progress and improve the provision of goods or services provided that such agreements do not restrict competition in a manner that is more than essential for achieving the beneficial objectives and do not eliminate competition in a significant part of the relevant market. It is interesting to note that where this provision is included in the competition laws of many other countries, it provides that the exempt agreement must also provide consumers with a fair share of the resulting profits but in the Law it is stated that the agreement will be exempt 'even if' consumers – subscribers and users – have a reasonable share of the resulting benefit.[132] Before deciding whether an act or omission constitutes anticompetitive conduct, the TRA must do all of the following: notify the licensed operator that it is conducting an investigation; provide reasons on the basis of which it believes that a breach has occurred or is about to occur; detail any information which it requires from the operator in order to complete its investigation; explain, where necessary, how the operator could remedy the alleged breach; and give the operator a reasonable period within which to make representations in response. Where a violation of the prohibitions contained in Article 65 of the Law is found, the Authority can direct the licensed operator to do or refrain from doing certain things in order to remedy, reverse or prevent the breach and can impose a fine not exceeding 10 per cent of the annual revenues of the licensed operator. Finally, the Article authorises the TRA to issue regulations for the purposes of maintaining efficient competition in the telecommunications market and may also issue guidelines explaining what anticompetitive conduct entails.

In September 2004 the Regulation on Mergers and Acquisitions was issued and came into effect in October of the same year. A number of consultations were conducted prior to issuing the Regulation for the purposes of making sure that it was fair and in line with international practices. The aim of this Regulation is to protect the interests of consumers and competitors when mergers, acquisitions and joint ventures take place. The TRA has the power to analyse these transactions before they occur to ensure that they do not have an adverse effect on competition in the telecommunications market, which will in turn disadvantage consumers. Where this is found to be the case, the Authority can prohibit the transaction or impose conditions to remove the anticompetitive aspects.

---

[132] See Art. 65(c) of the Law.

II. Brazil

The National Telecommunications Agency, *Nacional de Telecomunicações* (ANATEL) was created by the General Telecommunications Law, *Lei Geral de Telecomunicações* (LGT) in 1997 to bring about the end of state-legalised monopolies in the Brazilian telecommunications services market. ANATEL was charged with overseeing and regulating the telecommunications sector in Brazil in accordance with two fundamental principles of the LGT: universalisation and competition.[133] Though ANATEL has authority to autonomously act to combat anticompetitive practices and institute preliminary investigations and administrative proceedings,[134] the procedures it adopts must always be informed to the Administrative Council for Economic Defence, *Conselho Administrativo de Defesa Econômica* (CADE), a key authority in the country's competition law regime.

In practice, ANATEL and CADE work in tandem in this sector by combining their efforts to monitor concentration acts and to investigate anticompetitive practices, assisting in the production of supporting evidence in the respective proceedings. As a result of this particular procedure, transactions carried out in the telecommunications sector need to be notified to CADE and to ANATEL in two copies instead of notification in three copies to CADE, the Secretariat of Economic Law (SDE) and the Secretariat for Economic Monitoring (SEAE), which is required for transactions carried out in other industry sectors. ANATEL effectively takes over the role of SEAE and performs its duties in the same way as the former does, conducting an economic analysis of the markets affected by the concentration act and preparing a non-binding report to be sent to CADE. However, unlike the SEAE (or even the SDE), ANATEL does not have a specified period of time in which it must report the conclusions from its analysis of the economic aspects of the transaction, which may result in the case being under ANATEL's analysis for quite a long period of time; sometimes longer than a year whereas if the matter were to be handled by the SEAE, the SEAE would be obliged to issue a report within 30 days. Furthermore, once the report is actually concluded by ANATEL's technical staff, it is sent to

---

[133] ANATEL's participation in competition law regulation is provided for in LGT – Law No. 9.472, 16 July 1997 and in an agency rule (Decree No. 2.338, 7 October 1997). See also the draft paper: *Competition and Globalization: Brazilian Telecommunications Policy at Crossroads* available at: http://arxiv.org/ftp/cs/papers/0109/0109094.pdf which discusses the fundamental principles of the LGT.

[134] See Norm No. 7/99, approved by Resolution No. 195, 7 December 1999.

ANATEL's Superintendence, which then has a 60-day period to review and approve the opinion delivered by ANATEL; only once the Superintendence's Board approves the report can it be sent to CADE, together with the case files, for the final judgment of the case. The involvement of ANATEL, as a sector-specific regulator, in determining competition questions should not be mistaken for deference by CADE of its duties as a competition authority: on reviewing the case files forwarded by ANATEL together with ANATEL's report, CADE makes it own conclusions within a 60-day period and this decision forms the basis of the final decision on the matter at hand. However, that being said, given the technical issues involved in transactions in the telecommunications sector, there is a greater likelihood – when compared to other sectors of activities – that CADE will follows ANATEL's opinion, but this is a not a rule set forth under Brazilian competition law.

III. Egypt

Egypt's former belief in the desirability and necessity of state control in the telecommunications sector was neither exceptional nor short lived; indeed, this belief dates back to 1854 with the initiating of the telegraph service between Cairo and Alexandria. However, with the new policy of liberalisation and structural reform ushered in the 1990s, the government embarked in 1998 on reform in the telecommunications sector. The government's aim was twofold: to restructure the sector and to open it to private investment. An important step taken in this regard was the creation of the National Telecommunications Regulatory Authority (NTRA), which was armed with the power to grant licences to entities aiming to provide different telecommunications services and which occurred following the enactment of Law No. 19, a hugely important instrument which effectively instituted a new regime in the telecommunications sector. This Law, among other things, brought about a structural separation in relation to the entities carrying out the regulatory and operational functions. Pursuant to Presidential Decree No. 101 issued two months later, in May 1998, the NTRA was given an independent status, having a ten-members board of directors headed by the Minister of Communications as it assumed responsibility for regulatory functions. The creation of NTRA was followed by that of the Ministry of Communications and Information Technology (MCIT) according to Decree No. 387 in October 1999. Finally, the revolution of regulation in the sector culminated on 4 February 2003, when the Egyptian Parliament passed the

Law on the Organization of the Telecommunications Sector,[135] which sets fundamental principles such as transparency, non-discrimination, neutrality of public operators towards competitive services, provision of universal service and unity of the network from a functional point of view to ensure equality of access. The Law also gives NTRA a more autonomous status, the power to impose sanctions, to establish a universal service fund, the freedom to set rules and regulations to properly manage and administer the proper organisational structure necessary to carry out all regulatory functions entrusted to the regulatory authority. Unlawful acts related to telecommunications sector activities are prohibited and will attract a court sentence of imprisonment or fine according to the severity of the violation in question.

Article 24 of the Law on the Organization of the Telecommunications Sector requires the NTRA to determine the necessary rules that would prohibit monopolistic practices; accordingly NTRA developed a 'Competition Policy Framework', which was implemented even prior to the adoption of a specific competition law in Egypt, namely Law No. 3/2005 concerning the Protection of Competition and the Prohibition of Monopolistic practices. Through this Framework, NTRA sets out the practices that should not be exercised by the licensee entities in their conduct of business. These include restrictions on abusing a dominant position, such as the prohibition of refusal to supply and entering into restrictive vertical agreements. However, now that a specific competition law has been adopted and a competition authority, the Egyptian Competition Authority, established it is not clear whether or not the work of both entities will overlap. In addition, despite these developments, the telecommunications sector is still widely considered as featuring price-fixing practices exercised by the existing two mobile operators and a lack of competition in the fixed line and international calls market.

IV. Indonesia

Until 1995 the telecommunications sector in Indonesia was monopolised by the government though two main carriers – PT Telekon and PT Indosat – and their predecessors but the inefficiencies[136] this created

---

[135] Law No. 10/2003.
[136] For instance, in 1992, only 1.5 million connected telephone lines were serving a population of 190 million.

and the commitments[137] undertaken by the Indonesian government paved the way for gradual change in the sector. In the early 1990s the first wave of reform began with the partial privatisation of PT Telekon and PT Indosat in 1994 and 1995 respectively and by 1997 the second wave of reform began with the Blueprint of Telecommunication 1999 and Telecommunication Law 1999,[138] both of which governed the government's policy for the following years. The Blueprint profiled the future of Indonesian telecommunications services and the Telecommunication Law provided guidelines for industry reforms, particularly focusing on liberalisation and the facilitation of new entrants.[139]

Under the authority of Article 4 of the Telecommunications Law, the Communications Minister, by Ministerial Decree, established the Indonesian Telecommunication Regulatory Board (BRTI) in 2003.[140] Before BRTI was established, the sector was governed by the Directorate General of Post and Telecommunications (DGPT), which operated under the Department of Communications. BRTI was charged with the supervision of competitive behaviour in the telecommunications sector and mandated to secure transparency, independence and fairness in the telecommunications network and service operations. BRTI began its operations in 2004 and it is comprised of the Telecommunication Regulatory Committee and the director. The Committee members consist of a chairman – the Director General of Posts & Telecommunications – and four experts in technical matters.[141] It is interesting to note the absence of any telecommunications association representatives from the Committee's membership and this coupled with the presence of the Director General of Posts & Telecommunications as chairman casts doubts on the Committee's independence because, though the Committee is authorised to make decisions through consensus or voting, final decisions require the approval of the Director General him or herself.

The spheres of activity of BRTI and Indonesia's competition authority, the KPPU, inherently have the potential to overlap: the KPPU is

---

[137] Namely, to GATT/WTO. See *Trade Policy Review-Indonesia*, WTO Doc WT/TPR/S/ 117 (2003) 92.

[138] Law No. 136 of 1999, the Telecommunications Law.

[139] See A. Young, S. Rahaju and G. Li, 'Regulatory Multiplicities in Telecommunications Reforms in Indonesia and China' (2005) *Macquarie Journal of Business Law* 135.

[140] Decree of Minister of Communication No. KM 31/2003 (11 July 2003).

[141] These matters include: (i) telecommunication and information technology; (ii) legal; (iii) economics; and (iv) other social sciences.

charged with the task of protecting competition and fighting anti-competitive behaviour and conduct as well as regulating harmful mergers and BRTI is responsible for economic competition (in terms of non-discriminatory access to input and pricing policy) and technical regulation in the telecommunications sector. The risk of problems arising from the potential overlap of jurisdictions seems to have been resolved through a process of coordination between the two authorities with KPPU acting in accordance with its 'Policy Harmonisation Mechanism' by which it identifies industrial policies it believes to effect competition and then initiates discussions as may be required. Working together in this way, the hope is that KPPU and BRTI will be able to internalise a competition culture and competition values in the telecommunications sector whilst not detracting from the special considerations needed to effectively manage the telecommunications sector.

Despite the fact that the Telecommunication Law contained competition provisions, for instance Article 10 of the Law which specifies that a merger or acquisition may be concluded provided that the transaction will not cause a monopolistic practice and unfair business competition, the biggest step taken to complete the reform agenda as envisaged by the Telecommunication Law and Blueprint was not taken until the government announced what has come to be known as the March 2004 Telecommunications Package. The Package consisted of eight Ministerial Decrees which among other things regulated contentious issues.[142] It is worth noting Decree No. 33/2004[143] in this regard as it deals with the issue of abuse of dominance in the sector. Article 4 of the Decree prohibits telecommunication firms from any of following: (i) abusing their dominant position to undertake monopolistic practices or unfair business competition; (ii) dumping or selling or operating their business at a lower tariff than cost and/or providing or selling their services at a price above the tariff formula which has been stipulated in accordance with the prevailing provisions; (iii) using their revenue for subsidising the operation cost of fixed networks and the provision of other competitive basic telephony

---

[142] For example, Decree No. 32/2004 on Interconnection Tariff; Decree No. 34/2004 on Universal Service Obligations; and Decree No. 35/2004 on the Operations of Fixed Local Wireless.

[143] See Decree of Minister of Communication No. KM 33/2004 (11 March 2004) regarding the Supervision over Fair Competition and the Operation of Fixed Networks and Provisions of Basic Telephony Services.

services operated by them not having dominant position in the market; (iv) requiring or directly or indirectly forcing their users or subscribers only to use certain networks and basic telephony services (controlled by them); and (v) not providing interconnection service or applying discriminatory terms to other operators of fixed networks and providers of basic telephony services who request interconnection. Decree No. 33/2004 stipulates that the telecommunications operator or provider will be considered to have a dominant position if its business, coverage area and revenue represent a 'majority' of the market. However, the Decree fails to provide a specific description of the percentage of the business, coverage area and revenue representing a majority of the market. In the absence of these provisions, one must assume that the general definition of dominant position contained in the national competition law is to be used as the general rule of interpretation in this case concerning the telecommunications sector.[144] Nonetheless, having a dominant position in the majority market in the telecommunications sector is not prohibited, as far as the dominant operator does not abuse this position.

V.   Jordan

The relevant authority in charge of regulating the telecommunications sector in Jordan is the Telecommunications Regulatory Commission (TRC), established under the Telecommunications Law 1995, as amended.[145] Due to the fact that competition issues assume considerable importance in the work of the TRC, the *Instructions on Competition Safeguards in the Telecommunications Sector* were adopted in February 2006.[146] The Instructions provide a binding framework within which competition analysis in the telecommunications sector must be conducted. This covers cases of abuse of dominance, anticompetitive behaviour and harmful mergers and acquisitions; the power to conduct this analysis is reserved to the TRC. The adoption of the Instructions therefore in effect meant that the TRC and the Competition Directorate, the relevant competition authority in the country (and the Ministry of Industry and Trade) have dual jurisdiction in relation to competition issues arising in the telecommunications sector. Therefore, firms

---

[144] See Law No. 5 Concerning Prohibition of Monopolistic Practices and Unfair Business 1999.
[145] See the Telecommunications Law No. 13 of 1995, as amended.
[146] See TRC Board Decision No. 1–3–2006 of 14 February 2006.

operating in the sector will have to comply with both the Telecommunications Law and the Instructions and deal with the TRC on the one hand and comply with the Competition Law No. 33/2004 and deal with the Competition Directorate on the other. The existence of a dual system should not itself be objectionable especially given that the authorities have made their interest in coordinating their work very clear. What is concerning however is the fact that the Instructions do not adequately deal with all issues, which may arise in an effort to conduct competitive analysis or seek to protect competition in the sector. In particular, the Instructions are silent on procedural issues dealing with submission of complaints about the anticompetitive behaviour or abusive conduct of licensees and the type of actions, which may be taken by the TRC when identifying a competition problem. As a result therefore the exact role of the TRC when dealing with competition problems in the telecommunications sector is not known given that neither the Telecommunications Law nor the Instructions nor the Competition Law offer any helpful indication in this regard.

VI. Kenya

From the formation of the Kenya Posts and Telecommunication Corporation (KPTC) in 1948 to its liquidation in 1999, the KPTC was the sole governmental corporation in Kenya to provide both postal and telecommunications services and infrastructures. The first steps towards economic liberalisation and restructuring were taken by the Kenyan government in 1996, when it adopted a policy framework paper – Economic Reforms 1996–1998 – following support and contributions from the World Bank and the IMF. Part of that framework included the Kenya Communications Act 1998 and the Postal Corporation Act 1998; once implemented these acts officially separated telecommunications services and postal services through the restructuring of the KPTC: Telecoms Kenya Limited and Kenya Postal Corporation were each created to operate in the market and the Communications Commission of Kenya (CCK) was established to act as a licensing and regulatory authority.

The Kenya Communications Act 1998 and its Regulations require the CCK to develop, maintain, promote and enforce effective competition.[147] In performing its duties, the CCK has broad powers. Specifically,

---

[147] Section 23(1)(b) of the Kenya Communications Act 1998 and Reg. 5(1) of the Kenya Communications Regulations 2001.

it may investigate, on its own initiative, any licensee whom it has reason to believe has engaged in 'unfair competition'. Acts of unfair competition specifically include: 'the effectuation of anticompetitive changes in the market structure and in particular, anticompetitive mergers and acquisitions in the telecommunications sector'.[148] Regulation 5(2)(d) extends the definition to 'any other practices or acts that are prohibited under any other written law', thus creating potential for the CCK's activities to overlap with those of the national competition authority – the Price and Monopolies Commission – which enforces the Trade Practices, Monopolies and Price Control Act. When complaints are made to the CCK about the anticompetitive practices of telecommunications operators and service providers, the Telecommunications Licence Enforcement Unit – an affiliate of the CCK – conducts the relevant investigation. The operator or service provider is given notice of the investigation and it should cooperate by providing any information that is requested. Once an investigation is complete and the CCK has decided that the operator is acting in 'conflict' with the principle of fair competition it may issue an appropriate order, which may include a penalty depending on the case at hand. The CCK can order the infringer to 'cease and desist' from engaging in the practice, to take corrective steps to negate the harmful effects of the practice, and order the payment of a fine of 500,000 shillings per month until the anticompetitive activity ceases.

VII. Nigeria

The colonial administration first established telecommunications facilities in Nigeria in 1886 and until deregulation in 1992 a succession of state monopolies controlled the telecommunications sector.[149] Deregulation was motivated by, amongst other things, a need to attract foreign investment and the reality that the government was unable to continue funding what had become a highly inefficient industry. The Nigerian Communications Commission (NCC) was inaugurated in 1993 as the independent national regulator for the telecommunications sector.[150] The NCC's functions specifically include 'the promotion of

---

[148] See www.cck.go.ke/.
[149] Between 1960 and 1985 these were the Post and Telecommunications and Nigerian External Communications Limited; in 1985 Nigerian Telecommunications Limited took over both monopolies until deregulation.
[150] See Decree No. 75 of 1992.

fair competition in the communications industry and protection of communications services and facilities providers from misuse of market power or anticompetitive or unfair practices' and one of its stated objectives is to 'ensure fair competition in all sectors of the Nigerian communications industry'.[151]

Chapter VI, Part I of the Nigerian Communications Act 2003 contains far-reaching competition provisions, furnishing the NCC with 'exclusive competence to determine, pronounce upon, administer, monitor and enforce compliance of all persons with competition laws and regulations' in respect of the telecommunications sector.[152] Section 91 of the Act prohibits licensees from engaging in several types of anticompetitive conduct, which covers: any activity which has the purpose or effect of 'substantially lessening competition' in the sector;[153] entering into agreements or understandings concerning typical cartel behaviour;[154] and tying/bundling.[155] Section 92 of the Act on the other hand regulates the activities of those licensees deemed to hold a dominant position in the market. The NCC is also given authority to review potential mergers between licensees under section 93 of the Act, which requires such licensees to apply for prior authorisation in respect of any conduct that may result in the substantial lessening of competition.

The NCC has wide powers of investigation under Chapter V of the Act. The NCC may initiate an investigation itself or following receipt of a written complaint;[156] the NCC is given discretion to perform an investigation in any manner it thinks fit but the person being investigated must, generally, be given the opportunity to submit written representations to the NCC.[157] Following its investigation, the NCC will deliver a report outlining the subject matter of the investigation, its findings and the evidence on which those findings were based, along with any other matters arising out of the investigation that the NCC thinks fit to divulge.[158] In the course of an investigation, the NCC has the power to obtain information (including accounts and records) and to require persons believed to have relevant information to give

---

[151] See www.ncc.gov.ng/. [152] See Nigerian Communications Act No. 19 of 2003, s. 90.
[153] See s. 91(1) of the Act.
[154] Such as rate-fixing, market allocation and types of exclusionary behaviour. See s. 91(3) of the Act.
[155] See s. 91(4) of the Act. [156] See ss. 61 and 62 of the Act.
[157] See s. 63 of the Act. [158] See s. 63(6) of the Act.

evidence.[159] Under section 65(1) of the Act failure to provide evidence or the provision of misleading or inaccurate evidence is punishable by fine or imprisonment, provided that the person knew or had reason to believe that this was the case. When confronted with an infringement, the NCC may seek an interim injunction to cover the period between its investigation and a court action.[160] Furthermore, to strengthen the enforcement of the competition components of the Act private persons are permitted to bring private enforcement actions against an infringer provided that such persons obtain a certificate of leave from the NCC.[161]

The provisions of the NCA have been expounded in the NCC's Competition Practices Regulations 2007, which were created to provide a solid regulatory framework for the protection of fair competition. The Regulations, among other things, provide guidance on how the NCC will determine a substantial lessening of competition or a position of dominance and explains the merger review procedure followed by the NCC when assessing merger operations. It is clear from the Regulations that the interests of consumers is an important consideration for the NCC, for instance Regulation 6 provides that the impact on consumers in terms of choice and price and the degree of interference with competition that may result in identifiable harm to consumers are key factors that must be taken into account when determining whether there has been a substantial lessening of competition. The Regulations provide that a breach of a provision may result in a fine, sanction or penalty, as determined under the Enforcement Process Regulations 2005[162] and that an abuse of a dominant position or anticompetitive practices falling within the prohibition contained in Communications Act itself entitle the NCC to, among other things, issue a direction to 'cease and desist', take remedial action, pay compensation to those who have suffered due to the activity in question and issue a public apology in a newspaper the NCC selects.[163]

The regulation of competition within the telecommunications sector in Nigeria has been undertaken in a very sensible manner; even though the draft competition bill in the country has yet to be finalised, concerns regarding the consistency of the bill's provisions and the sector rules have been acknowledged by the NCC and since the Communications

---

[159] All information given to the NCC is deemed to be true, accurate and complete, as stipulated under s. 62(2) of the Act.
[160] See s. 94(1) of the Act.   [161] See s. 94(2) of the Act.
[162] See Reg. 33.   [163] See Reg. 34.

Act and the NCC's Regulations are already in operation it appears that any inconsistencies will be resolved by amending the draft bill itself.[164]

Although the NCC is an independent body, it still has to take account of the government's National Telecommunications Policy (NTP)[165] and concerns have arisen as to the weight attached by the NCC to the NTP, particularly in respect of the pricing of mobile telecommunication services which is widely regarded as excessive. Chapter 6 of the NTP states that 'competitive market forces [are] the best determinant of the appropriate and sustainable levels of prices charged' and despite Chapter 6 going on to acknowledge that in the transition to instituting a competitive industry the NCC should prevent dominant operators from unduly controlling prices, the NCC has failed to take any action.

VIII. Oman

Oman had to open its telecommunications sector to the private sector to satisfy the obligation placed upon it by the WTO, of which it has been a member since 2000, and to allow foreign telecommunications companies to enter the Omani market. For this purpose, the Telecommunications Regulatory Act was promulgated by Royal Decree No. 30/2002 and established the Telecommunications Regulatory Authority[166] for the purpose of regulating the telecommunications sector and introducing competition therein. According to the Act, the duties of the Authority include, among others, creating a competitive environment among licensees to ensure the provision of 'world standard telecommunications services', taking the necessary steps to enable service providers to compete internationally and taking the necessary measures to examine the activities which prevent competition in the telecommunications sector. Articles 40 and 41 stipulate the rules of competition. According to these, any act or omission of a licensee that prevents or restricts competition in the telecommunications sector is prohibited. These actions or omissions include: abuse of a dominant position; the conclusion of agreements excluding or limiting competition in the market; as well as merger operations leading to changes in the structure of the market as a result of which competition will be prevented or restricted. With the approval of the Minister of

---

[164] See the *Report of the Public Inquiry on Competition Practices Regulations* available at www.ncc.gov.ng/index1.htm.
[165] See NTP 2000 Chapter 3.1.4.1.   [166] See www.tra.gov.om.

Transport and Communications, the Authority may issue further rules relating to the acts or omissions that prevent or restrict competition and it also has the task of deciding whether an act or omission does in fact lead to the prevention of competition. Before reaching a decision on this, the Authority must carry out the necessary investigations.

The *Executive Telecommunications Regulations* produced by the Authority further elaborate upon the behaviour and conduct which is prohibited pursuant to Articles 40 and 41 of the Act. Clause 14.1 of the Regulations provides a whole list of activities which players within the sector must refrain from, including: entering into a contract which is in restraint of trade; monopolisation of any service; practices which reduce competition in the market; discriminating in pricing; and other similar practices harmful to competition. Clause 14.2 of the Regulations prohibit three types of arrangements between two or more service providers, namely arrangements which: fix prices or other terms or conditions of services in the telecommunications sector; determine the result of a contract or business opportunity; and divide, share or allocate telecommunications markets among the service providers themselves or other service providers. Clauses 14.3 and 14.4 of the Regulations deal with abuse of dominance. According to the former provision, a licensed operator will be declared dominant by the Authority if it enjoys 'significant market power'. In deciding this, the Authority will take into account market shares and other 'appropriate factors'. A comprehensive list is contained in Clause 14.4 of the activities which will constitute abuse of a dominant position. These include, among others, inducing a supplier not to sell to a competitor, failing to supply facilities to a competitor within a reasonable time or on reasonable terms, bundling of services and supplying competitive services at a price below the average costs. The Authority is empowered to investigate, on its own initiative or on application from any person, whether the activities of a dominant service provider amount to an abuse of its position within the meaning of Clause 14.4 of the Regulations and whether they amount to an anticompetitive practice according to Article 40 of the Act. Under certain circumstances, it may be held that an activity does not constitute abuse of a dominant position or an anticompetitive practice and where this is done reasons for such a decision must be given and be consistent with 'evolution of a competitive market-based telecommunications sector'. Where an abuse of a dominant position or anticompetitive practice is found – whether under the Telecommunications Regulatory Act or the

Regulations – the Authority may impose such fines as it considers appropriate and require the offender to take one or more of the following actions: cease the anticompetitive activities immediately or within a specified time in line with certain conditions; make specific changes to eliminate or reduce the impact of the anticompetitive conduct; meet with those affected by the offenders' actions to determine remedies to prevent the continuation of such actions and resolve any disputes pursuant to Chapter XII (on dispute resolution) of the Regulations; publish an apology of their actions in one or more newspapers as specified by the Authority; and provide periodic reports to the Authority to enable it to examine whether the anticompetitive actions are continuing and determine their impact on the telecommunications market, competitors and users. Where there has been a repeated breach of a decision issued by the Authority, the Authority may order the offender to divest itself of ownership of some lines of business or carry out that business in a separate entity with a separate account, after it has given the offender specific notice that such a decision will be made, providing it with the opportunity to put across its arguments and if the Authority considers that such a decision is an effective means of deterring the continuation of anticompetitive practices.

IX.   The Philippines

Like many other countries, the Philippines' telecommunication sector was monopolised for a long time by a single firm: the Philippines Long Distance Telephone Company. However, unlike other countries this firm was initially a private entity in foreign ownership. Nevertheless, in 1990 the government decided, as part of its National Telecommunications Development Plan (1990–2010) to liberalise the sector and it enacted the Public Telecommunications Policy Act (PTPA) to this end. The PTPA governs 'public telecommunications entities' in the Philippines, which is defined rather broadly to refer to any person, firm, partnership or corporation, government or private, engaged in the provision of telecommunications services to the public for compensation. The National Telecommunications Commission (the NTC) is the sectoral regulator and principal administrator of the PTPA, taking the necessary measures to implement the policies and objectives the PTPA endorses; the objectives of the PTPA include the fostering of a 'healthy and competitive environment'. The NTC was established in 1972 as an independent government agency under the supervision of the Department of Transportation and Communication (as an affiliated/attached agency) and it has quasi-judicial functions as well as regulatory functions.

Under the PTPA the NTC is responsible for, among other things, protecting consumers against misuse of a telecommunications entity's monopoly or quasi-monopolistic powers by, but not limited to, the investigation of complaints and exacting compliance with service standards from such an entity. In this regard, the NTC may exempt any specific telecommunications service from its rate or tariff regulations if that service has sufficient competition to ensure fair and reasonable rates or tariffs. Nonetheless, the NTC retains residual powers to regulate rates of tariffs in cases where 'ruinous competition' results or when a monopoly, cartel or combination in restraint of free competition exists with the effect of distorting rates or tariffs or making them unable to function freely and this adversely affects the public; in such circumstances, the NTC is empowered to establish a 'floor' or 'ceiling' on the rates of tariffs.

The provisions in the PTPA are not the sole basis on which the NTC may intervene in the telecommunications sector in respect of competition matters; in fact, regulation of the sector – as the regulation of competition in the country as a whole – is fragmented and the NTC also derives authority to act under the numerous *memorandum circulars* it has issued. One such circular established the *Implementing Rules and Regulations Governing Community Antenna/Cable Television (CATV) and Direct Broadcast Satellite (DBS) Services* (CATV/DBS Regulations) in 2003.[167] The CATV/DBS Regulations intend to promote fair and healthy competition in the cable/satellite television market by preventing monopolies or any combination in restraint of trade or unfair competition and to provide the country with the widest possible access to sources of news, information, entertainment and data available. As a general rule, exclusive contracts which grant or have the effect of granting sole or exclusive rights to air or broadcast programmes or content to one or some CATV/DBS operators to the exclusion of other operators, or any behaviour that is tantamount to exclusivity (such as discrimination in the supply of programmes or content), between CATV/DBS operators and programme/content providers are presumed to be anticompetitive and contrary to sound public policy.[168]

---

[167] See NTC Memorandum Circular No. 10-10-03, 1 October 2003.
[168] See section 2 of NTC Memorandum Circular No. 10-10-03.

Any CATV/DBS operators seeking to execute such a contract can however avail themselves of an exemption by submitting a petition to the NTC which is determined by the NTC's Legal Department at a hearing.[169] Interested parties are given an opportunity to comment on and submit their grievances in respect of a petition before the hearing and at the hearing the onus is on the petitioner to show that the contract is not anticompetitive or contrary to public policy or that it serves the public interest so as to obtain an order granting the petition; failure to discharge these obligations will render the exclusivity provisions (not the whole contract) void.[170] Violations of any provisions of the CATV/DBS Regulations entitle the NTC to impose fines as well as other sanctions and penalties, such as the suspension or revocation of existing authorisations.[171] The CATV/DBS Regulations are only a temporary measure aimed at promoting competition and diversity in the cable/satellite market as the prohibition on exclusive contracts and the approval requirement automatically expires ten years from the date on which the Regulations became effective, provided they are not expressly extended or still considered necessary to promote competition, diversity or to protect the public interest and welfare.[172]

X. Saudi Arabia

The size and significance of the telecommunications sector in Saudi Arabia – along with the government's desire to facilitate competitiveness and enterprise in the local economy as a whole – are worth noting. The Kingdom has taken important steps towards creating an open and competitive environment, encouraging investment (both local and foreign) and protecting local consumers. Among these steps are: the partial privatisation of the telecommunications sector; the adoption of the Telecom Act[173] (which establishes the framework for regulating

---

[169] See sections 3 and 4 of NTC Memorandum Circular No. 10–10–03. The NTC does not entertain petitions unless it is shown: (a) that all the parties to the contract have agreed to submit any dispute pertaining thereto to the jurisdiction of the competent Philippine authorities; and (b) that all foreign and local programme or content providers have registered with the NTC and in the case of a foreign provider, it must also appoint a local agent to whom notices and other official correspondence may be sent.

[170] See section 4 of NTC Memorandum Circular No. 10–10–03.

[171] See section 9 of NTC Memorandum Circular No. 10–10–03.

[172] This would be 2013. See section 10 of NTC Memorandum Circular No. 10–10–03.

[173] Issued under Council Resolution No. 74 of 27 May 2001 and approved pursuant to Royal Decree No. M/12 of 3 June 2001. Chapter 6 of the Telecommunications Act establishes the framework for regulating competition in the telecommunications sector.

competition in the telecommunications sector) and the *Telecommunication Bylaws* (which develop the substance of the competition provisions in the Telecom Law and stipulate the remedies available for abuse of dominance and anticompetitive practices); and the creation in 2001 of an independent Communications and Information Technology Commission as a body responsible for regulating the sector. Since its creation the Commission has been active in opening the sector to greater competition and moving closer to its declared objective of ultimately achieving full market liberalisation.[174] The desire of the government to take such crucial steps appears to be motivated by the quest to join the WTO (in which it succeeded in 2006), to meet the legitimate expectations of firms and consumers and the general drive within the country for economic prosperity.

Competition appears to have begun to develop in the past two years in the telecommunications sector in Saudi Arabia, especially in relation to the provision of mobile phone services with beneficial results; the Commission has noted an improved product quality and the availability of more choice for consumers in the market. These important developments however have helped highlight various new strategic matters related to market liberalisation and protection of competition. As a response, the Commission has begun a review of its regulatory tools for the purposes of adapting those to the changing nature of practices of firms active in the sector and the prevention of possible anticompetitive practices and abusive conduct.

XI. Sudan

The Three-Year Economic Salvage Programme (1990–1993) adopted by the Sudanese government advocated opening the telecommunications market to the private sector to end 'monopolistic environment' prevailing in the sector. Accordingly in 1993 the government undertook to reform the telecommunications sector. The state-owned Sudan Telecommunications Public Corporation (STPC) was turned into Sudan Telecommunications Company (Sudatel). In addition, in 2001 the Telecommunications Act was enacted, which established the

---

Article 24 prohibits agreements or practices which would create a dominant operator or prevent, restrict or distort competition. Article 25 requires the approval of the CITC for mergers and the acquisition of more than 5% of the shares of another licensed operator. Article 26 prohibits abuse of a dominant position.

[174] Notable in this regard is the issuing of four licences for the provision of telecommunications services via satellite (VAST) and the issuing of three licences in the mobile phones sector to enable new operators to provide cellular services.

National Telecommunications Corporation (NTC) as the regulatory authority for the information and telecommunications sector. The objectives of the NTC are to regulate and promote the telecommunications sector to conform to 'development and globalisation', encourage investment in the telecommunications sector and to 'ensure and diffuse free and constructive competition ... in the field of telecommunications'. Article 41 of the Act provides that 'public telecommunications services shall be provided through free competition'. As a result of the transformation it has undergone, Sudan's telecommunications sector is held to be the most modern in Africa.

XII.   United Arab Emirates

The United Arab Emirates (UAE) came to witness incredibly fast and radical transformation in almost all aspects of its economic environment over a short period of time. In relation to the telecommunications sector, a serious shift has occurred in the government's previously hostile stance towards a free market economy and its policy of limiting competition and making entry by foreign firms into the market virtually impossible: the UAE opened the telecommunications sector to competition in 2003 with the adoption of its Telecom Law.[175] Furthermore, in its most recent National Telecommunication Policy, the gradual introduction of sustainable competition and a regulatory framework that is conducive to protecting the rights of market players and consumers were both highlighted as key policy objectives.[176]

Article 6 of the Telecom Law established the Telecommunications Regulatory Authority (TRA), whose mission includes 'safeguarding competition' and 'providing fair access to the domestic infrastructure'.[177] Article 14(3) gives the TRA the power to issue regulations, instructions, decisions and rules regulating and ensuring competition in the sector and thus far the TRA has not shirked its responsibilities, for instance, under the *Price Control Regulatory Policy Regulations* licensees are prohibited from instituting anticompetitive prices or prices which could have the effect of restricting, preventing or distorting competition in

[175] See Law Decree No. 3 of 2003, as amended.
[176] See paragraphs 3.1.1 and 3.1.2 of the National Telecommunication Policy, Supreme Committee for the Supervision of the Telecommunication Sector Resolution No. 13 of 2005.
[177] See www.tra.ae/vision_mission_values.php.

the short term or long term.[178] However, given the government's previous attraction to price regulation as opposed to the facilitation of competition, these Regulations may not necessarily be the best indicator of a true move towards fully embracing competition in the telecommunications sector.

10. Comments

The challenges facing different developing countries vis-à-vis the competition law question fall within different categories. As can be seen from the discussion above, four of these categories may be conveniently identified as: institutional; behavioural; regulatory; and structural. Ensuring that these challenges are faced in the right manner and given proper attention is a vital step in building better competition law regimes in different developing countries. Moreover, it is of crucial significance to recognise that competition law and policy cannot, and in fact do not, exist in isolation. Competition law and policy are interwoven with the general economic policy and political climate prevailing domestically and to a lesser extent the culture and social patterns of the relevant country. For this reason, a meaningful change in the field of competition law and policy may sometimes require, among other things, a change or at least some form of shift in position in the wider economic approach and policy adopted by the relevant government. It would be helpful to offer in this part of the chapter a number of thoughts and highlight several areas in which action would be highly recommended concerning the further development of competition law and policy in developing countries.

(A) The trade policy arena

The competition law scene within developing countries appears to be highly influenced by external trade relations concluded by the domestic governments of these countries. In the case of some countries, almost exclusively, the government's desire to accommodate foreign interests appears to determine the parameters of competition and competition policy in these countries. This is a deeply troubling situation given that the domestic competition law regime would not under these

---

[178] See Price Control Regulatory Policy Regulations (23 September 2008).

circumstances be afforded the opportunity to take its natural course for development and progress, including ensuring effective and impartial enforcement within the regime. This problem remains regardless of how 'perfect' or 'watertight' the relevant competition rules of the relevant law are in terms of drafting and wording. Hence, what is required in this case is a more sensitive government approach to competition and competition policy and a recognition that an almost *unconditional* offer to foreign firms and their home governments to participate in local markets is not necessarily in the relevant country's best interest and the interest of its consumers; nor is this unconditional offer in fact necessary in order to have participation by foreign firms in local markets: it would be reasonable to expect such participation to emerge even on a 'conditional' basis given that many of these firms need developing countries as much as (perhaps even more) than the latter need them.

(B) Scope and content of the competition rules

As previous parts of the chapter made clear, the competition *rules* of developing countries usually suffer from two major problems: the bundling of competition law and non-competition law provisions and the substantive and procedural law gaps. It is arguable that the best and easiest course of action, in both the short and the long term, would be to sever the *competition* provisions of the relevant law and develop them into an independent competition law. It is quite inevitable that some form of action will eventually have to be taken on the relevant law and that sooner or later the relevant government will need to turn its attention to this matter as can be seen from the experience of a number of developing countries who moved towards having laws which deal specifically and exclusively with competition. A continued existence of the bundled competition law and non-competition law provisions within the competition rules of developing countries is bound to hinder the future development of competition law and policy in these countries. This undesirable position will only become more difficult with the use of many of the provisions of the rules in such form. Hence, it is always suitable to recommend a clarification of the wording and scope of the different competition provisions within the rules with suitable amendments to be made in order to fill the gaps and loopholes created as a result of bundling.

(C)   Institutional structure

The institutional structure within the competition law regimes of developing countries in most cases calls for careful and serious attention. Specifically, the composition and status of local competition authorities in these countries are considered in most cases to be highly controversial and problematic. Among other things, the view is consistently taken that: the competition authority should be independent from the government with a separate budget and sufficient resources given to it; and the actual composition of the competition authority should not be at an extremely high level: a high level composition means that competition law and policy issues are bound to be sidelined and possibly even overshadowed by non-competition matters, which the members of the competition authority have responsibility for.

There are several alternatives regarding institutional structure and composition which may be suitable for developing countries. A particularly suitable option to pursue would be to create the position of a *chairman* of the authority along with an advisory board who could be made up of representatives of both the public and private sector. The chairman would be a person who enjoys expertise in competition-related fields and would be responsible for the running of the competition authority. Another possibility would be to have a board of directors or commissioners in place but to assign to it the responsibility of policy formulation. A position of *director of competition* could then be created within the competition authority who would be a qualified person responsible for the day-to-day operations of the authority. However, one should still recommend the creation of an advisory committee made up of representatives of different sectors to advise the director. In relation to all of these options, competition officials should operate within independent and autonomous units which are clearly identifiable from the relevant ministry (which has competition relevance) and the government more generally. With regard to the involvement of a minister in the field of competition law, it would be sensible to recommend that decisions by the competition authority should not be subject to approval by such a minister,[179] though it may be made possible for ministerial authorisation to be sought in cases where the parties disagree with the decision of the competition authority. Such authorisation

---

[179] See how decisions of the National Commission for the Defence of Competition (CNDC) of Argentina are ratified by the Secretariat of Domestic Commerce within the Ministry of Economy.

may be made possible on *narrow* grounds such as those of international competitiveness or economic development.[180]

(D) Capacity building and technical assistance

Competition authorities in the developing world need to be adequately staffed with lawyers, economists, investigators and case-handlers. The current number of staff within many existing competition authorities of developing countries (which in some cases is as few as four!) is simply insufficient for these authorities to be able to handle the competition work developing within the framework of the relevant competition law. Some of the countries are vast in geographical terms and the size of the population, which may be very diverse, necessitates the existence of competition authorities with adequate size to be able to execute their responsibilities. Furthermore, and equally important, competition expertise needs to be injected within the competition authorities of developing countries. In many cases such action is rather urgent. Expertise can be achieved in one of two ways, preferably using both simultaneously: First, through training sessions aimed at equipping staff of these competition authorities with a good understanding of competition law and policy including sessions dealing with competition law practice within key jurisdictions around the world and those dealing with appropriate case studies on how different provisions of the law are applied including a consideration of the analysis – in both legal and economics terms – which often need to conducted. Secondly, the relevant competition authority should seek to establish close relations with foreign competition authorities both within and beyond the relevant region within which its home country is located. As we saw from the examination of the competition law regimes of the EU and USA, competition authorities within these regimes and other ones around the world offer technical assistance and capacity building programmes aimed at assisting other young(er) competition authorities especially those of developing countries. These programmes usually take the form of secondments of officials from the former

---

[180] The mechanism of ministerial authorisation is found in the German competition law regime in the area of merger control: where merging parties disagree with a decision of the German cartel office blocking their mergers, the parties may seek ministerial authorisation on certain recognised grounds. If such an application for authorisation is accepted this will lead to the decision of the German cartel office being in effect overruled in the circumstances.

authorities to the latter and also having staff from the latter carry out visits to the former in order to experience first-hand how competition cases are handled in practice. Finally, the training should be extended to members of the judiciary who are likely to end up handling competition cases.[181] It is perfectly acceptable for this particular training to be integrated within the training programmes described here.

[181] See as an example here programmes run by UNCTAD. For an account on UNCTAD and its activities, see pp. 141–149 above.

Chapter 7

Regional competition law and policy

This chapter offers a 'global' overview of competition law and policy as they have come to be developed at regional levels (beyond Europe)[1] around the world. The chapter considers competition law initiatives within different regional communities as well as the inclusion of competition law as an element within regional free trade agreements. The aim here is not to offer an isolated treatment of every single effort at regional level but rather to consider the 'idea' of regional cooperation in an international context.

In recent years, considerable efforts have been made in relation to developing competition law and policy regionally. A review of these efforts will be given in the chapter with special attention being devoted to the following: Middle Eastern developments (with and without EU involvement); African developments: the *Economic and Monetary Community of Central Africa* (CEMAC), the *Common Market for Eastern and Southern Africa* (COMESA), the *West African Economic and Monetary Union* (UEMOA or WAEMU), the *Southern African Customs Union* (SACU), the *East African Community* (EAC) and the *Southern African Development Community* (SADC); in Asia: the creation of the *Association of South East Asian Nations* (ASEAN), the *South Asian Association for Regional Cooperation* (SAARC), and the *Asia-Pacific*

---

[1] The EU competition law regime was discussed in chapter 4; within which we also considered the European Economic Area (EEA) and the Association of European Competition Authorities (ECA). It may be also worth noting here the *Nordic Agreement on Cooperation in Competition Matters* entered into between Denmark, Iceland and Norway on 16 March 2001; Sweden joined the Agreement on 15 February 2004. The Agreement provides for notification of information concerning cases of interest and exchange of information between the parties. The exchange of information extends to confidential information; however when the latter is exchanged, the Agreement provides for: an *obligation of secrecy* on the part of the receiving party (i.e. the receiving competition authority); *restrictions on use* and restriction on *further distribution*. It is understood that a degree of cooperation between the parties has happened in practice within the framework of the Agreement in relation to conducting simultaneous raids in cartel investigations.

Economic Cooperation (APEC); in the Americas and the Caribbean: the creation of the *Southern Common Market* (MERCUSOR), the *Andean Community, Caribbean Community and Common Market* (CARICOM), the *North American Free Trade Agreement* (NAFTA), the *Central America-Dominican Republic-United States Free Trade Agreement* (CAFTA-DR) and the various Latin American Free Trade Agreements.

Within most of these initiatives and forms of cooperation, competition law has come to receive particular attention; in relation to some of these, competition law provisions feature rather prominently and in fact highly important and impressive steps have been taken towards building a supranational competition law regime in the relevant region(s). This chapter will focus on these competition law 'components' and will consider a number of interesting questions, which seem to arise when regional cooperation is viewed within an international setting. Chief among these questions are the following: why these different forms of regional cooperation *simply have not worked*; what their main contribution is whether regionally or in the field of competition law and policy globally; and what unique features, advantages or disadvantages they have in comparison to the EU, which is the most (and arguably the only) successful example of regional cooperation in the field of competition law and outside it.

1. Setting the scene

There are a number of reasons as to why competition law has been considered and developed within a regional cooperation setting. Perhaps the most obvious of these are the following: the fact that competition law is seen as complementary to rules on trade which regional cooperation often if not always includes; the fact that it is considered to be a natural component of economic cooperation, which is usually sought when regional cooperation is adopted; the fact that there is sometimes particular interest to enhance the status and importance of competition law domestically through creating a 'centre of gravity' at regional level; and the fact that such regional solutions can be seen as necessary to solve cross-border competition law problems. In relation to the last point in particular – as demonstrated so succinctly by the EU experience in the field – regional cooperation (or more accurately the creation of a regional competition law regime) can help in achieving more effective competition law enforcement both domestically and regionally. Previous chapters have made it clear how, with an increasing degree of globalisation and trade liberalisation, markets have become even more easy to access and as a result easier to monopolise and commit anticompetitive practices within them. With such cross-border economic activities in a global climate any resulting anticompetitive behaviour, conduct or transactions increasingly have significant regional and international consequences or implications. Through regional cooperation, such anticompetitive situations will be easier to confront and address (and where relevant regulate) more effectively. Indeed, in relation to some of these situations – most notably the regulation of cross-border merger operations – regional cooperation in this instance can have enormous benefits for firms whether in terms of harmonisation of substantive and procedural rules, reducing costs or enhancing legal certainty and minimising the risk of inconsistent findings by more than one competition authority.[2]

Regional cooperation in the field of competition law can have considerable advantages. These advantages appear to be underscored by the fact that those countries – especially developing ones – which lack effective domestic competition law regimes (and which have no form of regional cooperation in the field) will find it much harder to address anticompetitive behaviour, conduct or transactions with a cross-border dimension. By contrast, the existence of an effective competition law regime at a regional level – as is the case with the EU – can mean that such situations may be caught and regulated. There are important advantages therefore underpinning regional cooperation. It is important to be aware however of the difficulties facing countries in their efforts to build successful regional competition law regimes. In many parts of the world where regional cooperation has not been very fruitful or slow progress has been made in this respect, serious regional issues appear to dominate domestic as well as regional agenda, such as: bitter conflicts; poverty; and natural disasters and diseases; not to mention the absence of sufficient competition law expertise and resources which would be absolutely vital in any effort to build a viable regional cooperation framework. The existence of these serious hurdles means that fields

---

[2] One of the ways this is achieved is through using a one-stop-shop principle, under which when a transaction is regulated at the higher regional level it will be excluded from the jurisdiction of competition authorities at the lower national level. See the existence and the operation of this principle under Regulation 139/2004 in the EU competition law regime, chapter 4, note 10 (and accompanying text).

such as competition law would be pushed not to the *fore* but to the *background*.[3] Moreover, it must be appreciated that the journey from formulating the idea of regional cooperation to bringing the relevant initiative to fruition is long and features extremely tough terrain. Even if it were assumed that the destination would eventually be reached, realising coherent and practicable enforcement within a regional framework is a highly challenging task. Among other things, it would be important for domestic competition laws to exist in the relevant countries and for those countries to have in place practical mechanisms to ensure that the regional framework and the domestic regimes would operate in harmony and support each other in a way that would prevent possible conflicts, whether in terms of actual outcomes of cases or at a policy formulation level and avoid having one regime undermining the other. This would mean that there must be an appropriate tool in place defining the relationship between the regional and domestic level as well as between the national competition law regimes of the countries concerned.

Achieving success in building meaningful regional cooperation in the field of competition law very much depends on the exact aims to be achieved through regional cooperation. Broadly speaking, regional cooperation can be of different types. The first is where the cooperation will be used as a 'forum' for consultation and experience sharing which would facilitate the building of effective domestic competition law regimes and support these regimes through technical assistance and capacity-building channels. The second type is much more ambitious and much more 'long term' and complex: it involves building a mechanism for effective enforcement which could be handled by a number of authorities, including those which may operate at regional level. The most high-profile example in existence around the world of the latter is the European Competition Network (ECN), which brings together the European Commission and national competition authorities of the 27 Members States.[4] A third type of regional cooperation may revolve around achieving convergence and harmonisation – whether in substantive or procedural terms – among the domestic competition law regimes of the countries concerned.

The following part of the chapter will review the various ideas, efforts and initiatives which have emerged over the years seeking to develop

---

[3] See the discussion in the previous chapter, which considered the experience of developing countries in the field of competition law and the challenges facing them in building domestic effective competition law regimes.

[4] See pp. 194–198 above.

regional cooperation in the field of competition law in different parts of the world.

2. The Middle East

An (unsettled) debate has evolved over the years over how to define the region known as the 'Middle East' in geographical terms. This debate has spanned different academic, political and diplomatic circles though there will be no attempt here to contribute to it. For the purposes of this part, the 'Middle East' is taken to include the following countries: Algeria, Bahrain, Egypt, Iran, Israel, Jordan, Kuwait, Lebanon, Libya, Morocco, Oman, Palestine, Qatar, Saudi Arabia, Sudan, Tunisia, Turkey, United Arab Emirates and Yemen. Some of these countries have enacted competition law and others are going through the process.[5] A number of the counties with competition law regimes have adopted competition legislation only following the signing of their respective Association Agreements with the EU and as a result of the 1995 Barcelona Declaration, which stated that the signatory countries should make their competition legislation compatible with that of the EU. In the case of some of these countries, the enactment of competition legislation has been a pre-condition for accession to the World Trade Organisation (WTO)[6] and the result of a domestic realisation that doing so would enable the country in question to catch up with the process of globalisation and benefit more from international trade.[7]

Judged objectively, various Middle Eastern countries have been making admirable efforts in the field of competition law through instituting competition law regimes and seeking to build a 'portfolio' of effective enforcement. However what is remarkably striking is that – despite the huge similarities in cultural, religious, political and social terms shared by most of them – these countries have made little progress towards concluding a regional cooperation agreement with a noticeable competition law dimension. Obviously the fact that the region is regrettably embroiled in bitter conflict and division, and confrontation between regional (and world) powers has been the order of the day has not helped in this respect. Unfortunately countries in the Middle East have been

---

[5] See M. Dabbah, *Competition Law and Policy in the Middle East* (Cambridge University Press, 2007).
[6] See, for example, the Syrian experience with adopting domestic competition law.
[7] See p. 290 above for an example.

more inclined to create division and engage in confrontation rather than to forge deep and meaningful regional economic cooperation. Arguably however, the optimists would contend that in recent years the scene has come to change and the chances for regional cooperation in economic terms in general and the field of competition law in particular, though formerly perceived as an impossible dream now look to be, although distant, a possibility. To assess these chances it would be necessary at any rate to consider the different attempts made over the years to achieve regional cooperation, whether those have some or exclusive competition law relevance, in the Middle East.

(A) The League of Arab States

I. Historical background

Establishing the League of Arab States, or the Arab League as it is known more commonly, represents the oldest attempt to achieve regional cooperation in the Middle East. The League came into existence in 1945 and aimed to coordinate the economic affairs of its members, which at present stand at 22. Throughout most of its existence however the League has been dominated by lack of consensus and deep divisions between its members over policy positions and impasse is often reached when attempts have been made to reach binding common positions let alone implement them in practice. These dominating factors – one way or another – foretold the little impact the League would have and contributed towards most of the outcomes of its meetings and work being merely declaratory in nature.

II. GAFTA

Nonetheless, one of the major achievements made by the League was creating a pact aiming at the establishment of a Greater Arab Free Trade Area (GAFTA) in 1997. One of the main objectives of the GAFTA is the creation of the Pan Arab Market, a complete economic community in the Arab world which would follow the lines of the common market established within the EU. The deadline originally set for full implementation of the free trade area for the higher income countries was 2005 and less-developed members were given a transition period of up to 2010. GAFTA came into effect on 1 January 2005, covering 17 League members whose trade volume represented 94 per cent of the total intra-Arab trade. However, studies have shown that the level of trade is low and it has been suggested this is due to policy-induced factors including the dominance of the public sector, delays and costs in customs clearances and high transportations and communication costs.[8]

III. The competition Regulations

With the support of the League's Economic and Social Council, a draft set of Arab Competition Regulations has been prepared. However, little progress has been made in approving the draft and activities appear to have stalled; given that the work GAFTA has so far achieved is quite unimpressive, one ought not to raise expectations with regard to the future implementation of the Regulations. A purported final draft was produced in summer 2002 following receipt of comments from all Arab countries and the intention at that time was to submit that draft to the Economic and Social Council of the Arab League.[9] This draft would benefit from further thinking and work however, and it would be fitting to describe the draft as no more than a good first attempt. Although bearing the word 'Regulations', the Regulations are not intended to have the binding force of the Law and therefore their role is to serve as a set of guidelines. The fact that this is so can be expected to *limit* the influence the Regulations can have in practice. The Regulations contain 26 Articles and it could be said that they essentially take the form of a 'competition law', the provisions of which have been informed by three sources: EU competition rules;[10] the competition laws of the relevant Arab countries; and UNCTAD's Set of Multilaterally Agreed Equitable Principles and Rules for the Control of Restrictive Business Practices.[11] The declared aim of the Regulations is to protect and encourage competition and to supervise monopolistic practices for the purposes of increasing economic activity. The Regulations apply to collusion between persons,[12] abuse of

---

[8] See A. Dennis, *The Impact of Regional Trade Agreements and Trade Facilitation in the Middle East North Africa Region* (World Bank (Policy Research Working Paper 3837), 2006).

[9] It is understood that a detailed set of explanatory notes is being drafted and will also be submitted to the Council for approval. This set of explanatory notes is intended to serve as an accompanying document to the Regulations for the purposes of explaining the different provisions in the Regulations and their application.

[10] See chapter 4 above.

[11] The Set was discussed above at pp. 144–146.

[12] A person is defined in Art. 2 as a 'natural or legal person, or any other legal entity regardless of its form'.

Article 4 of the Regulations prohibits any agreement, which has an object or effect to distort free competition. The Article lists as examples of such agreements those which

dominance[13] and harmful mergers, though acts involving the sovereign or the exercise of prerogatives of public powers or the exercise of public tasks and activities fall outside the scope of the Regulations.[14] The scope of the Regulations also extends to concentrations[15] creating a dominant position.[16] The Regulations however are not intended to create a supranational enforcement mechanism. Rather, they provide for its rules to be

involve: price-fixing; market or customers sharing; refusal to deal with particular suppliers or customers; collusive tendering; hindering the entry or exit of products from markets and illegal stocking; and limitation of output, production and distribution activities. An 'agreement' is defined in Art. 2 of the Regulations to include a contract or arrangement whether written or oral, express or implied between two or more persons. The Regulations do not provide whether the prohibition applies to both horizontal and vertical agreements, though the intention of the draftsmen was that this is the case.

[13] Article 5 of the Regulations deals with abuse of dominance and prohibits conduct on the part of a dominant firm with an object or effect harming competition in particular conduct involving discrimination; refusal to supply without objective justification; predatory pricing; tying between products; complicating the activities of competitors; and engaging in acts leading to unfair or artificial pricing.

Dominance for the purposes of the Regulations can be of two types: single firm dominance and collective dominance. According to Art. 2 a dominant position is a position enabling a person or group of persons to control or affect market activities.

[14] See Art. 3 of the Regulations.

It is also important to note that either of the prohibitions above however would bite in the circumstances covered under Art. 6, under which the possibility for exemption is provided. According to the Article an exemption is possible in three situations. First, where the behaviour or conduct furthers the public interest and leads or is likely to lead to reduction in costs or improvement in production and distribution or technical progress. Secondly, where the conduct or behaviour is required by law or is necessary for the purposes of implementing or applying a provision within any law. The third situation concerns practices of selling below cost. The Article provides that selling below cost is caught within the net of the prohibitions, except where the practice is carried out in a situation in which one of the following prevails: the relevant products have short expiry date; such sale is ordered by court; the purpose behind the sale is to 'get rid' of old stock in order to make way for new products; or the products have 'special characteristics' and are subject to supervision and control by the state.

[15] A concentration is defined in Art. 2 as an operation involving a merger or acquisition. An acquisition, according to the Article, occurs where there is a transfer of total or partial ownership from one or more persons to another whether through shares, assets or any other means giving such person the ability to influence the strategic decision making of the former. Although the Article does not mention 'control' specifically, the understanding is that the 'transfer' and 'influence' referred to therein concern control.

[16] Chapter 3 (Arts 8–10) of the Regulations deals with concentrations in a rather brief manner. Article 8 provides for prior notification by any person intending to merge with or acquire another where the operation leads to the creation of a dominant position. The Article is silent on when this prior-mandatory notification must be effected. It does state however that concentrations must be reviewed within a strict (apparently non-extendable) 90 days. According to Art. 9 a decision to clear a concentration may be

enforced by competition authorities[17] at a domestic level. To achieve this, the Regulations provide for the creation of a competition authority within each Arab country which is to be armed with a wide range of powers and responsibilities enabling such an authority to effectively enforce the competition rules domestically.[18]

Considering the competition law regimes in existence within Arab countries at present, it is important to note that the provisions of the Regulations on enforcement are markedly different from some of those regimes. The Regulations acknowledge the differences in this regard and therefore provide that the substantive provisions which are contained in Chapter 4 are without prejudice to the right of individual countries to determine the nature of the authority created under the relevant competition law regime, its composition and its operation.[19] The right reserved to countries over enforcement can be seen specifically in the context of penalties: the Regulations provide for penalties to be determined by individual countries.[20]

The Regulations present a significant step in creating some form of regional cooperation mechanism in the Arab world. Prior to commencing the drafting process of the Regulations, there was a debate on whether they should serve as a blueprint for a regional competition law to be enforced at a supranational level within the Arab League or as guiding principles for members of the Arab League to follow for the purposes of adopting competition law in their domestic legal systems or modifying their existing rules according to the wording and spirit of the Regulations. Of course at the time this debate emerged a dissimilar

---

revoked at a later date where it turns out that the information supplied was false. Article 10 makes it clear that a concentration giving rise to competition concerns may be cleared if it is shown that the concentration contributes to economic progress in a way that would compensate for the competition harm.

[17] Under Art. 2 of the Regulations, an authority is defined as the competent body with responsibility to implement and enforce the Regulations in accordance with the internal rules in operation within each member state, i.e. each Arab country.

[18] See Chapter 4 (Arts 12–23) of the Regulations. Among the powers listed in Art. 12 are: conducting investigations (including searches); reviewing notified concentrations; engaging in competition advocacy and building a culture of competition; cooperation with foreign competition authorities; preparing annual reports to be submitted to the relevant bodies or persons in the country; and making decisions. Other provisions in Chapter 4 worth noting are those dealing with issues such as the expertise and qualifications of individuals to be appointed as competition officials (Art. 13), the obligation on officials to observe confidentiality in proceedings within the authority (Art. 22) and the obligation on those officials to avoid conflict of interest (Art. 21).

[19] See Art. 23.   [20] See Art. 24.

position to the present one had existed throughout the Arab world, namely that competition law and policy were absent from the vast majority of Arab countries.[21] In the end the *sensible* decision was made to follow the latter option.[22] It would have been futile and controversial to opt for a regional model that could have resulted in a 'top-down' as opposed to a 'bottom-up' approach to competition law and policy. Those in favour of the top-down model had one good argument however: the idea was to avoid a situation where some countries would unnecessarily or unavoidably delay the enactment of domestic competition rules and the creation of a regional competition law regime, which would have been beneficial for the purposes of addressing 'cross-border' competition problems. Additionally, through following this model it would have been possible to guarantee that the same standards, rules and policy and the same competition culture and approach would flourish as opposed to a situation where the rules would have to be 'adjusted' to a common approach at a later stage. Nonetheless, opting for this model would have been problematic. Apart from the fact that the model represents an ambitious attempt which requires political approval at the level of heads of states, in the Arab world domestic competition problems outnumber those with cross-border elements and thus the regional model would have had limited impact on such problems. Furthermore, there is a lack of a sufficiently robust and widespread competition culture in all Arab countries in particular and to a large degree insufficient recognition of competition or even an understanding of it. A regional model would have contributed very little to building such culture given the daunting task that the regional competition authority would have had to deal with and the differences that exist between the countries concerned. It should be clear therefore that the regional competition law regime would not have offered a good substitute for domestic competition law regimes in the different countries.

The Regulations can still be expected to make an important contribution on several fronts, starting from the fact that they provide a centre of gravity to which all domestic competition law regimes of Arab countries would be linked, to the fact that they would open a new chapter in the regional development of competition law and policy in the Arab world

---

[21] At that time, Jordan, Saudi Arabia, Egypt and Qatar had not adopted their competition laws and so only Algeria, Morocco and Tunisia had domestic competition legislation.

[22] In fact the decision was reached because of political objection to the regional approach. From a competition law perspective however, the correct outcome was reached.

and the Middle East more generally. The drafting of the Regulations has placed competition law and policy on the regional map. Whether the contribution made by this important document will translate into concrete steps depends to a large extent on the political support individual countries are willing to offer in this regard. There is no doubt that the fact that recently competition law has come to be introduced in Saudi Arabia, Egypt, Jordan, Qatar, Kuwait and Syria[23] and the fact that Lebanon and UAE are at an advanced stage of their competition law projects offer hope for this to occur; competition law would have been unthinkable in all of these countries even as recently as six years ago – something that makes these important developments of huge significance.

(B) The Agadir Agreement

The Agreement for the Establishment of a Free Trade Zone between the Arabic Mediterranean Nations (Agadir) was signed in 2004 by Egypt, Jordan, Morocco and Tunisia. The Agreement aimed to create a free trade area among these countries and one of its goals was to facilitate competition among its members. Agadir came into force in March 2007 and it is open to further membership by all members of the Arab League and Arab Free Trade Zone who are linked to the EU through an Association Agreement or Free Trade Agreement. The EU 'link' here takes its roots from the close proximity to the EU and the support it receives from the latter, which considers it as an attempt that can potentially be a key contribution to the objectives of the Barcelona process[24] and the establishment of a Euro-Mediterranean Free Trade Area. The EU support to Agadir has included financial funding in furtherance of its Neighbourhood Policy[25] for the period 2004–08 being given to the Agadir Technical Unit, established under Article 27 of the Agreement to deal with matters pertaining to the Agreement; further financial support is expected to be offered in the near future. Such financial support by the EU is hugely important and coupled with its technical support – as well as the proactive approach being adopted by the Agadir Technical Unit itself – it appears that Agadir is set for opening a new chapter in the cooperation among the relevant Middle Eastern countries. It is not unrealistic to expect that the close relationship with

---

[23] It is important to note here that Syria in fact gave important attention to the Regulations in preparing its competition law.
[24] See pp. 378–380 below.   [25] See pp. 379–380 below.

the EU in developing Agadir is likely to lead to some form of regional, harmonising, measures directed at competition law eventually coming into existence. The road ahead however is still long and considerable efforts will have to be made in order to achieve the desired harmonisation within Agadir in the field of competition law. At present, the four member states of Agadir are at varying stages of competition law developments and more crucially their domestic competition law regimes feature some sharp differences, especially in enforcement and procedural rules.

(C)   The Cooperation Council of the Arab States of the Gulf (GCC)

The GCC was created in 1981 and brings together the Gulf States of Bahrain, Kuwait, Oman, Qatar, Saudi Arabia and the UAE; Yemen is currently in negotiations for GCC full membership and expects to join by 2016. The GCC contains many economic objectives and in recent years it has edged closer to realising some of these; in comparison to GAFTA (which was discussed above) it has a far 'tighter' timetable. In 2001 the GCC Economic Agreement was signed to establish a Customs Union and the harmonisation of economic, financial and monetary policies; the aim is to provide for more economic integration through the establishment of the Gulf Common Market (GCM) and the Gulf Monetary Union. By 2003 the Customs Union was established; in January 2008 the GCM was launched; and the Monetary Union – which will introduce a single currency – is now hoped to be established in 2010.

As far as competition law is concerned, there are no provisions seeking to protect competition or calling for fighting anticompetitive situations within GCC framework. Thus there is a clear absence of any meaningful reference to competition law and policy in both the GCC's documents and its stated objectives; the phrases 'protection from unfair competition', 'avoidance of harmful competition' and 'increased competition' have been bandied around in describing disparate areas, such as economic cooperation in the oil and gas sector, the Model Regulation Law for the Promotion of Foreign Investment and the envisaged economic impact of GCC Customs Union. Without any real commitment to implementing competition law and policy it is hard to see how supranational competition regulation at the GCC level could ever emerge. Furthermore, this absence of commitment is odd given the importance bestowed upon economic development and cooperation among GCC members when competition law and policy are intrinsically linked to such aims.

(D) Cooperation through the European Commission

The EU and the European Commission specifically have – as we saw in chapter 4 above – made positive efforts in promoting regional cooperation beyond the EU in several ways. Of particular note is the work embarked upon as part of the Barcelona Process and the developments made with the EU's European Neighbourhood Policy.

The Barcelona Process, or the Euro-Mediterranean Partnership as it has also been known more recently, began with the Barcelona Declaration in 1995 when 15 EU Members and 14 Mediterranean Partners sought to establish a framework in which both bilateral and regional relations could be founded so as to transform the Mediterranean into a common area of peace, stability and prosperity and to encourage closer ties among countries in the Mediterranean and the Middle East. In 2008 the Partnership was re-launched as the Union for the Mediterranean and today 17 'partners' are involved, namely: Albania, Algeria, Bosnia and Herzegovina, Croatia, Egypt, Israel, Jordan, Lebanon, Libya, Mauritania, Monaco, Montenegro, Morocco, Palestine, Syria, Tunisia and Turkey. The work undertaken by the EU has allowed the countries involved to establish and engage in a dialogue in four different areas: politics and security; economics and finance; sociocultural matters; and migration.[26] Competition law and policy is not specifically addressed by the Economic and Financial Partnership, its natural home; rather, this particular Partnership seeks to promote shared economic development by introducing a Euro-Med free trade area, reforming individual key sectors such as energy through harmonisation, capacity building and the development of infrastructures; and by working with other international organisations, including the World Bank and the International Monetary Fund, to favour economic conditions of growth.

The idea behind the original Barcelona Process was to offer a 'neutral' platform on which regional cooperation could be forged in a meaningful way. A major incentive for including competition law and policy in this idea would be the wealth of competition law expertise available within the European Commission and its impressive 'know-how' in providing

---

[26] Migration was added as a fourth pillar in 2005 at the Barcelona Summit.

technical assistance and capacity building activities.[27] However, the realisation of such an idea which includes competition law and policy requires a strong commitment by the Commission and an even stronger commitment by the individual 'partner' countries and it has come to be seen that such a commitment is not realistic. Looking at the Barcelona Process (and its regional approach), achievements under the Process appear to have been modest. To a large extent, the regional approach embodied in the Process fell short of achieving its declared goals. The causes for this appear to be the significant differences in the stages of developments of the partner countries, the lack of common interest uniting them and the difficulty in achieving convergence in their individual interests. The 'one size fits all' approach of the Process triggered reservation on the part of the more developed partner countries over the real benefits they could reasonably expect to reap from the Process. In some cases these reservations reduced the political will of those countries to further or deepen their involvement within the Process, for instance the Turkish Competition Authority in particular adopted a policy which aligned itself closer to Western counterparts and it has not been particularly enthusiastic about engaging with other competition authorities in the Middle East.

With the enlargement of the EU in 2004, the European Neighbourhood Policy (ENP) was established to avoid the emergence of new dividing lines and to secure the prosperity, stability and security of the parties involved; the ENP has also taken over the role of building and managing bilateral relationships with the EU's neighbours. The countries involved in the ENP are the EU's immediate neighbours by land or sea: Algeria, Armenia, Azerbaijan, Belarus, Egypt, Georgia, Israel, Jordan, Lebanon, Libya, Moldova, Morocco, Occupied Palestinian Territory, Syria, Tunisia and Ukraine. The EU and each neighbour formulate ENP Action Plans which set out an agenda for political and economic reforms, having both short- and medium-term priorities. The Action Plans build upon existing agreements between the neighbours, i.e. Partnership and Cooperation Agreements and Association Agreements, and as a result Belarus, Libya and Syria are not technically 'active' within the ENP because no such agreements are in place for these countries. In more ways than one, the move on the part of the European Commission towards the ENP (with its *differential* bilateral approach) should be seen as an action taken for the purposes of filling the gaps in the Barcelona Process, particularly as to the

---

[27] See pp. 225–226 above.

inadequacies of the 'one size fits all' approach. Comparing the two ideas together, the ENP has a clear advantage in light of the fact that its work with each neighbour is tailored in light of that country's specific needs and characteristics. Nonetheless, the ENP suffers from several shortcomings as a suitable tool to further *regional* cooperation in the field of competition law amongst its neighbours. First, since the ENP has as its legal basis the Partnership and Cooperation Agreements and the Association Agreements concluded by the Commission with individual partners/neighbours over the years,[28] these Agreements have in fact contributed very little towards enhancing regional cooperation. Many of the provisions contained in these Agreements are vague with the competition provisions having not been implemented. Secondly, the Action Plans introduced within the framework of the ENP (and the Association Agreements) cover a wide range of areas, extending far beyond competition law and policy. These areas include justice and home affairs matters, science and technology issues and contact between peoples. With all of these areas being given particular importance, it is not clear what impact the Action Plans will have on the field of competition law or indeed how likely they are to contribute to furthering cooperation in the field. Thirdly, the ENP framework is not purely bilateral in nature or scope: a regional dimension is identifiable in light of the Commission's intention to apply the rules and standards within the framework regionally. Apart from the fact that this is bound to lead to a situation in which the lowest common denominator will be used, the Commission's approach could be said to be not entirely clear with regard to how the ENP fits with the Barcelona Process; as it stands, the ENP is stated to be a 'complementary' policy to that of the Barcelona Process and now Union for the Mediterranean. All of these points show that the terrain facing an effort to implement this type of regional cooperation is of an extremely difficult nature.

3. Africa

Africa has – like the neighbouring Middle East – been the victim of serious problems and crises. Admirably however, the continent and its people have developed a wonderfully positive approach to regional cooperation, which looks to solve the continent's problems and advance the interest of different African nations. This cooperation has been

---

[28] See pp. 208–223 above for a discussion on association and partnership and cooperation agreements.

particularly strong in the economic arena and has extended to the field of competition law itself; though the question of how fruitful this co-operation has been in practice remains highly debatable. The following discussion will assess this question and attempt to answer it in light of the different efforts seeking to establish regional cooperation in the field of competition law in Africa.

(A)   The Economic and Monetary Community of Central Africa (CEMAC)[29]

The Economic and Monetary Community of Central Africa (CEMAC) is comprised of five member states: Cameroon, Chad, Democratic Republic of Congo, Equatorial Guinea and Gabon. CEMAC is the product of two different unions: the Economic Union of Central Africa and the Monetary Union of Central Africa. It was set up with the conclusion of the Treaty establishing the Economic and Monetary Community of Central Africa in 1994 and came against the backdrop of successive African economic crises. The principle objective behind CEMAC is to establish a closer union between its member states, including the creation of an internal market and the abolition of obstacles to trade.

CEMAC contains a 'community' competition law mechanism, which features in Regulation 1/99 UEAC-CM-639 and Regulation 4/99 UEAC-CM-639. The relevant rules provide for anti-cartel regulation, prohibition on abuse of dominance and the regulation of merger operations. The rules are intended to apply where anticompetitive situations affect trade between member states; something that shows the similarity with the EU regime in this regard. The rules are 'enforced' by a Competition Monitoring Body (CMB), which includes the Executive Secretariat and the Regional Competition Council. Essentially, the CMB monitors the implementation of the rules within the domestic regimes of member states whereas the Council is the decision-making body; it decides on infringements and its decisions are subject to appeal to the Arbitration Court.[30]

Developments in practice have revealed concerns which have been raised as to the capacity of member states to implement CEMAC competition rules. Although the necessary political will can be said to be present, the member states suffer from institutional weaknesses which

---

[29] From its French name *Communauté Économique et Monétaire de l'Afrique Centrale*.
[30] See Art. 24 of Regulation 1/99 UEAC-CM-639.

directly impact on their capacity to implement the rules; indeed Cameroon is the only member state with a domestic competition law and authority in place.

(B) Common Market for Eastern and Southern Africa (COMESA)

The Treaty establishing the Common Market for Eastern and Southern Africa (COMESA) was signed on 5 November 1993 in Uganda and was ratified a year later in Malawi. It replaced the *Preferential Trade Area Treaty* of 1982 which envisaged a common market in Eastern and Southern Africa. COMESA has a fairly broad regional membership base, which includes: Angola, Burundi Comoros, Democratic Republic of Congo, Eritrea, Ethiopia, Kenya, Madagascar, Malawi, Mauritius, Namibia, Rwanda, Seychelles, Sudan, Swaziland, Tanzania, Uganda, Zambia and Zimbabwe.

COMESA may be considered to be an umbrella community given that it covers other regional organisations, including the East African Community (EAC) and the Southern African Development Community (SADC).[31] COMESA has very good working relations, formally and informally, with all the regional organisations on the continent. These relations can be seen in light of the *Memorandum of Understanding* signed with the EAC under which the EAC has agreed to adopt and implement the COMESA trade liberalisation and facilitation programme and the *Joint Task Force* established with SADC in order to harmonise their programmes.

Within the COMESA framework, member states are tasked with the responsibility to provide the conditions for economic integration, which is understood in a broader (European) sense as extending from creating a common legislative framework to the mutual recognition of standards and qualifications. Competition law is a foundation stone of economic integration under COMESA and it has been recognised as a key economic tool in any sustainable development agenda.[32] This particular emphasis on competition law is quite remarkable but appears to be chosen because of the belief that the economic transition experienced by most of the member states shows the need for competition law: in

---

[31] The EAC and SADC are discussed below.
[32] See *Aide Memoire: Trade Capacity Building: Strengthening the COMESA Trade Region Through a Culture of Competition* (COMESA, 2008).

these member states many former state monopolies have been replaced by private ones thus raising concerns at both national and regional levels as to the concentration of economic power in the hands of a few economic operators. Such transition and development appear to have highlighted and helped articulate the need for a regional framework to confront possible anticompetitive situations.[33]

A few COMESA countries have domestic competition laws, but these were considered to be inadequate to deal with complex cross-border and multi-jurisdictional competition issues. It was acknowledged that co-operation at bilateral level could resolve and redress some of these issues, but a regional framework was perceived to be a more consistent and sustainable way of addressing regional issues. A number of COMESA member states, including Kenya, Zambia and Zimbabwe, openly acknowledged prior to the creation of COMESA that national competition rules were insufficient to combat restrictive practices manifested at a regional level.

I.   The COMESA competition framework

COMESA competition law and policy incorporate a mechanism for achieving *harmonisation* among the competition rules and policies of member states in order to minimise and preferably avoid conflicts. Sectoral regulation[34] was also provided for and it was stated that the Council of Ministers will adopt rules to regulate the relevant sector(s); the first sector covered under these rules was air transport.

Under Article 55(3) of the COMESA Treaty, regional competition law was adopted in the form of the COMESA *Competition Regulations*. This occurred in late 2004 after being approved by the Council of Ministers. The Regulations are considered to be an independent mechanism designed to meet the aims and objectives of COMESA and *not* just an instrument for building a unified common market. Crucially, the Regulations are intended to enhance COMESA's rule-based trading system by promoting economic efficiency, the predictability of the trading regime, and good corporate governance among economic operators and consumers throughout the COMESA region.

---

[33] See *Competition Provisions in Regional Trade Agreements: How to Assure Development Gains* (UNCTAD, 2005)

[34] This refers to regulation of the special sectors; see pp. 338–361 above for a discussion on sectoral regulation (in the telecommunications) sector in different developing countries.

The Regulations deal with competition issues of a regional as opposed to domestic type, i.e. those which involve or have an impact on more than one COMESA member state. This means that it is open to COMESA to assert jurisdiction where anticompetitive situations have cross-border elements;[35] situations with a pure domestic element must be addressed at the national level. In becoming members, COMESA member states are deemed to have voluntarily agreed to cross-border situations being addressed at a regional level without surrendering their rights as sovereign countries to deal with any competition issues which may arise within their domestic boundaries. There is therefore concurrent jurisdiction in existence with the COMESA Commission[36] and national courts of member states being able to apply the Regulations. However because the Regulations are considered to have supremacy over national laws, in the case of conflict the Regulations must prevail over the conflicting national law.[37] In practice such conflict is avoided through ensuring that the Regulations are applied consistently and that the COMESA Commission and member states cooperate, as well as through member states paying close attention to Article 5 of the COMESA Treaty: according to this Article, member states undertake to make every effort to plan and direct their development policies with a view to creating conditions conducive to achieving the aims of the common market and the implementation of the COMESA Treaty and they also undertake to refrain from adopting any measures likely to jeopardise this. This idea of supremacy and obligation on member states not to undermine the COMESA rules has been borrowed from the EU regime: like the latter, the COMESA Regulations constitute 'a new legal order of international law', under which member states have limited their sovereign rights in some fields;[38] the subjects of this new order include the nationals of the member states.

The Regulations have a wide scope and provide for, among other things, the notification and control of mergers and acquisitions and

---

[35] It may be worth noting that Art. 55(1) of the COMESA Treaty although in fact based on Art. 101(1) TFEU, omits a specific reference to collusion which may 'affect on trade between Member States'. Nonetheless, UNCTAD considers that the impact of cross-border trade is an *implicit* prerequisite in light of the wording of the Regulations.

[36] See below for a discussion of the Commission and its role.

[37] According to Art. 5(2), the Common Market is to enjoy primacy over national law.

[38] See p. 165 above.

the control of anticompetitive business practices; and there are strong consumer protection provisions. By contrast with the EU competition law regime, the Regulations arguably provide for a somewhat broader concept of consumer protection, which is not merely concerned with providing safeguards for consumers, but also benefits traders by encouraging business transactions. This is especially the case with ethical traders, whom consumers are unable to distinguish from unscrupulous traders.

II.   Institutional structure

Article 6 of the COMESA Regulations provide for the creation of a specific competition body, the COMESA Competition Commission. The Commission is a corporate body with an international legal personality operating within the COMESA legal framework. Within the territory of each member state it has the legal capacity needed to perform its duties under the COMESA Treaty, including the power to acquire or dispose of moveable and immoveable property in accordance with national laws.

The Commission is expected to work closely with national competition authorities in the implementation of competition law and policy across the region. Under Article 7 of the Regulations, the Commission is given the function of applying the Regulations and it has the power to do a number of things, including: monitor and investigate anticompetitive practices within the common market; mediate disputes between member states concerning anticompetitive conduct; help member states promote their domestic competition laws and strengthen their institutions; and harmonise national laws with the Regulations. The Commission does not need to be notified, or have a complaint made to it, to be able to initiate a competition investigation.

The Commission includes a Board of Commissioners which reviews the initial determinations by the Commission and hears appeals. It can delegate its functions to another COMESA Agency established to coordinate and regulate a specific sector. The Board of Commissioners was appointed in September 2007 in Kenya by the Bureau of Council. In May 2008 the first training session for the Board took place so as to provide it with a good understanding of competition law and policy within the COMESA context. Decisions adopted by the Board of Commissioners can be appealed to the COMESA Court of Justice, which can conduct a judicial review of the acts of COMESA institutions.

(C)   West African Economic and Monetary Union (UEMOA[39] or WAEMU)

The West African Economic and Monetary Union (WAEMU) was established in 1994 as a union between eight African countries: Benin, Burkina Faso, Côte d'Ivoire, Guinea Bissau, Mali, Niger, Senegal and Togo. It has general economic objectives, which include the elimination of all tariff barriers on intra-Community trade; this has been achieved through a series of reforms started in 1996.

WAEMU establishes a regional competition regime, which, among other things, rests on two important pillars: precedence of 'community law' over national law and the direct and immediate applicability of community law within domestic legal regimes. Thus, member states are required to make necessary adjustments to their domestic laws to comply with the supranational character of the WAEMU. These two pillars are supported by a number of key Articles and the specific competition rules of WAEMU. In particular, it is important to highlight Articles 88–90. Article 90 gives the WAEMU Commission competence to apply the competition rules,[40] subject to the control of the Court of Justice which has jurisdiction to rule on all decisions issues and fines imposed by the Commission.[41] To facilitate the implementation[42] of these Articles, in 2002 the WAEMU Council of Ministers adopted the *Community Competition Law*, which has five elements, all of which came into force in January 2003: control of anticompetitive behaviour within WAEMU;[43] rules and procedures relating to the control of cartels and abuse of dominant position within WAEMU;[44] the control of state aid

---

[39] Acronym for the French name *Union et Monétaire Ouest Africaine.*

[40] The Commission acts through the Department of Fiscal Customs and Trade Policies, particularly the Trade and Competition Authority. It monitors compliance with WAEMU competition rules at national level and hence: receives complaints directly through national structures; initiates and investigates legal actions; and takes provisional measures, deciding on restrictions and fines. Before the Commission acts, it seeks advice from the Competition Advisory Committee.

[41] The Court of Justice enjoys the power to hear legal actions launched by WAEMU bodies and appeals against Commission decisions, which can be amended or annulled as the Court of Justice sees fit.

[42] All member states contribute to the implementation of the rules via their involvement in the deliberations of the Regional Advisory Committee, the supranational administrative body in charge of enforcement. The Committee is composed of two representatives from each member state and its role is to provide advice on the Commission's draft decisions.

[43] See Regulation 02/2002/CM/UEMOA.   [44] See Regulation 03/2002/CM/UEMOA.

within the WAEMU;[45] transparency of the financial relationship between members states and public enterprises on the one hand, and between public enterprises and international or foreign organisations on the other;[46] and cooperation between the WAEMU Commission and national authorities in the enforcement of the Law.[47] These five elements are supplemented by a non-exhaustive list of prohibited practices which was produced in order to facilitate greater clarity and legal certainty in relation to what type of situations are caught within the scope of the relevant rules. This list is based on a 'global' perspective of the most common practices in the field as well as on the distinctive features of the WAEMU.

The WAEMU competition rules apply to practices that have an intra-regional effect. In principle, the application of the rules is not exclusively reserved to the WAEMU Commission in all cases: member states that do not have domestic competition law in place can apply the rules within their own boundaries.[48] However in cases where an intra-regional effect exists, the Commission has exclusive authority to implement the rules;[49] it is for domestic authorities of member states to enforce domestic laws when they exist, but in areas covered by WAEMU rules, the latter will be considered to be supreme and as a result national laws cannot be applied. It should not be understood however that the two sets of regimes – community and domestic – within WAEMU operate in isolation without interaction. Indeed in practice such interaction is likely. For example, when there is an investigation, formal and informal cooperation between the Commission and each domestic authority occurs; this cooperation is facilitated by the presence of two representatives from each member state in the Commission.[50]

(D) Southern African Customs Union (SACU)

The Southern African Customs Union (SACU) is the world's oldest customs union. It was established in 1889 as a Customs Union

---

[45] See Regulation 04/2002/CM/UEMOA.   [46] See Directive 01/2002/CM/UEMOA.

[47] See Directive 02/2002/CM/UEMOA.

[48] Benin, Niger, Togo and Guinea-Bissau all apply WAEMU competition rules domestically though they have been asked to adopt competition law in conformity with the WAEMU Regulations.

[49] This was clarified by the Court of Justice in 2000; see Opinion 003/2000/CJ/UEMOA.

[50] Currently, different options are being explored in order to deepen the cooperation between the Commission and domestic authorities of member states. One of the proposals under consideration suggests establishing a network linking all of these authorities so as to strengthen cooperation between them.

Convention between the British Colony of Cape of Good Hope and the Orange Free State Boer Republic and today has all of the following African countries as its members: Botswana, Lesotho, Namibia, South Africa and Swaziland. Together these countries form a single customs territory, which has a single tariff applicable throughout it and no customs duties between these five African nations. Historically, South African interests dominated the SACU: under the 1910 and 1969 SACU Agreements South Africa had sole decision-making responsibility for customs and excise policies as the administration of SACU was on a part-time basis with meetings of the Customs Union only being held annually and there was no real check on South Africa's exercise of power; further-more, South Africa commonly entered into self-serving preferential agreements with non-SACU traders which had little or no benefit for other SACU members. The current SACU Agreement was signed in 2002 and came into effect in 2004; under this Agreement a joint decision-making process was put in place with the creation of several independent bodies – including an independent Administrative Secretariat to oversee SACU – so as to ensure that member states participate equally. The Agreement also recognised that, in respect of agreements with non-SACU members, there was a need to develop strategies which enhanced the political, economic, social and cultural integration of the region without jeopardising the economies of the smaller states.

SACU has a fairly developed institutional structure under the 2002 Agreement with a Commission, Council of Ministers, a Tribunal and a Trade and Industry Liaison Committee. The Commission is made up of senior officials from the ministries of finance and trade from each member state. It is responsible for the implementation of the 2002 Agreement and facilitates the implementation of the Council's decisions. The Council of Ministers consists of ministers of finance and trade from each member state and it is the supreme decision-making authority in SACU matters. The Tribunal is intended to be ad hoc and reports directly to the Council. Its aim is to adjudicate on any issue concerning the application of the 2002 Agreement or any dispute arising under it, but only at the request of the Council. Its decisions are final and binding. Finally, the Trade and Industry Liaison Committee assists in the devel-opment of policies and instruments to facilitate cooperation with regard to the field of competition among Member States.

There are two provisions that address competition within the SACU framework. Article 40 of the 2002 Agreement provides that member states agree that there shall be competition policies in each member state and that they will cooperate with each other in respect of competition enforcement. The second provision, Article 41, addresses unfair trading practices between member states by providing that the Council, on the advice of the Commission, shall develop policies and instruments to address them. These policies are annexed to the agreement.[51] Beyond these two key provisions, competition relevance within the SACU framework also derives from a cooperation agreement concluded with the European Free Trade Association (EFTA)[52] in 2006 which is known as the SACU–EFTA Agreement.[53] Article 15(1) of the Agreement states that the parties recognise that anticompetitive practices can hinder the fulfilment of the objectives of the Agreement. Article 15(2) provides that a party who considers that the Agreement is being hindered by a practice referred to in Article 15(1) may request the party in whose territory the practice originates to cooperate so as to end the practice or its effects. Cooperation includes the exchange of information available to the parties to the extent that it is permitted by the relevant law. Finally, Article 15(3) states that where the use of Article 15(2) does not offer a solution, the affected party can request consultation in the Joint Committee[54] with the aim of reaching a mutually satisfactory solution.

(E)   East African Community (EAC)

The Treaty for the Establishment of the East African Community (EAC) was signed in November 1999 and came into force in July 2000 and since then it has been revised on two occasions, once in 2006 and then again in 2007. The EAC Treaty is not however the sole governing legal document, a Protocol on the Establishment of the East African Community

---

[51] At the time of writing, the draft annexes to the agreement on unfair trade practices and cooperating mechanisms in competition law and policy had been prepared but were yet to be finalised. The indication available was that they are planned to be tabled before the Council of Ministers in June 2009 for adoption and implementation.

[52] See pp. 204–208 above for an account on EFTA.

[53] The Agreement was entered into in accordance with Art. 31 of the 2002 SACU Agreement, which provides that no SACU member state may enter into a preferential trade arrangement with a third party without the consent of other members. The SACU-EFTA Agreement is available at: www.efta.int/~/media/documents/legal-texts/free-trade-relations/southern-african-customs-union-sacu/sacu-fta-toc.ashx.

[54] The Joint Committee was established under Art. 33 of the SACU-EFTA Agreement. Each party is represented in the Committee and it is jointly chaired by representatives from an EFTA state and a SACU state. Under Art. 34 the Committee takes decisions by consensus and it has the power to set up sub-committees so as to delegate its work.

Customs Union (the 'Protocol') was signed in 2004 and serves to elucidate and build upon the provisions of the Treaty. There are five members within the EAC: Burundi, Kenya, Rwanda, Tanzania and Uganda.

The EAC's foundation in competition law and policy can be found in two different provisions. First, Article 75(1)(i) of the EAC Treaty stipulates that competition is one of the areas in which member states need to develop a joint protocol. Secondly, Article 21 of the Protocol prohibits 'any practice that adversely affects free trade ... which has as its objective or effect, the prevention, restriction or distortion of competition within the Community'. In February 2008, the work undertaken by the EAC to build on these foundations took its final form with the enactment of the EAC Competition Act. Section 37(1) of the Act established the EAC Competition Authority to enforce competition at a regional level; however, the authority is to only 'operate on an *ad hoc* basis' for a five-year initial and transitional period.[55] Amongst other things, Part IX of the Act gives the Committee the competence to investigate and impose sanctions and remedies.

The EAC has consistently been entertaining highly ambitious ideas for creating an almost fully fledged regional competition law regime. In its first meeting in 2001, the EAC's Council of Ministers considered that a competent, strong, independent and autonomous regional authority should be established to implement EAC competition law and policy.[56] To achieve this, the 'modernised' enforcement mechanism within the EU competition law regime has been used as source of consultation, albeit with notable modifications.[57] The belief is that the existence of autonomous and fully functional national competition authorities is thought to be fundamental to the success of the EAC authority as national authorities will enforce the decisions of the EAC authority.[58] This relationship of offering support by national authorities and complementarity does not, however, affect the supremacy[59] which EAC rules are to have over

---

[55] See s. 37(2) of the EAC Competition Act 2008.

[56] Some of the key competition officials of EAC member states have argued that the authority should also be more transparent in its work and follow an impartial approach to resolving conflicts at national level as it is inherently more objective. See, for example, the contribution by Kenya to UNCTAD: *Regional Cooperation on Competition Policy and Law: the East African Community Experience* (UNCTAD, 2006).

[57] See above for the modernisation programme within the EU competition law regime.

[58] Under s. 43 of the Act, EAC member states are obliged to mutually cooperate with and support the Authority in the application of EAC competition rules.

[59] Also in relation to the doctrine of supremacy, the influence of the EU regime – which (as we saw in chapter 4) stands on a pillar of supremacy of EU law – is apparent.

conflicting national provisions. To facilitate this supremacy, the competition laws and policies of member states should be harmonised with those of the EAC. The EAC framework however recognises that competition issues with national dimension should be left to the member states; EAC competition policy should be limited in respect of cross-border restraints and restraints from outside the EAC.[60]

Interestingly, a distinction has been drawn between competition as process and the protection of consumers within the EAC competition framework: EAC competition policy is not directed towards consumers as such but rather towards the protection of competition.

(F)   Southern African Development Community (SADC)

The Southern African Development Community (SADC) was established in 1992 with the signing of a declaration and treaty which transformed it from a loose alliance to an organisation with a recognisable legal character. SADC brings together all of the following countries: Angola, Botswana, Democratic Republic of Congo, Lesotho, Malawi, Mauritius, Mozambique, Namibia, Seychelles, South Africa, Swaziland, Tanzania, Zambia and Zimbabwe. The primary objective of the SADC is to promote economic growth and development, to alleviate poverty, to enhance the standard and quality of life of the people in the region and to support the socially disadvantaged through regional integration. SADC's plan towards progress rests on the aim of having a free trade area established first, followed by a custom union, followed by a common market and finally a monetary union. This agenda has made the need for regional competition policy even more necessary because the interconnectedness of 'competition', 'trade' and 'investment' is considered to translate into a policy nexus that poses considerable obstacles to policymakers. SADC contains no provisions on specific competition law at present however except for Article 25 of the *SADC Protocol on Trade* which states that 'Member States shall implement measures within the Community that prohibit unfair business practices and promote competition'. No procedure has been put in place for implementing Article 25.

One particular issue that has received considerable emphasis in seeking to set up a SADC competition framework has been the issue of cooperation. The SADC Secretariat has stated that it would establish a

---

[60] EAC rules embrace a doctrine of extraterritoriality based on an effects doctrine. For a discussion of the doctrine in the field of competition law see chapter 8.

standing *Competition and Consumer Policy and Law Committee* (CCOPOLC) in order to facilitate the creation of a mechanism for cooperation. The CCOPOLC is intended to have a competition mandate that would enable it to take into account the development needs and existing commitments on competition of member states. Among its specific aims are: fostering cooperation and dialogue among domestic competition authorities to encourage soft convergence;[61] facilitating and coordinating assistance programmes for the development and implementation of competition and consumer law and policy of member states; cooperating with other relevant regional and international institutions and where appropriate seeking convergence in approaches to competition and consumer protection; and assisting in preparing and conducting studies on, among other things, constraints on regional and international competitiveness, the benefits of competition law and policy for consumers, the link between competition policy and investment, and the effect of international cartels on the development of developing countries.

4. Asia (excluding the Middle East)

In the field of competition law and policy, Asia has had a most fascinating experience. At one end of the spectrum, several Asian countries have come to adopt specific competition legislation only recently (though the local economies of some of these countries have been very competitive internationally). At the other end of the spectrum, in some parts of Asia very effective and advanced competition law regimes are in operation, most notably in Japan and South Korea.

At a regional level, a number of Asian initiatives and communities have been established. The following are worth noting.

(A) Association of South East Asian Nations (ASEAN)

The Association of South East Asian Nations (ASEAN) was established in 1967 in Bangkok; since then the Association has grown from its five original member nations to ten: Brunei Darussalam, Cambodia, Indonesia, Laos, Malaysia, Myanmar, Philippines, Singapore, Thailand and Vietnam. ASEAN member states committed to 'effective cooperation' early on in the process, doing so under the 1976 Treaty of Amity

---

[61] See pp. 86–87 above for a discussion of this concept; also pp. 569–578 below.

and Cooperation in Southeast Asia (TAC). This bold and vague declaration has come to be clarified with the particular emphasis placed on 'three pillars': security; sociocultural integration; and economic integration.[62] In practice, the third of these pillars has come to dominate the regional agenda and it is the area in which ASEAN member states have made most progress. This can be seen in light of the proposal to establish the ASEAN Economic Community (AEC), which aims 'to create a stable, prosperous and highly competitive ASEAN economic region in which there is a free flow of goods, services, investment and freer flow of capital, equitable economic development and reduced poverty and socio-economic disparities'; the hope and expectation is for the AEC to become a reality by 2015.[63]

The AEC is founded in the ASEAN Free Trade Area (AFTA). The original 1992 AFTA agreement was signed by the then six members (collectively known as the ASEAN-6): Brunei, Indonesia, Malaysia, the Philippines, Singapore and Thailand. The primary goals of the AFTA seek to increase ASEAN's competitive edge by eliminating ASEAN tariff and non-tariff barriers; and attract more foreign direct investment to ASEAN countries. A Common Effective Preferential Tariff (CEPT) scheme has been chosen to meet these ends. The AFTA is now considered to be virtually established by the ASEAN,[64] but near completion is only amongst the ASEAN-6. The newer member states (Cambodia, Laos, Myanmar and Vietnam) are yet to fully comply with all aspects of the scheme, especially with regard to bringing down tariffs for almost all the relevant goods to the CEPT level.

Although several specific references are made to competition law and policy within the various ASEAN documents and output[65] and steps have been taken towards establishing some form of regional

---

[62] Interestingly, ASEAN seems to be have been perceived in different ways by different people: ranging from a loose political association to an economic community.

[63] See Bali Concord II (2003); originally the date of establishment for the AEC was 2020 but in January 2007 the ASEAN Leaders decided at the 12th ASEAN Summit to speed it up by five years.

[64] See www.aseansec.org/12021.htm.

[65] See, for example, para. 41 of the *ASEAN Economic Community Blueprint 2007* which provides that all member countries 'endeavour to introduce competition policy ... by 2015'. The paragraph also provides for the establishment of 'a network of authorities or agencies responsible for competition policy to serve as a forum for discussing and coordinating competition policies' and encouraging 'capacity building programmes/ activities for ASEAN Member Countries in developing national competition policy'. The Blueprint is available at: www.aseansec.org/21083.pdf.

cooperation – or at least in the short term regional guidelines[66] – dealing with competition law and policy, a proper framework for this purpose has yet to emerge.[67] Several public statements and actions have suggested that competition law is high on the ASEAN's agenda; in practice however very modest progress has been made towards achieving this. This can be seen in light of three *non*-developments: the 1999 Hanoi Plan of Action 'to explore the merits of common competition' which has remained merely a plan; the first conference on competition law and policy was not held until 2003; and the subsequent formation of the Consultative Forum for Competition (ACFC), which intended to be a way for domestic competition authorities or relevant bodies to plan and facilitate specific regional work to enhance competition law and policy, has yet to yield any significant results. Moreover, only five of the ten member nations of ASEAN have enacted competition law. They are: Indonesia, Philippines, Singapore, Thailand and Vietnam.[68] The influence of ASEAN in the adoption (or the potential adoption) of competition law and policy domestically within the remaining five nations appears to be negligible at best in respect of some member states.[69] Perhaps the lack of real influence for ASEAN in this case is caused in part by the lack of concrete provisions within the ASEAN framework pertaining to the

---

[66] The idea here was to develop a 'regional guideline on competition policy based on country experiences and international best practices with a view to creating a fair competition environment'. See para. 41 of the *ASEAN Economic Community Blueprint 2007.*

[67] It is worth noting that to date no official ASEAN authority has been established which could ensure cooperation, or at the least exchange of experience between different domestic competition authorities, not to mention the non-establishing proper norms on competition law and policy which the domestic authorities could follow. Nonetheless, in 2007, an agreement was reached by all ASEAN leaders to establish a network of local competition authorities which could serve as a forum for holding discussions and facilitating coordination on competition law and policy and also developing a regional policy framework. To this end, a group of experts was set up – the ASEAN Experts Group on Competition (AEGC) – which was given the task of studying and make recommendations on competition law policy including enforcement on a regional level. The group has focused on issues such as capacity building within domestic competition authorities, competition advocacy, establishing new competition authorities, and sorting out the priorities of such authorities.

[68] However, it should be noted that in the case of Thailand, the majority of the Competition Act 1999 is considered to be unenforceable due to failure to put in place all proper implementing regulations.

[69] It would be correct to say however that ASEAN's influence has not been totally negligible in the adoption of competition law within all member states. For example, with regard to Singapore ASEAN could be seen to have played a role.

adoption of competition law and policy at the domestic level in the member states. It is not quite clear whether the future will be particularly bright with regard to building a meaningful competition law agenda within ASEAN. Judged on the basis of developments and the progress made so far, realising this goal faces enormous legal, political and also socio-economic constraints. These constraints are likely to be fuelled by the differences existing between different ASEAN countries: other than the fact that only half of these countries have enacted specific competition law, it seems that all of the countries concerned do not share the unified vision of how a regional competition law framework can be developed and what purpose this framework can serve within the overall objective of economic integration of ASEAN.

(B) South Asian Association for Regional Cooperation (SAARC)

The South Asian Association for Regional Cooperation (SAARC) was established in December 1985 by India, Pakistan, Bangladesh, Sri Lanka, Nepal, Maldives and Bhutan; this membership expanded to eight when Afghanistan joined in 2007.

In 2004 the South Asia Free Trade Agreement (SAFTA) was signed and it came into force in 2006. Under Article 3(b) one of the objectives of SAFTA is 'promoting conditions of fair competition in the free trade area, and ensuring equitable benefits to all Contracting States'. Under Article 8, which sets out additional measures, rules for fair competition are mentioned as complementary to SAFTA. It is uncertain how significant the impact of these provisions are in practice however given that the understanding is that only if SAFTA makes good progress and deepens trade cooperation can the countries then consider developing a regional competition policy; in fact it is envisaged that competition law and policy will then be demanded in this case.[70] However, SAFTA took 11 years to be developed as it was originally in 1993 that SAARC countries signed a Preferential Trade Agreement to lower tariffs gradually. This delay – like current SAARC problems in general – are attributed to the standoff between Pakistan and India: the relationship between these two countries is difficult and adds to the existing uncertainty over the future directions of SAARC and SAFTA and their competition law agenda.

---

[70] See *Competition Provisions in Regional Trade Agreements: How to Assure Development Gains* (UNCTAD, 2005).

(C) Asia-Pacific Economic Cooperation (APEC)

The Asia-Pacific Economic Cooperation (APEC) is the largest regional community in existence; though it is wider than an Asian organisation: indeed it is Australasian. It is a forum for 21 members to discuss regional economy, cooperation, trade and investment. It is based on the 'liberalisation and facilitation of trade and investment' and 'technical and economic cooperation'. The members of APEC include: Australia, Brunei, Canada, Chinese Taipei, Hong Kong, Indonesia, Japan, Korea, Malaysia, New Zealand, Philippines, Singapore, Thailand, United States, China, Mexico, Papua New Guinea, Chile, Peru, Russia and Vietnam.

APEC has given particular focus to competition law and policy. It established a Competition Policy and Deregulation Group (CPDG) in 1996 which seeks to enhance the region's competitive environment. The CPDG operates under the guidance of the Committee of Trade and Investment (CIT) to develop an understanding of regional competition laws and to identify areas for technical cooperation among APEC members.[71] These competition-specific efforts were followed in 1999 with the endorsement of the APEC *Principles to Enhance Competition and Regulatory Reform*. These Principles are non-binding in nature, like APEC's other output, and are to be implemented voluntarily. Flexibility is particularly emphasised in the implementation process due to the realisation that a 'top-down, one size fits all' approach is not suitable for the diverse circumstances of the different member states.

The Principles are aimed at competition in a wider sense because they go beyond promoting competition and extend to promoting *regulatory reform*. They do not provide any suggestions as to substantive law however: they illustrate the ideal environment in which competition law and policy should be developed. This includes highlighting the significance of two major things: guaranteeing non-discrimination in the application of competition and regulatory principles – which includes transparency and the accountability of national administrations – and the comprehensiveness of such principles; and fostering confidence by promoting competition advocacy[72] and building expertise in domestic competition authorities and adequately resourcing them.

---

[71] In 2007 it was decided that CPDG would no longer report to CIT but to the Economic Committee.

[72] See pp. 65–70 above for an account on competition advocacy.

Beyond these initiatives and steps, APEC provides assistance to member states through training courses on competition policy and has created a Competition Policy and Law Database which allows member states to share their experiences and provide updates and developments on their competition laws and policy.

(D)   Trans-Pacific Strategic Economic Partnership Agreement

A Trans-Pacific Strategic Economic Partnership Agreement was entered into in 2005 between Singapore, Chile, Brunei and New Zealand. It is worth noting Article 9.4 of this Agreement which provides for a 'notification' obligation on the part of a party to the Agreement to other parties of any enforcement activity undertaken by the former against anticompetitive situations where: it considers that the important interests of another party is liable to be substantially affected; the anticompetitive situation is liable to have direct and substantial effect in the territory of the other party(ies); or the situation takes place principally in the territory of the other party(ies).

5.   The Americas and the Caribbean[73]

(A)   Southern Common Market (MERCOSUR)

The Southern Common Market (MERCOSUR) was founded in 1991 by the Treaty of Asuncion, which was later amended by the Treaty of Ouro Preto in 1994. At the heart of this initiative stands a regional free trade agreement between Argentina, Brazil, Paraguay and Uruguay; Venezuela signed a membership agreement and is currently awaiting ratification by the Brazilian and Paraguayan parliaments before being formally admitted as a 'full' member state. Bolivia, Chile, Colombia, Ecuador and Peru have the status of 'associate' member states.

MERCOSUR seeks to promote free trade and the free movement of people, goods and currency. Within the field of competition law, an attempt has been made to achieve harmonisation between the domestic competition policies of member states. This particular attempt emerged following the Asuncion Treaty and was seen as a necessary step towards regional integration. However little progress was made in practice until

---

[73] Some recent works have dealt exclusively with competition law and policy in certain parts of the Americas; see, for example, E. Fox and D. Sokol, *Competition Law and Policy in Latin America* (Hart Publishing, 2009).

1996,[74] when Argentina, Brazil, Paraguay and Uruguay adopted the *Fortaleza Protocol*[75] within the MERCOSUR framework under which they agreed to form a common institutional framework to address competition. However, despite the Protocol having been formally in force since 2000, it has yet to be actually implemented in practice.[76] The Protocol deals with practices which restrict, limit, falsify or distort competition or access to the market or which constitute an abuse of a dominant position in the relevant goods or services market; the Protocol however applies where such practices affect trade between member states. The Protocol established that each member state would have a competition law that would apply to all sectors of the economy and an autonomous competition authority to enforce the law. In those cases where extraterritorial application of relevant competition law is sought, the Protocol advocates the use of cooperation between the member states. For this purpose, the Protocol created a number of tools for cooperation between domestic competition authorities. It also advocates greater harmonisation between the domestic competition law regimes of MERCOSUR countries in the areas of merger control and anticompetitive conduct and behaviour.

Responsibility for adjudication and enforcement of the Protocol was placed in the hands of the MERCOSUR Trade Commission (TC), which is composed of national representatives, and the Committee for the Defence of Competition (CDC), which is intended to be composed of

---

[74] Some pre-1996 developments however had promising competition relevance. This includes the *Ouro Preto Protocol* signed in 1994 which provided for the resolution of disputes arising in any committee through a dispute settlement mechanism. Until 2004 these disputes were settled by ad hoc arbitration chambers formed to deal with specific matters, whose decisions could then be appealed to the TC. From July 2004 a permanent tribunal was created that could come to resolve competition disputes, but this still could only be used in Argentina and Brazil.

[75] See www.cade.gov.br/internacional/Protocolo_de_Ouro_Preto.pdf

[76] The *Protocol* has not been ratified by all of the member states; neither Argentina nor Uruguay has ratified it. Furthermore, only Brazil and Argentina have a competition law for both merger and conduct analysis and fully dedicated competition authorities. Although full ratification has not occurred, it is worth noting that some form of informal 'network' exists between the domestic competition authorities of member states. One can find examples from practice supporting this. For example in 2007 the Brazilian CADE decided to block the merger between Saint Gobain and Owens Corning because of the likely adverse effect on competition in the relevant markets due to risks of concentrations in these markets (especially the glass manufacturing market) in Brazil. The CADE took the step of informing competition authorities of relevant MERCOSUR member states.

national competition authorities when it is finally set up. These two bodies are not really supranational however; indeed there is no supranational body within the MERCOSUR framework with authority in the field; the agreement merely provides a mechanism for cooperation and the exchange of information between national authorities on transnational issues.[77] The CDC was intended to take charge of intra-regional investigations, which are handled in three stages: proceedings begin before the competition authority of each member state at the request of an 'interested' party which after a preliminary determination considering whether there are MERCOSUR implications decides whether to submit the case to the CDC for a second determination; at the second stage the CDC must decide whether the conduct violates the Protocol and recommend that sanctions and/or other measures be imposed; finally, through a directive, the CDC ruling is submitted to the TC for final adjudication.

There has been lack of sufficient progress within the Protocol however.[78] Therefore, an effort has been made to 'compensate' for this, namely the approval of a *Memorandum of Understanding* in 2003 by the Technical Committee on Competition which was intended to enhance cooperation within the MERCOSUR framework. The Memorandum addresses all of the following issues: notification procedures; exchange of information; and technical assistance. The Memorandum has been implemented within the legal systems of MERCOSUR member states.[79]

(B) The Caribbean Community and Common Market (CARICOM)

The Caribbean Community and Common Market (CARICOM) is a regional organisation of 16 Caribbean nations and dependencies seeking economic integration in the form of a single market across all member

---

[77] See M. C. Andrade, 'Competition Law in Mercosur: Recent Developments' (2003) *Global Competition Review* 1.

[78] In 2004, the TC requested a revision of the Protocol which was intended to finally create the CDC. The revision was also intended to enhance cooperation between domestic competition authorities and provide technical assistance by Argentina and Brazil for Uruguay and Paraguay; see B. Rosenberg and M. Tavares de Araújo, 'Implementation Costs and Burden of International Competition Law and Policy Agreements' in P. Brusick, A. M. Alvarez and L. Cernat (eds.), *Competition Provisions in Regional Trade Agreements: How to Assure Development Gains* (United Nations, 2005).

[79] See F. Jenny and P. Horna, 'Modernization of the European legal system of competition. law enforcement: lessons from other regional groupings' in Brusick, Alvarez and Cernat, note 78 above.

states.[80] The main purpose behind establishing it was to promote economic integration and cooperation among its members. This economic cooperation and integration extends to the creation of a regional common market for many of the CARICOM member states: the CARICOM Single Market and Economy (CSME), the origins of which extend to the Treaty of Chaguaramas 1973, which established the Caribbean Community and Common Market and the Revised Treaty of Chaguaramas (the Revised Treaty) of 2001.

The roots of CARICOM competition law and policy can be said to originate from the original Treaty of Chaguaramas.[81] In the Second Special Consultation among CARICOM heads of state on the CSME in 2000 competition policy and consumer protection were identified as 'support' areas to the main areas of free movement of goods, services and capital, and the right of establishment. Over the past nine years however some impressive progress has come to be made to turn the creation of a regional competition law regime from an idea into a reality. Principally, Chapter VIII of the Revised Treaty provides for the development of *Community* competition policy, which has the objective of ensuring that anticompetitive practices do not prevent the benefits anticipated from the establishment of the CSME. Chapter VIII requires member states to enact specific rules on competition and to establish domestic competition authorities to implement and enforce these rules.

The substantive CARICOM competition rules are quite comprehensive in their scope. They cover, among other things, agreements, decisions and concerted practices that have as their object or effect the prevention, restriction or distortion of competition and abuses of a dominant position in the market; the rules do not cover the field of merger control however. They also provide various legal and economic exemptions. These include situations where there is minimal effect on trade in the CSME; or where the behaviour or conduct has the effect of promoting technical or economic progress provided the restriction in question is indispensible to the attainment of these objectives and competition is not eliminated in a substantial part of the relevant market.[82]

---

[80] CARICOM members include: Antigua and Barbuda, Bahamas, Barbados, Belize, Dominica, Grenada, Guyana, Haiti, Jamaica, Montserrat, St Kitts and Nevis, St Lucia, St Vincent and the Grenadines, Suriname and Trinidad and Tobago.

[81] See, for example, Art. 30 which included competition policy provisions.

[82] Obviously, these are requirements which are modelled on Art. 101(3) TFEU; see p. 161 above for an account on the latter Article.

An institutional structure has been set up for the CARICOM competition law regime. Under Article 171 of the Revised Treaty the Community Competition Commission (CCC) was inaugurated in January 2008 as the regional body designated to have competence in relation to CARICOM competition policy; the CARICOM institutional structure also includes the Caribbean Court of Justice (CCJ), which serves as the final court of appeal for all CSME matters. Among the main functions the CCC is intended to carry out are: applying the competition rules; promoting and protecting competition, coordinating the implementation of CARICOM competition policy; monitoring anticompetitive situations; promoting the establishment of national competition institutions; and harmonising any existing competition laws of different member states.[83] Beyond these intended activities, the CCC will advise the Council for Trade and Economic Development (COTED) – which promotes trade and the economic development of CARICOM – on competition and consumer protection policies.

The CCC however does not enjoy *supranational* 'legal' authority under the Revised Treaty. This has direct impact when it comes to the initiation of an investigation which in practice is an extremely complex exercise, the main features of which may be summarised as follows: following a formal request of the CCC, the relevant domestic authority must undertake a preliminary examination of the matter; if the outcome of this preliminary assessment suggests that further investigation is justified the domestic authority shall consult with the CCC to determine who should have jurisdiction to fully investigate. In the case of disagreement as to who should conduct the investigation the CCC must cease any further examination of the matter and refer it to COTED for a decision. It is for the domestic authority to ensure that the determinations of the CCC are enforceable in its jurisdiction.

Obviously the deliberate decision not to accord to the CCC supranational status in a liberal sense is manifested in the reluctance of member states to surrender their sovereignty.[84] It is arguable that such a decision or reluctance is controversial because this attitude essentially constrains the CCC in its operation and subjects it to the decision-making powers of COTED, which is a political institution. Member states therefore are able to determine the CCC's mandate and actual work in practice.[85] This

---

[83] See Arts 173–74.   [84] See pp. 89–92 above for the doctrine of sovereignty.
[85] See A. Smith-Hillman, 'First a Glimmer, now a ...? The Prospect of a Caribbean Competition Policy' (2006) *Journal of World Trade* 405.

includes preventing the CCC from conducting an investigation into a situation even though the CCC may perceive it to be anticompetitive.

The operation of the CARICOM rules in practice is subjected to a tight time-schedule. Under the Revised Treaty, all legislation, agreements and administrative practices inconsistent with the rules of competition had to be notified to the COTED within 24 months. Within 36 months the member states had to establish a programme providing for the termination of proscribed legislation, agreements and administrative practices. It is questionable whether such a tight schedule is workable given that authorities have been established in only two CARICOM member states, namely Jamaica and Barbados. Interestingly, the lack of competition authority in all CARICOM countries has not been considered to be a problem within the framework of CARICOM given that CARICOM institutions and competition rules are able to function in place of the local authorities and rules of those CARICOM countries without competition law regimes. In this respect, a 'dual' function is envisaged for CARICOM institutions and rules. Obviously having such function has been thought to be necessary for the purposes of dealing with all types of anticompetitive situations, whether ones purely domestic in character or ones with a cross-border element. However, the real value of this in practice is highly questionable because of the lack of appropriate funding for the CCC to conduct its activities and its failure to match expectations.

Finally, it is worth noting that a dispute settlement mechanism in competition cases was created under the Revised Treaty. The scope of this mechanism however remains the subject of speculations: specifically it is not clear who can initiate actions under the mechanism. The question is relevant given that the Revised Treaty provides for the use of the mechanism in disputes between member countries. In practice, it may be possible for both individuals and member states to launch competition actions, which the CCC can investigate. In taking action, the CCC may seek an order from the CCJ to enforce the desired remedy, though it may be possible for the firm concerned to appeal such order.[86]

(C)   The Organisation of Eastern Caribbean States

The Organisation of Eastern Caribbean States (OECS) was formed in 1981 with the signing of the Treaty of Basseterre. It aims to promote

---

[86] S. A. McDonald, 'The Caribbean Court of Justice: Enhancing the Law of International Organizations' (2004) *Fordham International Law Journal* 930.

cooperation among its members by helping them maximise the benefits 'from their collective space' and to promote economic integration in the global economy. A dominant thought behind creating the OECS was to strengthen the position of its member states – who are relatively small countries – through the process of globalisation and liberalisation; many of these member states are also members of CARICOM.

Despite the OECS member states being small economies however, competition law and policy have been pushed to the fore. A number of proposals have emerged in recent years seeking to develop some form of regional competition law framework. The most recent and important proposal has been to establish a sub-regional competition commission to act as a *domestic* competition authority for its members. Interestingly, this has some implications for the CARICOM competition law regime and the latter's Community Competition Commission which will be reflected upon below.

(D)   The North American Free Trade Agreement (NAFTA)

The North America Free Trade Agreement (NAFTA) is a trade bloc in North America created by the USA (during the Clinton Administration), Canada and Mexico. The Agreement has two supplements: the North American Agreement on Environmental Cooperation and the North American Agreement on Labour Cooperation; both came into effect in 1994.

NAFTA's competition provisions feature in Chapter 15 of NAFTA entitled *Competition Policy, Monopolies and State Enterprises*. It provides that each party shall adopt or maintain measures to proscribe and take appropriate enforcement action against 'anticompetitive activities'; this includes cooperation in enforcement. Only the obligations relating to the notification of, and non-discrimination with regard to, state enterprises and monopolies, are subject to dispute settlement. A *Working Group* of competition and trade officials from the three countries is also provided for. The Agreement contains no further rules – whether general or specific – dealing with competition. The three members however have domestic competition law regimes in place and bilateral cooperation agreements have been entered into.[87]

---

[87] See chapter below on bilateral cooperation.

(E)   Central America–Dominican Republic–United States Free Trade Agreement (CAFTA-DR)

The Central America–Dominican Republic–United States Free Trade Agreement (CAFTA-DR) was signed in 2004 by the USA, Costa Rica, Dominican Republic, El Salvador, Honduras, Guatemala and Nicaragua and it has, as of 2007, been ratified by all of these countries. The aim of this Agreement is – as can be gleaned from its name – the creation of a free trade area covering these seven nations.

There is no specific competition chapter in the CAFTA-DR, but Chapter 13.4.2 on telecommunications states that each party 'shall maintain appropriate measures for the purpose of preventing suppliers, who, individually or collectively, are a major supplier in its territory from engaging in or continuing anticompetitive practices'. Chapter 13 however is neither relevant nor applicable to all the parties: Costa Rica, for example, was exempted from the commitments under the chapter because it has its own set of commitments reflecting its social aims in the telecommunications sector.

(F)   Latin American Free Trade Agreement

The Latin Free Trade Association (LAFTA) was created in 1960 by the Treaty of Montevideo; it was reorganised into the Latin American Integration Association (LAIA) in 1980 which nowadays includes among its member states: Argentina, Bolivia, Brazil, Chile, Colombia, Cuba, Ecuador, Mexico, Paraguay, Peru, Uruguay and Venezuela. The change of name was accompanied by a change of agenda, which became more realistic.

The main hope behind creating LAFTA was to create a common market in Latin America. The LAFTA Agreement did not provide for a coordination of policies, and when compared to other associations or communities seeking to establish a common market – such as the EU – it appears extremely limited in terms of its scope and *modus operandi*. When it was inaugurated, LAFTA was intended gradually to eliminate most barriers to intra-regional trade over a 12-year period. However, this eventually turned out to be an over-ambitious target, particularly because of the reluctance of major countries like Brazil and Argentina to liberalise trade quickly due to their high degree macro-economic instability.

With regard to the field of competition law, the change of name and agenda had no effect: there was still no mention of competition law and policy. In 1990, following a recommendation by a consultative organisation (the Group of Rio) that deemed the LAIA ineffective, the LAIA Council of Ministers approved guidelines on a stronger role for the Association though this did not include any consideration of competition law and policy. Obviously such past developments do not particularly signal a positive future for LAIA in the field of competition law or any possible role for LAIA to play in achieving regional integration more generally.

(G)   The Andean Community

The Andean Community was created in 1969 by the Cartagena Agreement. It was largely formed because of dissatisfaction with the Latin Free Trade Association (LAFTA), which was considered to have delivered more benefits to the largest member states, namely Brazil, Mexico and Argentina than the smaller member states. The Community is made of Bolivia, Columbia, Ecuador and Peru; Chile quit in 1973 and Venezuela withdrew in 2006.

One of the first *real* achievements of the Andean Community in building a regional community was the elimination of tariffs which happened in 1993 with the creation of a free trade area. A reversal of this pro-regionalism approach occurred in 1997 when reforms were introduced to the Cartagena Agreement. As a result of these reforms, 'leadership' was placed in the hands of the Presidents of member states and the Andean Councils of Presidents and Foreign Ministers became part of the Community's institutional structure. Arguably, such reforms have opened the gates even wider for heavy political influence to be exerted over the developments of the Community.

A competition law framework has been established within the Andean Community which is based on the *Andean Community Commission Decision 608*,[88] and which has been modelled on the basis of EU competition law regime.[89] This Decision regulates free competition in the

---

[88] *Decision 608* replaced in 2005 an earlier decision, *Decision 285* of 1991. *Decision 285* was a first attempt to establish common rules within the Andean Community to deal with anticompetitive situations. It was replaced because the latter was considered to suffer from weaknesses: among others, the standard used in Decision 285 was more of anti-dumping than competition standard which meant that the focus was on harm to competitors rather than harm to competition when determining whether a situation was anticompetitive.

[89] See J. Tavares de Araujo and L. Tineo, 'Competition Policy and Regional Trade Agreements' in M. Rodriguez Mendoza, P. Low and B. Kotschwar (eds), *Trade Rules in the Making: Challenges in Regional and Multilateral Negotiations* (Brookings Institute, 1999).

Community. It prohibits and sanctions practices restraining free competition[90] which affect the Community and which are exercised within the territory of one or more member state or a country *outside* the Andean Community through the effects doctrine; thus jurisdictions may be exercised extraterritorially.[91] Practices that originate or affect a single member state are dealt with under national competition laws. Underpinning Decision 608 are the principles of non-discrimination, transparency and due process.[92]

The investigative arm of the Andean Community is controlled by its General Secretariat, which has the power to start an investigation on its own initiative or at the request of a domestic authority, consumer organisations, natural or legal persons under public or private law, or other entities provided there is evidence that the behaviour could restrain competition. The first phase of an investigation is carried out jointly with the relevant domestic authorities of the member states. Hearings may be held, agreements executed and precautionary measures made. On conclusion of an investigation, the General Secretariat prepares a report made available to the parties, so as to hear their arguments, and to the *Committee on the Protection of Free Competition* (the adjudicative arm), which is made up of one high level representative from each member state, so as to receive their recommendations. When making the final decision, the General Secretariat delivers an opinion regarding the recommendation that has been made. The judicial arm of the community is the Andean Community Tribunal of Justice.

Corrective measures, such as undertakings, and sanctions can be imposed but the relevant governments of member states are responsible for their execution. This means that there is no need for involvement by domestic competition authorities and in practice member states nominate the responsible authority. Indeed some of the member states lack competition law regimes and such authorities. This includes Bolivia and Ecuador.[93] Nonetheless, Decision 608 does apply to these countries in the same way as both have competent bodies – part of the national government – to execute relevant corrective measures or sanctions.

---

[90] Practices restraining free competition include abuses of a dominant position or agreements which have the intent or effect of substantially restricting, affecting or distorting 'market supply and demand conditions'.

[91] The following chapter deals with the doctrine of extraterritoriality.

[92] See Art. 3 of the Decision.

[93] Ecuador has identified the Ministry of Trade, Industrialisation, Fish and Competitiveness as the relevant authority and Bolivia has identified the Vice Ministry of Trade and Exports.

One may wonder however about the prospects of such an approach to achieve successful implementation. In practice the implementation of Decision 608 has faced various problems, including the inability of designated domestic authorities of member states to implement the decisions of the Secretariat and to introduce necessary changes so as to comply with Decision 608.

In substantive terms, Decision 608 covers the areas of anticompetitive behaviour[94] and abuse of dominance quite comprehensively. For example, in relation to the former, the scope of the rules extend to bid-rigging which is quite unusual within regional settings whilst in relation to the latter the rules extend to a variety of situations, including predatory pricing.[95] Nonetheless, the Decision does not cover the area of merger control, which is left within the exclusive jurisdiction of individual member countries.

(H)   Ibero-American Forum on the Protection of Competition

The Ibero-American Forum on the Protection of Competition was created in 2002 in Madrid by Argentina, Brazil, Chile, Spain, Peru and Portugal. The main objective of the Forum was to establish itself as a centre of debate and reflection on competition issues but a working group made up of representatives from the Spanish, Portuguese, Panamanian and Brazilian competition authorities was established at the Forum's third meeting to study and analyse its projects involving cooperation and technical exchange. Notable work has also been achieved with the Ibero-American School for the Protection of Competition, which is financed by Spain's Tribunal for Competition Defence. This School provides training to officials in public administration within the participating countries.

6.   The Commonwealth of Independent States

The Commonwealth of Independent States (CIS) brings together all of the following countries: Azerbaijan, Armenia, Belarus, Georgia,

---

[94] It is important to note however that exemptions and exclusions from the prohibition on anticompetitive behaviour are left within the competence of individual member countries who are entitled to grant these.

[95] The abuse of dominance provisions within the Decision also cover situations of creation of barriers to entry.

Kazakhstan, Kyrgyzstan, Moldova, Russia, Tajikistan, Turkmenistan, Ukraine and Uzbekistan. Cooperation within the CIS framework rests on bilateral and multilateral cooperation between the countries concerned. Of particular relevance is the *Interstate Agreement on the Implementation of the Coordinated Antimonopoly Policy* which was concluded in December 1993 in Turkmenistan.[96] The Agreement contains the main principles of coordination and cooperation among CIS countries. Its primary objective is to create a legal basis for the prevention, limitation and elimination of monopolistic activities and unfair competition among firms operating in the common CIS economic area. The Agreement also provides for close cooperation among the domestic competition authorities of CIS countries, in particular through: coordination of joint efforts and activities; harmonisation of national competition laws to the extent necessary for the purposes of implementing the Agreement; creating favourable conditions for the development of competition, effective functioning of the goods markets and consumer rights protection; and elaboration of common procedures for the investigation and evaluation of anticompetitive situations.

An Interstate Council for Antimonopoly Policy[97] has been established within the CIS. Meetings of the Council occur at least twice a year. The Council functions on a project-oriented basis. The main focus of the Council in its work is placed on the need to coordinate – in a wide sense – the activities of CIS countries in the field of competition law (including achieving harmonisation between the rules within the CIS framework) and to promote the creation of conditions for the development of fair competition.

In 2007 CIS countries agreed to establish procedures for exchanging information between their domestic competition authorities and jointly investigated the air transportation market in the CIS.[98]

---

[96] A new edition of the Agreement was signed on 25 January 2000.

[97] At present the representatives of the following 11 CIS member states are the members of the Interstate Council on Antimonopoly Policy (ICAP): Republic of Azerbaijan, Republic of Armenia, Republic of Belarus, Georgia, Republic of Kazakhstan, Kyrgyz Republic, Republic of Moldova, the Russian Federation, Republic of Tadzhikistan, Republic of Uzbekistan and Ukraine.

[98] Domestic competition authorities started joint research of the market of passenger air carriage, including international flights between the CIS countries. The findings will be included in the *Final Report on Analysis of Air Carriage Market in the CIS States*, which will also contain recommendations on improving competitive environment on the air transportation market. The Final Report was put before the CIS Economic Council in 2008 but does not yet seem to have been published.

7.   Comments

A number of comments are worth making about the different competition law efforts which have been made around the world within different regional organisations and communities.

(A)   The high number of initiatives

Perhaps the most obvious comment relates to the relatively high number of initiatives seeking to develop a regional approach to competition law and policy; as we saw, these initiatives – like the communities within which they were launched – are at different stages of development. The fact that so many regional communities around the world have devoted particular attention to competition law and policy is highly interesting, not least because several of their individual *member states* actually lack competition law and most lack *effective* competition law regimes and sufficient expertise in the field of competition law domestically.[99] Obviously, one explanation for pushing for regional cooperation notwithstanding this is that there may be an interest to develop a top-down approach. Thus, through a strong and advanced regional competition law framework, the relevant countries could strengthen their own domestic regimes; doing so in a way that would ensure harmonised standards in those regimes. It is questionable whether this is a sound approach however, given that achieving such a desired outcome would – at any rate – be undermined by the fact that competition law is simply lacking in some of the countries concerned; the future looks very uncertain with respect to how much attention is likely to be given to the field of competition law in different African, Middle Eastern, Asian and American countries (especially within government circles) and whether national governments would favour a strong competition law framework and enforcement at a regional level given that this is likely to impact both on the way in which their national firms operate and the possibilities of attracting foreign direct investment by foreign firms, which may not necessarily favour effective competition enforcement;[100] not to mention the great uncertainty over the real intentions of different countries to limit their sovereignty in favour of autonomous regional authorities over

---

[99] See *Competition Regimes in the World: A Civil Society Report* (CUTS International, 2006).

[100] See Brusick, Alvarez and Cernat, note 79 above.

which they may have little control. Furthermore, it is questionable whether this approach would actually help achieve the intended result of support being offered by an established regional competition law regime to domestic competition law regimes and securing complementarities between the two.

(B) Harmonisation

A second comment worth making concerns the express desire of many of the communities discussed to achieve harmonisation between the domestic competition rules of the countries concerned. Equally worth noting however is that even with a comprehensive regional approach to harmonisation, success can never be guaranteed when major discrepancies exist in the legal, political and economic regimes and circumstances among the different countries concerned. Looking at all of the countries which are members of regional communities or organisations, it is obvious that significant differences exist between them and this is bound to make any harmonisation initiative difficult, if not virtually impossible, to undertake. Moreover, the countries within one and the same community may be at different stages of economic development and enjoy varying degrees of economic and trade strengths. Any attempt to achieve harmonisation – regardless of the mechanism used in this case – is likely to result in one or a small group of countries 'dominating' the process and this is likely to trigger objection on the part of weaker countries.

(C) Competition advocacy

What seems to be lacking within the different regional initiatives discussed in this chapter is a proper competition advocacy mechanism which could be used to enhance awareness on the part of individual countries in the field of competition law and perhaps help the countries concerned build a competition culture domestically and proper competition law agendas, which suit their own circumstances and which could help them develop the field in harmony with developments in the wider economic, social and political arena.

(D) Division in competence

The different regional communities seem to lack the necessary tools to deal with all situations concerning the exercise of jurisdiction and the likely problems following the exercise of jurisdiction by the relevant regional authorities,[101] most notably: the division in competence between the 'community' level and 'national' level; the exact role to be fulfilled by regional authorities especially in the arena of enforcement (for example, whether they will have the ability and if they do how to access and gather information in actual cases from firms operating in the different countries); and the necessary safeguards needed to be in place to deal with a possible expansion of the workload of regional authorities to an extent that they are no longer able to handle such workload (for example, whether in this case national competition authorities may become involved).

(E)   Overlap in membership

An ambiguity is created by the fact that some countries are parties to more than one regional community: the situation is open to too much speculation over whether an individual country in this case will give priority to the competition law framework of one community over another. It is probably safe to assume that the existence of overlap in membership is something that actually undermines the real prospects for creating a proper competition law regime at regional level and is very likely to lead to failure in turning the declared objectives of the relevant community into a reality. The likelihood of failure is enlarged considerably due to the overambitious goals set by some of the communities for themselves.

There is a particular need to clarify the relationship and define the interplay between many of the communities in the same region. For example, looking at the Americas, as we saw the Competition Commission of CARICOM has jurisdiction in cases with cross-border effects.[102] However, the interplay between it and the proposed OECS Competition Commission (OCC) needs to be assessed.[103] If OECS acted as a national authority, it is unclear whether OECS members would still be required to establish their own domestic authorities as required by the CARICOM Treaty. Although the justification behind the OECS may be understandable, the formation of an OCC does not look like it will advance the state of cooperation in the field of competition law in the

---

[101] See *The Attribution of Competence to Community and National Competition Authorities in the Application of Competition Rules* (UNCTAD, 2008).
[102] See pp. 399–402 above.   [103] See pp. 402–403 above for a discussion on the OECS.

CARICOM region as whole. The OECS is more likely to add further bureaucracy than help address competition law matters more effectively and expediently. It is also unclear how OECS member states would detect anticompetitive situations in domestic markets without having a domestic competition authority. Moreover, the overlap in membership has one serious implication concerning funding. Most if not all of the regional communities established around the world lack sufficient resources. This means that in practice countries which are members of more than one organisation will naturally be forced to prioritise with regard to which community their (limited) funds should go. There is considerable ambiguity surrounding the choice made by the country(ies) concerned and what factors or considerations are likely to guide or influence them in making their decision.

(F)   Copying the EU experience

Looking at the different regional communities established around the world, it is clear that there has been too much borrowing from the EU experience and at the same time extremely little – if any – consultation on the experience of other regions in the field of competition law. Interestingly, some of the communities have set themselves extremely overambitious goals to achieve in ten years what took the EU 50 years to achieve (and probably it is correct to say what the EU continues to achieve after 53 years of its existence). No doubt it is good for the different regional communities to be inspired by EU experience. However what is important to note is that it has neither been suitable nor useful to copy the EU in some cases when the circumstances and history are so different. As we saw in chapter 4, the experience in the field of competition law in the EU has been 'European'. Interestingly, when studying the experience with those regional communities which have opted to copy the EU experience one sees a paradox: on the one hand by following the EU model these communities have opted for a far-reaching form of regionalism whilst on the other the countries within these communities have been very reluctant to surrender sovereignty and to transfer competence to the regional level (as has been the case with the EU).[104]

---

[104] Although one must acknowledge that in the case of the EU, some of the founding member states reluctantly accepted the limitation of sovereignty and many of them questioned and continue to question the whole legitimacy of limitation on their sovereignty.

(G)   Lack of clear direction

Most of the regional efforts launched in the field of competition law have in essence been attempts to identify directions in which regional cooperation could be pushed. Much of what has been achieved could be considered to have been largely *exploratory* in nature and shows a degree of uncertainty in relation to what can be realistically expected. This can be seen in light of how considerable hopes were attached to a number of regional initiatives when these were first introduced though in practice little progress has been made and in the case of some initiatives resources have been wasted on never-ending discussions on revising these initiatives.

In many respects, it is difficult to imagine how regional cooperation can be advanced in certain parts of the world. Thus far, in most cases a large part of the discussion on regional cooperation has been merely academic. Considerable efforts need to be made in these cases in order to promote the regional cooperation agenda. In particular, 'implementation' at the domestic level of the regional rules or principles in many cases is extremely crucial for this purpose and this necessitates instituting domestic competition law regimes in the countries concerned.[105] Until now this has not happened and in some cases the regional cooperation agreement appears to be largely ineffective. Moreover, it is important to note that bureaucracy is a major constraint facing all regional organisations and this is likely to make the task of setting a clear future direction for the regional cooperation and achieving effective implementation much harder.[106]

The problems noted above actually mushroom when taking into account the point that many of the communities are difficult to classify in terms of where the emphasis is actually placed: whether on economic goals or political goals. As a result, these communities have been quite fragmented, especially when it comes to the economic arena. Regardless of whether the relevant community rests on political and/or economic foundations, it is important to realise that regional cooperation in the field of competition law cannot be seen through purely competition law lenses; in particular it cannot be seen as detached from wider

---

[105] For example, in relation to the MERCOSUR Protocol, implementation here would require the introduction of competition law regimes and the setting up of domestic competition authorities in Uruguay and Paraguay, two of the member states.

[106] Establishing a proper institutional structure at domestic level with sufficient financial resources and expertise is important to ensure successful implementation.

political and economic issues. This means that such cooperation is not as straightforward as might be first thought, nor does it stand in isolation. In almost all cases it depends on the wider political and economic circumstances prevailing in the region and the individual countries concerned.

(H)   Capacity constraints

Many of the regional communities suffer from capacity constraints. The country members of these communities are generally small economies which lack the necessary resources to be able to establish effective domestic competition law regimes, let alone devote resources to a regional competition law regime; the latter having the potential to be extremely high. Many of these countries suffer from serious economic, social and political problems which means that allocating resources for competition law – whether at a domestic or regional level – may not be deemed to be a national priority for some of the countries.[107]

(I)   Sub-regional cooperation

In some regions around the world, countries have opted for building 'sub-regional' cooperation, which represents a longer route for establishing a regional framework in the field of competition law rather than going for a comprehensive regional cooperation. A particularly notable example of sub-regional cooperation can be found in the Middle East,[108] in the case of the Gulf Cooperation Council and the Agreement for the Establishment of a Free Trade Zone between the Arabic Mediterranean Nations (Agadir). It is doubtful however to what extent this type of cooperation will be beneficial in the field of competition law especially given that not all of the countries in the relevant region would be part of the relevant sub-regional cooperation agreement. Furthermore, not all of the countries party to the sub-regional cooperation have domestic competition law regimes in existence. As a result, a sub-regionalism option is likely to be regarded as objectionable. Indeed, in some parts of the world, countries have been highly reluctant to subscribe to the idea of sub-regionalism in the field of competition law (especially the idea of creating

---

[107] See T. Stewart, 'Is Flexibility Needed When Designing Competition Law For Small Open Economies? A View From the Caribbean' (2004) *Journal of World Trade* 725.
[108] See pp. 370–380 above.

a sub-regional competition authority).[109] Sub-regionalism may also be considered to be problematic if the overall objective of the countries concerned is to achieve harmonisation in the competition law regimes of 'all' the countries in the region.

(J) Bilateral cooperation

In relation to the regions considered in this chapter there is a noticeable absence from the competition law scene of specific (intra-region) bilateral cooperation agreements. This is interesting given the strong ties enjoyed between many of the countries in these regions. One explanation for this absence may be that competition law came to be introduced only recently in the different countries and therefore competition enforcement has not matured to such an extent as to make the conclusion of such agreements possible. However, there is quite strong 'cross-border' or inter-regional trade within the relevant regions and there are international firms operating in the different countries of the individual regions. The likelihood of anticompetitive behaviour or abusive conduct or merger transactions with a cross-border element is therefore a realistic prospect.

Nonetheless, bilateral free trade agreements have been concluded between different countries within one and the same region. Some of these agreements contain competition relevance. However these agreements are not the most suitable medium for bilateral cooperation in the field of competition law to be established. The lack of formal or specific competition bilateral cooperation agreements between the different countries does not mean, however, that cooperation is virtually non-existent in the field: as will be seen in chapter 9, different forms of bilateral cooperation can be found, such as those involving joint meetings between competition officials and training seminars and workshops which may occur on an informal basis.

(K) Why regional cooperation has not worked?

The experience with the different initiatives launched at regional level around the world shows that building regional cooperation in the field of competition law is considered – especially by those pushing for this

---

[109] See, for example, the views expressed by some MERCOSUR countries; see *Competition Law and Policy in Brazil: A Peer Review* (OECD, 2005).

cooperation – to have several key benefits including: addressing market access problems;[110] adequately addressing competition problems with cross-border dimension; facilitating the provision of technical assistance between the different (participating) competition authorities and enhancing capacity building; harmonisation in national rules and standards which is desirable especially from the perspective of businesses who are interested in reducing their costs, having greater legal certainty and operating in similar regulatory environments;[111] and creating economically enhancing tools enabling firms to improve their operations and to achieve diversification in products and enhancing consumer interests.

On the whole, however, it is indisputable that regional cooperation in the field of competition law on the whole simply has not worked. This is perhaps an obvious conclusion though one that raises a number of questions. The most basic yet fundamental question revolving around regional cooperation is whether such cooperation is really necessary especially in regions where competition law in individual countries is not advanced or has not been introduced at all. Notwithstanding the importance attached to regional cooperation as noted in the previous paragraph, it is possible to question the benefits this cooperation has actually brought to the relevant countries, the relevant region as a whole and to the internationalisation of competition law more generally.

At present, the chances for comprehensive regional cooperation in the field of competition law in the different parts of the world covered in this chapter appear to be extremely slim. It does not seem realistic for any effort to attempt to opt for a fully fledged regional competition law framework without at least undertaking some preliminary steps. At a basic level, there are serious political obstacles and as a first step these need to be removed. Looking at those regional communities within which specific focus has been given to competition law, it is very noticeable that an extremely demanding timeframe has been 'self-imposed' on the countries concerned, especially in relation to implementation. This however has triggered a negative reaction on the part of countries and appears to have reduced their willingness to commit to a comprehensive regional agenda in the field of competition law and seems to have, in many cases, created a situation of 'postponing' compliance by the countries concerned with the various obligations or commitments under the

---

[110] See chapter 11 below which deals with the issue of market access.
[111] See pp. 106–110 above for a discussion on the interests and concerns of firms.

relevant regional framework.[112] Moreover, building a regional agenda in the field of competition law does depend on the success achieved by the countries concerned in the wider arena of economic integration and, because of the highly complex nature of the latter, political disagreements are very likely to emerge which, in turn, are likely to easily spill over into the field of competition law. In some cases, there is even heated rivalry between the relevant countries in terms of attracting foreign direct investment and tourism which makes regional cooperation harder to achieve. However, even if the enormous political hurdles to having a fully fledged regional competition law regime are to be ignored or removed, 'functional' constraints present serious problems because of the huge differences which exist between the countries concerned in terms of their experience in the field of competition law, including differences in institutional structures and enforcement approaches and tools used by the relevant competition authorities. It is therefore probably premature to embrace this option given that the focus in the first place should be to reach a stage where competition law is incorporated domestically in the countries concerned. A comprehensive form of regional cooperation would have little relevance in practice if only some of the countries concerned have domestic competition laws or effective competition law regimes while in others competition law and policy are remarkably absent or the competition law regimes in existence are weak. In this respect, it is probably best that competition law and policy in different regions around the world be developed from the bottom up by each country devising its own competition law regime and making some progress in the field of competition law. Progressing in this way is more conducive to creating a competition culture in the relevant region because it is more likely to be accepted by consumers and industry and is more promising when seeking to achieve meaningful regional cooperation between all the countries concerned.

---

[112] See A. F. Zago de Azevedo, 'Mercosur: Ambitious Policies, Poor Practices' (2004) *Revista de Economía Política* 4.

Chapter 8

The unilateral option: extraterritorial assertion of jurisdiction

In this and the following two chapters of the book, the 'options' of internationalisation[1] of competition law will be explored. The chapter will focus on the doctrine of extraterritoriality. It will provide a full and comprehensive account of the doctrine including an examination of the legal basis of the doctrine, the issue of sovereignty and the various case law developments that have occurred in different regimes, most notably the EU and USA.

When discussing competition law in an international context, the doctrine of extraterritoriality merits special treatment, not least because of the difficult issues it has triggered over the years and the difficult questions its application often gives rise to in real cases in practice. Reference has already been made more than once during the course of the discussion in this book as to the fact that enforcement by several competition authorities around the world has become 'extraterritorial' over the years. In light of this, it should not be difficult to see that an examination of such an activity is of crucial importance in the context of the present book.

The chapter is structured as follows. The first part considers the question of jurisdiction under public international law. The second part evaluates some fundamental issues underlying extraterritoriality. It advocates the view that the difficulties with extraterritoriality reside not only in the conflicts it has caused between countries, but also in the search for a compelling definition of it. The third part gives an account of developments in the EU and US competition law regimes in the area. The fourth part deals with the responses of countries which have been generated by reliance on extraterritoriality by other countries. The fifth part provides some reflections on extraterritoriality. It examines, among other things, the role of the judiciary in asserting extraterritorial

---

[1] See chapter 2.

418

jurisdiction in competition policy. The sixth part examines and offers some proposals on how to avoid or minimise conflicts triggered by extraterritoriality. Finally, the seventh part concludes.

1. Sovereignty and the principle of territoriality under public international law

In an examination of the doctrine of extraterritoriality under competition law it would be very helpful to begin with a look at the concept and doctrine of state sovereignty, something that has in fact already been done in this book.[2] In considering the latter doctrine one would gain a better understanding of a crucial principle of public international law, namely the territoriality principle the existence of which – although being a principle that would appear to negate and deprive the doctrine of extraterritoriality of any legitimacy – has actually facilitated the creation of the doctrine.

(A) The traditional approach

As we saw in chapter 2, a fundamental attribute of sovereignty resides in the fact that an individual country is competent to enact laws that are binding upon persons as well as regulating situations within its national boundaries.[3] The ability of a country to act in this way rests primarily on two grounds of assertion of jurisdiction. The first is *subject-matter jurisdiction*, also known as legislative or prescriptive jurisdiction. According to this type of jurisdiction, a country has competence to enact laws (which include all rules made through legislative, executive and judicial branches) concerning situations coming within its jurisdiction under public international law. The second is *enforcement jurisdiction*. This type of jurisdiction covers a country's ability to enforce its laws: that is the power of a country to give *effect* to a general rule or a decision by means of substantive implementing measures which may include even the use of force by the relevant authorities for the purposes of ensuring compliance with the rule or decision.

---

[2] See pp. 89–92 above.
[3] See Opinion of Advocate General Darmon in Case 114/85, *A. Ahlström Osukeyhtiö v. Commission* (*Woodpulp*) [1988] ECR 5139; [1988] 4 CMLR 901 at 923. This case is discussed below in the context of the EU competition law perspective on extraterritoriality.

The fundamental attribute of sovereignty arises from the principle of territoriality.[4] On the basis of this principle, a country is able to enact and enforce laws within its national borders. This was considered to give countries a *positive* right to assert jurisdiction and this is how 'positivists' in the field of public international law came to view the principle and its operations. An alternative way however was also developed in which the principle may be viewed as a *negative* right: the aim of the principle was said to limit the exercise of jurisdiction by countries to their domestic territories, thus holding that they were *not* entitled to assert jurisdiction beyond their national boundaries. Whether the territoriality principle was to (and should) be viewed as a positive or negative right, it was abundantly clear that if a country seeks to assert jurisdiction over acts committed beyond its borders it might infringe the sovereignty of other countries, and as a result would risk having its action amount to a violation of public international law.

Interpreting the principle of territoriality in this way was a 'traditional' approach to the issue of exercise of jurisdiction. However, at some point, what began to be clear was that the principle came to sit uncomfortably with the way in which public international law itself evolved and developed: in particular it came to be seen that placing a limitation on exercise of jurisdiction by countries in this manner itself was an 'infringement' of the sovereignty of those countries especially in light of the harm their interests may suffer due to conduct or behaviour occurring outside their boundaries. As a result, it became apparent that exceptions to the principle were inevitable and in fact necessary; it seems that this type of reasoning was influential in the development of a number of exceptions to the principle which came to be recognised under public international law. Introducing these exceptions meant that the competence of countries was considered to be possible to extend to certain situations

---

[4] See P.M. Brown, 'The Codification of International law' (1935) *American Journal of International Law* 25; I. Brownlie, *Principles of Public International Law* (Oxford University Press, 1998); R. Jennings and A. Watts (eds.), *Oppenheim's International Law* (Longman, 1996), vol. I, pp. 456–88; F.A. Mann, 'The Doctrine of Jurisdiction in International Law' (1964) 111 *Recueil des Cours* 9; M. Akehurst, 'Jurisdiction in International Law' (1972–3) *British Yearbook of International Law* 145; D.E. Rosenthal and W.M. Knighton, *National Laws and International Commerce: the Problem of Extraterritoriality* (Routledge, 1982); A.V. Lowe, *Extraterritorial Jurisdiction: an Annotated Collection of Legal Materials* (Grotius, 1983); C.J. Olmstead, *Extraterritorial Application of the Laws and Responses Thereto* (Oxford University Press, 1984); B.E. Hawk, *United States, Common Market and International Antitrust* (Prentice-Hall Law and Business, 1993).

beyond their national boundaries: that in certain cases countries were 'entitled' to assert jurisdiction 'extraterritorially'.

The four exceptions which came to be developed are as follows.

I. The nationality principle

The nationality principle allows a country to assert jurisdiction over its nationals regardless of their geographic location. Thus, even if they were to be abroad a country can still exercise jurisdiction in this case. Indeed a number of cases have arisen over the years which came to establish that under customary international law, a country is able to enforce its laws against its nationals, even when these laws have some effects beyond national borders.[5]

II. The protective principle

Under the protective principle of jurisdiction a country is entitled to regulate offences occurring beyond its national boundaries which target its national security, such as its political independence or territorial integrity.

III. The passive personality principle

According to the passive personality principle, an exercise of jurisdiction by countries should cover situations in which an act is committed beyond their national boundaries that harm their nationals abroad.

IV. The objective territoriality principle

The fourth exception, namely the objective territoriality principle, may be invoked when an act is commenced outside the boundaries of a country but concluded within its territory. Examples that are frequently used by international lawyers to illustrate the operation of this principle include situations where one person obviously abuses a medium such as postal services and sends poison from one country to another or where such a person stands a few metres away from the 'border' and fires a gun across the border killing or injuring another on the other side of the border.

---

[5] See *France v. Turkey ('S.S. Lotus')* (1927) PCIJ 9, 19; *Denmark v. Germany (North Sea Continental Shelf)* (1968) ICJ 3, 44–5.

(B) Mere assertion of jurisdiction v. enforcement

Beyond the principle of territoriality and its exceptions, the competence of a country to assert jurisdiction over situations outside its territory, especially those involving foreign individuals, is highly questionable. It is very possible that in such situations more than one country may assert jurisdiction. For example one may foresee this being done by at least two countries: the foreign country and the one in whose territory the conduct is occurring. Obviously, this may have a number of consequences and implications, perhaps chief among which is the conflict that is likely to arise between these countries. Nevertheless, and indeed very interestingly, generally it is thought that as long as a country does not attempt to apply its laws to conduct performed within the territory of another country (i.e. to seek enforcement), a *mere* assertion of the subject-matter jurisdiction by the former over individuals in the latter may not lead to any conflict between the countries concerned or to a violation of principles of public international law. The position would change radically however where the former does seek enforcement. In this case the possibility of conflict and violation of principles of public international law becomes obvious and a real prospect.[6]

(C) The (in)adequacy of the traditional approach in areas of economic law

The four exception principles to that of territoriality discussed above were initially developed in the context of physical conduct: for example, the scenario of the poison or the fired shot. Among the key purposes behind their creation – it may be argued – was the need to ensure that an appropriate mechanism would be in place to enable a country to deal with and punish all forms of 'criminal' activities effectively and comprehensively. Having such a 'physical' conduct flavour seems to have ruled out the possibility of the exceptions being seen as adequate to deal with economic conduct – for example, in the case of a business, behaviour or conduct on the part of firms or individuals. Whether the exceptions could be invoked in this particular context proved to be a seriously difficult conundrum, which lasted for a considerable time. There were those who argued that such an extension of the use of the exceptions would be 'inadequate' because these principles did not seem to be

---

[6] See Rosenthal and Knighton, note 4 above.

sufficient to address questions of economic conduct, since they emerged with physical conduct in mind. Those in favour however, argued that such an extension was perfectly 'adequate' and they had a suitable suggestion for a foundation on which such extension could be built: a country could assert jurisdiction over acts committed beyond its borders on the basis that these acts produced economic effects within its territory.

2.   The 'effects' doctrine

(A)   General

Regardless of the respective strengths of the views in favour and against extending the application of the four exceptions to the principle of territoriality to cover areas of economic law, it seems that the conundrum outlined above came to be eventually solved, though largely this has been by countries themselves taking action *unilaterally*. Under this solution, harmful economic effects were considered to be equivalent to effects of unlawful physical conduct originating from the territory of one country but concluded in another. In many ways, this represented a sharp shift in position which until the present day is not clear to what extent it has been recognised under public international law; as we noted, the shift received recognition in the jurisprudence of certain countries. Those countries came to believe that it was imperative to address all forms of economic harm whether originating within or outside their national boundaries even though this may require them to adopt an expansive concept of competence or jurisdiction.[7] Ultimately, according to these countries, the guiding compass here must be the occurrence of economic 'effects'. It was this particular philosophy that led to the birth of the doctrine of 'effects', which has served as the bedrock to the doctrine of extraterritoriality almost globally in the field of competition law.

(B)   The justification

Whether the adopting of an expansive concept of jurisdiction by certain countries as outlined above is fully compatible with public international law or not, it would only be fair to ask whether, objectively, the effects doctrine is nonetheless justified and what might such an objective justification be.

---

[7] See D. Gerber, 'The Extraterritorial Application of German Antitrust Law' (1983) *American Journal of International Law* 756.

It would not require a great deal of imagination to see how the territoriality principle falls short of guarding the legitimate interests of countries whether in areas of physical activities or economic relations.[8] It is because of this shortcoming that public international law itself came to see the *necessity* for developing the four exceptions. Among other things, these exceptions show that individual countries should be entitled to assert subject-matter jurisdiction to ensure proper protection is afforded to their citizens and national security and interests. Holding that a country's national economic order is a stone's throw away as opposed to a mile away from the 'boundaries' of the concept of national security and interests would not be an unreasonable proposition at all. The field of competition law is an integral part of a country's economic order and its general commercial interests; not to mention its relevance in some cases to issues of national security. Hence – and in light of the increasing interdependence between countries and the significance of international trade for the welfare of countries – it is difficult to disagree with the logic behind adopting an effects doctrine. Following the territoriality principle but not its exceptions in an area of economic law, such as competition law, would have serious and possibly damaging consequences. Among these consequences the possibility of firms being able to evade national regulation in some cases ranks high.[9] It would not be difficult to see how *strict* territoriality may afford some firms the opportunity to engage in harmful anticompetitive conduct, which will go largely undetected and unpunished; not to mention the serious risk of transforming certain countries into competition law 'havens'. Allowing this to happen may well result in harm to consumers and competitors of those firms. Firms would therefore be able to engage in harmful economic conduct without being subjected to any form of supervision, since their acts would have been committed 'beyond' national boundaries.[10]

There is therefore a need to recognise that some logic is built into the doctrine of effects. Nonetheless it is equally important to recognise that the existence of this element of logic does not mean that countries should have an almost *absolute* right to deploy the doctrine whenever they want to as a tool for fighting what they might perceive as harmful foreign

[8] See D. F. Turner, 'Application of Competition Laws to Foreign Conduct: Appropriate Resolution of Jurisdictional Issues' (1985) *Fordham Corporate Law Institute* 231.

[9] See Gerber, 'Afterword: Antitrust and American Business Abroad Revisited' (2000) *Northwestern Journal of International Law and Business* 307.

[10] See T. W. Dunfee and A. S. Friedman, 'The Extraterritorial Application of United States Antitrust Laws: a Proposal for an Interim Solution' (1984) *Ohio State Law Journal* 883.

conduct. Among other things, such a situation would fall foul of public international law, under which an assertion of jurisdiction by an individual country needs to satisfy a requirement of a sufficiently close or reasonable link between the 'foreign' acts and its domestic territory – a view that in fact is inherent in the exceptions to the principle of territoriality itself.[11] Countries cannot assert jurisdiction if the minimum requirement of such 'nexus' is not met. What this means in the present context is that the effects doctrine can be regarded as a legitimate basis to assert jurisdiction over acts committed abroad which adversely impact upon domestic situations but this can only happen *under certain circumstances*. This is being emphasised because there is no reason why, in principle, the validity of the effects doctrine should not be questioned, if the country relying on it fails to take into consideration the sovereign interests of other countries or in asserting its jurisdiction extraterritoriality such country undermines the interests of other countries. The most effective way of taking account of such interests would be for countries to adhere to the principles of public international law. It seems, therefore, that although the effects doctrine may constitute a legitimate basis for asserting jurisdiction, such assertion cannot be absolute, i.e. it is subject to certain conditions, which seem to be imposed under international law. As such, a country that seeks to assert its jurisdiction extraterritorially will need to satisfy these conditions.[12] This is particularly so if any risk of conflict with other countries is to be minimised or eliminated – an aim that surely all countries should strive to achieve.

The use of the doctrine of extraterritoriality in different competition law regimes can be said to have recognised this limitation and the need for 'nexus' between the foreign situation and the domestic market. In particular the different cases involving extraterritorial assertion of jurisdiction – which will be discussed below – confirm that jurisdiction in the field of competition cannot be asserted without the presence of 'direct, substantial and foreseeable' anticompetitive effects;[13] this would furnish sufficient proof that the effects doctrine can be said to meet the requirement of reasonable link under public international law; in some of the cases in practice the extraterritorial action may be against behaviour, conduct or transactions in which domestic firms are also involved. As a

---

[11] See Mann, note 4 above.
[12] See R. Alford, 'The Extraterritorial Application of Antitrust Laws: the United States and the European Community Approaches' (1992) *Virginia Journal of International Law* 1.
[13] See p. 448 below.

matter of interest however it may be worth noting here that public international law offers no definition or guidance of the requirement of direct, substantial and foreseeable effects and that in practice interpreting and applying this requirement has been done by individual countries according to their own perception; in the case of some competition law regimes the perception has been that of the domestic national competition authorities and courts.

3. The doctrines of 'implementation' and 'single economic entity'

It is worth noting that the effects doctrine does not enjoy universal recognition in different competition law regimes as the sole basis for establishing jurisdiction extraterritorially. In the EU competition law regime two doctrines have come to be introduced and relied on for the purposes of giving the rules in the regime an extraterritorial reach, namely those of 'single economic entity' and 'implementation'. These doctrines will be discussed further below and the differences between the effects and implementation doctrines will also be examined;[14] the question of whether it can be said that the doctrine of effects has no presence in the EU competition law regime will also be considered.

4. Extraterritoriality: some fundamental issues

(A) The question of definition

Despite the incredible amount of attention poured on the issue of extraterritoriality in competition law literature, there has been little attempt to ask whether the concept is susceptible to some kind of definition and if it is how should it be defined. To be fair, it is very possible that this has been directly caused by the fairly well-recognised difficulty in finding a definition that could be compelling and on which general consensus would emerge. Perhaps the definition that can be considered to be closest to fitting such description is that extraterritoriality concerns the application of domestic competition law in specific cases containing 'foreign elements'. However even such fairly neutral and (arguably) very wide definition itself would need further definition, in particular the concept of 'foreign elements', which at any rate would defy a general definition,

---

[14] See pp. 432–452 and 453–469 below.

especially in areas of economic law. For this reason, it would be more appropriate, instead of searching for a definition of the doctrine in the field of competition law, to focus on identifying or describing situations of extraterritoriality using adequate examples.

(B)   The scenarios

Broadly speaking a number of scenarios can be identified which can be said to come within the scope of the doctrine of extraterritoriality:

- *Scenario 1*: when the competition rules of country A are applied by the judiciary and competition authorities of country A to conduct, behaviour or transactions occurring in the territory of country B but which produce effects in country A;
- *Scenario 2*: when country A applies its competition rules in situations occurring beyond its boundaries which affect its firms in foreign markets;
- *Scenario 3*: when the same rules are applied by the judiciary and competition authorities of country A to situations within its territory which affect firms operating in country B or more broadly where the rules are applied to *local* behaviour, conduct or transactions which affect foreign markets or consumers;
- *Scenario 4*: when the judiciary and competition authorities of country A apply its competition rules to conduct, behaviour and transactions in country B affecting foreign firms, consumers or markets in country B.
- *Scenario 5*: when the competition rules of country A are applied by the judiciary and competition authorities of country B in situations falling within the latter's territory which produce effects within and/or beyond national boundaries.

The most common among these scenarios as has come to emerge in practice is *the first scenario*, under which a country applies its domestic competition law to the behaviour and activities of foreign firms taking place beyond its national boundaries but which produce effects on local markets. This of course is distinguished from the scenario in which a country applies its domestic competition rules to behaviour and activities of its national firms occurring on foreign soil. According to the review of the principle of territoriality and its exceptions conducted above this latter scenario seems to be a recognised principle under public international law; unlike the former scenario which does not seem to have equal recognition, and thus it has given rise to some serious difficulties and conflicts in the field.[15] The first scenario is also different from the fourth one, which *normally* would not come within the scope of the competition rules in this particular context because these rules place emphasis on the need to demonstrate *effect* on competition and/or trade in the relevant jurisdiction, i.e. *locally*.[16] This means that situations affecting competition and/or trade in foreign markets are beyond the scope of the local competition rules. Finally, with regard to the second scenario this can be considered to be a variant of extraterritoriality which can be termed 'outbound' extraterritoriality: an application of domestic competition law in order to, for example, deal with market access problems relating to the efforts of domestic firms to penetrate foreign markets.[17]

(C)   Sources of extraterritoriality

The sources of extraterritorial assertion of jurisdiction by competition authorities and courts around the world differ from one regime to the next. In some regimes, the basis is clearly statutory and the relevant competition law either explicitly,[18] or implicitly makes it clear that the rules apply in an extraterritorial fashion; the latter is often seen in the use of wide wording such as: the relevant law applies to all types of conduct or behaviour regardless of where they occur. In other regimes, the competition rules are silent on the issue of extraterritoriality but the courts took the lead in establishing that they do apply extraterritorially.[19] In some regimes the sources may be of a 'soft' type and extraterritorial jurisdiction is established in guidance published by the relevant competition authority(ies).[20]

---

[15] See V. Lowe, 'The Problems of Extraterritorial Jurisdiction: Economic Sovereignty and the Search for a Solution' (1985) *International and Comparative Law Quarterly* 724.

[16] Numerous examples can be found in practice of this emphasis; see in particular the EU and US competition law regimes.

[17] The issue of market access is discussed in chapter 11 below in the context of the relationship between competition and trade policies.

[18] See the examples furnished by Brazil (Art. 2 of the Federal Antitrust Law 1994); Egypt (Art. 5 of the Law on the Protection of Competition and the Prohibition of Monopolistic Practice 2005); Jordan (Art. 3 of the Competition Act 2004); Canada (s. 46 of the Competition Act 1986); and Singapore (s. 33(1) of the Competition Act 2004).

[19] See for example Arts 101 and 102 TFEU; the Articles are mentioned and discussed at p. 161 above.

[20] See the US Department of Justice Antitrust Division *Antitrust Enforcement Guidelines for International Operations* (1995), discussed further below at pp. 450–452. According to the Guidelines an extraterritorial reach exists in the case of s. 7 of the Clayton Act 1914

Notwithstanding the difference in the types of sources, different competition law regimes are *united* in their approach and policy to apply their rules in order to deal with business phenomena – whether domestic or foreign – that affect competition and markets domestically. This can be seen especially in the area of anti-cartel enforcement: several international cartels have been prosecuted in competition law regimes around the world and the participation of foreign firms in these cartels has led to punishment in these regimes.[21]

(D) Extraterritoriality and the internationalisation of competition law

The process of internationalisation of competition law was discussed in chapter 2 above. As may be recalled, the doctrine of extraterritoriality was labelled an option or example of internationalisation. It would be helpful at this stage to consider the specific links between the doctrine of extraterritoriality and this process.

It seems that a number of strong links exist here which arguably have been established by the fact that in both theory and practice extraterritoriality concerns situations, which extend beyond the national level and move more towards the international plane. As an option or example however an extraterritorial assertion of jurisdiction when compared with the other option of cooperation – whether bilateral, regional or international – is not usually seen under a positive light. Put simply, it could be said that relying on extraterritorial application of domestic competition laws would reduce the incentives of countries for the internationalisation of competition law in a 'bilateral' or 'pluralist' sense. If, by relying on its own competition rules, a country is independently able to control activities beyond its boundaries, then its willingness to cooperate with other countries on the international plane will not be particularly strong, unless it could achieve better results through cooperation.[22] The situation may be much worse if such a country would opt for extraterritorial assertion of

though the reference is to any person 'engaged in commerce or in any activity affecting commerce'; s. 7 is discussed at p. 244 above.

[21] Notably, see the *Vitamins* cartel and the *Marine hose* cartel.

[22] This point can be illustrated with reference to the USA and its 'vision' on cooperation. As the discussion in chapters 5 and 10 shows, the USA, while expressing its views in favour of cooperation, has delivered major blows to the efforts to internationalise competition law through binding multilateral avenues, especially in the 1940s and 1950s; more recently it has shown enormous objections to concluding a binding multilateral agreement within the WTO.

jurisdiction in an aggressive way, which is seen by other countries as amounting to an intrusion into their national sovereignty. In this case such reliance on the doctrine may trigger conflicts between the countries concerned. The frictions which such conflicts may cause can seriously damage the relationship between the countries in an increasingly globalised world in which different countries are supposed to operate as trading partners and they have the potential of diminishing any hope or calls for meaningful cooperation in the field; not to mention that such situations may become perceived as ones of national competition law 'imperialism' – with strong countries imposing their standards on others. Claims of such imperialism have on a number of occasions over the years surfaced against US reliance on extraterritorial assertion of jurisdiction which many countries saw as an attempt to impose respect for US competition law on the entire world in order to promote national interests.[23]

At the same time it ought to be recognised that a country's motive for making use of the doctrine of extraterritoriality may well be to protect its national interests and guard its national sovereignty; however it is unlikely that other countries will not see this particular use as an infringement of their own national sovereignty.[24] An attempt to address harmful *extraterritorial* situations through extraterritorial assertion of jurisdiction – particularly when it is unlikely that the same could be achieved in another way – presents an example of competition law being internationalised. This means that an unusual relationship exists between the doctrine and the process of internationalisation: though in a narrow situation the doctrine can be seen as an option of the latter the prevailing view is that a reliance on the doctrine of extraterritoriality represents a step in the opposite direction to opting for a meaningful internationalisation of competition law.

(E)   Is there a political dimension to extraterritoriality?

Viewing extraterritoriality through the lenses of the principle of territoriality and its exceptions and in terms of situations of foreign elements

---

[23] See D. Rishikesh, 'Extraterritoriality Versus Sovereignty in International Antitrust Jurisdiction' (1991) *World Competition* 33.

[24] See Justice Holmes in *American Banana* (discussed further below) where he wrote at p. 356 of the judgment that the lawfulness of an act 'must be determined wholly by the law of the country where the act alone is done'. Otherwise, according to Justice Holmes, the assertion of jurisdiction would be unjust and would be an interference with the sovereignty of another country, which the other country 'justly might resent'.

and their control using domestic laws may give the impression that the doctrine (and more importantly the conflicts its use can give rise to) is a question of mere assertion of jurisdiction – on a legal basis – under public international law. This is especially so since the exceptions to the territoriality principle have facilitated the creation of the 'extra' in coining the doctrine of extraterritoriality. The actual recognition of the doctrine however emerged in national legal systems of different countries and *not* under public international law. As such, one may agree that there is a legal basis to the doctrine; or to put the point the other way: there is no argument that the doctrine is illegal.

Whilst it is no doubt true the doctrine has grown from roots found within such setting, nevertheless, extraterritoriality lies in the crossroads between law and politics. In particular the application of the doctrine reveals that it has not been purely about legal considerations; in addition, political factors do have their place in the operation of the doctrine. Therefore the doctrine and the problems it has given rise to are not necessarily purely legal in nature. In more ways than one, the problems here can be seen as ones, which concern international relations: the relations of one country with other countries. It would not be that difficult to imagine a situation arising which reveals a country attaching national interests to the existence of a cartel arrangement or another type of practice normally considered to be anticompetitive;[25] nor is it inconceivable for a situation to arise in which such a country attaches considerable interest to its national firms not being subjected to any form of control, regulation or liability, not having to reveal certain information,[26] and not having to comply with a particular kind of remedy order, which may all arise as a result of another country applying its competition law extraterritorially.[27] An attempt to safeguard national interests in these cases is likely to (if not inevitably) trigger serious problems. These problems concern important political questions,[28] such as: who can make and enforce rules regulating behaviour of businesses with

---

[25] See D. E. Rosenthal, 'What Should be the Agenda of a Presidential Commission to Study the International Application of US Antitrust Law?' (1980) *Northwestern Journal of International Law and Business* 372.

[26] See D. Papakrivopoulos, 'The Role of Competition Law as an International Trade Remedy in the Context of the World Trade Organization' (1999) *World Competition* 45.

[27] See generally J. H. Shenefield, 'Thoughts on Extraterritorial Application of the United States Antitrust Laws' (1983) *Fordham Law Review* 350.

[28] See H. G. Maier, 'Extraterritorial Jurisdiction at a Crossroads: an Intersection Between Public and Private International Law' (1982) *American Journal of International Law* 280.

cross-border dimension.[29] Put differently, the nature and content of the doctrine is as much political as legal.[30] Consequently, it is important to recognise that there is an important political dimension to extraterritoriality. This is all the more so when it comes to considering possible solutions or alternatives to the use of the doctrine in the field.[31]

5.   Developments in the USA and the EU

Discussing extraterritoriality without actual and adequate reference to its use in different competition law regimes would be pointless. It is crucial therefore that a review of the experience with the doctrine in some regimes is offered in order to facilitate a better understanding of the doctrine, how it has been developed in those regimes and the exact function it has been performing in practice. The present part will therefore offer a comprehensive examination of the doctrine under the US and EU competition law regimes. Other than the fact that these two are the world's most important competition law regimes, two different perspectives have purportedly been developed on the extraterritoriality question on both sides of the Atlantic; although this remains to be examined.

(A)   The American perspective

I.   US jurisprudence

Beginning the discussion here with the US perspective would be in order. In addition to being the oldest of the two regimes, the USA was amongst the first countries to recognise the 'effects' doctrine in the field of competition law;[32] though it was believed at one point that US

---

[29] See chapter 2.

[30] Several writers have argued – quite incompletely – that the problem of extraterritoriality is one of legal conflict. Against this, some writers have argued that disputes arising as a result of extraterritoriality are not simply about legal theory; they are equally disputes about the policy objectives the law should serve. See J. W. Bridge, 'The Law and Politics of United States Foreign Policy Export Controls' (1984) *Legal Studies* 2.

[31] See further below on the solutions to extraterritoriality.

[32] See Stroock, Stroock and Lavan, 'Convergence of Trade Laws and Antitrust Laws: Unilateral Extraterritorial US Antitrust Enforcement – Can it Work to Open Japan's Markets?' in H. B. Coretesi (ed.), *Unilateral Application of Antitrust and Trade Laws: Toward a New Economic Relationship Between the United States and Japan* (The Institute, 1994), p. 114.

The origins of the doctrine of extraterritoriality are illustrated in several laws in the USA: the Sherman Act 1890, the Clayton Act 1914, the Federal Trade Commission Act

competition law did not apply to activities occurring outside national boundaries.[33] This was the position adopted in an important case, *American Banana Co.* v. *United Fruits Co.* (1909) in which the Supreme Court explicitly ruled out an extraterritorial reach to the country's oldest competition legislation, the Sherman Act 1890, stating that the Act did not apply to activities outside the USA. Justice Oliver Wendell Holmes in particular expressed the importance of not violating the 'universal rule' against 'interference with the authority of another sovereign, contrary to the comity of nations, which the other state concerned justly might resent'.[34]

This was an important statement by the highest court of the land, though it did not survive for too long: in *United States* v. *Sisal Sales Corporation*, the Supreme Court decided to take a different approach to the question of extraterritoriality and in doing so it ruled that jurisdiction under US competition law may be asserted in relation to conduct taking place *within* and *outside* the borders of the USA alike.[35] The *Sisal* judgment was obviously crucial and as it turned out it paved the way for a line of judicial pronouncements in favour of extraterritoriality. Some of these pronouncements were more far reaching than others. Perhaps the most notable example of a far-reaching pronouncement in the early years of US competition law jurisprudence on extraterritoriality was the one given nearly 20 years later after *Sisal* in the famous case of *United States* v. *Aluminium Co. of America (Alcoa)*, in which Judge Learned Hand *crafted* the proposition that the USA can assert jurisdiction over a cartel agreement concluded outside its territory by foreign firms, with the US firm not being party to the agreement. He famously stated that:

> It is settled law ... that any State may impose liabilities, even upon persons not within its allegiance, for conduct outside its borders which

---

1914, the Robinson-Patman Act 1936 and the Hart-Scott-Rodino Antitrust Improvements Act 1976. See pp. 247–248 above for a discussion of these Acts.

[33] See *American Banana Co.* v. *United Fruits Co.*, 213 US 347 (1909).

[34] At 356. It is worth asking to what extent this outcome in *American Banana* can be interpreted as a total rejection by the Supreme Court at that time of the doctrine of extraterritoriality in the field of competition law given the involvement of the government of Costa Rica in the case: the government in the case had seized property belonging to American Banana, though allegedly United Fruit was behind this. Thus there was a state involvement in the case and this can be said to have been influential. See pp. 487–488 below for further discussion on state involvement.

[35] 274 US 268 (1927).

has consequences within its boarders which the State reprehends; and
these liabilities other States will ordinarily recognize.[36]

Whether – especially at that early stage – the extraterritoriality question
was 'settled law' can be considered to have remained – up to the present
day – 'not settled'. In his reasoning as to why US competition law has
extraterritorial reach, Judge Hand believed that it was irrelevant under
the circumstances that the agreement was of a completely foreign nature:
such an agreement could still be declared unlawful because a country
may punish an economically harmful act, which it may reprehend, even
if committed by individuals beyond its borders.[37] In the years that
followed *Alcoa*, several important judgments have come to deal with
the extraterritoriality question and a very extensive body of literature has
come to emerge in which the doctrine has been analysed and debated;
these two developments have contributed a great deal towards making
the US competition law regime – and the USA more generally – a very
rich source for understanding extraterritoriality.

II. From *Alcoa* to *Timberlane*

In a way, one might say that huge importance should not be attached to
Alcoa but to post-*Alcoa* case law for the purposes of establishing whether
the extraterritoriality question was 'settled' under US competition law.
There is no doubt that the judgment itself was not warmly received
around the world and perhaps more seriously it ushered in a period of
quite extensive extraterritorial assertions.[38] *Alcoa* gave rise to conflicts
between the USA and other countries,[39] many of whom considered the
judgment to be a sea of controversy and fundamentally wrong. Some of
the voices expressing deep concerns over the *Alcoa* proposition appear
to have been *heard* by US judges sitting to hear extraterritoriality actions
in the years that followed. This can be seen in light of how later
formulations of the effects doctrine by US courts were more carefully

---

[36] Ibid., 148 F 2d 416 (2nd Cir., 1945), 444.   [37] Ibid., 443.

[38] See W. L. Fugate, *Foreign Commerce and the Antitrust Laws* (Little Brown, 1958).

[39] See K. Brewster, *Antitrust and American Business Abroad* (McGraw-Hill, 1958); N. de
B. Katzenbach, 'Conflicts on an Unruly Horse: Reciprocal Claims and Tolerance in
Interstate and International Law' (1956) *Yale Law Journal* 1087; D. E. Rosenthal,
'Relationship of US Antitrust Laws to the Formulation of Foreign Economic Policy,
Particularly Export and Overseas Investment Policy' (1980) *Antitrust Law Journal* 1189;
J. B. Sandage, 'Forum Non Conveniens and the Extraterritorial Application of United
States Antitrust Laws' (1985) *Yale Law Journal* 1693.

worded.[40] Some of these formulations fell only short of harshly criticising *Alcoa*. An illustration here can be found in the case of *Timberlane I*, which concerned a 'conspiracy' by US and foreign firms – with the involvement of officials of foreign governments. The US Court of Appeals for the Ninth Circuit held that the effects doctrine as enunciated in *Alcoa* is 'by itself ... incomplete because it fails to consider other nations' interests. Nor does it expressly take into account the full nature of the relationship between the actors and this country.' In effect, this particular statement in *Timberlane I* ushered in a new approach to extraterritoriality in particular one embracing a principle of judicial comity. The term comity here is taken to describe a general principle that a country should take other countries' important interests into account in its law enforcement in return for their doing the same. This seems to conform with the actual definition of the term given by the US Supreme Court – well before the USA came to introduce competition legislation – as 'the recognition which one nation allows within its territory to the legislative, executive or judicial acts of another nation, having due regard both to international duty and convenience, and to the rights of its own citizens'.[41] In some cases the Court was even more specific, ruling that 'the central precept of comity teaches that, when possible, the decisions of foreign tribunals should be given effect in domestic courts, since recognition fosters international cooperation and encourages reciprocity, thereby promoting predictability and stability'.[42] This interpretation of comity seems to put the concept in its special *hybrid* context and shows that the concept should not be viewed along the lines of legal obligations, nor along the lines of simple acts of good manners and courtesy.[43]

The judgment of the Court of Appeals in *Timberlane I* – following the spirit of the jurisprudence of the US Supreme Court – opened the door for a 'jurisdictional rule of reason' approach on the basis of the principle of comity to be adopted by US courts when dealing with the doctrine of

---

[40] See *Timberlane Lumber Co. v. Bank of America National Trust and Savings Association*, 549 F 2d 597 (1976), 611–12.

[41] See *Hilton v. Guyot*, 159 US 113, 163–4 (1865).

[42] See also *Laker Airways Ltd. v. Sabena, Belgian World Airlines*, 731 F 2d 909, 937 (1984), See H. Yntema, 'The Comity Doctrine' (1966) *Michigan Law Review* 1.

[43] See in this regard judicial pronouncements to this effect produced in some parts of the world, most notably perhaps the judgment of the Supreme Court of Canada in *Morguard Invs. v. De Savoye* (1990) SCR 1077.

extraterritoriality.[44] This approach however does not seem to be wholly the result of judicial invention in the field of competition law, but appears to be an adaptation of a contribution of a prominent American scholar, Kingman Brewster, in the late 1950s who advocated a 'jurisdictional rule of reason' principle to be applied through a balancing exercise between national and foreign interests in a broad sense.[45] The *Timberlane I* jurisdictional rule of reason approach or balancing exercise rested according to the Court on a number of factors that must be taken into account:

> [T]he degree of conflict with foreign law or policy, the nationality or allegiance of the parties and the locations or principal places of business of corporations, the extent to which enforcement by either state can be expected to achieve compliance, the relative significance of effects on the US as compared with those elsewhere, the extent to which there is explicit purpose to harm or affect American commerce, the foreseeability of such effect, and the relative importance to the violations charged of conduct within the US as compared with conduct abroad.[46]

Whilst this appears to furnish a ground for a *broad* balancing exercise between domestic and foreign interests in competition law cases, the purpose clearly was to devise a *narrower* approach to the doctrine of extraterritoriality than the one established in *Alcoa*.[47] Under this approach, extraterritorial application of US competition rules required not only the existence of a significant effect within the USA whether actual or intended, but also a balancing of the respective interests of the USA in asserting jurisdiction, and of any other country which might be offended by such assertion.[48] The Court of Appeals came to follow this approach – albeit arguably with *some modification* – in its second *Timberlane* case, *Timberlane II*, in which the Court held that in asserting extraterritorial jurisdiction, a court should examine: '(1) the effect or intended effect on the foreign commerce of the United States; (2) the type and magnitude of the alleged illegal behaviour, and (3) the

---

[44] A similar approach – showing a judicial move towards use of comity – is possible to identify in Canada; see in particular the case of *Hunt* v. *T&N plc* (1993) SCR 289.

[45] See Brewster, note 39 above.   [46] 549 F 2d 614.

[47] In spite of this narrowing of the scope of the doctrine, however, other countries still held the view that the doctrine offended against common principles of public international law. See generally A. D. Neale and D. G. Goyder, *The Antitrust Laws of the United States of America: a Study of Competition Enforced by Law* (Cambridge University Press, 1980).

[48] See E. Fox, 'Extraterritoriality and Antitrust – is Reasonableness the Answer?' (1986) *Fordham Corporate Law Institute* 49.

appropriateness of exercising extraterritorial jurisdiction in light of considerations of international comity and fairness'.[49] Another example of a *modified approach* can be seen from the judgment of the Third Circuit Court in *Mannington Mills, Inc.* v. *Congoleum Corp.*[50] The Court advocated that the following facts should be taken into account: whether a remedy was available in the relevant foreign jurisdiction; whether the authorities in this jurisdiction had launched proceedings, which were pending at the time; whether there was any potential harm to US foreign policy from the assertion of jurisdiction extraterritorially in the circumstances; whether an order for relief would be more effective if issued in proceedings in the USA; whether in a case where an order for relief is made in the relevant foreign jurisdiction this would be acceptable to US authorities and courts; and whether international rules or agreement governed the relevant situation. The approach adopted by some US courts around the same time these judgments were delivered was not merely modifying however: in some key cases, the effectiveness of the *Timberlane I* factors were simply questioned. A notable example here is *Laker Airways Ltd* v. *Sabena, Belgian World Airlines* in which it was held that comity 'has not gained more than a temporary foothold in domestic law'.[51]

III. From *Timberlane* to *Hartford Fire*[52]

The judgments of the Court of Appeals in the *Timberlane* cases was not to be the final word on the question of extraterritoriality under US competition law, and perhaps it is good that this was not so: after all what the case seems to have confirmed was the existence of a heated debate among the judiciary on a hugely important doctrine in the US competition law regime. Hence it would have been useful and in fact necessary for the US Supreme Court to enter once again this debate and to hopefully follow and confirm *Timberlane I*. The case of *Hartford Fire* offered the opportunity for the Supreme Court to do the former, though the Court appears to have rejected the opportunity to do the latter. Before considering the facts of the case and the judgment it would be helpful to mention an important development which occurred in 1987, namely the

---

[49] *Timberlane Lumber Co.* v. *Bank of America National Trust and Savings Association*, 749 F 2d 1378, 1382 (1984).

[50] *Mannington Mills, Inc.* v. *Congoleum Corp.*, 595 F.2d 1287, 1294–95 (1979).

[51] See *Laker Airways Ltd* v. *Sabena, Belgian World Airlines*, 731 F.2d 909, 950 (1984).

[52] See *Hartford Fire Insurance Co.* v. *California*, 113 S. Ct. 2891 (1993).

adoption of the Restatement (Third) of Foreign Relations Law of the United States by the American Law Institute. The Third Restatement embraced the ruling in *Timberlane*. It emphasised the importance of comity and set out a number of factors determining when an extraterritorial assertion of jurisdiction would be (un)reasonable as follows:

> (a) the link of the activity to the territory of the regulating state, i.e., the extent to which the activity takes place within the territory, or has substantial, direct, and foreseeable effect upon or in the territory; (b) the connections, such as nationality, residence, or economic activity, between the regulating state and the person principally responsible for the activity to be regulated, or between that state and those whom the regulation is designed to protect; (c) the character of the activity to be regulated, the importance of regulation to the regulating state, the extent to which other states regulate such activities, and the degree to which the desirability of such regulation is generally accepted; (d) the existence of justified expectations that might be protected or hurt by the regulation; (e) the importance of the regulation to the international political, legal, or economic system; (f) the extent to which the regulation is consistent with the traditions of the international system; (g) the extent to which another state may have an interest in regulating the activity; and (h) the likelihood of conflict with regulation by another state.[53]

Hartford Fire involved a not particularly complicated set of facts. In 1988, several US and UK insurance firms were alleged to have breached the Sherman Act 1890 by entering into agreements to alter certain terms of insurance coverage they offered and not to offer certain types of insurance coverage. In particular under the agreements reinsurance was to be offered to US firms only on jointly agreed terms. In their response to the allegations, the UK-based firms argued that the US courts should not assert jurisdiction over conduct that occurred in another jurisdiction and was lawful there, even if the conduct in question produced effects in the USA: UK insurance law regulated the situation in question and so it was perfectly legal; a position supported by the UK government. The case was brought initially before the District Court which considered the question of extraterritorial jurisdiction and came to the conclusion that it could assert jurisdiction over the conduct of the UK firms under the Sherman Act 1890 because their decision to refuse to provide reinsurance or retrocessional reinsurance to cover certain types of risks in the USA had a direct *effect* on the availability of primary

---

[53] See *Restatement (Third) of Foreign Relations Law of the United States*, ss. 401 and 403 (1987).

insurance *in the USA*.[54] In dealing with the international comity point, the Court, referring to *Timberlane II*, held that extraterritorial assertion of jurisdiction *in the case* should not give way to international comity considerations. On appeal, the Court of Appeals however took a different view: whilst agreeing with the District Court on the existence of effects within the USA, it reversed the former's ruling with respect to the international comity consideration.[55] This particular situation paved the way for the Supreme Court to become involved which it did on appeal. The Supreme Court however was divided on the question of extraterritoriality. Delivering another of its famous 5–4 judgments, the Court held that the Sherman Act 1890 does apply to foreign conduct that was meant to produce and did in fact produce some substantial effect in the USA.[56] Regarding international comity considerations, the Court held that there was no need to decide this question, and that in any case, 'international comity would not counsel against exercising jurisdiction in the circumstances alleged', even if asserting jurisdiction over foreign acts usually gives way to international comity considerations.[57]

An important point made in the judgment that is worth mentioning relates to the argument of UK firms and government that the challenged conduct was not contrary to UK law and policy. The Court responded to this argument by saying that there was no 'true conflict' between UK and US laws on this point.[58] The Court referred to section 415 of the Third Restatement, holding that there cannot be a 'true conflict' if the firm, subject to the laws of two jurisdictions, can comply with both. As there was no 'true conflict' in this case, held the Court, there was no need to consider whether a US court should, on the basis of international comity, refrain from asserting jurisdiction.

The judgment was hugely important and it did sound a number of alarms both within the USA as well as around the world. In deciding in this way, the Supreme Court raised several questions, some of which are of crucial significance.[59] Perhaps the most important question concerns the

---

[54] See *In re Insurance Antitrust Litigation*, 732 F. Supp. 464, 484 (1991).

[55] See *In re Insurance Antitrust Litigation*, 938 F 2d 919, 932, 934 (1991).

[56] See 509 US 764, 796 (1993), per Justice Souter. [57] Ibid., 798. [58] Ibid., 798–9.

[59] Many of these questions have been noted in the literature on the case. See V. Gupta, 'After *Hartford Fire*: Antitrust and Comity' (1996) *Georgetown Law Journal* 2287; J. A. Trenor, 'Jurisdiction and the Extraterritorial Application of Antitrust Laws after *Hartford Fire*' (1995) *University of Chicago Law Review* 1583; K. Dam, 'Extraterritoriality in an Age of Globalization: the *Hartford Fire* Case' (1993) *Supreme Court Review* 289; L. Kramer, 'Extraterritorial Application of American law After the Insurance Antitrust

view of the majority that for a 'true conflict' to exist, compliance with US law should lead to a violation of the law of another country – a proposition that many found difficult to accept. Indeed, in the case itself, Justice Scalia, delivering the judgment for the minority, described this view as a 'breath-takingly broad proposition'.[60] It was of no surprise therefore that such a view, it was considered, would trigger conflicts in the application of US competition law between US interests and the legitimate interests of other countries. Interestingly in this regard is the Court's specific reference to the Third Restatement as a source of support for its view whereas it seems that the Court's view does not sit comfortably with the approach of the Third Restatement. This can be seen in light of an account offered by the principal author of the part of the Restatement on which the Supreme Court relied in its judgment who reflected on the judgment using the following hypothetical but 'in-point' example:

> In determining whether state A exercises jurisdiction over an activity significantly linked to state B, one important question, in my submission, is whether B has a demonstrable system of values and priorities different from those of A that would be impaired by the application of the law of A. I am not suggesting that, if the answer to the question is yes, A must stay its hand. The magnitude of A's interest, the effect of the challenged activity within A, the intention of the actors, and the other factors that I hope will disappear from view remain important. But, conflict is not just about commands: it is also about interests, values and competing prio-rities. All of these need to be taken into account in arriving at a rational allocation of jurisdiction in a world of nation-states.[61]

It is arguable that possibly the only conclusion the Court should have drawn from invoking the Third Restatement is that it would be prefer-able for the US courts to *refrain* from asserting jurisdiction over foreign situations if such an assertion is unreasonable. In the case, Justice Scalia

---

Case: a Reply to Professors Lowenfeld and Trimble' (1995) *American Journal of International Law* 750; P. R. Trimble, 'The Supreme Court and International Law: the Demise of Restatement Section 403' (1995) *American Journal of International Law* 53; P. M. Roth, 'Jurisdiction, British Public Policy and the Supreme Court' (1994) *Law Quarterly Review* 194; E. Fox, 'US Law and Global Competition and Trade – Jurisdiction and Comity' (1993) *Antitrust Report* 3; S. Calkins, 'The October 1992 Supreme Court Term and Antitrust: More Objectivity than Ever' (1994) *Antitrust Law Journal* 327.

[60] At 820 of the judgment.
[61] See A. F. Lowenfeld, 'Conflict, Balancing of Interests and the Exercise of Jurisdiction to Prescribe: Reflections on the Insurance Antitrust Case' (1995) *American Journal of International Law* 42.

applied section 403 of the Third Restatement and the factors therein[62] to the facts of the case and concluded that these factors went against the application of US competition law. According to Justice Scalia, the relevant actions took place primarily in the UK, and the defendants were UK firms whose principal place of business was outside the USA. He thought it was beyond imagination to consider that an assertion of jurisdiction in the case would be reasonable, and therefore it was inappropriate to assume, in the absence of statutory indication to the contrary, that Congress had made such an assertion.[63]

Laying the issue of *claimed* misinterpretation of the Third Restatement by the Supreme Court to one side, the Court's emphasis on the need for a 'true conflict' did not coincide with the specific emphasis it came to place in previous decisions on the importance of taking into account the interests of foreign countries,[64] as well as on the need to carefully inquire into the reasonableness of the assertion of jurisdiction in competition law cases.[65] Furthermore it has been noted that cases had arisen prior to *Hartford Fire* which show that even the existence of a 'true conflict' would not guarantee that there will be no extraterritorial assertion of jurisdiction; especially when substantial effects are found to be produced in US markets or the claimants are US firms in the situation.

Another difficult question the judgment raised concerned the use of what is known as the sovereign compulsion defence.[66] This defence calls for denial of jurisdiction by US courts in cases where an explicit law of another country *compels* the persons committing the anticompetitive acts – who would face sanctions should they not comply – to do so. This is based on the assertion that sovereignty includes the right of a country to regulate commerce within its boundaries; therefore when such country compels a particular practice, firms there have no choice but to obey. In this way, acts of firms are considered to become *essentially* acts of the country concerned. In the USA, the Sherman Act 1890 does

---

[62] For s. 403 and its factors see p. 438 above.   [63] At 819.

[64] See *Doe* v. *United States*, 487 US 201, 218 (1988); *Société Nationale Industrielle Aérospatiale* v. *United States District Court*, 482 US 522 (1987).

[65] See *Asahi Metal Indus. Co.* v. *Superior Ct.*, 480 US 102, 115 (1987).

[66] See *InterAmerican Refining Corporation* v. *Texaco Maracaibo, Inc.*, 307 F. Suppl. (1970); *Mannington Mills Inc.* v. *Congoleum Corp.*, 696 F 2d 1287, 1293 (1979); *Timberlane Lumber Co.* v. *Bank of America National Trust and Savings Association*, 549 F 2d 597 (1976); *United States* v. *Watchmakers of Switzerland* 1963 Trade Cas. (CCH) 70,600 (1962). See also J. J. Leidig, 'The Uncertain Status of the Defence of Foreign Sovereign Compulsion: Two Proposals for Change' (1991) *Virginia Journal of International Law* 321.

not confer jurisdiction on US courts over acts of foreign countries. By its terms, it prohibits only anticompetitive practices of natural persons and firms. In the judgment itself the requirement of 'true conflict' between local and foreign laws which would translate into a requirement that the conduct in question which is prohibited under the former must be compelled under the latter appears to confuse the exercise of judicial discretion in the context of international comity with the evidence necessary to establish the affirmative defence of foreign sovereign compulsion. Had the UK firms established that their conduct was compelled under UK law, they would have been able to escape the mischief of section 1 of the US Sherman Act by virtue of the foreign sovereign compulsion defence; this would have happened without the need for any analysis of international comity. The majority opinion in *Hartford Fire* leaves open the question whether international comity could require a US court to consider abstaining from exercising jurisdiction in the absence of a true conflict and, if so, under what circumstances.[67]

IV.   Post-*Hartford Fire*

Some of the difficulties raised in the judgment in *Hartford Fire* came to be reflected in its post-case law. In particular that case law was divided on the issue of comity. Some subsequent cases noted that *Hartford Fire* 'did not question the propriety of the jurisdictional rule of reason or the seven comity factors in *Timberlane I*',[68] and in several cases the courts have struck out claims after finding 'true conflicts' with foreign law,[69] whilst in other cases the courts refused to dismiss claims on the basis of international comity.[70] In this respect, it was difficult to judge where *Hartford Fire* has left the principle of international comity within the overall framework of the doctrine of extraterritoriality.[71] Perhaps a good illustration here can be found in *United States* v. *Nippon Paper Industries Co.*[72] The case involved a Japanese firm, Nippon Paper, charged by the

---

[67] See J. P. Griffin, 'Extraterritoriality in US and EU Antitrust Enforcement' (1999) *Antitrust Law Journal* 159.

[68] See *Metro Indus. Inc.* v. *Sammi Corp.*, 82 F 3d 839, 846, (1996) note 5.

[69] See *Filetech SARL* v. *France Telecom*, 978 F. Supp. 464 (1997); *Trugman-Nash Inc.* v. *New Zealand Dairy Board*, 945 F. Supp. 733, 736 (1997).

[70] See, for example, *Caribbean Broad Sys.* v. *Cable and Wireless Plc*, 1998–2 Trade Cas. (CCH) 72,209 (1998).

[71] See J. P. Griffin, 'Extraterritorial Application of US Antitrust Law Clarified by United States Supreme Court' (1993) *Federal Bar News and Journal* 564.

[72] 109 F 3d 1, 8–9 (1997). For a commentary on the case see A. Gluck, 'Preserving *Per Se*' (1999) *Yale Law Journal* 913.

USA with participating in a conspiracy with other firms to fix prices in the USA contrary to section 1 of the Sherman Act 1890. The District Court dismissed the charge and held that criminal prosecution under US competition law could not extend to wholly extraterritorial conduct. On appeal, the Court of Appeals reversed the District Court decision, holding that the US government could prosecute Nippon Paper for conspiring to fix prices in the USA. The Court stated that there was no compelling reason why principles of comity should exempt Nippon Paper from prosecution. According to the Court, a finding in Nippon Paper's favour would encourage firms to use illegal means to influence markets in the USA, rewarding them for erecting as many territorial firewalls as possible between cause and effect.

It is difficult to estimate the far-reaching effect of *Nippon Paper*, especially since the Supreme Court did not give leave to Nippon Paper to appeal. However, it may be appropriate to agree that in the light of post-*Hartford Fire* case law[73] in general, and in *Nippon Paper* in particular, US competition authorities have continued to be zealous in their reliance on extraterritoriality, and comity considerations appear to have had little impact on outcomes in actual cases. This approach by the authorities will be examined further below, but before doing so it would be important to look at one final piece in the jigsaw supplied by two cases: *Hoffman-La Roche* v. *Empagran* and *Intel Corp.* v. *Advanced Micro Devices*.

V.   Hoffman-La Roche v. Empagran

This case arose from the famous vitamins cartel, which was investigated on both sides of the Atlantic, and some of its members, in particular Hoffman-La Roche, were punished severely. The plaintiffs in the case (non-US firms) were selected buyers of vitamins, which were intended to be sold outside the USA. They brought a class action against Hoffmann-La Roche for damages on the ground of a price-fixing conspiracy in breach of the Sherman Act 1890. The US Court of Appeals (Washington DC) – reversing the judgment of the District Court – held that US courts had the authority to hear an action of damages such as the one in question, namely where the plaintiff, defendant and the conduct of the

---

[73] See *United States* v. *Cerestar Bioproducts BV*, 6 Trade Reg. Rep. (CCH) 45,098 (1998); *United States* v. *Heeremac*, 6 Trade Reg. Rep. (CCH) 45,097 (1997) (Case Nos. 4323–4); *United States* v. *Hoffmann-La Roche*, 6 Trade Reg. Rep. (CCH) 45,097 (1997) Case Nos. 4277–8 .

defendant were all foreign; Hoffman-La Roche had sought to contest the action on the ground that the plaintiffs were foreign buyers who had purchased the vitamins in question outside the USA.

This was an important judgment which gave rise to division within the US courts themselves as well as to causing discomfort on the part of foreign countries. The judgment however was appealed to the US Supreme Court and the latter decided to overturn it. Justice Breyer delivered the 'opinion' of the Court; the entire bench, other than Justice O'Conner who did not participate in hearing or deciding the case, agreed with this opinion.

The judgment of the Supreme Court offered a very thoughtful review of relevant previous case law and the Foreign Trade Antitrust Improvements Act (FTAIA) 1982.[74] Considerable emphasis came to be placed on the interpretation that must be given to the wording of the Act and its legislative history in this regard. Importantly, the Court stated in very clear terms that FTAIA came perhaps to limit but not stretch the application of the Sherman Act to foreign commerce. This was a key statement in the whole approach of the Court because amongst other things it cancelled any attempt to give exaggerated weight to the previous case law, which had sought to expand as opposed to limit the extraterritorial reach of the Sherman Act.

The judgment also shows that due regard must be had to principles of public international law and the need to interpret 'ambiguous' US laws in a way that would avoid unreasonable interference with the sovereignty of other nations; in fact a position some US courts came to embrace almost a century before competition law was introduced in the country.[75] The Court explained that this method of statutory interpretation came to caution US courts 'to assume that legislators take account of the legitimate sovereign interests of other nations when they write American laws. It hereby helps the potentially conflicting laws of different nations work together in harmony – a harmony particularly needed in today's highly interdependent commercial world.'[76] Remarkably, the Court acknowledged that the extraterritorial application of US competition rules can interfere with the sovereignty of other countries, but the Court noted with approval that the judicial position of US courts has always been to regard this application as being reasonable and

---

[74] See pp. 447–449 below for an account on this Act.

[75] See *Murray* v. *Schooner Charming Betsy*, 2 Cranch 64 (1804).

[76] See p. 8 of the judgment.

compatible with the principle of comity, in so far as the rules are the result of legislative efforts to deal with harm caused in domestic markets by foreign anticompetitive behaviour. The Court emphasised the harm must be *domestic* however; and this has provided it with the basis to question the validity of an action where the harm was foreign (or even if it had a domestic element as well that element was independent of the foreign harm). The answer given by the Court on this point was in the form of a rhetorical basic question:

> Why is it reasonable to apply this law to conduct that is significantly foreign *in so far as that conduct causes independent foreign harm and that foreign harm alone gives rise to the plaintiff's claim?* We can find no good answer to the question.[77]

The Court felt that offering this view is important to give due weight to the principle of comity and would be a sensible interpretation of FTAIA, a piece of legislation – the Court reflected – that can (and was enacted to) play a major role in enabling the USA to show leadership in ideas and policy formulation in the field of competition law. The Court noted:

> Where foreign anticompetitive conduct plays a significant role and where foreign injury is independent of domestic effects, Congress might have hoped that America's antitrust laws, so fundamental a component of our own economic system, would commend themselves to other nations as well. But if America's antitrust policies could not win their own way in the international market place for such ideas, Congress, we must assume, would not have tried to impose them, in an act of legal imperialism through legislative fiat.[78]

One question that the judgment raised was whether the action in the case would have succeeded had the plaintiffs been the US government and not private. It might be argued that this should make no difference given that the action would still be brought against 'foreign injury', something according to Hoffman-La Roche and the US Solicitor General had never been allowed in US courts. The Court did take note of a number of cases however,[79] in which action on the basis of foreign injury was admissible and it felt that the situation would be different in case the action is brought by the government. It stated:

---

[77] See p. 9 of the judgment; italics in original.   [78] See p. 13 of the judgment.

[79] The cases cited before the Court included three which came before the Supreme Court: *Timken Roller Bearing Co.* v. *United States*, 341 YS 593 (1951); *United States* v. *National Lead Co.*, 332 US 319 (1947); and *United States* v. *American Tobacco Co.*, 221 US 106 (1911).

> A government plaintiff, unlike a private plaintiff, must seek to obtain the relief necessary to protect the public from further anti-competitive conduct and to redress anti-competitive harm. And a Government plaintiff has legal authority broad enough to allow it to carry out this mission ... Private plaintiffs, by way of contrast, are far less likely to be able to secure broad relief.[80]

Another question the judgment seems to have raised is whether an action in these circumstances would succeed where actual domestic effects were produced in the USA as a result of which foreign injury was caused. It is arguable that the judgment seems fairly reliably to indicate that FTAIA would not be interpreted in a way to capture such a situation and as a result the chances for success in such actions appear to be slim.

It is interesting to observe whether, in light of this view by the Court, the judgment actually represents a sufficiently clear 'limitation' being placed on the US exercise of extraterritoriality. Arguably, the Court – whilst right in dismissing the action in question – has left the boundaries of extraterritoriality in the same place as before the action arose.

VI.   Intel Corp. v. Advanced Micro Devices[81]

Advanced Micro Devices (AMD) Inc. brought an action against Intel Corp. which sought the production by Intel Corp. of certain documents relating to competition law proceedings against the firm in the USA: AMD had complained to the European Commission against Intel[82] and was intending to use the relevant documents in the proceedings on the European side of the Atlantic; the Commission had stated its refusal to seek these documents itself. Intel resisted this action on the ground that the documents were at any rate not discoverable in the European proceedings as foreign proceedings; notwithstanding the fact that the European Commission can be considered to be a qualified 'foreign tribunal' for a US court to invoke its discovery powers. Intel relied on the European Commission's apparent concern that US claimants may engage in fishing expeditions when launching such competition actions

---

[80] See p. 14 of the judgment. The Court cited with approval some previous judgments 'in favour' of allowing such government actions, most notably *United States* v. *E. I. Du Pont de Nemours & Co.*, 336 US 316 (1961) in which the Court held that it was 'well settled that once the Government has successfully borne the considerable burden of establishing a violation of law, all doubts as to the remedy are to be resolved in its favour'.

[81] See *Intel Corp.* v. *Advanced Micro Devices, Inc.*, 542 US 241 (2004).

[82] See the Commission's findings following its investigation and the heavy fine imposed on Intel, mentioned in chapter 1, note 18.

in Europe. The Supreme Court however does not appear to have found Intel's arguments convincing. It felt that non-US bodies (including the European Commission) might sometimes be interested in receiving judicial assistance and cooperation from US courts.[83] The Court stated that US courts had the power to examine the nature of the foreign proceedings in question and consider the 'receptivity' of the foreign government or the court or authority abroad to such assistance. The approach taken by the Supreme Court in the case seems to differ from that adopted in *Empagran* in that the majority in the case can be said to have established that it is possible, perhaps preferable, to adopt a case-by-case approach when dealing with such situations as opposed to developing broad or general approach to be applied in different cases concerning the actual scope of US law; the latter approach seems to be the favoured approach in *Empagran* with the Court clearly stating that proceeding on a case-by-case basis was 'too complex to prove workable'.

VII.   The legislative approach

The US Constitution itself clearly provides for government regulation of conduct affecting interstate or foreign commerce, regardless of the place where this conduct occurs.[84] If compared to the 'effects' doctrine formulated by US courts over the years, it would seem that this clause in the Constitution provides a considerably wider basis for extraterritorial assertion of jurisdiction. This wide basis however should not be considered to be unlimited: the fundamental principle of due process – itself recognised in the fifth and fourteenth Amendments to the Constitution – means that any such assertion of jurisdiction would indeed require a minimum link between foreign defendants and US laws or jurisdiction.[85] Nonetheless, the constitutional or legal basis is there for the USA to adopt laws, which has extraterritorial reach.

The USA is one of the very few countries in the world in which the legislature regularly intervenes in the domestic competition law regime to 'improve' the operation of the regime without necessarily leaving it to courts always to take a lead on the matter.[86] Often such intervention is necessary and helpful, though sometimes it may happen that the

---

[83] It is worth noting here the later proceedings in *Re Microsoft* (428 F. Supp. 2d 188, 195–96 (2006)). In this case the District Court emphasised the importance of rejecting an action which may undermine as opposed to 'foster' the cooperation with the European Commission and 'violate established principles of comity'.

[84] See the *Commerce Clause of the Constitution*, clause 3 in Art. 1, s. 8.

[85] See *Burger King* v. *Rudzewicz*, 471 US 462, 476–77 (1985).   [86] See pp. 102–103 above.

intervention goes in the opposite direction. It is of particular interest to inquire which of these opposing outcomes was achieved when Congress decided to intervene in 1982 in the question of extraterritoriality by adopting the Foreign Trade Antitrust Improvements Act (FTAIA).

The enactment of FTAIA came to simplify the operation of the doctrine of extraterritoriality in the field of competition law by setting out the extraterritorial reach of US competition rules.[87] Arguably it was intended to amend the extraterritorial feature of the Sherman Act and as a result leave little room for a judicial role in marking the territorial boundaries of US competition law. As post-FTAIA case law shows however, US courts have continued to play a major role in expanding and narrowing the scope of territorial reach of the Sherman Act and it seems that the particular approach and language used in FTAIA have enhanced the scope for a judicial role. The Act established a uniform test, whereby jurisdiction could only be asserted over conduct that has a 'direct, substantial, and reasonably foreseeable'[88] effect on US domestic or (certain) export commerce. The approach adopted to the issue of extraterritorial jurisdiction under the Act is highly interesting: the Act provides for a specific exclusion of the application of the Sherman Act 1890 'to conduct involving trade or commerce ... with foreign nations', but allows intervention by way of exceptions for conduct that significantly harms imports, domestic commerce, or the trade or commerce of a US export competitor (what is referred to in section 15 of the Act as 'export trade or export commerce with foreign nations, of a person engaged in such trade or commerce in the United States'). FTAIA seeks to remove any doubt that the Sherman Act does not prohibit any anticompetitive behaviour or conduct on the part of US firms engaged in export or US firms engaged in export or other commercial activities occurring outside the USA, as long as the adverse effect in the situation is felt in foreign markets. If effect in the situation is produced within the USA however, the situation will be within the scope of the Sherman Act.

The language and particular approach of *exclusion–inclusion* or literally more accurate *exclusion–exception* of FTAIA however are highly technical, and have been used by parties in competition law actions who believed the wording of the Act was ambiguous to favour their position;

---

[87] The Act amended the Sherman Act 1890 and the Federal Trade Commission Act 1914 in regards to export commerce and wholly foreign conduct, but not with respect to import commerce; see pp. 238–245 above for an account on both Acts.

[88] See s. 6 of the Act.

this happened in *Hoffman-La Roche* v. *Empagran* which we considered in the previous section.[89]

Whilst offering a helpful formulation of the ground on which the doctrine of extraterritoriality may be invoked, FTAIA contributed very little to clarifying the role played by the 'jurisdictional rule of reason' principle, which came to be recognised by some US courts, most notably by the Court of Appeals in *Timberlane I*. Indeed it appears that there was a designed intention for the Act to remain neutral in relation to this principle as can be seen from the legislative history of the Act, which shows the Act was intended neither to prevent nor to encourage additional judicial recognition of the special international characteristics of transactions and that it would have no effect on the courts' ability to employ notions of comity or otherwise to take account of the international character of transactions where a court determines that the requirements of subject-matter jurisdiction were met.[90] In this way, FTAIA appears to fall somewhere in the middle between the two outcomes mentioned above.

A specific legislative recognition of the principle was however given four years later within the Third Restatement of the Foreign Relations Law 1986. Looking at sections 402, 403 and 415 of the Restatement, it is abundantly clear that the Congress adopted a 'jurisdictional rule of reason' type of approach.[91] The Restatement considered that a balancing approach, derived from the principle of judicial comity, was necessary by virtue of principles of public international law.[92]

The case law dealing with FTAIA however shows that the principle of comity has a role to play within FTAIA's framework. How small or large this role is something that can be difficult to quantify because of the 'difficult' nature of the case law. For example in *Hartford Fire*, it seems that the Supreme Court was at difficulty in precisely establishing how FTAIA fitted within the previous case law on extraterritoriality and as a result seems to have given a widened scope to FTAIA while marginalising the principle. In *Hoffman-La Roche* on the other hand the Court seems to have narrowed the scope of FTAIA considerably, giving the principle a particularly large role to play in reaching the conclusion that the action could not succeed.

---

[89] See in particular Part V of the judgment.   [90] See H. R. Rep. No. 97–686 (1982), 10.

[91] See D. T. Murphy, 'Moderating Antitrust Subject Matter Jurisdiction: the Foreign Trade Antitrust Improvements Act and the Restatement of Foreign Relations Law (Revised)' (1986) *University of Cincinnati Law Review* 779.

[92] See p. 435 above.

VIII. Guidelines of the enforcement authorities

The third strand of the examination of the US competition law perspective on extraterritoriality is furnished by the guidance published by the US competition authorities, the Department of Justice, Antitrust Division and the Federal Trade Commission. As chapter 5 showed, these two authorities play a key role in the regime and often their approach to competition law questions is highly influential, though many times lacks sufficient consistency. The approach of the authorities to the question of extraterritoriality offers considerable support in this regard.

To fully understand the authorities' approach, it would be helpful to start with what is now their old approach to extraterritorial application of US competition rules, namely the view held in the late 1970s and early 1980s as reflected in the *Guidelines on International Operations* (1977). At that time, the Department of Justice Antitrust Division's 'official' approach to extraterritoriality was that the main purpose of the doctrine was to protect US export and investment opportunities abroad against private restrictions involving foreign firms in foreign markets. The Guidelines showed the Division's desire to 'protect American export and investment opportunities against private imposed restraints'. In this way, the Division's particular concern was over 'market access' problems: it believed that each US-based firm exporting goods, services or capital should be allowed to compete and not be kept out of foreign markets by some restriction introduced by stronger or less-principled firm(s) operating in those markets.[93] Needless to say, this particular approach to extraterritoriality raised many eyebrows in other countries around the world. Indeed the Division itself at that time had little plausible explanation for why this should be the particular approach to extraterritoriality and hardly any convincing answers for how this approach fitted with even the most outspoken judgment by the courts in favour of extraterritoriality. It is hardly surprising therefore that a few years later the Division seems to have abandoned this concern and came to deploy the consumer welfare objective as the focal point in its use of the doctrine of extraterritoriality and its work in the international arena. This can be seen from the Division's *Antitrust Enforcement Guidelines for International Operations* (1988) in which it stated in unequivocal terms in footnote 159 that:

---

[93] See US Department of Justice Antitrust Division, *Antitrust Guidelines for International Operations* (1988), p. 5.

> Although the FTAIA extends jurisdiction under the Sherman Act to
> conduct that has a direct, substantial and reasonably foreseeable effect
> on the export trade or export commerce of a person engaged in such
> commerce in the United States, the Department is concerned with
> adverse effects on competition that would harm US consumers by redu-
> cing output or raising prices.[94]

Such concern with consumer harm brought the Division to give its
specific reaction to the jurisdictional rule of reason and the test of
reasonableness as established by US courts, namely that in taking enforcement actions against export restraints that harmed consumers in the
USA and its exports, the idea of reasonableness was a matter of 'prosecutorial discretion' rather than law.

Early in the 1990s however footnote 159 was pushed further down and
finally off the page all together: it was repealed. The most recent explanation offered by the Division at that time was that Congress did not intend
US competition law to be limited to cases based only on direct harm to
consumers, arguing that when both imports and exports are of importance to the US economy, the Division would not limit its concern to
protecting competition in only half of US trade. This different line of
policy was later inserted into the *Antitrust Enforcement Guidelines for
International Operations* (1995) adopted jointly by the Division and the
Federal Trade Commission which stated that the authorities may, in
appropriate cases, take enforcement action against anticompetitive conduct, wherever occurring, that restrains US exports, if: first, the conduct
has a direct, substantial and reasonably foreseeable effect on exports of
goods or services from the USA, and secondly, the US courts can obtain
jurisdiction over persons or firms engaged in such conduct.[95] Along this
new line of policy, the authorities agreed to consider legitimate interests
of other countries in accordance with the relevant recommendations of
the Organisation for Economic Cooperation and Development (OECD)
and various bilateral cooperation agreements entered into by the USA
with other countries in the field of competition law.[96] The Guidelines

---

[94] Ibid., footnote 159. See M. Lao, 'Jurisdictional Reach of the US Antitrust Laws: Yokosuka
and Yokota, and "Footnote 159" Scenarios' (1994) *Rutgers Law Review* 821.

[95] See Guidelines (1995), note 73.

[96] Ibid. By way of extension, note 74 of the Guidelines mentions a number of factors which
the authorities would take into account when considering the legitimate interests of
other countries. These factors have been derived partly from previous international
guidelines and partly from the 1991 Cooperation Agreement between the USA and the
EU; for the latter, see pp. 501–505 above.

further explain that the Divisions would take into consideration, as a matter of 'prosecutorial discretion', comity beyond whether there is a conflict with foreign law.[97] The Division has emphasised however that it does not believe that it is the role of the courts to 'second guess' the competition authorities' judgment as to the proper role of comity concerns under such circumstances.[98] Although controversial, such comments seem to make it clear that the USA remains determined to tackle foreign conduct that harms its exports, but would do so only after some account has been taken of any possible reaction by foreign countries to this policy approach.

(B) The European Union perspective

As we saw from chapter 4, the European Union (EU) competition law regime differs in many fundamental respects from its US counterpart; though both regimes also share some important similarities. One of the differences in perspectives has been in relation to the question of assertion of jurisdiction and the 'basis' for application of the competition rules in an extraterritorial context; as will be seen below, one might wonder however whether a real difference of perspective exists here or whether the difference is nothing but a superficial one.

I. The early cases

The issue of whether EU competition law is capable of extraterritorial application arose as early as 1964 before the European Commission, in the case of *Grosfillex*,[99] in which the Commission considered the 'effects' doctrine. In the case the Commission felt that the whole spirit, letter and operation of EU competition rules were actually compatible with such a doctrine: the territorial scope of EU competition law is determined neither by the domicile of the firm nor by where the agreement is concluded or carried out, and the sole and decisive criterion is whether an agreement 'affects' competition within the Common Market or is

---

[97] The Guidelines provide, at p. 20, that as part of a traditional comity evaluation, the Antitrust Division would consider whether one country encourages a certain course of conduct, leaves firms free to choose among different strategies or prohibits some of those strategies. In addition, the Antitrust Division would take into account the effect of its enforcement activities on related enforcement activities of a foreign competition authority.

[98] See pp. 21–22 of the Guidelines.   [99] See *Grosfillex-Fillistorf* [1964] 3 CMLR 237.

designed to have this 'effect'. *Grosfillex* therefore made clear that the Commission embraced fully the doctrine and this position was later confirmed by a statement made by the Commission in its 11th *Report on Competition Policy* in which it referred to *Grosfillex* and stated that it was one of the first competition authorities to have applied the internal effect theory to foreign firms.[100]

II.   *Dyestuffs* and the single economic group

The first occasion that arose for the European Court of Justice (ECJ), the EU's highest to express its view on the matter came as early as 1972 in its *Dyestuffs* judgment.[101] The ECJ however avoided the extraterritoriality question in the case and simply declined to accept the suggestion of Advocate General Mayers to adopt the effects doctrine. Instead it held that jurisdiction should be asserted in this case on the basis of the principle of territoriality by relying on the existence of a single economic group or the 'economic entity' doctrine: because the parent (non-EU) firm enjoyed control over the strategic business behaviour of its subsidiary (EU-based) firm, the participation of the latter in an illegal conduct was attributed to the former. On that basis the ECJ found that Article 101 TFEU[102] applied and it seems to have felt that the question of extraterritoriality was not relevant in the facts of the case.

III.   The 'implementation' of *Wood Pulp*

(a) The doctrine of implementation   However much enthusiasm the Commission seems to have had for a US-style effects doctrine, it later became clear that this enthusiasm was not shared at all by the ECJ. The opportunity to demonstrate this lack of enthusiasm and a strong desire on the part of the ECJ to coin a different doctrine for establishing jurisdiction in competition cases presented itself in the case of *Wood Pulp*.[103]

Wood Pulp reached the ECJ via an appeal action against the decision of the Commission in the case in which it had stated that EU competition law does apply extraterritorially where conduct outside the EU produces

---

[100] See Commission, 11th *Report on Competition Policy* (1981), p. 36. See also *Aniline Dyes Cartel* [1969] 8 CMLR D23, at D33.

[101] See Cases 48/69 etc., *ICI* v. *Commission* [1972] 3 ECR 619; [1972] CMLR 557. See L. Brittan, *Competition Policy and Merger Control in the Single European Market* (Grotius, 1991). See F. A. Mann, 'The *Dyestuffs* case in the Court of Justice of the European Communities' (1973) *International and Comparative Law Quarterly* 35.

[102] See p. 161 above.   [103] [1988] ECR 5193; [1988] 4 CMLR 474.

adverse economic *effects* within it.[104] The Commission thus followed its earlier approach to the question. The ECJ, on the other hand, declined to address this issue, but held that Article 101(1) TFEU would apply where a price-fixing agreement is *implemented* within the EU.[105] This particular statement ushered in an implementation doctrine within the EC competition law regime under which the behaviour or conduct of a non-EC based firm would be caught not on the ground that it produces effects within the EC but simply because it has the effect of implementing the infringement therein through, among others, the firm's own subsidiaries or agents. Clearly one major significance of the ECJ's conclusion is that the ECJ can be said to have rejected the US-style effects doctrine.[106]

(b) **The impact of** *Wood Pulp* One major consequence of the ECJ judgment in *Wood Pulp* was felt in the Commission's decisional practice following in the case in which the Commission seems to have largely – but arguably not exclusively – followed the implementation doctrine. Two particular Commission decisions delivered shortly after *Wood Pulp* can be mentioned as examples to illustrate this. In the first case, *PVC*,[107] the Commission conducted an investigation into an alleged price-fixing cartel in which the Norwegian manufacturer of PVC participated. In asserting jurisdiction in the case – over the actions of this non-EU based firm – and eventually ruling that there was an infringement of

---

[104] At pp. 499–500. For a general discussion of these issues see L. Whatstein, 'Extraterritorial Application of EU Competition Law – Comments and Reflections' (1992) *Israel Law Review* 195.

[105] In contrast to what was said above about the position of the Commission, it has been argued that the ECJ remains dedicated to 'an objective territoriality principle', which requires that a foreign firm engage in a 'consummating act' within the EU in order to extend jurisdiction and to further the goal of single market integration when dealing with competition cases. See J. P. Griffin, 'EC and US Extraterritoriality: Activism and Cooperation' (1994) *Fordham International Law Journal* 353.

[106] See s. 46 of Canada's Competition Act 1986 which states that a 'corporation, wherever incorporated, that carries on business in Canada and that implements, in whole or in part in Canada, a directive, instruction, intimation of policy or other communication to the corporation or any person from a person in a country other than Canada who is in a position to direct or influence the policies of the corporation, which communication is for the purpose of giving effect to a conspiracy, combination, agreement or arrangement entered into outside Canada that, if entered into in Canada, would have been in contravention of section 45, is, whether or not any director or officer of the corporation in Canada has knowledge of the conspiracy, combination, agreement or arrangement, guilty of an indictable offence and liable on conviction to a fine in the discretion of the court.'

[107] (1990) *Official Journal* L-74/1; [1990] 4 CMLR 345.

Article 101(1) TFEU the Commission relied on the doctrine of implementation. In the second case, *LdPE*,[108] the Commission also employed the implementation doctrine to bring an action against several manufacturers of thermoplastic low-density polyethylene for fixing prices and engaging in other forms of collusion. Interestingly, however, the Commission singled out Rapsol, the Spanish firm, because unlike the Austrian, Finnish and Norwegian firms, Rapsol did not 'implement' its agreement in the EU, but rather in Spain, before the latter acceded to the EU: Spain joined the EU in 1986. The Commission stated that this fact did not immunise Rapsol from legal action. Thus, according to the Commission, it was entitled to assert jurisdiction to the extent that Rapsol's involvement in the cartel affected competition within the EU. Hence, it may be observed that the Commission seems to have moved beyond the implementation doctrine, in this particular instance, towards an effects doctrine.[109]

More recently the Commission referred to the implementation doctrine in one of its high-profile cartel decisions, the *Lysine cartel*.[110] In its decision in this case, the European Commission imposed fines totalling €110m on four firms, Archer Daniels Midland (USA), Ajinomoto (Japan), Kyowa Hakko (Japan), Cheil Jedang (Korea) and Sewon (Korea) for operating a worldwide price-fixing cartel during the first half of the 1990s. The firms Ajinomoto and Sewon received a 50 per cent reduction in the amount of the fine for fully cooperating with the Commission and the firms Cheil Jedang and Kyowa Hakko were rewarded with a 30 per cent reduction in their fines because they furnished the Commission with limited evidence, which qualified them for this lenient treatment.

IV.   The Guidelines on effect on trade

The *Guidelines on effect on trade between Member States* were adopted as part of the Commission's Modernisation package in 2004.[111] The Commission provides in the Guidelines that:

---

[108]   (1989) *Official Journal* L-74/21; [1990] 4 CMLR 382.

[109]   Quite interestingly, former (late) EU Commissioner for competition, K. van Miert, seems to have indicated on several occasions that in asserting jurisdiction in extraterritorial situations the Commission will make use of the 'effects' doctrine. See K. van Miert, 'Global Forces Affecting Competition Policy in a Post-Recessionary Environment' (1993) *World Competition* 135.

[110]   See *Amino Acids* (2001) *Official Journal* L-152/24.   [111]   See pp. 163–164 above.

Article 81 and 82 [now Articles 101 and 102 TFEU] apply to agreements and practices that are capable of affecting trade between Member States even if one or more of the parties are located outside the Community. Articles 81 and 82 apply irrespective of where the undertakings are located or where the agreement has been concluded, provided that the agreement or practice is either implemented inside the Community, or produce effects inside the Community. Articles 81 and 82 may also apply to agreements and practices that cover third countries, provided that they are capable of affecting trade between Member States.[112]

V.   Merger cases

All of the cases mentioned in the previous two sections concerned situations of collusion under Article 101 TFEU. The issue of extraterritoriality however also assumes huge significance in the context of other types of business phenomena, principally merger operations. Indeed it can be argued that the question here has a greater significance especially with the existence of an *ex ante* type of regulation of merger operations in many competition law regimes, including the EU regime. The use of this type of regulation – which receives expression in a requirement of mandatory pre-merger notification – can give a competition authority an opportunity to assert jurisdiction over what many consider pure 'foreign mergers'. The issue therefore must be addressed in this context of merger operations and the EU regime in this case furnishes an excellent case study.

(a) **The concept of 'Community dimension'**   The relevant instrument which deals with merger operations in the EU, Regulation 139/2004 commonly referred to as the Merger Regulation, includes in Article 1 a concept of Community dimension. This concept is expressed in the form of turnover thresholds and gives the European Commission the power to assert jurisdiction over merger operations (concentrations), which satisfy the thresholds stipulated in Article 1.

Arguably, the concept of Community dimension gives the Commission the power to exercise almost unfettered jurisdiction over purely foreign mergers, i.e. those operations in which the parties are foreign and non-EU based. This means that the possibility is open for a merger operation to fall within the net of the concept even if there is no *effect* produced within the EU or possibly – although this effect is produced – it is extremely minimal approaching *no-effect*. To many,

---

[112] See para. 100 of the Guidelines, (2004) *Official Journal* C-101/81.

this possibility has already been turned into reality on a number of past occasions and they often cite supporting examples such as: the 1993 Satellite joint venture merger operation between the Japanese firms JCSAT and SACAT; the 1999 joint venture between Nestle Pillsbury and Haagen Dazs;[113] and the (in)famous 1997 merger between US aircraft manufacturers Boeing and McDonnel Douglas.[114] It has been argued that all of these cases without exception make it abundantly clear that an effects doctrine was used; possibly an aggressive form of it especially in the case of *Boeing/McDonnel Douglas*.

An important issue that arises in light of such claims and cases is of course how they can be reconciled with the way in which jurisdiction should according to the ECJ be asserted under the regime: the implementation doctrine itself. Obviously this is a difficult question which one might think reveals that the *doctrine* is possibly not compatible with the operation of an instrument such as Regulation 139/2004, which can only be applied with an *effects* doctrine. Whether this is so is something that needs to be examined.

A special feature of merger transactions as guided by an *ex ante* form of regulation is that when dealing with these transaction a separation must be made between two inherent stages: the first is the stage at which the merger agreement or contract is reached or the merger in the case of a public bid is announced and the second is the one that follows clearance by the competition authority when the merger is *implemented*. What is clear is that Regulation 139/2004 applies to both of these stages. To return to the original question asked above however: does this show that the Regulation is compatible with the ECJ's doctrine of implementation? Answering this question requires a consideration of some of the key merger cases on jurisdiction decided over the years.

(b) *Gencor* v. *Commission* Perhaps the most important example of a merger case dealing with the question of extraterritorial jurisdiction in the EC regime is that of *Gencor* v. *Commission*;[115] not least because the case reached the General Court of the EU (GCEU) and in more than one respect the latter delivered a highly crucial judgment on the issue of extraterritoriality. The case was decided within the framework of the old (and first) Merger Regulation, Regulation 4064/89, the predecessor of the current Regulation 139/2004. This important fact however

---

[113] Case No IV/M.1689 (6 October 1999).   [114] (1997) *Official Journal* L-336/16.
[115] Case T-102/96, [1999] ECR II-753; [1999] 4 CMLR 971.

does not impact on the issue of assertion of jurisdiction in light of the fact that the concept of Community dimension under both Regulations is identical.

Gencor v. *Commission* concerned a proposal to create a joint venture between Gencor, a firm incorporated in South Africa, and Lonrho, a firm incorporated in the UK. At the relevant time, Gencor was active mainly in the mineral resources and metal sectors. It held a stake of 46.5 per cent in Implats, a firm also incorporated in South Africa, which brought together Gencor's activities in the Platinum Group Metal (PGM) sectors. Lonrho, on the other hand, was active in the mining, metals, agriculture, hotels and general trade sectors. It controlled 73 per cent of Eastern Platinum Ltd and Western Platinum Ltd (LPD), both incorporated in South Africa, which brought together Lonrho's activities in the PGM sector. Gencor controlled the remaining 27 per cent of LPD. The proposal was for Gencor and Lonrho to acquire joint control of Implats. As a result of the operation, the shares of Implats were intended to be divided as follows: the public was expected to hold 36 per cent, Gencor 32 per cent and Lonrho 32 per cent. The parties notified their proposed operation to both the South Africa Competition Board and the European Commission. While the former approved the proposed operation, the latter decided to block it because the Commission thought that the operation was incompatible with the Common Market. The European Commission believed that the proposed operation would have created a dominant position as a result of which effective competition would have been significantly impeded in the Common Market.

The case assumed great significance because, among other things, it addressed very important questions with regard to the ability of the Commission to assume jurisdiction in the case and because conflicting decisions on the same facts were reached by two different competition authorities: the Commission and the South Africa Competition Board. The case also witnessed political intervention at a high level by the Government of South Africa in order to persuade the Commission that the operation should be allowed to proceed; although none of the political figures who actually intervened attempted to contest the decision of the Commission or question the legality of its actions. The parties, in particular Gencor, however did not believe that the Commission was entitled to exercise jurisdiction in the case and therefore sought annulment of the decision by the GCEU. In its submission before the latter, Gencor tried to argue that the Commission lacked jurisdiction under the Regulation since the operation was carried out outside the EU. The firm also argued in the alternative that if the Regulation was applicable and the Commission could exercise jurisdiction, this exercise of jurisdiction was unlawful and therefore inapplicable pursuant to Article 277 TFEU (formerly Article 241 EC).

However convincing such arguments may appear to be, the GCEU refused to accept them and dismissed the application for judicial review of the Commission decision accordingly. The GCEU held that the Regulation was in fact applicable to the proposed operation, even if consummated in South Africa. It specifically explained that the jurisdictional thresholds of the Regulation as appear under the concept of Community dimension in Article 1 were consistent with the judgment in *Wood Pulp*. Thus, according to the GCEU it was possible to reconcile between the wording and operation of the concept of Community dimension and the doctrine of implementation: in effect the *implementation* doctrine was equivalent to the turnover thresholds in the Article. The Court emphasised that there was no requirement in Article 1 of the Regulation that the firms concerned must be incorporated or established in the EU or that the production facilities covered by the operation must be carried out within the EU. On that basis, the Court held that the Commission will have jurisdiction in a case such as the one at hand.

Turning to the question of consistency between the Commission's assertion of jurisdiction under the Regulation and international law, the GCEU felt that there was nothing to indicate that such inconsistency did not exist. According to the Court, as a matter of public international law, there could be no objection to the assertion of jurisdiction on the part of the Commission under the Merger Regulation in relation to an operation outside the EC, provided that its *effects* within the EU would be immediate (meaning in the medium term), substantial and foreseeable. The Court explained at paragraph 90 of the judgment that the application of the Regulation is justified under public international law when it is foreseeable that a proposed concentration will have an immediate and substantial *effect* in the Community. The GCEU also opined at paragraph 98 of the judgment that in the case of an operation or transaction which substantially *affects* competition within the Common Market by creating a dominant position, the Commission cannot be prevented from asserting jurisdiction over such operation or transaction by reason of the fact that, in a world market, other parts of the world are affected by the operation or transaction. On the fact of the case, the Court decided that the activities of the firm concerned – although carried out outside the EU – have the *effect* of creating or strengthening a dominant position as a result of which effective competition in the Common Market or in a substantial part of it will be significantly impeded.

Although it had emphasised the compatibility of the concept of Community dimension with the doctrine of implementation, it is obvious that all of these points show that the GCEU in the case clearly departed from the implementation doctrine and embraced that of effects. The parties themselves viewed this as particularly alarming given that in their view, asserting jurisdiction in this manner would be a breach of the doctrine of proportionality. The GCEU's response here however was this was unlikely because on the facts of the case there was no 'genuine conflict'. According to the Court, the South Africa Competition Board only decided that the parties can merge. It neither asked nor *compelled* them to merge and as such a genuine conflict between EU law and South African law did not exist.[116]

(c) *GE, Honeywell* v. *Commission*[117]   Another high-profile merger case on the question of jurisdiction can be found in the failed merger between the US firms General Electric (GE) and Honeywell International. On 3 July 2001, the European Commission decided to block the proposed merger on the ground that this operation would have led to the creation of a dominant position on several markets as a result of the combination of Honeywell's leading positions on these markets with GE's financial strength and vertical integration into aircraft purchasing, financing, leasing and aftermarket services. The Commission held that the merger was incompatible with the Common Market. Later on appeal to the GCEU, the latter on the whole confirmed the Commission's decision.

The merger, however, was cleared in the USA; and this factor contributed to the unprecedented level of publicity and interest the case attracted. Furthermore, the fact that the Commission blocked the merger led to very severe and harsh criticism by the USA of the practices of the European Commission. In particular, the Commission was accused of

---

[116] It may be worth noting an apparently similar approach adopted in *Wood Pulp* in which the ECJ stated that there was no conflict between the positions under US competition law and EU competition law because in the circumstances under the former there was merely an exemption given to US firms under the export cartel exemption mechanism under the Webb-Pomerene Act 1918. Thus according to the ECJ there was no obligation on the firms in question under US law to enter into or operate the cartel which was illegal under EU law.

[117] See Cases T-209/01 and 210/01, *General Electric Company* v. *Commission* [2005] ECR II-5575.

being concerned with the interest of competitors as opposed to consumers, a claim the European Commission has consistently denied.

In substantive terms, the case opened up fresh and serious questions about the differences in the test used at that time on either side of the Atlantic when deciding whether to clear or block a merger. In the USA, the test which is in use – contained in section 7 of the Clayton Act 1914 – is that of 'substantial lessening of competition' (SLC). According to this test, a merger will be prohibited if it will lead to SLC. In the EU, on the other hand, the test that was used is that of creating or strengthening a dominant position as a result of which competition will be significantly impeded in the Common Market or in a substantial part of it.[118] The test is commonly referred to as the 'dominance' test. This particular test however was modified under Regulation 139/2004 and clarified considerably: in particular by converting the question of dominance from being the sole scenario to the main scenario. The new test is therefore of significant impediment to effect competition in particular as a result of the creation or strengthening of a dominant position.

Beyond substantive issues, the decision in *GE/Honeywell* is also important given that it seems to have marked a continuation of the Commission's approach to asserting jurisdiction in merger cases in which none of the firms involved are incorporated or have their production facilities within the EU – as has been witnessed under previous decisions, most notably *Gencor* v. *Commission*. For this reason, and others, the decision is a remarkable one.

(C) Comments on the EU and US perspectives

Considering the European Commission's own approach to the question of extraterritoriality, it is very arguable that this approach, corresponds precisely with the US' understanding of appropriate jurisdiction and with the US' understanding of the effects doctrine. The Commission's decisions in the landmark merger cases discussed above – along with the judgment of the GCEU in *Gencor* v. *Commission* – only confirms that this is the case. At one level, one might welcome this consistency of approach to one of the most difficult issues in the international competition law sphere. As the US and EU experience succinctly demonstrates the doctrine of extraterritoriality is very much alive and there appears to be no indication – not in the slightest – that the position is likely to change in

---

[118] See Art. 2 of (old) EC Regulation 4064/89.

the future. At another level however, the particular kind of use that has come to be made of the doctrine on both sides of the Atlantic may well be seen as controversial, often being quite an aggressive pursuit of foreign situations and at any rate within the two regimes individually it is a use that has lacked sufficient consistency.

Looking at the position in the EU first, it is clear that whilst the Commission has shown it is willing to move closer to the position of the USA,[119] the ECJ has shown its reluctance to endorse such a move and so far seems to have remained committed to territorial requirements. The gulf between the ECJ and the Commission here may be seen as damaging to the Commission's assertion of jurisdiction and may invite speculations that the doctrine plays a very weak role within the EU regime.[120] It is unlikely to be true that the doctrine plays a weak role in the regime however as can be seen from the field of merger control. Nonetheless, the 'development' of the doctrine seems to be wrapped up with some uncertainty. For example, it is difficult to judge the exact reason for the apparent rejection by the ECJ of the effects doctrine: whether it was motivated or related to the ECJ's commitment to the goal of market integration, to which it accords primacy;[121] whether it feels that US-type solutions are not necessarily sensitive or suitable to conditions within the EU; or whether the ECJ has not really needed to make a finding on this matter in its judgments on the topic, in particular *Dyestuffs* and *Wood Pulp*. The approach of the ECJ is nonetheless problematic given that the ECJ has not completely ruled out the possibility that the effects doctrine could be used in the application of EU competition law.[122]

---

[119] See P. M. Roth (ed.), *Bellamy & Child: European Community Law of Competition* (Oxford University Press, 2008); K. Stockman, 'Foreign Application of European Antitrust Laws' (1985) *Fordham Corporate Law Institute* 251; K. M. Messen, 'Antitrust Jurisdiction Under Customary International Law' (1984) *American Journal of International Law* 783; J. F. Bellis, 'International Trade and the Competition Law of the European Economic Community' (1979) *Common Market Law Review* 647.

Some writers have argued that the Commission has supplemented its integration agenda with the US notion of comity. See B. Pearce, 'The Comity Doctrine as a Barrier to Judicial Jurisdiction: a US–EU Comparison' (1994) *Stanford Journal of International Law* 525.

[120] See A. J. Himmelfarb, 'International Language of Convergence: Reviving Antitrust Dialogue Between the United States and the European Union With a Uniform Understanding of "Extraterritoriality"' (1996) *University of Pennsylvania Journal of International Economic Law* 909.

[121] See chapter 4.

[122] See W. D. Collins, 'The Coming of Age of EC Competition Policy' (1992) *Yale Journal of International Law* 249.

The apparent lack of full harmony in approach between the ECJ and the Commission can also be seen with regard to the issue of comity between nations. The general approach adopted by the EU seems to show respect for the principle of international comity, and the EU has acknowledged the OECD Recommendations on the matter.[123] As we saw in chapter 3, these Recommendations state that member countries recognise the need to give effect to the principles of international law and comity and to use moderation and self-restraint in the interest of cooperation in the fight against anticompetitive practices. The Commission however does not seem to embrace this view unconditionally: it has made clear that the assertion of jurisdiction does not give way to international comity in the application of EU competition law where EU law does not require the foreign firms concerned to act in breach of their domestic law and its application does not adversely affect the important interests of a third country. In any case, according to the Commission, the interests of third countries must be so important in order to prevail over the fundamental interest of the EU in maintaining a system of undistorted competition throughout the common market.[124] Unlike the Commission, the ECJ has offered a limited explanation regarding its position on international comity. Over the years, it has only occasionally touched on the issue. In the case of *IBM*, for example, in response to the argument of IBM that the Commission should have considered international comity before initiating its proceedings and formulating its decisions, the ECJ held that the Commission need not do so.[125] This brevity of the ECJ in dealing with the matter can also be seen in light of *Wood Pulp*. In the judgment, the ECJ devoted only a few lines to its position regarding the application of international comity, holding that in relation to the argument on disregard of international comity, it was sufficient to observe

---

[123] See p. 138 above.

[124] See *Aluminum Imports from Eastern Europe* (1985) *Official Journal* L-92/1, p. 14. In the case, the Commission seems to have implicitly recognised that in certain cases EU fundamental interest of ensuring undistorted competition has to give way to comity considerations.

  Former Commissioner for Competition, Sir Leon Brittan stated that the Commission considers itself obliged to have regard to comity when exercising its jurisdiction in competition cases involving foreign elements. See Brittan, p. 16, note 101 above.

[125] Cases C-60/81 and 190/81, *IBM* v. *Commission* [1981] ECR 2639, 2655. According to Griffin this even suggests that the ECJ considers international comity an issue within the Commission's discretion, at least in facts similar to *Wood Pulp*, i.e. the challenged conduct was not compelled by foreign law as the remedy does not require the firms to act in any way contrary to their national law. See Griffin, pp. 358–9, note 105 above.

that it amounted to calling into question the EU's jurisdiction to apply its competition rules to conduct such as that which was found to exist in that case and that, as such, that argument had already been rejected.

Turning to the GCEU judgment in *Gencor v. Commission*, the particular account by the GCEU on the question of assertion of jurisdiction may seem to be confusing. Even if it were to be accepted that in its judgment the GCEU upheld the doctrine of implementation, the fact that much of its account is worded using the language of effects would be considered to be contradictory. In fairness however perhaps the explanation should be that the GCEU seems to have created a structure for assertion of jurisdiction in merger cases which consists of two different levels: at the first, procedural level the GCEU seems to have held that this carries the doctrine of implementation whereas at the second, substantive level the GCEU seems to have introduced the effects doctrine. But this approach can give rise to problems especially in light of the generous margin of discretion the Commission enjoys here and given the fact that this means that in the case of foreign mergers the Merger Regulation would apply (and the Commission will be able to assert jurisdiction) even in absence of any *effects* produced by such operations. Obviously problems would not arise in two different situations: at one end of the spectrum, where the foreign merger produces no effects within the EU and does not satisfy the notification thresholds in Article 1 of the Merger Regulation; at the other end of the spectrum, where the merger operation produces effects and does fall within the scope of Article 1 of the Regulation. The difficulty however concerns the group of situations that fall somewhere in the middle between these two extremes: where the operation produces no effects but does satisfy the notification thresholds. The GCEU seems to have recognised this group of situations though it felt that this does not constitute a problem given that according to the GCEU it was necessary for the Commission to receive a notification in order to determine the existence or absence of effects within the EU. In other words the road to the second level of substantive appraisal and the 'effects' doctrine was via the first level of procedural matters and the doctrine of 'implementation'. One might wonder however whether this type of approach satisfies the doctrine of proportionality, which the EU recognises and respects. Indeed, the EU position here would appear to be questionable when compared with the US position, which accepts an exemption for foreign mergers in certain cases.

It is worth asking where has the judgment of the GCEU in *Gencor v. Commission* left the question of extraterritoriality. An answer to the question however does not seem to be readily available. On the one hand, there can be no question that the European Commission or another competition authority should be entitled and able to control problematic and harmful merger operations even if doing so through recourse to the doctrine of extraterritoriality. As we noted before, the problem (if one exists) can be seen as residing in the actual doctrine. On the other hand, the use of the doctrine has been expansive and in some cases controversial. So perhaps *Gencor* v. *Commission* has left the question in need of further clarification by the EU courts; it would be sensible to suggest here that this clarification may be provided by the EU courts embracing a 'reasonableness' approach to the question, namely taking into account not only the interests of foreign countries under the umbrella of a 'jurisdictional rule of reason', but also the interests of merging parties themselves who often face considerable uncertainty and costs when their merger operation is subjected to multi-jurisdictional review. Indeed at this juncture one may reflect on the perceived difference between the case of purely foreign and purely-EU wide mergers. In relation to the former, being caught within the purview of Article 1 of the Merger Regulation often means having to obtain the regulatory approval of an *additional* competition authority – not necessarily a desirable prospect. In relation to the latter however, coming within the scope of Article 1 of the Regulation can have enormous benefits, chief among which is the highly desirable prospect of possibly having to obtain the regulatory approval of *fewer* competition authorities.

A more important issue relates to how the Commission will act in cases which are not covered under the implementation doctrine. It is of interest to see whether the Commission will remain faithful to the implementation doctrine, whether it will utilise the effects doctrine in those cases or whether it will rely on the positive comity principle as covered in the EU–US bilateral agreement.

The USA, on the other hand, has come to build a particularly strong experience and reputation as a formidable advocate of promoting extraterritoriality. This can be evidenced through developments occurring within the three branches of: jurisprudence, legislation and guidance by the Antitrust Division and the Federal Trade Commission. These developments within the different branches however have shown that the USA's position on extraterritoriality does not seem to be entirely consistent, as more than one standard appears to have emerged in the application of the doctrine.[126] For example, one standard that has emerged within the first

---

[126] See V. D. Sharma, 'Approaches to the Issue of Extra-territorial Jurisdiction' (1995) *Australian Journal of Corporate Law* 45.

branch is the common law test of whether, in the light of international comity concerns, jurisdiction should be exercised on the particular facts. In this context, it would be useful to reflect on the impact of *Hartford Fire*. The Supreme Court in *Hartford Fire* adopted a wide formulation of the extra-territorial scope of US competition law. It has been argued that in doing so, the Supreme Court has ignored the limits placed on the US jurisdiction by public international law. Moreover, it has forgone the opportunity to place the US approach to extraterritoriality upon the same principles as those which underpin other competition law regimes in the world, in particular the EU regime. It may be appropriate here to contrast this approach with that of the European Commission and the GCEU in cases such as *GE/Honeywell* and *Gencor* v. *Commission* which seem to have brought the EC position on extraterritoriality closer to that of the USA.

The second standard that has emerged under the regime for assertion of extraterritorial jurisdiction is the 'direct, substantial, and reasonably foreseeable' test of the FTAIA, under which the position is not clear with regards to whether comity considerations are always taken into account as an adequate substitute for the criteria of 'direct, substantial, and reasonably foreseeable'. These criteria appear to focus exclusively on establishing a sufficiently close link with the USA to justify the assertion of jurisdiction, without reference to international comity.[127] Finally, one may identify a third standard which appears to be a cocktail standard. This has emerged in the enforcement authorities' guidance on the topic. For example, in the *Antitrust Enforcement Guidelines for International Operations* (1995) the US competition authorities make it clear that they will continue to assert jurisdiction under the effects doctrine in accordance with both *Hartford Fire* and the 'direct, substantial, and reasonably foreseeable effect' test under the FTAIA. On the other hand however, they seem to have signalled some willingness to seek to cooperate with competition authorities in other jurisdictions

---

[127] It has been argued that the nature and intensity of the US' interest in regulating extra-territorial conduct cannot alone determine the proper limits on extraterritorial jurisdiction. See 'Predictability and Comity: toward Common Principles of Extra-Territorial Jurisdiction' (1985) 98 *Harvard Law Review* 1310, 1320 (Notes section). See also Messen, pp. 784–5, note 119 above, stating that this was exactly the view adopted in *Timberlane Lumber Co.* v. *Bank of America*, 549 F 2d 597 (1976), which established that although a country may have jurisdiction whenever a sufficient number of connecting factors are present, it should nevertheless refuse to exercise jurisdiction if the regulatory interests it is pursuing are outweighed by the interests of one or more foreign countries, who are likely to be seriously injured by the assertion of such jurisdiction.

to address cross-border anticompetitive behaviour.[128] Nevertheless, the 1995 Guidelines make it clear that the possibility of a unilateral action by the US competition authorities is not ruled out, especially in cases where foreign countries fail to take action or take only inadequate action to address anticompetitive behaviour of private firms, which the USA condemns within its boundaries.

The existence of different tests may cause inconsistency and lack of uniformity in how US competition law and policy in relation to extra-territorial assertion of jurisdiction will develop;[129] as we have noted and as the various cases discussed above amply illustrate, this has already been happening. Indeed it may be said that the real difficulty with the use of the doctrine of extraterritoriality in the US regime is not so much the aggressive pursuit of it rather the lack of inconsistency and clarity in approach which are crucial to enable other nations, their competition authorities, courts and firms to understand the ambit of the US doctrine and its functioning in practice. Looking at *Alcoa*, for example, it can be said the Supreme Court did not establish that, when applying US competition law extraterritorially, actual effect in the USA must be proved; rather the Court seems to have suggested that it would be sufficient in such cases to show 'intent' to produce such effect. This cannot be said to have been maintained in post-*Alcoa* decisions, in which the focus was placed more on effect than on intent.[130] In these decisions some US courts clearly stated that the Sherman Act can catch conduct occurring in foreign markets 'but only when the conduct has an effect on American commerce'.[131] More recently in *Hartford Fire*, the Supreme Court seems to have developed an integrated approach when it reinstated the issue of 'intent' whilst also referring to actual effect. The Court stated that 'it is well established that the Sherman Act applies to foreign conduct that was meant to produce and did in fact produce some substantial effect in the United States'.[132] Whether the Court meant to say that both intent and actual effects are required or either of these would be sufficient is something that many consider open to debate.

---

[128] See US Department of Justice, Press Release, 'Justice Department Closes Investigation into the way AC Nielsen Co. Contracts its Services for Tracking Retail Sales' (3 December 1996).

[129] See L. Rholl, 'Inconsistent Application of the Extraterritorial Provisions of the Sherman Act: a Judicial Response Based Upon the Much Maligned "Effects" Test' (1990) *Marquette Law Review* 435.

[130] See *Dee-K Enterprises, Inc.* v. *Heveafil Sdn. Bhd.*, 299 F.3d 281, 288 (2002).

[131] See *Matsushita Elec. Indus.* v. *Zenith Radio Corp.*, 475 US 574, 582 n.6 (1986).

[132] At p. 796.

Moreover, the particular use of extraterritoriality as displayed in *Hartford Fire* offers a perfect recipe for triggering conflicts between the US and other nations around the world, including with the EU.

Finally, it may be appropriate to end the reflections here with several comments on the scope of the differences and similarities between the developments on either side of the Atlantic. Perhaps the most obvious point of distinction relates to the effects and implementation doctrines.[133] Any practical importance of the distinction between anticompetitive conduct outside the EU 'implemented' within it and the 'effect' of such conduct seems to be limited to a few, rare cases. This preference towards limiting the areas of application of the implementation doctrine has been expressed by some commentators who have argued that it was necessary for the EU to exclude certain competition law prohibitions from its jurisdictional purview, if the implementation doctrine was to remain consistent with the expressed will of the ECJ to assert jurisdiction on the basis of the territoriality principle.[134] Still, it is not very clear which areas should be included and which should be excluded in this case. It has been recommended that anticompetitive practices, such as refusal to buy from, or supply to, firms established within the EC, should be covered under the implementation doctrine,[135] whilst others have argued that this would stretch the current jurisprudence of the ECJ. A second difference to be identified between the two regimes concerns the issue of comity: the EU and the USA do not share

---

[133] It may be of interest to observe in this regard the view expressed by the US Antitrust Division that the 'implementation' test adopted in the ECJ usually produces the same result as the US effects doctrine employed in the USA. See *Antitrust Enforcement Guidelines for International Operations* (1995).

Against this, it has been argued that this view cannot be accepted, since the ECJ has consciously rejected the effects doctrine. See P. Torremans, 'Extraterritorial Application of EU and US Competition Law' (1996) *European Law Review* 280; W. Van Gerven, 'EC Jurisdiction in Antitrust Matters: the *Wood Pulp* Judgment' (1989) *Fordham Corporate Law Institute* 451.

In practice, the ECJ's notion of 'implementation' will be sufficient to catch most agreements concluded outside the EU which seriously harm competition within it; however, there may be some cases which would not be caught under the 'implementation' doctrine, but would be under the 'effects' doctrine: for example, a refusal by non-EU firms to supply goods or services to EU firms.

[134] Alford, p. 36, note 12 above.

[135] See T. Christoforou and D. B. Rockwell, 'European Economic Community Law: the Territorial Scope of Application of EEC Antitrust Law' (1989) *Harvard International Law Journal* 195; J. P. Santos, 'The Territorial Scope of Article 85 of the EEC Treaty' (1989) *Fordham Corporate Law Institute* 571.

the same concept of comity principles. Such differences in perspective of the EU and the USA raise a number of issues and difficulties concerning their respective positions and the furtherance of competition law in the international realm. In relation to the former, it may be anticipated that differences between the two regimes will impact on their positions with respect to their relationship. For example, in the bilateral cooperation agreement between them, whilst the comity rights granted in Articles V and VI of the agreement apply to both parties, it seems that the benefits to both parties will be disproportionate in light of the differences in their approach to extraterritoriality and the issue of comity. In relation to the latter, the differences between the two regimes exemplify the difficulties that are bound to appear in both the interaction between competition policy and public international law and in bringing the EU and US systems of competition law closer together which, in turn, will have a major impact on the internationalisation of competition law.

With regard to similarities, a mutual liberal extraterritorial application of competition law between the two regimes does not necessarily mean the elimination of all the difficulties associated with extraterritoriality. Nor does it mean that such a mutually expansive scope for the laws of one jurisdiction will be free of friction. However, taken in parallel with the above description of the extraterritorial reach of US competition laws, the ruling by the GCEU in *Gencor* v. *Commission* and the decision of the Commission in *GE/Honeywell* make it clear that there is a particular need to seek ways towards a meaningful internationalised competition law, albeit in limited areas, such as mergers.

6. Responses to extraterritoriality

Understanding the doctrine of extraterritoriality requires more than an examination of its foundation under public international law and its use under different competition law regime. Doing just that would no doubt help in understanding the doctrine, but that understanding will be incomplete. A crucial component in ensuring a complete understanding of extraterritoriality is the reaction the application of the doctrine by certain countries has triggered on the part of other countries. It would be safe to say that over the years there have been a number of these reactions, some of which were particularly vehement and perhaps the harshest reactions came in response to the US reliance on the doctrine. The USA seems to have been singled out for various reasons. Principally, this has been due to:

its aggressive pursuit in this area on occasions; the relatively high number of cases in which it came to rely on the doctrine; and the perceived disregard on its part of the relevance and importance of other countries' sovereignty and national interests. Objections to extraterritorial assertion of jurisdiction by the USA have in some cases been based on what was seen as an encouragement to other jurisdictions to follow suit and adopt the 'effects' doctrine under their competition law regimes.[136]

Over the years, the number of countries which have 'resisted' the US position on extraterritoriality within the field of competition law has increased piecemeal.[137] A number of countries have developed a particularly strong reputation as advocates against the US use of the doctrine extraterritoriality in the field. This includes one of the USA's closest allies over many years: the UK. UK judges in particular came to develop a remarkable antithesis for what they considered to be an approach by US judges that was a flagrant breach of principles of public international law. The position which the UK has often maintained against the US use of the doctrine was particularly damning in those cases where the US assertion of jurisdiction occurred in relation to what the USA perceived to be foreclosed foreign markets or refusal to adopt US technical standards in those markets. Foreclosure in foreign markets has been recognised in the USA as sufficient to establish the requisite 'effect' for US competition law to apply; occasionally this has been referred to as 'outbound extraterritoriality', which is different from 'inbound extraterritoriality' where the basis for assertion of jurisdiction is effects produced in local markets. According to the UK, such line of policy showed US competition rules being used as a trade policy tool to open markets perceived as closed to US firms – a highly objectionable and inappropriate use of competition law.[138] The UK however has not been the only

---

[136] An OECD Report entitled *Restrictive Business Practices of Multinational Enterprises*, produced in 1977, concluded at para. 120 that at that time 13 competition law regimes had embraced the 'effects' doctrine. Today, the number is considerably higher with many competition law regimes in existence around the world. The doctrine features even in fairly young regimes of some developing countries.

[137] See J. P. Griffin, 'Foreign Governmental Reactions to US Assertion of Extraterritorial Jurisdiction' (1998) *George Mason Law Review* 505. For an account of the position of the Pacific countries vis-à-vis US extraterritoriality see S. W. Chang, 'Extraterritorial Application of US Antitrust Laws to Other Pacific Countries: Proposed Bilateral Agreements for Resolving International Conflicts Within the Pacific Community' (1993) *Hastings International and Comparative Law Review* 295.

[138] Comments of the UK government on the *Antitrust Enforcement Guidelines for International Operations* (1995) December 1994; see J. P. Griffin, 'International

jurisdiction to react in this particular way to the US use of extraterritoriality. In the EU, the European Commission has noted in the past that the *accent* on unilateral action by the USA in the field of competition law was contrary to, on the one hand, the commitment to respect comity principles and, on the other hand, the efforts needed to support international cooperation.[139] Criticisms against the USA have also been made by the Swiss government during the US competition law proceedings against the Swiss Watchmaking Industry.[140] The Swiss government claimed that the application by the USA of its competition law in the case would give rise to treble effect of: infringing the national sovereignty of Switzerland; violate international law; and harm the international relations of the USA.

(A)   The three ways

The exact type and form of responses by certain countries to the use of extraterritoriality by others has been largely guided by the relevant facts of the situation at hand and the particular relationship between the – asserting and responding – countries in question. Over the years, three types of (non-mutually exclusive) responses have come to emerge in this area. These are: diplomatic protest, blocking through statutes and blocking through case law.

I.   Diplomatic protest

Diplomatic protest by foreign governments against extraterritorial application of domestic competition laws has been the most common and immediate reaction; perhaps one could also say the most *diplomatic* type of reaction. On numerous occasions intense diplomatic dialogues, at the highest level, have occurred between different world capitals – often between Washington DC and other capital cities – as a result of extraterritorial assertion of jurisdiction.[141] At the heart of these diplomatic dialogues usually stands the protest that such assertion adversely affected the interests of the countries concerned and amounted to an intrusion

---

Antitrust Guidelines Send Mixed Message of Robust Enforcement and Comity' (1995) *World Competition* 5.

[139] Comments of the European Commission Services February 1995 concerning the *Antitrust Enforcement Guidelines for International Operations* (1995).

[140] See *United States* v. *Watchmaking of Switzerland Information Centre, Inc.*, 133 F. Supp. 40 (1955).

[141] See J. Davidow, 'Extraterritorial Antitrust and the Concept of Comity' (1981) *Journal of World Trade Law* 500; M. Weiner, 'Remedies in international transactions: a case for flexibility' (1996) *Antitrust Law Journal* 261.

into their own domestic affairs. With perhaps extremely few exceptions, there is little evidence available however that these diplomatic protests (and the diplomatic dialogues within which they are usually expressed) lead to any fruition.[142] For this reason, some have questioned the usefulness or effectiveness of diplomatic protest in serving the interests of foreign countries in their extraterritoriality conflicts, particularly with the USA in light of the uncertain position of comity considerations and the role they can be expected to play in the US competition law regime.[143]

II. Responding by legislation

The limited effectiveness of diplomatic protest and the uncertain and unproductive nature of diplomatic dialogues had one specific consequence: it brought certain countries to believe in the need to respond to extraterritorial assertions of jurisdictions by the USA in particular through taking unilateral steps to block what they came to see sometimes as an unacceptable intrusion into matters within their own jurisdictions. One of the options these countries came to pursue in this regard was to erect legal barriers in the form of blocking laws to thwart such intrusion.[144,145] These blocking laws – frequently referred to as blocking statutes – aim at prohibiting (i.e. blocking) acts by persons who are 'subjects' of competition law investigations by foreign authorities from complying with requests or orders issued by the latter. The scope of the prohibition in this case can be extremely wide covering the disclosure, copying, inspection or removal of documents located in the territory of the *enacting* country. Effectively therefore through a blocking law an

---

[142] In some cases diplomatic efforts have been fruitful in the past; see J. R. Atwood, *Antitrust and American Business Abroad* (McGraw-Hill, 1981); M. Sennett and A. I. Gavil, 'Antitrust Jurisdiction, Extraterritorial Conduct and Interest Balancing' (1985) *International Lawyer* 1185.

[143] See below for a discussion on comity considerations.

[144] Case 48/69, *ICI Ltd.* v. *Commission* [1972] ECR 619; [1972] CMLR 557.

[145] See the Ontario Business Records Protection Act 1947, enacted as a result of the discovery order in *In re Grand Jury Subpoena Duces Tecum*, 72 F. Supp. 1013 (1947), the first of such legislation. See also P. C. F. Pettit and C. J. D. Styles, 'The International Response to the Extraterritorial Application of United States Antitrust Laws' (1982) *Business Lawyer* 697; A. J. Carroll, 'The Extraterritorial Enforcement of US Antitrust Laws and Retaliatory Legislation in the United Kingdom and Australia' (1984) *Denver Journal of International Law and Policy* 377. For a good overview of these instruments see A. V. Lowe, 'Blocking Extraterritorial Jurisdiction: the British Protection of Trading Interests Act 1980' (1981) *American Journal of International Law* 257; A. h. Hermann, *Conflicts of National Laws with International Business Activity: Issues of Extraterritoriality* (Howe Institute, 1982).

attempt by a foreign country or its authorities (in this context often the USA) seeking to apply domestic competition rules extraterritoriality would be frustrated and rendered meaningless.

A question that has arisen on occasions is whether adopting a blocking law by a country is a proportionate response to another country asserting its jurisdiction extraterritorially. The concern over such response is that it appears to be a drastic measure and a perfect recipe for triggering a serious conflict between the countries concerned. For example, the asserting country may see this as an offensive move by the blocking country which seeks to deprive it of its 'right' to address situations it deems to be harmful to its interests (including competition in its local markets). It is not clear how convincing this view is, especially since adopting a blocking law shows the kind of desperation that the blocking country feels in the face of what it may regard as a highly intrusive extraterritorial assertion of jurisdiction.

A number of blocking laws came to be adopted by countries over the years. The UK has developed a particularly strong reputation as a blocking country with the adoption of two such laws over the years.[146] The *first* was the Shipping Contracts and Commercial Documents Act 1964, enacted in reaction to the US investigations of the liner conferences. This Act had a fairly narrow scope of application which required demonstrating an infringement of UK jurisdiction. It came to be replaced in part by the *second* Act – the Protection of Trading Interests Act 1980 – which has a considerably broader scope extending to all cases of damage to the commercial interests of the UK;[147] these commercial interests include but are not narrowly limited to the field of competition law. The 1980 Act empowers the Secretary of State to prohibit compliance with foreign measures for regulating or controlling international trade and the supply of any commercial documents or information in response to the requirements of a foreign authority which are outside its jurisdiction.[148] Beyond this prohibition, the Act contains a number of important provisions, some of which have serious implications in practice. These provisions include: section 1 which gives the power to the Secretary of State to issue

---

[146] For an overview see M. L. Novicoff, 'Blocking and Clawing Back in the Name of Public Policy: the United Kingdom's Protection of Private Economic Interests Against Adverse Foreign Adjudications' (1985) *Northwestern Journal of International Law and Business* 12.

[147] See A. K. Huntley, 'The Protection of Trading Interests Act 1980: Some Jurisdictional Aspects of Enforcement of Antitrust Laws' (1981) *International and Comparative Law Quarterly* 213.

[148] See s. 2 of the Act.

orders to a UK person to notify him of orders adopted in foreign jurisdictions which affect international trade or threaten to harm UK trading interests as well as the power to forbid the firms concerned from complying with these measures;[149] section 3 which states that a failure to comply with orders under sections 1 and 2 will attract penalties; section 4 which states that in cases where UK sovereignty would be infringed as a result of a discovery process involving a foreign body a UK court should decline any request for assistance by such a body; finally sections 5 and 6 which deal with foreign multiple damages,[150] which according to the former awards of these are not enforceable in the UK and where paid by a UK firm or individual in proceedings against it in the foreign jurisdiction it may launch a UK action – usually referred to as claw-back – to recover any excess above the amount of compensation this firm or individual were required to pay.

It should be clear from the discussion above why the UK's reputation as a resisting country has been particularly strong. Nonetheless other countries have resisted extraterritoriality through blocking laws. A good example can be found in the case of France which introduced legislation that made it a criminal offence to communicate documents relating to commercial or technical matters for use in foreign proceedings, except pursuant to a treaty or international agreement.[151] Other countries which have introduced similar laws include Australia, Canada, South Africa and New Zealand. Some of these countries reinforced their legislation by amending them under the influence of the UK legislation. For example, Australia replaced its previous legislation with the Foreign Proceedings (Excess of Jurisdiction) Act 1984; the same can be seen in relation to Canada which passed its Foreign Extraterritorial Measures Act 1984 and South Africa which adopted its Protection of Business Amendment Act 1984.[152] The year 1984 is of course remarkable because a number of domestic firms of these countries were involved in the

---

[149] See SI 1983/900, the Protection of Trading Interests (US Antitrust Measures) Order 1983.

[150] An example of these is the treble damages award in the USA. See further below.

[151] See Law No. 80–538 16 July 1980, J.O., p. 1799.

[152] See *In re Uranium Antitrust Litigation: Westinghouse Elec. Corp.* v. *Rio Algom Ltd.*, 617 F 2d, 1248 (7th Cir. 1980). See also J. P. Griffin, 'Possible Resolutions of International Disputes Over Enforcement of US Antitrust Law' (1982) *Stanford Journal of International Law* 279; M. Harvers, 'Good Fences Make Good Neighbours: a Discussion of Problems Concerning the Exercise of Jurisdiction' (1983) *International Lawyer* 784; M. Joelson, 'International Antitrust: Problems and Defences' (1983) *Law and Policy in International Business* 1121; D. A. Sabalot, 'Shortening The Long Arm of

investigations and proceedings in the USA in the uranium cartel.[153] Adopting these laws by the countries concerned was considered necessary in order to protect their own firms and their interests.

III.   Responding by case law

The third type of response some countries have deployed to block an aggressive reliance on the doctrine of extraterritoriality by US courts in particular is through case law. Obviously due to its nature, this method would require judicial intervention and action in the resisting country. In comparison to the second method of blocking laws, this particular method has one key advantage: it affords the resisting country the opportunity to avoid engaging in diplomatic wars or political confrontation and to claim that the action in this case is purely a 'discourse' between the judges of the two countries.

Under this method, the UK has also been a pioneer in blocking efforts. The earliest attempt made by a domestic UK court to derail the extra-territorial application of US competition laws arose in 1952 in *British Nylon Spinners* v. *Imperial Chemical Industries (ICI)*.[154] In the case the UK Court of Appeal ordered ICI not to comply with a court order from the USA, requiring ICI to reassign certain patents to Du Pont.[155] The Court of Appeal disregarded an earlier order by Judge Ryan in an action brought by the US government against ICI[156] to dispose of industrial property abroad because it was said that this constituted an attempt to assert extraterritoriality which UK courts did not recognise.[157] Referring to the statement in Judge Ryan's opinion that it is not an infringement of the authority of a foreign country for a US court to order harmful effects on US trade to be removed,[158] the Master of the Rolls famously stated:

> If by that passage the learned Judge intended to say (as it seems to me that he did) that it was not an intrusion on the authority of a foreign sovereign

American Antitrust Jurisdiction: Extraterritoriality and the Foreign Blocking Statutes' (1982) *Loyola Law Review* 213 (includes table of different states with blocking statutes).

[153] See p. 483 below.

[154] [1954] 3 All ER 88.

[155] *British Nylon Spinners Ltd.* v. *ICI* [1953] I Ch. 19. See O. Khan-Freund, 'English Contracts and American Antitrust Law: the *Nylon Patent* Case' (1955) *Modern Law Review* 65.

[156] See *United States* v. *Imperial Chemical Industries (ICI)*, 100 F. Supp. 504, 592 (1951).

[157] See *British Nylon*, at 24, note 155 above.

[158] See *United States* v. *ICI*, 105 F. Supp. 215, 229 (1951).

to make directions addressed to that foreign sovereign or to its courts or to nationals of that foreign power effective to remove (as he said) 'harmful effects on the trade of the United States', I am bound to say that, as at present advised, I find myself unable to agree with it.[159]

At the time, this particular approach by the Court of Appeal and the Master of Rolls was considered to be an isolated case. However the case of *Rio Tinto Zinc* v. *Westinghouse Electric Corp.* that would arise 25 years later established that this was far from being so.[160] In that case a similar objection to the US extraterritorial approach was expressed, this time by the House of Lords. Lord Diplock submitted that the use by the US government of US judiciary as a means to investigate activities of UK firms taking place outside the USA on the basis that those activities infringed US competition laws amounted to an unacceptable invasion of the sovereignty of the UK.[161] The case was connected to the US investigation into allegations that a cartel was operating in the uranium sector. A request for assistance in the discovery process in the US Court of Appeals was made on the basis of the Evidence (Proceedings in Other Jurisdictions) Act 1975 which the House of Lords rejected because of concerns over improper extraterritorial assertion of jurisdiction. Although the Act lays down an obligation on UK courts to assist where requests for discovery are made, it is possible for the relevant UK court to avoid this by relying on statutory exceptions.

It may be worth noting – in addition to the support UK courts can be said to enjoy from statute in resisting foreign extraterritorial assertion of jurisdiction – that UK courts have discretion at common law enabling them to curtail, among other things, situations where such assertions may be considered to be a possibility. This can be seen from the position taken by the Court of Appeal in *Midland Bank plc* v. *Laker Airways plc*:[162] in this case Laker Airways was ordered to halt its US action against Midland Bank which would have led to US competition law being applied extraterritorially.

---

[159] See *British Nylon*, at 24, note 155 above.

[160] [1978] 1 All ER 434.

[161] Ibid., at 639. For a good discussion of this case see G. J. Newman, 'Potential Havens From American Jurisdiction and Discovery Laws in International Antitrust Enforcement' (1981) *University of Florida Law Review* 240. See also the similar view expressed in the same case by Lord Wilberforce, at p. 448, that 'it is axiomatic that in antitrust matters the policy of one state may be to defend what is the policy of another state to attack'.

[162] [1986] 1 All ER 526.

(B)   Assessing the responses

There are two opposing ways in which the responses to extraterritoriality discussed above can be assessed. On the one hand, it may be possible to argue that looked at within the actual timeframe in question of over 80 years (since the first time the USA made use of the doctrine) the different responses have arisen only infrequently and occasionally. This may bring one to submit that asserting countries such as the USA are unlikely to give particular attention to such responses, the first of which (diplomatic protest) naturally suffers from an inherent limitation of ineffectiveness; diplomatic protest does not get the protesting country that far where the assertion of extraterritoriality is taking place within the domestic courts of the asserting country. On the other hand, one may put forward the view that the USA or another asserting country should take these responses seriously and regard them as a reflection of serious concerns and interests of foreign countries. Especially this must be so in the case of the USA: the responses have come from the USA's closest allies and trading partners and they have been shaped at the highest level, within the judicial and executive branches of these allies and partners. A decision by the USA to take action under its competition laws in situations *beyond* its national boundaries should be sensitive to any potentially negative consequences to both: relations with other countries as part of its foreign policy and its efforts to promote cooperation with US and foreign competition authorities.[163] Over the years, however, this sensitivity has not been clearly demonstrated.

A due regard for the sovereignty and independence of other countries in matters relating to their own trade and national interests requires *restraint* on the part of countries attempting to impose their own laws and methods of regulating economic conditions outside their own territorial boundaries. Whilst countries have an absolute sovereign right to deal with acts committed within their borders which infringe their laws, a desire to apply their laws beyond their boundaries – and even their absolute belief that their own laws and methods are ideal for all jurisdictions – cannot justify an *absolute* assertion of extraterritorial jurisdiction over economic activities involving foreign firms. US President Eisenhower in his first inaugural speech famously spoke of nine fixed principles that must guide the USA in its conduct. The fourth of these

---

[163] See B. Born, 'Recent British Responses to the Extraterritorial Application of United States Law: the *Midland Bank* Decision and Retaliatory Legislation Involving Unitary Taxation' (1985) *Virginia Journal of International Law* 91.

principles he expressed as follows: 'we shall never use our strength to try to impress upon another people our own cherished political and economic institutions'.

7. Comments

The doctrine of extraterritoriality and the way it has developed in the field of competition law has been highly fascinating. Without needing to rehearse some of the points made by way of justification, there should be no argument against extraterritoriality as an idea *per se*; nor perhaps should (but in any case can) there be an argument against its use. The discussion above if anything has shown that the doctrine is well established (and in the field of merger control in particular is inherent) in competition law. Any hope that this position might change in the future is likely to prove unfounded. One ought to be realistic that in the years to come, competition law enforcement is likely to remain extraterritorial in relevant situations; perhaps we might witness an expansion in this regard as more countries enact, and strengthen, their domestic competition laws and new branches of competition enforcement grow: such as that of private enforcement and private actions for damages.

One might however choose to question the manner in which the doctrine has been applied and observe a possible lack of safeguards against its use. In fairness, it is necessary to acknowledge that there is a difficulty associated with extraterritoriality.[164] How serious this difficulty is and whether it calls for serious action to address it very much depends on one's perspective. At one end of the spectrum, one may argue that when balanced against the purpose served by the doctrine (to deal with

---

[164] The literature identifying problems associated with extraterritoriality (and more importantly suggesting solutions to solve these problems) is abundant. See K. R. Feinberg, 'Economic Coercion and Economic Sanctions: the Expansion of United States' Extraterritorial Jurisdiction' (1981) *American University Law Review* 323; M. Dabbah, *The Internationalisation of Antitrust Policy* (Cambridge University Press, 2003), ch. 8; J. M. Grippando, 'Declining to Exercise Extraterritorial Jurisdiction on Grounds of International Comity: an Illegitimate Extension of the Judicial Abstention Doctrine' (1983) *Virginia Journal of International Law* 395; B. Grossfeld and C. P. Rogers, 'A Shared Values Approach to Jurisdictional Conflicts in International Economic Law' (1983) *International and Comparative Law Quarterly* 931; B. E. Hawk, 'International Antitrust Policy and the 1982 Act: the Continuing Need for Reassessment' (1982) *Fordham Law Review* 201; J. Mirabito and W. Friedler, 'The Commission on the International Application of the US Antitrust Laws: Pulling in the Reins' (1982) *Suffolk Transnational Law Journal* 1.

harmful situations that might otherwise escape being caught) the use of the doctrine should be considered to be reasonable; especially since – even in the USA – the use of the doctrine has not been as frequent as many might think and relatively the number of extraterritorial cases has not been particularly high. Extraterritoriality can be a valid basis for asserting jurisdiction, since traditional territoriality rules are inadequate to deal with acts of an economic nature. At the other end of the spectrum, it is arguable that it would be sufficient for the doctrine of extraterritoriality to be applied only on one or a few occasions for there to occur considerable damage in terms of undermining principles of public international law and intrusion into the sovereignty of other nations, not to mention a possible serious derailment of any promising effort towards internationalisation of competition law based on cooperation. Furthermore, there is an objection to extraterritoriality on the ground that it represents techniques of the nineteenth century and so it is not necessarily suitable or even sensitive to conditions and developments of the twenty-first century.

(A)   Extraterritoriality as an act of aggression

At a very basic level, extraterritoriality can be described as a situation in which country A seeks to extend its jurisdiction over behaviour, conduct or transaction occurring in country B. Such an attempt may well amount to a breach both of the law of country B and of international comity, and it may well be viewed by the former as an act of aggression.[165] In the field of competition law – particularly as far as the USA is concerned – this has been an act of judicial aggression.[166] Whether everyone would agree with this assessment however is very much open to debate. Many of the cases discussed in the chapter seem to confirm the existence of a well-established understanding on the part of many courts – both in the USA and the EU – that in the absence of a clear domestic law to the contrary they must apply and enforce the principles of public

---

[165] See D. P. Wood, 'The Impossible Dream: Real International Antitrust' (1992) *University of Chicago Legal Forum* 277.

[166] See *Timken Roller Bearing Co.* v. *United States*, 341 US 593 (1951); *United States* v. *Minnesota Mining and Mfg. Co.*, 92 F. Supp. 947 (1950); *United States* v. *Imperial Chem. Indus. Ltd.*, 100 F. Supp. 504 (1951); *Holophane Co.* v. *United States*, 352 US 903 (1956); *United States* v. *Watchmakers of Switz. Info. Ctr., Inc.*, 1963 Trade Cas. (CCH) 70,600 (1962), order modified, 1965 Trade Cas. (CCH) 71,352 (1965).

international law.[167] One such principle is that the domestic laws of an individual country cannot extend beyond its own territories, except so far as regards its own nationals. The judgment of the ECJ in *Wood Pulp* for example can be cited as an appropriate illustration of how a court recognises that its jurisdictional competence is governed by this (objective) territoriality principle.[168] Some courts in the USA, however, through ignorance or disregard of this principle seem to seek to address the extraterritorial behaviour of foreign firms over which they have obtained jurisdiction according to US rules; on occasions through a misinterpretation of these rules.[169] These cases demonstrate a basic misconception regarding the competence of the courts under public international law, to proceed against foreign firms under their domestic laws. If a country can assume extraterritorial jurisdiction over acts by foreign firms because they have 'consequences' within its territory and because it 'reprehends' such acts, the door will definitely be opened to an almost unlimited extension of this jurisdiction. Clearly, there is a need to know where to draw the line. Therefore, examining the role of law courts seems to be the logical next step in this analysis.

But one must acknowledge that in some cases courts have a duty to establish or approve extraterritorial assertion of jurisdiction generally,[170] including in the field of competition law.

(B) The role of courts

One 'positive' consequence of the developing of the doctrine of extraterritoriality in the field of competition law policy has been highlighting two remotely related things: the lack of sufficient safeguards in use of extraterritoriality by courts and the courts can play in paves the way for achieving harmonisation in the field. In relation to the lack of sufficient safeguards, this can be seen in light of a case like *Empagran*: the judgment of the US Court of Appeal in the case could have had serious

---

[167] See *The Schooner Channing Betsy*, 2 Cranch 64, 118 (1804).

[168] Also courts in Canada (including the Supreme Court of Canada) have upheld the view that there should be a real and significant link between the assertion of jurisdiction and the subject matter. See *Tolofson* v. *Jensen* (1994) SCR 1022, 1049; *Morguard Invs., Amchem Prods., Inc.* v. *British Columbia Workers' Comp. Board* [1993] SCR 897.

[169] See, for example, the interpretation of the US Court of Appeal in *Hofmman-La Roche* v. *Empagran* given to FTAIA 1982.

[170] See Art. 5(XXXV) of the Brazilian Constitution for an example of a duty of jurisdiction on the state.

implications if it was not reversed by the Supreme Court on appeal; a final stage in the judicial procedure in the USA that is not always likely to be reached.

With regard to the issue of harmonisation, the manner in which the US courts have applied the doctrine of extraterritoriality raises several questions with regard to the role of the judiciary in the context of international comity. It is not clear whether it is a proper task for the judiciary to decide extraterritoriality cases in this context.[171] It seems that in practice, US courts have not been completely objective in their analysis, tending to give more weight to domestic than foreign interests.[172] Arguably, it is difficult to expect domestic courts to arrive at an impartial balance between national interests and those of other countries. The balancing of these interests, as may be observed in the case of the USA, is not confined to the discipline of law as such, but seems to take place within the context of other domains,[173] most notably international comity. For this reason, the balancing may in some cases be more a *political* than a legal exercise. Some commentators have argued that such balancing of interest by the courts is neither appropriate nor workable because it requires balancing sensitive political and diplomatic concerns traditionally considered 'non-justiciable'. In the absence of herculean detachment, there is inevitably a risk of a 'home town' decision merely by virtue of the fact that US courts have a different perspective from courts in other jurisdictions.[174]

The use of the doctrine of extraterritoriality within many US courts can also give rise to uncertainty in law and policy, in general, and for firms, in particular; and there seems to be an indication that the practice of the courts in the past has been confusing and contradictory;[175] not to

---

[171] See J. S. Stanford, 'The Application of the Sherman Act to Conduct Outside the United States: a View from Abroad' (1978) *Cornell International Law Journal* 195.

[172] See H. G. Maier, 'Interest Balancing and Extra-territorial Jurisdiction' (1983) *American Journal of Comparative Law* 579; D. W. Bowett, 'Jurisdiction: Changing Patterns of Authority Over Activities and Resources' (1982) *British Yearbook of International Law* 1.

[173] See generally L. L. Jaffe, 'Standing to Secure Judicial Review: Public Actions' (1961) *Harvard Law Review* 1265.

[174] See A. E. Ehrenzweig, 'The *Lex Fori* – Basic Rule in the Conflict of Laws' (1960) *Michigan Law Review* 637.

[175] See J. S. McNeill, 'Extraterritorial Antitrust Jurisdiction: Continuing the Confusion in Policy, Law, and Jurisdiction' (1998) *California Western International Law Journal* 425; J. H. Shenefield, 'Extraterritoriality in Antitrust' (1983) *Law and Policy in International Business* 1109; J. W. Ongman, '"Be no longer chaos": Constructing a Normative Theory of the Sherman Act's Extraterritorial Jurisdictional Scope' (1977) *Northwestern University Law Review* 733.

mention the lack of consistency between courts at different hierarchy in the case.[176] As a result it is understandable why often foreign firms operating outside the USA find it difficult to predict whether their conduct or behaviour may potentially give rise to liability under US competition law.[177] Some of these firms may not feel that US courts are the best forum to address these questions even when they opt for the 'jurisdictional rule of reason' approach. In *Laker Airways*, for example, Laker Airways had serious reservations about the jurisdictional rule of reason because it considered US courts ill-equipped to balance national interests of the USA and those of foreign nations, submitting that such an exercise normally revolves around 'purely political factors which the court is neither qualified to evaluate comparatively nor capable of properly balancing'.[178] The jurisprudence of US courts in general, and the decision of the majority in the Supreme Court in *Hartford Fire* in particular, increases this uncertainty; though the judgment of the Supreme Court in *Empagran* has provided some comfort.[179]

In light of this, it might be worth asking or considering whether it would be better or more appropriate for extraterritoriality questions to be dealt with solely using inter-governmental consultation and negotiation; possibly to leave it to competition authorities.[180] It is fairly safe to say that questions of extraterritoriality should be treated as an

---

[176] *Hartford Fire* and *Empagran* are two cases in point. In the former the District Court had decided in favour of extraterritorial assertion of jurisdiction, the Court of Appeal reversed this, and finally the Supreme Court effectively reinstated the decision of the District Court. In the latter, there was a District Court decision against admissibility of the action, a judgment by the Court of Appeal in favour and finally a judgment by the Supreme Court reversing that of the Court of Appeal.

[177] See also the view expressed by some commentators that there are serious doubts that courts are an appropriate forum for evaluating conflicting national and foreign interests on a case-by-case basis. See Turner, p. 233, note 8 above.

[178] See at pp. 949–50.

[179] Also, note the existence of the treble damages remedy increases the dangers in US litigation, hence the enhanced risk for foreign firms. See below.

[180] Former Australian Attorney General P. Durack once argued that law courts should not decide on the justification of law and policy in extraterritoriality conflict, stating that in this kind of conflict an important matter is the question of the impact of the conflict upon foreign relations which is not justiciable, as it falls within the realm of diplomatic negotiations. See P. Durack, 'Extraterritorial Application of US Antitrust Law and US Foreign Policy', address before the ABA Section of International Law (12 August 1981), Library of Congress, File 1055; J. L. Snyder, 'International Competition: Towards a Normative Theory of United States Antitrust Law and Policy' (1985) *Boston University International Law Journal* 257.

international as opposed to national competition law issue and that as a result the matter is really a manifestation of a policy conflict between countries. In such cases, it is more appropriate to resolve any conflict that might arise through means of consultation and negotiation. It is thought that if the courts in one country seek to resolve the conflict in favour of that country by invoking domestic competition law, this may not be seen entirely as an application of the rule of law but rather a pure policy drive – albeit in judicial guise – in favour of promoting national interests.[181] In an area which is the juxtaposition of law and politics, it is doubtful whether judges are in the best position to assess the impact that any decision they make will have on foreign relations.[182] Furthermore, there is always the risk that this would compromise their independence. If the national legislature has not given a clear signal regarding its aim to regulate activities beyond national borders,[183] it is questionable whether courts are justified in interfering.[184]

Another important advantage of confining extraterritoriality questions to the medium of competition authorities is flexibility. Among other things, a competition authority handling the question may feel particularly encouraged to consider the ability of other competition authorities to deal with anticompetitive acts committed beyond its own

---

[181] Support for this point can be found in the case of *Laker Airways* v. *Sabena*, 731 F 2d 909 (1984).

[182] See D. G. Blair, 'The Canadian Experience' and M. R. Joelson, 'The Department of Justice's Antitrust Guide for International Operations' in J. P. Griffin (ed.), *Perspectives on the Extraterritorial Application of US Antitrust and Other Laws* (ABA, Section of International Law, 1979). Interestingly, some US courts have shed some doubt on the competence of the courts to handle issues of this nature. See *In re Uranium Antitrust Litigation*, 480 F. Supp. 1138, 1148 (1979).

[183] It has been argued that if the US Congress has not expressed its views on the matter, US courts in dealing with the extraterritorial scope of US competition law should proceed on the presumption that Congress did not intend to violate principles of international law. See generally Trenor, note 59 above.

The case of *Baker* v. *Carr*, 369 US 186, 198–200 (1962) seems to establish that a court should refrain from dealing with an action based on a federal statute unless the prohibition constituting the subject matter of the action has been declared unlawful by Congress. See W. L. Craig, 'Extraterritorial Application of the Sherman Act: the Search for a Jurisdictional Standard' (1983) *Suffolk Transnational Law Journal* 295.

[184] It is interesting to observe the attitude of the US Court of Appeals in the *Uranium* case, where the Court described the foreign countries, despite the encouragement of the US Antitrust Division to them to submit their arguments to the US courts, as 'surrogates' for absent defendants, adding that 'shockingly to us, the governments of the defaulters have subserviently presented for them their case against the exercise of jurisdiction'. *In re Uranium Antitrust Litigation*, at 1256, note 152 above.

484 INTERNATIONAL AND COMPARATIVE COMPETITION LAW

boundaries and within the latter's jurisdiction, before it should seek extraterritorial enforcement of its own competition laws.[185] The authority would also be in a good position to examine whether its concerns can be addressed more effectively by its counterparts in other jurisdictions. There seems to be sufficient evidence in recent times showing some developments – including within the US competition law regime – mirroring such a proposal, albeit to a limited extent.[186] For example, the *Antitrust Enforcement Guidelines for International Operations* (1995) make it clear that the US authorities *may* consult with interested foreign countries to attempt to eliminate anticompetitive effects in the USA instead of bringing their own enforcement actions. There is no doubt that this is a helpful position to adopt, not only for the purposes of dealing with extraterritoriality cases as they may arise in practice but also for the purposes of enabling mutual trust and confidence between competition authorities to flourish. This is also bound to have long-term positive effect in terms of paving the way for bilateral cooperation. Ironically, the disadvantages of extraterritoriality are one reason why considerable emphasis has been put in recent years on the development of mechanisms for bilateral, regional or even global cooperation between countries in the field of competition law.

Against these arguments, however, stand other arguments supporting a judicial involvement in the context of extraterritoriality and comity.[187] In particular, it has been noted that analysing comity considerations is a proper exercise for the courts and that the involvement of foreign elements or foreign relations does not *ipso facto* render the courts incompetent to deal with the matter. It has also been said that it should not be supposed that a case touching or concerning foreign relations lies beyond judicial cognisance.[188] In fairness, this view carries substantial merit. Nonetheless, it would be sensible to advocate in this case that greater weight should be given by US courts to principles of international

---

[185] See D. A. Valentine, 'Building a Cooperative Framework for Oversights in Mergers – the Answer to Extraterritoriality Issues in Merger Review' (1998) *George Mason Law Review* 525.

[186] See C. G. Lytle, 'A Hegemonic Interpretation of Extraterritorial Jurisdiction in Antitrust: From *American Banana* to *Hartford Fire*' (1997) *Syracuse Journal of International Law and Commerce* 41.

[187] See S. A. Burr, 'The Application of US Antitrust Law to Foreign Conduct: has *Hartford Fire* Extinguished Considerations of Comity?' (1994) *University of Pennsylvania Journal of International Business Law* 221.

[188] See *Baker* v. *Carr*, 369 US 186, 211, 211–12 (1962).

law, in particular the principle of international comity to enable them to resolve conflicts of extraterritoriality in a more objective manner without tipping the balance in favour of national interests and national firms at the expense of interests of other countries and their firms. Such view therefore calls for a more careful balance of interests exercise to be undertaken by US courts.[189] Within this exercise, courts should take into account interests of foreign countries beyond the confines of national laws and policy goals.[190] As a result, it would be expected that fewer intrusions into the sovereignty of other countries would arise and this would ensure more respect for the principles of public international law, such as those aiming to safeguard non-intervention in the affairs of other countries by one country.[191]

When entertaining or putting forward such thoughts caution is needed however because of the unique nature of cases in the field of competition law which in respect of different jurisdictions many times concern local markets, which have their own characteristics. This means that the approach adopted in one jurisdiction concerning a particular case (such as settling this case) may not necessarily be possible to take into account when the competition authorities or courts in another jurisdiction formulate their own approach in the same case.

(C)   Viable alternatives to extraterritoriality

It is fairly clear from the examination of the US and EC experience on the topic that extraterritoriality may be used in two scenarios: the first is where the foreign situation produces effects within the domestic markets of the asserting country and the second (the controversial one) is where the asserting country through the doctrine attempts to deal with foreign situations it perceives as hindering the access of its national firms to foreign markets.[192] Whilst as we noted there is probably no scope for

---

[189] See generally E. Rosic, 'The Use of Interest Analysis in the Extraterritorial Application of United States Antitrust Law' (1983) *Cornell International Law Journal* 147.

[190] See the proposal suggested by some writers for the courts to substitute juridical factors of *forum non conveniens* for political decision-making in resolving extraterritorial antitrust cases; see Sandage, pp. 1707–14, note 39 above.

[191] See the *Uranium* case and *US* v. *General Electric Co.*, 170 F. Supp. 596 (1959).

[192] See J. C. Farlow, 'Ego or Equity? Examining United States Extension of the Sherman Act' (1998) *Transnational Lawyer* 175.

arguing in favour of eliminating the doctrine, one may propose other effective means to take its place. One alternative means could be to employ trade policy to deal with the second scenario mentioned here, namely, market foreclosure stemming from anticompetitive behaviour taking place beyond national boundaries.[193] The merit of this suggestion lies in the fact that if implemented competition law would not be used at all. Thus, any problem concerning the gathering of necessary evidence, the existence of a suitable remedy and the possibility of jurisdictional conflict would not arise. The matter in this case will be left in the hands of trade agencies who will be able to undertake empirical analysis and market access evaluation into foreign market restraints. Indeed, a suggestion along these lines has come from the heart of US competition law practice with some competition law practitioners arguing that such an inquiry would help identify large markets where there are few or no imports, identify where there are no exports from one major country to another and identify where persistent and dramatic price differentials exist between markets.[194]

Although very attractive, such a proposal seems to be problematic in many ways. In addition to the confusion that may be added to the roles of competition and trade policy, imbuing trade agencies with what effectively is a competition law task does not seem to be appropriate. Apart from the lack of expertise of trade agencies in competition law matters, it is likely that this would complicate competition law enforcement itself and result in uncertainty. On the other hand, whilst it would be appropriate to recommend involving trade and competition policy experts in transnational competition policy matters, it is less appropriate to suggest the exclusion of the latter.[195] The International Competition Policy Advisory Committee (ICPAC)[196] in its report argued against applying the trade methodology to practices of firms beyond US borders.

---

[193] Chapter 11 deals with competition and trade policies with respect to market access-restraining private anticompetitive behaviour.

[194] See Report of the International Competition Policy Advisory Committee (ICPAC) (2000), p. 249. See pp. 487–491 for ICPAC and its report. Note that a similar proposal seems to have come from some firms. The Eastman Kodak Co. proposed during 1999 that an independent body make a finding that a restrictive practice is taking place on foreign markets and thus constitutes a hindrance to market access; this will then be used as a presumption on the part of antitrust authorities that it is necessary to initiate an enforcement action. See www.kodak.com.

[195] See further chapter 11.   [196] See pp. 266–267 above.

ICPAC stated there is a risk that firms operating within the USA and others in foreign markets will be subjected to different standards with the consequence being adverse for the latter. The report also warned of the risk that applying different standards would trigger parallel actions by other countries, something that US firms are very certain to contest.[197]

(D) Extraterritoriality in most exceptional circumstances

In view of the difficulty with the proposal in the previous section to suggest possible alternatives to extraterritoriality in some instances, it would be worth asking whether a suggestion could be put forward to confine the assertion of extraterritoriality to exceptional circumstances. These circumstances could be when it will be first apparent that there is a link between the anti-competitive behaviour taking place beyond national boundaries and the commerce of a country and the conditions of competition therein and secondly, only in the absence of the ability of other competition authorities to deal with the matter themselves.[198] Thus, extraterritorial application of competition law in this instance should be confined to cases in which cooperation with other competition authorities is not possible. This would present an improvement on previous positions adopted by the USA under which the USA applied its competition laws to foreign activities that had a 'direct, substantial, and foreseeable' anticompetitive effect on its commerce regardless of whether the activities in question were sanctioned by other competition authorities or not.

However it would not be fair to say that US courts have not taken on board the interests of other countries at all. Arguably, they have and this can be seen in light of the different devices[199] created over the years,

---

[197] See ICPAC, p. 251, note 194 above. See, however, the *MCIWorldcom/Sprint* case ((2000) *Official Journal* L-300/1) for a good example of real cooperation between the USA and the EU, with the USA leaving EU matters to the European Commission to handle.

[198] See *United States* v. *Watchmaking of Switzerland Information Centre, Inc.*, 133 F. Supp. 40 (1955).

[199] For a good discussion of these instruments see J. P. Griffin, 'United States Antitrust Law and Transnational Transactions: an Introduction' (1987) *International Lawyer* 307; P. Areeda and L. Kaplow, *Antitrust Analysis: Problems Text, Cases* (Little Brown, 1988).

including (in addition to the principle of comity and the jurisdictional rule of reason): the act of state doctrine;[200] the sovereign immunity;[201] and the foreign sovereign compulsion defence.[202]

However, a proposal in favour of extraterritoriality in exceptional cases has limitations. It is very doubtful whether other countries would regard such a proposal as sufficient to address their extraterritoriality concerns, even in light of the fact that the assertion of jurisdiction in this case is occurring in the most exceptional circumstances. Furthermore, more than one claim can be made against the adequacy of defences such as the foreign compulsion defence. It seems to be very odd and inappropriate for a country to try to get other countries to regulate their domestic economy by 'compulsion' especially when the former is in favour of reducing public intervention in the marketplace. Such an attempt amounts to an intervention in the way the latter countries elect to operate their socio-economic systems and to handle their domestic affairs.

In addition to the criticism just made, the defences seem to be applied in a political rather than a legal context. Consequently they seem to be, in essence, discretionary 'politically oriented' devices. US courts appear to have the discretion to attach relative weights to every factor considered under each device and then weigh them against one another. To complicate matters even further, the US Department of Justice has insisted that US courts should refrain from the use of comity in order to dismiss actions brought by US competition authorities. According to the US

---

[200] Under the act of state doctrine, US courts would refrain from questioning the legality of acts adopted by other countries within their jurisdiction. This is because a sovereign country is bound to respect the independence of every other sovereign country and the courts in one country will not sit in judgment on the acts of a government of another country done within its own territory. See *Underhill* v. *Hernandez*, 168 US 250 (1897). See also D. Gill, 'Two Cheers for *Timberlane*' (1980) *Swiss Review of International Competition Law* 7.

[201] Under the sovereign immunity defence, a country should not be made a defendant in US courts with regard to its political activities, as opposed to commercial activities. See *The Schooner Exch.* v. *M'Faddon*, 11 US (7 Cranch) 116 (1812). See also H. C. Pittney, 'Sovereign Compulsion and International Antitrust: Conflicting Laws and Separating Powers' (1987) *Columbia Journal of Transnational Law* 403. In the USA, Congress enacted the Foreign Sovereign Immunities Act 1976, which gives US courts exclusive responsibility to decide when a foreign sovereign is entitled to immunity in US courts. Note that recently US Congress narrowed the immunity in 1976 by establishing that immunity does not extend to the commercial activity of foreign governments; see the Foreign Sovereign Immunities Act 1998.

[202] For comments on the sovereign compulsion defence see p. 488 above.

Antitrust Division, if the Division decides to pursue a competition law action, it amounts to determination by itself that the interests of the USA should be given priority over the interests of any foreign country and that the challenged conduct is more harmful to the USA than any injury to foreign relations that might result from the competition law action.[203] As we noted above,[204] this is in line with the stance the Division has continued to maintain that when it comes to determining the reasonableness of assertion of jurisdiction in cases of export restraints harmful to US consumers, reasonableness was a matter of 'prosecutorial discretion' rather than law.

Thus, although it seems an attractive way to minimise conflicts of extraterritoriality, in practice, this 'conflict of laws' proposal seems to fall short of reaching the desirable end of avoiding or minimising such conflicts. Indeed in *Empagran* the Supreme Court touched on such a possible approach and came to conclude that it would not be workable:

> The Sherman Act covers many different kinds of anticompetitive agreements. Courts would have to examine how foreign law, compared with American law, treats not only price fixing but also, say, information-sharing agreements, patent-licensing price conditions, territorial product resale limitations, and various forms of joint venture, in respect to both primary conduct and remedy. The legally and economically technical nature of that enterprise means lengthier proceedings, appeals, and more proceedings – to the point where procedural costs and delays could themselves threaten interference with a foreign nation's ability to maintain the integrity of its own antitrust enforcement system ... How could a court seriously interested in resolving so empirical a matter – a matter potentially related to impact on foreign interests – do so simply and expeditiously?[205]

Two points may be made in response to this particular view by the Supreme Court however. First, though one may appreciate the difficulty outlined by the Court, suggesting that US judges should also look at the relevant laws of foreign countries[206] is not just to advocate an exercise in judicial reciprocity or an attempt to establish a lowest common denominator in extraterritoriality. Rather, it is to argue that the judiciary should

---

[203] See Guidelines (1995), note 167.   [204] See pp. 450–452 above.

[205] See judgment at p. 12.

[206] See G. Quinn, 'Sherman Gets Judicial Authority to go Global: Extraterritorial Jurisdictional Reach of US Antitrust Laws are Expanded' (1998) *John Marshall Law Review* 141.

develop common international standards and promote harmonisation in the extraterritorial application of competition laws. Secondly, surely at this point in the development of competition law internationally, at a time when more and more countries are instituting competition law regimes with rules aimed at similar types of conduct, the judiciary in all countries should acknowledge that the question of applying their domestic laws to conduct entered into outside their national territories by firms not located in that territory cannot be answered purely by an analysis of the national law. Just as anticompetitive conduct of foreign firms can have an effect in a country's territories, so too can judicial decisions in the country affect persons and conditions outside it.

(E)   Abandoning treble damages

The final strand of reflections on the doctrine of extraterritoriality concerns the treble damages remedy, which has been unique to US competition law. Treble damages is in many cases considered to be three times more crucial than public enforcement in the US competition law regime. This remedy sits at the heart of the private enforcement branch within the regime and its perusal requires no prior action by the enforcement authorities; in some jurisdictions, injured parties may bring their own legal action but only after the country in question has condemned the conduct and even in those jurisdictions in which this is not the case private enforcement of any kind has been rather scarce.

The existence of the treble damages remedy under the US regime has given rise to a tension in the relationship between the USA and other countries.[207] The view held by several countries has been that it is not particularly appropriate for their national firms to be liable in treble damages in cases before US courts, especially since actions in these cases do not infringe their own domestic competition rules. This tension has been recognised by the US Supreme Court itself in its recent decision in *Empagran* as a point of illustration of how competition law regimes differ dramatically; though the Court offered no view on the remedy or the role it should play in the regime other than to recognise the arguments of those for and against the remedy. In the proceedings before the Court a

---

[207] See Report of the American Bar Association Sections of Antitrust Law and International Law and Practice on *The Internationalization of Competition Law Rules: Coordination and Convergence* (1999), pp. 21–2.

number of foreign countries made strong submissions against[208] treble damages which essentially argued that this remedy supersedes their national policy decisions, can potentially facilitate interference with the way they choose to regulate their markets, enable their firms to bypass their domestic scheme of remedies and undermine their own enforcement policies by discouraging cartel participants from 'confessing' to foreign competition authorities about their cartel arrangements in return for prosecutorial leniency.[209]

Despite the almost continuous protest over the years, the USA has maintained that the treble damages remedy is a useful means of combating domestic and foreign anticompetitive behaviour and for this reason it has emphasised that there is no consideration of abandoning this remedy. The reasons for this particular stance have been highlighted by ICPAC. First it noted that US competition law makes no distinction between 'domestic' and 'foreign' defendant firms against whom the remedy might be eventually ordered. Furthermore, whilst it is recognised that removing the treble damages remedy in export restraint cases might result in fewer conflicts with the laws of other countries, such a move would also reward jurisdictions that have consistently been against the extraterritorial application of US competition law. According to ICPAC, such an approach would result in foreign defendant firms gaining better treatment under US law than US defendants and could open floodgates regarding whether the offending conduct harmed 'imports' commerce or 'export' commerce. In ICPAC's view the case law record shows that a distinction between the two situations may itself be very difficult to make; most of the cases included claims involving both situations. The conclusion by ICPAC therefore was that in spite of the potential benefits from increased cooperation from foreign authorities and firms, it is not advisable to alter the treble damages remedy.[210]

---

[208] There were submissions made in favour of treble damages however primarily by economists.

[209] See, for example, the Briefs submitted by Canada, Japan and Germany in the case. In relation to the point about leniency, there is considerable truth in such argument which can be seen in light of the changes the European Commission came to introduce to its cartel leniency programme in December 2006. For the European Commission leniency notice see p. 164 above.

[210] See ICPAC, pp. 247–8, note 194 above. Further reasons for retaining the remedy are that it underpins 95 per cent of competition law litigation in the USA and is circumscribed by the antitrust injury requirement established in certain US cases which means that plaintiffs may only recover if they suffer losses flowing from the anticompetitive act

Regardless of how compelling this explanation is, the use of the treble damages remedy in some cases may be highly problematic. This includes situations where the remedy is employed to address restraints by foreign firms that may impede access by US firms to foreign markets. For example, though the authorities in the USA have begun to consider principles of comity before applying US competition rules extraterritorially, there is no obligation on private firms to do so.

Thus the question of whether abandoning the treble damages remedy would be considered a positive step forward is a relevant one to ask especially since not everyone (other than foreign governments) seems to be in favour of the remedy.[211] One of the reasons why abandoning treble damages is considered to be important is that although actions brought to claim such damages seem to advance the public policies enshrined in competition law, they actually represent personal interests as opposed to the public interest. These actions stand in complete contrast to public actions, which are brought in the name of the public interest. Hence, private parties have no responsibility to balance a broad range of public interest on whether they should initiate an action. It is not beyond logic to even suggest that private parties may intentionally contribute to widening the difference between their own country and other countries in antitrust policy in order to enhance their chances of receiving a favourable judgment. To this end, it seems that abandoning the treble damages remedy would be an effective way to minimise extraterritoriality conflicts. Nevertheless, it is difficult to force upon countries the elimination of treble damages, because public international law has no scope of application with regard to the way in which a country elects to organise its own economic, legal and political orders. It can only interfere in cases of competition law conflicts between countries, though even here the various cases on extraterritoriality show how limited if at all likely to occur such intervention may be.

The problem of extraterritoriality cannot be solved merely by jurisdiction or comity rules, whether judicial or of any other type. The problem is

itself. Hence, for example, if there was a firm thought to be failing but not in actual fact failing and a market leader merges with it, then another firm could not claim treble damages for subsequent losses arising from this merger as it had not suffered any competition law injury as such.

[211] See Rosenthal and Knighton, p. 88, note 4 above. However, other writers are not particularly optimistic about abandoning private treble damages. See J. Davidow, 'Treble Damage Actions and US Foreign Relations: Taming the "Rouge Elephant"' (1985) *Fordham Corporate Law Institute* 37.

far more considerable than that. It seems that an increase in bilateral and multilateral negotiations between countries in the field of competition law is required to resolve these issues.[212] Closer forms of cooperation between countries and their competition authorities should be fostered. The situation will only deteriorate if countries continue to exchange court orders and blocking statutes. The amount of animosity and friction produced by this issue can have very serious implications for relations between countries and effective efforts towards cooperation between them in the internationalisation of competition law. This problem needs to be solved in the most effective and expedient way possible.

---

[212] See L. Anderson, 'Extraterritorial Application of National Antitrust Laws: the Need For More Uniform Regulation' (1992) *Wayne Law Review* 1579.

Chapter 9

The bilateral option: cooperation between competition authorities

The focus of this chapter will be on bilateral cooperation between competition authorities: what can be termed the bilateral option. The mechanism of bilateral cooperation can be considered to be an old one in the field of competition law and a considerable amount of literature has been written on the topic. Among other things, the chapter will consider the different types of bilateral cooperation and their use in actual cases. The chapter will provide a critical analysis of the strategy including a look at its advantages and disadvantages and consider some examples of bilateral agreements that have come to be concluded over the years. The chapter will conclude with a look towards the future in order to consider possible directions for developing bilateral cooperation and offer a policy perspective in this respect.

1. Bilateral cooperation 'through' extraterritoriality

The previous chapter demonstrated, among other things, that the doctrine of extraterritoriality – regardless of its 'rights' or 'wrongs' as an option – is one means of international enforcement in the field of competition law. However it is a means that has serious limitations: even if one were to imagine a world built on extraterritoriality, the doctrine can be explosively problematic and is not necessarily capable of offering a solution to a perceived competition problem. Most notably, the doctrine suffers from serious limitation at the enforcement level. Ultimately, a country asserting extraterritorial jurisdiction would want to ensure that it would be able to enforce the finding reached in the case, whether by its judiciary or competition authority(ies). Experience in the field however shows that enforcement is not always guaranteed, unless cooperation would be forthcoming from the home competition authority of the firms in question or the authority in whose jurisdiction the assets of the firms are located. An example in point here is furnished by the

Rabies-Vaccines[1] merger case which was investigated by the US Federal Trade Commission (FTC). This case concerned the acquisition of the French firm, Connaught by Institute Merieux of Canada. Despite identifying competition concerns in the case, the firms had no assets in the USA and so the FTC needed the *cooperation* of the Canadian Competition Bureau in the circumstances. The shortcomings and problems of extra-territoriality – as exposed by this particular case and in the discussion in the previous chapter more widely – highlight and demonstrate the need for cooperation; particularly bilateral cooperation.

2.   Meaning and types of bilateral cooperation

It would be useful to consider the meaning of bilateral cooperation and the different types of bilateral cooperation which have emerged over the years. Bilateralism is an *evolving* concept that is conditioned by different developments both from within and outside the field of competition law. Moreover the exact meaning of the concept very much depends on the context in which it is used and the aim or objective sought behind bilateral cooperation. For this reason, it would be important to consider – in addition to the meaning and types of bilateral cooperation – the aims and objectives standing behind this form of cooperation.

(A)   Meaning of bilateral cooperation

The traditional meaning given to bilateral cooperation in the field of competition law has revolved around the existence of a bilateral cooperation agreement between *two* jurisdictions. It is true that such agreements – especially those incorporating a positive comity principle[2] – have become the dominant form of bilateral cooperation in the field in recent years. However, the term bilateral cooperation should be understood in a considerably wider sense than this in order to capture *all* situations in which the competition authorities of two jurisdictions are able to coordinate their activities, cooperate in various ways to enhance their respective enforcement efforts and strive to eliminate any risk of conflict in their lines of work. This cooperation can be achieved with or without a formal mechanism for cooperation, meaning with or without a formal agreement between the jurisdictions concerned. Bilateralism can be achieved in a

---

[1] Case No. 891 0098, 55 Fed. Reg. 1614 (1990).
[2] See pp. 498–499 below for an explanation of the concept of positive comity.

variety of ways, other than on the basis of a specific formal cooperation agreement, for example through: informal or *de facto* positive comity cooperation; free trade agreements; general economic cooperation agreements; association and partnership agreements;[3] and even links established with entire regions (such as the Euro-Med and Neighbourhood Agreements entered into between the European Commission and Mediterranean countries).[4] All of these types have enormous importance in practice and have actually contributed towards advancing competition law globally through bilateral mediums. Such interpretation of bilateralism can be said to go well beyond the traditional, narrow meaning of the term. However this wider interpretation is being and should be adopted specifically because the term is not at all traditional; nor is it in fact to be narrowly understood.

(B)   Types of bilateral cooperation

Under the narrow definition of bilateralism, three types of situation are usually identified, namely: agreements with positive comity; agreements with negative comity; and 'de facto' cooperation. These three types of cooperation will be discussed in turn. What unites these types is that they are situations of cooperation which are competition-specific; however as we noted in the previous section, under a wide definition of bilateralism other types of cooperation can be identified which are not competition specific: in these cases the competition law element is one element of a wider cooperation agreement or framework. These situations will be described briefly below.

I.   Agreements with negative comity: first generation agreements

The concept of comity was mentioned repeatedly in the previous chapter in the context of 'international comity'. Essentially, the concept means – to use the definition of an English language dictionary – mutual civility or courtesy shown by different sides. In the field of competition law, the concept was first developed in the context of bilateral cooperation around this definition. This therefore gave it the connotation of 'negative' comity: two parties showing mutual good manners, moderation and self restraint.

---

[3] See pp. 208–222 above for an account on the association and partnership and cooperation agreements entered into by the European Commission.
[4] See pp. 378–380 above.

The incorporation of this particular concept into formal cooperation agreements between countries made them first generation agreements.

It is unclear when the concept of negative comity in the context of bilateral cooperation in the field of competition law was actually coined, though the first occasion on which it was used in the context of a formal bilateral agreement arose in 1976 when the USA and Germany signed their *Antitrust Accord*;[5] other such agreements later emerged, such as the *US–Australia Agreement* 1982[6] and the *US–Canada Memorandum of Understanding* 1984.[7]

Generally, a bilateral agreement with negative comity provides that one party to the agreement should seek to take into account the important interests of the other party and notify the latter when its enforcement activities may have an impact on those important interests. The idea is that the 'other party' would not in this case be or is not in a position to conduct its own investigation. Thus, an investigation will be launched by one party only and this should normally be the party with the superior or more reasonable 'right' to assert jurisdiction, the main objective here being to prevent jurisdictional conflicts.

There is a mixed feeling in the field about the real value of negative comity agreements. On the one hand, these agreements offer an excellent forum for competition authorities to consult with each other and to exchange particular views on competition issues whether generally or as they arise in the case at hand. This forum for consultation may also include annual meetings between the officials of the competition authorities concerned intended to address conditions under which the parties will offer assistance to each other and possibly appropriate circumstances under which they may agree to coordinate their enforcement activities. Some people would argue, in addition, that these agreements have the potential to promote the flows of trade and investment between countries through enhancing market access and enhance the enforcement of

---

[5] *Agreement between the US and Germany Relating to Mutual Cooperation Regarding Restrictive Business Practices* (23 June 1976).

[6] *Agreement between the US and Australia Relating to Cooperation on Antitrust Matters* (23 April 1997); the agreement was reinforced in 1999 by a mutual enforcement assistance agreement.

[7] *Memorandum of Understanding between Canada and the US as to Notification, Consultation and Cooperation with Respect to the Application of National Antitrust Laws.* This Memorandum of Understanding was superseded in 1995 by the *Agreement between the US and Canada Regarding the Application of Their Competition and Deceptive Marketing Practices Laws* (23 April 1997).

competition law globally. On the other hand, it is unclear to what extent such forum is actually suitable to achieve the main aim behind such agreements, namely to resolve jurisdictional conflicts in particular due to their lack of binding force and fairly loose language, which tends to cloud the whole framework of the agreement with ambiguity.

II. Agreements with positive comity principle

In contrast with negative comity agreements, bilateral agreements incorporating a positive comity principle represent a second generation of bilateral cooperation agreements, which arguably came to emerge due to the inadequacy of the former agreements coupled with an increase in the complexity of competition law practice and enforcement, and an increase – in parallel – in the trust and confidence competition authorities came to develop between them. Positive comity agreements rest on a *positive* mechanism of actions, through which cooperation between competition authorities can be facilitated. The idea underlying this positive mechanism is quite simple to express: one party to the agreement (known as the requesting party) can ask the other party (known as the requested party) to address anticompetitive behaviour within the latter's boundaries which has effect on the interests of the former. The concept of positive comity therefore differs from that of negative comity in the context of bilateral cooperation in the sense that in the former situation the parties *do not* pursue a minimum objective of preventing jurisdictional conflicts which is the cornerstone of negative comity cooperation. The positive nature of comity here requires *positive actions* to be taken by the parties to achieve cooperation and offer reciprocal assistance within the framework of their agreement. These positive actions include – very crucially – a renunciation by one party of its right in favour of the other party, who would normally be in a better position to conduct an investigation in a given case.

Positive comity agreements have become far more common in the field than negative comity agreements although they have been purely a 1990s phenomenon. Several of these agreements have come to be concluded mainly by the EU and USA among themselves as well as with many other countries. This includes – perhaps the most famous example of such agreements – the US–EU agreement entered into in 1991 and followed by the second cooperation agreement signed in 1998; the US agreements with Brazil, Canada,[8] Israel, Japan

---

[8] Previously, the parties also entered into a cooperation agreement in 1995.

and Mexico entered into in 1999; the EU–Japan agreement; and EU–Canada agreement.[9]

The proliferation of positive comity agreements in the field of competition law has contributed to the huge significance the concept has come to acquire leading in particular to its utilisation in actual cases.[10] Nonetheless, to what extent the existence of these agreements actually influences the natural tendency of the relevant competition authorities not to take into account the effects of their decisions on the interests of other countries remains somewhat difficult to quantify. A positive comity agreement would be most useful in situations involving 'pure conflict' between competition authorities and it seems it is in these cases that recourse to the agreement would be made. It may be sensible to suggest however that the mechanism should be used within a broader context, including where a minimal conflict might arise as well as where a conflict is not likely; a use in fact that has been seen in the cooperation between the US and EU competition authorities in merger cases.[11]

III.   *De facto* cooperation (using primarily positive comity)

The final form which the mechanism of bilateral cooperation can take and that has arisen at times resides in what can be described as the *de facto* cooperation. The main scenario here is one in which a positive comity principle is used. In the absence of a formal cooperation agreement – whether competition specific or general – between two jurisdictions, it may still be possible for the competition authority in one jurisdiction to make for example a positive comity type of referral to the authority of another jurisdiction. Such a possibility has turned into a reality on a number of occasions, most famously in the *Kodak/Fuji*

---

[9] An agreement has also been entered into with Canada. See *Cooperation Agreement between Canada, the EC and the ECSC* (1999) *Official Journal* L-175/49; [1999] 5 CMLR 713.

[10] For example, a cooperative enforcement agreement between Canada and the EU provides for reciprocal notification and cross-border requests for enforcement action. Under the agreement, each side is required to take the other's interests into consideration. In addition to placing a high degree of emphasis on traditional comity, the agreement provides protection for the confidentiality of information collected during the enforcement process. Another example is the agreement reached between the USA and Israel, which provides for enforcement cooperation and coordination, notification of enforcement action and confidentiality protections. See the *US–Israel Agreement Regarding the Application of Their Competition Laws* (15 March 1999).

[11] See pp. 512–514 below.

case which is examined in detail in chapter 11. *Kodak/Fuji* arguably opened the door – despite the strong disagreement between the USA and Japan in the case – to formalising the cooperation between them which eventually happened in 1999, when they entered into a cooperation agreement for the enforcement of their competition laws. The agreement includes provisions on notification of enforcement and positive comity. Under this agreement, one party will inform the other of its enforcement activities and will consult with the other on matters arising under the agreement. However, the agreement does not strictly provide for a rigorous enforcement of the Japanese Anti-Monopoly Law 1947. Instead, the agreement was expected to be implemented in accordance with the existing laws of each party, which meant that the likely effect was surrounded by some uncertainty.[12]

IV.   Cooperation within a wider framework

A number of situations may be identified in which bilateral cooperation in the field of competition law exists within a wider framework of cooperation, whether a free trade agreement, general economic cooperation agreement or another type of agreement (such as association and partnership and cooperation agreements).[13] A number of examples of such situations can be found. Many free trade agreements contain competition chapters with commitments expected of the parties that vary from introducing competition law to specific cooperation along negative and positive comity lines. Such agreements – even when they have limited relevance in the field of competition law – are widely considered to be effective vehicles for facilitating specific competition bilateral cooperation agreements; some of them even explicitly provide for concluding such agreements.[14]

A particularly high-profile example of competition cooperation within a wider framework is the Australia–New Zealand cooperation which will be discussed below.

---

[12] See *Agreement Concerning US–Japan Cooperation on Anticompetitive Activities* (7 October 1999).

[13] See pp. 208–222 above.

[14] See, for example, the free trade agreements entered into by Singapore with Korea and Australia. The agreement with Korea provides in Art. 15.6 that '[w]ithin six (6) months from the coming into effect of [the Singapore Competition Act 2005], the Parties shall consult with a view to making a separate arrangement between their competition authorities regarding the scope and content of co-operation and co-ordination'.

3. Some case studies on bilateral cooperation agreements

Whilst it is important to 'categorise' bilateral cooperation in the manner done above, it would be crucial to offer some case studies as examples of bilateral cooperation in practice. In this section this will be done in relation to formal bilateral cooperation, focusing in particular on positive comity agreements; the same will be done in chapter 11 in relation to *de facto* bilateral cooperation.[15]

Perhaps the two most high-profile examples of positive comity bilateral cooperation agreements are the *EU–US cooperation* and the *Australia– New Zealand cooperation*. These examples represent situations of bilateral cooperation in a competition-specific and wider sense and would make highly interesting case studies. They are described and discussed in this section; in addition to the Canada–US and UK–US cooperation.

(A) The EU–US positive comity cooperation

There are a number of reasons why the bilateral cooperation between the EU and USA in the field of competition law is extremely important to study. Perhaps sitting at the apex of these reasons is the fact that the EU and US competition law regimes – as emphasised in this book – are the world's most important regimes with a well-established record of cooperation. The fact that perhaps the most important conflicts in competition decisions have concerned these two regimes nothing but enables such reasons to mushroom. Many in the field of competition law regard the EU–US cooperation as the most obvious example of bilateralism.

I.   The 1991 and 1998 Agreements

Historically – in the years preceding 1991, when the US and EU formally agreed for the first time to formalise their cooperation – the cooperation between them was informal and not particularly extensive. Very few cases indeed involved an attempt by the competition authority(ies) of one to 'explore' the possibility for cooperation, whether in a negative, positive or another form of comity sense. To be frank, the number of cases that might have required some form of cooperation during those years was not particularly high; not to mention the fact the favoured enforcement approach at the relevant time in the USA was to opt for extraterritorial assertion of jurisdiction. With the various developments

---

[15] See pp. 596–597 below.

that have come to occur – such as the instituting of a specific mechanism for merger regulation in the EU[16] and the increase in the number of competition cases with an international dimension in general in addition to changes in relation to extraterritoriality as noted in the previous chapter – it became clear that instituting formal cooperation between these two important trading parties was only a matter of time; this eventually emerged on 23 September 1991 when the EU and USA signed their first bilateral cooperation agreement. A brief description of the various provisions in the agreement may be helpful: Article I contains the objectives of the agreement; Article II deals with the obligation of reciprocal notification and talks about the need to notify the other party whenever it becomes apparent to one party that its enforcement activities are likely to affect the interests of the former; Article III deals with exchange of information between the parties and meetings between their officials;[17] Article IV deals with assistance (cooperation and coordination) of enforcement activities between the parties; Article V – the central pillar – deals with the important issue of positive comity;[18] finally the issue of negative comity is covered under Article VI.

The creation of the agreement facilitated many benefits for the parties, including affording them the opportunity to exchange views in all cases of mutual interest and, when appropriate, to coordinate their enforcement activities. The cooperation that has come to be witnessed under the agreement especially in the early years of its existence was generally quite close and productive.[19] And this has enabled the parties to identify ways

---

[16] See p. 162 above.

[17] See, for example, Art. III(3) which allows each party to provide the other with 'any significant' information that may come to its attention and that may warrant enforcement activity by the other party.

[18] See D. Conn, 'Assessing the Impact of Preferential Trade Agreements and New Rules of Origin on the Extraterritorial Application of Antitrust Law to International Mergers' (1993) *Columbia Law Review* 119, 148; C. D. Ehlermann, 'The International Dimension of Competition Policy' (1994) *Fordham International Law Journal* 833; see further below.

[19] In the period from January 1995 to December 1996, for example, there were varying degrees of cooperation in nearly 100 cases. See J. P. Griffin, 'EC and US Extraterritoriality: Activism and Cooperation' (1994) *Fordham International Law Journal* 353. Note, however, the *Boeing/McDonnell Douglas* case, which indicates that this has not always been the case ((1997) *Official Journal* L-336/16). Yet, the recent *MCIWorldCom/Sprint* (1999) case is a paradigmatic example of the European Commission and the US competition authorities working closer than ever before and sharing information constructively. See Commission Press Release, 'Commission Opens Full Investigation into the *MCIWorldCom/Sprint* Merger' (21 February 2000); see further p. 513 below.

in which the agreement can be improved; a step that was taken eventually in 1998 when they concluded their second cooperation agreement.[20] The road to the 1998 Agreement however was not a short one. It started with the initiation of a round of successful negotiations between the parties which resulted in a proposal adopted to build on the 1991 Agreement and to deepen the cooperation between them. The new agreement was intended and in fact came to bring many advantages to the parties. It contributed to advancing the principle of positive comity by refining it considerably and 'placed' the framework of the agreement on the aim to reduce adverse effects on competition and consumer welfare; it also confirmed the efforts of the parties to continue employing the principle and clarified the manner in which the principle will be implemented. The most remarkable innovation of the agreement however is the creation of a presumption that in certain circumstances one party, the party making the positive comity request will normally defer or suspend its own enforcement activities over a period not exceeding six months, where the anticompetitive behaviour is occurring principally in and directed principally towards the other party's territory.[21] This represents an important development because it shows a serious willingness on the part of the USA in particular to cooperate with respect to competition law enforcement rather than seeking to apply its competition rules extraterritorially. Article III of the Agreement shows that the circumstances under which this request may be made are particularly wide: it would be possible for the requesting party to do so even if the situation is not deemed to be illegal under its competition law. In other words, Article III of the Agreement shows that there is no longer a requirement of double illegality, i.e. for the behaviour or conduct in question to be 'illegal' under the laws of both parties. Clearly, this change was designed to facilitate the making of more positive comity requests.

II. Brief comments on the EU–US cooperation

Normally, one would expect little interest on the part of a 'strong' competition authority or the decision or policymakers in a 'dominant' competition law regime to move closer to another (rival) regime. However this has not

---

[20] (1998) *Official Journal* L-173/26; [1999] 4 CMLR 502.

[21] It would be important to note however that this change bringing in the 'presumption' does not apply in merger cases because the timeframe (of six months' suspension of investigation) and the operation of the presumption are not compatible with merger cases and the merger review process on both sides of the Atlantic which features strict time limits.

been the case as far as the EU and the USA are concerned: a mechanism of close bilateral cooperation has been introduced and actually used. The 1991 and 1998 Agreements have contributed significantly to bringing these two important systems of competition law closer to each other. Following the adoption of the agreements, the number of cases in which consultation and coordination of enforcement efforts have taken place grew phenomenally. The agreements also converted contacts between officials at the European Commission and the Antitrust Division of the US Department of Justice and the Federal Trade Commission from a matter of infrequent occurrence to something of a daily routine in the work of the three authorities. These daily contacts have been prominent in the area of merger control (but also in recent years in the area of cartel enforcement)[22] and have reached a very advanced level. This deserves a special emphasis given the fact that both parties apply different procedural and substantive rules in the field of competition law in general and the area of merger control in particular. There have of course been divergences in the same case and on the same facts between the three authorities.[23] Remarkably, however, these divergences have happened rarely. Without wishing to express an opinion on which party was wrong and which was right in those rare cases of divergences, it is sufficient to remember – as former senior EU and US competition officials who were involved in these cases consistently argued – that reasonable minds may reach different conclusions on the application of the same law to the same facts using the same body of evidence. In the case of the EU and the USA, at least, as has already been said, different rules are applied by each party.[24] It is therefore understandable that divergences may occur in some cases. What is important, however, is that both parties seem to be committed to fostering a more broadly based transatlantic dialogue in the field of competition law, identifying areas of convergence and seeking to narrow those of divergence. This has been the impression given in particular by successive EU competition Commissioners, Assistant Attorney-Generals for Antitrust and Chairmen of the Federal Trade Commission at collective meetings

---

[22] A number of high-profile cartel investigations can be mentioned as examples, including the *Marine hose* cartel and the *Vitamins* cartel. In the former cases, the coordination between the European Commission and the Antitrust Division of the Department of Justice was particularly close and extended to the investigations conducted by the Commission on the business premises of the members of the cartel in a number of EU member states.

[23] See, for example, the case of *GE/Honeywell*, discussed at pp. 460–461 above.

[24] See further chapters 4 and 5 above.

and in public, such as at competition law conferences and events.[25] It is indeed striking that the USA has committed itself to expanding and intensifying its bilateral cooperation with the EU in the field of competition law during the eight years of the Bush Administration, mostly so in light of hardly any 'cooperative' spirit shown by the Administration in other areas stretching from imposing tariffs on steel to others as diverse as the Middle East and the creation of the International Criminal Court.

(B)   The Australia–New Zealand 'closer' cooperation

Australia and New Zealand entered into their Closer Relations Agreement in 1983. This agreement came to establish a free trade area covering the entire territory of these two close allies. The idea behind the agreement is to eliminate barriers between the countries to ensure the creation and later full-functioning of a Trans-Tasman market.

The agreement has a particular relevance in the field of competition law and has had a positive impact on the relationship between the parties in the field: in particular it facilitated an impressively long process of extensive convergence that continues to unfold until the present day; and which is expected to continue in the years to come. This convergence has been particularly noticeable in the field of merger control with New Zealand taking important steps to bring its regime 'closer' to that of Australia. The type and extent of cooperation between the competition authorities of the parties, the Australia Competition and Consumer Commission (ACCC) and the New Zealand Commerce Commission have been meaningful and deep: under the agreement, one competition authority is entitled to demand information from persons based in the jurisdiction of the other authority. Cooperation has also come to emerge between the national courts of the two countries with the courts in one being able to issue orders addressed to persons located in the other.

The agreement has been a huge success in practice. This success however may be explained with reference to factors, which are 'unique' to the parties; some of which extend beyond the field of competition law itself. Among these factors are: the highly similar and to some extent common culture prevailing in the two countries; their analogous levels of economic development; the existence of mutual trust and confidence

---

[25] See, for example, the outcome of the meeting between former EU Commissioner for Competition Mario Monti, former Assistant Attorney-General Charles James and former Chairman of the Federal Trade Commission Tim Muris on 24 September 2001.

between their administrative authorities and courts; and in the field of merger control in particular, the existence of similar substantive rules.

In 2007 Australia and New Zealand concluded a cooperation agreement.[26]

(C) Canada–US cooperation[27]

Canada and the USA enjoy an extremely important and close relationship as major trading partners. In addition to geographic proximity, this factor has been influential in building meaningful bilateral cooperation between the two countries in the field of competition law. Originally, the parties entered into a *Mutual Legal Assistance Treaty* (MLA) in 1990.[28] The MLA was intended to allow either party to request assistance from the other party in enforcing its criminal laws; the scope of the laws here covered criminalisation of anticompetitive situations. A significant step was taken five years later to formalise cooperation between Canada and the USA when the two parties concluded their 1995 *Agreement Regarding the Application of their Competition and Deceptive Marketing Practices Laws*. The agreement was intended to introduce negative[29] and positive comity[30] principles in the relationship between the parties in the field as well as impose a mutual obligation on the parties to avoid or minimise jurisdictional conflicts.[31] In the latter context, the agreement provides that each party must give careful consideration to the important interests of the other party at all stages of its enforcement efforts.

From Canada's perspective, cooperation with the USA in the field of competition law is extremely important. Indeed the Canadian authorities

---

[26] See the table of bilateral agreements at p. 532 below.

[27] It is worth noting that the cooperation between Canada and the USA in the field of competition law extends to cooperation between the Canadian competition Bureau and public bodies in the USA (other than US competition authorities). For example, the Bureau concluded a cooperation arrangement with the US Postal Inspection Service in Washington on 2 April 2008 which seeks to enhance competition law enforcement in relation to different types of deceptive marketing practices – such as mass marketing fraud – which has a cross-border element.

[28] Whenever an opportunity presents itself the parties and specifically the Canadian government and authorities take particular care to stress that bilateral cooperation between them dates back to the early years of the twentieth century when 'they jointly investigated and prosecuted a cartel involving newsprint that operated in both countries'. See the Canadian Brief submitted in *Hoffmann La-Roche* v. *Empagran*; see pp. 443–446 above for a discussion of the case.

[29] See Art. VI of the Agreement.   [30] See Art. V of the Agreement.

[31] See Art. VI of the Agreement which provides for avoidance of conflicts.

have consistently viewed the 1995 Agreement as the most important bilateral cooperation agreement Canada has with another jurisdiction. Such feelings seem to be reciprocated by the USA and its competition authorities. In line with such mutual interest to strengthen bilateral cooperation, in 2004 the parties concluded a second cooperation agreement which has consolidated the principle of positive comity contained in Article V of the 1995 Agreement.[32] Other than seeking to prevent impediment as a result of anticompetitive situations to the flows of trade and investment between the parties and competition and consumers in their local markets, Article I of the Agreement also lists among the objectives of the Agreement the goal of establishing 'cooperative procedures to achieve the most effective and efficient enforcement of competition law, whereby the competition authorities of each Party will normally avoid allocating enforcement resources to dealing with anticompetitive activities that occur principally in and are directed principally towards the other Party's territory, where the competition authorities of the other Party are able and prepared to examine and take effective sanctions under their law to deal with those activities'. The clarification which the Agreement delivers to the principle of positive comity and use can be seen from Article III of the Agreement which states that the 'authorities of a Requesting Party may request the competition authorities of a Requested Party to investigate and, if warranted, to remedy anticompetitive activities in accordance with the Requested Party's competition laws. Such a request may be made regardless of whether the activities also violate the Requesting Party's competition laws, and regardless of whether the competition authorities of the Requesting Party have commenced or contemplate taking enforcement activities under their own competition laws.'

(D) UK–US cooperation

The relationship between the UK and the USA in the field of competition law is worth describing in a few lines because it sheds useful light on the functioning of mutual assistance treaties (MLATs) and extradition treaties. These treaties offer an additional example of a wider framework as described above for cooperation, which may extend to competition law;

---

[32] *Agreement between the Government of Canada and the Government of the United States of America on the Application of Positive Comity Principles to the Enforcement of Their Competition Law* (2004).

though more commonly competition law is actually excluded from these treaties and in many cases there is a requirement for double criminality,[33] meaning that the offence needs to be criminalised under the laws of both parties – obviously, this is highly restricting in cases where criminalisation is possible under the competition law of one but not both parties.

The UK and the USA have not concluded a specific competition cooperation agreement.[34] Nonetheless, a MLAT was concluded between the parties in 1994 which concerns criminal matters. Originally, the MLAT provided for exclusion of competition law from its scope. This exclusion was removed however in 2001. This was an important step towards facilitating meaningful bilateral cooperation between the UK and the USA. However, arguably the more significant change in this respect has been the criminalisation of cartels in the UK under section 188 of the Enterprise Act 2002 which has created double criminalisation. Furthermore, the parties have also concluded an extradition treaty which now extends to the field of competition law.[35]

In 2008 the UK House of Lords (now the Supreme Court) delivered its important ruling in the case of *Norris*.[36] Norris, an executive of the firm Morgan Crucible was the subject of price-fixing charges in the USA and the question arose whether he could be extradited to the USA in order to face these charges. The House of Lords came to the conclusion that this should not be possible because of the lack of double criminalisation. Prior to the coming into force of Enterprise Act 2002, criminalisation of cartels was technically possible in the UK by invoking the common law offence of 'conspiracy to defraud'. According to the House of Lords however price-fixing during those days was not quite within the scope of the rules here because it did not – of itself – amount to a criminal offence; unless the price-fixing was accompanied by aggravating factors such as deception or misrepresentation in which case it would have constituted a criminal offence at common law.

---

[33] These two elements are considered to hinder the potential of such treaties as cooperation instruments in the field of competition law. See the report by the Cartels Working Group of the International Competition Network (ICN) on *Cooperation between Competition Agencies in Cartel Investigation*, submitted to the ICN Annual Conference 2007, at pp. 15–16.

[34] See the *International Antitrust Cooperation Guide of the American Bar Association* (2004).

[35] See *Extradition Treaty between the Government of the United States of America and the Government of the United Kingdom of Great Britain and Northern Ireland* (31 March 2003).

[36] See *Norris* v. *Government of the United States of America* (2008) UKHL 16.

This development with regard to the UK–US MLAT shows that in actual cases for such cooperation instruments to realise their potential of facilitating bilateral cooperation in the field of competition law, it is important for there to be no exclusion of competition law under the relevant MLAT and where the latter concerns criminal matters it is essential that criminalisation extends to competition law under the domestic regimes of the parties.

4. The importance of bilateral cooperation

The fact that certain countries have been turning their attention to and entering into a steadily increasing number of bilateral cooperation agreements shows the particular importance attached to this type of cooperation; a fact that arguably has been enforced considerably over the years with the successive guidance published by the Organisation for Economic Cooperation and Development (OECD) on the topic; key guidance here includes the 1967, 1979, 1986[37] and 1995 *Recommendations*.[38] The importance of bilateral cooperation resides in the use of this form of cooperation to achieve a number of aims in practice. These aims have been dressed up as the different 'benefits' of bilateral cooperation which most famously the OECD has attempted to advocate. Among the key benefits that have been mentioned are the fact it: facilitates convergence and harmonisation in both procedural and substantive terms within different competition law regimes; offers a good alternative to extraterritorial assertion of jurisdiction (in many cases it is far preferable);[39] is realistic and possible to achieve; carries no legal obligation on competition authorities and thus leaves discretion in their hands to choose their avenue(s) of enforcement; includes no threat, nor intrusion into the sovereignty of countries; has a real potential to eliminate conflicts between countries; and provides an appropriate forum for consultation to take place between competition authorities and an opportunity for the parties to improve their

---

[37] See *Recommendation of the Council for Cooperation between Member Countries in Areas of Potential Conflict between Competition and Trade Policies* (OECD, 1986). The 1986 OECD *Recommendation* revised earlier versions issued on: 5 October 1967 and 25 September 1979.

[38] See *Revised Recommendation of the Council Concerning Cooperation between Member Countries on Anti-Competitive Practices Affecting International Trade* (OECD, 1995).

[39] Despite this it may be possible to regard bilateral cooperation, especially within an increasingly globalised competition law context, not as a substitute but rather as a complimentary tool to the unilateral option of extraterritoriality.

enforcement mechanism and practices. Added to this host of benefits one may mention other practical benefits such as the removal of many difficulties associated with access to information and other evidentiary matters which have come to frequently surface in competition cases.[40] In many ways, bilateral cooperation can ensure that the relevant competition authority and the relevant situation will be brought together, i.e. that the relevant authority – the one that is better placed – will be able to conduct an investigation into the situation. The benefits of bilateral cooperation can also be seen against the backdrop of the fact that firms will be relieved from the burden of duplicated enforcement and inconsistent conclusions which may be reached by different competition authorities – a benefit that has considerable weight particularly for firms involved in transnational merger operations.[41] Finally, bilateral cooperation may facilitate more meaningful discussions between countries in the context of practices of private firms restraining market access, as a result of which better access to markets may be ensured leading to growth of flows of trade and investment in the global economy. Many of these benefits have been recognised by the OECD in its careful consideration of bilateral cooperation through the actual experience of many OECD members. Beyond the OECD recommendations mentioned above, the *Recommendations on cartels*[42] have identified six potential benefits of a positive comity approach to cross-border enforcement. The benefits include improved effectiveness in remedying illegal conduct, improved efficiency in investigations, reduced need for sharing confidential and other information, avoidance of jurisdictional conflict, prevention of damage to the requested country's interests and protection for other legitimate interests of the protected country.

The importance of bilateral cooperation can also be seen in its absence in some cases. These cases demonstrate how useful bilateral cooperation can be, but more seriously and how problematic its absence can be. For example, in 2004 the Turkish Competition Board opened an investigation into the seized coal market following the receipt of complaints about a significant increase in the retail prices of coal which apparently was caused by an 'artificial' increase in the price of imported coal. The Board found that a price-fixing cartel was in operation by two subsidiaries of Glencore International AG, Glencore Istanbul Madencilik Ticaret A.Ş. and Minerkom Mineral ve Kati Yakitlar Tic. A.Ş., Krutrade AG and Mir Trade AG. Whilst the former two firms were established in Turkey the latter two were not: Krutrade

---

[40] See WTO *Annual Report* (WTO, 1997), p. 31.   [41] See pp. 106–110 above.
[42] See p. 138 above.

AG was established in Austria and Mir Trade AG was established in Switzerland. In its conclusion of the investigation however the Board was unable to establish a breach of Article 4 of the Law on the Protection of Competition 1994 by Mir Trade AG: it needed to obtain the necessary documents to support its investigation and findings which proved impossible in practice. The Board attempted to rely on Articles 17 and 23 of the Turkey–European Free Trade Association (EFTA) States Free Trade Agreement 1991 and made a request to Switzerland seeking cooperation to facilitate access to such documents. This request however was rejected by Switzerland citing the impossibility of enforcing Swiss competition rules in this case. With regard to Krutrade AG, the Board was able to find a breach by the firm of Article 4 of the Law though the Board failed to reach a final decision due to the failure to communicate its finding officially and properly to the firm. Interestingly, the Board had sought the cooperation of the Austrian authorities in relation to two aspects: establishing a breach of Article 4 of the Law and communicating its pre-decision finding to Krutrade AG. In relation to the first aspect – which the Board aimed to conduct within the framework of the Customs Union Agreement (CUA) under the EU–Turkey Association Agreement – the request was transferred by the Austrian authorities to the European Commission. On its part the Commission could not answer the Board in the positive on the grounds that there were no implementation rules for the competition law provisions within the CUA;[43] restrictions of confidentiality existed;[44] and there was in any case lack of anticompetitive effect in the EU. Indeed the absence of cooperation is considered to have a more far-reaching consequence beyond the facts of individual cases. Increasingly, such absence is considered to be an obstacle preventing developing countries[45] as well as those countries with young competition law regimes from realising effective enforcement in cross-border competition cases.[46]

---

[43] Apparently the Commission found Art. 43 of the association agreement between the parties to be *insufficient* as a legal basis for the cooperation sought in the case. The Article provides that one party under the Agreement may request the other party to initiate enforcement action if the conduct carried out in the territory of the latter adversely affects the interests of the former. Under para. 3 of the Article however the requested party enjoys *complete* discretion in deciding to answer the request in the positive.

[44] See pp. 525–526 below in relation to such restrictions.   [45] See further chapter 6 above.

[46] For example, in Singapore – which introduced specific competition legislation in 2005 – the view that seems to be held by competition officials, policymakers and practitioners is that the absence of cooperation agreements is a hindrance to efforts by the Singapore Competition Commission to launch actions against foreign firms involved in international cartels in particular.

No given list of benefits of bilateral cooperation however can ever be said to be closed as other benefits may be found. One crucial benefit flowing from bilateral cooperation not mentioned above is convergence and harmonisation. Convergence deserves particular emphasis because, among other things, it is a long-term benefit that goes beyond focusing on individual cases or isolated instances of cooperation *towards* building a policy perspective on the whole exercise of understanding and applying competition law.[47] To put things in context, convergence supports the role of bilateral cooperation as one of the strategies to internationalise competition law; the other notable strategies we identified earlier in the discussion were multilateral cooperation and to a lesser extent extraterritoriality. It is this aspect of bilateral cooperation that deserves particular focus and it is here that future directions are worth considering; this is something we will return to later in the discussion. At this stage however – in order not to present the discussion of the 'other' benefits identified above in the abstract and as stand-alone – it would be vital to furnish evidence of practice of these benefits and to weigh them against the limitations or shortcomings, which may be identified in relation to bilateral cooperation. These issues will be examined in turn.

5. Bilateral cooperation in practice

As was noted above, it is crucial to support the points identifying the various benefits of bilateral cooperation with examples from practice in order to ensure that the discussion would not otherwise amount to mere academic indulgence. To this end, this part will mention and discuss a number of instances in which bilateral cooperation had a positive impact on the relationship between the parties, their respective enforcement mechanisms and the actual outcome in the relevant cases; the latter of course is usually hugely important to firms themselves. Most of the cases mentioned here concern the topic of merger control; though some concern other areas within the field of competition law.[48] The discussion of the cases will be presented around the benefits that cooperation brought about.

(A) Coordination of enforcement efforts

One of the major benefits of the US–EU cooperation has been the creation of framework for their competition officials to coordinate their enforcement

---

[47] The following chapter contains a detailed discussion of convergence in a multilateral context.
[48] See the discussion below on the case of *CRS/SABRE* at pp. 514–516 below.

efforts. This can be seen for example in the light of the Administrative Agreement on Attendance which was entered into between the European Commission and the Antitrust Division of the Department of Justice in 1999. Under this agreement, the competition officials of one authority are able to *attend* proceedings within the other. Such attendance has happened in a number of important merger cases, including: *BOC/Air Liquide* (2000)[49] in which officials of the Federal Trade Commission attended an oral hearing within the European Commission; and *MCIWorldCom/Sprint* (1999)[50] in which officials of the European Commission attended the 'pitch' meeting between the Antitrust Division of the Department of Justice and the merging parties. For many people, the case represents a very good example of true comity being practised between the USA and the EU.

Coordination of enforcement efforts between the EU and USA however has not been limited to attendance and has extended to exchange of information, discussing substantive issues in the relevant case and taking note of decisions adopted in the other regime. For example, in the case of *Exxon/Mobil* (1999),[51] there was close coordination between the European Commission and the US Federal Trade Commission on their appraisal of the transaction. This included exchanging information, including confidential information since the parties in the case waived their right to confidentiality. Similar cooperation can be seen in cases such as *Allied Signal/Honeywell* (1999)[52] and *AstraZeneca/Novartis* (2000).[53] In the former case the coordination between the Antitrust Division of the Department of Justice and the European Commission ensured that they were able to discuss issues of market definition and the suitability of the divestiture remedies proposed by the merging parties; discussing the latter was particularly important since the largest chunk of the assets in questions were located in the USA. In the latter case, there were particularly helpful discussions between the US Federal Trade Commission and the European Commission concerning the issue of remedies in the case. In a more recent case, *Oracle/PeopleSoft* (2004)[54] there was a highly important example of *interaction* between the two

---

[49] Case No. COMP/M.1630 (20 January 2000).   [50] (2000) *Official Journal* L-300/1.

[51] *Exxon/Mobil* (1999) *Official Journal* C-127/2.

[52] *United States* v. *Allied Signal Inc. and Honeywell Inc.*, No. 99–2959, 2000 (2000) and *Allied Signal/Honeywell* Case No. COMP/M.1601 (1 December 1999) (European Commission).

[53] No. 001 0082; Docket No. C-3979 (US) and Case No, COMP/M.1806 (26 July 2000) (European Commission).

[54] Case No. C 04–0807 VRW (US) and Case No. COMP/M.3216 (26 October 2004) (European Commission).

regimes with the European Commission taking into account developments in the case on the other side of the Atlantic. Although the Antitrust Division had decided to object to the merger – in line with a view taken by it and the European Commission that the merger was likely to give rise to competition problems in the relevant market, the market for software applications for automated financial management systems and human resources processes – this was rejected by the US District Court because it found gaps in the definition of the relevant market adopted by the Division. The European Commission embraced the views of the District Court and decided to clear the merger. The existence of the bilateral cooperation agreement between the US and the EU meant that the Commission was able to take into account evidence gathered as part of the proceedings before the District Court; something that doubtfully would have been possible in the absence of the agreement and the enforcement coordination it facilitated.

Obviously these cases show that the coordination has created many linking points for the competition authorities on both sides of the Atlantic to make their bilateral cooperation as effective and as meaningful as possible. This is bound to be of benefit not only to the authorities themselves but also to the firms, who – as we saw – may have a number of concerns when their conduct, behaviour or transactions are investigated by more than one competition authority.[55] For example in 2002 the authorities published – within their Merger Working Group – the *Best Practices on Cooperation in Merger Review*,[56] a highly important step that opened the door to synchronisation of the merger review timetable on both sides of the Atlantic; exchange of information and analytical data on matters such as market definition, effects on competition and merger efficiencies. The Best Practices also include directions for merging parties themselves such as those aiming to encourage them to consider waiving their right to confidentiality in order to enable the authorities to exchange confidential information between themselves which many times can be very useful to the parties themselves.

All of the above cases concern merger situations. It would be helpful therefore to shed some light on the cooperation that has come to emerge between the parties outside the area of merger control. A good example in which such cooperation actually occurred and was seen as important is the *CRS/SABRE* case which arose in 1997. In this case, the US Department of

[55] See pp. 106–110 above for an account of these concerns.
[56] Available at www.usdoj.gov/atr/public/international/docs/200405.htm.

Justice requested the European Commission to investigate activities within the computer reservation system markets that were suspected of hindering the ability of US firms active in these markets from competing effectively in the EU. A claim was made by SABRE, which is owned by American Airlines, that the anticompetitive behaviour of the three large airline owners of Amadeus – Lufthansa, Air France and Iberia Airlines – on the European side of the Atlantic, the leading firms in computer reservation system markets, impeded its ability to penetrate markets in Europe and expand its presence on those. SABRE alleged that a collaboration existed between the three airline owners and their travel agents in which they agreed to refuse to supply SABRE with the same fare data as they supplied to Amadeus, in addition to denying the former the ability to carry out the various booking and ticketing functions available to the latter. The US Department of Justice made a positive comity request to the Commission on the basis of the cooperation agreement between the EU and the USA. Senior officials within the Antitrust Division felt that the Commission was in the best position to investigate this conduct because it occurred within the EU and consumers there are the ones who are principally at risk if competition has been distorted.[57] By contrast, senior competition officials within the European Commission, believed the case was 'important psychologically'. In its investigation, the Commission treated this as a priority case because it was aware of the fact that how it handles US positive comity referrals will certainly determine largely how the US competition authorities will handle its referrals.[58] In 1997 it began an 'initial inquiry', which lasted for two years. This was followed in March 1999 by opening formal proceedings against Air France. The Commission stated, on the basis of its initial inquiry, that Air France had discriminated against SABRE to favour Amadeus.[59]

The case had a particularly positive impact in enhancing the confidence of the EU and the US competition authorities regarding the effectiveness of the principle of positive comity. This was an important development because it came to occur at a relatively early stage in the formal cooperation between the parties and because it won the support of US politicians to the whole concept of bilateral cooperation and the mechanism of

---

[57] See Press Release of the Antitrust Division, 'Justice Department asks European Communities to Investigate Possible Anticompetitive Conduct Affecting U.S. Airlines' Computer Reservation Systems' (28 April 1997).

[58] See European Commission Press Release, 'EU Gives Priority to US Airline Reservation Case' (9 September 1997).

[59] See European Commission Press Release, 'Commission Opens Procedure Against Air France for Favouring Amadeus Reservation System' (15 March 1999).

positive comity. Indeed some US legislators were fairly quick to welcome the European Commission's response to the Antitrust Division's request for enforcement and its efforts in the case. Senator Herb Kohl of the *Antitrust, Business Rights and Competition Sub-committee* stated in the wake of the Commission's investigation that it was becoming obvious that the USA's most important positive comity agreement, with the EU, was beginning to pay off.[60] Such positive statements by leading US politicians have not been the norm however and occasionally were replaced by severe criticisms of the European Commission and its practice. This was the case following the Commission's decision in *GE/Honeywell*.[61] In fairness however, even in this exceptional case, cooperation between the European Commission and the Antitrust Division was very evident; as it has been in other cases.[62]

(B)   Convergence

It is highly arguable that the most important of the benefits resulting from the US–EU bilateral cooperation has been the impressive degree of convergence achieved between the two regimes. This convergence has been made possible because the bilateral cooperation between the parties enabled them better to understand each other's competition law and policy, strengthen their individual enforcement efforts and avoid unnecessary divergence(s) in their decisional practice that might lead to conflict. This can be seen especially in the area of merger control with the European Commission's more economic-based approach in the appraisal of mergers and the use on occasions of US competition authorities of important EU-based concepts such as that of dominance.[63]

---

[60] See 'Senate Sub-Committee Focuses on International Enforcement, Positive Comity' 76 *Antitrust & Trade Reg. Rep.* (BNA) 482 (6 May 1999).

[61] See above for a discussion of the case.

[62] In addition to the cases mentioned above, see the closely coordinated parallel investigations in cases such as, *CVC/Lenzing* (2001) *Official Journal* C-141/13 (European Commission/FTC), *Alcoa/Reynolds* (1999) *Official Journal* C-339/14 (European Commission/Antitrust Division) and *Compaq/HP* (2001) *Official Journal* C-374/68 (European Commission/FTC).

[63] For example, in the case of *Office Depot/Staples* (1997), the Federal Trade Commission utilised the concept of 'dominance' in its opposition to the proposed merger between the parties: according to it the merger would have created a dominant entity in the office supply market. This is highly notable given that the dominance test does not *stricto senso* feature in the substantive test of s. 7 of the Clayton Act 1914 which refers to mergers leading to 'substantial lessening of competition or tending to create a monopoly'. As we saw in chapter 4 above, the substantive test featuring in Art. 2 of the EU Merger Regulation 139/2004 refers to 'creation or strengthening of a dominant position'.

Convergence between the EU and US regimes also can be said to exist notably in relation to the *modus operandi* of EU and US competition authorities. The benefit of coordination of enforcement efforts as discussed above can be considered to contain an element of convergence in the way competition authorities on both sides of the Atlantic have come to *operate*, particularly in the area of merger control.

Such convergence however should be viewed in light of the divergence and disagreements that sometime, do arise; this issue will be considered further below.

6. Limitations, shortcomings and criticisms of bilateral cooperation agreements

To offer a balanced view of the real value of bilateral cooperation it would be important to highlight the shortcomings and limitations of this option and assess in practical terms whether these are of such a weight that they would cancel the enormously huge and real benefits identified above.

Several serious shortcomings or limitations may be identified.

(A) Use of confidential information

One shortcoming of bilateral cooperation relates to the exclusion of provisions on the exchange of confidential information. Competition authorities are unable to share confidential business information amongst themselves without the consent of the firms involved or a clear authorisation under their local laws or a binding international treaty. Obviously, the issue of exchange of confidential information is a very difficult and sensitive issue in practice. On the one hand, firms themselves may benefit from waiver of the right to confidentially when their transactions are being reviewed by two authorities, who have a bilateral cooperation agreement between them. The lack of ability on the part of such authorities to exchange confidential information therefore might affect the interests of these firms because this may make it very difficult if not impossible for these authorities to conduct comprehensive investigations.[64] Indeed, even in the USA – the country with the strongest tendency to opt for unilateral actions in the field of competition law – such a situation has been recognised. In 1994, the US Congress passed the International Antitrust

---

[64] See D. E. Rosenthal, 'Equipping the Multilateral Trading System With a Style and Principles to Increase Market Access' (1998) *George Mason Law Review* 543.

Enforcement Assistance Act which permits the US competition authorities to obtain and exchange with foreign competition authorities, where relevant, confidential information. Under the Act, the USA is allowed to enter into what are referred to as 'Antitrust Mutual Assistance Agreements'.[65] The Act provides that US authorities may open proceedings to obtain such information from US nationals on behalf of foreign authorities, subject to them being satisfied that the latter will safeguard the confidentiality of the information and undertake to ensure reciprocity. Essentially what the Act enables US and the relevant foreign authorities to do is to carry out joint investigations without necessarily having to seek the consent of the owners of confidential information. It is doubtful however whether such 'benefit' is really practical: the adoption of the Act has not led to what was expected to be a large number of mutual assistance agreements with foreign jurisdictions.[66]

On the other hand, waiver of right to confidentiality by firms may involve certain risks for this in cases where this information ends up in the hands of competitors or customers who might then abuse it or use it to launch their own actions against such firms. These risks are particularly high in competition law regimes, such as that of the USA which allows for and favours private enforcement; such risks however are nevertheless possible to address with the existence of adequate binding commitments by the receiving competition authority regarding the manner in which it would handle confidential information received by them within the framework of the bilateral cooperation agreement.

The prohibition on exchange of confidential information exists even in the case of the closest cases of bilateral cooperation; and often this proves to be a hurdle in the face of having cooperation in individual cases. For example, notwithstanding its close cooperation with US competition authorities and strong interest to cooperate closely within these authorities and within the framework of the Canada–US cooperation agreement,[67] the Canadian Competition Bureau is prevented under section 29 of the Competition Act 1986 from sharing confidential information with 'third parties', except where one of the following situations exists: the disclosure of information by the Bureau is to Canadian law enforcement agencies; the information in question has entered the public domain; the owner of the

---

[65] See pp. 507–509 above in relation to the US–UK cooperation.
[66] See however the 1999 bilateral cooperation agreement, mentioned in note 6 above, between the USA and Australia which was based on this Act.
[67] See pp. 506–507 above.

information consents to the disclosure; and where the disclosure is within what is worded in general language: the 'purposes of the administration or enforcement of the Act'. In 2007 the Bureau published its *Confidentiality and Mutual Assistance in Enforcing Competition Laws Bulletin* which reflects the Bureau's thinking on the issue of confidentiality and section 29. The Bulletin clearly shows the importance the Bureau attaches to cooperation and recognises that exchange of confidential information within the framework of this cooperation is sometimes necessary, notwithstanding that the decision to do so is never 'taken lightly'.[68] In relation to section 29, the Bulletin provides that while the Bureau respects the requirements of the section, it may 'communicate information in specific circumstances to foreign authorities to address a matter under the Act. In all cases where confidential information is communicated to a foreign authority, the Bureau seeks to maintain the confidentiality of the information through either formal international instruments or assurances from the foreign authority. The Bureau also requires that use of the confidential information by the foreign authority will be limited to the specific purposes for which it is provided.'[69]

Notwithstanding the limitation it imposes, section 29 shows the importance of having cooperation agreements in the field. In the Bureau's own words the existence of such agreements – whether bilateral or multilateral cooperation instruments – enhances significantly the prospects of disclosure of information under section 29. According to the Bulletin:

> Generally, where there is no bilateral or multilateral cooperation instrument in force, the Bureau does not communicate information protected by section 29 unless it is fully satisfied with the assurances provided by the foreign authority with respect to maintaining the confidentiality of the information and the uses to which it will be put.

Another example worth citing can be found in the case of the EU and Turkey which have an Association Agreement between them and have a relationship of a 'regional organisation' (the EU) and 'legitimate candidate' for accession talks to join this organisation (Turkey); not to mention of course Turkey's serious interest in cooperating with the EU and its important steps in following EU rules and standards in the field of competition law. In 2004 the Turkish Competition Board opened a cartel investigation into the electrical equipment market. The European Commission had collected material to which the Turkish Competition Board was hoping to gain access. The Board made a request to the Commission for

---

[68] See section 4.2.2 of the Bulletin.   [69] See section 4.2.2.2 of the Bulletin.

cooperation but the latter rejected the request on grounds of confidentiality: the Commission felt that the information could not be disclosed due to the prohibition contained in Article 28 of EU Regulation 1/2003[70] which provides that 'without prejudice to the exchange and to the use of information foreseen in Articles 11, 12, 14, 15 and 27, the Commission and the competition authorities of the Member States ... shall not disclose information acquired or exchanged by them pursuant to this Regulation and of the kind covered by the obligation of professional secrecy'. In response to the point raised by the Board that exchange of information between the parties was possible under Article 36 of the Customs Union Agreement between Turkey and the EU, the Commission relied on the limitation in the Article, namely that such exchange was subject to the requirements of professional and business secrecy.

(B)   Solving disputes

Beyond the limitation concerning exchange of confidential information, bilateral cooperation agreements fall short of offering a proper forum to deal with or solve disputes, which may arise between the competition authorities concerned in certain cases;[71] though they may be however – as we noted before – a suitable vehicle for avoiding conflicting outcomes in competition cases. The latter highly desirable outcome of course cannot be guaranteed in every case and sometimes divergences do occur. One may wonder therefore about a shortcoming that might be inherent in the very nature of the mechanism of bilateral cooperation to enable the competition authorities concerned to reach agreed competition rules or standards, especially in highly difficult areas such as the treatment of conglomerate mergers, vertical restraints in agreements between non-competitors and abuse of dominance. Arguably, although as a result of bilateral cooperation agreements the practices of competition authorities are brought closer together, even in the case of highly divergent competition law regimes, the agreements are unlikely to replace the need to agree on basic principles relating to their enforcement. It is very likely that commercial frictions may remain unresolved in the absence of a mechanism or procedure for dispute resolution in the relevant bilateral cooperation agreement.

---

[70] See pp. 194–197 above.

[71] It is worth noting here that the OECD in its 1995 recommendation (mentioned in note 38 above) attempts to offer an option to competition authorities in case of a dispute: to approach and make use of its 'good offices'.

(C)   The double illegality requirement

In a way, the shortcoming identified in the previous section is related to the narrowness in scope bilateral agreements may have due to the need in many cases for the situation in question to *affect* the domestic markets of both authorities. In the absence of this double effect, it is unclear to what extent the competition authority of the jurisdiction with no effect will invest its resources into investigating a situation that affects the conditions of competition and interests of another country. For example, in relation to cartels – which rank top of the list of serious competition offences for many competition authorities – an exemption may exist under the laws of one party to a bilateral cooperation agreement with regard to export cartels.[72] One may wonder in this case, what value a request by the other party to the agreement would have in relation to such cartels given that the requested party would not be able to act against the situation; notwithstanding that the export cartel may have adverse effects within the boundaries of the requesting party. Other than the bilateral agreement likely to be rendered meaningless in this case, it can be said that bilateral agreements have the potential of giving rise to discrimination between the parties to the agreement.

Additionally, the possibility may exist for the positive comity principle to be strategically utilised in requests to shift the burden of investigations to the requested party enabling the requesting party to save its resources.

(D)   Long-term nature of the bilateral cooperation strategy

Other limitations from which bilateral cooperation agreements appear to suffer include the inherently long-term nature and high cost of entering into this type of agreements; let alone building a framework of cooperation between competition authorities and development of a globally comprehensive principle of positive comity. At present, the number of agreements with positive comity is relatively small and they show clear exclusion of developing countries; indeed also a lack of proper role for firms to play within the framework of the agreements which one may envisage could be particularly helpful to the relevant competition authorities.

Concluding a bilateral cooperation agreement is not the exclusive monopoly of the competition authorities of the relevant parties. In some

---

[72] See, for example, the discussion at p. 460 above concerning the *Wood Pulp* case and existence of an exemption for export cartels under US competition law regime.

cases more than one government body must approve the agreement and it can be extremely difficult to convince officials who work in different ministries and who have different orientation and priorities and who talk and understand completely different terms when it comes to establishing international bilateral links.

(E) Confidence in comity

The overall view of the principle of comity within the framework of most if not all bilateral agreements in existence is that it is weak and remains to develop into a solid and mature principle. There is a noticeable degree of uncertainty among many communities in the field over how much the principle is actually used in practice especially since the principle does not limit the discretion of the relevant competition authorities to choose to take any action they deem fit to protect competition and consumers in their jurisdictions. The different bilateral cooperation agreements which have been concluded in the field of competition law show that the parties have discretion whether to take action and what action to take when receiving a (positive comity) request from the other party. At the same time, the agreements usually do not prevent the latter – notwithstanding the request – from taking action with respect to the anticompetitive situation in question.

(F) Soft law nature of bilateral agreements

Bilateral cooperation agreements are more seen as having a soft law nature than instruments which produce binding obligations. This seems to lower the interest in concluding these agreements. In competition authorities' circles the emphasis is put on 'cooperation' and not necessarily on 'bilateral agreements'. Many authorities feel that informal cooperation is a better alternative – largely because of its de facto nature and lack of cost – to concluding bilateral agreements, which although formal has a soft law nature. In practice informal cooperation is understood to be very extensive though difficult to quantify.

7. Contribution to the internationalisation of competition law

It may be helpful to reflect on the type of contribution bilateral cooperation could make in furthering the process of internationalisation of competition law. It is difficult to imagine the emergence of a level playing field in this process if this were to be founded only on a category of inevitably hetero-geneous bilateral agreements. Furthermore, the scope of these types of cooperation is constrained by differences remaining in competition law and its enforcement in different jurisdictions. For example, in the light of the discussion in previous chapters, it is clear that the goals of the compe-tition laws of different jurisdictions are not identical and the priorities of different competition authorities do not always coincide. Differences between competition law regimes are bound to lead to differences in approach, especially with respect to areas, such as vertical restraints, export cartels, abuse of market dominance and mergers (principally conglomer-ate ones).

8. Assessing the status quo

The above discussion on bilateral cooperation – particularly the comments made on the EU–US cooperation and the Australia–New Zealand closer relation – show a positive outlook in relation to bilateral cooperation. However one must conduct a critical assessment of bilateral cooperation in order to verify whether this outlook is indeed positive.

The most remarkable feature of the EU–US cooperation in particular is not how impressive this bilateral cooperation has been; nor is the fact that it has brought two very different regimes together. Rather what is remarkable is that this successful example of cooperation belongs to a group of examples which together have been the exception rather than the rule. The EU–US example is a good one to inspire others to follow it (if they can), but it is far from being *representative* of the common approach to bilateral cooperation in the field.

Assessing whether the outlook of bilateral cooperation in general is positive requires widening the lenses to be able to look at a number of key issues.

(A) Fulfilling the objectives behind bilateral cooperation

It is not clear whether there is full consensus that bilateral cooperation between competition authorities – wherever it exists in the form of an agreement – has achieved its objectives. Even if one takes the EU–US example, many people have pointed to the shortcoming of the 1991 and 1998 agreements in 100 per cent fulfilling the aim of avoiding likely conflicting outcomes in competition cases, let alone offering a proper forum to deal with or solve disputes when they actually arise. Critics of this important example of bilateral cooperation often point to the never disappearing and unavoidable possibility of conflict between the two regimes.

It is difficult to dispute this point: divergences do and can occur between the EU and the US as can be seen from cases such as *GE/ Honeywell International* (2001), *Boeing/McDonnell Douglas* (1997) and *Ciba-Ceigy/Sandoz* (yr). It would be important to appreciate nonetheless that cases of divergence have been extremely few indeed and on the whole can be explained with reference to the nature of the merger review process (prediction of future impact of operations), the use of different theoretical models and possible differences in outlook concerning the assessment of merger remedies. For example, *GE/Honeywell* showed, among other things, the European Commission's concern over conglomerate effects, which were not taken into account by the Antitrust Division of the Department of Justice. In *Ciba-Ceigy/Sandoz*, the Federal Trade Commission and the European Commission diverged not on the question whether the merger was likely to create adverse effect in the market for crop protection and animal health (on which in fact they agreed), but rather on the extent of the remedies the parties needed to propose in order to eliminate all competition concerns. In the case, the Federal Trade Commission felt that the remedies proposed by the parties were not sufficient to address its concerns whilst the European Commission was satisfied in the circumstances. Nonetheless, what these cases show is that the possibility of divergence is always present and this can lead to serious consequences in practice.[73]

(B) Extent of bilateral cooperation

In most cases of bilateral cooperation between competition authorities, the extent of cooperation appears to be clouded with ambiguity. Generally there is an abundance of 'reporting' – especially in the form of statements and speeches by competition officials – that cooperation took place in certain cases without however detailing in what respect(s) the cooperation ensued and how extensive it was. For example, in the famous *Vitamins* cartel, following the announcement of investigation

---

[73] A number of other examples of divergences can be found around the world. See, for example, the merger between Colgate Palmolive and American Home Products (the *Kolynos-Colgate* merger) (1995) in relation to which there was divergence between the USA and Brazil.

by US competition authorities against Hoffmann-La Roche, Basf Aktiengesellschaft and Aventis (now Rhône-Poulenc) for cartel practices in the vitamins market, several competition authorities opened their own cartel investigations; this included the Secretariat of Economic Law (SDE) of Brazil. The SDE widely reported that cooperation took place with the US competition authorities but no detail was given as to the extent of the cooperation. Another example is the *Lysine* cartel. Here too the Brazilian SDE reported that a 'great deal' of documents were obtained with the cooperation of the US Department of Justice without specifying however what documents were obtained.

In *Oracle/PeopleSoft*, although the European Commission made it clear that it cooperated closely with the Antitrust Division of the Department of Justice in reaching its clearance decision, it never disclosed in what regard the authorities cooperated.

(C) Scope of bilateral cooperation

There is a clear lack of certainty whether – where the cooperation extended to exchange of information – this covered all information in the possession of the relevant competition authority(ies). If one listens to the declaration of competition authorities who cooperate bilaterally, it is consistently made clear that even if documents were disclosed to other competition authorities this never included confidential information (without the consent of the parties that is). This is not something however on which practitioners in the relevant regime can agree with confidence. Practitioners who deal with more than one competition authority sometimes form the impression that an exchange of confidential information must have taken place. This is something often ascertained from the nature and type of questions or issues raised by a competition authority to whom no disclosure of information was made.

The issue of confidential information is a very difficult and sensitive one. It has been repeatedly said that a major shortcoming or limitation from which bilateral cooperation seems to suffer relates to the exclusion of provisions allowing the exchange of confidential information; competition authorities are unable to share confidential information amongst themselves without the consent of the firms involved or a clear authorisation under law.

On the one hand, firms themselves may benefit from waiver of the right to confidentiality when their transactions are being reviewed by two authorities, who have a bilateral cooperation agreement between them; *Exxon/Mobil* which was mentioned above could be cited as a good example here. The lack of ability on the part of such authorities to exchange confidential information therefore might affect the interests of these firms because this may make it very difficult if not impossible for these authorities to conduct comprehensive investigations. Indeed, even in the USA – the country with the strongest tendency to opt for unilateral actions in the field of competition law – such situation has been recognised as can be seen from the adoption of the International Antitrust Enforcement Assistance Act 1994 which was discussed above. A similar position exists in the Dutch competition law regime under which the Netherlands competition authority can exchange confidential information obtained during the course of an investigation with foreign competition authorities.[74] However the authority may do so only where the following are satisfied:

- the confidentiality of the information is sufficiently protected;
- adequate assurance is given that the information will not be used for purposes other than the enforcement of the foreign competition law; and
- if disclosure of the information in question is in the interest of the Dutch economy.

On the other hand, waiver of right to confidentiality by firms – as we saw above – may involve certain risks for them in cases where this information ends up in the hands of competitors or customers who might then 'abuse' it or use it to launch their own actions against such firms; risks that are particularly high in competition law regimes which have a private enforcement strand.

(D) Existence of cooperation v. lack of cooperation

In practice the cooperation agreements entered into by some competition authorities have resulted in virtually no instances of actual cooperation as stipulated under the relevant agreement. Indeed in the case of certain competition authorities an extensive web of bilateral agreements has been established though the actual cooperation in practice has not gone beyond being academic.[75] On the other hand, there are instances in

---

[74] Other examples can be found in Art. 29 of the Malta Competition Act 1994 and the Competition Ordinance of Pakistan 2010.

[75] See, for example, Ukraine which has entered into agreements with Georgia, Azerbaijan, the Russian Federation, Lithuania, Poland, Hungary, Bulgaria, the Czech Republic among other countries.

which – notwithstanding the absence of a formal agreement – competition authorities have opted for full and meaningful cooperation, which has included exchanging of information in actual cases.[76] In these cases the chances of meaningful cooperation – notwithstanding the absence of an agreement – including exchange of information will be enhanced enormously by the existence of: *general laws* in the country(ies) concerned;[77] *bilateral agreements of general economic nature*;[78] and *international treaties.*[79] Additionally, especially important here is whether 'compatibility' exists between the laws of the countries concerned with regard to the nature of competition offences, most importantly whether they are considered to be of a civil or criminal nature.

9. Cooperation and comity: a relationship of harmony?

Whether the mechanism of cooperation and the principle of comity sit comfortably with one another seems to be open to question. One of the major pillars of cooperation is considered to be exchange of information between the authorities concerned. When information is disclosed to the other party this can be expected to enhance the efforts of the receiving authority to conduct an effective investigation. It is unclear whether comity will have a role to play when two investigations may end up being conducted in these cases and ultimately leading to conflicting outcomes or at least differences in how the same situation is viewed.

---

[76] A notable example here is the cooperation between Chile and the USA witnessed on some occasions.

[77] See, for example, Act 24,767 in Argentina which governs international cooperation in relation to criminal prosecution, adjudication and application of penalties and makes it an obligation on Argentina to provide assistance to any country offering reciprocity or having ratified an international treaty to this effect.

[78] Such as the Japan–Philippines Economic Partnership agreement which was entered into in September 2006. Although no specific cooperation agreement in the field of competition exists between the parties, the Agreement provides for cooperation between them in the field.

[79] A few notable examples can be found here including: the *Inter-American Convention on Mutual Assistance in Criminal Matters* which makes it a binding obligation on parties to render to one another mutual assistance in relation to criminal investigations, proceedings and prosecutions; the *Civil, Commercial, Labour and Administrative Cooperation Protocol (Las Leñas Protocol)* within which Argentina, Brazil, Uruguay and Paraguay have undertaken to provide mutual assistance and wide cooperation in civil enforcement matters; the *Inter-American Convention on the Taking of Evidence Abroad*, adopted under the auspices of the Organisation of American States, which governs the execution of letters rogatory and establishes a framework for cooperation between the parties; and the *Hague Convention on the Service Abroad of Judicial and Extrajudicial Documents in Civil or Commercial Matters* 1965.

Moreover, bilateral cooperation has quite often been seen as a means for strong jurisdictions to achieve harmonisation by weaker jurisdictions with their competition rules and practice. This itself does not sit comfortably with the idea of comity, which as we saw above rests on the need to take into account foreign interests.

10. Looking to the future: a policy perspective

The various points made above serve to show that while there are important benefits attached to bilateral cooperation, serious shortcomings, limitations and ambiguity surround this cooperation most of which have not until now been addressed properly. There is room therefore for considering how one can address the various shortcomings and limitations. One basic comment that should be made about the factors giving rise to the shortcomings, limitations and ambiguity surrounding bilateral cooperation is that these cannot be grouped together when thinking about possible solutions or suggestions for improvement. For example, the issue of confidential information cannot be coupled with that of conflicting outcomes and dispute resolution. The former may simply be addressed under national law or international treaty whereas the latter would require a mechanism, such as a forum to resolve the dispute. More importantly however there is room for considering how one can move forward towards promoting bilateral cooperation and enhancing their effectiveness as an international strategy and its desirable outcome of convergence and advancing competition law. All of the shortcomings, limitations and ambiguity notwithstanding, bilateral cooperation has been a highly important 'option' through which competition law has come to be considerably internationalised over the years. Bilateral cooperation has emerged in recent years as a phenomenally important topic in the field of competition law generally, and in practice it has been playing a significant role in the application and enforcement of competition rules in different parts of the world.

Looking ahead however, it would be appropriate to encourage competition authorities to opt for bilateral cooperation where possible, particularly ones that most vigorously enforce their competition rules today; this is especially important, in the absence of a realistic possibility of adopting preferable methods of addressing competition issues in the global economy – such as adopting a multilateral approach with binding commitments. Moreover bilateral cooperation is widely seen as the most important form of cooperation from the point of view of furthering and safeguarding legal relations between countries; something that is seen from the attitude of some of the world's most advanced competition authorities, such as those of the Canada, the EU and the USA. It was also noted above that a bilateral strategy could offer an effective solution to the use of 'aggressive' strategies – such as extraterritoriality – by certain countries in ways that could lead to undermining fairness in a global economy and the exploitation of other countries. Adopting the EU–US agreement as a model, and building on the efforts of competition authorities which have entered into similar agreements, seems to be a sensible step to take.

Indeed it can be said that globally there is nowadays overwhelming support for cooperation. This is seen even in countries such as the USA, which for many years was sceptical about cooperation. For example, in April 2007, the US Antitrust Modernisation Commission (AMC) published its findings, which made clear recommendation to the US government to pursue more cooperation agreements in the field of competition law based on comity principles with trading partners and make greater use of the comity in existing bilateral cooperation agreements with other jurisdictions.[80]

It seems that bilateralism has a huge potential that remains unfulfilled in relation to its role as a strategy for internationalising competition law and this has mainly been so for two reasons: first, the lack of a *centre of gravity* that could pull the different strands of bilateralism together and ensure that a coherent long-term vision is built with regard to how the vehicle of bilateralism can and should be driven along the 'internationalisation' of competition law route; and secondly, the lack of sufficient knowledge about the extent of bilateral cooperation at present and the prospects for developing it further.

(A)   A centre of gravity

Until now, bilateralism has been mainly developed in the following way: through initiatives taken by some competition authorities to forge bilateral links with other competition authorities and an occasional notable involvement by the OECD, through publishing recommendations and offering a platform for some competition authorities to meet and collaborate in various respects. As such, bilateralism has ended up being a highly limited tool in scope; confined to certain competition authorities; and not widely used in practice.

---

[80] See in particular recommendation 41 of the AMC; for a discussion on the AMC and its report see pp. 268–272 above.

This situation however can be improved *dramatically* if bilateralism can be injected more concretely within an international organisation with a wide base. The International Competition Network (ICN) would be a suitable forum to do this because of its unique membership and the credibility it enjoys as an organisation with sole emphasis on soft-law convergence.[81] Building a bilateralism platform within the ICN would fit very well with the emphasis the organisation puts on convergence.

A number of ideas may be advanced here. Chief among these is building an initiative to develop the bilateral cooperation's long-term benefit of convergence. This would somehow shift the exclusive focus on bilateralism from that of its overwhelming perception at present as a specific tool to be introduced only where the parties come to realise they have many commonalities, which are created most obviously by overlap of jurisdiction, i.e. as has been the case with the EU–US cooperation. With such shift, attention will come to be given to the contribution bilateral cooperation could make towards advancing competition law, especially at policymaking level and achieving crucial convergence and harmonisation among different rules and standards.

Essentially, therefore, what is being proposed here is advancing the actual mechanism inherent in bilateral cooperation. As was noted above, the whole idea of bilateral cooperation – which was started in the 1960s – originally developed around agreements with negative comity: the good manners, courtesy, 1970s and 1980s, *first* generation agreements. This was followed by the 1990s development and the introduction of positive comity agreements: the *second* generation agreements. What the idea being described here does is advocate the developing of *third* generation bilateral agreements, '3G', through using a centralised international platform. These 3G agreements will not be limited to cooperation in actual isolated cases. The focus will be on creating wide channels of cooperation through which all of the following can flow: hosting competition law events in the form of conferences and seminars; arranging training programmes; and holding general consultations aiming at advancing expertise and achieving convergence.

(B) *Lack of knowledge*

The second reason for the *unfulfilled* potential of bilateral cooperation has been simply the lack of knowledge of the extent of this form of

---

[81] See pp. 573–578 below.

cooperation in practice and lack of familiarity with the prospects for developing it.

It is unclear whether it is known exactly how many bilateral agreements actually exist in the field, let alone how many of these are positive comity agreements, negative comity agreements or mixed (with positive and negative comity principles). This shows lack of knowledge about the extent of bilateral cooperation as a *network* in practice. The other face to the same coin is that many competition authorities themselves are uncertain about what prospects really exist for them to build a bilateral strategy. There are many competition authorities who are keen to enter into bilateral cooperation (not necessarily for purposes such as avoiding jurisdictional conflict), but they simply do not know how to go about it, who would be interested and who would be a suitable partner. The picture is made all the more bleak by the perceived inherently long-term nature and cost of entering into this type of agreements. At present, the number of bilateral agreements is perhaps not as large as it should be, the sole focus has come to be given to positive comity and they show clear exclusion of developing countries; this is in addition to the lack of a proper role for firms to play within the framework of the agreements which one may envisage could be particularly helpful to the relevant competition authorities. Building a centralised platform – in the form of a centre of gravity as mentioned earlier – would have an important role to play in changing this situation dramatically. Often these authorities need to be educated on how bilateral cooperation can help them build their expertise and how to go about achieving it. With a centralised platform shifting the focus on bilateralism from that of a purely national affair to a strategy with an international component, it will be much more realistic to achieve the objective of promoting competition law understanding and furthering those efforts seeking to realise meaningful convergence. This is perhaps the particular future direction – a change in policy perspective – with regard to how bilateral cooperation is approached and utilised that is worth giving some thought to.

Table of bilateral agreement   The table below outlines the cooperation in existence in a variety of bilateral agreements between different jurisdictions. The table is not fully exhaustive; for example it does not include situations where bilateral cooperation between two jurisdictions manifests itself in an informal manner (in the form of *de facto* cooperation) or those in which bilateral cooperation is based on general economic cooperation or free trade agreements. The table does however cover most bilateral competition-specific agreements – including those with both positive comity and/or negative (traditional) comity principles – which are in existence around the world.

Party 1	Party 2	Agreement	A brief description
Australia	Korea	Cooperation Arrangement (2002)	The agreement provides for the sharing of information and assistance and cooperation in enforcement activities.
Australia	New Zealand	Cooperation Agreement (2007)	The agreement provides for the exchange of information, assistance and general coordination and cooperation in activities.
Australia	Taiwan	Cooperation and Coordination Agreement (2002)	Australia and Taiwan undertake to provide information, notify enforcement activities within each other's domain and provide assistance where needed.
Australia	United Kingdom	Cooperation Agreement (2003)	Notification, cooperation and communication in enforcement, avoidance of conflicts and confidentiality provisions are included.
Bosnia and Herzegovina	Croatia	Cooperation Agreement (2007)	The agreement provides for the permanent exchange of data, information and

			documents relevant for market competition, provision of expert opinions, and coordination of activities relevant for market protection.
Bosnia and Herzegovina	Macedonia	Memorandum of Understanding	Mutual cooperation is directed at the exchange of legal norms and other legal sources for the implementation of competition activities.
Canada	Brazil	Cooperation Agreement (2008)	The agreement has provisions regarding notification of enforcement activities, exchange of information, avoidance of conflicts and confidentiality.
Canada	Chile	Memorandum of Understanding	Provisions relate to mutual technical assistance and the application of competition rules.
Canada	Costa Rica	Free Trade Agreement	The agreement contains provisions concerning the exchange of information and a system of consultation and technical assistance.
Canada	Japan	Cooperation Agreement (2005)	The agreement deals with notification, confidentiality and deferral of investigations.

Canada	Korea	Cooperation Agreement (2006)	Canada and Korea have agreed to cooperate by way of notifying each other of certain enforcement activities, by sharing information (whilst maintaining confidentiality) and by avoiding conflicts of interest.
Canada	Mexico	Cooperation Agreement (2001)	The agreement covers issues relating to positive comity, technical assistance, notifications and consultations.
Canada	New Zealand	Cooperation Agreement (2003)	Notification, cooperation and communication in enforcement, avoidance of conflicts, exchange of information and confidentiality provisions are included.
Canada	Taiwan	Cooperation Agreement (2002)	Notification, cooperation and communication in enforcement, avoidance of conflicts, exchange of information and confidentiality provisions are included.
Canada	United Kingdom	Cooperation Agreement	Notification, cooperation and communication in enforcement and confidentiality provisions are included.

Canada	United States of America	Agreement on the Application of Competition and Deceptive Marketing Practice Laws, 1995, as amended by the Agreement on the Application of Positive Comity Principles to the Enforcement of Competition Laws (2004)	The agreement deals with notification, coordination, avoiding conflicts, consultations and confidentiality.
Croatia	Romania	Cooperation Agreement	The agreement provides for the permanent exchange of data, information and documents relevant for market competition, provision of expert opinions, and coordination of activities relevant for market protection.
EU	Australia	Cooperation Agreement	Notification, cooperation and communication in enforcement and confidentiality provisions are included.
EU	Canada	Cooperation Agreement (1999)	The agreement provides for notification, coordination of enforcement activities and rendering of assistances, deferral and the exchange of information.

EU	Japan	Agreement Concerning Cooperation on Anticompetitive Actions (2003)	The agreement provides for notification of cases under investigation, the possibility of coordination, deferral, exchange of information and regular meetings.
EU	United States of America	Cooperation Agreement (1991) and Positive Comity Agreement (1998)	The provisions of the agreements relate to notification, cooperation and coordination of actions, and the use of positive and traditional comity.
El Salvador	Chile	Cooperation Agreement (2007)	The agreement is based on the principles of reciprocity and mutual benefits; it has the objective of cooperation and coordination between the respective national competition authorities.
El Salvador	Cost Rica	Cooperation Agreement (2007)	The agreement is based on the principles of reciprocity and mutual benefits; it has the objective of cooperation and coordination between the respective national competition authorities.
El Salvador	Spain	Cooperation Agreement (2007)	The agreement is based on the principles of reciprocity and mutual benefits; it has the

			objective of cooperation and coordination between the respective national competition authorities.
Greece	Albania	Protocol of Cooperation (2006)	The specific areas of cooperation include the exchange of information about new decisions, the organisation of seminars, the implementation of joint programmes and common conferences and the creation of a Permanent Contact Commission which is responsible for the implementation of the joint activities.
Greece	Cyprus	Protocol of Cooperation (2006)	The Protocol covers the exchange of information about new decisions, the organisation of seminars, the implementation of joint programmes and common conferences and the creation of a Permanent Contact Commission which is responsible for the implementation of the joint activities.

Japan	Philippines	Economic Partnership Agreement (2006)	Both nations agreed to cooperate in the field of competition, though the extent to which this cooperation will manifest is currently unknown.
Korea	United States of America	Free Trade Agreement (2007)	Provisions on mutual cooperation, notification, conference, and exchange of information regarding competition law policy and enforcement are included in the agreement.
Korea	Turkey	Memorandum of Understanding (2005)	The parties intend to develop cooperation in the field of applying competition rules, aimed at ensuring efficiency in the functioning of markets for goods and services.
New Zealand	Taiwan	Cooperation Agreement (2002)	Notification, cooperation and communication in enforcement, avoidance of conflicts, exchange of information and confidentiality provisions are included.
New Zealand	United Kingdom	Cooperation Agreement (2003)	Notification, cooperation and communication in enforcement, avoidance of conflicts and confidentiality provisions are included.

Taiwan	France	Cooperation Agreement	Exchanging information, notification, consultation and confidentiality are all provided for in the agreement.
Turkey	Romania	Memorandum of Understanding (2005)	The parties envisage the exchange of information and documents in respect of particular matters.
United States of America	Australia	Agreement on Mutual Antitrust Enforcement Assistance (1999)	Australia and the USA exchange evidence on a reciprocal basis for use in competition law enforcement. Both positive and negative comity procedures are used.
United States of America	Brazil	Cooperation Agreement (2003)	The countries have agreed to exchange information and experience in the antitrust subject, either concerning acts and contracts or administrative procedures and preliminary investigations. In cases of violations of the economic order, the agreement enables the authorities to communicate among themselves, including the exchange of public agents to assure

			the effectiveness of investigations.
United States of America	Germany	Cooperation Agreement (1976)	The agreement deals with the provision of information, requests for assistance and confidentiality.
United States of America	Israel	Cooperation Agreement (1999)	The agreement provides for the coordination of enforcement activities, the use of positive comity principles, and measures relating to the avoidance of conflicts, consultations and confidentiality.
United States of America	Japan	Cooperation Agreement (1999)	The agreement governs notifications, requests for assistance, coordination of enforcement activities and consultation.
United States	Mexico	Cooperation Agreement (2000)	The agreement provides for notification, coordination of enforcement, technical cooperation and measures aimed at avoiding conflicts.

Chapter 10

The multilateral option: cooperation through binding and non-binding commitments

This chapter will examine the third of the three internationalisation options in the field of competition law: the multilateral option, namely the desire and efforts to develop a collective approach by countries in the field. The focus in the chapter will be on specific forms which this option can take and which may be conveniently grouped together under two headings: 'binding' obligations and 'non-binding' obligations. The main forms of the former – as they have come to emerge over the years – include: concluding a binding multilateral agreement; drafting an international competition law code; and building an international competition law regime with an independent institutional apparatus and capabilities and competence to handle competition cases. The latter heading, on the other hand, covers multilateral instruments introduced within a loose institutional framework, extending to mainly but not exhaustively guidelines, best practices and recommendations produced at a supranational level, i.e. by international organisations active in the field; the International Competition Network (ICN), the Organisation for Economic Cooperation and Development (OECD) and the United Nations Conference on Trade and Development (UNCTAD) have all developed and produced such instruments over the years.

The chapter will in particular shed light on the usefulness of the multilateral option as a means to address competition problems in the global economy, and assess the realistic future prospects of pursuing this option through binding and non-binding obligations on countries and highlight the difficulties surrounding each of these two endeavours.

1. Multilateralism through binding obligations

A term that has in recent times been used to describe multilateral instruments resting on binding obligations is that of 'hard law' instruments.[1]

(A) Past developments

The idea of multilateralism was originally developed within the context of binding obligations. We are in fact not far from a centenary since the first time the whole idea emerged and was seriously discussed;[2] in this regard, it is important to note that, contrary to the impression formed by many people in recent years, the debate around this idea (not least in terms of origins) is not really purely academic.[3] The birth of the idea resulted from some remarkable developments that came to unfold around the first quarter of the twentieth century including a noticeable antipathy around that time towards anticompetitive practices, most notably the phenomenon of cartels. This antipathy can be seen from the way the League of Nations (replaced in 1945 by the United Nations) considered cartels as 'an enemy of world trade'; a slogan that was given a stronger emphasis in the early 1930s. During those years, cartels were employed by several countries, notably Germany, Italy and Japan, as a means for mobilising for what became the Second World War;[4] in particular German cartels[5] and Japanese *zaibatsu*[6] were viewed as harmful practices in the face of free trade between countries and they contributed significantly towards efforts to introduce a global prohibition on cartels, notably the *Draft Havana Charter*.

---

[1] The chapter will use the terms of 'binding commitments', 'binding obligations' and 'hard law instruments' interchangeably and in the same manner the terms 'non-binding commitments', 'non-binding obligations' and 'soft law instruments'.

[2] A distinction here is made between efforts to build an international competition law initiative and those aiming at promoting free trade internationally; the latter is considered to have been started in the 1800s.

[3] It is fair to say however that since the 1990s in particular the debate has had a strong academic flavour and academic leadership has on a number of occasions provided the 'fuel' for its continuation – see, as a notable example, the Munich Group's Initiative (p. 87 above and pp. 545–547 below) and also arguably the launch of the International Competition Network (p. 149 above).

[4] See chapter 1 for a discussion on the historical perspective of competition law.

[5] See the I. G. Farben cartel as an (in)famous example.

[6] Zaibatsu were powerful, family-owned industrial conglomerates which until the end of the Second World War were the dominant market players in the Japanese economy (during this time there was no competition law in the country: Japan adopted its Anti-monopoly Law in 1947).

I. The Draft Havana Charter

In an attempt to address international cartels and anticompetitive practices in general, the *Draft Havana Charter* was introduced under the auspicious of the 'new' United Nations. The Draft Charter aimed to, among other things, establish an International Trade Organisation (ITO) and introduce provisions dealing with restrictive business practices.[7] The Draft Charter imposed an obligation on member countries of the *proposed* ITO to prevent firms from engaging in activities which may 'restrain competition, limit access to markets or foster monopolistic control in international trade' where these restraints interfered with the trade-liberalising aims of the Draft Charter.[8] Among the specific practices brought within the scope of the prohibition were: price-fixing; restrictions on terms and conditions of supply; market sharing; discrimination; limiting production or fixing quotas; unjustified or unlawful use of intellectual property rights; and preventing the development of particular technologies. The Draft Charter stated that members could bring complaints about such restraints to the ITO. The latter would then be entitled, under Article 48 of the Draft Charter, to investigate and recommend action to the home countries of the firms engaged in restrictive practices. By all accounts, this was an impressive effort to create an agenda for developing international competition rules and principles and for building a global initiative in the field. The initiative however came to prove to be a distant dream, mainly due to US objection to it, which meant that the ITO never actually materialised and the Draft Charter was deemed to fail.[9] This result may be considered to be surprising, particularly in light of the USA's hostility at that time towards restrictive practices, especially those with international reach and influence.[10] The serving US President at that time, President Franklin Roosevelt spoke privately and publicly about the US 'tradition' to oppose monopolies and how competition law was 'as much part of the American

---

[7] See *Havana Charter for an International Trade Organization*, UN Doc. E/Conf. 2/78 (1948); printed in C. Wilcox, *A Charter for World Trade* (Macmillan, 1949). See also G. Bronz, 'The International Trade Organisation Charter' (1949) *Harvard Law Review* 1089; R. R. Wilson, 'Proposed ITO Charter', (1947) *American Journal of International Law* 879.

[8] See Art. 46 of the Havana Charter.

[9] See A. F. Lowenfeld, *Public Controls on International Trade* (Matthew Bender, 1983).

[10] See T. Arnold, *Bottlenecks of Business* (Reynal & Hitchcock, 1973); C. D. Edwards, *Control of Cartels and Monopolies: an International Comparison* (Oceana Publications, 1967), pp. 228–30; B. E. Clubb, *United States Foreign Trade Law* (Little Brown, 1991).

way of life as the due process clause of the Constitution'. He made it clear on more than one occasion that the way forward to fighting international cartels in particular 'can be achieved only through collaborative action'.[11]

II. The ECOSOC draft convention

The failure of the Draft Havana Charter however did not derail the entire multilateralism project completely. Five years later, the United Nations Economic and Social Council (ECOSOC) recommended the inclusion of a draft convention that would have established a new international agency endowed with the responsibility to receive and investigate complaints of restrictive business practices. This was in fact an initiative originating from President Roosevelt's vision of utilising the United Nations to pursue the collaborative effort he had famously spoken about, as mentioned in the previous section. However, the USA rejected the draft convention because it felt that disparities in domestic policies and practices were so substantial that they would render an international organisation ineffective.[12] The USA also was not in favour of a provision in the draft under which each country enjoyed one vote, believing that this would have afforded certain countries the chance to abuse this provision and use it in a hostile manner towards the USA and its interests.

III. Engaging the GATT

The fate met by the ECOSOC draft convention dealt another serious blow to the multilateralism effort which – though was not a fatal blow – it virtually eliminated any chance for real progress to be made for the next five years, until 1958 that is: when a General Agreement on Tariffs and Trade (GATT)[13] *Experts Group* was set up to address the topic of restrictive practices of private firms and make some recommendations. Among the key findings reached by this group was the finding that there was a particular *lack of necessary consensus among countries* and insufficient experience in the field of competition law (or restrictive business practices to use the dominant terminology around that time) and this

---

[11] See letter from Franklin Roosevelt to his Secretary of State at the time (the Franklin Roosevelt Library, New York, File 277).

[12] D. P. Wood, 'The Impossible Dream: Real International Antitrust' (1992) *University of Chicago Legal Forum* 277, 284–5.

[13] See pp. 550–562 below for a discussion of the GATT and its successor, the WTO; also pp. 120–130 above.

made it particularly difficult – and quite unrealistic – to try to reach any form of multilateral agreement on how to deal with restrictive business practices with an international component.[14] The group noted that for this purpose and to enhance the prospects for building an international strategy in the field, it would be essential first for regimes to be instituted around the world in order to deal with these harmful practices domestically. This latter point made considerable sense and clearly was designed to avoid a 'top-down' approach, under which competition law would be imposed on countries as opposed to being allowed to *grow* from domestic roots. The group's recommendations were followed by a 1961 report in which the GATT recommended that in case of a dispute, the parties to the dispute should engage in consultation with each other on the control of restrictive business practices.[15] The report particularly recognised that practices of firms 'which restrict competition in international trade may hamper the expansion of world trade and the economic development in individual countries and thereby frustrate the benefits of tariff reductions and of the removal of quantitative restrictions or otherwise interfere with the objectives of the GATT'. Arguably, this conclusion can be seen as an improvement on the 1958 recommendation, which was considered to be a result of a *tacit acceptance* that international cartel activities did not present – conclusively in the eyes of all countries and people – a serious problem that required addressing as well as a *realisation* that there was enormous opposition to any attempt to limit the national sovereignty of countries.

IV. The Munich Group's code

Little progress however came to be made after 1961 until 1993, when a group of 12 competition law expert scholars – branded widely as the Munich Group – decided to take a small step that had the potential of translating into a giant leap towards building an international competition law framework.[16] At the heart of their initiative, stood the (eventually completed) task of drafting a *multilateral competition law code*,

---

[14] GATT Resolution 5 November 1958 cited in D. Furnish, 'A Transnational Approach to Restrictive Business Practices' (1970) *International Lawyer* 317. See also M. E. Janow, 'Competition Policy and the WTO' in J. Bhagwati and M. Hirsh (eds.), *The Uruguay Round and Beyond* (University of Michigan Press, 1998).

[15] GATT Resolution, BISD 28 (9th Supp., 1961).

[16] International Antitrust Code Working Group, Draft International Code as a GATT–MTO Plurilateral Trade Agreement (10 July 1993).

which included substantive rules and principles,[17] in the form of a multilateral agreement. The responsibility of 'administering' the *Draft Code* – primarily to ensure compliance by countries with its provisions but also to request domestic courts and competition authorities to initiate investigations to deal with competition problems – was intended to be that of an independent international body, possibly an autonomous competition authority; thus the idea of incorporating the Draft Code within the soon-to-be-created WTO was clearly envisaged. The vision for operating the Draft Code was highly interesting. The Draft Code had what may be termed as a 'hybrid' nature: on the one hand, countries would join the Code (when finalised and adopted) *voluntarily* whilst on the other hand they had to ensure the application of their domestic competition rules would *comply* with Code.[18] Whilst its rules were intended to deal with competition cases with a cross-border element, the *Draft Code* actually recognised that the domestic competition laws of countries would be the applicable law. This was designed to effectively make the provisions of the Draft Code enforceable by domestic competition authorities in their respective jurisdictions. The intended operation of the Draft Code foresaw the possibility of disputes arising and in this regard the approach chosen by the group was that such disputes should be heard by a permanent international competition panel, forming part of a wider dispute settlement mechanism.

The Draft Code was prepared using a very open-textured language and it seems this was deliberately used in order to make the Draft Code as inclusive as possible in terms of 'accommodating' the different circumstances of countries, their varying experiences in the field of competition law and the particular needs of different competition authorities. Nonetheless, the basic concept underlying the Draft Code was remarkably ambitious: creating a set of international competition rules and principles to be implemented through the enforcement actions of domestic competition authorities, with supervisory and dispute resolution functions given to an autonomous international body, under the

---

[17] The substantive rules included in the Draft Code dealt with a variety of business phenomena stretching from cartels to mergers. The principles of the Draft Code on the other hand covered many of those principles which have come to feature in the WTO agreements, such as the national treatment principle.

[18] What this means is that the system intended to be created under the Draft Code was to be operated on the basis of ideas originating at the national level as well as on the basis of understanding international politics and international economic issues; and some appropriate recourse to principles of public international law.

auspices of which the Draft Code was to be *administered*. Yet this ambitious approach appears to have been by design: the idea was to facilitate the emergence of a global perspective to competition cases with an international dimension to ensure that among other things the risk of inconsistent decisions being reached by competition authorities – which is inherent in competition law practice particularly in an area such as merger control – would be eliminated. To realise this idea, a pragmatic approach was suggested: an incorporation of international competition rules and principles within domestic competition law regimes without interfering with the sovereignty of countries, whether through demanding they modify their domestic rules or limiting their power of domestic competition authorities or minimising the scope for domestic enforcement.

Despite these major efforts by the group to enhance the 'selling points' of the Draft Code and show particular sensitivity towards the issue of sovereignty, the Draft Code came to face a number of criticisms, which effectively meant it would not advance beyond the proposal stage. Primarily, the broad and open-textured language of the Draft Code was perceived to be vague and ambiguous and questions were raised that this would do away with its value as opposed to enhance the latter. The perceived vague nature of the wording of the Draft Code was considered to have a negative contributory effect to the wide role of the proposed international body. A mixture of the two was considered likely to trigger difficulties in ensuring accountability by this body and add more bureaucracy to enforcement of competition cases. Additionally, it was uncertain whether the purported pragmatic approach underpinning the Draft Code was actually workable for three reasons: the existence of major differences between countries in the field of competition law, let alone the lack of proper and functioning competition law regimes in some countries; the serious likelihood that the Draft Code would be impossible to implement without alterations being made by countries to their domestic competition rules; and the fact that although it was intended that actual enforcement *powers* would remain in the hands of domestic competition authorities, the operation of the Draft Code would have impacted on the *discretion* of competition authorities.[19]

---

[19] The issue of discretion of competition authorities has huge importance in the field; see M. Dabbah, *The Internationalisation of Antitrust Policy* (Cambridge University Press, 2003), ch. 4.

V.   Towards the WTO option

Perhaps the final ring in the chain of past developments that should be mentioned is the effort to integrate a competition law agenda within the World Trade Organisation (WTO) framework which came to surface in 1995. In a way, this effort may be considered to be a current one, notwithstanding the serious obstacles it has come to reach since its initiation. The effort will be discussed in greater detail below.[20]

(B)   Reaching the present

The various (and almost distant past) developments surveyed above carried hope and frustration for the proponents of the multilateral option of internationalisation of competition law through binding commitments. On the one hand, the developments showed that there were merits to the debate on the use of an international strategy to deal with restrictive business practices and this, among other things, encouraged the proponents of the option to continue the debate and formulate different ideas for converting it into concrete steps. There was therefore hope, which came to spread its wings to what – from the standpoint at the time – looked like a development in the distant future: the creation of the WTO and the conclusion of a competition agreement within its framework. On the other hand, the developments gave rise to an element of frustration: whilst it was abundantly clear that countries on the whole were willing to explore options for building a multilateral strategy in the field of competition law, they lacked a sufficiently strong political will to take concrete steps in that direction. Furthermore – in fairness to the sceptics and opponents of the idea – it was equally clear that in practical terms countries were not *ready* to take any step in this regard: other than the lack of sufficient competition law expertise and proper institutional structure to enforce the rules in different countries, it is not clear that a general consensus actually existed among countries on the value of competition and whether competition was considered desirable and worthy of protection. Some countries had deep misgivings about competition as a concept, a phenomenon and a process, and on the whole believed that it had no benefit to offer them but harm. Much of those years (of the twentieth century) saw a remarkable tendency in many parts of the world to favour a tradition of exerting strict government control

---

[20] See pp. 550–562 below.

over the planning and management of domestic economies, and only in a few countries were there any material steps taken in the opposite direction. This situation paved the way for one of the twentieth century's most heated debates: the debate between capitalism and communism which in many ways stood on the question over the desirability of competition in the marketplace. As it is almost historical knowledge these days however, the debate is widely regarded to have remarkably settled in favour of the market mechanism. This can be seen in light of the dramatic changes that came to occur as represented by among other things the move on the part of many countries from monopolisation to de-monopolisation and from state control and planning to liberalisation and privatisation. These changes enormously contributed to the growing recognition that, on the whole, competition can be regarded as an effective tool for enhancing innovation, furthering economic growth and safeguarding the economic welfare and social development of countries. The desirability of competition has been enhanced phenomenally therefore, and as a result this has made the current position remarkably different from that which existed for most of the twentieth century.

(C) Contemplating the future

When discussing multilateral cooperation and the option of building it through binding obligations, it is helpful to review past (and relevant present) developments. This is what the discussion above aimed to do. Equally crucial however, it is vital to assess what chances there are for this strategy in the future, whether in the short or long term. This assessment calls for awareness of the various options as they stand at present. This part of the chapter therefore will not attempt simply to 'propose' options or models for pursuing this option of multilateralism. It is probably the case that it would be more helpful not to do so at any rate but rather to exhaust the discussion on the options we already have.

In contemplating the future, the discussion here will not aim at an assessment of specific individual suggestions or proposals that have been put forward over the years. Rather the chapter will opt for an assessment to be conducted in *broad* terms under which these proposals will be grouped together according to type or category. This is done with the commonalities between the different proposals in mind of course.

Looking at the various proposals which have emerged over the years and which have been 'imagined' as suitable ways to push for multilateralism in the field of competition law on the basis of binding obligations, two broad categories may be possible to identify: achieving this through a top-down approach or through a bottom-up approach. Under the former approach, what has been contemplated is essentially an option along the lines of the Munich Group's international competition code: a multilateral agreement of some form with a type of international institutional framework. The latter approach, on the other hand, is one that would cover ideas, such as convergence and harmonisation among the competition law regimes of different countries in order to emerge with some common standards in the field internationally. It is true that under this bottom-up approach a multilateral agreement might be in existence to achieve this and that therefore ideas under it should at least be considered as falling into both categories. Nonetheless, the distinction made here – between the two approaches – rests on where the emphasis on multilateralism is placed and where the actual 'operation' of the latter is. Under the top-down approach, emphasis and operation are at the *higher international level* whereas the bottom-up approach demands these two to exist at the *lower, domestic* (or where appropriate *regional*)[21] level.

I. Proceeding on the basis of a multilateral agreement

For many years, the question was asked whether the way forward in advancing competition law at the international level was through the conclusion of some form of a binding multilateral agreement. Towards the end of the 1990s however this question seems to have shifted in its emphasis to become *what form of binding multilateral agreement was suitable to pursue a multilateral strategy in the field.* In this way, considerable consensus came to emerge that a multilateral agreement was, if not absolutely necessary, at least highly desirable. Those in favour of this option have repeatedly confirmed their position that this perhaps is the best way forward in order to enable the global competition law community – particularly competition authorities and firms – to operate in a more effective way and to contribute to advancing competition law and policy and their understanding in a meaningful way: for the former (competition authorities) to enhance their ability to deal with increasingly international competition problems caused by the latter (firms) while for the latter to be relieved of an increasingly heavy burden caused by high costs and legal uncertainty resulting from current multi-investigations or multi-enforcement by different competition

---

[21] See chapter 7 for an examination of regionalism in the field of competition law.

authorities. The proponents of this option received momentum with the arrival of the new millennium which witnessed *encouraging* progress made at the 4th WTO Ministerial Conference held in Doha in November 2001 and the outstanding preparations, which came to be made for the 5th WTO Ministerial Conference held in Cancun in 2003. The (well-documented) desertion by participants in Cancun of negotiations to 'go to the beach' instead has rendered the multilateral agreement option in need of serious revival. The lack of this for the past six years however has come to confirm the doubts expressed for a long time by the opponents of the option.

Whilst it has been effectively pulled down (some might say removed from) the global competition law agenda, realistically speaking the question appears to have reverted back to its original form: whether the way forward in internationalising competition law is through the binding multilateral agreement option. One major consequence of this development has been that the competition law community globally has been effectively forced to pedal back to the former position of debating the need for this serious step in the field. Obviously, if the step of adopting such agreement is to be taken, it is widely believed that the most appropriate forum at present is the WTO. Essentially therefore, the debate over the desirability and realistic prospects of adopting a binding multilateral agreement is over the desirability and realistic prospects of a WTO competition law option: the question is to what extent in the short or long term competition law should become part of any multilateral trade negotiations between countries at the WTO.

Any view in favour of including competition law within the WTO must be clear on what should be considered – in terms of rules and principles – in those future negotiations. This includes clarity on whether there is a set of comprehensive competition rules extending beyond the core prohibition on cartels and serious abuses of dominance to business phenomena such as mergers and vertical restraints;[22] whether at any rate these rules should be subject to dispute settlement procedures; whether the rules should be operated within a framework of various WTO principles, such as those on transparency, non-discrimination and national treatment;[23] whether a specifically contextualised approach to competition law should be adopted within WTO obligations to remove

---

[22] Vertical restraint issues have already arisen in the WTO context – see the *Kodak/Fuji* case, discussed at pp. 609–614 below.

[23] See pp. 607–608 below for a discussion of these principles.

hindrances to market access;[24] and more importantly, whether there is a need to determine the appropriate role for the WTO over the longer term in the field.

In discussing this vision for the future, it would be helpful to set out the arguments *in favour* and *against* of a WTO agreement in the field of competition law and to consider the views of different countries on pursuing the multilateral strategy through binding obligations and on the appropriate role of the WTO in this regard; countries play a crucial and leading role in this context given that their political agreement is needed to discuss competition law within the WTO framework and to reach such an agreement.[25]

The discussion below will explore these three strands; without looking at the origins of the WTO competition law initiative, which was discussed above.[26]

(a) **Arguments in favour**   In proposing the idea of building a WTO competition law agenda on the basis of a multilateral agreement – consisting of substantive rules to deal with competition cases with an international element and an international institutional framework to monitor compliance by countries with these rules – the *Singapore Group*[27] broadly had the EU competition law regime as a suitable model in mind. In proposing this, the Group had the clear backing of the EU itself, and other important WTO players, including: Canada, Korea and Japan among others.[28] The Group was also encouraged by what many came to perceive as key strengths enjoyed by the WTO which put in a 'favourite' position as the place in which to bring to life what was by then considered to be virtually an impossible dream. These strengths effectively came to be widely recognised as the arguments in favour of WTO competition policy. Some of these arguments rested on the actual *structure and operation* of the WTO. This included the fact that the WTO enjoyed a broadly inclusive membership of 154 participants representing the developed and developing world. Such broad membership base

---

[24] See chapter 11 for a discussion on the relationship between competition and trade policy, specifically in the context of the 'market access' principle.

[25] See pp. 100–111 above for a discussion on the role of key actors including countries in the process of internationalisation.

[26] See in particular pp. 123–130 above.

[27] See pp. 123–124 above for an account on the background of the Singapore Group.

[28] See however below for an account on the specific views of these countries on the WTO competition option.

would give any WTO competition law agreement unquestionable legitimacy: the agreement would be the result of negotiations between all of these countries and would only be reached once their consensus or approval has been secured. Beyond the advantage of the wide base, the WTO operates in a way that is considered to afford important flexibility to countries seeking to implement their WTO obligations: implementation of such obligations may be undertaken by developed countries in the immediate term to be followed by implementation by developing countries following that. This could be of crucial significance in the context of a WTO competition law agreement, in facilitating a gradual approach of countries implementing their obligations according to a timeframe suited to their own domestic circumstances and needs. A third advantage to be mentioned concerns the WTO's well-established dispute resolution mechanism. Through this mechanism the WTO has been able to demonstrate important credibility to solve disputes between countries, most crucially in an efficient manner.

The other arguments in favour concern the *content* of important WTO provisions and the *relevant expertise* it enjoys. Competition concepts and language are not totally absent from WTO agreements, protocols and papers. Notable examples of WTO provisions dealing with competition issues include: Article VIII and IX of the *General Agreement on Trade in Services* (GATS);[29] Articles 8 and 40 of the *Trade-Related Intellectual Property Rights* (TRIPS) agreement;[30] and Article 40 of the *Reference Paper on Telecommunications*.[31] Additionally, competition cases have been handled by the WTO Appellate Body in the *Kodak/Fuji* case (1998), and competition-based considerations have been applied by the WTO dispute settlement bodies, most notably in the *Mexico-Telecommunications* case (2004).[32] In this latter case, the USA had complained to the WTO against Mexico's international long-distance rules, which it claimed were incompatible with the Reference Paper on Telecommunications. In finding in favour of the USA, the WTO Dispute Settlement Body followed what may be regarded as a competition analysis-based approach, which included defining the relevant market.

These advantages – as highlighted in the *arguments in favour* – serve as important indicators that when it comes to considering its suitability to pursue competition policy issues, the WTO may be considered to be suitable, or at least not totally unsuitable. This suitability can be

---

[29] See pp. 603–604 below. [30] See pp. 604–605 below. [31] See pp. 605–606 below.
[32] Both of these cases are discussed in the following chapter; see pp. 609–616 below.

considered to be enhanced when one takes into account the positive attitude of important international bodies – notably the World Bank, UNCTAD and the ICN – towards the WTO in regard to its involvement in the field of competition law and the likely support these organisations will offer to the WTO in this involvement. However to assess the real value of any argument in favour of WTO competition policy in practice, it would be important to consider them in light of the arguments to the contrary.

(b) **Arguments against**   The WTO is a trade organisation. This fact on its own to many people presents a major hurdle in the face of a proposal advocating the conclusion of a WTO multilateral agreement in the field of competition law. The basis of this view appears to be informed by the gulf that can exist between competition and trade policy issues and the possible lack of harmony between them in practice.[33] To be frank, one wonders however about the merit of this argument given that great similarities exist between the two policies and the fact that there is a close nexus between the WTO objectives of trade liberalisation and open markets, and the commitment of an increasing number of countries – most of whom are members of the WTO family – to instituting competition law regimes and reinforcing existing ones. This, in addition to the fact that the WTO enjoys important capabilities of offering an *integrated* trade and competition enforcement approach,[34] is a factor in favour of developing a competition law agenda at the WTO. Nonetheless, one cannot ignore the huge weight of the fact that the WTO is what it is (a trade body) and its use by highly influential WTO members to highlight some of the disadvantages a WTO competition law option suffers from.[35]

The WTO's field of competence is not the only factor to be raised in the form of an argument against involvement in the field of competition law. In fact some of the perceived key strengths of the WTO have been identified as major weaknesses too. For example, the WTO's wide membership may be considered to be problematic in terms of achieving convergence among the interests of its different members. To put the point a different way, a level playing field is clearly lacking between

---

[33] See pp. 589–595 below for the complementarities and conflict between competition and trade policy.

[34] This integrated approach is most valuable in the case of hindrances to market access which are hybrid in nature, meaning ones resulting from private and public involvement. See pp. 587–588 below for an account of such hindrances.

[35] See pp. 556–557 below for an account on the views of USA.

different WTO members, with some possessing considerable competition law experience whilst others have either little or no experience at all in the field. In pushing for 'universal' competition rules to be implemented by countries in such differing positions, there is a real risk that the lowest common denominator will be opted for – an approach both groups of members are likely to reject for different reasons. The result therefore might be a set of substantive rules suffering from major weaknesses and ineffectiveness to be considered adequate to deal with competition problems in a globalised economy. This seems only to cement in the position of those countries who at any rate appear reluctant to accept any form of binding obligation in the field of competition.

However even if one were to consider these arguments as *answerable*, possibly by submitting that the flexibility of the WTO approach could cater for this through affording countries with less experience in the field the opportunity to develop this experience within a generous framework for implementing their obligation, other difficulties will immediately present themselves. Among these is the manner in which disputes are handled within the WTO framework and which is remarkably adversarial and runs along a dividing line – that has the prospect of turning into a major gulf – between *exporting* and *importing* countries. The primary objective behind hearing the case is to establish who is right and who is wrong. Such an approach – whilst suitable for trade disputes – would be questionable if it were to be followed in competition cases. Often – if not always – there is no right or wrong party among competition authorities in these cases in terms of asserting jurisdictions; though there might in some cases be right or wrong – but many times in between – concerning the substantive conclusion by competition authorities in cases. A confrontational or adversarial way of seeking a solution could cause frictions, possibly more than those triggered occasionally at present when competition authorities disagree in one and the same case. Furthermore, a WTO body sitting to hear a competition dispute would not necessarily be guaranteed to have a sufficiently global perspective, which would pull all the interests of the countries concerned together and anchor a policy approach that could offer future useful guidance.

(c) **The views of different countries**   It was remarked above that building a future vision in the field of competition that is based on a binding multilateral WTO agreement requires an understanding of three different strands. The discussion above considered the first two of these. Thus it remains for us to consider the third strand, the views of different countries on this vision. Over the years, the Singapore Group has received various 'communications' from many WTO members on the WTO competition law question and the issue of binding commitments-based multilateralism in the field more generally. These views have been extremely divergent and in the case of individual WTO members sometimes even inconsistent. The views have ranged from regarding the WTO as being of crucial significance in developing competition law at the international level, to advocating that the WTO option was subject to certain (and serious) limitations, to showing scepticism about the whole idea of a binding multilateral competition law agreement, let alone within the WTO.

(i) The US scepticism The position of the USA on the appropriateness of the WTO as a forum for negotiating competition rules has been inconsistent, but on the whole highly sceptical. Whilst the USA has actively supported efforts within the Singapore Group, it has also expressed some reservation on the practical value of using the WTO for the purposes of developing a multilateral competition law agreement. The USA has raised several concerns with respect to the WTO venturing into the field of competition law. These concerns have been repeatedly voiced by US competition officials who have argued that the case has not been made as yet for a binding multilateral agreement in the field of competition law. In particular, they have cited the lack of necessary knowledge on whether and to what extent key competition and trade policy issues may benefit from an integrated approach, let alone the difficulty of developing consensus on these issues. The WTO's principal concern with governmental trade-restraining practices has been considered to give rise to a serious limitation on its ability to deal with competition issues (even those arising in the context of hindrances to market access) because not all competition and trade policy problems overlap.

The view offered by US competition officials has been that forcing the issue nonetheless would fuel a perceived inherent risk in the WTO mechanism that the WTO would second-guess prosecutorial decision-making in complex evidentiary contexts – a task in which the WTO is considered to have no experience and for which it is not suited. Reflecting the general views of the USA, the International Competition Policy and Advisory Committee (ICPAC)[36] has argued that the traditional mandate of the WTO – negotiation of rules, which are then made subject to dispute settlement – may be inappropriate for handling competition

---

[36] See pp. 266–267 above.

issues, which should rather be discussed broadly and in a consultative manner. Such an approach of negotiating rules was also considered as something that would inevitably 'politicise' competition law and its enforcement in ways that are unlikely to improve either the economic rationality or the legal neutrality of decision-making in the field.[37]

Such concerns have only consolidated the US position that the main ingredient for furthering competition law internationally should be provided through the conclusion of bilateral agreements between different competition authorities and where relevant pursuing a multilateral strategy using soft law measures;[38] though this would not herald the demise of the unilateral option of asserting jurisdiction extraterritoriality. In the USA's views, prior to reaching the stage at which a binding multilateral agreement would be concluded, countries need to develop a culture of sound and effective competition law enforcement to be based on shared experience, bilateral cooperation and the provision of technical assistance to countries that are introducing or about to introduce domestic competition rules as well as those with young competition law regimes in existence. At least at one point however, the particular emphasis placed by the USA on bilateral cooperation did not sit quite comfortably with the positive signals that emerged from the attitude of the USA with regard to negotiating a multilateral agreement on competition law within the WTO as came to be seen in light of the support the USA has given to the text produced at the Doha Conference in 2001.

(ii) The EU enthusiasm The European Union – specifically the European Commission – has consistently been in favour of a 'more' internationalised competition law. As we saw in chapter 4, the European Commission has moved beyond placing a heavy emphasis on the importance and effectiveness of bilateral cooperative agreements between different competition authorities to champion the idea of a multilateral agreement, to be introduced within the WTO. This position can be seen in light of the original push by the EU in 1995 to establish the Singapore Group as well as the different statements made by successive EU commissioners for competition; some made very recently indeed and in the aftermath of the fatal outcome of the negotiations at Cancun: if one were to ask senior

---

[37] See address given by Joe Klein, former assistant attorney general for antitrust before the OECD Conference on Trade and Competition (30 June 1999) entitled: 'A Reality Check on Antitrust Rules in the WTO, a Practical Way Forward on International Antitrust'.
[38] See below.

competition officials in the EU – even at this point in time – about the best option of internationalisation, they would vote overwhelmingly in favour of the multilateral option and the conclusion of a binding agreement.

The EU vision of a multilateral agreement has had some alterations made to it over the years, albeit perhaps cosmetic ones. In actual substance however, this vision has remained unchanged and the 'roadmap' it revealed shows careful thinking by the European Commission on such a difficult issue. For example, the Commission has recommended what may be seen as a 'step-by-step' approach, to begin with preliminary negotiations, looking at: the different types of business phenomena giving rise to competition problems; ensuring adequate and transparent competition law enforcement in different jurisdictions; and building international cooperation through exchange of non-confidential information and through incorporating notification and positive comity provisions.[39] The Commission has explicitly excluded from its proposal any suggestion to pursue in the short term convergence among the substantive provisions of the competition laws of different countries, stating that such wider convergence could be reached over time. It has however suggested that a dispute-settlement mechanism should be included, though initially to be limited to deal with breaches of common principles or rules relating to the developing of competition law regimes at the national level. Dispute settlement, according to the Commission, might also be used for alleged patterns of failure to enforce competition law in cases affecting the trade and investment of other WTO members.[40]

This position of the EU has won some support by a number of WTO countries, including Australia, Canada and Japan, although these countries have not endorsed the proposal *verbum verbatim*. For example, Japan appears in favour of a multilateral agreement in the field but also has concurred with developing countries, particularly from the Asia-Pacific region, by emphasising that multilateral negotiations on competition must include anti-dumping issues.[41]

(iii) The educational approach of African countries   Chapter 7 above dealt with regional competition law and policy. It demonstrated, among

---

[39] See pp. 498–499 above for an account on positive comity.
[40] See the proposals of the Group of Experts (the wise men group): 'Competition Policy in the New Trade Order: Strengthening International Cooperation and Rules' COM (95) 359; see pp. 223–224 above.
[41] See Communications from Japan, WT/GC/W/308 (25 August 1999).

other things, the enormous interest of African countries in adopting a
collective approach in the field, albeit at a regional level. African countries however have also shown remarkable interest in WTO developments in the field of competition law and some of them have expressed
interesting views on the matter focusing in particular on the need to
adopt an educational approach and to protect the interest of developing
countries.

Kenya is one of the few African nations that have spoken on the idea of
concluding a binding multilateral agreement in the field of competition
law. It has submitted its own views to the WTO as well as offering views
on behalf of the group of African countries.[42] At the heart of Kenya's own
views stood a concern that a binding multilateral agreement in the field
may have an adverse effect on comparatively stronger firms of developing countries – by 'clipping the wings' of these firms – so that they are
not able to compete with strong firms of the developed countries.[43] To
address this concern, Kenya proposed that any multilateral agreement
on competition law should include a code of conduct for multinational
firms.[44] This specific proposal was aimed at introducing an educational
element to the process of internationalisation of competition law which
Kenya and African countries in general argued should extend to enhancing the technical assistance offered to developing countries. It was
emphasised that the existence of domestic competition law regimes,
including effective competition authorities to enforce competition law,
was not common to all African countries and most countries around the
world more generally. This meant that it was crucial for a WTO agenda
in the field of competition law to include activities to conduct educational, exploratory and analytical work focusing on the needs of developing countries.

The position developed by Kenya – especially on behalf of the African
countries – has been amplified by South Africa who also believed that it
would be crucial to embark on a thorough educational process that

---

[42] See Communications from Kenya on behalf of the African Group, WT/GC/W/300
(6 August 1999).

[43] See Communications from Kenya, WT/GC/W/233 (5 July 1999).

[44] The idea of a code of conduct had already been introduced (and tested) within
UNCTAD (the *Set of Multilaterally Agreed Equitable Principles and Rules for the
Control of Restrictive Business Practices*). As the discussion at pp. 144–146 above showed
the UNCTAD Set has not been a particular success. Note however, that efforts toward
reaching consensus between developed and developing countries for such a code failed
previously at the UN.

would better prepare developing countries for any future competition negotiations within the WTO.[45] Indeed South Africa has been an African champion on the topic of competition law education and has always welcomed and provided for an opportunity for foreign specialists to become involved in actual (usually a few selected) cases, which are handled within the ranks of its competition law regime through offering advice on the competition analysis conducted in these cases.

According to South Africa, an educational process is a necessary condition for negotiating multilateral rules on competition within the WTO due to the fact that developing countries have not had the same opportunity to prepare for such negotiations, which means that developing countries are therefore not on a level playing field whether vis-à-vis themselves or developed countries and cannot be expected to present a well-researched position. In particular, South Africa called for further analysis of the strengths and weaknesses of reaching a multilateral agreement in the field, and has made it clear that it would be desirable for UNCTAD and the World Bank to offer some assistance in engaging in this debate and conducting such analysis; but also crucially for this assistance to be offered to competition authorities in developing countries. According to South Africa, this assistance should extend beyond the *traditional* support offered to competition authorities in terms of passing domestic competition laws and their enforcement, and should include scrupulous assessment of the expected outcomes and the implications for developing countries of having a multilateral agreement. To ensure fruitful results from this educational initiative, South Africa has suggested that process should extend over a period of at least two years. It has also recommended that resources be provided to developing countries in order to allow them to participate in the formal negotiations on a multilateral agreement in a meaningful manner.

(iv) Korea's vision of internationalisation through transition   Korea has generally supported the conclusion of some form of a multilateral agreement in the field of competition law with an effective dispute-settlement mechanism.[46] This particular position in favour of internationalisation through multilateralism has been based on Korea's belief in the need for enhancing international cooperation among competition authorities

---

[45] See Communications from the Republic of South Africa, WT/WGTCP/W/138 (11 October 1999).

[46] See Communications from Korea, WT/GC/W/298 (6 August 1999).

given that this will lead to better enforcement of competition law in different jurisdictions. Korea has encouraged opening a discussion within the WTO on how to incorporate the principle of positive comity[47] into a multilateral framework to impose greater discipline on cross-border anticompetitive behaviour and conduct and help reduce unnecessary costs and the risk of conflicts where appropriate. In its communication of its various views to the WTO on the question of multilateralism in the field of competition law, Korea has singled out international mergers as an area in which it cautioned that it may not be feasible to harmonise substantive rules of merger control in different jurisdictions; though in its view it remains worthwhile to *examine* possible means of enhancing cooperation among competition authorities on issues such as common procedures for review of mergers, harmonisation of merger notification forms and notification deadlines, and the establishment of a common body to which international mergers may be notified. Korea expressed a similar caution in the context of exchange of confidential information, arguing that dealing with such exchange of information within the framework of a multilateral agreement is premature at this stage, given the differences in the national competition laws governing the exchange of information in member countries of the WTO.

In supporting the case for building a multilateral framework in the field of competition law, Korea has recommended, however, transitional periods for the application of the rules under the framework according to the level of economic development in each country and other domestic conditions.[48] It has recommended that, given the progressive liberalisation of trade worldwide and the fact that as a result developing countries are no longer able to resort to the export-oriented economic growth policy through protection of domestic industries, competition law should be introduced from the early stage of economic development in countries. According to Korea, greater competition will lead to the best allocation of economic resources, help small and medium firms to grow and will enable the country in question to respond proactively and promptly to fast-changing economic conditions within and outside national boundaries.

---

[47] See pp. 498–499 above.

[48] Also Turkey has recommended that a multilateral framework within the field should include provisions for transitional periods in order to allow members at different stages of development to observe and adhere to their commitments. See Communications from Turkey, WT/GC/W/250 (13 July 1999).

(v) Norway's almost unconditional support for multilateralism   Norway
has been in favour of negotiating and establishing a multilateral competition law framework within the WTO, covering conduct of a private and
public nature, and containing, among other things, a list of objectives,
core principles, dispute settlement procedures as well as providing for
international cooperation between competition authorities. Norway has
also recommended that the negotiations should include an examination
of the need to develop rules on anticompetitive conduct, including hardcore cartels. In this way, Norway has shown almost unconditional support for a fully fledged multilateral approach in the field of competition
law to be adopted within the WTO framework; though it has however
advocated the proposition that the negotiations should take due account
of the special needs of countries at different stages of development
through implementation of transitional arrangements and the provision
of technical assistance, therefore bringing its position closer to that of
Korea and to a certain extent the African group as discussed in the
previous two sections.[49]

II.   Convergence

Being a *future* means through which the multilateral option (based on
binding obligations) in the field of competition law may be pursued,
does not mean that convergence and harmonisation does not exist at
present. Indeed the process has been unfolding one way or another, most
notably in the international arena in recent years through non-binding
obligations.[50] During the last two decades or so, domestic competition
laws of different countries have been converging. This process has been
facilitated by several factors. Perhaps the most obvious one is the process
of – formal and informal – bilateral cooperation between domestic
competition authorities. The discussion in the previous chapter in particular offered several examples of how domestic competition authorities
have, albeit to a limited extent due to restrictions on exchange of confidential information, increasingly engaged in informal consultations
among themselves in enforcement matters in cross-border competition
cases. As we saw, cooperation has been particularly common in merger
cases between EU and US competition authorities who quite frequently
exchange views on their analytical approaches on issues such as market
definition and economic analysis in general in these cases. Furthermore,

[49] See Communications from Norway, WT/GC/W/310 7 (5 September 1999).
[50] See below.

a number of mature competition authorities have offered valuable technical assistance to countries with economies in transition and others with little experience of using the concept of competition and competition law. This process of technical assistance has generated many benefits, perhaps the most important of which has been promoting convergence and furthering common understanding in the field. Other benefits have included clarifying differences between different competition law regimes, such as the EU and US regimes as well as differences between what mature competition law regimes offer and what those countries (mostly developing countries) with little experience in the field think is appropriate for their economic and political conditions. The benefits of cooperation and technical assistance can be observed in the case of a number of African, Asian and Middle Eastern countries, in which competition authorities have relied heavily on information from other jurisdictions when interpreting, applying and enforcing their laws.

Convergence of competition laws may be observed in different fora, including in the EU,[51] in the USA and even in the OECD. Some commentators have argued that convergence is a prerequisite to any move towards comprehensive internationalisation of competition law, including the creation of an international competition law code to achieve this outcome. Whether this is a valid argument or not depends on certain factors as well as on the advantages and disadvantages associated with convergence.

(a) **Advantages**   A number of advantages are attached to the convergence of competition laws of different countries around the world. Some of these advantages are considered beneficial to countries and their competition authorities; others are considered to be of benefit to firms. Obviously, the fact this is so makes convergence a highly attractive option.

(i) Sovereignty and related considerations   An obvious argument that can be advanced in favour of convergence is that from the perspective of many countries this form of internationalisation is preferable to the conclusion of a binding multilateral agreement with an international institutional framework as discussed in the previous section above. This is because, unlike the latter, it does not present a serious threat to the sovereignty of countries nor does it interfere with the enforcement prerogatives of different competition authorities.

---

[51] See chapter 4 above.

(ii) The needs of countries with no competition law Another argument in favour of convergence is that efforts aiming at concluding a multilateral agreement for the creation of an international competition law regime are frankly quite ambitious for the moment. For this reason, it is more sensible and realistic to focus on important intermediate steps. Convergence, in this regard, is seen as such an important step, which can help countries with no competition law to introduce this law domestically and to build a suitable enforcement mechanism.

(iii) Relief for firms Convergence of different competition laws offers substantial benefits to firms operating in international markets. In particular, firms would be offered relief from the burden of having to deal with competition law regimes that are different in both substantive law and the procedures used.[52] The net result would be that the cost of their operations and compliance would be substantially reduced which is a highly desired outcome that could have considerable positive results in terms of enhancing efficiency in the marketplace. Moreover, it is guaranteed that, with convergence, uniformity of approach by different competition authorities will be more likely than otherwise. This is especially so in the area of merger control.

(iv) Removing hindrances to market access Convergence is likely to enhance the flows of trade and investment between countries by removing market access-restraining private anticompetitive behaviour. This is especially valuable in the case of those countries which have not been tough enough on private anticompetitive behaviour within their own boundaries and thus have impaired the entry to domestic markets by foreign firms and in the case of countries with no competition laws.

(b) Disadvantages Offsetting these advantages are some disadvantages associated with convergence of domestic competition laws which must be mentioned.

(i) An inherently long process It would not be difficult, especially in the light of the discussion on the EU experience in the field,[53] to point out the fact that convergence of different competition laws is a very slow process, and as a matter of fact its success cannot be guaranteed. In the EU, despite the increasing strength of the EU competition law regime and the

---

[52] See pp. 108–109 above.   [53] See pp. 187–192 above.

EU more generally and its influence on the domestic competition law regimes of EU member states, harmonisation and convergence have been developing for over 50 years without reaching full maturity. On the basis of this situation, it is difficult to imagine that better progress, or even an equal one, will be made in the convergence of different competition law regimes around the world. Countries do not share common competition law traditions. Furthermore, their seriousness in enforcing their competition laws differs, not to mention the fact that many countries do not even have competition laws in place at the moment or have at best infant competition law regimes.

(ii) Different forms and different goals of competition law   Those countries with competition law differ with regard to the form of their laws and what goals should be sought when enforcing their laws. Whilst some countries have opted for economic goals, others have used their competition laws to further social and even political goals.[54] Of course, an attempt to converge competition laws with different goals risks collision between them.

Various views have been put forward over the years advocating that these concerns should not be particularly problematic because there may be convergence in the goals of competition law towards certain 'core' principles. According to these views, convergence is to be expected, as countries increasingly look to one another for lessons and, as an increasing number of countries seek to become partners in the global trading system. Such an approach is in use already, albeit in a limited form, in certain jurisdictions and international organisations.[55]

The difficulty associated with a convergence approach, however, is that it may not be possible to succeed in making these goals coincide.[56] It could be argued convergence is not possible when different goals are claimed in the name of competition law and when competition policy is dynamic and constantly evolving. For example, how can one arrive at the 'core' of competition law's purpose by convergence of goals covering

---

[54] See pp. 40–44 above.

[55] See, for example, the work of the OECD Committee on Competition Law and Policy (CLP): *Interim Report on Convergence of Competition Policies* (1994); the work of the US Federal Trade Commission: *Anticipating the 21st Century: Competition Policy in the New High-Tech Global Marketplace* (1996); and the work of UNCTAD: *Draft Commentaries to Possible Elements for Articles of a Model Law of Laws* (1995). Chapter 4 contains some discussion of this issue in relation to the EU.

[56] See M. L. Azcuenaga, 'The Evolution of International Competition Policy: a FTC Perspective' (1992) *Fordham Corporate Law Institute* 1.

economic efficiency (economics) and others dealing with generic concepts such as fairness and justice (social) and those dealing with integration within regional economies (politics)? The fear is that certain goals, not to mention the fact that they are adopted by strong countries, will prevail over other goals; those 'other goals' may, of course, be advocated by weaker countries.[57] For example, in developed countries, a primary goal of antitrust law is to enhance an efficient allocation of resources and maximise consumer welfare in the traditional economic sense. In contrast, many developing countries tend to have a broader goal for competition law, namely building a market economy and securing the political acceptance necessary for this.[58] In this case if convergence is to be pursued, it might lead to benefiting some countries at the expense of others – a factor which may minimise the prospects of success in achieving meaningful convergence; although the opposite of this view has been argued by some countries with advance competition law regimes. For example, in the USA the view has been expressed that the convergence of goals will lead to a lowest common denominator, whereby countries with strong competition law regimes will be forced to accept weaker goals advocated by other countries with less advanced competition law regimes.

Even if convergence is both possible and effective and an agreement on the goals of competition law amongst different competition law regimes may be reached, there can still be great disparity between countries regarding the means of convergence and regarding how the means to achieve these goals is perceived.[59] This can be illustrated by the way in which different countries consider competition law should be enforced. Assume that *country A*, *country B* and *country C* share identical goals for competition law. A fundamental cause of divergence between them would be that the means of achieving those goals may be differently conceived by each country. This divergence of perception may be attributed to lack of agreement between the countries over the optimal means of achieving identical goals which is generally caused by differences in the circumstances prevalent in each country. For example, culture may affect the optimal means of achieving a particular goal and thus, the choice of competition law and policy.[60] This is reflected by the fact that

[57] See A. Guzman, 'Is International Antitrust Possible?' (1998) *New York University Law Review* 1501.
[58] See the discussion in chapter 6.   [59] See p. 565 above.
[60] See L. Haucher and M. Moran, *Capitalism, Culture and Economic Regulation* (Oxford University Press, 1989).

competition law tradition may differ from one jurisdiction to the next. A central feature of the EU competition law tradition – as we saw in chapter 4 – has been the idea that competition law is special and that using law to protect competition moves outside the discipline of law. In light of this view, EU competition law has been considered to be a unique type of law,[61] which deals with problems for which traditional legal mechanisms are not suitable, and thus it requires correspondingly non-traditional methods and procedures. This contrasts sharply with the approach under US competition law regime, which relies primarily on traditional legal forms and institutions in protecting competition.[62] It is therefore important to realise that there is no single coherent framework which binds the competition laws of more than one jurisdiction together. Neither competition law nor competition policy exists in the abstract. Different competition laws reflect different concerns, values and goals. As was noted in chapter 1, competition law has now been adopted in almost 120 countries, whose economies and economic development may be very different. It would be quite unrealistic to imagine that the competition rules within each regime will be concerned with, and pursuing, identical goals.[63]

In addition to these differences, there are other ones which could be mentioned, in particular those which relate to factors such as the size of the country. Such factors may also affect the choice of competition law and policy and may lead to divergences with respect to the goals of competition law.

(iii) Defining competition   It is not clear whether countries agree on how the concept of competition should be defined and understood. The discussion in chapter 1 above considered the concept of competition in some detail.[64]

(D)   Comments

The discussion above demonstrated that the idea of pursuing the multilateral strategy through binding commitments and obligations on countries has been seriously considered on a number of occasions. Several

---

[61] See p. 164 above.
[62] See D. Gerber, *Law and Competition in Twentieth Century Europe* (Oxford University Press, 1998).
[63] See WTO *Annual Report* (WTO, 1997), p. 34.   [64] See pp. 20–30 above.

proposals have been made. As we saw, one of these is to establish an international variant of existing competition law regimes, most notably the EU regime. The idea here is to develop through the support of the WTO structural features of a competition law regime. Within such a framework, the WTO would create a set of rules with a dispute settlement mechanism, which would require countries to introduce competition laws in their jurisdictions. Needless to say however, this proposal – and the idea of convergence – for involving the WTO is not the only one that has surfaced over the years. Different proposals have been formulated for involving the WTO. One of these has been to develop general principles, both procedural and substantive, of competition law. The OECD and the World Bank have been seeking for a number of years to develop a 'Global Corporate Governance Forum'.[65] The OECD has also developed a set of 'best practices' principles on corporate governance, which complement its joint projects with the World Bank. The joint initiative has been hosting meetings and workshops attended by representatives of the business community and governments of countries.

Regardless of the form of the proposal for involving the WTO, one thing has become abundantly clear since the Cancun experience in 2003: the fresh hopes created at Doha in 2001 for a serious mandate to take foothold within the WTO have been nothing but almost totally erased. This has seriously affected the prospect for pursuing the multilateral option though binding obligations, whether in the form of a multilateral agreement or convergence. In fairness, such development is probably not as bad it sounds and perhaps the question must be asked again whether pursing the option through the WTO is a sensible step under all circumstances. As things stand at present, countries are at enormously different stages of economic development and at different stages on the 'competition law ladder', with the first step involving the mere adoption of some form of competition law and the last step involving the existence of an effective competition law regime, with strong institutional framework and credible enforcement. Very few countries have made it to the top of the ladder, several have just climbed to the first step and many are scattered on the way; crucially however, the majority of countries have not started climbing at all and their legal systems lack specific competition rules. Additionally, even in areas where the case for a binding multilateral agreement can arguably be considered to exist, most notably that of merger control, competition law is closely interwoven with important domestic policies such as

---

[65] See www.gcgf.org.

industrial policy, public interest and social security. Taking into account the extreme reluctance of certain countries to relinquish their powers in favour of an international body or to become subject to any form of binding obligations, these factors show the major difficulties with pursuing multilateralism through binding commitments. Competition law in general and certain aspects of it carry hugely important economic, social and political considerations for countries. In many ways, the power to apply competition law is considered to be a definition of the commercial identity of countries and an expression of their economic independence. The chances of an international body being able to assume the responsibility to do this in an international setting do not appear to be particularly realistic. Experience within many regions of the world demonstrates this succinctly. For example, in the EU considerable difficulties were raised when an attempt was made to introduce a specific mechanism for regulating mergers.[66] Despite the fact that member states had been confirmed to have limited their sovereignty in the field of competition law, some of them wanted to safeguard their national interest and attempt to reserve the power to themselves to be able to handle certain mergers, even if they had a 'Community dimension';[67] hence the inclusion of the EU Merger Regulation 139/2004 (like its predecessor Regulation 4064/89) of a specific provision, Article 21(4), which enables member states nonetheless to review such mergers. If one were to transfer this to a global setting, the fundamental problems raised here will only be inflated in a serious way.

2. Multilateralism through non-binding commitments

The discussion in this part of the chapter will in one way complement that in the previous part by examining the option of pursuing the multilateral strategy through non-binding obligations. This part will focus in particular on the option of convergence and harmonisation – whether at substantive or procedural levels – and provide a detailed account and analysis of the contribution made by key international bodies and organisations such as UNCTAD, the OECD and the ICN.

(A) Assessing the chances non-binding multilateralism

One of the main conclusions drawn in the previous part was the fact that not all countries are necessarily prepared to be legally bound by a

---

[66] See p. 162 above. [6] See p. 162 above.

multilateral agreement in the field of competition law. As we saw, this reluctance has, among other things, contributed to the demise of this particular option of multilateralism. A legitimate question that is worth asking however, is whether the multilateral option can still be successfully pursued on the basis of non-binding obligations. In answering this question it would be helpful to clarify what cooperation through non-binding commitments actually entails and the advantages it has over cooperation through binding commitments.

I. Form

The idea of pursuing multilateralism through non-binding commitments primarily revolves around the use of recommendations, guidelines and best practices which themselves carry no binding obligations for countries. This means that countries are obliged neither to subscribe to them, nor to take any steps to implement them within their existing competition law regimes (or legal systems more widely).

II. Reasons for 'popularity', advantages etc.

There are a number of reasons to indicate that despite their lack of binding force, success is possible to achieve in using this option of multilateralism; most notably the fact that this option has been taking foothold in recent years. If this experience is a reliable way to ascertain success, the chances of this option appear to be real. Additionally, there seems to be a recognition that countries may be prepared to cooperate in meaningful ways in building a multilateral strategy but without any binding obligations. As we shall see further below, there is ample evidence supporting this from the work of the International Competition Network (ICN) which forms the backbone in a discussion on multilateralism through non-binding obligations. But evidence can also be found outside the boundaries of the ICN. For example, the Asia-Pacific Economic Cooperation Forum (APEC) has been built on this recognition,[68] that it is possible to advance some harmonisation of practices outside a framework of binding legal instruments. Also the proposed global competition law initiative of the International Competition Policy Advisory Committee (ICPAC)[69] is built on the premise that countries can usefully explore areas of cooperation in the field and facilitate further convergence and harmonisation. Countries seem to prefer developing a common understanding through consultations and non-binding

---

[68] See pp. 396–397 above for a discussion on APEC.   [69] See pp. 266–267 above.

principles. Success can also be considered to be likely due to important advantages non-binding commitments enjoy especially when compared to binding commitments. Among the main features of the latter are: the lack of flexibility; the length of time it takes for countries to negotiate and agree; and the particular difficulty in amending them following their adoption. Non-binding commitments by contrast appear to have a high degree of flexibility and the approach underpinning them – as the ICN experience shows – can be extremely pragmatic. These commitments also are less time consuming and they neither pose a limitation on national sovereignty nor difficulty when seeking to amend them following their adoption. Finally, there is no doubt that the support of the USA for this option of multilateralism has been highly influential in building its popularity especially with the important work carried out by the US Antitrust Division and Federal Trade Commission when establishing the ICN in 2001.[70]

III. Disadvantages

The existence of important advantages in the case of non-binding commitments however does not mean that these instruments do not suffer from any shortcomings. In fact they do and some of the key advantages underpinning them can be said to have inherent shortcomings. For example, the fact that non-binding commitments lack binding force may make it particularly difficult to predict whether, when and how they will be implemented by countries; as a result they may appear to offer only a low level of legal certainty, something that could be fuelled by the considerable discretion left in the hands of countries and their competition authorities over implementation of the commitments. Furthermore, the fact that non-binding commitments are formulated in quite general language means that determining their real benefit and effectiveness is only possible when their implementation within domestic competition law regimes occurs. Obviously these shortcomings are serious. Nonetheless, experience with non-binding commitments shows they are not impossible to overcome. This is a point which the discussion will consider below.

(B) The evolution of non-binding multilateralism so far

The idea of building multilateral cooperation through the use of non-binding obligations is not a new one. It dates back to the 1960s and 1970s

---

[70] See p. 149 above.

during which years the OECD and UNCTAD began to pave the way for this option. It was not until considerably later however – precisely until the creation of the ICN – that this option began to attract wider global appeal, in both the developed and developing world and was seen as an option enjoying credibility. In the interim, the option came to witness gradual evolution. Arguably, various developments – especially in the field of merger control[71] – strengthened the case for creating multilateral instruments based on non-binding commitments.

To understand all of these points fully, it would be useful to look at these developments closely from the perspectives of UNCTAD, the OECD and the ICN and to reflect the various developments carefully.

I.   UNCTAD

UNCTAD's involvement in the field of competition law was discussed in chapter 2. It was noted that the centrepiece of this involvement has been the *Set of Multilaterally Agreed Principles and Rules for the Control of Restrictive Business Practices*, which was described as having, in effect, a two-tiered structure of rules and principles addressed to countries and firms. The non-binding force of the Set was no doubt one of its most important features, though utilising it in practice proved to be a particularly difficult task to discharge in light of the fact that the Set came to safeguard the interest of developing countries, many of whom at the time did not have competition law on their statute books.

II.   OECD

As we saw above, the OECD has been playing a leading role in publishing recommendations and best practices in the field of competition law.[72] These have been mainly addressed to competition authorities; though many concern a wider audience. Through its impressive output, the OECD has maintained the goal of achieving a variety of benefits for competition authorities, firms and consumers in different OECD countries and to some extent non-OECD countries.

---

[71] Especially worth mentioning here are: the increasing number of merger cases being subjected to multi-jurisdictional merger review and the desire on the part of EU and US competition authorities to bring their regimes closer together and to eliminate cases of conflict. The few cases of divergence between the EU and US regimes were particularly influential here.

[72] See pp. 137–140 above which among other things give details of some of the most notable recommendations and best practices produced over the years.

III. The ICN

One of the key differences between the ICN and other international bodies and organisations – as identified in chapter 2 – is the fact that it is a 'virtual' network, though in practice not all of the ICN operations are conducted in the virtual environment. This feature – along with the other ones highlighted above, such as the uniqueness of its membership and emphasis on consensus building – have armed the ICN with key advantages in its pursuit of multilateralism through non-binding commitments in the field.

The work of the ICN has been of particular orientation and focus, determined by the aim and project at hand. This has enabled it to achieve greater consensus and to develop two advantages, namely the *credibility* of its output due to the large number of competition authorities – from both the developing and developed worlds – engaged in its work and the *incentives* it offers to countries to implement its recommendations and best practices especially in light of its pragmatic approach and no threat to national sovereignty. Neither the OECD nor UNCTAD could rival the ICN in this respect: the former suffers from a lack of a sufficiently broad membership base, which at any rate excludes developing countries and the latter – whilst enjoying a broad membership base – seems to fall short of providing an incentive to countries to implement its Set.[73]

The benefits brought about by the ICN cannot be overstated. They have encompassed within their scope competition authorities and firms. The work of the ICN has been extremely precise and well-focused on particular projects in areas in which convergence and harmonisation are considered to be possible and desirable to achieve. The ICN has proceeded on the basis of a realistic and non-ambitious agenda. Its operation – using the model of steering and working groups[74] – has enabled it to give different competition authorities the opportunity to play a role in contributing to the ICN output but at the same time the opportunity to learn and benefit from the often useful discussions within these groups.

Among the areas in which the ICN's work has been a huge success is that of merger control. Since its creation, the ICN has produced a number of important best practices, recommendations and guiding principles dealing with different aspects of merger control. These aspects include: conflict of jurisdiction situations in cases of multi-jurisdictional merger review; thresholds for merger notification; review period in merger cases by competition authorities; form(s) used by firms to notify

---

[73] See p. 144 above. [74] See pp. 151–152 above.

their mergers to competition authorities; procedural matters; merger remedies; and powers enjoyed by competition authorities. The work of the ICN in relation to some of these aspects is worth highlighting.

(a) **Conflict of jurisdiction principles**   The ICN recognised at a very early stage of its existence that the issue of multi-jurisdictional merger review was a hugely important one because it brings into play the question of which authority or authorities are entitled to exercise jurisdiction over a merger operation. In its deliberation on the matter, the ICN established an important principle for determining the question of jurisdiction seeking thus to avoid situations of conflict of jurisdiction between different competition authorities, namely the *principle of appropriate nexus*. According to this principle, a competition authority should assert jurisdiction in cases where an appropriate nexus or link is established between its jurisdiction and the relevant merger operation. In practice, this was considered to exist where the operation produces appreciable effects within the relevant jurisdiction. According to the ICN guidance on the matter, appreciable effects should normally be considered to exist where in the relevant jurisdiction(s), at least two of the merging firms are engaged in economic activities *or* the acquired firm or business exists. The idea behind such an approach is to reduce the number of competent competition authorities: specifically to exclude those competition authorities in whose jurisdiction the merger operation produces minimal effects from reviewing the operation.

(b) **Merger notification principles**   Anyone who is familiar with the area of merger control will appreciate the inherent difficulty in determining the 'thresholds' for merger notifications. Obviously this is an issue which is related to that of exercising jurisdiction, as discussed in the previous section. This difficulty is caused by the fact that determining thresholds depends on a number of factors, such as the size of the economy in the relevant jurisdiction and the other socio-economic and sociopolitical factors which are unique to the jurisdiction in question. This means it is understandable that in practice there are significant differences between merger control regimes around the world over the type and size of the notification thresholds. Equally, this means that bridging such differences through convergence or harmonisation may not be possible to achieve; one may even wonder whether this is in fact desirable to do given the outcome is bound to be recommended thresholds, which are either too high for small jurisdictions or too low for large ones.

In its work on this matter, the ICN has realised the 'sensitivities' involved and for this reason it chose to offer general guidance on how notification thresholds should be set. Specifically, the ICN has recommended that such thresholds should be: clear and understandable and based on objective and quantitative criteria. This means that the preference expressed by the ICN shows that it favours a loose framework giving different ICN members the discretion necessary to determine the notification thresholds but to do so on the basis of 'common criteria'.[75]

(c) **Merger review period principles** The issue of review period in merger appraisal by competition authorities is another hugely important one in the area of merger control. It is also a difficult issue because determining it in practice requires striking a balance between two important sets of interests: the interest of competition authorities to spend long enough reviewing merger operations in order to ensure that proper appraisal is conducted and the interest of merging firms to wait for as short a time as possible in order to avoid any unnecessary harm to their interests.

Being aware of the need for such balancing exercise, the ICN recommend that a merger review period should be a reasonable period. Obviously, this is too general as a recommendation. Nonetheless, the ICN has stated that up to six months would fit within this description; though it has not ruled out the possibility of such period being extended up to the same length in relation to those merger operations meriting this.

(d) **Notification form principles** Looking around the world, one is able to see significant differences in existence between merger control regimes with regard to the form used to notify merger operations to competition authorities. The ICN realised this fact means that it is difficult to achieve full convergence and harmonisation and for this reason it has opted for neutral guidance. Specifically, the ICN has given particular attention to the interests of merging parties and has recommended that the type of notification form and crucially the information required as part of it

---

[75] Such preference towards loose framework on the part of the ICN can also be seen from how it recommended expanding the spectrum of events triggering notification of a merger operation by firms to include situations in which they have demonstrated 'good faith intention' to merge; i.e. without necessarily needing to have concluded a binding merger agreement prior to notification.

should not impose an unnecessary burden on them. It recommended the use of a requirement for submission of minimal core of information initially in order to enable the competition authority to determine whether the relevant operation falls within its jurisdiction. More widely, the ICN proposed the use of one of three different models regarding form and content of notification in merger cases: *model one*: the use of long and short notification forms (the former to be used for complex merger operations and the latter for simple and fairly straightforward ones); *model two*: a method of requiring detailed information with a discretionary power given to the competition authority to waive some of the information requested; and *model three*: a method of requiring limited information initially with the power given to the competition authority to request the submission of additional information. Needless to say, the value of such a recommendation for the purposes of achieving convergence and harmonisation is very doubtful though one should appreciate that such an approach is highly pragmatic nonetheless.

(e) **Merger remedies principles** The ICN has produced some useful principles concerning the topic of merger remedies, which has come to receive particular attention in recent years.[76] The ICN has emphasised the importance of operating a regime for merger remedies which is transparent and efficient. In particular, the ICN recommended that transparency must exist in relation to crucial issues such as: types of remedies available and the deadline for their submission; remedies must be easily administrable and effective to address anticompetitive outcomes of merger operations; sufficient time must be given to merging parties to discuss and evaluate proposals for remedies; and competition authorities should enjoy the power to monitor remedies and where necessary seek enforcement through the appropriate channels.

(f) **Procedural principles** The ICN has formulated a number of important procedural principles which seek to enhance confidentiality, procedural fairness, effectiveness, transparency, efficiency and predictability of merger control regimes of ICN members. The ICN has attached particular significance to the need to facilitate a proper 'dialogue' between a competition authority and merging parties.

The ICN has also produced a set of principles advocating the need to arm competition authorities with the necessary powers to be able to conduct

---

[76] See p. 152 above.

merger reviews, including the power to open investigations; the power to block or clear merger operations (including conditional clearance); and the power to opt for enforcement actions, especially in relation to remedies. The ICN has also advocated the need for competition authorities to be independent: obviously the existence of the powers mentioned here in practice goes a long way to show such independence.

(C) Comments

It is highly arguable that the most significant development in recent times concerning the multilateral option in the field of competition law has been the use of non-binding commitments and their outcome of soft convergence. Such convergence has emerged with regard to mainly substantive but also procedural issues. For example, in the field of merger control one is able to see significant evidence of the former in particular. Such soft convergence has resulted primarily from the increasing reliance and emphasis on economic analysis in the application of competition law in the vast majority of jurisdictions around the world. It is the universality of economic analysis that has been an important force driving convergence. This point is worth emphasising because it can be easily (wrongly) assumed that the only driving forces behind such convergence are: political and juridical forces;[77] demands for the adoption of international codes; desires to regulate multinational enterprises; and desires by certain countries – most notably developing countries – to alter the global trading order.

The ICN experience in particular (and to some extent that of the OECD)[78] has tremendously increased mutual learning between different competition law regimes and their authorities. This no doubt has helped establish that convergence is possible to achieve through the implementation of soft principles into hard law instruments. For example, a number of competition authorities have altered their practices in

---

[77] It is important to note however that in the case of the ICN, the *will* of key competition authorities – notably the European Commission, the US Antitrust Division and the US Federal Trade Commission – has been important in creating the Network in the first place and ensuring the success of its work.

[78] UNCTAD – by comparison to the ICN and the OECD – has in recent times been seen as far less active in pushing the global multilateral agenda on the basis of non-binding commitments. This actually is quite remarkable because of the origins of UNCTAD and its long history in the field. As noted above however, there is no doubt that the impression that has been formed about UNCTAD – as an organisation for developing countries – has contributed to its inactivity.

the field of merger control in light of the work of the ICN. This includes the introduction of 'good faith intention' as a triggering event for notification of merger operations in the EU regime; the adoption of the principle of appropriate nexus of jurisdiction in Brazil; the greater transparency US competition authorities have come to facilitate through the publication of reasoned explanation of decisions approving mergers where the decision establishes a precedent; and the use of short and long notification forms in a number of jurisdictions, most notably the EU regime. Such outcomes are particularly worth noting because they show that there has been implementation by even some of the world's most advanced competition law regimes.

The remarkable success of the ICN has created serious expectations that the process of soft convergence is set to continue for the foreseeable future especially given that the fairly wide consensus that this process has – in a short period of time of nine years – led to greater trust and confidence between different competition authorities (not seen before 2001), a reduction in the costs of firms involved in cross-border merger transactions and greater effectiveness and efficiency on the part of different competition law regimes, within both the developed and developing world. At the same time, such development has arguably rendered merely academic if not historic any proposal of a multilateral approach that is based on binding commitments. In a reverse manner, it is arguable that the failure of the latter – especially within the WTO context – has paved the way for the use of non-binding commitments and soft convergence.

A final point worth reflecting on concerns the question of whether soft convergence – notwithstanding the use of non-binding commitments – suffers from a problem of accountability, namely ensuring that an international body which produces these instruments remains accountable to its subjects. Some people have argued that the use of non-binding instruments is not totally free from limitation of sovereignty and actually involves some form of coercion: bringing countries to accept commitments produced at the higher level.[79] It is doubtful whether in the field of competition law this should be considered to be problematic, especially when one considers the important benefits following from soft convergence which surely should be considered as outweighing any such concern.

---

[79] See B. Kingsbury, N. Krisch and R. B. Stewart, 'The Emergence of Global Administrative Law' (2005) *Law and Contemporary Problems* 15; J. Cohen and C. Sabel, 'Global Democracy?' (2005) *New York University Journal of International Law and Politics* 736.

Chapter 11

Competition and trade policy

This chapter is concerned with a specific and highly important topic, namely the relationship between competition policy and trade policy. This topic assumes particular significance in the context of the present book as well as any discussion or debate on the international dimension of competition law and policy. Among the issues which will be examined in this chapter are: the aims and objectives of these policies; the differences between them; the similarities or even complementarities between them; and the lessons one may learn from each of these policies individually which may be helpful in particular for the purposes of developing competition law and policy inter- nationally. One of the major issues which will be examined in the chapter is that of market access, which is found at the heart of the phenomenon of hindrances – of different types – that may impede the ability of foreign firms to enter the domestic markets of countries. The issue of market access and hindrances to it are therefore of primary importance when discussing the relationship between the two policies: it provides a 'meeting' or 'linkage' point between competition and trade policy. The chapter will specifically address the possible approaches currently available under competition and trade policy which can be used to address market access concerns involving anticompetitive behaviour of private firms, mainly hybrid hindrances, which in addition – as we saw in the previous chapter – have a public involvement. The chapter will outline the shortcomings of these approaches in both the short and long term. The chapter will also consider how trade policy and competition policy can support each other at an international level within the context of the market access principle and examine in detail the chances for developing competition policy within the WTO.

1. Overview

Examining the relationship between competition and trade policy is both interesting and challenging almost in equal measures. It is of considerable interest to ask whether 'linkage' exists between the two policies which could be exploited in a positive way in order to advance competition law and policy globally and offer a 'comprehensive' response to the different competition problems or issues with an international dimension; i.e. the kind of problems we identified in chapter 1 above.[1] Perhaps it should be noted at this stage that – at least at first glance – the trade and competition communities are not necessarily ones that can be considered to be living in total harmony and in fact one may go further and express reservation about an attempt to bring the two communities closer together: the trade community tends to be dominated by political rhetoric and protectionism that sometimes go in the opposite direction of opening markets to foreign participation and building global competition. Perhaps one here need not go beyond citing recent examples from the 2008 US elections and the 'race' among candidates in those elections to oppose the North American Free Trade Agreement (NAFTA) and bilateral free trade agreements between the USA and other countries. Obviously, such stance might be problematic when seeking to internationalise competition law and policy which among other things requires an enormous amount of consensus-building work and cooperation.

Nonetheless, there are a number of reasons as to why examining the relationship between competition and trade policies can be vital. In the context of the present book, the main reason for this lies in the phenomenon of 'hindrances' and the related concept of 'market access', namely *hindrances* which might impede the *access* by foreign firms to domestic markets. Such a situation may give rise to serious concerns, which in turn may give rise to a number of issues in terms of the relationship between competition policy and trade policy. Among these issues are the 'linkage' between the two policies and how the two policies should interact in an integrated and liberalised global economy. These issues themselves raise some important questions in the internationalisation of competition law.[2]

Whilst – as we shall see – hindrances may be of different types, the focus in this chapter will be on hindrances caused by the anticompetitive behaviour of domestic private firms to market access by foreign firms. In particular, the chapter will examine the roles that competition

---

[1] See pp. 80–82 above.

[2] See H. M. Applebaum, 'Antitrust and the Omnibus Trade and Competitiveness Act of 1998' (1989) *Antitrust Law Journal* 557; C. D. Ehlermann, 'The International Dimension of Competition Policy' (1994) *Fordham International Law Journal* 833.

and trade policies play in addressing this situation and the factors which may limit the role of either policy in this regard. The discussion considers the relationship between competition and trade policy, since, as will be seen, there are implications for both policies, especially in the case of 'hybrid' hindrances. The purpose of the chapter, however, is not to give a detailed analysis of both policies independently, but rather to examine how they interact in this particular context, since what is important for us is to evaluate the implications and lessons which one policy holds for the other.

(A) Anticompetitive behaviour and its effect on the flows of international trade and investment

One of the major efforts by the international community to liberalise trade globally has been dedicated to removing hindrances to the flows of trade and investment erected by countries in the form of tariffs, quotas, taxes, restrictions on foreign direct investment and other trade-hindering measures.[3] These efforts have been mainly in the form of agreements between countries. Both internationally and regionally, countries have concluded agreements or treaties seeking to lower trade barriers and to facilitate greater cross-border trade and investment. Internationally, this can be seen in light of the General Agreement on Tariffs and Trade (GATT) which served as a tool to liberalise trade in the post-1950s era. Other efforts can be seen in the light of the events leading to the birth of the World Trade Organisation (WTO) in the 1990s. Regionally, as we saw in chapter 7 – a number of agreements aiming at trade liberalisation have come to be concluded, most notably, the European Union (EU), the North American Free Trade Agreement (NAFTA) and the Asia-Pacific Economic Cooperation (APEC) Forum. All of these efforts have undoubtedly facilitated (and contributed) to the growth seen over the years in the flows of trade and investment worldwide. Nonetheless, it is clearly the case that the lowering of barriers between countries came to expose hindrances caused by the anticompetitive behaviour, conduct and transactions of private firms which can cause serious impediment to these flows. Increasing attention has been devoted to the desirability of the removal of such hindrances especially

---

[3] See C. T. Fedderson, 'Focusing on Substantive Law in International Economic Relations: the Public Morals of GATT's Article XX(A) and "Conventional Rules of Interpretation"' (1998) *Minnesota Journal of Global Trade* 75.

since governmental hindrances have decreased in significance. The consensus that came to develop therefore has been that these flows could be enhanced and further growth could be facilitated if these hindrances were to be completely removed.[4] As early as 1960, the GATT recognised that anticompetitive practices of firms may hinder the expansion of world trade and economic development in individual countries, frustrate the benefits of tariff reductions and removal of quantitative restrictions thus undermining the aims and objectives of GATT.[5]

(B) The concepts of 'market access' and 'hindrances'

It would be helpful to explain the important terms of market access and hindrances here.

I. Market access

The concept of 'market access' is one with which many competition specialists are familiar though the understanding of the concept by such specialists is in a 'relevant market context';[6] this is obviously different from the understanding trade policy experts have of the concept which stretches along the lines of access by foreign firms to local markets. Market access is a controversial issue in the field of competition law and that of trade policy. The exact meaning of the concept very much depends on one's understanding and perspective, as well as on the context in which it is used. It should not be that surprising therefore that there is no universal consensus on what the meaning of concept should be.[7]

In the present discussion, market access is taken to connote the conditions associated with the entry of firms into a particular market in order to sell goods and provide services. To an extent, this definition is similar to that given by the WTO. According to the WTO, market access describes the extent to which goods or services can compete with locally made products in another market. In the WTO framework the term

---

[4] See statement of former US assistant attorney general for antitrust, Joe Klein at the Hearings on 'Antitrust Enforcement Oversight', before the US House of Representatives, Committee on the Judiciary, 105th Cong., 1st Session (5 November 1997).

[5] See S. W. Waller, 'Can US Antitrust Laws Open International Markets'? (2000) *Northwestern Journal of International Law and Business* 207; E. Fox, 'Foreword: Mergers, Market Access and the Millennium' (2000) *Northwestern Journal of International Law and Business* 203.

[6] See above for an account on the issue of market definition in competition cases.

[7] See H. Hauser, 'Proposal for a Multilateral Agreement on Free Market Access (MAFMA)' (1991) *Journal of World Trade Law* 77.

stands for the totality of government-imposed conditions under which a product may enter a country under non-discriminatory conditions. The emphasis on the concept of market access within the WTO context has a clear trade policy perspective given its focus on government involvement.

It is essential to note, however, that the definition given here of market access is not intended to be comprehensive about what market access is in reality, but rather an explanation in order to facilitate a better understanding of the issues at hand.

II. 'Hindrances'

The term 'hindrance' is used occasionally in the field of competition law when talking about hindering the process of competition. As a concept however, a term that can be regarded as a synonym in the field is foreclosure; or that of 'barriers to entry', in itself a misunderstood concept. It may be of interest to observe the way different scholars have defined 'barriers to entry'. One the one hand, a barrier to entry has been considered to exist in situations where the firm seeking to enter the market faces a higher cost than that faced by the incumbent firm, the one already in the market.[8] On the other hand, the concept has been defined as anything that makes it difficult for a firm to enter a market.[9]

Putting the issue of definition to one side, it may not be easy in practice to draw a clear line between what amounts to hindrance and what does not. Hindrance to market access can be caused by *practices of firms* (i.e. the result of anticompetitive behaviour, conduct or transactions), *practices of countries* (in the form of government measures or laws or regulations) and in some cases *practices of both* – known as 'hybrid' or 'mixed' practices.[10] If the hindrance is of the first type, one can expect it to be addressed under competition law. If, on the other hand, the

---

[8] See, for example, the approach adopted by Chicago School scholars who gave a very restrictive view of the concept focusing on exclusionary practices, i.e. practices designed by a firm in the market to keep competitors out of the market. See R. H. Bork, *The Antitrust Paradox: a Policy at War with Itself* (Basic Books, 1978), ch. 16.

[9] A particularly detailed account of the concept of barrier to entry is offered by Bain, whose work has done much to popularise the concept. He listed among barriers to entry such things as economy of scale, capital requirements and product differentiation, arguing that virtually any impediment to market entry should be regarded as a barrier. See J. Bain, *Barriers to New Competition* (Harvard University Press, 1956), pp. 114–15.

[10] Several complaints about private or hybrid practices have surfaced over the years. See, for example, claims by the American Electronics Association about restraining practices in the Japanese electronics market (Submissions to the US Trade

hindrance is of the second type, then one can expect that trade policy and its tools will become relevant. However, if the hindrance is of the third type, the position becomes less clear. In this case, one can expect that there will be implications for both competition and trade policy. Using this division of types of hindrance, the responsibility for hindrance to market access may not always be easily apportioned between private firms or countries. There may be cases in which the responsibility may have to be attached to both firms and countries, since the restraints may be 'mixed' or 'hybrid' in nature.

(a) Hindrance caused by anticompetitive situations: practices of firms[11]

(i) Horizontal agreements Horizontal agreements – those entered into between firms operating at the same level of the market – amongst domestic firms can hinder access to domestic markets by foreign firms if the former, for example, agree to refrain from purchasing or distributing products imported by or from the latter, or to withhold from the latter materials, services, supplies or other necessary inputs. For example, if firms X, Y and Z in country A, which enjoy a position of economic strength, decide to stop importing a specific product of country B, the consequence of this agreement may prevent those domestic firms handling that product in country B from penetrating the domestic market of country A. Other examples which may be cited are where X, Y and Z share markets between them or engage in pricing practices designed to keep foreign firms out of country A.

(ii) Vertical agreements Agreements between domestic firms at different levels of the economy, for example, between a supplier and a distributor, may have the effect of hindering the ability of a foreign firm to develop a distribution network, which it needs in order to access the domestic market; such firm may also be prevented from expanding its presence in the local firm as a result of the vertical agreement.[12] Normally, this is the case in exclusive distribution agreements and exclusive purchasing agreements containing clauses preventing the distributor from handling the product(s) of the foreign competitor; such

---

Representative (USTR) in 1991) and complaints from auto parts makers in Europe and the USA about similar practices in Indonesia and Korea. See www.ustr.gov. A more high-profile example is the *Kodak/Fuji* case which is examined below; though the case is generally classified as an example of private hindrance.

[11] See also the general discussion in relation to these practices at pp. 32–36 above.
[12] See below the discussion on the *Kodak/Fuji* situation.

agreements can substantially raise barriers to entry by foreign firms. It is interesting to observe, on the other hand, how also in an international context, vertical agreements and restraints have been regarded as important for enhancing access to foreign markets because firms – regardless of their overall size and power – may not necessarily enjoy the required expertise or familiarity with different foreign markets and so they may choose to conclude vertical agreements with local distributors to enhance their prospects of entering these markets. Obviously there is a link between these two 'opposing' perspectives on vertical agreements: a vertical agreement between two local firms may hinder the ability of a foreign firm from entering into a vertical agreement or expanding its existing vertical network in the relevant local market.

(iii) Abuse of dominance   Hindrance to market access by foreign firms may occur in the case of dominant domestic firms which engage in abusive conduct. Such conduct can be in the form of refusal to supply or deal, discounts and rebates, abuse of intellectual property rights, predatory pricing[13] and selective price-cutting[14] which are all designed with the aim of excluding foreign firms from domestic markets.

(iv) Mergers   A merger between firms may generate anticompetitive effects beyond the borders of the country or countries where the merger is taking place; this for example can be in the form of causing foreclosure. The development of national champion firms through domestic mergers

---

[13] In simple terms, predatory pricing involves selling below cost (i.e. selling at a loss). A dominant firm may engage in such a practice for the purposes of excluding competitors: the firm will in these circumstances lower its price to below cost level for a period of time (until the firm would have 'dealt' with competitors) after which the firm will raise prices to a higher level than that prevailing previously in order to recoup its losses. In real cases, establishing the existence of predatory pricing is not a straightforward matter and requires handling complex cost concepts, such as *Average Variable Cost* and *Average Total Cost* (or the concepts of *Average Avoidable Cost* and *Long-run Average Incremental Cost*, as the European Commission states in its *Guidance Paper* on Article 102 TFEU; the *Guidance Paper* was referred in chapter 4 above, at note 43.

[14] Selective price-cutting arises in a situation where the dominant firm selects a particular customer and offers such a customer a price cut. This offer will not be extended to other customers of the firm. The cut in price in this case will not be to below cost level. The idea behind the practice is to 'protect' the position of the dominant firm in relation to those customers who may be actual or potential target for competitors of the firm. This way the firm will be able to ensure that such competitors will be kept away from such customers, i.e. excluded.

can hinder the ability of potential foreign firms to penetrate domestic markets.[15]

(b) Hindrance caused by practices of countries   There are several ways in which practices by countries may directly or indirectly impair market access by foreign firms. The following two points illustrate how countries could be held accountable for hindering market access by foreign firms.

(i) Exemptions under competition law   Countries may directly exempt the anticompetitive behaviour of domestic firms from the application of their domestic competition laws. This issue has for many years been subjected to close scrutiny[16] but is relevant to the present discussion on the effect of practices of countries on market access because exemptions from those countries' competition laws may have consequences beyond their domestic borders in general, and for foreign firms aiming to access the market in those countries in particular. The concern about exemptions in this case is a serious one, especially since there is no indication of willingness on the part of countries unilaterally to confine the scope and application of exemptions from their domestic competition laws. The reluctance of countries to abandon their existing exemptions and exclusions can be seen from the OECD *Recommendations on Hardcore Cartels.*[17] Despite the willingness of OECD members, as expressed in the Recommendations, to cooperate on enforcement action against hardcore cartels, the Recommendations did not attempt to impose any binding rules on exemptions by countries. As a result, an extensive use of exemptions could easily lead to a substantial amount of economic activity around the world avoiding the competition laws of different jurisdictions.

(ii) Strategic application of domestic competition law   Countries may indirectly strategically apply their domestic competition laws in order to promote 'national champions' or protect local firms at the expense of foreign firms. A country may undertake strategic measures for the protection of anticompetitive behaviour of domestic firms because it gains more from those measures than foreign countries. In a tactical

---

[15] See D. I. Baker and W. T. Miller, 'Antitrust Enforcement and Non-Enforcement as a Barrier to Imports' (1996) *International Business Law* 488.

[16] See R. P. Inman and D. L. Rubinfeld, 'Making Sense of the Antitrust State Action Doctrine: Balancing Political Participation and Economic Efficiency in Regulatory Federalism' (1997) *Texas Law Review* 1203.

[17] See p. 138 above.

application of its domestic competition law, a country may immunise private anticompetitive behaviour by virtue of different measures, such as the 'state action' doctrine.[18]

(c) **Hindrances with public and private elements**   As outlined above, restraints on market access can be mixed or hybrid in nature. This is, for example, the case where the practices of a country facilitate the anticompetitive behaviour of private firms.[19] The following examples may be used as an illustration.

(i) Limiting foreign direct investment   One way in which a foreign firm may access a market is through foreign direct investment. An action by a country to give an association of firms in a particular domestic industry the power to decide, for example, whether or not to grant licences to individual firms, can mean that the association may use this power in an exclusionary manner against foreign firms.

(ii) Standardisation   Standardisation in industries by standard-setting bodies, especially in the hi-tech sector, such as telecommunications and information technology, can offer considerable advantages to domestic firms. In a global market, the activities of standard-setting bodies have the potential of exerting an impact on the flows of trade between countries. Such bodies may opt for technological standards, as a result of which a foreign standard will not prove to be compatible with technologies available in the local market. Such action can tilt the development of those technologies towards a domestically selected standard with the outcome that the ability of a foreign firm, which does not have any presence in the standard-setting body, to access the domestic market may be hindered.

(iii) Lack of enforcement by competition authorities   Anticompetitive behaviour or conduct by private firms may also be encouraged by the lack

---

[18] See E. Fox, 'The Problem of State Action that Blesses Private Action that Harms "the Foreigners"' in E. Zach and C. M. Correa (eds.), *Towards WTO Competition Rules: Key Issues and Comments on the WTO Report (1998) on Trade and Competition* (Kluwer Law International, 1999), p. 325. See further chapter 8, note 200 and accompanying text.

[19] An example of repeated allegations of hybrid restraints may be found in the history of the Japanese passenger vehicle industry. See generally J. F. Rill and C. S. Hambers, 'Antitrust Enforcement and Non-Enforcement as a Barrier to Import in the Japanese Automobile Industry' (1997) *Empirica* 109. Another example of hybrid restraint is found in the US Corn Refiners Association complaint to the US Trade Representative about the practices of the Mexican government; See p. 619 below.

of enforcement by their domestic competition authorities. Such lack of enforcement may give an indication to those firms that their anticompetitive behaviour or conduct is permissible. Policymakers in one country may even adopt a more active role by encouraging local firms, for example, to divide markets, thinking that this will lead to stabilisation in a domestic industry in its early stage of development or infancy.[20]

(d) Comments In the case of hybrid restraints, anticompetitive behaviour, conduct or transactions by private firms may hinder market access because this may be facilitated by some supportive action by the country. The fact that this matter – mainly due to the involvement of public and private elements – cannot be addressed satisfactorily under competition or trade policy separately, blurs the lines of accountability of countries and firms. As a result, one can expect that economic and political tensions will materialise between countries and between countries and firms.

The involvement of countries in hybrid restraints is a matter of particular significance when it comes to analysing these restraints under competition and trade policy. Interestingly, however, that legal significance differs under the two policies. As far as competition policy is concerned, the involvement of a country means that the behaviour of a private firm, which would otherwise be considered anticompetitive and possibly prohibited, may escape being caught by competition law.[21] Thus, a restrictive or anticompetitive behaviour or conduct of a firm may escape being caught by the provisions of competition law because it has been authorised by a country as part of a clearly formulated policy to displace competition with regulation and where the government of the country concerned supervises the behaviour in question.[22] Under trade policy, on the other hand, the involvement of a country in the manner just described means that catching hybrid restraints is more possible.[23] Still, whereas active participation by a country in hybrid

---

[20] See generally M. Dabbah, 'Measuring the Success of a System of Competition Law: a Preliminary View' (2000) *European Competition Law Review* 369.

[21] See generally American Bar Association Antitrust Section, *Antitrust Law Developments 1049* (1997). A good example is provided in the light of various doctrines such as the foreign sovereign compulsion doctrine, and the foreign sovereign immunity doctrine and the Act of state doctrine; see above.

[22] See *Parker* v. *Brown*, 317 US 341 (1943) and *Southern Motor Carriers Rate Conference* v. *US*, 471 US 48 (1985).

[23] The USA, for example, argued that the market access-restraining practices in the *Kodak/ Fuji* case were orchestrated by the Japanese government and on that basis fell foul of WTO rules; see pp. 609–614 below for a discussion on the case.

practices may be caught by trade policy, for example by the WTO rules, there is less certainty whether a lesser role for countries – such as sanctioning or tolerating the private practice – can be caught.[24]

During the last two decades, market access-restraining hybrid practices have become a distinct new element in the competition and trade policy debate. Whilst there has been no comprehensive empirical study with economic or statistical analyses in this important debate, there seems to be an increasing recognition and sufficient indication that the effect of private anticompetitive practices on trade and investment flows between countries can be as serious as hindrances solely caused by the behaviour of countries. Equally, there seems to be a growing recognition that the anticompetitive behaviour or conduct of private firms may be blessed by actions of countries, policies and practices.[25] Under many of these factual patterns an important question raised is whether, and to what extent, the resulting problems from market access-restraining hybrid practices are attributable to the country as opposed to the private firms concerned.

A final important comment that should be made concerns the place of the concept of 'market access' under competition and trade policy. Whilst the removal of artificial impediments to market access is perhaps the most obvious goal of trade policy, especially post-1945, it is not apparent that ensuring market access has been recognised as an appropriate goal for competition policy internationally. In order to understand these differing perspectives on the place of the concept of market access under both policies, one should consider their differences in general.

2. The perspectives of competition and trade policies: differences

Competition and trade policies have different perspectives.[26] These perspectives mean that on the whole major differences exist between the two policies; but some similarities can be said to exist however. Among these differences is the difference in scope between the two policies, which address economic distortions of different kinds.

---

[24] See how the US Congress, for example, has attempted to reach such lesser government roles through the concept of 'toleration' within the meaning of s. 301 of the Trade Act 1974; see pp. 616–620 below.

[25] US firms in different industries have repeatedly argued that their access to Japanese markets is hindered by the behaviour of Japanese private firms; see pp. 609–614 below.

[26] For a general comparison of competition and trade policy, see H. M. Applebaum, 'The Interface of the Trade Laws and the Antitrust Laws' (1998) *George Mason Law Review* 479.

Competition policy is primarily concerned with anticompetitive behaviour, conduct and transactions of firms.[27] Competition law and policy are nationally determined and their primary focus is on protecting competition in the marketplace, local consumers and the operation of domestic markets.[28] Trade policy, on the other hand, is principally focused on the behaviour of countries. It is internationally determined and its main aim is to remove acts and practices by countries that foreclose access by foreign firms to domestic markets. The difference in outlook – national v. international – between the two policies runs parallel to the difference in basis: the legal basis of competition law enforcement is wider than that of trade policy which some would argue is because trade policy is decided through more political than legal processes;[29] one may wonder however whether in relation to politicisation, there is a difference of kind or degree between competition and trade policy.[30] It is difficult to claim that competition policy channels are totally free from the influence of politics, though it is indeed the case that trade policy has to be based on the political consent of those who win or lose from the expansion of trade and hence a greater weight is given to 'producer interests'.[31] Competition policy, on the other hand, tends to be more concerned with consumer interests than trade policy.[32] Another difference is that not all competition policy concerns are relevant to trade policy. For example, the procedural and substantive features of multi-jurisdictional merger control are not matters customarily considered under trade policy. In addition, international cartels appear to be a serious problem for individual countries and the global economy which give rise to serious competition policy issues but do not, directly at least, influence trade policy issues. Finally, when there is an overlap in competition and trade policy issues, different conclusions regarding the effects

---

[27] Note, however, the existence of state aid rules in the competition law chapter in EU competition law regime; see pp. 161–162 above.

[28] See R. E. Hudec, 'A WTO Perspective on Private Anti-Competitive Behavior in World Markets' (1999) *New England Law Review* 79.

[29] See B. Doern, *Competition Policy Decision Processes in the European Community and United Kingdom* (Carleton University Press, 1992).

[30] See B. Doern and S. Wilks, *Comparative Competition Policy* (Oxford University Press, 1996).

[31] See G. Feketekuty, *Reflections on the Interaction between Trade Policy and Competition Policy: a Contribution to the Development of a Conceptual Framework* (OECD, 1993).

[32] See J. M. Finger (ed.), *Antidumping: How it Works and Who Gets Hurt?* (University of Michigan Press, 1993); T. M. Boddez and M. J. Trebilcock, *Unfinished Business: Reforming Trade Remedy Laws in North America* (C. D. Howe Institute, 1993).

of a particular restraint may be reached. Judging a restraint from a competition policy perspective means that its effects have to be considered in terms of efficiency and consumer welfare and other goals of competition law mentioned in chapter 1 of the present book,[33] whilst a trade policy perspective will mainly consider whether the restraint adversely impacts on the flows of trade and investment between countries and access to markets by keeping foreign firms out of those markets. Interestingly, from a trade policy perspective, the restraint can still be condemned even if it has positive effects on efficiency and the welfare of those participants in the domestic market.

3. Substitutability between competition policy and trade policy

A highly interesting question relates to whether there is any substitutability between competition policy and trade policy, especially whether one policy can obviate the need for the other policy in the case of hybrid restraints of market access.

First, regarding the substitutability of competition policy by trade policy, it is important to note that whilst trade policy tools remove public impediments to access to domestic markets by foreign firms, such tools do not tackle private impediments caused from within domestic markets. This means that it is possible to be sceptical about the claim in favour of trade policy rendering competition policy unnecessary, even if this result is achievable. This is because while a free trade stance greatly reduces the scope of the task facing competition authorities, it does not imply that competition law and policy have no purpose to serve. Free trade must be complemented by the freedom of entry of firms, including the possibility to contest markets, in particular through foreign direct investment, especially in the services sector and as far as products confined to domestic markets are concerned.[34] This view is in line with another on the potential role of competition policy in addressing private restraints that may arise in international trade. One of the driving forces of globalisation is liberalisation of trade and investment. Removing barriers

---

[33] See pp. 40–44 above.

[34] See B. Hoekman and P. C. Mavroidis, 'Linking Competition and Trade Policies in Central and East European Countries', Policy Research Working Paper 1346 (World Bank, 1994); W. F. Shughart, J. Silverman and R. Tollison, 'Antitrust Enforcement and Foreign Competition' in F. S. McChesney and W. F. Shughart (eds.), *The Causes and Consequences of Antitrust: the Public Choice Perspective* (Chicago University Press, 1995).

to trade and investment does not necessarily ensure access to markets. A progress report produced within the OECD and submitted at its 1993 Ministerial Meeting argued that globalisation was expected to lead to more efficient production and marketing, lower prices and improved product quality and variety, but that it will fail to do so unless market access and competition can be preserved and enhanced.[35] As firms attempt to improve or maintain their competitive position in an increasingly global environment, they may take actions aimed at effectively keeping foreign competitors out of their domestic market. While the dividing line between meeting competition and restricting or defeating it by hindering access can admittedly be a fine one, it nonetheless emphasises the potential contribution of competition policy to addressing problems of access to and presence in domestic markets encountered by foreign firms.[36] Thus the conclusion to be drawn from these points is that there is a need for competition policy in the global economy, and that the existence of trade policy does not affect this conclusion.

Using competition policy to combat private anticompetitive practices affecting international trade and hindering market access may be desirable. Nevertheless, its effectiveness as a remedy in this instance gives rise to several concerns. First, there is little awareness of the nature of similarities or differences between competition and trade policies with regard to market access. Secondly, it is not clear whether a commonly understood competition law which is applicable to market access-restraining practices exists. Thirdly, there is a risk that countries may be drawn into deep market access disputes of a competition law nature. Countries do not often seem to have confidence in the ability of the institutions of one another to resolve such disputes, something that is likely to trigger differences between countries over dispute resolution.[37] Finally, it is worth noting that problems may arise from the way domestic competition policy of a country is formulated: where such policy is inadequately framed – to the extent that it permits anticompetitive practices which preclude effective market access or an effective market

---

[35] See Joint Progress Report on Trade and Competition Policies submitted by the Committee on Competition Law and Policy and the Joint Group on Competition and Trade.

[36] See A. Zampetti and P. Sauve, *New Dimensions of Market Access: an Overview* (OECD, 1995).

[37] See Fox, 'Competition Law and the Agenda for the WTO: Forging the Links of Competition and Trade' (1995) *Pacific-Rimely Law and Policy Journal* 1.

presence by foreign firms – this may be an impediment in itself especially to the flows of trade and investment between countries.

The flip side concerns the possibility of competition policy substituting trade policy. This matter requires particular attention be given to the scope and goals of competition law. These two issues determine – in no small measure – the extent to which substitution may occur. *On the one hand*, with regard to the issue of scope, it was argued above that domestic competition law may be limited by the existence of exemptions.[38] A particular example of how exemptions can diminish the effectiveness of domestic competition law to address trade policy issues is the case of export cartels, which usually benefits from some form of exemption under the competition rules of different regimes.[39] At a more general level, the scope of a domestic competition law can also be limited in terms of its enforcement. The importance of the issue of enforcement may be observed in three different contexts. First, the extent to which foreign firms can have a private right of action to complain about anticompetitive practices and seek enforcement under the domestic competition rules of the host country. The position here rests on two factors: one factor is whether the relevant domestic competition law regime provides for rights of foreign firms to complain to the domestic competition authority and the second factor is whether foreign firms have *locus standi* or launch private actions in domestic courts in the host country if they are neither incorporated nor have another form of legal presence therein. Secondly, the extent to which domestic competition authorities and courts will act in cases where foreign interests are involved: the scope of national competition law and policy to respond to trade concerns of foreign countries can be limited by a possible non-enforcement of the competition rules of the host country. This issue triggers formidable difficulties, especially since enforcement of competition law falls within the discretion of national competition authorities. Thirdly – and this is a point that arises due to the political nature of trade policy – the extent to which domestic competition authorities are immune from political pressures: the effectiveness of domestic competition law in resolving trade policy issues will depend upon the independence of domestic competition authorities. Ensuring such adequate independence is likely to encourage and enable competition authorities to initiate and deal with

---

[38] See pp. 46–47 above.
[39] See U. Immenga, 'Export Cartels and Voluntary Export Restraints Between Trade and Competition Policy' (1995) *Pacific-Rimely Law and Policy Journal* 93.

cases involving alleged anticompetitive practices that adversely affect foreign interests.

On the other hand, regarding the issue of goals of competition law, as we saw in the course of the discussion in chapter 1, it is clear that domestic competition laws in different jurisdictions serve different goals. In the USA, the main generally accepted objective of competition law is economic efficiency and consumer welfare. In the EU, on the other hand, other goals have equal status such as furthering market integration. It seems that economic goals of efficiency and consumer welfare are regarded as more favourable to the use of competition law as a trade remedy, than those relating to social and political objectives. This is because the former goals are neutral, whilst the latter goals might be used to support domestic firms to the detriment of foreign firms and consumers. Wider political goals are likely to undermine the role of competition law and policy as an effective means to combat market access-restraining practices. It is interesting to observe in this regard the first recital of the WTO agreements which sets out the objectives of the multilateral trading system. The recital refers to 'raising standards of living' and 'optimal use of the world's resources in accordance with the objectives of sustainable development' which seems to indicate that promoting efficiency and welfare in a global economy are among such objectives.

4. Consistencies between competition policy and trade policy

The discussion in the previous section indicated that recognising economic efficiency and consumer welfare as the goals of competition law enhances the prospects of substitution between competition and trade policy. It is not totally clear however that this can make the two polices 'coincide' in practice with regard to how concerns relating to market access should be handled. It is probably not the case in all circumstances. Arguably, however, this should not present a problem provided that market access hindrances are considered from a shared perspective, competition and trade policy. It is true that the differences between the two policies – as outlined above – may affect an attempt to develop such shared perspective. Nonetheless, one must also recognise the existence of consistencies between the two policies: competition and trade policies are compatible as far as concerns relating to market access are concerned. This can be seen in the context of the free movement and competition law provisions in the EU, where the two sets of provisions have always been considered complementary in achieving the goals of the EU including promoting a continuous, harmonious and balanced development of economic activities.[40] The aim of both policies is to improve the efficient allocation of resources. Trade policy contributes to efficiency by removing barriers that impede the ability of foreign firms to access new markets. Competition policy contributes to efficiency by preventing firms from harming competition. This shows actual and potential consistencies between the two policies.

5. The different approaches under competition policy and trade policy

There are a number of *existing* approaches under competition and trade policy which may be adopted to deal with hindrances resulting from anticompetitive situations (whether in whole or partly) involving private firms.

(A) Approaches under competition policy

I. Relying on extraterritoriality

As we saw in chapters 2 and 8, the doctrine of extraterritoriality – however controversial – can be viewed as a type of internationalisation. The discussion in chapter 8 in particular offered a comprehensive examination of the doctrine and demonstrated how many competition law regimes incorporate a mechanism for extraterritorial assertion, which receives expression mainly in the form of the doctrine of effects in the competition rules of those regimes. In the case of some regimes, this mechanism has – in the eyes of several countries – sometimes been used aggressively by the competition authorities and courts in those regimes; primarily to attempt to deal with situations where they consider the anticompetitive behaviour of domestic firms of other countries hinders the entry of their firms into the domestic market of the latter. In such a case, the doctrine of extraterritoriality would be used by the home country of the foreign firms to open such 'domestic' markets.[41]

---

[40] See pp. 209–210 above.

[41] The use of extraterritoriality to open foreign markets was refereed to in chapter 8 as 'outbound' extraterritoriality. This as we noted was practiced most notably by the USA: see, for example, *United States* v. *Pilkington plc*, 59 Fed. Reg. 30604 (1994), in which the US Antitrust Division challenged restrictions imposed by Pilkington in the UK that prevented US firms from exporting to the UK.

Whether, however, such an attempt will be met with success very much depends on the circumstances of the case at hand; at any rate success may not be guaranteed given that such attempts may not necessarily enjoy sufficient impact to address competition concerns beyond domestic markets. On the contrary, extraterritorial assertion of jurisdiction in the field of competition law – particularly in such cases – may give rise to considerable problems and can aggravate conflicts between countries and lead to a serious friction in the interface between competition and trade policy.[42] These points were highlighted in the discussion during chapter 8 but may also be illustrated using a hypothetical example. Suppose that country A and country B both have effective competition law regimes. Imagine that the anticompetitive behaviour of firm X in country A does not harm either conditions of competition or other firms in the market in country A (the local market), but rather it is preventing firm Y of country B from penetrating that market. Of course, the primary concern of country A's competition authority would be to protect conditions of competition (and possibly competitors) in country A's market. The fact that no harm is caused to conditions of competition, consumers or competitors in the local market, may lead the authority to conclude that the relevant competition rules do not apply on the basis of lack of competitive harm locally; even if harm is done to firm Y. However, country B's competition authority or court, being concerned about the lack of action on the part of country A's competition authority, may try to apply the competition law of country B extraterritorially in order to open the market in question for firm Y. The fact that more than one competition authority is involved and may reach different conclusions over one and the same matter will lead to conflicts between country A and country B and may trigger uncertainty; let alone the objection that may be voiced by country A on grounds of interference by country B with its sovereignty and prerogatives.

II. Bilateralism

Another option that may be available under competition law and which we discussed in chapter 9 is that of bilateral cooperation between competition authorities. In more ways than one, bilateral cooperation – whether achieved through formal positive or negative comity or *de facto* positive comity cooperation *or* as part of general, wider economic

---

[42] See Papakrivopoulos, 'The Role of Competition Law as an International Trade Remedy in the Context of the World Trade Organization' (1999) *World Competition* 45.

cooperation – offers considerable advantages over the unilateral option of extraterritoriality, which as we noted suffers from several problems. In particular, bilateral cooperation may eliminate conflicts between countries in practice and remove many problems associated with access to information and other evidentiary matters which frequently surface in competition cases. The benefits of cooperation should also be seen against the backdrop of the fact that firms will be relieved from the burden of duplicated enforcement and the risk of inconsistent conclusions which may be reached by the relevant competition authorities.[43] In the context of practices of private firms restraining market access of foreign firms, bilateral cooperation could offer an added value for providing a platform for dialogue and negotiation between the competition authorities concerned and this is likely to enhance market access and promote the growth of flows of trade and investment in the global economy.

(B)   Approaches under trade policy

I.   International trade law: the WTO option

(a) **General**   As we saw above,[44] competition law is not included in the WTO framework and as a result the Organisation's rules do not cover the anticompetitive behaviour or practices of private firms. Those rules are meant to address governmental practices as opposed to the practices of private firms; the latter in general are not directly addressed under any type of international rules. Nevertheless, the idea of pursuing a WTO 'option' in the field of competition law dates back as we saw to as early as the inauguration of the Organisation itself. This idea became very promising in 2001 in the run up to the Doha WTO round and as a result gained legitimacy and momentum. Shortly afterwards however the situation came to change dramatically and the idea witnessed a sharp transition from being promising to becoming highly questionable and controversial. Indeed probably a single word used in the 2007 WTO Annual Report would best describe the current state of affairs concerning the option: that Report describes the WTO working group on the interaction between trade and competition as 'inactive'.

---

[43] See pp. 106–108 above.

[44] See in particular the discussion in chapter 2, but also the discussion in chapter 10, especially pp. 548–562.

The fact that work on exploring a competition option within the WTO has been put on hold seems to have done nothing but encourage the development of creative thinking on how – despite this – a competition 'link' can be established with the WTO framework. In other words the question is whether the possibility exists for extending the scope of some WTO rules to deal with the behaviour and practices of firms, albeit indirectly within a competition law context. Anyone familiar with the debate on internationalising competition law in general would appreciate this indeed is a difficult question and answering it in the positive might prove to be controversial. However, answering it in the negative may not be totally accurate given that realistically speaking such possibility can be said to exist. It may be worth noting here the view of the WTO itself as expressed over ten years ago that the number of areas where the multilateral trading system is already addressing competition issues has increased with the result of the Uruguay Round and the subsequent work of the WTO.[45] In fairness, the way in which the global trading system has developed and the fact that practices, behaviour and transactions of firms easily transcend national boundaries and can directly impact on international trade naturally place competition policy within an international trade setting, making it very arguable that competition law and policy are effectively inseparable from trade policy.[46]

A few possibilities may be identified through which the WTO rules may address situations involving private firms. There are several WTO provisions and mechanisms within the WTO framework of rules and principles which are of possible relevance here: the consultation and cooperation arrangements under each of the main WTO agreements; the general rules of the WTO relating to non-discrimination and transparency; the areas where the WTO already provides for some minimum standards that governments are to follow in combating or regulating anticompetitive practices (notably in the area of basic telecommunications); the provisions which allow for remedies to enterprise practices, notably in the area of anti-dumping; and the WTO dispute-settlement mechanism.

The WTO framework of rules and principles is extremely complex and detailed, running into thousands of pages. Out of these, the following

---

[45] See in particular the outcome of the WTO 4th Ministerial Conference held in Doha in November 2001.

[46] See S. D. Amarasinha, 'WTO Core Principles and Trade/Competition Policies' and F. Jenny, 'Competition, Trade and Development Before and After Cancun' (2004) *Fordham Corporate Law Institute* 711 and 631 respectively.

have particular competition-related relevance and significance: the *Agreement on Technical Barriers to Trade*; the *Agreement on Government Procurement*; the *General Agreement on Tariffs and Trade*; the *General Agreement on Trade in Services*; the *Trade Related Intellectual Property Rights*; the *Telecommunications Reference Paper on Regulatory Principles of the Negotiating Group on Basic Telecommunications*; and *the Understanding on Commitments in Financial Services* (UCFS). Beyond these WTO agreements, competition-related matters and issues have come to feature in some WTO cases; though to date the number of these cases remains remarkably low, presumably due to the fact that the competition-related relevance of WTO rules as seen in light of these agreements themselves lacks sufficient concentration and is largely fragmented and dispersed.[47]

(i) The Agreement on Technical Barriers to Trade Under the Agreement on Technical Barriers to Trade of the WTO, member countries are required to take such reasonable measures as may be available to them to ensure that non-governmental standard-setting bodies comply with the Agreement's Most-Favoured-Nation (MFN), national treatment and other requirements.[48] The purpose behind this is to prohibit the use of standard setting for the purpose of impeding market access. The Agreement also provides that as to certain of its requirements, member countries shall formulate and implement positive measures and mechanisms in support of the observance by bodies other than central government bodies.[49] These prohibitions have not been properly tested in practice however.

(ii) The Agreement on Government Procurement As a plurilateral agreement within the WTO framework, the Agreement on Government Procurement[50] is not binding on all members of the WTO: currently 40 members are parties, including member states of the EU, the USA, Canada and China to name but a few; 19 WTO

---

[47] See F. Souty, 'Is there a need for additional WTO competition rules promoting non-discriminatory competition laws and competition institutions in WTO members?' in E. U. Petersmann (ed.) *Reforming the World Trading System* (Oxford University Press, 2005), p. 305.

[48] See below for a discussion of these principles.

[49] See Annex 1A, at Arts 3.1, 3.5 and 8.1 of the *Marrakesh Agreement Establishing the WTO* (15 April 1994).

[50] See *ibid.*, Annex 4(b).

members hold observer status under the Agreement. The Agreement directly requires its parties to subject government procurement[51] to international competition by inserting the key principle of non-discrimination into national rules, practices and procedures relating to government procurement and its tendering processes. Parties to the Agreement and their entities are required to implement the WTO's national treatment principle[52] when dealing with government procurement: they must give 'no less favourable' treatment to the products, services and suppliers of any other party to the Agreement than they would give to their domestic products, services and suppliers and they may not discriminate among goods, services and suppliers of other parties.[53] The Agreement also indirectly facilitates competition by promoting transparency in that it requires the parties to publish laws, regulations, judicial decisions, administrative rulings and any procedures regarding government procurement.[54]

Disputes arising out of the Agreement can bring into action the WTO's *Dispute Settlement Understanding*.[55] As the Agreement is plurilateral, a number of special rules or procedures are applicable: for instance, the 'cross-retaliation' provision in the Understanding is not applicable to disputes arising out of the Agreement and the Dispute Settlement Body has authority to authorise consultations among parties to a dispute in respect of remedies when a violating measure cannot be withdrawn.[56] For the competitive tendering process, the parties to the Agreement are required to establish an independent domestic 'challenge procedure' giving recourse to suppliers who believe that a procurement has not been carried out within the requirements of the Agreement.[57]

Though government procurement was initially carved out from the scope of the main multilateral trade rules, during the Tokyo Round of Trade Negotiations (1973–79) this was considered to be an unacceptable

---

[51] The Agreement does not automatically apply to all government procurement: each party's coverage is determined by reference to the Appendix I Annexes. Annexes 1 to 3 cover central and sub-central government entities as well as other bodies, such as public utilities. Generally, all goods are covered by the Agreement and Annexes 4 and 5 specify each party's covered services and construction services. For each party, the Appendix I Annexes will also state the threshold value above which individual procurements are covered.

[52] See below.   [53] See Arts 3.1 and 3.2.   [54] See Art. 19.1 and Appendix IV.

[55] See Art. 22. To date, there have only been three disputes between parties to the Agreement on Government Procurement. See: www.wto.org/english/tratop_e/gproc_e/disput_e.htm.

[56] See Arts 22.7 and 22.3.   [57] See Art. 20.

gap in the multilateral trading system since, in most countries, governments and the agencies under their control are together the biggest purchasers of goods of all kinds – from basic commodities to pharmaceuticals – and there is no doubt that pressure is exercised politically to favour domestic suppliers over foreign competitors thus hindering international competition. However, government procurement is still not included in the main commitments of the General Agreement on Trade in Services, which is examined below.

(iii) The General Agreement on Tariffs and Trade   Several articles of the General Agreement on Tariffs and Trade (GATT) are relevant to the field of competition law. These include Articles II:4,[58] III, XVII, XI,[59] XX(d),[60] and XXIII.[61]

Article III of the GATT has been interpreted and applied on several occasions by WTO Panels especially within the context of the national treatment principle. In one of the most notable rulings, *the Japan-Taxes on Alcoholic Beverages (Japan-Alcoholic Beverages II)*, the WTO Appellate Body declared that the broad and fundamental objective behind the Article was to avoid protectionism, namely 'to ensure that internal measures [are] not to be applied to important or domestic products so as to afford protection to domestic production'. The Appellate Body emphasised that Article III comes to protect expectations of 'the equal competitive relationship between imported and domestic products'.[62]

Article III:4 applies to 'all laws, regulations and requirements affecting internal sale, offering for sale, purchase, transportation, distribution or use' of products of national origin. The phrase 'laws, regulations and requirements' has been interpreted to include 'any laws or regulation which might adversely modify the conditions of competition between domestic and imported products' on domestic markets;[63] the phrase also covers laws, regulations and requirements of both substantive and procedural types.[64]

---

[58] The Article concerns the existence of an import monopoly and the prohibition on illegal protectionism and discrimination.

[59] The Article prohibits quantitative restraints and unjustifiable import monopolies.

[60] This Article contains a similar prohibition to that found in Art. XI.

[61] See below.

[62] See *Japan-Taxes on Alcoholic Beverages (Japan-Alcoholic Beverages II)*, WT/DS8/AB/R, WT/DS10/AB/R, WT/DS11/AB/R (1 November 1996).

[63] See *Italian Discrimination against Imported Agricultural Machinery (Italy Agricultural Machinery)* (23 October 1958), BISD 7S/60.

[64] See *United States-Section 337 of the Tariff Act of 1930 (US-Section 337 Tariff Act)* (7 November 1989).

Article XVII[65] contains the principle of non-discrimination in relation to state trading enterprises and mandates that such enterprises make purchases or sales in accordance with commercial considerations and allow enterprises of other WTO members the ability to compete. Specifically, paragraph 1 of the Article provides:

> (a) Each Member undertakes that if it establishes or maintains a State enterprise, wherever located, or grants to any enterprise, formally or in effect, exclusive or special privileges, such enterprise shall, in its purchases or sales involving either imports or exports, act in a manner consistent with the general principles of non-discriminatory treatment prescribed in this Agreement for governmental measures affecting imports or exports by private traders.
>
> (b) The provisions of subparagraph (*a*) of this paragraph shall be understood to require that such enterprises shall, having due regard to the other provisions of this Agreement, make any such purchases or sales solely in accordance with commercial considerations, including price, quality, availability, marketability, transportation and other conditions of purchase or sale, and shall afford the enterprises of the other Members adequate opportunity, in accordance with customary business practice, to compete for participation in such purchases or sales.

Another provision of the GATT that has particular importance is Article XXIII on nullification and impairment. This Article concerns measures adopted by governments of WTO members which nullify or impair 'agreed' market access or the fulfilment of the objectives underpinning the GATT. The Article may be used by WTO members as a launch pad for complaints against measures adopted by other members impeding the access of products or firms of the former to the local markets of the latter; arguably this includes the competition rules of the latter as well as the manner of enforcement of these rules. The use of Article XXIII as a competition law tool was attempted on more than one occasion, most notably in the *Kodak/Fuji* case.[66] This has, among other things, encouraged competition specialists to argue that the competition rules of WTO members were within the scope of the WTO dispute settlement system which meant that such rules must comply with WTO standards.[67] Such arguments have come to 'flourish' as a result of some subsequent

---

[65] See below for the application of the Article in the USA–Canada dispute in the *Wheat/grain* case.

[66] See below.

[67] See C. D. Ehlermann and L. Ehring 'WTO Dispute Settlement and Competition Law: Views from the Perspective of the Appellate Body's Experience' (2002) *Fordham International Law Journal* 1505.

WTO rulings. Notable here is the Panel's ruling in the EU's complaint against the US Anti-Dumping Act 1916[68] in which the Panel stated that 'the scope of the WTO Agreement does not exclude *a priori* restrictive business practices'. According to the Panel this meant that a domestic competition law would not per se be excluded from the application of WTO rules. The Panel clearly had in mind past precedents on the issue as it noted that 'panels under GATT 1947 and the WTO have addressed various aspects of restrictive business practices initiated by governments when such practices had the effect of impeding market access of foreign products or entry of foreign enterprises'.

(iv) The General Agreement on Trade in Services Two particular provisions of the General Agreement on Trade in Services (GATS) carry competition relevance: Article VIII and Article IX which deal specifically with the obligations of WTO members to address the trade-restricting business practices of dominant firms and those which supply exclusive services as well as firms which offer other services; it is also important to note the *GATS Annex on Telecommunications*.[69]

Article VIII deals with monopolies and exclusive service suppliers. Of particular importance is paragraph 2 of the Article which provides for a clear obligation on WTO members within their commitments to ensure there is a prohibition on abuse of a monopoly position to act in their territory in a manner inconsistent with such commitments where a supplier of the WTO member 'competes, either directly or indirectly or through an affiliated company, in the supply of a service outside the scope of its monopoly rights and which is subject to that Member's specific commitments'.

Article IX on the other hand deals with the case of non-monopolies. According to paragraph 1 of the Article, competition may be restrained and trade in services may be restricted as a result of certain business practices of non-monopoly service providers. According to paragraph 2, where such practices exist relevant WTO members are required to enter into consultations with a view to eliminating such practices.

The importance of these articles of GATS lies in the recognition underpinning them that certain business practices may restrict competition and hinder trade in services. Indirectly therefore the Articles can be

---

[68] See *United States Anti-Dumping Act of 1916-Complaint by the European Communities* DS136/R (31 March 2000).

[69] See below in the context of the discussion on the *Mexico–Telecom* case, pp. 615–616 below.

said to lay down an obligation on WTO members to ensure that their domestic services markets remain competitive and to address any anticompetitive situation.

(v) The Understanding on Commitments in Financial Services The Understanding on Commitments in Financial Services allows certain WTO members (namely those who participated in the Uruguay Round) to take on further commitments in respect of financial services over and above those commitments outlined in GATS by way of negotiation. In addition to Article VIII of GATS – the prohibition on abuse of monopoly position (discussed in the previous section) – members are obliged under the Understanding to list in their schedules existing monopoly rights and to 'endeavour to eliminate them or reduce their scope', thus putting a positive obligation on members to open domestic financial services markets to competition.[70]

Members also agree to endeavour to remove or limit non-discriminatory measures which have a 'significant adverse effect' on the supply of financial services of other members, which specifically includes any measure adversely affecting the ability of foreign suppliers to operate, compete or enter the member's domestic market provided that this does not unfairly discriminate against domestic service suppliers.[71]

(vi) The Trade Related Aspects of Intellectual Property Rights The relationship between competition law and intellectual property rights is one of the most difficult and interesting relationships between the different branches of law. The WTO Agreement on Trade Related Aspects of Intellectual Property Rights (TRIPS) did not come into effect to address this relationship but rather to attempt a harmonisation of intellectual property rights globally. Nonetheless the competition relevance of the TRIPS Agreement is obvious in light of a number of its key provisions, in particular Articles 8, 31 and 40. Article 8 shows the importance of prohibiting anticompetitive situations resulting from the use of intellectual property rights. For example, Article 8.2 states that 'appropriate measures, provided that they are consistent with the provision of this Agreement, may be needed to prevent the abuse of intellectual property rights by right holders or the resort to practices which unreasonably restrain trade or adversely affect the international transfer of technology'.

---

[70] See section B.1 of the Understanding.   [71] See section B.10 of the Understanding.

The second of the three provisions, Article 31, concerns the situation of compulsory licensing; what amounts according to its title to 'other use without authorisation of right holder'. According to the article, compulsory licensing is one possible option to deal with cases in which anticompetitive practices related to patent use may occur. Finally, Article 40 concerns the issue of intellectual property licensing and provides a declaration expressing WTO members' agreement that licensing practices which may restrain competition may produce an adverse effect on trade and may impede the transfer and dissemination of technology.

(vii) The Telecommunications Reference Paper on Regulatory Principles of the Negotiating Group on Basic Telecommunications Negotiating the Telecommunications Reference Paper on Regulatory Principles of the Negotiating Group on Basic Telecommunications by WTO members has been one of the major competition law successes achieved by the WTO in its early years. In particular, section 1 of the Reference Paper has direct competition relevance and significance making it in the eyes of different commentators a 'multilateral' agreement in the field of competition law.[72]

The idea of branching out within the WTO negotiations towards the telecommunications sector stems from a number of reasons. Among these was the considerable importance the sector assumes globally and the huge scope it carries for national telecommunications operators to 'abuse' their power through, for example, denying access by foreign operators to their local networks, thus undermining one of the important values of the WTO. It is worth noting that none of the existing WTO rules or agreements were considered to be sufficient to address all the particular characteristics of the sector; this includes the GATS itself and specifically Article VIII thereof.[73] Thus, with the widening curve of liberalisation which the sector came to witness since the mid-1990s and its opening up to competition and foreign investment, there is little wonder that specific efforts came to be directed to negotiating a specific agreement on telecommunications within the WTO which eventually came to be adopted in February 1997 by 69 WTO members. This essentially became the Reference Paper on Telecommunications. The new agreement or Reference Paper – which was not supposed to stand

---

[72] See L. A. Sullivan, 'The US, the EU, the WTO, the Americas, and Telecom Competition' (1999) *Southwestern Journal of Law and Trade in the Americas* 63.
[73] See p. 603 above for an account on this Article.

alone but rather as one part of the GATS – was intended to extend to basis telecommunications, which stretches from local and long distance services to international services for public and private uses provided through any of the following technologies: cable, satellite and wireless.

The Reference Paper has a number of objectives, all of which revolve around the issue of market access, in particular, the idea of ensuring effective market access and foreign investment commitments through WTO-based safeguards in the domestic laws of WTO members. Sections 1–6 of the Paper provide its six guiding principles which include: having competitive safeguards in the telecommunications sector; allocation and use of scarce resources; having independent regulation; having publicly available licensing criteria; establishing universal services; and building interconnectivity in services. In setting out to achieve its declared objectives and in following these guiding principles, the Paper contains an explicit prohibition on anticompetitive practices, especially of the types mentioned in section 1.2 of the Paper: anticompetitive cross-subsidisation; not making available to other service providers on a timely basis technical information about essential facilities and commercially relevant information which is necessary for them to gain access; and the use of information obtained from competitors with anticompetitive results.

A good case in which the WTO Appellate Body had the opportunity to offer an account on the application of the WTO rules in the telecommunications sector is the Mexico-Telecoms case, which is discussed below.

(b) **Comment**   The general and specific reference to competition issues in all of the WTO instruments mentioned above makes it at least arguable that the basis for stretching WTO rules to deal with anticompetitive situations is possible and can be said to be already evident within the WTO framework. Hence, it probably is not wholly unrealistic or unreasonable for the WTO to become involved in addressing such situations by addressing a request to each of its members to create and enforce a regime dealing with private anticompetitive practices; as we noted in chapter 1, an obligation on countries seeking to join the WTO to enact a competition law is something that is found in practice.[74] A request by the WTO in this case could take one of several forms. One possibility could be for the WTO to insist on adopting general principles, such as those covered in the General Agreement on Trade in Services (GATS), which

---

[74] See p. 290 above.

the country concerned must follow. A second possibility would be for the WTO to lay down detailed substantive provisions, such as those provided in the Agreement on Trade Related Aspects of Intellectual Property Rights (TRIPS). A third possibility would be to introduce a requirement to set up and maintain a procedure in the domestic legal order of WTO members for foreign firms to complain about market access issues where these are the result of anticompetitive practices of domestic firms and enforce their rights under domestic competition law regimes.

(c) **The principles** A number of well-established WTO principles have competition relevance. These feature in several of the WTO provisions and instruments mentioned above; they have also been invoked on many occasions by WTO members in their actions against fellow members. They include the national treatment principle and the most favoured nation principle; together these two principles form key components of the overarching WTO non-discrimination principle. These principles form a cornerstone of the entire WTO system.

(i) National treatment principle The national treatment principle is of crucial significance within the WTO framework and has been invoked on numerous occasions by WTO members in their complaints against other members. The principle comes to ensure that foreign goods, services or persons receive equal (i.e. not less favourable) treatment to that given to domestic goods, services and persons. At the heart of the principle therefore stands the object of preventing discrimination against goods, services or persons of foreign origins by putting them at a competitive disadvantage vis-à-vis their domestic counterparts. In this way, the principle enables one to decide whether the rules and laws of WTO members are consistent with the WTO framework by highlighting the sometimes blurred divide between the legitimate powers and prerogatives of WTO members *and* mere acts of national protectionism.

The national treatment principle does not have 'universal' application however: it is subject to what may be considered serious limitations. For example, under GATT the principle applies to goods but not to producers; nor does it apply to measures concerning security matters under Article XXI of the GATT and Article XIVbis of the GATS.

(ii) Most favoured nation The most favoured nation (MFN) principle is an important companion of the national treatment principle. The underlying objective of the principle is to prohibit discriminatory

treatment among different WTO members by providing that favourable treatment offered to one WTO member must unconditionally be extended to other members. The typical situation in which the principle is expected to operate is where within a bilateral relationship one WTO member grants favourable treatment to the other in the form of low tariffs or other trade concessions; in this case – through the operation of the principle – such favourable treatment is expected to become 'multi-lateralised' within the WTO framework. The MFN principle however does not have absolute application. Exceptions to it have been recognised, primarily in the case of customs unions, common markets and free trade areas because of the special circumstances of these.

(d) **The Trade Policy Review Mechanism** An important feature of the WTO system is the Trade Policy Review Mechanism (TPRM), which enables the WTO General Council – the Trade Policy Review Body[75] – to 'monitor' various domestic trade-related policies and practices of WTO members in particular to evaluate their compatibility with and impact on the global trading system.[76] The underlying purpose behind the Mechanism is to enhance the adherence and compliance with the WTO framework by its members and ensure greater transparency in their domestic trade policies and practices. The TPRM has in a way a peer review function though the actual review is not conducted by WTO members themselves. The TPRM was initially introduced in 1988 within the Uruguay Round on a provisional basis; it came to be introduced on a permanent basis within the Marrakesh Agreement establishing the WTO. This in itself shows the remarkable importance WTO members have come to attach to the Mechanism, though in non-WTO circles little is known about it as an activity.[77]

The TPRM lacks legally binding force. Perhaps it would be appropriate to describe its effect as peer pressure taking the form of diplomatic

---

[75] See pp. 120–123 above for an account on the constitutional and institutional structure of the WTO.

[76] See Annex 3, Art. A(i) of the Marrakesh Agreement.

[77] See D. Keesing, *Improving Trade Policy Reviews in the World Trade Organisation* (Institute for International Economics, 1998). Certainly, as far as the field of competition law is concerned, when discussing peer review or country review the OECD would be the sole international organisation that would come to most people's minds. In the context of the TPRM however this is understandable given that the Mechanism exists within a purely trade body without a competition mandate or concrete agenda in the field, namely the WTO.

persuasion using an inducement and reason approach.[78] This appears to be sufficiently recognised within the framework of the key provision of the *Marrakesh Agreement*, namely Article A(i) of Annex 3 which provides that the Mechanism neither serves as a ground for enforcing WTO obligations or dispute settlement, nor as a tool to introduce new policy commitments on WTO members. It is of course highly arguable whether this particular 'soft-law' nature and approach of the TPRM is an advantage as opposed to a disadvantage and commentators have been divided on this.[79] As far as the WTO itself is concerned, it has consistently advocated the importance of the TPRM as a mechanism, which enjoys a unique place within the WTO system in furthering non-confrontational discussion on major trade policy questions.

(e) **Some notable cases**   A number of cases have over the years arisen before the WTO in which different WTO provisions were considered in a competition context.

(i) Kodak/Fuji: USA–Japan dispute[80]   *Kodak/Fuji* is arguably the most high-profile example of a hybrid hindrances to market access case. The case arose out of a complaint by US firm, Kodak in 1995 that as a result of Japanese firm, Fuji's behaviour (with the backing of the Japanese government) it was unable fully and fairly to access the photographic film and paper market in Japan and as a result suffered harm. This was essentially a petition by Kodak under section 301 of the US Trade Act 1974 to the US government.[81] Kodak made a number of claims, one of them was that Fuji enjoyed an exclusive relationship with all leading wholesalers in the Japanese market and that it relied on a number of vertical restraints, including resale price maintenance[82] with its partners (local distributors). As a result of these, Kodak claimed its access to the Japanese market was impeded.

---

[78] See V. Curzon Price, 'New Institutional Developments in GATT' (1992) 1 *Minnesota Journal of Global Trade* 87.

[79] See, for example, J. H. Jackson, *Restructuring the GATT System* (Council on Foreign Relations, 1990) expressing scepticism about the Mechanism and S. Laird, 'The WTO's Trade Policy Review Mechanism-From Through the Looking Glass' (1999) *The World Economy* 741 arguing in favour of the Mechanism and highlighting its key strengths.

[80] See *Japan-Measures Affecting Consumer Photographic Film and Paper (Japan-Film)*, WT/DS44/R (22 April 1998).

[81] See pp. 616–620 below for a discussion of s. 301.   [82] See p. 16 above.

After a period of intensive lobbying by Kodak in Washington, the USA complained to the WTO about the situation arguing that the practices of the Japanese authorities and Fuji amounted to unreasonable hindrances to market access by foreign firms like Kodak to the Japanese markets;[83] it also engaged the Japanese government and specifically the Japanese Fair Trade Commission (JFTC) in a bilateral manner.[84] The JFTC looked into the case, but determined that Fuji's behaviour was not contrary to the Japanese competition rules. The JFTC found that access to the relevant market, including channels of distribution, was adequately available to all firms, whether foreign or domestic. This conclusion by the JFTC was reached after what many termed a superficial investigation. The WTO Dispute Resolution Panel also rejected the US complaint. Several voices were heard within the USA expressing dissatisfaction with the outcome in the case and specifically serious concerns about cooperation between the USA and Japan in the field of competition law, especially since at that time the USA was considered to be making good progress in its bilateral relationship with the EU under their cooperation agreements.[85] The reason for such concerns seemed to go beyond the actual outcome of the case, and involved other factors, such as the US lack of confidence at that time in Japan's commitment to fight and eradicate anticompetitive behaviour and the JFTC's enforcement of Japanese competition rules. The fact that Japan relied on administrative guidance and informal enforcement rather than a formal decision-making process

---

[83] See Press Release of the USTR, 'US Launches Broad WTO Case under GATT, GATS against Japan on Film' (June 1996); also J. M. Ramseyer, 'The Costs of the Consensual Myth: Antitrust Enforcement and Institutional Barriers to Litigation in Japan' (1985) *Yale Law Journal* 604; J. P. Trachtman, 'International Regulatory Competition, Externalization, and Jurisdiction' (1993) *Harvard Journal of International Law* 47, 54–5;. W. L. Fugate, 'Antitrust Aspects of US–Japanese Trade' (1983) *Case Western Reserve Journal of International Law* 505.

[84] In its reference to the JFTC, the USTR expressed an interest in opening a dialogue with the JFTC on the matter. The USTR also stated that the USA intended to discuss with Japan what it felt amounted to significant evidence of anticompetitive activities that it had uncovered in this sector, and to ask the latter to take appropriate action. The USTR confirmed the willingness of the USA to supply the JFTC with any necessary information that may assist the latter in its investigation. See Office of the USTR, Press Release, 'Acting US Trade Representative Charlene Barshefsky Announces Action on Film' (13 June 1996). The US Antitrust Division of the Department of Justice, for its part, said it was willing to assist the JFTC in its competition analysis in the case.

[85] See, for example, remarks by some members of the US Senate: 'Senate Sub-Committee Focuses on International Enforcement, Positive Comity' (6 May 1999).

seemed to be another factor, which seems to have given rise to this lack of confidence.[86]

The heart of the dispute in the case was the alleged lack of competition enforcement by Japan in the situation which was considered to have given Fuji an advantage over Kodak in the Japanese market. The case shows that the involvement by a government in a vertical restraint situation can be a major complicating factor. For one thing, this means that using competition law itself may not be possible or fruitful to address the situation, not to mention the fact that in such a case competition law can be easily pushed to the side by political confrontation and frictions and trade disputes between the countries concerned. It is important however not to exaggerate the extent of the problem arising in this situation because one could say strictly speaking *Kodak/Fuji* is an exceptional case: at best disputes concerning vertical restraints in international markets have been very much US–Japanese. Probably, there is little scope therefore for saying that vertical restraints present a serious problem in international markets which would require addressing within a body such as the WTO. A number of supporting points can be made. First, competition law enforcement around the world has been strengthened in recent years and many competition authorities have come to embrace the view that hindering the access of foreign firms to local markets may harm competition and consumers in these markets. Secondly, many competition authorities (and their governments more generally) have come to realise that the way they apply their competition rules to deal with complaints by foreign firms seeking to access local markets will determine the way the home countries of these firms and their competition authorities will apply their own competition rules when the situation is reversed. Thirdly, the belief in trade liberalisation has grown worldwide. Finally, it is important to note that for a vertical restraint strategy by local firms against foreign ones to succeed, among other things, the local market of these firms must be substantially non-competitive. This last point is particularly interesting to consider in the context of the *Kodak/Fuji* dispute because it allows one to reflect on the extent to which the behaviour of the complaining firm (Kodak) contributes to the resulting problem complained of.

---

[86] See generally J. Haley, 'Administrative Guidance Versus Formal Regulation: Resolving the Paradox of Industrial Policy' and I. Hiroshi, 'Antitrust and Industrial Policy in Japan: Competition and Cooperation in Law and Trade Issues of the Japanese Economy' in G. Saxonhouse and K. Yamamura (eds.), *Law and Trade Issues of the Japanese Economy: American and Japanese Perspectives* (University of Washington Press, 1986).

For many years, Kodak and Fuji enjoyed mirror positions: each enjoyed a market share of 70 per cent in its home market and 10 per cent in the other's market. Prior to the creation of Fuji, Kodak operated in Japan and had an established relationship with four major local wholesalers (Kashimura; Ohmiya; Asanuma; and Misuzu). After the Second World War things began to change. Principally, various tariffs and quotas came to be imposed by the Japanese government, which also limited foreign investment. Kodak changed its business strategy however and began to operate through a single wholesaler (Negase & Co). Some wholesalers who were previously major distributors of Kodak apparently were offended by being abandoned by Kodak and did not like the idea of having to obtain Kodak products from Kodak's sole wholesaler. They shifted to Fuji. And Kodak – in parallel – shifted to start selling technology, a market in relation to which – it is worth noting – Kodak boasted more than once that it was not concerned about competition from its Japanese rivals! With the easing of tariffs and quotas by the Japanese government in the 1970s, Kodak's business came to flourish. The firm was content with trading with only a single wholesaler (Negase). In line of its strategy, it established a subsidiary to support this wholesaler and later formed a join venture with it. Its success was due to its policy of aggressive price cuts and introducing new attractive products in the 1980s. In this period there was very aggressive competition between Kodak and Fuji and the latter seems to have enjoyed an advantage due to its innovation with Kodak lagging behind. For example, Fuji marketed a single use camera in 1987, which Kodak only managed to produce a year later. Nonetheless, even research conducted by Kodak showed that its products were on the shelves of about 54 per cent of outlets in Tokyo.

It is legitimate to ask whether in the situation – in light of these facts – there was indeed a problem which Kodak was entitled to complain about. Nonetheless, assuming this was the case one wonders whether Kodak conducted itself in the right manner in all the circumstances. A few things can be mentioned here: Kodak itself chose – when changing its business strategy – to deal with one trading partner; there were times that Kodak appeared more interested in questionable tactics designed to annoy the Fuji management (such as the buzzing of the Fuji Tower in Tokyo with its blimp carrying the 'Go Kodak' words); and the Kodak management can be said to have lost focus in conducting the important business of the firm with so much attention given to lobbying and politics: Kodak deliberately – it seems – wanted this to be a trade not a competition issue and chose initially not to complain to the

JFTC. It believed in the idea of having the US government help it in international markets. This eventually put the case before the WTO, which decided to reject the US complaint. This particular outcome seems to have fuelled the uncertainty and scepticism that had been felt for so many years prior to the case about the real prospects for the WTO to play a role in the field of competition law. At any rate, the outcome in the case can be said to have confirmed the unsuitability of the WTO to solve such cases. It is unclear however whether the case can be said to have established that involving trade officials as adjudicators in competition cases (and those dealing with vertical restraint issues specifically) is controversial because these officials are guided by different considerations and operate within a framework different from that of competition. Nonetheless, what the case does clearly show is that there can be a real difficulty in the setting-up of a WTO panel to hear competition-related cases. In this case it took three months to form a panel, which at the end had to be imposed by the WTO Director-General.

At the same time, probably one ought not to exaggerate the significance of the case in light of the fact that it dealt with a unique topic, namely vertical agreements. As widely known, the treatment of the topic in the field of competition law has such a jurisdiction-specific flavour. This flavour is political and economic in its source as much as it is legal. To this short list however one must add a crucial item which has often been ignored: the business source. When considering the treatment of vertical agreements specific attention must be given to the way firms build their business strategy in international markets. This last point deserves particular emphasis especially when one takes into account how firms react to competition enforcement. For example, aggressive enforcement by a competition authority in the area of vertical agreements may cause firms to switch (if this is possible in principle) to alternatives such as vertical integration. The uniqueness of the topic can also be seen in light of its treatment within one and the same jurisdiction. In many parts of the world, this treatment has changed rather radically sometimes,[87] and there is no reason why this should not continue to be the case in the future. These have a far-reaching policy implication at the international level because they illustrate the difficulty in achieving convergence between different competition law regimes. It is important to emphasise in this context that achieving meaningful convergence will not necessarily be guaranteed when all competition law regimes will

---

[87] See as a notable example the EU competition law regime.

consistently across the board view every single restraint in a vertical agreement – whether resale price maintenance, export ban or another – through the same lenses, as either something to be assessed *per se* or through a *rule of reason* approach.[88] This is because there are aspects relating to the regulation of vertical agreements which are time sensitive and very susceptible to subjectivity. One of them is the exercise of market definition.[89] The experience of Kodak itself is highly interesting to consider in this regard. In the USA the firm was for many years the subject of two consent decrees which, among other things, restricted its distribution practices in US markets. However, in 1994 the restrictions imposed on Kodak were removed by the US District Court[90] (as confirmed by the US Court of Appeals),[91] because it was considered that Kodak's vertical restraints had been rendered obsolete due to changes in the market: the market was considered to be global and no longer national. The court agreed that Kodak possessed no power in this market, which was considered to be competitive. This point shows that in relation to vertical agreements – in particular those with an international dimension – divergence, as opposed to convergence, between different competition law regimes can easily arise. This can be seen from deliberations and discussions within the OECD and the ICN. Looking at these deliberations, there is no doubt that many similarities can be identified in how different competition authorities regulate vertical restraints and no doubt these similarities have increased in recent years. Nonetheless, there are some key issues in relation to which key differences exist. One of these issues concerns the question of whether the size of the economy has an impact on the seriousness of market access problems facing foreign firms resulting from vertical agreements entered into between local firms. Some competition authorities seem to believe that this seriousness is greater in the case of smaller economies whilst others appear to believe this is not so. Such differences in position and outlook are no doubt important to take into account especially when considering the utilising of an international mechanism such as the WTO to deal with vertical agreements in a market access context and when considering the issue of convergence of approach to vertical agreements between different competition law regimes more generally.

---

[88] See pp. 239–242 above for an account on these two approached.
[89] For the exercise of market definition, see pp. 70–77 above.
[90] See *United States v. Eastman Kodak Co.*, 853 F. Supp. 1454, 1487–88 (1994).
[91] See *United States v. Eastman Kodak Co.*, 63 F.3d 95, 102 (1995).

(ii) Mexico–Telecoms: USA–Mexico dispute[92]   The case arose out of a complaint by the USA to the WTO in 2002 against Mexico's international telecommunications long-distance rules, which specifically: required US telecommunications carriers to *interconnect* with Mexican telecommunications operators in order to terminate calls into Mexico; prevented US carriers from obtaining leased lines to terminate calls into the Mexican market and failed to ensure that US telecommunications operators would have reasonable and non-discriminatory access to and use of public telecommunications networks and services; and gave the dominant telecommunications operator in Mexico, Teléfonos de México (Telmex) exclusive authority to negotiate termination rates into Mexico on behalf of all national telecommunications carriers. In relation to this last point, the rates for terminating international calls were considered to be higher than the ones applied in countries with competitive telecommunications sector. The USA claimed a failure on the part of Mexico to ensure that Telmex provides interconnection at rates and on terms and conditions which were reasonable and to stop Telmex from acting in an anticompetitive manner.

The complaint centred around allegations that the Mexican measures were anticompetitive and discriminatory and amounted to toleration of private practices which impeded access by US firms to the local telecommunications market. Basically, the USA claimed that in the case there were both problematic *actions* and *inactions* on the part of Mexico which fell foul of a number of WTO provisions, specifically those of GATS and the Telecommunications Reference Paper.

The WTO Dispute Resolution Panel delivered its report in April 2004, reaching the conclusion that Mexico had committed a breach of its WTO obligations; except in relation to one aspect of the allegations.[93] Among the breaches committed by Mexico: its breach of Articles 5(a) and (b) of the GATS Annex on Telecommunications (because of its failure to ensure reasonable and non-discriminatory access to and use of telecommunications networks in the country); its breach of Article 2.2(b) of the Telecommunications Reference Paper (due to its failure to ensure interconnection at 'cost-oriented' rates for the cross-border supply of

---

[92] See *Mexico – Measures Affecting Telecommunication Services* (2 April 2004).

[93] This concerned the cross-border telecommunications services supplied on a *non-facilities* basis in Mexico. In relation to these, the WTO Dispute Resolution Panel found that Mexico did not violate its WTO obligations because it had not entered into commitments for these services.

facilities-based basic telecommunications services); and its breach of Article 1.1 of the Telecommunications Reference Paper (due to its failure to maintain appropriate measures to prevent anticompetitive practices by Telmex). This particular outcome led to Mexico changing its policy and practices and on that basis the findings of the Panel were complied with. Obviously, this shows that the WTO is able to adopt competition-relevant measures and to engage in competition-related work with material results.

(iii) *Wheat/Grain: USA–Canada dispute*[94]   The *Wheat/Grain* case is often cited as a strong example of the argument that the actual decisional practice of the WTO seems to have dismissed the suitability or appropriateness of conducting competition law analysis in WTO cases. In the case, the WTO Appellate Body considered Article XVII:1 of the General Agreement on Tariffs and Trade 1994[95] and concluded in paragraph 145 of its report that there was 'no basis for interpreting that provision as imposing comprehensive competition-law-type obligations'. This case can be said to carry a greater weight when considered alongside the *outcome* in *Kodak/Fuji*. However, it should also be looked at in light of evidence available of the WTO's ability to conduct competition-law-type analysis and the outcome in the *Mexico–Telecoms* case as discussed in the previous section.

(B) Domestic trade laws

The other way to reach private access-hindering practices in foreign markets is by using the trade laws of individual countries. However, better success cannot be guaranteed here than with the previous (WTO) option since no domestic trade law directly reaches such practices. However, in theory at least, such practices may be reached indirectly. One example is found in the case of the US Trade Act 1974. This piece of legislation offers the US government a tool to deal with perceived hindrances to US firms when attempting to penetrate foreign markets. The Act is a trade measure and is designed to address such hindrances where these are caused by foreign governments. In other words the Act is directed at public hindrances. Nonetheless – theoretically at least – the

---

[94] See *Canada – Measures Relating to Exports of Wheat and Treatment of Imported Grain*, WT/DS276/AB/R (27 September 2004).

[95] See p. 602 above for an account on this Article.

possible scope of the Act can be said to extend to hindrances with private elements.[96] Achieving this in practice may prove however to be a difficult task, the fulfilment of which requires quite a journey to be covered, mainly to interpret one key provision of the Act, section 301, in such a way to render this possible.

According to subsection 301(a)(1), the United States Trade Representative (USTR) shall take action as authorised in subsection (c) against situations which in the USTR's determination amounts to: (a) denial of the rights of or benefits to the USA under any trade agreement; or (b) an act, policy or practice of a foreign country which is in violation of or inconsistent with the provisions of any trade agreement or which is unjustifiable and burdens or restricts US commerce. Subsection (b)(1) provides, on the other hand, that the USTR may take action where 'an act, policy, or practice of a foreign country is unreasonable or discriminatory and burdens or restricts United States commerce'. By virtue of the definitions and special rules contained in subsection 301(d), unreasonable acts, policies, and practices of foreign countries include, but are not limited to, those which, among other things, deny fair and equitable 'market opportunities, including the toleration by a foreign government of systematic anticompetitive activities by enterprises or among enterprises in the foreign country that have the effect of restricting, on a basis that is inconsistent with commercial considerations, access of United States goods or services to a foreign market'.

In light of this particular wording of the section, USTR has come to argue that the hindrance to market access by private practices may be considered 'unreasonable foreign practices' within the meaning of the section. Section 301 tackles practices or policies of foreign countries that are 'unfair', 'unjustifiable', 'unreasonable', 'burden or restrict US commerce' and which constitute *toleration* of 'systematic anticompetitive practices'. This includes practices or policies that are contradictory to international norms and principles, such as the principle of most favoured nation (MFN).[97] For the purposes of the section, where the access by US firms to the market of a foreign country is hindered by one or more firms in the country behaving 'systematically' in an anticompetitive manner that 'burdens or restricts US commerce', then that country

---

[96] See A. D. Smith, 'Bringing Down Private Trade Barriers – an Assessment of the United States' Unilateral Options: Section 301 of the 1974 Trade Act and the Extraterritorial Application of US Antitrust Law' (1994) *Michigan Journal of International Law* 241.

[97] See pp. 607–608 above.

will be taken to have tolerated that behaviour personally by failing to enforce its domestic competition laws.[98]

The Act can be said to give the doctrine extraterritoriality a statutory expression[99] because it expands the scope of the doctrine in dealing with anticompetitive situations. However, the Act is not a competition law. Moreover, in practice the effectiveness of section 301 to be used as a tool for dealing with situations involving anticompetitive practices is limited for three main reasons. First, the Act, in general, and section 301 in particular, do not offer any definition of the terms 'toleration', 'anticompetitive' or 'systematic'.[100] Secondly, the USTR – which is in charge of administering the Act – enjoys full discretion regarding whether or not to initiate an action in a given case. Finally, a proceeding under the section does not involve litigation, adjudication and ultimately a remedy. It is true that the Act refers to initiation of action, an investigation, a hearing and possibly trade 'retaliation'. But, in practice it seems that all these elements do not always feature in a section 301 proceeding. Hence, it would be more appropriate to regard section 301 as a medium for the USTR to *negotiate* with authorities in foreign countries for the removal of any practices having the consequence of hindering access by US firms to the markets of these countries. Even when it comes to retaliation, it seems that in the majority of cases, section 301 proceedings lead to negotiated resolutions rather than trade retaliation. Two fundamental reasons can be identified for this view. First, retaliation as a last resort seems to be damaging to the US petitioning industry (i.e. the industry or firm(s) who petition the US government to take action), except for rare cases in which there is two-way trade in the product as to which market

[98] It is interesting to note that there also exists a 'special section 301' under s. 182 of the Act which applies to intellectual property rights (IPRs). Under this section, the USTR is required to identify countries that deny sufficient and effective protection of IPRs which are established under international agreements, such as the WTO Trade Related Aspects of Intellectual Property Rights (TRIPS), or which deny fair and equitable market access for persons that rely on IPR protection. If the USTR considers that a trading partner is an offending country it can designate that country as a 'Priority Foreign Country'; this will lead to an automatic triggering of a section 301 action where negotiations under special s. 301 fail to remove the IPR violation or practices. In effect, s. 182 of the Act relies on s. 301 for enforcement.

[99] This is obviously in addition to the expression given by the Foreign Trade Antitrust Improvements Act 1982 (FTAIA), which is discussed at pp. 447–449 above.

[100] In 1988, US trade law was brought closer to its competition law by making 'unreasonable' practices or behaviour under s. 301 also applicable to those governmental actions that constitute systematic toleration of anti-competitive activities by foreign firms that restrict market access. See Applebaum, at 483, note 26 above.

access problems exist. In those rare cases the retaliatory trade restrictions would benefit the petitioner in the US market. Apart from those rare cases, however, the US industry or firms do not gain anything from trade retaliation. In most cases, the problematic practice in the market of the foreign country, which is the petitioner's problem, remains unresolved and the retaliatory action taken provides the petitioner with no offsetting benefit. Moreover, it is not absolutely clear that certain industries or firms may prefer retaliation because they may lose even more from possible counter retaliation by the relevant foreign governments. Secondly, in cases where the practice is considered 'unreasonable', the USTR might run the risk of violating WTO rules if retaliatory measures are taken. One can expect a foreign country to take the matter to the WTO in response to the retaliation. This of course involves a high degree of probability that the USA will be ordered by the WTO to cease the retaliation.

It is not clear, however, if the USA will refrain from retaliation. For example, between 1992 and 2000, the Clinton administration's policy was that trade retaliation in section 301 proceedings would be adopted in certain cases even if this would trigger a strong reaction from relevant countries or ultimately the WTO. Arguably, a similar position was adopted by the Bush Administration between 2000 and 2008. There is no reason however, why – now that the two administrations are no longer in power – one cannot doubt the validity of such statements. In the *Kodak/Fuji* dispute, for example, as was mentioned above, the USTR ultimately decided not to follow a section 301 route and instead referred the complaint to the WTO with regard to the claims of government unfair practices and turned to launching a dialogue with the Japanese government and the Japan Fair Trade Commission in dealing with the private anticompetitive practices.[101] In light of this, it must be questioned whether future cases involving market access disputes will witness heavy use of the section. Nevertheless, it will be of some interest to

---

[101] See p. 610 above.

It is worth noting another case of US allegation of hybrid restraint that was the subject of a proceeding under s. 301: the *Corn Refiners case* (1999). This concerned an alleged government-approved concerted refusal to deal in Mexico. In 1998, the US Corn Refiners Association complained to the USTR about the practices of the Mexican government, which was alleged to have supported a restrictive agreement between the Mexican sugar producers' association and the major Mexican soft drink bottling companies. The petition claimed that the parties agreed to limit the amount of high fructose corn syrup (HFCS) they would buy.

observe how the current Democratic administration under the presidency of Barack Obama will formulate its policies under section 301 and the US trade and competition laws more generally.

(C)   Reflections

The above options of competition policy and trade policy in terms of substance may have the *potential* in the long run to be used as an effective means of combating market access-restraining private practices. However, this does not detract from the fact that currently each option suffers from certain limitations in respect of its approach. For example, the doctrine of extraterritoriality seems to raise more concerns than it actually solves. As far as the mechanism of bilateral cooperation between competition authorities is concerned, this mechanism suffers from an inherently prolonged process of developing an adequate global framework for it and at any rate bilateral cooperation agreements do not offer answers to questions of market access hindrances when these hindrances involve (in)actions on the part of countries. The limitations facing trade policy options, on the other hand, are more obvious and primarily relate to the fact that these options do not directly address the anticompetitive behaviour of private firms; or to put it more accurately, trade policy options may lead to results in some cases, primarily where the market access hindrance involves both public and private elements but obviously success here cannot be guaranteed. The issue of market access-restraining private practices therefore remains. To effectively address the concerns raised by it, arguably a proper international approach needs to be developed under competition law and policy. Obviously this is an idea which rests at the heart of the whole process of internationalisation of competition law: in seeking to internationalise competition law a fundamental aim is to address all competition problems with an international dimension properly and effectively; hindrances to market access involving anticompetitive practices of firms is one big example of a competition problem with an international dimension.[102] It is suggested that one should proceed under competition policy as opposed to trade policy when developing an international approach because *it is* in the field of competition law that *action is necessary* and because trade policy is international in its orientation. The focus of trade policy is on the

---

[102] See E. Fox, 'Toward World Antitrust and Market Access' (1997) *American Journal of International Law* 1.

interests of foreign firms as it is on local ones: in seeking to liberalise trade and open markets (which are among the main goals of trade policy) the idea is to open local markets to foreign firms. Under competition policy, there is no such attention given to the interests of foreign firms: in fact it is not acceptable to most if not almost all countries – most notably the USA – to consider the adverse effects on foreign firms or foreign economies when applying their domestic competition rules; nor is this possible within the scope of the rules because of the domestic orientation of competition law and policy. An illustration can be found in relation to even the most neutral goals of competition law, namely economic efficiency and consumer welfare: when considering these goals, competition authorities address the role of foreign firms (as they do for domestic firms) from the standpoint of their contribution to the efficiency of the marketplace and the maximisation of consumer welfare locally.[103] Such an approach does not leave room for any consideration of whether those foreign firms suffer adverse effects from the practices of domestic firms.[104] This means that the possibility exists in material terms that the anticompetitive behaviour of domestic firms will be exonerated where, on balance, it benefits domestic consumers and enhances market efficiency, notwithstanding the harm such situation may produce for foreign firms (including hindering their access to local markets). As a result, the possibility exists for foregoing an opportunity for competition authorities and countries more generally to promote global welfare and the creation of a fair and free global system of trade because a market access hindrance problem in one country means a limitation on the exports of other countries. It is no wonder therefore that views have been put forward expressing dissatisfaction with such a state of affairs especially in light of the relentless globalisation the world has been witnessing.[105] Among the most vocal voices here have been those of the OECD and the WTO. A report produced within the OECD in 1995 stated:

> As trade policy should be made much more responsive to the interests of consumers, so should competition policy probably take international

---

[103] See, for example, the US case of *Northern Pacific Railway v. United States*, 356 US 1, 4 (1958).

[104] See the EU Communication to the WTO Working Group on the Interaction between Trade and Competition Policy (24 November 1997).

[105] See D. I. Baker, 'Antitrust and World Trade: Tempest in an International Teapot?' (1974) *Cornell International Law Journal* 16.

considerations and the interests of both producers and consumers beyond domestic jurisdictions greater into account.[106]

This particular view of the OECD is worth considering in the context of the extensive work conducted by the Organisation on the relationship between competition policy and trade policy. Since the creation of its joint group on trade and competition (JGTC),[107] the OECD has produced several reports dealing with the relationship between competition policy and trade policy.[108] The reports cover a wide range of topics concerning this relationship. Particular emphasis, however, has been placed on the consistencies and inconsistencies between the two policies. Some of these reports emphasised that differences between the two policies still remain, especially on both perspective and approach.[109] However, the reports have failed to identify how differences between the two policies hinder the operation of one or the other policy. Remarkably, the reports – despite realising the existence of important differences between the two policies – have reached the important conclusion that the two policies are broadly compatible. It has been said that the two policies are complementary with basically the same goals: free trade and free competition are mutually supportive.[110] As far as the issue of market access is concerned, some of the reports – especially the Hawk report produced on behalf of the JGTC and the Competition Law and Policy Committee (CLP)[111] – explained how market access is related to the enforcement of domestic competition rules. For example, the Hawk report argued that strengthening domestic competition laws in this respect would help minimise or alleviate trade policy disputes arising as a result of market access-restraining private anticompetitive behaviour. The report noted that this would also help reduce the need for

---

[106] See *New Dimensions of Market Access in Globalizing World Economy* (OECD, 1995), p. 254.

[107] See pp. 134–135 above.

[108] It should be noted however that the OECD produced an important report on this relationship in 1984: *Report on Competition and Trade Policy: their Interaction*. This was the product of the Committee of Experts on Restrictive Business Practices. The Report examined the possible approaches to developing an improved international framework for dealing with problems arising at the frontier of competition policy and trade policy.

[109] See *Consistencies and Inconsistencies between Trade and Competition Policies* (OECD, 1999).

[110] See *Trade and Competition Policy for Tomorrow* (OECD, 1999).

[111] See *Antitrust and Market Access* (OECD, 1996). For an account on the CLP see pp. 133–134 above.

extraterritorial assertion of jurisdictions by competition authorities and courts.

The WTO has expressed a similar view to that of the OECD, arguing that:

> Even where the criteria of allocative efficiency are solely applicable, the fact that such criteria are generally applied in respect of efficiency and welfare within the jurisdiction in question and may not take into account adverse effects on the welfare of producers and consumers abroad may lead to situations where the enforcement of national competition law will not adequately take into account the interests of trading partners.[112]

Clearly, such views of important international organisations carry considerable weight for the purposes of shifting the focus of domestic competition authorities from national to global welfare and from local efficiencies to global ones. It is less clear, however, whether there is a prospect in the foreseeable future that this can win the support of different countries and their domestic competition authorities, or at least of the USA and its competition authorities. Also, one should take into account the general reservations on the part of various bodies and organisations about the whole process of internationalisation of competition law in the form of a multilateral agreement or the introduction of competition policy within an international trade agenda.[113] Nonetheless, it is worth asking: whether reservations or even objections to the idea of shifting the focus of competition authorities and countries from 'local' to 'global' setting notwithstanding, one should not at least consider proposing solutions for 'improvement' because artificial barriers caused by anticompetitive practices lead to market foreclosure and in turn cause trade tensions. Arguably, it is both desirable and necessary to do so. As we saw – especially in the context of the discussion in the previous chapter – there has been no shortage of proposals especially for the purposes of developing an international dimension to competition law. These proposals however have not been focused on the issue examined throughout this chapter: hindrances to market access.[114]

---

[112] See WTO *Annual Report* (WTO, 1997), p. 75.   [113] See pp. 87–89 above.

[114] It is worth mentioning here the joint report produced in January 2000 by the Antitrust and International Trade Sections Task Force of the American Bar Association on *Private Anticompetitive Practices as Market Access Barriers*. The report urged countries to take action against private anticompetitive practices that restrain market access by foreign firms in ways that substantially distort competition in the markets within an individual country's jurisdiction. The task force did not suggest that countries agree on

It would be interesting to consider the idea of developing a universal market access principle under competition policy – as a counterpart to the market access principle under trade policy. Doing so would perhaps secure a greater likelihood of effectively addressing market access-restraining private practices which is desirable from a competition policy perspective. This is also desirable from a trade policy point of view: for example, a country that has undertaken trade liberalisation measures has every interest in ensuring that the welfare and efficiency benefits arising from such measures are not lost due to anticompetitive practices by firms. Avoiding the nullification or impairment of trade liberalisation commitments, as a result of such practices, is also a matter of legitimate concern for members of the global trading family. Competition law and policy do not normally have specific trade objectives, such as promoting market access. However, in pursuing the goals of promoting economic efficiency and consumer welfare, an effective application of competition law is essential for tackling barriers to entry set up by firms in the market or other anticompetitive practices, which affect both foreign and domestic firms. Furthermore, adopting a market access principle under competition policy would not only lead to a growth in the flows of trade and investment, but also provide more consistency in the application of competition policy tools as a complement to trade policy. This can then be followed by the fostering of international cooperation, which seems to be desirable from a trade policy perspective: it seems that all countries would benefit from the effective application of competition law to anticompetitive practices which hinder access to markets. The substantial removal of hindrances to the flows of trade and investment globally erected by countries has greatly contributed to enhanced conditions of competition in different countries. At the same time, in the absence of an effective competition law, firms may have an incentive to engage in anticompetitive behaviour with a view to protecting their position on the domestic market against foreign competition. The risk

the details of substantive competition law or procedure. Instead, it recommended that countries take actions consistent with the principles of national treatment and most favoured nation (MFN), as well as provide a fair, transparent process, accessible to foreign firms where complaints can be made of market access-denying practices and a resolution will be reached within a reasonable period of time. The American Bar Association took no position as to what, if any, dispute resolution mechanism should be established to deal with the situation where one country is aggrieved by another country's failure to take action against foreclosure caused by private practice to the former's firms or consumers. Also, the report did not offer a view on the appropriate role of the WTO.

of conflicts of jurisdiction arising from the application of the competition laws of countries can also have repercussions for the global trading system. The scope for such conflicts is greater if competition authorities pursue trade policy goals by seeking to apply domestic competition law to anticompetitive practices affecting exports and which do not have a substantial impact on the domestic market.[115] There is also a risk that, in the absence of effective remedial action under competition law, pressure could grow for the unilateral use of trade sanctions or of such bilateral trade agreements that may run counter to the principles established and observed by the global trading family. Clearly in these instances the sensible thing to do would be for a country to apply its domestic competition law to practices which are both contrary to domestic welfare and the legitimate interests of other countries and to seek ways for cooperation with other countries. Enhanced international cooperation in competition policy would therefore lead to significant gains from both the competition and trade policy perspectives.

A market access principle under competition policy would prohibit all forms of anticompetitive practices – including all those involving private and public elements – which hinder the ability of foreign firms to penetrate domestic markets. Including private and public practices avoids the difficulty associated with the existence of hybrid restraints. Such principle could be introduced initially within the WTO, for the benefit of securing a wider agreement on it among countries. When introduced, the principle could then be adopted in the domestic regimes of different countries, who would assume the responsibility of this task. Countries would be required to provide effective enforcement mechanisms, tools for discovery, procedural enforcement and fair process with a principle of non-discrimination and sufficient remedies to countries and direct actions to firms within the national legal systems. The WTO would be responsible for monitoring whether countries are adopting and enforcing the principle.

Obviously, it would be over-ambitious, and possibly naive, to argue that a market access principle under competition policy should be adopted in the first instance regarding all types of anticompetitive situations, including cartels, vertical restraints, abuses of dominance and mergers. It would be sensible therefore to consider adopting the principle first regarding some of these situations and then as it develops and its familiarity increases with time, it can be extended to cover other business

---

[115] This is what, as we saw in chapter 8, is referred to a situation of 'outbound' extraterritoriality.

phenomena. For example, it seems sensible to begin with hardcore cartels and mergers first, as opposed to vertical restraints and abuses of dominance. There is consensus internationally that cartels deserve immediate attention. Furthermore, merger control also seems to be an issue of some urgency and importance. Both cartels and merger operations have become increasingly international in recent years and very often give rise to market access issues. On the other hand, vertical restraints are an issue of some difficulty. This point should be clear in the light of the discussion above in relation to the *Kodak/Fuji* case. It is highly debatable whether vertical agreements should be included within the scope of the proposed market access principle in the immediate, *or* the medium or long term. On the one hand, there is the view that the position in relation to the regulation of vertical agreements within individual jurisdictions has not featured consistency or sufficient clarity and for this reason it may be appropriate to recommend that the position with regard to the regulation of vertical agreements in individual jurisdictions must first be clarified and consolidated before examining the prospect of including it within the scope of a market access principle. On the other hand, vertical agreements can as we saw in the context of the *Kodak/Fuji* case give rise to market access problems (or at least questions). Arguably, the same argument and counter argument may be rehearsed in relation to the issue of abuse of dominance. It may be possible to argue that this topic does not seem to be a matter of considerable need for immediate attention especially in a market access context, though as we saw in relation to the International Competition Network (ICN) and its work, recently attention has come to be given to this topic in an international context.

BIBLIOGRAPHY

Books and Articles

Achy L. and Sekkat L., *Competition, Efficiency and Competition Policy in Morocco* (International Development Research Centre, 2005)

Akehurst M., 'Jurisdiction in International Law' (1972–3) *British Yearbook of International Law* 145

Albors-Llorens A. and Goyder J., *Goyder's EC Competition Law* (Oxford University Press, 2009)

Alford R., 'Subsidiarity and Competition: Decentralized Enforcement of EU Competition Laws' (1994) *Cornell International Law Journal* 275

Alford R., 'The Extraterritorial Application of Antitrust Laws: the United States and the European Community Approaches' (1992) *Virginia Journal of International Law* 1

Amarasinha, S. D., 'WTO Core Principles and Trade/Competition Policies' and Jenny F., 'Competition, Trade and Development Before and After Cancun' (2004) *Fordham Corporate Law Institute* 711

Amato G., *Antitrust and the Bounds of Power* (Hart Publishing, 1997)

Anderson L., 'Extraterritorial Application of National Antitrust Laws: the Need for More Uniform Regulation' (1992) *Wayne Law Review* 1579

Andrade M. C., 'Competition Law in Mercosur: Recent Developments' (2003) *Global Competition Review* 1

Applebaum H. M., 'Antitrust and the Omnibus Trade and Competitiveness Act of 1988' (1989) *Antitrust Law Journal* 557

Applebaum H. M., 'The Coexistence of Antitrust Law and Trade Law with Antitrust Policy' (1988) *Cardozo Law Review* 1169

Applebaum H. M., 'The Interface of the Trade Laws and the Antitrust Laws' (1998) *George Mason Law Review* 479

Areeda P. and Kaplow L., *Antitrust Analysis: Problems, Text, Cases* (Little Brown, 1988)

Areeda P., Kaplow L. and Edlin A. S., *Antitrust Analysis: Problems, Text, Cases* (Aspen Publishers, 2004)

Arnold T., *Bottlenecks of Business* (Reynal & Hitchcock, 1973)

Atwood J. R., *Antitrust and American Business Abroad* (McGraw-Hill, 1981)

Auerbach P., *Competition: the Economics of Industrial Change* (Blackwell, 1988)

Azcuenaga M. L., 'The Evolution of International Competition Policy: a FTC Perspective' (1992) *Fordham Corporate Law Institute* 1

Bailey E. E., 'Contestability and the Design of Regulatory and Antitrust Policy' (1981) *American Economic Review* 178

Bain J., *Barriers to New Competition* (Harvard University Press, 1956)

Baker D. I., 'Antitrust and World Trade: Tempest in an International Teapot?' (1974) *Cornell International Law Journal* 16

Baker D. I., 'To Indict or Not to Indict: Prosecutorial Discretion in Sherman Act Enforcement' (1977–8) *Cornell Law Review* 405

Baker D. I. and Miller W. T., 'Antitrust Enforcement and Non-Enforcement as a Barrier to Imports' (1996) *International Business Law* 488

Bator F., 'The Autonomy of Market Failure' (1958) *Quarterly Journal of Economics* 351

Baumol W., Panzar J. and Willig R., *Contestable Markets and the Theory of Industry Structure* (Harcourt Brace Jovanovich, 1988)

Bechtold R., 'Antitrust Law in the European Community and Germany – an Uncoordinated Co-existence?' (1992) *Fordham Corporate Law Institute* 343

Bellamy C., 'Some Reflections on Competition Law in the Global Market' (1999) *New England Law Review* 15

Bellis J. F., 'International Trade and the Competition Law of the European Economic Community' (1979) *Common Market Law Review* 647

Bengoetxea J., *The Legal Reasoning of the European Court of Justice* (Oxford University Press, 1993)

Bhattacharjea A., 'The Case for a Multilateral Agreement on Competition Policy: a Developing Country Perspective' (2006) *Journal of International Economic Law* 293

Bishop B. and Bishop S., 'Reforming Competition Policy: Bundeskartellamt – Model or Muddle' (1996) *European Competition Law Review* 207

Blair D. G., 'The Canadian Experience' and Joelson M.R., 'The Department of Justice's Antitrust Guide for International Operations' in Griffin J. P. (ed.), *Perspectives on the Extraterritorial Application of US Antitrust and Other Laws* (ABA, Section of International Law, 1979)

Blässar M. and Stragier J., 'Enlargement' (1999) *European Community Competition Policy NewsLetter* 58

Boddez T. M. and Trebilcock M. J., *Unfinished Business: Reforming Trade Remedy Laws in North America* (C. D. Howe Institute, 1993)

Bork R. H., 'Legislative Intent and the Policy of the Sherman Act' (1966) *Journal of Law and Economics* 7

Bork R. H., *The Antitrust Paradox: a Policy at War with Itself* (Basic Books, 1978)

Bork R. H., 'The Role of the Courts in Applying Economics' (1985) *Antitrust Law Journal* 2

Bork R. H., *The Tempting of America* (Sinclair-Stevenson, 1990)

Born B., 'Recent British Responses to the Extraterritorial Application of United States Law: the *Midland Bank* Decision and Retaliatory Legislation Involving Unitary Taxation' (1985) *Virginia Journal of International Law* 91

Bos P-V., 'Towards a Clear Distribution of Competence Between EC and National Competition Authorities' (1995) *European Competition Law Review* 410

Botteman Y. and Burnside A., 'Networking Amongst Competition Agencies' (2004) *International Trade Law Review* 1

Bourgeois J., 'EC Competition Law and Member States Courts' (1993) *Fordham International Law Journal* 331

Bowett D. W., 'Jurisdiction: Changing Patterns of Authority Over Activities and Resources' (1982) *British Yearbook of International Law* 1

Boza B., 'Tailor Made Competition Policy in a Standardised World: a Study From the Perspective of Developing Economies' in IDRC Report, *Tailor-made Competition Policy in a Standardising World: The Experience of Peru* (Instituto Apoyo and Ciudadanos al Día, 2005)

Brewster K., Jr, *Antitrust and American Business Abroad* (McGraw-Hill, 1958)

Bridge J. W., 'The Law and Politics of United States Foreign Policy Export Controls' (1984) *Legal Studies* 2.

Brittan L., *Competition Policy and Merger Control in the Single European Market* (Grotius, 1991)

Brodley J. F., 'The Economic Goals of Antitrust: Efficiency, Consumer Welfare, and Technological Progress' (1987) *New York University Law Review* 1020

Bronz G., 'The International Trade Organisation Charter' (1949) *Harvard Law Review* 1089

Brown P. M., 'The Codification of International Law' (1935) *American Journal of International Law* 25

Brownlie I., *Principles of Public International Law* (Oxford University Press, 1998)

Buchanan J. M., 'Rent Seeking and Profit Seeking' in Buchanan J. M., Tollison R. D. and Tullock G. (eds.), *Toward a Theory of the Rent Seeking Society* (Texas A. and M. University, 1980)

Budzinski O., *The Governance of Global Competition: Competence Allocation in International Competition Policy* (Edward Elgar Publishing, 2008)

Burnside A. and Crossley H., 'Cooperation in Competition: a New Era?' (2005) *European Law Review* 234

Burr S. A., 'The Application of US Antitrust Law to Foreign Conduct: Has *Hartford Fire* Extinguished Considerations of Comity?' (1994) *University of Pennsylvania Journal of International Business Law* 221

Calkins S., 'The October 1992 Supreme Court Term and Antitrust: More Objectivity Than Ever' (1994) *Antitrust Law Journal* 327

Canenbley C. and Rosenthal M., 'Co-operation Between Antitrust Authorities In and Outside the EU: What Does it Mean for Multinational Corporations?: Part 2' (2005) *European Competition Law Review* 178

Carlin W., Fries S., Schaffer M. and Seabright P., *Competition and Enterprise Performance in Transition Economies: Evidence From a Cross-Country Survey* (Centre for Economic Policy Research, 2001)

Carlin W., Haskel J. and Seabright P., 'Understanding the Essential Fact About Capitalism: Markets, Competition and Creative Destruction' (2001) *National Institute Economic Review* 67

Carroll A. J., 'The Extraterritorial Enforcement of US Antitrust Laws and Retaliatory Legislation in the United Kingdom and Australia' (1984) *Denver Journal of International Law and Policy* 377

Carstensen P. C., 'Antitrust Law and the Paradigm of Industrial Organization' (1983) *University of California, Davis Law Review* 487

Celnicker A. C., 'The Federal Trade Commission's Competition and Consumer Advocacy Programme' (1988–9) *Saint Louis University Law Journal* 379

Cernat L. and Holmes P. (eds.), *Competition, Competitiveness and Development: Lessons From Developing Countries* (UNCTAD, 2004)

Chang S. W., 'Extraterritorial Application of US Antitrust Laws to Other Pacific Countries: Proposed Bilateral Agreements for Resolving International Conflicts Within the Pacific Community' (1993) *Hastings International and Comparative Law Review* 295

Chetty V., *The Place of Public Interest in South Africa's Competition Legislation* (ABA, Section of Antitrust Law, 2005)

Christoforou T. and Rockwell D. B., 'European Economic Community Law: the Territorial Scope of Application of EEC Antitrust Law' (1989) *Harvard International Law Journal* 195

Clark J. M., *Competition as a Dynamic Process* (Brookings Institution, 1961)

Clark J. M., 'Towards a Concept of Workable Competition' (1940) *American Economic Review* 241

Clubb, B. E., *United States Foreign Trade Law* (Little Brown, 1991)

Cohen J. and Sabel C., 'Global Democracy?' (2005) *New York University Journal of International Law and Politics* 736

Collins W. D., 'The Coming of Age of EC Competition Policy' (1992) *Yale Journal of International Law* 249

Conn D., 'Assessing the Impact of Preferential Trade Agreements and New Rules of Origin on the Extraterritorial Application of Antitrust Law to International Mergers' (1993) *Columbia Law Review* 119

Cook P., Fabella R. and Cassey L., *Competitive Advantage and Competition Policy in Developing Countries* (Edward Elgar, 2007)

Cova B. and Fine F., 'The New Italian Antitrust Act *vis-à-vis* EC Competition Law' (1991) *European Competition Law Review* 20

Craig P. P. and De Burca G., *EU Law* (Oxford University Press, 2009)

Craig W. L., 'Extraterritorial Application of the Sherman Act: the Search for a Jurisdictional Standard' (1983) *Suffolk Transnational Law Journal* 295

Crampton P., 'Alternative Approaches to Competition Law: Consumer's Surplus, Total Welfare and Non-efficiency Goals' (1994) *World Competition* 55

Cumming G., 'Assessors, Judicial Notice and Domestic Enforcement of Articles 85 and 86' (1997) *European Competition Law Review* 370

Curzon Price V., 'New Institutional Developments in GATT' (1992) 1 *Minnesota Journal of Global Trade* 87

Dabbah M., *Competition Law and Policy in the Middle East* (Cambridge University Press, 2007)

Dabbah M., 'Conduct, Dominance and Abuse in "Market Relationships": Analysis of Some Conceptual Issues Under Article 82 EC' (2000) *European Competition Law Review* 45

Dabbah M., *EC and UK Competition Law: Commentary, Cases and Materials* (Cambridge University Press, 2004)

Dabbah M., 'Measuring the Success of a System of Competition Law: a Preliminary View' (2000) *European Competition Law Review* 369

Dabbah M., 'The Development of Sound Competition Law and Policy in China: an (Im)Possible Dream?' (2007) *World Competition* 341

Dabbah M., 'The Dilemma of Keck – the Nature of the Ruling and the Ramifications of the Judgment' (1999) *Irish Journal of European Law* 84

Dabbah M., *The Internationalisation of Antitrust Policy* (Cambridge University Press, 2003)

Dabbah M., 'The Internationalisation of Competition Law and MNEs as Non-State Actors in the Process' (2003) *Non-State Actors and International Law* 1

Dabbah M., 'The Internationalisation of EC Competition Policy' in Akopova I., Bothe B., Dabbah M., Entin L. and Vodolgin S. (eds.), *The Russian Federation and European Law* (Hopma, 2001)

Dabbah M. and Hawk B., *Anti-cartel Enforcement Worldwide* (Cambridge University Press, 2009)

Dabbah M. and Lasok P., *Merger Control Worldwide* (Cambridge University Press, 2005)

Dam K., 'Extraterritoriality in an Age of Globalization: the *Hartford Fire* Case' (1993) *Supreme Court Review* 289

Damro C., 'EU Delegation and Agency in International Trade Negotiations: a Cautionary Comparison' (2007) *Journal of Common Market Studies* 883

Damro C., 'Multilateral Competition Policy and Transatlantic Compromise' (2004) *European Foreign Affairs Review* 269

Davidow J., 'Extraterritorial Antitrust and the Concept of Comity' (1981) *Journal of World Trade Law* 500

Davidow J., 'Treble Damage Actions and US Foreign Relations: Taming the "Rouge Elephant"' (1985) *Fordham Corporate Law Institute* 37

De Mello L. R., 'Foreign Direct Investment in Developing Countries and Growth: a Selective Survey' (1997) *Journal of Development Studies* 1

Dennis A., *The Impact of Regional Trade Agreements and Trade Facilitation in the Middle East North Africa Region* (World Bank (Policy Research Working Paper 3837), 2006)

Deringer A., 'The Distribution of Powers in the Enforcement of the Rules of Competition and the Rome Treaty' (1963) *Common Market Law Review* 30

Dewey D., 'The Economic Theory of Antitrust: Science or Religion?' (1964) 50 *Virginia Law Review* 413.

Dignam A., 'The Role of Competition in Determining Corporate Governance Outcomes: Lessons From Australia's Corporate Governance System' (2005) *Modern Law Review* 68

Dignam A. and Galanis M., *The Globalisation of Corporate Governance* (Ashgate Publishing, 2009).

Dilorenzo T., 'The Origins of Antitrust: an Interest-Group Perspective' (1985) *International Review of Law and Economics* 73

Dima A. M., Musetescu R. and Paun C., 'Trade and Competition Policies at the Crossroads: Conflicts and Synergies on the Long Run' (2008) *Journal of International Trade Law and Policy* 79

Doern B., 'Canadian Competition Policy Institutions and Decision Processes' in Doern B. and Wilks S., *Comparative Competition Policy* (Oxford University Press, 1996)

Doern B., *Competition Policy Decision Processes in the European Community and United Kingdom* (Carleton University Press, 1992)

Doern B. and Wilks S., *Comparative Competition Policy* (Oxford University Press, 1996)

Dolan R. C., 'Price Behavior in Tight Oligopoly' (1984) *Review of Industrial Organization* 160

Dornbusch R., 'The Case for Trade Liberalisation in Developing Countries' (1992) *The Journal of Economic Perspectives* 73

Drexl J., 'International Competition Policy After Cancun: Placing a Singapore Issue on the WTO Development Agenda' (2004) *World Competition* 419

Dunfee T. W. and Friedman A. S., 'The Extraterritorial Application of United States Antitrust Laws: a Proposal for an Interim Solution' (1984) *Ohio State Law Journal* 883

Dunning J. H., *The Globalization of Business: the Challenges of the 1990s* (Routledge, 1993).

Dutz M. and Hayri A., 'Inappropriate Regulation and Stifled Innovation in the Road Freight Industry: Lessons for Policy Reform' in Amato G. and Laudati L. L. (eds.), *The Anticompetitive Impact of Regulation* (Edward Elgar, 2001)

Easterbrook F. H., 'The Limits of Antitrust' (1984) 63 *Texas Law Review* 1

Eden L., 'Bringing The Firm Back in: Multinationals in International Political Economy' in Eden L. and Potter E. (eds.), *Multinationals in Global Political Economy* (Macmillan, 1993)

Edwards C. D., *Control of Cartels and Monopolies: an International Comparison* (Oceana Publications, 1967)

Edwards S., 'Openness, Growth and Trade Liberalisation in Developing Countries' (1993) *Journal of Economic Literature* 1358

Ehlermann C. D., 'Implementation of EC Competition Law by National Antitrust Authorities' (1996) 17 *European Competition Law Review* 88

Ehlermann C. D., 'Reflections on a European Cartel Office' (1995) *Common Market Law Review* 471

Ehlermann C. D., 'The Contribution of the EC Competition Policy to the Single Market' (1992) 29 *Common Market Law Review* 257

Ehlermann C. D., 'The European Community, its Law and Lawyers' (1992) *Common Market Law Review* 213

Ehlermann C. D., 'The International Dimension of Competition Policy' (1994) *Fordham International Law Journal* 833

Ehlermann C. D. and Ehring L. 'WTO Dispute Settlement and Competition Law: Views From the Perspective of the Appellate Body's Experience' (2002) *Fordham International Law Journal* 1505

Ehlermann C. D. and Laudati L. L. (eds.), *European Competition Law Annual 1997: Objectives of Competition Policy* (Hart Publishing, 1998)

Ehrenzweig A. E., 'The *Lex Fori* – Basic Rule in the Conflict of Laws' (1960) *Michigan Law Review* 637

Elzinga K. G., 'The Goals of Antitrust: Other Than Competition and Efficiency, What Else Counts?' (1977) 125 *University of Pennsylvania Law Review* 1191

Farlow J. C., 'Ego or Equity? Examining United States Extension of the Sherman Act' (1998) *Transnational Lawyer* 175

Faull J., 'Effect on Trade Between Member States and Community: Member States Jurisdiction' (1989) *Fordham Corporate Law Institute* 485

Faull J. and Nikpay A., *The EC Law of Competition* (Oxford University Press, 2007)

Fedderson C. T., 'Focusing on Substantive Law in International Economic Relations: the Public Morals of GATT's Article XX(A) and "Conventional Rules of Interpretation"' (1998) *Minnesota Journal of Global Trade* 75

Feinberg K. R., 'Economic Coercion and Economic Sanctions: the Expansion of United States' Extraterritorial Jurisdiction' (1981) *American University Law Review* 323

Feketekuty G., *Reflections on the Interaction between Trade Policy and Competition Policy: a Contribution to the Development of a Conceptual Framework* (OECD, 1993)

Fernandez Ordonez M. A., 'Enforcement by National Authority of EC and Member States' Antitrust Law' (1993) *Fordham Corporate Law Institute* 629

Fidler D. P., 'Competition Law and International Relations' (1992) *International and Comparative Law Quarterly* 563

Fiebig A., 'A Role for the WTO in International Merger Control' (2000) *Northwestern Journal of International Law and Business* 233

Finger J. M. (ed.), *Antidumping: How It Works and Who Gets Hurt?* (University of Michigan Press, 1993)

Fingleton J., Fox E., Neven D. and Seabright P., *Competition Policy and the Transformation of Central Europe* (CEPR, 1995)

First H., 'Antitrust Law' in Morrison A. B. (ed.), *Fundamentals of American Law* (Oxford University Press, 1996)

Fisher F. M., 'Transnational Competition Law and the WTO' (2006) *Journal of International Trade Law and Policy* 42

Flynn D. O. and Giraldez A., 'Born Again: Globalization's Sixteenth Century Origins (Asian/Global Versus European Dynamics)' (2008) *Pacific Economic Review* 359

Flynn J. J., 'Antitrust Jurisprudence: a Symposium on the Economic, Political and Social Goals of Antitrust Policy' (1977) 125 *University of Pennsylvania Law Review* 1182

Flynn J. J., 'The Reagan Administration's Antitrust Policy, "Original Intent" and the Legislative History of the Sherman Act' (1988) 83 *Antitrust Bulletin* 259

Forrester I. S. and Norall C., 'The Laicization of Community Law: Self-Help and the Rule of Reason: How Competition Law is and Could be Applied' (1984) *Common Market Law Review* 11

Fox E., 'Competition Law and the Agenda for the WTO: Forging the Links of Competition and Trade' (1995) *Pacific-Rimely Law and Policy Journal* 1

Fox E., 'Extraterritoriality and Antitrust – is Reasonableness the Answer?' (1986) *Fordham Corporate Law Institute* 49

Fox E., 'Foreword: Mergers, Market Access and the Millennium' (2000) *Northwestern Journal of International Law and Business* 203

Fox E., 'Global Problems in a World of National Law' (1999) *New England Law Review* 11

Fox E., 'International Antitrust: Cosmopolitan Principles for an Open World' (1998) *Fordham Corporate Law Institute* 271

Fox E., 'The Battle for the Soul of Antitrust' (1987) *California Law Review* 917

Fox E., 'The Modernization of Antitrust: a New Equilibrium' (1981) *Cornell Law Review* 1140

Fox E., 'The Politics of Law and Economics in Judicial Decision Making: Antitrust as a Window' (1986) *New York University Law Review* 554

Fox E., 'The Problem of State Action that Blesses Private Action that Harms "the Foreigners"' in Zach E. and Correa C. M. (eds.), *Towards WTO Competition Rules: Key Issues and Comments on the WTO Report (1998) on Trade and Competition* (Kluwer Law International, 1999)

Fox E., 'Toward World Antitrust and Market Access' (1997) *American Journal of International Law* 1

Fox E., 'US Law and Global Competition and Trade – Jurisdiction and Comity' (1993) *Antitrust Report* 3

Fox E. and Sokol D., *Competition Law and Policy in Latin America* (Hart Publishing, 2009)

Fox E. and Sullivan L. A., 'Antitrust – Retrospective and Prospective: Where are we Coming From? Where are we Going?' (1987) *New York University Law Review* 936

Fox E., Sullivan L. A. and Peritz R. J., *Cases and Materials on United States Antitrust in Global Context* (Thomson West, 2009)

Francis B. P. B., 'Subsidiarity and Antitrust: the Enforcement of European Competition Law in the National Courts of Member States' (1995) *Law and Policy in International Business* 247

Frazer T., 'Competition Policy After 1992: the Next Step' (1990) *Modern Law Review* 609

Frederickson A., 'A Strategic Approach to Multi-Jurisdictional Filings' (1999) *European Counsel* 23

Fugate W. L., 'Antitrust Aspects of US–Japanese Trade' (1983) *Case Western Reserve Journal of International Law* 505

Fugate W. L., *Foreign Commerce and the Antitrust Laws* (Little Brown, 1958)

Furnish D., 'A Transnational Approach to Restrictive Business Practices' (1970) *International Lawyer* 317

Furse M., 'Competition Law Choice in China' (2007) *World Competition* 323

Furse M., *Competition Law of the EC and UK* (Oxford University Press, 2008)

Gal M., *Competition Policy in Small Market Economies* (Harvard University Press, 2003)

Gal M., 'Does Size Matter: the Effects of Market Size on Optimal Competition Policy' (2001) *The University of South Carolina Law Review* 1437

Galloway J., 'Moving Towards a Template for Bilateral Antirust Agreements' (2005) *World Competition* 589

Gavil A. I., Kovacic W. E. and Baker J. B., *Antitrust Law in Perspective: Cases, Concepts and Problems in Competition Policy* (Thomson West, 2008)

Gelhorn E. and Kovacic W. E., *Antitrust Law and Economics in a Nutshell* (Thomson West, 2004)

Gerber D., 'Afterword: Antitrust and American Business Abroad Revisited' (2000) *Northwestern Journal of International Law and Business* 307

Gerber D., 'Competition Law and the WTO: Rethinking the Relationship' (2007) *Journal of International Economic Law* 707

Gerber D., *Law and Competition in Twentieth Century Europe* (Oxford University Press, 1998)

Gerber D., 'The Extraterritorial Application of German Antitrust Law' (1983) *American Journal of International Law* 756

Gerber D., 'The Transformation of European Community Competition Law' (1994) *Harvard International Law Journal* 97

Gerber D., 'The US–European Conflict Over the Globalisation of Antitrust Law' (1999) *New England Law Review* 123

Gifford D. J. and Raskind L. J., *Federal Antitrust Law: Cases and Materials* (Anderson Publishing Co., 2002)

Gill D., 'Two Cheers for *Timberlane*' (1980) *Swiss Review of International Competition Law* 7

Gilpin R., *Political Economy of International Relations* (Princeton University Press, 1987)

Gluck A., 'Preserving *Per Se*' (1999) *Yale Law Journal* 913

Goyder J., *EC Competition Law* (Oxford University Press, 2002)

Granovetter M., 'Economic Action and Social Structure: the Problem of Embeddedness' in Granovetter M. and Swedberg R. (eds.), *The Sociology of Economic Life* (Westview Press, 1992)

Green A. W., *Political Integration by Jurisprudence: the Work of the Court of Justice of the European Communities in European Political Integration* (Sijthoff, 1969)

Griffin J. P., 'EC and US Extraterritoriality: Activism and Cooperation' (1994) *Fordham International Law Journal* 353

Griffin J. P., 'Extraterritorial Application of US Antitrust Law Clarified by United States Supreme Court' (1993) *Federal Bar News and Journal* 564

Griffin J. P., 'Extraterritoriality in US and EU Antitrust Enforcement' (1999) *Antitrust Law Journal* 159

Griffin J. P., 'Foreign Governmental Reactions to US Assertion of Extraterritorial Jurisdiction' (1998) *George Mason Law Review* 505

Griffin J. P., 'International Antitrust Guidelines Send Mixed Message of Robust Enforcement and Comity' (1995) *World Competition* 5

Griffin J. P., 'Possible Resolutions of International Disputes Over Enforcement of US Antitrust Law' (1982) *Stanford Journal of International Law* 279

Griffin J. P., 'United States Antitrust Law and Transnational Transactions: an Introduction' (1987) *International Lawyer* 307

Griffin J. P., 'What Business People Want From a World Antitrust Code' (1999) *New England Law Review* 39

Grippando J. M., 'Declining to Exercise Extraterritorial Jurisdiction on Grounds of International Comity: an Illegitimate Extension of the Judicial Abstention Doctrine' (1983) *Virginia Journal of International Law* 395

Grossfeld B. and Rogers C. P., 'A Shared Values Approach to Jurisdictional Conflicts in International Economic Law' (1983) *International and Comparative Law Quarterly* 931

Gupta V., 'After *Hartford Fire*: Antitrust and Comity' (1996) *Georgetown Law Journal* 2287

Guzman A., 'Is International Antitrust Possible?' (1998) *New York University Law Review* 1501

Guzman A., 'The Case for International Antitrust' (2004) *Berkley Journal of International Law* 355

Haley J., 'Administrative Guidance Versus Formal Regulation: Resolving the Paradox of Industrial Policy' in Saxonhouse G. and Yamamura K. (eds.), *Law and Trade Issues of the Japanese Economy: American and Japanese Perspectives* (University of Washington Press, 1986)

Hall D. F., 'Enforcement of EC Competition Law by National Courts' in Slot P. J. and McDonnell A. (eds.), *Procedure and Enforcement in EC and US Competition Law* (Sweet & Maxwell, 1993)

Halverson J., 'Harmonization and Coordination of International Merger Procedures' (1991) *Antitrust Law Journal* 531

Hancher L. and Moran M., *Capitalism, Culture and Economic Regulation* (Oxford University Press, 1989)

Hannay W. M., 'Transnational Competition Law Aspects of Mergers and Acquisitions' (2000) 20 *Northwestern Journal of International Law and Business* 287

Harvers M., 'Good Fences Make Good Neighbours: a Discussion of Problems Concerning the Exercise of Jurisdiction' (1983) *International Lawyer* 784

Hauser H., 'Proposal for a Multilateral Agreement on Free Market Access (MAFMA)' (1991) *Journal of World Trade Law* 77

Hawk B. E., *Antitrust and Market Access* (OECD, 1996)

Hawk B. E., 'Antitrust in the EEC – the First Decade' (1972) *Fordham Law Review* 229

Hawk B. E., 'International Antitrust Policy and the 1982 Act: the Continuing Need for Reassessment' (1982) *Fordham Law Review* 201

Hawk B. E., *United States, Common Market and International Antitrust* (Prentice-Hall Law and Business, 1993)

Hay D. 'Competition Policy' (1986) *Oxford Review of Economic Policy* 1

Hay D., 'The Assessment: Competition Policy' (1993) *Oxford Review of Economic Policy* 1

Held S., 'German Antitrust Law and Policy' (1992) *Fordham Corporate Law Institute* 311

Hermann A. H., *Conflicts of National Laws with International Business Activity: Issues of Extraterritoriality* (Howe Institute, 1982)

Hiljemark L., 'Enforcement of EC Competition Law in National Courts – the Perspective of Judicial Protection' (1997) *Yearbook of European Law* 83

Himmelfarb A. J., 'International Language of Convergence: Reviving Antitrust Dialogue Between the United States and the European Union with a Uniform Understanding of "Extraterritoriality"' (1996) *University of Pennsylvania Journal of International Economic Law* 909

Hiroshi I., 'Antitrust and Industrial Policy in Japan: Competition and Cooperation in Law and Trade Issues of the Japanese Economy' in Saxonhouse G. and Yamamura K. (eds.), *Law and Trade Issues of the Japanese Economy: American and Japanese Perspectives* (University of Washington Press, 1986)

Hodgson G. M., *Economics and Institutions* (Cambridge University Press, 1988)

Hoekman B. and Kee H. L., *Imports, Entry and Competition law as Market Disciplines* (Centre for Economic Policy Research, 2003)

Hoekman B. and Mavroidis P. C., *Linking Competition and Trade Policies in Central and East European Countries* (World Bank (Policy Research Working Paper 1346), 1994)

Hood N. and Young S., *The Economics of the Multinational Enterprise* (Longman, 1979)

Hoppner T., *Abuse of Market Dominance: The Refusal to Supply Competitors under Article 82 EC* (VDM Verlag Dr. Muller Aktiengesellschaft & Co. KG, 2009)

Hovenkamp H., *Federal Antitrust Policy: the Law of Competition and its Practice* (Thomson West, 2005)

Howse R. and Nicolaidis K., 'Legitimacy and Global Governance: Why Constitutionalizing the WTO is a Step Too Far?' in Cottier T. and Mavroidis P. C. (eds.) *The Role of the Judge in International Trade Regulation: Experience and Lessons for the WTO* (University of Michigan Press, 2003)

Hudec R. E., 'A WTO Perspective on Private Anti-Competitive Behavior in World Markets' (1999) *New England Law Review* 79

Huntley A. K., 'The Protection of Trading Interests Act 1980: Some Jurisdictional Aspects of Enforcement of Antitrust Laws' (1981) *International and Comparative Law Quarterly* 213

Hutchings M. and Levitt M., 'Concurrent Jurisdiction' (1994) *European Competition Law Review* 123

Immenga U., 'Export Cartels and Voluntary Export Restraints Between Trade and Competition Policy' (1995) *Pacific-Rimely Law and Policy Journal* 93

Inman R. P. and Rubinfeld D. L., 'Making Sense of the Antitrust State Action Doctrine: Balancing Political Participation and Economic Efficiency in Regulatory Federalism' (1997) *Texas Law Review* 1203

Jackson J. H., *Restructuring the GATT System* (Council on Foreign Relations, 1990)

Jackson J. H., *The Jurisprudence of GATT and the WTO* (Cambridge University Press, 2000)

Jacquemin A., 'The International Dimension of European Competition Policy' (1993) *Journal of Common Market Studies* 91

Jaffe L. L., 'Standing to Secure Judicial Review: Public Actions' (1961) *Harvard Law Review* 1265

Jakob T., 'EEA and Eastern Europe Agreements with the European Community' (1992) *Fordham Corporate Law Institute* 403

Janow M. E., 'Competition Policy and the WTO' in Bhagwati J. and Hirsh M. (eds.), *The Uruguay Round and Beyond* (University of Michigan Press, 1998)

Jennings R. and Watts A. (eds.), *Oppenheim's International Law* (Longman, 1996), vol. I

Jenny F., 'French Competition Law Update: 1987–1994' (1995) *Fordham Corporate Law Institute* 203

Jenny F. and Horna P., 'Modernization of the European Legal System of Competition. Law Enforcement: Lessons From Other Regional Groupings' in Brusick P., Alvarez A. M. and Cernat L. (eds.), *Competition Provisions in Regional Trade Agreements: How to Assure Development Gains* (United Nations, 2005)

Joelson M., 'International Antitrust: Problems and Defences' (1983) *Law and Policy in International Business* 1121

Jones A. and Sufrin B., *EC Competition Law: Text, Cases and Materials* (Oxford University Press, 2007)

Katzenbach N. de B., 'Conflicts on an Unruly Horse: Reciprocal Claims and Tolerance in Interstate and International Law' (1956) *Yale Law Journal* 1087

Keesing D., *Improving Trade Policy Reviews in the World Trade Organisation* (Institute for International Economics, 1998)

Kennedy D. and Webb D. E., 'The Limits of Integration: Eastern Europe and the European Communities' (1993) *Common Market Law Review* 1095

Kerse C., *EC Antitrust Procedure* (Sweet & Maxwell, 1994)

Kerse C., 'The Complainant in Competition Cases: a Progress Report' (1997) *Common Market Law Review* 230

Khan-Freund O., 'English Contracts and American Antitrust Law: the *Nylon Patent* Case' (1955) *Modern Law Review* 65

Khemani R. S., 'Competition Policy: an Engine for Growth' (1997) *Global Competition Review* 20

Kingsbury B., Krisch N. and Stewart R. B., 'The Emergence of Global Administrative Law' (2005) *Law and Contemporary Problems* 15

Kintner E. K., *An Antitrust Primer* (Macmillan, 1973)

Kirchner C., 'Competence Catalogues and the Principle of Subsidiarity in a European Constitution' (1997) *Constitutional Political Economy* 71

Kitzinger U. W., *The Politics and Economics of European Integration: Britain, Europe, and the United States* (Basic Books, 1963)

Korah V., *An Introductory Guide to EC Competition Law and Practice* (Sweet & Maxwell, 1994)

Korah V., *An Introductory Guide to EC Competition Law and Practice* (Hart Publishing, 2007)

Korah V., 'Tetra Pak II – Lack of Reasoning in Court's Judgment' (1997) *European Competition Law Review* 98

Kovacic W. E., 'Capitalism, Socialism and Competition Policy in Vietnam' (1999) *Antitrust* 57

Kovacic W. E., 'Getting Started: Creating New Competition Policy Institutions in Transition Economies' (1997) *Brooklyn Journal of International Law* 403

Kovacic W. E., 'Merger Enforcement in Transition: Antitrust Controls on Acquisitions in Emerging Economies' (1998) *University of Cincinnati Law Review* 1075

Kramer L., 'Extraterritorial Application of American Law After the Insurance Antitrust Case: a Reply to Professors Lowenfeld and Trimble' (1995) *American Journal of International Law* 750

Krueger A. O., 'The Political Economy of Rent-Seeking Society' (1974) *American Economic Review* 291

Kwoka J. E. and White L. J., *The Antitrust Revolution: Economics, Competition, and Policy* (Oxford University Press, 2003)

Laird S., 'The WTO's Trade Policy Review Mechanism – From Through The Looking Glass'(1999) *The World Economy* 741

Lande R. H., 'Wealth Transfers as the Original and Primary Concern of Antitrust: the Efficiency Interpretations Challenged' (1982) *Hastings Law Journal* 65

Lao M., 'Jurisdictional Reach of the US Antitrust Laws: Yokosuka and Yokota, and "Footnote 159" Scenarios' (1994) *Rutgers Law Review* 821

Leidig J. J., 'The Uncertain Status of the Defence of Foreign Sovereign Compulsion: Two Proposals for Change' (1991) *Virginia Journal of International Law* 321

Lerner M. (ed.), *The Mind and Faith of Justice Holmes: His Speeches, Essays, Letters, and Judicial Opinion* (Random House, 1943)

Liakopoulos T., 'New Rules on Competition Law in Greece' (1992) *World Competition* 17

Lipsey R. and Chrystal A., *An Introduction to Positive Economics* (Oxford University Press, 1995)

Lipsey R. and Chrystal A., *Principles of Economic Law* (Oxford University Press, 1999)

Locke J., *Two Treatises of Government* (Cambridge University Press, 1988)

Lloyd P. J., 'When Should New Areas of Rules be Added to the WTO?' (2005) *World Trade Review* 275

Lloyd P. J. and Vautier K. M., *Promoting Competition in Global Markets: a Multi-National Approach* (Edward Elgar, 1999)

Lowe A. V., 'Blocking Extraterritorial Jurisdiction: the British Protection of Trading Interests Act 1980' (1981) *American Journal of International Law* 257

Lowe A. V., *Extraterritorial Jurisdiction: an Annotated Collection of Legal Materials* (Grotius, 1983)

Lowe A. V., 'The Problems of Extraterritorial Jurisdiction: Economic Sovereignty and the Search for a Solution' (1985) *International and Comparative Law Quarterly* 724

Lowenfeld A. F., 'Conflict, Balancing of Interests and the Exercise of Jurisdiction to Prescribe: Reflections on the Insurance Antitrust Case' (1995) *American Journal of International Law* 42

Lowenfeld A. F., *Public Controls on International Trade* (Matthew Bender, 1983)

Lytle C. G., 'A Hegemonic Interpretation of Extraterritorial Jurisdiction in Antitrust: From *American Banana* to *Hartford Fire*' (1997) *Syracuse Journal of International Law and Commerce* 41

Maher I., 'Alignment of Competition Laws in the European Community' (1996) *Yearbook of European Law* 223

Maier H. G., 'Extraterritorial Jurisdiction at a Crossroads: an Intersection Between Public and Private International Law' (1982) *American Journal of International Law* 280

Maier H. G., 'Interest Balancing and Extra-territorial Jurisdiction' (1983) *American Journal of Comparative Law* 579

Mann F. A., 'The Doctrine of Jurisdiction in International Law' (1964) 11 *Recueil des Cours* 9

Mann F. A., 'The *Dyestuffs* Case in the Court of Justice of the European Communities' (1973) *International and Comparative Law Quarterly* 35

Marceau G., 'The Full Potential of the Europe Agreements: Trade and Competition Issues: the Case of Poland' (1995) *World Competition* 44

Marenco G., 'The Uneasy Enforcement of Article 85 EEC as Between Community and National Levels' (1993) *Fordham Corporate Law Institute* 605

Maresceau M. and Montaguti E., 'The Relations Between the European Union and Central and Eastern Europe: a Legal Appraisal' (1995) *Common Market Law Review* 1327

Marsden P., *A Competition Policy for the WTO* (Cameron May, 2003)

Marsden P., '"Antitrust" at the WTO' (1998) *Antitrust* 28

Martinzez Lage S. M., 'Significant Developments in Spanish Antitrust Law' (1996) *European Competition Law Review* 194

Mason E., 'Monopoly in Law and Economics' (1937) *Yale Law Journal* 34

Massey P., 'Reform of EC Competition Law: Substance, Procedure and Institutions' (1996) *Fordham Corporate Law Institute* 91

Matsushita M., 'Reflections on Competition Policy/Law in the Framework of the WTO' (1997) *Fordham Corporate Law Institute* 31

May J., 'Antitrust Practices in the Formative Era: the Constitutional and Conceptual Reach of State Antitrust Laws, 1880–1918' (1987) *University of Pennsylvania Law Review* 495

McChesney F. S., 'In Search of the Public Interest Model of Antitrust' in McChesney F. S. and Shughart W. F. (eds.), *The Causes and Consequences of Antitrust: the Public Choice Perspective* (Chicago University Press, 1995)

McChesney F. S., 'Talking 'bout My Antitrust Generation: Competition for and in the Field of Competition Law' (2003) *Emory Law Journal* 1401

McDonald S. A., 'The Caribbean Court of Justice: Enhancing the Law of International Organizations' (2004) *Fordham International Law Journal* 930

McGowan L. and Wilks S., 'The First Supranational Policy in the European Union: Competition Policy' (1995) *European Journal of Political Research* 141

McNeill J. S., 'Extraterritorial Antitrust Jurisdiction: Continuing the Confusion in Policy, Law, and Jurisdiction' (1998) *California Western International Law Journal* 425

Meade J., 'Decentralisation in the Implementation of EEC Competition Law – a Challenge for the Lawyers' (1986) *Northern Ireland Law Quarterly* 101

Meessen K. M., 'Antitrust Jurisdiction Under Customary International Law' (1984) *American Journal of International Law* 783

Mendes M. M., *Antitrust in a World of Interrelated Economies: the Interplay between Antitrust and Trade Policies in the US and the EEC* (Editions de l'Université de Bruxelles, 1991)

Mirabito J. and Friedler W., 'The Commission on the International Application of the US Antitrust Laws: Pulling in the Reins' (1982) *Suffolk Transnational Law Journal* 1

Muchlinski P. T., *Multinational Enterprises and the Law* (Oxford University Press, 2007)

Mueller D. C., *Public Choice* (Cambridge University Press, 1979)

Murphy D. T., 'Moderating Antitrust Subject Matter Jurisdiction: the Foreign Trade Antitrust Improvements Act and the Restatement of Foreign Relations Law (Revised)' (1986) *University of Cincinnati Law Review* 779

Neale A. D. and Goyder D. G., *The Antitrust Laws of the United States of America: a Study of Competition Enforced by Law* (Cambridge University Press, 1980)

Newman G. J., 'Potential Havens from American Jurisdiction and Discovery Laws in International Antitrust Enforcement' (1981) *University of Florida Law Review* 240

Nicoliades P., 'For a World Competition Authority' (1996) *Journal of World Trade Law* 131

Noonan C., *The Emerging Principles of International Competition Law* (Oxford University Press, 2008)

Norberg S., 'The EEA Agreement: Institutional Solutions for a Dynamic and Homogeneous EEA in the Area of Competition' (1992) *Fordham Corporate Law Institute* 437

North D. C., *Institutions, Institutional Change and Economic Performance* (Cambridge University Press, 1990)

Novicoff M. L., 'Blocking and Clawing Back in the Name of Public Policy: the United Kingdom's Protection of Private Economic Interests Against Adverse Foreign Adjudications' (1985) *Northwestern Journal of International Law and Business* 12

Ohmae K., *The Borderless World: Power and Strategy in the Interlinked Economy* (Harper-Collins, 1994)

Olmstead C. J., *Extraterritorial Application of the Laws and Responses Thereto* (Oxford University Press, 1984)

Olson M., *The Logic of Collective Action* (Harvard University Press, 1965)

Ongman J. W., '"Be No Longer Chaos": Constructing a Normative Theory of the Sherman Act's Extraterritorial Jurisdictional Scope' (1977) *Northwestern University Law Review* 733

Orland L., 'The Paradox in Bork's Antitrust Paradox' (1987) *Cardozo Law Review* 115

Pakaphan N. S., 'Indonesia: Enactment of Competition Law' (1999) *International Business Lawyer* 491

Palim M. R. A., 'The World Wide Growth of Competition Law: an Empirical Analysis' (1998) *Antitrust Bulletin* 105

Papakrivopoulos D., 'The Role of Competition Law as an International Trade Remedy in the Context of the World Trade Organization' (1999) *World Competition* 45

Pearce B., 'The Comity Doctrine as a Barrier to Judicial Jurisdiction: a US–EU Comparison' (1994) *Stanford Journal of International Law* 525

Pera A. and Todino M., 'Enforcement of EC Competition Rules: a Need for Reform?' (1996) *Fordham Corporate Law Institute* 125

Peritz R. J. R., *Competition Policy in America, 1888–1992: History, Rhetoric, Law* (Oxford University Press, 1996)

Peters G., 'United States Policy Institutions: Structural Constraints and Opportunities' in Doern G. B. and Wilks S., *Comparative Competition Policy* (Oxford University Press, 1996)

Petersmann E. U., 'International Competition Rules for the GATT–MTO World Trade and Legal System' (1993) 7 *Journal of World Trade Law* 35

Petersmann E. U., 'Legal, Economic and Political Objectives of National and International Competition Policies: Constitutional Functions of WTO "Linking Principles for Trade and Competition"' (1999) 34 *New England Law Review* 145, 155

Petersmann E. U., 'Proposals for Negotiating International Competition Rules in the GATT–WTO World Trade and Legal System' (1994) *Aussenwirtschaft* 231

Pettit P. C. F. and Styles C. J. D., 'The International Response to the Extraterritorial Application of United States Antitrust Laws' (1982) *Business Lawyer* 697

Pitofsky R., 'The Political Content of Antitrust' (1979) *University of Pennsylvania Law Review* 1051

Pittney H. C., 'Sovereign Compulsion and International Antitrust: Conflicting Laws and Separating Powers' (1987) *Columbia Journal of Transnational Law* 403

Porter M. E., *The Competitive Advantage of Nations* (Macmillan, 1989)

Posner R. A., 'The Federal Trade Commission' (1969) *Chicago-Kent Law Review* 48

Pryce R., *The Politics of the European Community* (Butterworths, 1973)

Quinn G., 'Sherman Gets Judicial Authority to Go Global: Extraterritorial Jurisdictional Reach of US Antitrust Laws are Expanded' (1998) *John Marshall Law Review* 141, 158

Rahl J. A., 'An International Antitrust Challenge' (1989) *North Western Journal of International Law and Business* 98

Ramseyer J. M., 'The Costs of the Consensual Myth: Antitrust Enforcement and Institutional Barriers to Litigation in Japan' (1985) *Yale Law Journal* 604

Ratliff J. and Wright E., 'Belgian Competition Law: the Advent of Free Market Principles' (1992) *World Competition* 33

Rennie J., 'Competition Provisions in Free Trade Agreements: Unique Responses to Bilateral Needs or Derivative Developments in International Competition Policy?' (2009) *International Trade Law Review* 57

Rennie J., 'The Evolution of Competition Law in Singapore and Thailand and its Implications for Bilateral Competition Policy in SAFTA and TAFTA' (2009) *International Trade Law Review* 1

Reynolds M. and Mansfield P., 'Complaining to the Commission' (1997) *European Counsel* 34

Rholl L., 'Inconsistent Application of the Extraterritorial Provisions of the Sherman Act: a Judicial Response Based Upon the Much Maligned "Effects" Test' (1990) *Marquette Law Review* 435

Riley A. J., 'More Radicalism, Please: the Notice on Cooperation Between National Courts and the Commission in Applying Articles 85 and 86 of the EEC Treaty' (1993) *European Competition Law Review* 93

Rill J. F. and Hambers C. S., 'Antitrust Enforcement and Non-Enforcement as a Barrier to Import in the Japanese Automobile Industry' (1997) *Empirica* 109

Rishikesh D., 'Extraterritoriality Versus Sovereignty in International Antitrust Jurisdiction' (1991) *World Competition* 33

Rittler R., Braun D. and Rawlinson F., *EEC Competition Law – a Practitioner's Guide* (Kluwer, 1991)

Rodger B. J. and MacCulloch A., *Competition Law and Policy in the EC and UK* (Routledge-Cavendish, 2009)

Romani F., 'The New Italian Antitrust Law' (1991) *Fordham Corporate Law Institute* 479

Rosenberg B. and Tavares de Araújo M., 'Implementation Costs and Burden of International Competition Law and Policy Agreements' in Brusick P., Alvarez A. M. and Cernat L. (eds.), *Competition Provisions in Regional Trade Agreements: How to Assure Development Gains* (United Nations, 2005)

Rosenthal D. E., 'Equipping the Multilateral Trading System with a Style and Principles to Increase Market Access' (1998) *George Mason Law Review* 543

Rosenthal D. E., 'Relationship of US Antitrust Laws to the Formulation of Foreign Economic Policy, Particularly Export and Overseas Investment Policy' (1980) *Antitrust Law Journal* 1189

Rosenthal D. E., 'What Should be the Agenda of a Presidential Commission to Study the International Application of US Antitrust Law?' (1980) *Northwestern Journal of International Law and Business* 372

Rosenthal D. E. and Knighton W. M., *National Laws and International Commerce: the Problem of Extraterritoriality* (Routledge, 1982)

Rosic E. A., 'The Use of Interest Analysis in the Extraterritorial Application of United States Antitrust Law' (1983) *Cornell International Law Journal* 147

Roth P. M. (ed.), *Bellamy & Child: European Community Law of Competition* (6th edn, Oxford University Press, 2008)

Roth P. M., 'Jurisdiction, British Public Policy and the Supreme Court' (1994) *Law Quarterly Review* 194

Rowe F. M., 'The Decline of Antitrust and the Delusions of Models: the Faustian Pact of Law and Economics' (1984) 72 *Georgetown Law Journal* 1511

Sabalot D. A., 'Shortening the Long Arm of American Antitrust Jurisdiction: Extraterritoriality and the Foreign Blocking Statutes' (1982) *Loyola Law Review* 213

Sandage J. B., 'Forum Non Conveniens and the Extraterritorial Application of United States Antitrust Laws' (1985) *Yale Law Journal* 1693

Santos J. P., 'The Territorial Scope of Article 85 of the EEC Treaty' (1989) *Fordham Corporate Law Institute* 571

Scherer F. M. and Ross D., *Industrial Market Structure and Economic Performance* (Houghton Mifflin, 1990)

Schumpeter J., *Capitalism, Socialism and Democracy* (Allen and Unwin, 1976)

Schwartz L. B., '"Justice"; and Other Non-Economic Goals of Antitrust' (1979) *University of Pennsylvania Law Review* 1076

Sennett M. and Gavil A. I., 'Antitrust Jurisdiction, Extraterritorial Conduct and Interest Balancing' (1985) *International Lawyer* 1185

Shaffer G. C., *Defending Interests Public-Private Partnerships in WTO Litigation* (Brookings Institute, 2003)

Sharma V. D., 'Approaches to the Issue of Extra-territorial Jurisdiction' (1995) *Australian Journal of Corporate Law* 45

Shenefield J. H., 'Extraterritoriality in Antitrust' (1983) *Law and Policy in International Business* 1109

Shenefield J. H., 'Thoughts on Extraterritorial Application of the United States Antitrust Laws' (1983) *Fordham Law Review* 350

Shughart W. F., 'Be True to Your School: Chicago's Contradictory Views of Antitrust and Regulation' in McChesney F. S. and Shughart W. F. (eds.),

The Causes and Consequences of Antitrust: the Public Choice Perspective (Chicago University Press, 1995)

Shughart W. F., Silverman J. and Tollison R., 'Antitrust Enforcement and Foreign Competition' in McChesney F. S. and Shughart W. F. (eds.), *The Causes and Consequences of Antitrust: the Public Choice Perspective* (Chicago University Press, 1995)

Simons H. C., *A Positive Program for Laissez Faire: Some Proposals for a Liberal Economic Policy* (Chicago University Press, 1934)

Singh A. and Dhumale R., *Competition Policy, Development and Developing Countries* (South Centre Working Papers, 1999)

Siragusa M. and Scassellati-Sforztine G., 'Italian and EC Competition Law: a New Relationship – Reciprocal Exclusivity and Common Principles' (1993) *Common Market Law Review* 93

Smith A., *The Theory of Moral Sentiments* (A. Millar, 1759)

Smith A. D., 'Bringing Down Private Trade Barriers – an Assessment of the United States' Unilateral Options: Section 301 of the 1974 Trade Act and the Extraterritorial Application of US Antitrust Law' (1994) *Michigan Journal of International Law* 241

Smith-Hillman A., 'First a Glimmer, Now a ...? The Prospect of a Caribbean Competition Policy' (2006) *Journal of World Trade* 405

Snyder J. L., 'International Competition: Towards a Normative Theory of United States Antitrust Law and Policy' (1985) *Boston University International Law Journal* 257

Sosnick S. H. 'A Critique of Concepts of Workable Competition' (1958) 72 *Quarterly Journal of Economics* 380

Souty F., 'Is There a Need for Additional WTO Competition Rules Promoting Non-Discriminatory Competition Laws and Competition Institutions in WTO Members?' in Petersmann E. U. (ed.), *Reforming the World Trading System* (Oxford University Press, 2005)

Stanford J. S., 'The Application of the Sherman Act to Conduct Outside the United States: a View from Abroad' (1978) *Cornell International Law Journal* 195

Staniland M., *What is Political Economy?: A Study of Social Theory and Underdevelopment* (Yale University Press, 1985)

Steenbergen J., 'Legal Issues of Economic Integration: Modernisation and International Competition Law' (2005) *Legal Issues of European Integration* 219

Stewart T., 'Is Flexibility Needed When Designing Competition Law for Small Open Economies? A View From the Caribbean' (2004) *Journal of World Trade* 725

Stewart T., Clarke J. and Joekes S., *Competition Law in Action: Experience from Developing Countries* (International Development Research Centre, 2007)

Stigler G. J., 'A Theory of Oligopoly' (1964) *Journal of Political Economy* 44

Stockman K., 'Foreign Application of European Antitrust Laws' (1985) *Fordham Corporate Law Institute* 251

Stockmann K., 'Trends and Developments in European Antitrust Laws' (1991) *Fordham Corporate Law Institute* 441

Stopford J. M. and Strange S., *Rival States, Rival Firms* (Cambridge University Press, 1991)

Stothers C., 'Parallel Trade and Free Trade Agreements' (2006) *Journal of Intellectual Property Law and Practice* 578

Stragier J., 'The Competition Rules of the EEA Agreement and Their Implementation' (1993) *European Competition Law Review* 30

Stroock, Stroock and Lavan, 'Convergence of Trade Laws and Antitrust Laws: Unilateral Extraterritorial US Antitrust Enforcement – Can it Work to Open Japan's Markets?' in Cortesi H. B. (ed.), *Unilateral Application of Antitrust and Trade Laws: toward a New Economic Relationship between the United States and Japan* (The Institute, 1994)

Sturm R., 'The German Cartel Office in Hostile Environment' in Doern G. B. and Wilks S., *Comparative Competition Policy* (Oxford University Press, 1996)

Sullivan E. T. and Harrison J. L., *Understanding Antitrust and its Economic Implications* (LexisNexis, 2003)

Sullivan L. A., 'Economics and More Humanistic Disciplines: What are the Sources of Wisdom for Antitrust?' (1977) 125 *University of Pennsylvania Law Review* 1214

Sullivan L. A., 'The US, the EU, the WTO, the Americas, and Telecom Competition' (1999) *Southwestern Journal of Law and trade in the Americas* 63

Supanit S., 'Thailand: Implementation of Competition Law' (1999) *International Business Lawyer* 491

Swann D., *Competition and Consumer Protection* (Penguin, Harmondsworth, 1979)

Tarullo D. K., 'Norms and Institutions in Global Competition Policy' (2000) *American Journal of International Law* 478

Tavares de Araujo J. and Tineo L., 'Competition Policy and Regional Trade Agreements' in Rodriguez Mendoza M., Low P. and Kotschwar B. (eds.), *Trade Rules in the Making: Challenges in Regional and Multilateral Negotiations* (Brookings Institute, 1999)

Taylor M. D., *International Competition Law – A New Dimension for the WTO* (Cambridge University Press, 2006)

Temple Lang J., 'European Community Constitutional Law and the Enforcement of Community Antitrust Law' (1993) *Fordham Corporate Law Institute* 525

Torremans P., 'Extraterritorial Application of EU and US Competition Law' (1996) *European Law Review* 280

Trachtman J. P., 'International Regulatory Competition, Externalization, and Jurisdiction' (1993) *Harvard Journal of International Law* 47

Trenor J. A., 'Jurisdiction and the Extraterritorial Application of Antitrust Laws after *Hartford Fire*' (1995) *University of Chicago Law Review* 1583

Trimble P. R., 'The Supreme Court and International Law: the Demise of Restatement Section 403' (1995) *American Journal of International Law* 53

Turner D. F., 'Application of Competition Laws to Foreign Conduct: Appropriate Resolution of Jurisdictional Issues' (1985) *Fordham Corporate Law Institute* 231

Ullrich H., 'Harmonisation within the European Union' (1996) *European Competition Law Review* 178

Ulph A., 'Recent Advances in Oligopoly Theory From a Game Theory Perspective' (1987) *Journal of Economic Surveys* 149

Uruena R., 'The World Trade Organization and its Powers to Adopt a Competition Policy' (2006) *International Organisations Law Review* 55

Valentine D. A., 'Building a Cooperative Framework for Oversights in Mergers – the Answer to Extraterritoriality Issues in Merger Review' (1998) *George Mason Law Review* 525

Van Bael I., 'The Role of National Courts' (1994) *European Competition Law Review* 6.

Van der Esch B., 'The Principles of Interpretation Applied by the Court of Justice of the European Communities and their Relevance for the Scope of the EEC Competition Rules' (1991) *Fordham Corporate Law Institute* 223

Van Gerven W., 'EC Jurisdiction in Antitrust Matters: the *Wood Pulp* Judgment' (1989) *Fordham Corporate Law Institute* 451

Van Miert K., 'Competition Policy in Relation to the Central and Eastern European Countries – Achievements and Challenges' (1998) *European Community Competition Policy NewsLetter* 1

Van Miert K., 'Global Forces Affecting Competition Policy in a Post-recessionary Environment' (1993) *World Competition* 135

Varady T., 'The Emergence of Competition Law in (Former) Socialist Countries' (1999) *American Journal of Comparative Law* 229

Vernon R., 'Sovereignty at Bay: Ten Years After' (1981) *International Organisation* 517

Vernon R., *Sovereignty at Bay: the Multinational Spread of US Enterprises* (Longman, 1971)

Vissi F., 'Challenges and Questions around Competition Policy: the Hungarian Experience' (1995) *Fordham International Law Journal* 1230

Waller S. W., 'Can US Antitrust Laws Open International Markets'? (2000) *Northwestern Journal of International Law and Business* 207

Waller S. W., 'The Internationalization of Antitrust Enforcement' (1997) *Boston University Law Review* 343

Walters M., *Globalization* (Routledge, 1995)

Weiler J., 'Community, Member States and European Integration: is the Law Relevant?' (1982) *Journal of Common Market Studies* 39

Weiner M., 'Remedies in International Transactions: a Case for Flexibility' (1996) *Antitrust Law Journal* 261

Weintraub R. J., 'Globalization Effect on Antitrust Law' (1999) *New England Law Review* 27

Weiss F., 'From World Trade Law to World Competition Law' (2000) *Fordham International Law Journal* 250

Wesseling R., 'Subsidiarity in Community Law: Setting the Right Agenda' (1997) *European Law Review* 35

Wesseling R., 'The Commission Notices on Decentralisation of EC Antitrust Law: in for a Penny, Not for a Pound' (1997) *European Competition Law Review* 94

Wessman P., 'Competition Sharpens in Sweden' (1993) *World Competition* 113

Whatstein L., 'Extraterritorial Application of EU Competition Law – Comments and Reflections' (1992) *Israel Law Review* 195

Whish R., *Competition Law* (Oxford University Press, 2008)

Whish R., 'Enforcement of EC Competition Law in the Domestic Courts of Member States' (1994) *European Competition Law Review* 60

Widegren M., 'Competition Law in Sweden – a Brief Introduction to the New Legislation' (1995) *Fordham Corporate Law Institute* 241

Wilcox C., *A Charter for World Trade* (Macmillan, 1949)

Williams M. *Competition Policy and Law in China, Hong Kong and Taiwan* (Cambridge University Press, 2004)

Williamson O. E., *Antitrust Economics* (Blackwell, 1987)

Wilson R. R., 'Proposed ITO Charter' (1947) *American Journal of International Law* 879

Wood D. P., 'The Impossible Dream: Real International Antitrust' (1992) *University of Chicago Legal Forum* 277

Wood D. and Whish R., *Merger Cases in the Real World: a Study of Merger Control Procedures* (OECD, 1994)

Yntema H., 'The Comity Doctrine' (1966) *Michigan Law Review* 1

Young A., Rahaju S. and Li G., 'Regulatory Multiplicities in Telecommunications Reforms in Indonesia and China' (2005) *Macquarie Journal of Business Law* 135

Zago de Azevedo A. F., 'Mercosur: Ambitious Policies, Poor Practices' (2004) *Revista de Economía Política* 4

Zampetti A. B. and Sauve P., *New Dimensions of Market Access: an Overview* (OECD, 1995)

Reports, Guidelines, Codes and Studies

Aide Memoire: Trade Capacity Building: Strengthening the COMESA trade region through a culture of competition (COMESA, 2008)

Antitrust Modernisation Commission Report and Recommendations (2007)

Canadian Competition Bureau Information Bulletin on the Abuse of Dominance Provisions as Applied to the Telecommunications Industry (2008)

Competition Policy in the OECD Countries (OECD, 1986)

Competition Provisions in Regional Trade Agreements: How to Assure Development Gains (UNCTAD, 2005)

Competition Regimes in the World: A Civil Society Report (CUTS International, 2006)

Consistencies and Inconsistencies between Trade and Competition Policies (OECD, 1999)

Draft Multilateral Competition Law Code of the Munich Group (1993)

European Commission 11th Report on Competition Policy (1981)

European Commission 13th Report on Competition Policy (1983)

European Commission 15th Report on Competition Policy (1985)

European Commission 23rd Report on Competition Policy (1993)

European Commission 25th Report on Competition Policy (1995)

European Commission 28th Report on Competition Policy (1998)

European Commission's Guidance on Enforcement Priorities in Applying Article 82 [now Article 102 TFEU] of the Treaty to Abusive Exclusionary Conduct by Dominant Undertakings (2008)

European Commission's Guidelines for the Assessment of Horizontal Cooperation Agreements (2000) *Official Journal* C-3/2

European Commission Guidelines on Effect on Trade Between Member States (2004) *Official Journal* C-1010/81

European Commission Guidelines on Horizontal Mergers (2004) *Official Journal* C-31/5

European Commission Guidelines on Non-horizontal Mergers (2007) *Official Journal* C-265/7

European Commission Guidelines on the Application of Article 101(3) TFEU (ex Article 81(3)) (2004) *Official Journal* C-101/97

European Commission Guidelines on Transfer of Technology (2004) *Official Journal* C-101/2

European Commission Green Paper on Damages Actions for Breach of the EC Antitrust Rules (2005)

European Commission Notice concerning Cooperation between the Commission and Courts of the Member States with Regards to the Application of Articles 85 (now Article 101 TFEU) and 86 (now Article 102 TFEU) (1993) *Official Journal* C-39/6

European Commission Notice on Agreements of Minor Importance (De Minimis) (2001) *Official Journal* C-368/13

European Commission Notice on Cartel Leniency (2006) *Official Journal* C-298/17

European Commission Notice on Cooperation between the Commission and National Competition Authorities in Handling Cases Falling within the Scope of Article 85 and 86 EC (1996) *Official Journal* C-262/5

European Commission Notice on Cooperation between the Commission and National Courts (2004) *Official Journal* C-101/54

European Commission Notice on Cooperation within the Network of Competition Authorities (2004) *Official Journal* C-101/43

European Commission Notice on Handling of Complaints by the Commission (2004) *Official Journal* C-101/65

European Commission Notice on Informal Guidance Relating to Novel Questions (Guidance Letters) (2004) *Official Journal* C-101/78

European Commission Notice on Market Definition (1997) *Official Journal* C-372/5

European Commission White Paper on the Modernisation of the Rules Implementing Articles 85 [now Article 101 TFEU] and 86 [now Article 102 TFEU] of the EC Treaty (1999) *Official Journal* C-132/1

Guidelines for Multinational Enterprises (OECD, 1976)

New Dimensions of Market Access in Globalizing World Economy (OECD, 1995)

Recommendation of the Council for Cooperation between Member Countries in Areas of Potential Conflict between Competition and Trade Policies (OECD, 1986)

Regional Cooperation on Competition Policy and Law: the East African Community Experience (UNCTAD, 2006); contribution by Kenya

Relationship between Regulators and Competition Authorities (OECD, 1999)

Report of the American Bar Association Antitrust Section, *Antitrust Law Developments 1049* (1997)

Report of the American Bar Association Sections of Antitrust Law and International Law and Practice on the Internationalization of Competition Law Rules: Coordination and Convergence (1999)

Report of American Bar Association on Private Anti-Competitive Practices as Market Access Barriers (2000)

Report of the International Competition Policy Advisory Committee (ICPAC) (2000)

Report on Competition and Trade Policy: Their Interaction (OECD, 1984)

Revised Recommendation of the Council Concerning Cooperation between Member Countries on Anti-Competitive Practices Affecting International Trade (OECD, 1995)

Tailor-made Competition Policy in a Standardising World: The Experience of Peru (Instituto Apoyo and Ciudadanos al Día, 2005)

The Future of Transnational Antitrust – From Comparative to Common Competition Law Munich Series on European and International Antitrust Law (2003)

Trade and Competition Policy for Tomorrow (OECD, 1999)

US Department of Justice Antitrust Division *Antitrust Enforcement Guidelines for International Operations* (1988)

US Department of Justice Antitrust Division *Antitrust Enforcement Guidelines for International Operations* (1995)

US Horizontal Merger Guidelines (1992)

US Non-horizontal Merger Guidelines (1984)

White Paper on Damages Actions for Breach of the EC Antitrust Rules (2008)

World Development Report (WDR) 2000/2001: Attacking Poverty

World Trade Organisation Annual Report (WTO, 1997)

UNCTAD Report of Eminent Persons (1974)

UN Set of Multilaterally Agreed Equitable Principles and Rules for the Control of Restrictive Business Practices (1980)

INDEX